The Author

HANS P. GUTH, Ph.D. University of Michigan, is Professor of English at San Jose State College. He has published widely in professional journals and is the author or editor of several successful books in the field, including: *Words and Ideas* (1959), *Concise English Handbook* (1961), *Ideas and Image* (1962). His lectures on poetry, fiction, and drama have been broadcast over KPFA-FM San Francisco, KPFK-FM Los Angeles, Radio Frankfurt, and Radio Free Berlin.

English
Today
and
Tomorrow

PRENTICE-HALL INTERNATIONAL, INC., *London*
PRENTICE-HALL OF AUSTRALIA, PTY., LTD., *Sydney*
PRENTICE-HALL OF CANADA, LTD., *Toronto*
PRENTICE-HALL FRANCE, S.A.R.L., *Paris*
PRENTICE-HALL OF INDIA (PRIVATE) LTD., *New Delhi*
PRENTICE-HALL OF JAPAN, INC., *Tokyo*
PRENTICE-HALL DE MEXICO, S.A., *Mexico City*

Prentice-Hall, Inc., *Englewood Cliffs, New Jersey*

Hans P. Guth
*Professor
of English
San Jose
State
College*

English
Today
and
Tomorrow

A Guide for Teachers of English

Library of Congress Catalog Card Number: 64–12552

Printed in the United States of America

28301–C

English Today and Tomorrow is a book for teachers of English and for others who take an interest in the teaching of English in school or college. The book is intended both for the future teacher and for the teacher in service concerned with broadening his understanding of his craft.

Recent decades have seen much vigorous development in several areas of the discipline of English. Though in the long run these developments should give the teacher a firmer grasp of his subject, their novelty and diversity may at present bewilder rather than enlighten him. While specialized research and experiment continues, there is a need for taking stock of current trends, for trying to see them in perspective.

English Today and Tomorrow aims at a unified view of the discipline of English in its current state. It attempts to give a balanced account of such major areas of English as language, composition, and literature, and the relations existing between them. It explores the assumptions underlying current work in the study of language and literature and its implications for the work of the classroom teacher. It tries to relate recent developments in teaching techniques

Preface

and resources to a coherent rationale of the English teacher's work.

I hope that this book may prove useful as a textbook for courses, institutes, and workshops for teachers of English at all levels of instruction. At the end of each chapter, bibliographical notes and suggestions for exploration and analysis direct the reader to materials for further study. Both the chapter bibliographies and the final bibliography provide a structured program for additional reading. The book will have served its purpose if it clears up even a few of the questions that perplex the present or future teacher and if it confirms him in his dedication to English as the most challenging and rewarding of academic subjects.

This book owes an obvious debt to students, teachers, scholars, and textbook authors too numerous to mention. I am grateful to professional organizations that allowed me to make generous use of material from their publications. My special thanks are due to Robert M. Gorrell, University of Nevada, and Thomas H. Wetmore, Ball State Teachers College, who read the first draft of the manuscript and made many valuable suggestions. My greatest debt is to William Slothower of San Jose State College. His shrewd insights into pedagogical and professional problems have helped crystallize my thinking on many matters related to the central cause to which this book is dedicated: the cause of competent and meaningful work in the teaching of English.

H. GUTH

My special thanks are due to the following organizations for granting me permission to quote from their publications: The National Council of Teachers of English, The Modern Language Association of America, The College English Association, Speech Association of America, and the University of Michigan Research Club in Language Learning. I am further indebted to the following for permission to reprint copyrighted material:

The AAUP Bulletin for permission to quote from an editorial, a committee report, and an article by R. F. Fuchs.

Analysis for permission to quote from an article by Friedrich Waismann.

The American Scholar for permission to quote from articles by J. W. Krutch and Jacques Barzun. Copyright © 1955 and 1962 for Krutch, copyright © 1957 for Barzun by the United Chapters of Phi Beta Kappa. By permission of the publishers.

American Scientist and the author for permission to quote from an article by Anatol Rapoport.

Appleton-Century-Crofts, Inc. for permission to quote from Lewis Leary ed., *Contemporary Literary Scholarship,* copyright © 1958 by Appleton-Century-Crofts, Inc.; Charles C. Fries, *American English Grammar,* copyright © 1940 by Appleton-Century-Crofts, Inc.; and Albert H. Marckwardt and Fred G. Walcott, *Facts About Current Usage,* copyright © 1938 by Appleton-Century-Crofts, Inc.

Acknowledgments

A. P. Watt & Son, International Authors N.V., Cassell & Company, Ltd., and Willis K. Wing for permission to quote from Robert Graves, *Goodbye to All That.*

The Editor of the Aristotelian Society for permission to quote from an article by W. B. Gallie in the *Proceedings* of the Society.

The Atlantic Monthly for permission to quote from articles by Wilson Follett, John Braine, Valborg Anderson, A. C. Eurich, and Oscar Handlin.

Basil Blackwell & Mott, Ltd. for permission to quote from Otto Jespersen, *Growth and Structure of the English Language.*

Beacon Press for permission to quote from James Baldwin, *Notes of a Native Son,* copyright © 1955 by James Baldwin, reprinted by permission of the Beacon Press; and John Dewey, *Reconstruction in Philosophy.*

Kenneth Burke for permission to quote from *Counter-Statement* and *The Philosophy of Literary Form* (the latter now available in a Vintage paperback edition).

Claassen Verlag G.M.B.H. for permission to quote from Dolf Sternberger *et al.*, *Aus dem Wörterbuch des Unmenschen.*

Doubleday & Company, Inc. for permission to quote from *The Summing Up* by W. Somerset Maugham. Copyright © 1948 by W. Somerset Maugham. Reprinted by permission of Doubleday & Company, Inc.

Educational Testing Service and the author for permission to quote from an article by James G. Holland.

The English Leaflet for permission to quote from an article by James Sledd.

E. P. Dutton & Co., Inc. for permission to quote from H. G. Rickover, *Education and Freedom.*

Ernest Benn Limited for permission to quote from A. N. Whitehead, *The Aims of Education.*

ETC. for permission to quote from articles by Anatol Rapoport, S. I. Hayakawa, and Dona Worrall Brown.

James D. Finn for permission to quote from an article on instructional technology.

Fund for the Advancement of Education for permission to quote from John W. Meaney, *Televised College Courses.*

Funk & Wagnalls Company, Inc. for permission to quote from Margaret M. Bryant, *Current American Usage.*

G. & C. Merriam Company for permission to quote from *Word Study* and *Webster's Third New International Dictionary.*

George Allen & Unwin Ltd. for permission to quote from Otto Jespersen, *Language.*

G. P. Putnam's Sons for permission to quote from John Dewey, *Art as Experience.*

Hamish Hamilton Ltd. for permission to quote from an article by Alan S. C. Ross in Nancy Mitford ed., *Noblesse Oblige.*

Harcourt, Brace & World, Inc. for permission to quote from Stuart Chase, *Power of Words;* Edward Sapir, *Language;* Harold Whitehall, *Structural Essentials of English;* Paul Roberts, *English Sentences;* Charles C. Fries, *The Structure of English;* C. K. Ogden and I. A. Richards, *The Meaning of Meaning;* George Orwell, *Shooting an Elephant and Other Essays; Dickens, Dali and Others; Such, Such Were the Joys; Animal Farm;* Alfred Kazin, *A Walker in the City;* Alfred Kazin ed., *The Open Form;* R. P. Blackmur, *Language as Gesture;* T. S. Eliot, *Selected Essays, 1917–1932;* C. G. Jung, *Modern Man in Search of a Soul;* Dudley Fitts and Robert Fitzgerald, *The Oedipus Cycle;* Mark Schorer *et al.* eds., *Criticism;* I. A. Richards, *Principles of Literary Criticism;* J. W. Krutch, *The Modern Temper.*

Harold Matson Company, Inc. for permission to quote from J. B. Priestley, *Margin Released.* Copyright © 1962 by J. B. Priestley. Reprinted by permission of the Harold Matson Company, Inc.

Harper & Row, Publishers for permission to quote excerpts from "U and NON-U" by Alan S. C. Ross in Nancy Mitford ed., *Noblesse Oblige,* copyright © 1955 by Alan Strode Campbell Ross, reprinted by permission of Harper & Row, Publishers; E. B. White, *One Man's Meat;* J. B. Priestley, *Margin Released;*

Aldous Huxley, *Music at Night and Other Essays;* Thornton Wilder, *Three Plays;* J. W. Gardner, *Excellence.*

Harvard Educational Review and the author for permission to quote from an article by B. F. Skinner.

Harvard University Press for permission to quote from John B. Carroll, *The Study of Language,* and Jerome S. Bruner, *The Process of Education.*

S. I. Hayakawa for permission to quote from an article in *Poetry.*

Holt, Rinehart & Winston, Inc., for permission to quote from *Exercise Exchange;* and from *Complete Poems of Robert Frost.* Copyright © 1923 by Holt, Rinehart & Winston, Inc. Copyright renewed 1951 by Robert Frost. Reprinted by permission of Holt, Rinehart & Winston, Inc.

Houghton Mifflin Company for permission to quote from Irwin Edman, *Adam, the Baby and the Man from Mars,* and Archibald MacLeish, *Ars Poetica.*

The John Day Co., Inc. for permission to quote from Hugh Sykes Davies, *Grammar Without Tears.*

The Kenyon Review for permission to quote from an article by Harold Whitehall.

Alfred A. Knopf, Inc. for permission to quote from Donald J. Lloyd and H. R. Warfel, *American English in Its Cultural Setting;* H. L. Mencken, *The American Language* and *Happy Days, 1880–1892;* D. H. Lawrence, "Pornography and Obscenity"; Gilbert Highet, *The Art of Teaching.*

Joseph Wood Krutch for permission to quote from an article in *Saturday Review.*

Language for permission to quote from articles by R. B. Lees, Charles C. Fries, and D. L. Bolinger.

Linguistica Press for permission to quote from Robert A. Hall, Jr., *Linguistics and Your Language.*

Little, Brown and Company for permission to quote from Jacques Barzun, *Teacher in America,* and Walter Lippmann, *The Public Philosophy.*

Donald J. Lloyd for permission to quote from an article in *The American Scholar.*

McGraw-Hill, Inc. for permission to quote from Albert R. Kitzhaber, *Themes, Theories and Therapy.*

The Macmillan Company for permission to quote from Otto Jespersen, *Growth and Structure of the English Language;* Arthur M. Schlesinger, *Paths to the Present;* Robert E. Spiller et al. eds., *Literary History of the United States;* and A. N. Whitehead, *The Aims of Education.*

W. Somerset Maugham and William Heinemann, Limited for permission to quote from *The Summing Up.*

The M.I.T. Press, Massachusetts Institute of Technology, Cambridge, Mass., for permission to quote from Benjamin Lee Whorf, *Language, Thought and Reality.*

Mouton & Co. for permission to quote from Noam Chomsky, *Syntactic Structures.*

New Directions for permission to quote from *The Collected Poems of Dylan Thomas,* copyright © 1957 by New Directions; and from *Some Versions of Pastoral* by William Empson. All Rights Reserved. Both excerpts reprinted by permission of New Directions, Publishers. British rights for the excerpt by Dylan Thomas courtesy of J. M. Dent & Sons Ltd.

The New Yorker for permission to quote from an article by Dwight Macdonald.

New York Herald Tribune Syndicate for permission to quote from an article by John Crosby.

The New York Times and the authors or their representatives for permission to quote from articles by Saul Bellow, Frank O'Connor, and John Dewey. Copyright © by The New York Times. Reprinted by permission.

Northwestern University Press for permission to quote from Eliseo Vivas, *D. H. Lawrence.*

Oxford University Press for permission to quote from Douglas Bush, *English Literature in the Earlier Seventeenth Century;* Margaret Nicholson, *Dictionary of American-English Usage;* C. S. Lewis, *The Allegory of Love;* I. A. Richards, *The Philosophy of Rhetoric;* W. H. Gardner ed., *Poems of Gerard Manley Hopkins.*

The editor of *Preprints of Papers for the Ninth International Congress of Linguists* and the authors for permission to quote from articles by Noam Chomsky and Werner Winter.

Princeton University Press for permission to quote from Francis Fergusson, *The Idea of a Theater,* and A. Tate, ed., *The Language of Poetry.*

Rand McNally & Company for permission to quote from J. Lloyd Trump and D. Baynham, *Focus on Change.*

Random House, Inc. for permission to use excerpts from "The Slit," copyright © 1957 by Loren Eiseley, reprinted from *The Immense Journey,* by Loren Eiseley, by permission of Random House, Inc. From "The Unknown Citizen," copyright © 1940 by W. H. Auden, reprinted from *The Collected Poetry of W. H. Auden,* by permission of Random House, Inc. From "In Memory of W. B. Yeats," copyright © 1940 by W. H. Auden, reprinted from *The Collected Poetry of W. H. Auden,* by permission of Random House, Inc. From "Pure and Impure Poetry," copyright © 1943 by Robert Penn Warren, reprinted from *Selected Essays,* by Robert Penn Warren, by permission of Random House, Inc. From Ralph Ellison, *Invisible Man,* copyright © 1947, 1948, 1952, by Ralph Ellison. From Bergen and Cornelia Evans, *A Dictionary of Contemporary American Usage,* copyright © 1957 by Bergen Evans and Cornelia Evans.

The Reporter for permission to quote from articles by William Lee Miller, Alfred Kazin, and Spencer Klaw.

The Ronald Press Company for permission to quote from Albert R. Kitzhaber, Robert M. Gorrell, and Paul Roberts, *Education for College: Improving the High School Curriculum,* copyright © 1961 The Ronald Press Company; and from W. Nelson Francis, *The Structure of American English,* copyright © 1958 The Ronald Press Company.

Bertrand Russell for permission to quote from an article in the *Saturday Review.*

St. Martin's Press for permission to quote from Joshua Whatmough, *Language: A Modern Synthesis;* A. C. Bradley, *Oxford Lectures on English Poetry* and *Shakespearean Tragedy.*

Saturday Review for permission to quote from articles by John Van Druten, Clifton Fadiman, Edmund S. Morgan, Charles L. Todd, Marchette Chute, John

Ciardi, Judson T. Shaplin, Norman Cousins, James K. Feibleman, J. W. Krutch, and Bertrand Russell.

Scott, Foresman & Company for permission to quote from James H. Sledd, *A Short Introduction to English Grammar,* copyright © 1959 by Scott, Foresman & Company.

Charles Scribner's Sons and Odhams Press Limited for permission to quote from Winston Churchill, *My Early Life.*

Dorothy J. Shaw for permission to quote from Charles B. Shaw ed., *American Essays.*

The Society of Authors and the Public Trustee for permission to quote from George Bernard Shaw, *Man and Superman.*

Frank Sullivan for permission to quote from *A Rock in Every Snowball.*

The University of Chicago Press for permission to quote from Robert M. Hutchins, *The University of Utopia;* and from R. S. Crane ed., *Critics and Criticism.*

University of North Carolina Press for permission to quote from an article by Northrop Frye and from Cleanth Brooks, *Modern Poetry and the Tradition.*

University of Texas Press for permission to quote from an article by Archibald A. Hill.

The Viking Press for permission to quote from Phyllis McGinley, *A Short Walk from the Station;* Lionel Trilling, *The Liberal Imagination;* Carl Van Doren, *Three Worlds;* Arthur Miller, *Death of a Salesman;* and John Steinbeck, *The Grapes of Wrath.*

Wadsworth Publishing Company for permission to quote from Hans P. Guth, *Words and Ideas;* and from Hans P. Guth ed., *Literature.*

The Ward Ritchie Press for permission to quote from an article by Aldous Huxley.

Edmund Wilson for permission to quote from *Classics and Commercials.*

The World Publishing Company for permission to quote from *Webster's New World Dictionary* of the American Language, College Edition. Copyright © 1962 by The World Publishing Company.

Table of Contents

part one

The Discipline of English

The teaching of English seems simple from a distance but becomes more complicated as one takes a closer view. To many laymen, the English teacher is the person who teaches students how to spell, where to insert commas, and whether or not to split their infinitives. The more of an amateur the teacher of English is, the more he is likely to be forever preoccupied with the mere outward tokens of literacy. As he begins to take his professional responsibilities more seriously, he comes to realize how much more is involved. There is no point in teaching students how to spell words they do not know or care how to use. There is no point in punctuating sentences that were not worth writing. There is no point in teaching the finer points of linguistic etiquette to students who have not learned the first principles of articulate, mature, forceful expression.

Similar reservations apply to the more sophisticated popular concept of the English teacher as a guardian of our literary heritage. Between the outward tokens of familiarity with literature and a genuine and lasting relationship with it there is as much difference as between the unread leatherbound Works on the shelf and

A Preliminary View

the dog-eared paperback on the desk. We accomplish little if we instill a perfunctory and unavailing piety toward literary classics in students who are not making progress toward self-motivated, unassisted appreciation of a Shakespeare play, a George Eliot novel. Studying the biographies of Hawthorne and Whitman remains fruitless if our students as adults will never on their own read a serious contemporary American playwright, novelist, or poet. Truly to teach writing and reading, we must affect our students in ways that escape superficial observation and measurement.

The teacher interested in the larger implications of his task soon finds that there is no scarcity of relevant material calling for his attention. Scholarship, research, and teaching in English and American language and literature make up one of our major educational industries. In each major area of English, the material awaiting the inquisitive teacher on the library shelves is of staggering bulk. Moreover, aside from sheer volume, the teacher soon realizes that it is difficult to see in its mutual relations. It is hard to relate to a coherent general perspective. No one seriously investigating the present state of English can help being bewildered by conflicting emphases and approaches, by strong but contradictory claims.

Part of the difficulty is the growing tendency toward specialization that English shares with other academic fields. Often there is little communication between those interested in the workings of language and those interested in the workings of literature. Within such large divisions, the student of dialects may have little to say to the student of semantics; the Chaucer specialist may have little time to listen to the Faulkner specialist. Much material published in scholarly journals and monographs presupposes a degree of specialized interest that narrowly limits its appeal. As in other fields, so in English, the young scholar aiming at academic recognition typically proceeds not by developing the broadest possible interests but by staking out a relatively narrow area of language studies or of literary history for detailed investigation.

More serious than mere compartmentalization are differences in point of view, in attitude toward language, and in interpretation of educational responsibility. In his course work, in professional journals, and at professional conferences, the prospective English teacher is the object of much conflicting advice. The answer to the question "What is English?" varies widely, depending on the background of the speaker. Often, what at first seems a comprehensive interpretation of our task as teachers of English turns out to be but the lengthened shadow of a specialist's personal interest and commitment. In his bleaker moods, the English teacher foresees an ever new branching out of emphases and approaches, of movements and countermovements, until

> how many Grecian tents do stand
> Hollow upon this plain, so many hollow factions.
> —Shakespeare, *Troilus and Cressida,* Act I, Sc. 3.

The pessimist can claim with some justice that English teachers are united by a common label and divided by incompatible and mutually unintelligible interests, terminologies, and commitments.

Though the teacher may give in to such pessimistic reflections in his tired moments, his work from day to day must obviously be based on a different assumption. If English teachers are to function effectively in the classroom, they must be able to overcome the tendency of their profession toward fragmentation of effort. After the spokesmen of special areas and distinctive approaches have had their say, the teacher must be able to pick up the pieces and go back to his classroom with some coherent rationale of his discipline. He must be able to see current problems and controversies in perspective. He must discount what is faddish and polemical, just as he must discount what represents mere unexamined tradition and educational inertia. He must see the specialist in his true light as the expert on a limited subsection of a large dynamic discipline.

The Subject Matter of English

For the present and future teacher of English, the most urgent need is to form a conception of his discipline as more than a chorus of conflicting voices, as more than the sum of multitudinous unrelated parts. Between the popular stereotype of the English teacher as the Emily Post of language, and the disillusioned view of him as the advocate of the most unpredictable and diverse points of view, there is a view of English as a discipline whose various parts become meaningful as they support and illuminate each other. The subject matter of English is not an accidental accumulation of more or less remotely related areas of interest. It is unified by its concern with the workings of language—its purposes, functions, and effects. To counteract the effects of specialization and fragmentation, English teachers must define their discipline in such a way as to stress this underlying unity.

The teacher of English teaches students to understand and use language. Understanding language means having an informed awareness of how language works in utterances ranging from a simple everyday statement to a complex lyric poem. Competence in using language means being an articulate and responsible speaker and writer, but also being a perceptive, responsive listener and reader, able to deal with material ranging from utilitarian prose to complex and demanding imaginative literature. A firm grasp of the lexical and grammatical substance of a sentence is as essential in reading prose as in reading poetry, in reading Charles Beard as in reading James Joyce. Conversely, adequate response to the imaginative and emotional dimensions of language is as essential in reading a columnist as in reading a sonneteer. Typically, the English teacher's concerns range from the mechanical to the intangible, from the technical to the humane, from the trivial to the sublime. Without a firm grounding in the technical details of his discipline, his teaching becomes opinionated, improvised, superficial. Without a concern for the human relevance of his subject matter, his teaching becomes a barren inventory of technicalities.

To assure his technical competence, the English teacher must have a more or less thorough grounding in a number of subjects. He must have an understanding of the sound system of English. He must come to see how a limited number of variations in position and movement of tongue and lips and in the function of our vocal cords produce the rich and varied phenomenon of human speech. He must have an understanding of how "this wonderfully complex symphony" is represented in a writing system using "only the letters of the alphabet and a sprinkling of punctuation conventions"[1] and yet, in the hands of a master, is capable of trans-

[1] Henry Lee Smith, Jr., "The Teacher and the World of English," *The English Journal,* XLVII (April, 1958), 182.

scribing a wide range of human thought and emotion. The teacher needs
an extensive familiarity with the resources of English vocabulary, with
the ways of words and their meanings, concrete and abstract, popular and
technical, clearly conveyed or merely suggested. He knows how, in competent use of the language, context identifies among the multiple meanings of a given word the one intended, with an astonishing capacity for
economy and precision of expression, richness of implication, and subtlety
of nuance. He needs a knowledge of English **grammar,** of the features
that make the difference between pairs like

> Gentlemen prefer blondes.
> Blondes prefer gentlemen.
>
> The physician studied burns.
> The physician's study burns.
>
> The nurse neglected the patient.
> The nurse was neglected by the patient.

He needs to know how a limited stock of grammatical devices is used to
work words into structures ranging from simple subject-predicate statements to sentences of paragraph length.

While the grammarian charts the recurrent patterns, the principles of
arrangement and interdependence in sentences, the authority on **usage**
explores the significance of variations in pronunciation, vocabulary, and
grammar from individual to individual and group to group. He investigates our choices among *alternative* words, word forms, and constructions.
In the study of dialects, he explores regional variations; in the study of
the social implications of usage, he explores differences in language habits
associated with differences in education, prestige, or social status. In the
study of style, he notes the different kinds of language used by the same
person in different situations and for different effects. He explores the
reflection in language of formality and informality, seriousness and facetiousness, folksiness and exclusiveness. Usage is the general heading for a
study of the differences between "We ain't got none" and "We don't have
any"; between "You are requested to leave the premises" and "Get out";
between "I shew thee glad tidings" and "I bring you good news."

In all these areas, a knowledge of the history of the language is
needed to help the teacher see underlying relationships and to provide an
explanation for much that to the contemporary observer is merely capricious and bewildering. The English spelling system, a nightmare for the
observer of rational or practical bent, makes a certain amount of sense
when seen as a record of an earlier stage of the language. Thus, the spelling of *knight* and *light* preserves a stage of the language when these words
did not rhyme with modern *bite* but were much closer than they are now
to German *Knecht* and *Licht,* derived from the same Germanic ancestors.
Etymology, the study of word history and word roots, helps us master

large portions of English that employ recurrent Latin and Greek elements. Thus, awareness of the Latin *culpa*, "fault," helps us correlate *culpable, culprit,* and *exculpate;* awareness of the Greek *eu–*, "good, well," helps explain *eulogy, euphemism,* and *euphony.*

Characteristic features as well as apparent irregularities of English grammar become meaningful when seen as relics of or departures from grammatical patterns found in other Indo-European languages. Such apparently isolated features as the plural ending of *oxen,* the *–'s* of *sorcerer's apprentice* and *week's pay,* or the past forms in *sing–sang, ring–rang* are partial survivals of intricate systems of word forms still fully preserved in the oldest documents of English literature. Similarly, variations in usage can be more fruitfully discussed when one recognizes their historical dimension. Thus, when we point out that formal written English requires *this kind* rather than *these kind,* we should also know that *these kind* occurs in the work of writers from Sir Philip Sidney to Jane Austen. Since both are authors with eminently rational minds, we will hesitate to ascribe the lack of agreement in *these kind* to an illiterate disregard for logic.

If one way of making the technical workings of language meaningful is to see them in historical perspective, another is to relate them to the larger questions of purpose and effect. **Rhetoric** investigates the structure of prose discourse. By gradations more subtle than the traditional categories of description, narration, exposition, and argument, it ranges over the whole spectrum of writing that describes, reports, informs, explains, argues, convinces, persuades, suggests. Insofar as the structure of discourse reflects logical processes involved in the marshaling of information and ideas, the rhetorician must be a student of applied logic. Insofar as language is more than a rigorous translation of logical processes into words, the rhetorician must be a student of the kind of semantics that explores verbal resources, verbal pitfalls, and verbal strategies. Insofar as the rhetorician is concerned with effectiveness and appropriateness of manner, he must be a student of style.

Where the informative and expository uses of language shade over into the aesthetic and imaginative ones, the teacher becomes a student of **literary criticism** and literary theory. He needs an understanding of the role of imaginative experience in general, and of the ways in which literature in particular may mirror, explore, shape, and transform life. He needs to know the major genres and their particular conditions and limitations. In fiction, he must know something about the resources and technical requirements of the novel and short story; in drama, he must be able to deal with characteristic appeals of tragedy and comedy; in poetry, he must be familiar with some of the characteristic effects of lyric, satire, and epic. Regardless of the genre, understanding literature requires an awareness of the tools and devices that determine both the over-all structure and the line-by-line texture of a work: rhythm, metaphor, symbol, allusion, irony, paradox; the manifold elements that make for regularity and irregularity, variety and order, cogency of form and richness of implication.

As features of our language become meaningful when seen in historical perspective, so many features of our literature become meaningful when seen in their historical relations. The early novel owes many of its distinctive features to its kinship with a loosely jointed biographical narrative of travel and adventure. The modern novel in much of its narrative technique mirrors the preoccupation of writers like Henry James, James Joyce, and Virginia Woolf with problems of perspective, of point of view. The sonnet as a form grew out of a characteristic world of thought and feeling, just as the closed couplets of Dryden and Pope are not isolated phenomena but part of a tradition marked by distinctive assumptions and practices. The work of a writer becomes more intelligible as we begin to understand both the assumptions he accepted and those he rejected or modified. Much of the irony in the love poetry of John Donne is directed against earlier conventions of poems about love; the disillusionment of A. E. Housman and Thomas Hardy is in part a reaction against the more affirmative tone of their Victorian predecessors. No writer produces in a vacuum; he is typically influenced, in ways not always obvious, by a rich body of tradition and convention.

Though the study of literary history thus illuminates the literature both of the present and of the past, its primary function is to lead us to those writers whose work is of permanent significance. Certain writers are too central in our cultural heritage for the English teacher to have a mere nodding acquaintance with them. Certainly, he must in his study of literature reach the point where he can go back with pleasure and profit, and on his own, to Chaucer, Shakespeare, and Milton. But beyond these, there are other writers the English teacher must know more or less intimately if his teaching of literature is not going to be amateurish or capricious. Such writers are, in British fiction, Henry Fielding, Charles Dickens, George Eliot, James Joyce; in American fiction, Nathaniel Hawthorne, Herman Melville, Henry James, William Faulkner. Such writers are, among the poets, John Donne, William Blake, Emily Dickinson; Wordsworth, Coleridge, and Keats; Pound, Eliot, and Yeats. Such writers are, among the critics, Pope and Arnold; among the satirists, Swift and Twain and Shaw.

In dealing with the themes and forms of such writers, in coming to terms with the difficulties of interpretation and of judgment that they pose, the teacher develops that maturity of response to literature, and that familiarity with its essential qualities and paradoxes, that he needs to make his work in the classroom sound and fruitful. Their work provides him with the evidence against which to test proposed theories and definitions and approaches. It provides him with the background against which to see current preoccupations and current vogues.

The major problem faced by the teacher trying to assure his competence in his subject matter is how to combine an adequate grounding in detail with a sound and coherent over-all perspective. To the extent that linguist, rhetorician, critic, and historian go their separate ways, the classroom teacher must form his own estimate of how their contributions fit into a more comprehensive, more balanced picture. To earn the right to assess the specialist's contribution, the teacher must first learn to understand the specialist's language and thus meet him, at least within limits, on his own terms. But if instead of making this assessment the teacher merely takes the specialist's word for "what English is," he may find himself in the position of the blind man who felt the elephant's trunk and decided an elephant was an animal very much like a snake.

Major Current Trends

One preliminary contribution to the establishment of a unified concept of English is to map some of the territory for which the teacher of English is responsible. Another is to identify some major currents that affect the teaching of English and to relate them to a more general perspective. No matter how various such developments may seem on the surface, a number of major trends in the study and teaching of language and literature are clearly coming into their own. Though they have been developing for several decades, they have only recently begun to affect school and college in decisive ways. Whether or not they are "the wave of the future," no responsible teacher of English can afford to ignore them. Whether to the individual teacher they seem aggressively new or in part already stale, sound or superficially fashionable, congenial or alien to his training and temperament, they are leaving a profound imprint on the teaching of English at home and abroad.

Taking deliberately the long and comprehensive view, one can identify four major movements that in the last several decades have decisively affected what the teacher of English does in his classroom and what the scholar does at his desk. People in English vary greatly in how consciously they identify with a school of thought, in how deliberately they repeat the catchwords of a group or of a conference manifesto. And yet one can hardly pick up a textbook or a syllabus published in recent years that does not in some way reflect the influence of the four major developments here at issue.

The most concrete of these developments is the revolution in the study and teaching of grammar under the influence of **linguistics**. Claiming status as the most concrete of the social sciences, linguistic science developed separately from and sometimes in opposition to traditional

philology as taught in the graduate schools of most large universities. One
of its pioneers in the United States was Leonard Bloomfield, whose
Language appeared in 1933. Among the teachers and textbook authors
pioneering the application of linguistics to the teaching of English were
Charles C. Fries, Harold Whitehall, Paul Roberts, W. Nelson Francis, and
James H. Sledd.

Unlike much of nineteenth-century philology, linguistics developed
in application to languages such as those of the American Indian, *outside
the Indo-European language family.* Here the investigator, confronted
with radically new and different linguistic structures, was often forced to
forego familiar categories and preconceptions. Furthermore, he worked
with unrecorded spoken languages and was thus forced to deal directly
with the sounds of *speech,* rather than seeing language through its
secondary reflection in a written tradition. Finally, the traditional philologist had been typically interested in comparing a language with its
older historical forms and with the present and older forms of related
languages. In the work of the linguistic anthropologist, the emphasis was
necessarily on obtaining an accurate, reliable description of an unknown
or only imperfectly known language in its current form.

In the teaching of grammar, the development of applied English
linguistics meant new terms and categories, but above all a new attitude.
Traditionally, the teacher had treated the schoolroom grammar as if it had
been created on the eighth day. It was something known, something that
had been covered, something learned once and for all. One saw no need
to start from the beginning, to work it up all over again, to reconstruct it
from its foundations, using current speech as evidence and guide. One saw
no need to restore his original innocence in matters grammatical, to ask:
Where do we start if we wish to develop a system of grammar? What
standards do we apply; what procedures are reliable?

In trying to convince the teacher of the need for exactly such a reconstruction, the linguist relied on two familiar arguments. The established
school grammar was modeled on the traditional grammars of Latin and
Greek. It followed them, first in its arrangement of items and categories,
and second in the definition of their qualities. Discussing the noun, the
traditional grammarian mentally had before him the Latin:

Nominative	*vir*
Genitive	*viri*
Dative	*viro*
Accusative	*virum*
Ablative	*viro*

In some languages this pattern could be filled in with relative completeness and ease, as in the German:

Nominative	*der Mann*
Genitive	*des Mannes*
Dative	*dem Manne*
Accusative	*den Mann*

Even here, it will be noted, the ablative presented a problem. This problem appears in multiplied form in the English:

Nominative	*the man*
Genitive	*of the man*
Dative	*to the man*
Accusative	*the man*

Here, an analogue to Latin case structure has been created by simply repeating the same "plain" or all-purpose form *man* four times and by eking out the Latin scheme with prepositions translating relationships typically signaled by the case forms of Latin.

Similarly, the German *"Ich gehe—du gehst—er geht"* is a reasonably close parallel to the Latin *"amo—amas—amat"* pattern. But the list "I went—you went—he went—we went—they went," repeating the same form of the verb five times, is again an exercise in contrastive Indo-European grammar. The declensions and conjugations of traditional grammar may thus be said to have been haunted by linguistic ghosts. These were self-explanatory to the historical and comparative linguist but did not contribute to a simple and efficient description of the current language. Conversely, traditional grammar was likely to slight features for which Greek and Latin had no exact precedent, and thus no ready-made terms and categories. Thus, from the linguist's point of view, the first major drawback of the traditional grammar was that it attempted to fit English into a foreign mold.

Secondly, the traditional grammar defined its major categories in ambiguous terms. Summarizing the characteristic meanings of the major parts of speech, it relied on oversimplified "notional," or meaning-based, definitions. A verb like *to walk* "expresses action," but so does the noun *walk*. *To thieve* expresses action, but so does *theft*; as *to act* expresses action, so does the noun *action* itself. The various *ways* in which verb and noun refer to concepts involving action the traditional grammar was not equipped to differentiate. Similarly, the noun *redness* is the name of a quality, but so, in some sense not clearly ruled out by the familiar notional definition of the noun, is the adjective *red*. Apparently even someone who claimed to rely on the traditional definitions told nouns, verbs, and adjectives apart by other means.

The linguist's characteristic solution here was to abandon the attempt at semantic, meaning-based definition and to point instead to the concrete, tangible signals that distinguish one major category from the other. For school grammar, the most important of these are position and inflection, that is, word order and word form. The role of position can be graphically demonstrated by the use of test frames. In "The _____ gave a _____ to the _____," the forms filling the blanks, regardless of their meaning, would belong to the same major category. This category would include items whose appearance may typically be signaled by *a, an,* or *the;* which typically appear as subjects of verbs or as objects of verbs and prepositions. In "The evening was rather _____ but had a very _____ ending," the forms filling the blanks belong in a major category containing items that typically modify nouns or appear as complements of linking verbs, and that typically fit into positions after "intensifiers" like *very* or *rather.*

Inflection, or word form, helps group together words that appear with the plural or possessive *s,* or with the other less common plural forms: *boy, boy's, boys; man, man's, men; car, car's, cars.* Verbs typically have the third person singular *s* in the present tense: *asks, meets, walks.* Another major inflectional category includes words with the comparative *er* and the superlative *est: taller, tallest; greater, greatest; friendlier, friendliest.* By combining positional and inflectional criteria, the linguist could hope to substitute concrete and relatively foolproof description for the familiar definitions. Additional tangible signals he could draw on were characteristic word-forming suffixes (*–ment, –ness, –hood, –ance* for nouns, for instance) or contrasting stress (*cóntrast, contrást; óbject, objéct,* etc. to distinguish nouns and verbs). By moving in this general direction, the linguist was able to substitute formulas and test patterns that could be concretely manipulated for the more abstract and ambiguous concepts of conventional grammar.

The objections to the linguist's arguments, and more generally to his proposed reformation of English grammar, were many. Teachers satisfied with the tried and true protested that the "scientific" hairsplitting of the linguist was hardly needed in dealing with the elementary problems of their students. Humanists, alarmed by the concrete, mechanistic, scientific emphasis of the new grammars, feared that to surrender grammar to the scientist would be a mere prelude to the weakening of the humanist's position in other related areas. Interested in language as meaningful discourse, they justly feared that the linguist's preoccupation with the tangible would lead to a general shift of emphasis in language education.

In the encounter with skeptical or hostile colleagues, however, the linguist was aided by his having transformed grammar from a weary convention into an intellectually challenging, rapidly developing discipline. The alert and responsible teacher came to scoff and stayed to study and to learn. Today there is hardly a textbook or convention address that does not in some way—eagerly or reluctantly, aggressively or diplomatically—show the influence of the linguist's re-examination of English grammar.

In view of much vigorous and conflicting activity, it is unlikely that any one new system will in the near future become *the* widely adopted and taught grammar of English. Rather, we will for the foreseeable future have to adopt James Sledd's definition of a grammar as "one of several possible descriptions of a language."[2] In the meantime, the effect of applied English linguistics on the teaching of grammar will vary in detail but be broadly similar in its general results. First, *the school grammar will be a more authentically English grammar than it was in the past.* It will show the distinctive features of modern English as well as those it has in common with its Indo-European relatives and ancestors. Second, *the grammar taught in the schools will be more concrete, and to that extent more teachable, than it used to be.* It will be focused on things that can be shown, demonstrated, manipulated. Above all, grammar will cease to be a subject on which every educated person can assume to be his own expert. It will gain in academic status as it becomes, like other areas of our discipline, a field which requires of the teacher a continuing interest and a familiarity with current work.

The second major movement affecting the teaching of English, though it goes back several decades before recent developments in applied English linguistics, has been reinforced by them. Since the twenties, there has been a continual effort to modify the conventional schoolroom attitude toward usage. Characteristically, the schools have concentrated not on "What is language?" but on "What is right language?" The conventional answer given by the schools was that right English was the "correct" English considered the badge of the educated man. In practice, the teaching of correct English took the form of drilling the student in a collection of miscellaneous usages differing from those of his native speech and derived from a tradition of textbooks and handbooks of unexamined authority. The traditionally oriented teacher settled a question of *different than* as against *different from* by looking it up in Woolley or in Webster's, preferably in an earlier than the current edition.

In part, the traditional rulings on correctness were a legacy of centuries when English was increasingly replacing Latin as the language of education, scholarship, and serious literature. Neoclassical writers like Dryden and Swift tended to assume that language, like literature, had to be "reduced to rule" if it was to approach the beauty, clarity, and vigor of classical Latin. Like neoclassicists in other countries, they regarded the vernacular as a wild growth that had to be carefully pruned if it was to serve for literary purposes. In practice, such pruning took the form of ob-

[2] *A Short Introduction to English Grammar* (Chicago: Scott, Foresman & Company, 1959), p. 184. Copyright © 1959 Scott, Foresman & Company, Chicago.

jections to isolated usages that seemed to lack or violate classical precedent. Thus, when Dryden declared that the preposition at the end of
a sentence was a fault, he presumably was guided by his feeling for Latin
word order, which rules out such a construction. Similarly, comparison
with Latin rules for the uses of case forms led eighteenth-century grammarians to condemn the object form of a pronoun after a linking verb
(It's *me.*) and the subject form of the interrogative as the object of a verb
(*Who* did you ask?). In these and similar cases, rules constructed on the
model of Latin grammar led writers to condemn as errors or corruptions
expressions common in contemporary educated usage and, in some
notable instances, in their own writings.

As developed and codified by the authors of nineteenth-century textbooks, the rules of correctness became an inventory of objections to
familiar features of everyday speech. These objections were rationalized
on logical and rhetorical grounds. Etymology was taken to require that
between, etymologically related to *two,* refer to two of a kind. Redundancy was made the basis of objections to *cannot help but* and *reason is
because.* The need for accurate distinctions was said to require observing
the difference between *further* and *farther, fewer* and *less, if* and *whether,
each other* and *one another.* Confusion of grammatical categories was
objected to in the use of *like* as a conjunction, of *due to* as a preposition.
Logical consistency in grammatical relationships was said to require
"everybody took *his"* rather than "everybody took *theirs."* Many such
arguments reflected a concern with precise and logical expression. What
served to discredit them was their miscellaneous and unco-ordinated
nature. Too often they were clearly *ad hoc* arguments designed to discredit
a specific debated expression rather than part of a coherent and generally
applicable rationale of usage.

There never was any question that many usages taught as correct dif-
fered from the natural speech of the students; the teacher, in fact, never
tired of telling them so. Studies in the twenties and thirties documented
what was obvious to the alert listener: many usages conventionally listed
as incorrect were in current use by educated and influential people in all
walks of life. Examination of the work of great writers, both past and
recent, provided any alert reader with ample instances of alleged solecisms
and illiteracies.

Through the influence of studies such as those of Sterling A. Leonard,
of Marckwardt and Walcott, and of Charles C. Fries, and through textbooks such as those of Porter G. Perrin, the simple distinction between
right and wrong gradually gave way to a more flexible and realistic **liberal**
attitude toward usage. Teachers began to replace the alternative of correct
and incorrect with the distinction between standard and nonstandard—
the former the language of education, publishing, higher echelon business
and administration; the latter the natural speech of people with relatively

little formal education, often marked by some regional dialect features. *Within* standard English, teachers began to recognize the difference between a formal written standard and an informal conversational standard. Thus, many expressions once considered a sign of ignorance and ill manners were restored to their rightful status as characteristic of an informal, richly idiomatic current standard speech. The question no longer was what was simply and absolutely right but what was appropriate for the degree of formality indicated by the occasion. *Appropriateness replaced correctness as the criterion of "good English."*

It had long been suspected that traditional instruction, far from teaching students to use language with force and competent ease, had by and large had an inhibiting effect. Trying to escape from the constantly criticized patterns of their native speech, many students wrote a tortured no-man's-language, substituting a stilted, unnatural diction for the sweet sound of English undefiled. Even in adult life, their instinctive reaction to the approach of an English teacher was to "watch their language," that is, to lapse into a sheepish silence. The liberal position made it possible to try a more positive approach to usage: to sharpen the student's perception of meanings and implications, to develop in him a feeling for the color and variety of language, to help him choose suitable and effective expression for what he had to say.

Such don'ts as remained in this approach were based on a realistic appraisal of preferences and conventions that a writer ignores at the risk of alienating his reader. That in educated English certain types of sentence fragments are conventionally considered illogical and substandard is an observation the writer disregards at his peril. To split an infinitive may incur the avoidable displeasure of a teacher or editor taught to dislike that construction. The general tendency of educated American English toward informality and the spread, often largely unacknowledged, of liberal attitudes toward language have combined to reduce considerably the number and the seriousness of the shibboleths the student needs to know.

Many pioneers in applied English linguistics and the development of the new grammars had earlier participated in the movement to liberalize attitudes toward usage, and the two movements to some extent merged and went hand in hand. Nevertheless, the effect of linguistics on the treatment of usage has been two-sided. On the one hand, the linguists have scathingly attacked the theoretical shortcomings of the traditional doctrine of correctness. They have worked, often successfully, to restore the native speaker's confidence in his command of the language. In the schools, their influence has strengthened the general movement away from the obsessive overemphasis on correctness that used to keep teachers from attending to matters equally or more important.

On the debit side, there are only limited scientific means for recording the social repercussions of usage and the psychological effects of style. Responses to nuances of usage and style are subjective and depend on complex psychological and cultural variables. Authoritative treatment here requires the trained discrimination of the sensitive observer. In some areas, such as dialect geography, the student of usage receives substantial help from such "scientific" techniques as the careful gathering and evaluation of questionnaire responses. But such techniques are too blunt to register satisfactorily the nuances that are perceived by someone who uses language with discrimination and force and who has the feeling for language that comes from much patient listening and much experimenting with one's linguistic resources. As teachers concentrate on the growing body of concrete scientific knowledge about the signaling system of the language, there is a danger that we may come to neglect some of the most important things about language simply because they cannot be objectively measured.

Similar reservations concerning the growing influence of linguistics apply in regard to the third major movement of concern to today's teacher of English. Considered by some a passing fashion, this movement has nevertheless in the last twenty years or so profoundly affected the teaching of English in school and college. Though of the greatest human and educational importance, it never succeeded in gaining the prestige and perquisites that the academic world bestows on scholarly and scientific disciplines more safely and solidly limited in scope and method.

It had long been true that in his concern with concrete linguistic fact on the one hand and imaginative literature on the other the scholar and teacher of English had neglected a third major dimension of his subject: *the responsible use of language in everyday life.* Students who knew all about declarative, imperative, and interrogative sentences could not tell a plain statement of fact from casual conjecture, let alone from subtle innuendo. Distinguished historical linguists were painfully naive when confronted with any reasonably sophisticated kind of political polemics. English teachers let pass the opportunity of alerting future lawyers and judges and jurymen to the manifold hidden premises and suggestions lurking in a seemingly matter-of-fact announcement. The English teacher concerned to preserve "good English" was often no more aware of his human and political responsibilities than his European colleague who extolled the glories of classical Latin while leaving his charges the helpless prey of the grossest and most suicidal kind of chauvinistic rhetoric.

Semantics, in its various forms and applications, developed as an attempt to chart for the student the more important relations between word and referent, between language and the world. It started from the realization that language is always more than a code for the transmission of data. It is a complex, and often dangerously misleading, instrument of human relations. Far from merely passing on a message, it betrays the speaker—his attitudes, background, ambitions, hopes, and fears. Far from merely describing reality, it sets up the terms and categories according to which we interpret—and shape—reality. On the one hand, it is a source of power, enabling us to impose our wills on others through the magic of words. On the other hand, it hems us in and limits us, until we become the prisoners of our own terms and slogans.

Wherever teachers of English have recognized the central role of their subject in a liberal education, the concepts of semantics have influenced handbooks, rhetorics, and books of readings. At colleges and universities where the course in freshman English was firmly dedicated to the purposes of general education, semantics, whether or not so called, furnished much of the perspective and materials for the course. Students were trained to distinguish between report and judgment, and to recognize the implied imperatives in judgments of value. They thus became aware of the difficulties obscured by glib public promises to stick to the facts and look at the record. They were alerted to the honorific or derogatory connotations of many words that to the linguistically naive seem simply objective labels. Thus, they began to recognize the element of verbal manipulation in labels like *statesman* and *politician, labor leader* and *union boss, business leader* and *tycoon.* They became familiar with degrees of abstraction and levels of generalization and with the problem of keeping abstractions from becoming purely verbal by anchoring them to concrete referents.

Many students both in high school and college thus received elementary and much needed guidance in the art of distinguishing between sense and non-sense, between honest argument and verbal sleight-of-hand. Ideally, they thus became better prepared than some of their contemporaries to participate responsibly in the public dialogue without which a free society cannot survive. They learned more about the realities of political life in a single hour devoted to the semantic analysis of a newspaper editorial than from a series of lectures devoted to the structure of governmental institutions. They began to understand requirements of fruitful debate that have escaped the notice of eminent scholars and educators.

The scientific linguist, by temperament and training, was often poorly equipped to sympathize with this kind of instruction. He missed the commitment to a rigorous methodology and to rigorous standards of verification that he, like his colleagues in the social sciences, had adopted from the natural scientist. Attempts at a scientific semantics, reminiscent of developments in experimental and statistical psychology, proceed by isolating from a mass of complex variables those that can be more or less firmly controlled. As in experimental psychology, there is little prospect that the complexities of responsibility and human purpose can be in a significant and comprehensive way illuminated by scientifically acceptable means. In the meantime, as much as ever, our students need to be alerted to what is hinted as well as to what is said; as much as ever, they need to develop the skill of reading between the lines. What needs to be said, from the point of view of the expert on language, after a speech by a mob orator foreign or domestic will now as in the past have to be said by someone with wide experience, a quick ear, unusual linguistic sophistication, and a lively moral sense. To the development of these qualities such semanticists as S. I. Hayakawa have made a contribution not likely to be excelled by anyone committed to rigorous scientific standards.

Part of the attractiveness, but also part of the limitation of semantics has been that it has served the hard-pressed liberal in the classroom as a welcome weapon against various kinds of intellectual and political obscurantism. As Stuart Chase observed, "Semantics is the demagogue's worst friend."[3] However, the very effectiveness of semantics as a tool in controversy may tempt the teacher to abuse it in the pursuit of short-range objectives. His goal should be to give his students the kind of semantic sophistication that will make them knowledgeable and responsible users of language in their later lives. In order not to compromise this goal, the teacher must be careful not to apply to the verbal behavior of his intellectual or political opponents a kind of analysis that he would not apply to his own. He must further be careful not to confuse the identification of the emotional, communal, and generally extralogical elements in language with a crude debunking of them. In short, he must employ semantics to raise, rather than to shut off by premature and oversimplified answers, some of the most crucial questions about our dealings with language.

The fourth and last major movement to be discussed here brings us to what is usually the English teacher's first love—his concern for imaginative literature. The study and teaching of literature used to be modeled to a considerable extent on a type of philology taken over from the German universities. Discussion of an author meant extensive preliminary treatment of his biography. Much effort was devoted to establishing his social, economic, and cultural milieu. Much time was devoted to the study of sources, to detailed comparison of the author's work with earlier treatments of the same theme, to the search for precedents for his use of plot elements or features of style. Major stylistic epochs were defined in terms of predominant philosophical and stylistic trends. Much detailed philological work was done on etymologies, meanings, dialectal variants in earlier texts.

What has happened in the classroom and in the textbooks during the last few decades is a massive shift in emphasis from these important auxiliary disciplines to the no less important central activity toward which they all tend: *the close reading of the text itself.* Under the influence of the **new criticism,** discussion came to center more and more on close textual

3 *Power of Words* (New York: Harcourt, Brace & World, Inc., 1954), p. 235.

analysis with an eye toward the wholeness of the given work. College text-books like those by Cleanth Brooks and Robert Penn Warren, and dozens of others modeled on them, made it their business to make the student go back to the literary text for definite answers about its structure and form. A whole generation of students was taught to dwell on the implications of key metaphors, to trace the recurrence of a central symbol. They were alerted to crucial ironies, to paradoxes setting up thematic polarities, to conflicts solved in the dialectic of dramatic or poetic structure.

The phenomenal popularity of the short lyric and the short story as objects of study and teaching was due in part to their being perfect objects for a close and yet reasonably comprehensive analysis. In the short stories of Hemingway, Faulkner, and Joyce, the teacher could explore details of language and structure while at the same time relating them to the central situation or the central conflict that gave unity to the whole. He was thus able to maintain a Coleridgean perspective, stressing unity in variety, similarity in disparateness, order in spite of complexity. The symptoms of a change were obvious in course descriptions and in literature anthologies. Survey courses shifted from the cursory inventory of literary history to the close reading of selected major works. Period courses received increasing competition from courses in the literary genres, where emphasis was clearly on the literature rather than on the intellectual, cultural, and biographical milieu. Detailed discussion of what students had read began to rival the lecture as a means of sharpening their literary perception.

Fears that literature was increasingly being read in a truncated or inbred fashion, out of context, proved exaggerated. One way of alerting the reader of *Oedipus Rex* to the dramatist's attitudes toward priests, gods, and kings is to deliver an introductory lecture on Greek politics and religion. Another way, and perhaps one producing a more lasting impression, is to make the student pay careful attention to what attitudes toward priests, gods, and kings are revealed in the play itself. By keeping introductory materials to a minimum, the teacher decreases the danger of providing material that may prejudge the reader's response. If "the text is the thing," the student has a better than usual chance of approaching crucial problems of interpretation with an open mind.

Nor does such an approach go counter to the need for making the student conscious of characteristic differences of style. He is more likely to learn to know Byron well if he is encouraged to respond to Byron's characteristic idiom, in a spirit of "wise passiveness," than if he were to read him with preconceived ideas about Romantic and neoclassic elements in his style. Careful attention to "what is there" discourages the student from forcing an author into a preconceived framework; it gets the student used to conceding an author his own characteristic means of expression. A style consciousness thus inductively developed is likely to be a surer guide to literary appreciation than would be secondhand information, however authoritatively developed and effectively presented it is.

The temptations and pitfalls of a text-centered approach are familiar. Typically, the teacher brought to it a knowledge of the historical and biographical context that he could no longer take for granted in his students. Inevitably, he was tempted to present as derived from the text what he had actually derived from his knowledge of literary history. The more candid teacher, even though setting out to teach masterpieces and major writers, soon learned to arrange his course so that one major writer and one masterpiece would illuminate another. He learned to strike a balance between treating the work of literature as a unique construct, to be taken and interpreted on its own terms, and treating it as a document acquiring its full meaning only when seen in its biographical and historical relations.

When such a balance is missing, the text-centered approach encourages capricious and esoteric interpretation. The teacher must try very hard not to turn literary criticism into an arcane study in which the instructor, after appropriate abracadabra, produces the rabbit that the student is never able to find for himself. For all its emphasis on metaphor and symbol, the new criticism to some extent failed to provide firm criteria—and firm limits—for metaphorical and symbolic interpretation. Encouraged by the example of critics like Kenneth Burke and William Empson in an uncontrolled free-association technique, teachers made part symbolic of whole, quality symbolic of object, and object symbolic of anything associated with it in time, place, shape or previous literature, until every object in a literary work could mean everything except itself. Followers of an oversimplified Freudianism saw in every girl a Jocasta, in every straight object a phallic symbol. Jungians, unsatisfied with the poignant emotional impact of a representative human situation, felt impelled to go beyond it to the discovery of a mythical archetype of obscure human relevance. One exasperated short-story writer, when describing a character burying his old clothes, protected himself against symbolic interpretation by specifying in the story that the character was not symbolically burying his old self; he just had no more need for his old clothes.

Among the more balanced critics, emphasis on close textual study led to a general preference for what was stylistically difficult or sophisticated and thus especially rewarding when made the object of analysis. For instance, G. M. Hopkins' "The Windhover" and Franz Kafka's "Country Doctor" were again and again anthologized, explicated, analyzed, and taught—not only because they are first-rate pieces of "modern" literature, but also because their complexities and ambiguities present a challenge to the analyst. When carried to an extreme, such preoccupation with the technical aspects of literature threatens to obscure its more basic appeal as an illumination and criticism of life. Imaginative literature speaks to us first of all not as technicians, theorists, and critics, but, more directly and more relevantly than any other form of language, as human beings. Kafka's technique is fascinating because in uncanny fashion it shapes and projects basic human anxieties. Hopkins' "The Windhover" does more than invite analysis; it elevates and fills with joy. It is true that this joy is not accessible to someone who has not learned the complex skills involved in reading difficult poetry. It is just as true that this joy is not accessible to someone whose preoccupation with technique has blunted his feeling for literature as a living thing.

Especially in introductory courses, teachers were sometimes led to neglect the authors that are most effective in developing the student's lasting interest in literature. In graduate schools and scholarly publications, interest came to center on authors of great technical sophistication: Henry James, William Faulkner, James Joyce. It became fashionable to look somewhat condescendingly at writers less self-conscious and deliberate in matters of style, such as the masters of the great realistic tradition in the novel, from Thackeray and George Eliot to Thomas Hardy and Arnold Bennett. In American literature, the burgeoning critical interest in writers like Melville and Faulkner led to a certain neglect of the literature of social document and social criticism, in which the American tradition is especially rich.

The great realistic novel, the novel of ideas by Orwell and Huxley and Ellison, the social drama of Ibsen and Arthur Miller provide the teacher with literature that is humanizing and liberalizing because of its human sympathy, its intense conviction, its human relevance. In these and similar works the uninitiated student can, and often does, discover a more serious and more profound response to life than in the mercenary platitudes of popular entertainment. In introducing the student to works of increasing formal complexity, the teacher must know how to make formal analysis a clue to more rewarding reading, to a more adequate response to the author's purpose. In this way, greater critical and technical competence derived from a habit of close reading and analysis will bear fruit in teaching that is a genuine introduction to literature in its full human dimensions.

Later chapters of this book are designed to explore in greater detail the four movements here briefly sketched. They will examine some of their historical context as well as the theoretical and practical problems they bring with them. They will relate them to other, more traditional areas in the discipline of English. In the meantime, what do the four major developments here described mean for today's teacher of English? First, today's English teacher must be more critical, more aware of first principles and fundamental problems, than in the past. He can no longer absorb uncritically an established tradition, an established body of conventions. He must be prepared to make intelligent choices, to defend his point of view. He cannot help being a professional, who as a matter of course recognizes the need for continuing education in an always developing field. He will be more of a theorist than he used to be, aware of the need for a cogent and coherent rationale of his subject.

At the same time, the teacher will ideally have a more workmanlike familiarity with the concrete details of his craft. He will have been trained to pay full and detailed attention to the linguistic and formal "what's there" before he establishes the connections and formulates the conclusions that lead to the comprehensive interpretation of a text. The combination of theoretical awareness and technical, craftsmanlike competence will increasingly transform the teaching of English into a profession in the full sense of the word.

English in Context

Whatever the nature of major trends in the discipline of English, some of its basic features remain unchanged. English is a subject unlike any other. The teacher of English does not deal with a clearly limited subject matter that can be systematically taught, memorized, tested, and forgotten. Instead, he is trying to develop a lasting maturity and sophistication in the student's use of and response to language. As every practicing English teacher knows, such maturity is affected by many diverse conditions and influences. Some of the most crucial of these, such as intelligence or social and cultural background, are beyond the teacher's control. Others are subject to his influence only to a limited extent: interests and prejudices derived from previous experience, attitudes toward learning and toward English developed during previous schooling, lack of reinforcement of the teacher's work in the rest of the student's schoolwork and in his cultural environment. But even those factors that are more clearly part of the teacher's professional responsibility are complex and interrelated. Changes in the student's verbal ability and in his competence and discrimination as a reader are typically a matter of gradual growth over the years. It is true that the teacher can measure the student's understanding and retention of material covered and his progress in specific skills. However, the most important results of his instruction are not immediate, concrete, and predictable but long-range and uncertain.

It is true in any field that the success of a teacher depends to a large extent upon his personal qualities. It is truer than usual in English, where any judgment of the competence of either teacher or student is a judgment not only of his knowledge but also of his articulateness, maturity, sensitivity. Thus, when teachers of English protest against attempts to dilute the solid subject matter of their courses, that subject matter should not be taken to mean a body of facts and categories comparable to those recorded in an encyclopedia, nor a set of skills susceptible to measures of proficiency like shorthand or typing. In our use of language and our response to literature more of our full selves is involved than in other academic fields. The teacher of English must combine a detailed and workmanlike competence in the various areas of his discipline with an awareness of their relationship to each other as well as their human significance.

The teacher of English must be able to present the special premises and conditions of his discipline to his associates in education, and he must be prepared to do the same for the interested general public. Because of the central role language and literature play in life, he must expect to have his work scrutinized, and on occasion hampered, by his fellow citizens. The average layman has deeply ingrained attitudes toward language. They range from largely unconscious reactions to elaborate rationalizations. In the most diverse places and periods, variations from familiar language habits have served as tokens of what the members of a given group respond to as alien, undesirable, or inferior. A teacher trying to change language habits or attitudes toward language must realize that he is dealing with complicated and intimate psychological factors. When he concerns himself with some of the uses and abuses of language most typical of our society, his work is necessarily, and often quite rightly, taken as a criticism of established practices. What to the linguist, semanticist, or lexicographer may be matters for scholarly exploration may be to the layman issues charged with emotion.

Nor is the English teacher protected against controversy when he concerns himself with literature. The teacher is likely to see the elements of a literary work as part of a whole and in the full context of the work's historical relations. The layman is much more likely to notice even peripheral elements that go counter to his standards of good taste, of morality, of loyalty, of economic or religious right-thinking. Great literature is typically more searching, revealing, or disturbing than literature designed to confirm existing standards. As a result, the works the teacher finds most satisfying are the most likely to give offense to the self-righteous. Established literary classics, fortunately, are to some extent protected from one-sided or illiberal attacks both by conventions of piety toward the great dead and by difficulties of language and interpretation. Correspondingly more vulnerable, however, are modern works that seem to have topical significance or whose authors, as citizens and private human beings, have attracted unfavorable attention.

The routine teacher, teaching safe and sound materials in safe and sound ways, is not likely to be troubled by these and similar problems. As the National Council of Teachers of English indicates in its statement on "The Student's Right to Read," the victim of censorship pressures is often the outstanding teacher who tries to explore truly significant material with his students:

> The censorship pressures that get the most publicity are those of small groups that protest the use of a limited number of books with realistic elements: *Huckleberry Finn, The Scarlet Letter, Catcher in the Rye, Brave New World, 1984, The Grapes of Wrath,* to name a few. Frequently the victims are among our best teachers who, encouraged by the excellent literature newly accessible to students in inexpensive paperbacks, have ventured outside the narrow boundaries of conventional texts.

In the opinion of the Council, "because of outside pressures many English teachers cannot carry out their central responsibility: teaching the cultural heritage of Western civilization."[4]

How to counter such pressures is a question that remains largely unsolved. The individual teacher is of course responsible for giving his students the tools for a mature appraisal of literary works. As a member of vigorous, and if necessary aggressive, professional organizations, he can do his share toward making his task as a teacher understood and respected by the community.

To sum up, the teacher of English is engaged in difficult, important, and responsible work. To be professionally qualified, he needs sound and balanced training in the major areas of his discipline. Within the discipline of English, he must be able to see specialized interests and current developments in perspective. He must be able to relate them to a rationale that prevents the proliferation of movements and of efforts at cross-purposes with each other. Beyond technical competence, the teacher must respond to the human and humane dimension of his subject. He must realize that his work becomes truly meaningful at the point where more than the student's intellect begins to be engaged. Finally, the teacher of English must be an articulate spokesman for his profession. He should be able to explain, and if necessary defend, the nature and importance of his work to his colleagues in other fields, to administrators, and to the public.

[4] "The Student's Right to Read," National Council of Teachers of English (Champaign, Ill., 1962), p. 10.

For the teacher of English, the most important development in the last two or three decades has been the rise of linguistics. Linguistics is the study, according to rigorously defined methods or principles, of *language as a system*. The linguist is concerned, not with the listing of miscellaneous items, as in a dictionary, but with recurrent patterns and characteristic relationships. He investigates the terms on which the minimal significant elements in the linguistic code work together in meaningful statements. He aims at discovering the underlying regularities that introduce order and predictability into the complicated sounds of speech.

one

Taking the term in its most comprehensive sense, the **grammar** of a language is this system of regularities. The grammarian typically investigates even an apparently isolated or "capricious" linguistic element as potentially "a special case of general rules applying as well to many other items."[1] When so defined, the study of grammar deals not with the social status of isolated phrases or constructions but with the structure of language. It deals not with questions of linguistic etiquette but with the basic, architectonic relations that give language order and coherence.

Grammar

Many of the most essential features of the linguistic system are learned by the native speaker before adolescence. Even the five-year-old uses with perfect ease such constructions as "But what Virginia said wasn't really true," or "Michael won't stop riding my bike." Though he may still confuse *tooken* and *taken* and *seed* and *saw,* the basic structure of his sentences already shows a command of more grammar than his elders can easily analyze. Except for certain structures more common in writing than in speech, the conversation of the average teenager makes use of all the major grammatical resources of the language.

As a result, the student of his own language may be tempted to take

[1] Noam Chomsky, "The Logical Basis of Linguistic Theory," *Preprints of Papers for the Ninth International Congress of Linguists* (Cambridge, Mass.: 1962), p. 516.

grammar for granted. He may concentrate his attention on vocabulary or etymology, or on the history of the language more generally, its kinship with other languages and its own dialectal variations. His major interest may be in alternatives of usage or in the resources of style. Each of these pursuits, however, at one point or another involves an understanding of grammar. The meaning of a word varies with its grammatical functions. The historian of the language cannot describe changes unless he can meaningfully analyze what is changing into what. The stylist must identify the grammatical structures whose stylistic effects he proposes to describe. Any student or teacher of language willy-nilly operates with some system of grammar. To the extent that rhetorician and critic deal with language as a system, their understanding of it must be reasonably thorough and well informed. They will want to guard against having their studies vitiated by unexamined biases or outright misconceptions.

Assumptions of Language Study

Unfortunately, developing a working knowledge of grammar is no longer simply a matter of taking a standard treatment off the shelf. The student of grammar must be aware of conflicting assumptions in the study of language and of different systems of analysis to which they have led. In trying to identify such basic assumptions, it is helpful to place them first in a historical perspective. Our present attitudes toward language are in varying ways influenced by major historical trends.

It is not surprising that eighteenth-century grammarians should have looked in language for the clear and unambiguous light of universal Reason. An age that with Alexander Pope saw in nature

One clear, unchanged, and universal light

naturally tended to assume that language as well as literature was subject to rules that represented "nature methodized." It just as naturally tended to see the purest embodiment of such universal principles in the language of the revered authors of "learned Greece" and "immortal Rome." Confronted with the richly idiomatic and "irregular" complexity of current speech, it assumed that the underlying principles of grammar were necessarily more regular, more simple and elegant, than the "corruptions" of current usage. Eighteenth-century grammarians like James Harris and James Buchanan thus assumed the existence of a universal grammar founded in universal reason, and embodied in its purest state in the Greek and Latin of classical literature.

Similarly, it is not surprising that the Romantic rehabilitation of the Gothic and the revival of interest in a native literary and historical heritage coincided with a strong emphasis on the historical and comparative study of the vernacular in its earlier forms. What had earlier been considered the barbarous dialects of peoples lacking the true light of classical culture was now considered with a proprietary pride the authentic medium of native tradition. Emphasis in language study shifted from the normative and regulatory to the restorative and antiquarian. The same generation that built colleges and post offices in a style copied from fourteenth-century cathedrals taught students to read *Beowulf* in the original and to know the variants of a word in several major Anglo-Saxon dialects.

In the second half of the nineteenth century, the deterministic literary criticism of Hippolyte Taine purported to derive the character of literary works scientifically from the author's "race," "milieu," and "moment." It should not surprise us that a grammarian like Otto Jespersen, trained in the era of Taine, looked for "the relation of language to national character," if not the spirit of the race. He explored such qualities of English grammar as "masculine" vigor, "businesslike shortness," and "freedom from pedantry" and related them to factors like climate, manners, and political tradition.[2]

Many grammarians attracted to twentieth-century linguistics had been trained in a positivistic philology that emphasized the concrete and tangible aspects of language. They were used to conducting rigorously detailed and quantitative studies of the use of the dative in an Anglo-Saxon document or of the types of imagery in the work of a Romantic poet. It should not surprise us that they welcomed attempts to make language study rigorously scientific, agreeing emphatically that "only matters which can be quantitatively measured or described in physical terms can be the subject of objectively true statements."[3]

The importance of this statement lies in what it implies, not about the method of science, but about the kind of subject matter that can be profitably investigated by strict scientific method. What limits the subject matter of science is its commitment to making observation more rigorous and reliable than it is in ordinary experience. To achieve this end, science confines itself to what can be concretely identified and measured in physical, quantitative terms, with results that stay the same regardless of the private history and subjective preferences of the observer. In dealing with language, such a commitment leads one to concentrate on the physiological rather than the psychological. It leads one to deal with language first and foremost as a "muscular activity," taking place in the organs producing speech sounds, rather than as a mental activity, taking place in the language centers of the brain. As Leonard Bloomfield said in *Language* (1933), we have no way of determining what the speakers may "feel," no

---

2 *Growth and Structure of the English Language*, 9th ed. (New York: Doubleday & Company, Inc., 1956), pp. 1–17.

3 James B. McMillan, "A Philosophy of Language," *College English*, IX (April, 1948), 385–90, in *Readings in Applied English Linguistics*, Harold B. Allen, ed. (New York: Appleton-Century-Crofts, Inc., 1958), p. 204.

way of describing scientifically whatever mental events correspond to the concrete, tangible signals of speech. For him, the danger lay "in mentalistic views of psychology, which may tempt the observer to appeal to purely spiritual standards instead of reporting the facts."[4]

By adopting this perspective, linguistics identified itself as one of the behavioral sciences, putting the emphasis on concretely observable linguistic behavior, rather than on the mental processes to which such behavior is as the visible part of the iceberg is to the unfathomable whole. The scientific linguist is "scientific" first of all in the sense that he insists on the "recognizable linguistic forms" and leaves aside as unverifiable speculation whatever cannot be rigorously identified.[5] The "philosophical," to a generation of linguists, became identical with the subjective, and the subjective in turn with the impressionistic and unsound.

Only in relatively recent work have linguistic theorists protested against too narrow a commitment to linguistic "surface" fact and stressed the need "to formulate underlying principles and to concentrate on the kinds of data that shed some light on these." They have concluded that "the attempt to gain some insight into the range of data that we now have is likely to be far more fruitful than the attempt to make this data more firm, e.g. by tests for synonymy, grammaticalness, and the like." Recent re-evaluations of the premises of linguistic science reflect the conviction that procedures that "might soothe the scientific conscience" do not necessarily advance our understanding of the nature of language.[6]

It is a commonplace that the perspective and methods of the investigator circumscribe the results of the investigation. The eye of the beholder helps determine the picture on the retina. The investigator's battery of measuring and testing devices determines the kinds of phenomena he can record. Progress in the natural sciences has been due to the scientist's minimizing the influence of common-sense notions, intuitive certainty, emotional and aesthetic response, preference, and ulterior motive. The scientist owes both his successes and his limitations to his skill in bypassing the seething turmoil of psychological phenomena between stimulus and response, and in substituting a more rigorously controlled system of responding to experience.

Linguistic science has in the past owed its progress to its clear focus on what can be quantitatively measured and behavioristically verified. The humanist has tended to view it with suspicion, since he is convinced not only of the ultimate opaqueness of science in matters of preference and value, but also of its limited ability to do justice to the "feel" of experience, and to help chart the psychological complexities of human interaction. Where science makes progress by drastic specialization, the hu-

---

[4] *Language* (New York: Holt, Rinehart & Winston, Inc., 1933), p. 38.
[5] *Ibid.*, p. 5.
[6] Chomsky, "Logical Basis," *Preprints*, pp. 513, 528.

manist's ideal is that "a person must somehow be able to grasp the complexities of life as a whole." Like the philosophers refusing to look through the astronomer's telescope in Bertolt Brecht's play *Galileo,* humanists have been reluctant to look at linguistic findings derived from premises radically different from their own.

No matter where his initial sympathies may lie, the teacher of English can ill afford to choose sides between scientist and humanist. Rather, he must deplore the barriers, real and imagined, that have separated the representatives of "science" and "culture" since T. H. Huxley's and Matthew Arnold's time. Ultimately, no definition of culture will stand in which the scientist does not play an important and honored role. The student of language, perhaps more so than investigators in other fields, feels the need to see science in its organic relations with the total of human knowledge and civilization. Ideally, he must be able to deal authoritatively both with language as a signaling system subject to rigorously objective observation, and with language as the medium of complex human interaction. He will agree with Otto Jespersen that on the one hand "Nature has rendered it impossible for anyone to penetrate to the mind of anyone else except through its outer manifestations" and that it is consequently impossible to get at larger questions about language except through its sounds. On the other hand, there is the danger that linguistic sounds will be investigated in such a mechanistic way "as partly to dehumanize the study of language."[7] The teacher can help bridge the gap between the "two cultures" if he studies the picture of language presented by the behavioral scientist with a vivid awareness of the limitations imposed by the size of the frame.

Within the frame of a rigorously objective study of grammar, a number of difficult choices will for some time confront the classroom teacher. In spite of the vigor of controversies concerning usage, the basic difficulty in choosing an acceptable school grammar does not lie in deciding whether a given sentence is idiomatic English. Whatever their declared premises and methods, in practice grammarians of different persuasions "assume intuitive knowledge of the grammatical sentences of English and ask what sort of grammar will be able to do the job of producing these in some effective and illuminating way."[8] They may disagree on the appropriateness and permissibility of a given sentence, but not on whether it could actually have been produced in accordance with the linguistic habits of a native speaker. In short, apparent arguments over whether a sentence is "English" or not are typically not arguments over questions of fact but of preference and value. Current teaching practice helps the teachers steer clear of confusion here by treating the ques-

---

[7] *Language: Its Nature, Development, and Origin* (New York: Holt, Rinehart & Winston, Inc., 1922), p. 66.
[8] Noam Chomsky, *Syntactic Structures* (The Hague: Mouton & Co., 1957), p. 13.

tions of fact under the heading of grammar and the questions of appropriateness or permissibility under the heading of **usage.**

By and large, then, grammarians of different persuasions would agree on the idiomatic character of

> Laughing wildly, the museum director seized his cane and smashed the priceless *Song-cheng-wan* vase.

They would argue about the classification of *museum* and *priceless* and *Song-cheng-wan*. For instance, they would debate whether a category of "adjective" could be set up that would accommodate all three of these items, or whether the concept of "modification" can be defined in such a way as to do justice to the relations between these items and *director* or *vase* but so as to exclude a number of other grammatical relationships in this sentence. They would disagree on the relevance of case-terminology or Immediate-Constituent analysis. For instance, they would debate whether in looking for major elements we should make the first major cut in the traditional manner between subject and predicate or in the manner of Immediate-Constituent analysis between *wildly* and *the*. They would argue about different ways of relating the sentence to, or deriving it from, more elementary sentence models. Though at times they would discuss "mere differences in terminology," there would be just as many times when similarities in terminology would obscure differences in analysis. Typically, *the present differences between grammars of English exist between different systems of classifying identical phenomena*. The teacher of English must be aware of the most important of these systems. He must be able to estimate their most significant differences and the extent to which they are mutually compatible.

Structural Grammar

If we are aiming at certainty in a confusing field, we will be strongly attracted toward attempts to model our school grammar on a strictly empirical and inductive method. Such a method makes us begin by listening to the sounds of a language and, noticing recurrent patterns, gradually reducing them to order. Historically, this is the method appropriate for the linguistic anthropologist investigating a previously unrecorded language. In listening to two persons speaking together, we would parallel the procedure described by John B. Carroll in *The Study of Language:*

> We make a tape recording of the sounds we hear, and upon careful study of this recording it turns out that the sounds uttered by the two persons have at least some similarities. Though many of the sounds may seem strange to our ears, we can learn to recognize, fairly well, the vowels and consonants which occurred in the speech of our subjects. Suppose we find that the various vowels and consonants we recognize sound approximately the same

no matter which one of our subjects is talking, and that they occur on the average with about the same frequencies. . . . We analyze our tape recording further and find that the sounds often occur in similar sequences; if we listen carefully to the breaks between these sequences we might conclude that our subjects use many "words" in common. . . . We could go on in this way, making increasingly detailed analyses. We should want to study how the longer sequences of sounds are put together; we would try to discover certain constancies or invariances in the structure of our subjects' utterances.[9]

The great merit of such a method is its rejection of all preconceptions, its loyalty to "what is there." Its effectiveness, as Kenneth Burke observed in a more general reference to the scientific method, is that of "stooping to conquer," in that "it begins by *listening* rather than by *asserting.*"[10] The great strength of science as compared with various closed systems is its built-in commitment to self-correction. Edgar H. Sturtevant, in a graphic account of this self-correcting tendency, describes the man who walked down a hotel corridor and met another man walking in the opposite direction. When he bent his course somewhat to the left, the other man turned right by an equal amount; when he turned somewhat to the right, the other man turned somewhat to the left, making a collision inevitable unless they both stopped short. "Presently the man I had originally noticed revised his interpretation of the evidence: he was facing his own reflection in a mirror. So he walked off at a right angle to his original course. Just so science must frequently revise its conclusions."[11]

In emulating the methods of science, twentieth-century grammarians undertook to start over from the beginning and act on Bloomfield's statement that "the only useful generalizations about language are inductive generalizations."[12] Following in their footsteps, we would work our way from sound resources (phonetics) to significant sound contrasts (phonemics) and smallest meaningful units (morphemics). We would then proceed to grammar in the more limited sense, that is, the forms of words (morphology) and combinations of words in a sentence (syntax). Several grammars published in the fifties by grammarians often grouped together as **structural linguists** thus move "through the hierarchy of English structure, from the smallest elements, sounds, up to the largest elements, sentences."[13] In theory at least, the structural linguist typically aims at thus inductively developing an analysis of the *spoken* language before examining the writing system and its "secondary representation" of speech.

[9] John B. Carroll, *The Study of Language* (Cambridge, Mass.: Harvard University Press, 1959), p. 7.
[10] *The Philosophy of Literary Form* (Baton Rouge: Louisiana State University Press, 1941), p. 407.
[11] *An Introduction to Linguistic Science* (New Haven: Yale University Press, 1960), p. 1.
[12] Bloomfield *Language*, p. 20.
[13] Archibald A. Hill, *Introduction to Linguistic Structures: From Sound to Sentence in English* (New York: Harcourt, Brace & World, Inc., 1958), p. iii.

In the study of sound resources, much work had been done before the premises of modern scientific linguistics were formulated. Nineteenth-century **historical phonetics** had paid a great deal of attention to sound changes marking important stages in the history of the major Indo-European languages. Thus, "Grimm's law" summed up certain systematic sound changes that had a part in differentiating the early Germanic precursors of modern English and German from their Indo-European relatives. These changes accounted for differences like *p* in Latin *pater* and *f* in English *father, t* in Latin *tres* and *th* in English *three, g* in Latin *genus* and *k* in English *kin*. Investigation of apparent exceptions to such patterns of phonetic change led to refinements like "Verner's law," which traced different patterns of consonant change after accented and unaccented vowels. For the student of English literature, the most important sound change is the great vowel shift that in the fifteenth century changed the vowel sounds in *name, see, five, root,* and *down* from their Chaucerian values—that is, sounds close to "Continental" (German, Italian) *a, e, i, o, u* —in the direction of their Modern English values.

Apart from the detailed investigation of the phonetic resources of English, such studies had important implications for the investigator's view of language. To give one limited example, English spelling, chaotic to the layman, shows traces of system when one sees how it preserves in a fossilized state older ways of pronouncing English. If one goes back far enough, the different spellings of the same vowel in *clean, heap, sea* on the one hand and *meed, keep, see* on the other begins to reflect a difference in pronunciation. In Shakespeare's time, *meed* had its modern vowel but *clean* was close to modern *lane*. In Chaucer's time, *meed* was close to the vowel sound of *lane* but *clean* was close to the vowel sound of modern *there*. On a larger scale, the regularities of phonetic change impressed on the investigator's mind the fundamental concepts of language as typically in a state of constant, long-range change, and of language not as a collection of miscellaneous items but as an orderly system. As Edward Sapir said, "Nothing is perfectly static. Every word, every grammatical element, every locution, every sound and accent is a slowly changing configuration, molded by the invisible and impersonal drift that is the life of language." At the same time, phonetic changes were "regular"; phonetic laws "affect all examples of the sound in question or, if the phonetic change is conditional, all examples of the same sound that are analogously circumstanced."[14]

Where earlier scholars had seen in different languages a mere Babel of unrelated voices, the relations within the major language families could now be charted so as to exhibit a complex but orderly system of

14 *Language: An Introduction to the Study of Speech* (New York: Harcourt, Brace & World, Inc., 1949), pp. 171, 180.

correspondences. English could be seen in its relations to languages as diverse as Lithuanian and Armenian; modern languages could be seen in their relations to such remote predecessors as Gothic and Sanskrit. At the same time, such investigations kept the scholar constantly in touch with such basic linguistic processes as analogical change, as when historical, phonetically correct *elder—eldest* is to some extent replaced by *older—oldest*, formed in analogy to prevailing ways of forming comparatives and superlatives. Where etymology appealed in part to lovers of the curious or to the collector's instinct for isolated fact, insofar as it drew on historical phonetics it appealed to those with a methodical, scientific, systematizing turn of mind.

In the meantime, **comparative** or **contrastive phonetics** developed as a means of charting phonetic differences between major European languages, and between their major dialects. Studying positions of lips and tongue, for instance, a phonetician like the Frenchman Passy could pin down the differences between the English *t* in *try*, the German *t* in *tragen*, and the French *t* in *trois*. He could thus teach his students to go beyond imitating the sounds of a foreign language or a strange dialect by simply substituting the closest similar sound from their own language. For instance, by the simple expedient of bringing the tongue forward when speaking German, or twice as far, crowding against the upper teeth, when speaking French, the English or American student could experiment fruitfully with the possibilities of articulation that each language utilizes in its own way.

Ideally, phonetics could transform Eliza Doolittle from a Cockney flower girl into a fair lady who could pass as a duchess at an ambassador's garden party—or at least say "Walk! Not bloody likely" with all the phonetic characteristics of the prestige dialect. In practice, phonetics enabled the trained phonetician to spot with deadly accuracy the provincial origin of the newly elegant and the newly rich. In the teaching of foreign languages, it helped students escape from the curse of a heavily and unmistakably alien "foreign accent." Phonetics further taught students to consider spelling, especially English spelling, as a convention determined by historical accidents, in many ways an inefficient and misleading system of transcribing the sounds of speech. A practical result of this realization was the development of the International Phonetic Alphabet by such pioneers in phonetics as Passy, Henry Sweet, and Daniel Jones. Compared with ordinary spelling, a phonetic alphabet attempts to eliminate the use of a variety of symbols for the same sound (*me, see, sea, lief, Leigh*), and the use of an identical symbol to indicate different sounds (*rough, cough, bough, through, dough*). A phonetic alphabet further attempts to furnish some means of distinguishing closely related sounds so as to make possible the graphic indication of dialectal differences, for example. It thus may provide ways of indicating the glides that make diphthongs or "double vowels" of the vowels in *name, write,* and *bout.*

The modern linguist, trying to work his way inductively from the flow of speech sounds to the underlying principles of organization, could thus profit from the considerable spadework done by his precursors in historical and comparative phonetics. However, insofar as he was interested in structure, in system, he was hindered rather than helped by the great variety of speech sounds that phonetics had been charting. Not only is articulation different in English *try* and French *trois,* but there is a different *t* in English *team* and *steam;* a sound like English *l* is different in articulation and sound quality in *lip* and in *thrill.* Many other English consonants vary considerably in sound quality depending on their relative position in a word and depending on the sounds that precede and follow them. The linguist systematized the great variety of speech sounds of a given language by sorting them out into phonemes. A **phoneme** is a cluster, or bundle, of sounds that function in the language as the smallest signaling unit distinct from other such units. The ordinary person would recognize a difference in meaning between *pin* and *bin.* The letters *p* and *b* here symbolize a sound contrast that has phonemic value; *p* and *b* represent different phonemes. The ordinary person would *not* recognize a difference in meaning between *pin* and variations of *pin* using a slightly different *p*-sound as found, say, in *spin,* or *tip.* Such non-significant variants, or **allophones,** of *p* would be said to belong to the same phoneme. Contrasts between them are not utilized by the signaling system of the language to affect meaning. On the other hand, we recognize a difference in meaning when hearing *thy* and *thigh,* though the only difference is a variation in the sounds symbolized by *th.* The two distinctive sounds here symbolized by *th* would therefore be said to be different phonemes.

Many English consonant phonemes coincide with the bundle of variants conventionally transcribed by the corresponding letters: *b, p, d, t, v, f,* etc. Other letters, like the combination *th,* stand for several different phonemes; *g,* for instance, stands for three different phonemes in *good, gin,* and *rouge.* The English vowel phonemes are somewhat harder to identify. They are in some cases hard to distinguish reliably from each other, as in contrasting pairs like *merry—Mary, pawned—pond.* Like the pairs of sounds here illustrated, they may have confusing regional variants. Their rendering in conventional English spelling is notoriously varied and capricious. How incompletely the inventory of these vowel phonemes coincides with the basic *a, e, i, o, u* of the writing system may be inferred from a partial list including the vowel phonemes in *hit, head, hat, hot, hut,* and *hood.* The vowels in *hate, hide, heat, hoist,* and in *home, how, hoot* are usually analyzed as double vowels or diphthongs. They consist of the familiar vowel phonemes and one of two characteristic glides involving a raising of the tongue, forward in *hate* and *hoist,* backward in *how* and *home.* Characteristic variations in the system of vowels are among the most noticeable differences setting major American and British dialects off from each other.

Phonetic transcription attempts, within limits, to reproduce the distinctive sound quality of an utterance. *Phonemic transcription limits itself to those contrasts that are significant as part of the signaling system of a language.* Typically, structural linguists have used phonemic transcription in producing a written record of utterances under investigation.

In charting the phonemic structure of English, linguists concerned themselves with sound features that produce significant contrasts by being as it were superimposed on utterances otherwise consisting of the same phonemes. We recognize as significant—that is, as part of the linguistic code—the difference between the spoken equivalents of "Oh!" and "Oh?," "Prodúce!" and "Próduce!," "Donald Duck" and "Donald, duck!" Of the features of intonation here illustrated, the most familiar is **stress,** that is, relative prominence in such features as loudness and length. It accounts for the contrast in pairs like *prógress* and *progréss, súbject* and *subjéct;* it distinguishes *white hóuse* from *White House,* a *dancing téacher* from a *dáncing teacher.* Stress makes possible the meaningful variations in emphasis in pairs like

> He was very *good.*
> He *was* very good.
> John was awarded a *scholarship!*
> *John* was awarded a scholarship!

By regularizing the stress patterns of natural speech the poet produces the effect of predictable recurrence we call meter:

> Did this woman set in motion the Greek expedition to Troy?
> Was thís the fáce that láunched a thóusand shíps?

What matters for metrical analysis is relative stress, that is, whether a syllable has stronger stress than the ones that surround it. Linguists, on the other hand, distinguish one or two intermediate degrees of stress between the most and the least prominent. They usually identify four different degrees of stress in the typical pronunciation of a sentence like "Paul's in the bedroom." Proceeding from loudest to softest they may be labeled primary ($'$), secondary ($\land$), tertiary ($\grave{}$), and weak ($\breve{}$):

> Pâul's ĭn thĕ bédròom.

The second feature of intonation is **pitch,** which makes the difference between shrill, high-frequency sounds and their low-frequency, slow-vibration counterparts. Significant variations in pitch are seen most clearly in the rising pitch that distinguishes "John" and "John?" or "He is ill." and "He is ill?" These questions normally have the simple rising pitch of questions to be answered yes or no. The concluding portion of such questions rises from the second, or normal, to the third level of pitch and stays there:

²He is ³ill³?
²Are you coming ³back³?

A more complicated rising-falling pitch normally marks the concluding portion of statements and of questions requiring an answer other than yes or no. The concluding portion of such an utterance rises to the third level but then drops off to the first, or lowest, level of pitch:

²The dog chased the ³cat¹.
²Where are you ³going¹?
²When should I ³call him¹?

Beyond such basic pitch patterns, other characteristic pitch contours are our major devices for signaling alarm, incredulity, insistence:

²Am I planning to marry ⁴George²!

A third feature of intonation is often labeled **juncture**. There are different kinds of perceptible breaks in the flow of speech. These breaks are not simply pauses of varying lengths; they may involve retarding of tempo in the pronunciation of adjoining sounds as well as changes in their sound quality. They are correlated with typical patterns of stress and pitch. Shifting in the least noticeable of these breaks ("plus juncture" or "open transition") makes the difference between "a name" and "an aim"; betweeen "I scream" and "ice cream." Its presence makes the difference between *nitrate* and *night rate*. *Night rate* substitutes for the *–tr–* combination, with its characteristic transitional sound accompanying the movement of the tongue from *t* to *r,* the more clear-cut terminal *t* and initial *r* that we might hear at the end or at the beginning of a sentence. Open transition often, but not always, coincides with the divisions of utterances into words in conventional writing.

A more noticeable break ("single bar juncture" or "level juncture") corresponds to commas that do not signal a rise in pitch in sentences like, "Mr. Smith, the janitor, turned off the lights." Marked by a sharp terminal rise in pitch, the third type of juncture ("double bar juncture" or "rising juncture") is often heard before the commas in sentences like "Mr. Smith, who has served us many years, has decided to retire." Marked by a sharp drop in pitch and volume, the fourth type of juncture ("double cross juncture" or "falling juncture") terminates most utterances. Level, rising, and falling juncture are often grouped together as "terminals" distinguished by sustained (→), rising (↗), and falling (↘) pitch.

Detailed analysis of the possible variations in stress, pitch, and juncture is a relatively recent development. Controversy about the general scheme of classification and about difficult details continues among the

experts. Many currently influential textbooks base their treatment of
intonation and of phonemics generally on *An Outline of English Structure,* by George L. Trager and Henry Lee Smith, Jr., first published in
1951.[15]

Bloomfield classified such elements of intonation as degrees of stress
and pitch as "secondary phonemes" to distinguish them from primary
phonemes, that is, consonants and vowels. They are often called **supraseg-
mental** phonemes, since unlike vowels and consonants they typically involve relationships that go beyond the one-syllable segments sufficient for
phonemic analysis in pairs like *pin—bin, pin—pen, pin—pit.* By the same
token, they lead to a consideration of complete utterances and thus provide a bridge from phonemics to syntax.

Intonation at times helps establish grammatical distinctions not
otherwise clear or conclusive. Obviously, *upon* functions differently in the
following two sentences:

> Much responsibility was put *upon* him.
> He was much put *upon.*

The first *upon* is a preposition, governing the object-form of the
pronoun, but the second *upon* is something else, as is obvious from the
subject-form *He* at the beginning of the sentence. Students of intonation
patterns have pointed out that this distinction shows up in weaker stress
on the preposition than on its "adverbial" double in pairs like

> We took ín a show. (secondary stress on *in*)
> We sat ìn a car. (tertiary stress on *in*)

In combinations like "took in a show" and "sent in a request," *in* carries
the stress carried in the contrasting sentences by the simple verbs ("*sat* in
a car"). Open transition separates *took in* and *a show,* but *sat* and *in a car.*
The *in* in *took in* is therefore legitimately considered part of a phrasal,
or compound, verb rather than an ordinary preposition.

The teacher of writing will be intrigued by the partial correspondence between intonation and punctuation. Many a teacher has demonstrated the difference between restrictive and nonrestrictive modifiers by
reading the one with as level pitch and as even tempo as possible and the
other with exaggerated rising pitch at exaggerated breaks:

> Americans who do not speak French need not apply.
> Americans, who do not speak French, need not apply.

Similarly, the difference between coordinate and noncoordinate adjectives
can be heard as well as seen:

> an honest civil servant
> an honest, civil reply

[15] *An Outline of English Structure* (Washington: American Council of Learned
Societies, 1957).

In the discussion of sentence fragments it is useful to parallel the contrast between comma and period with the contrast between a level or rising juncture that, in Bloomfield's words, "promises continuation of the sentence," and the falling juncture that brings it to a full stop.[16] However, the teacher must not expect such partial and sometimes complicated correspondences to simplify miraculously the conventional uses of periods, semicolons, and commas. In the words of W. Nelson Francis, "the teacher who has made some study of intonation can thus teach students to punctuate 'by ear,' so far as this is possible. Beyond that, the conventions of punctuation must be taught in relation to grammar."[17]

Meanwhile, our inductive approach to grammar is clearly ready to proceed beyond the individual phoneme. The linguist will first stop to investigate the possible *combinations* of phonemes, showing, for instance, that some consonant clusters, like those at the beginning of German *Pflaume* and at the end of German *Herbst,* are un-English, not part of the signaling system of the language. We are then ready to study permissible or normal combinations of phonemes into the recurrent linguistic forms known as morphemes. If a phoneme may be defined as the smallest unit of signaling that *makes a difference* in meaning, a **morpheme** may be roughly defined as the smallest unit that by itself *carries* meaning. In a sample of text large enough for our inductive purposes, we will find recurrent combinations like *pin, seek, John,* and *grow.* These all carry meaning but cannot be split any further into meaningful subunits. Like variants of the same phoneme, different instances of the same morpheme are not necessarily identical in all respects; witness the different pronunciation of *the* in *the boat* and *the end.*

Soon our investigation will be concerned with recurrent combinations of several morphemes. Beyond the "base" morpheme, the inflectional ending in *Greeks* and *lives* carries the general meaning of "more than one," the derivational ending in *seeker* the meaning of "one who. . . ." Generally, familiar prefixes and suffixes, as well as the "root" words, would have the status of morphemes. The way such individual morphemes are combined has obvious repercussions as to their phonological quality. Notice for instance the change from *f* to *v* in *life—lives.* Notice the change from [k] to [s] to [š] from "logic" to "logicism" to "logician." The systematic study of such relationships has indeed led recent investigators to question the feasibility of phonemic analysis largely prior to and separate from attention to the way morphemes work together in words and sentences.

Pinned, redder, slowly, growth, modesty, prepare, postpone, etc., can all be split into their base morphemes, or roots, and other "bound" morphemes, meaningful and functional only when thus affixed to a base

---

[16] Bloomfield, *Language,* p. 92.
[17] *The Structure of American English* (New York: The Ronald Press Company, 1958), pp. 563–64. Copyright © 1958 The Ronald Press Company.

morpheme. Problems result when morphemic analysis goes beyond the obvious. The investigator must guard against taking shortcuts like identifying meaningful roots familiar to him from the history of the language. What influenced historical development is not necessarily operative in the present linguistic code. Thus, in English, *impresario* is a single morpheme, whatever meaningful subunits it may have had in its original Italian. The teacher thinking in traditional categories of roots and affixes may have trouble remembering that according to the linguist's definition of morpheme the plural-affix in *oxen* is a variant, or **allomorph,** of the plural-affix in *Greeks*. He may consider morphemic analysis artificial when it is applied where no combination of discrete elements takes place. Though it seems logical enough to analyze *walked* as "*walk* + the *ed* morpheme," it seems unilluminating to analyze a form like *ran* similarly as "*run* + allomorph of *ed*."

Nevertheless, morphemics furnishes us with the building blocks for grammar proper. We can now turn our attention to similar strings, or sequences, of morphemes and analyze their similarities. Suppose we collect a sampling of combinations like the following:

> the mountain climber
> the young mountain climber
> a very young mountain climber with warts
> the youngest mountain climber of all
> this very pretty freshman girl in my class
> the two prettiest freshman girls of Toledo

Noting that such clusters occur in varying length, with a word like *climber* or *girl* still present in their shortest versions, we could call *climber* or *girl* the **headword** of the cluster in which it appears. The most striking thing about the other elements in each cluster is the rigidity of sequence, that is, of **word order.** "A with very warts climber young mountain" is obviously not possible. But even minor variations are rigidly limited by word order, which we thus identify as our first major grammatical device: The meaning of each string depends on the relative position of the items it contains.

A second grammatical device is familiar to us from our discussion of morphemes: **Inflections** express the relationship between "two . . . girl*s*" and "young*est* . . . of all." Compared with highly inflected languages like Latin or Old English, Modern English obviously relies much less on inflection and much more on word order as a signal of grammatical relationships. Even a loan word exceptionally rich in inflectional endings, like *alumnus, alumni, alumna, alumnae,* has lost the many additional inflectional endings it would have in Latin: *alumno, alumnum, alumnorum, alumnis, alumnam,* and so forth.

Some words in each string have a relatively weak lexical and strong **grammatical,** that is, relational meaning: *the* and *a* prepare us for the appearance of a word like *climber* or *girl; of* ties *Toledo* to the rest of the string. We may thus follow those modern grammarians that list such words (articles, prepositions, conjunctions, and some others) as **function words** or structure words. These we identify as the third major device of English grammar for tying isolated words together into a meaningful sequence.

Setting up this category makes for convenience in listing the major grammatical devices of English: word order, inflection, function words, and intonation patterns. However, we cannot expect every grammarian to adopt this scheme, since "it is impossible to distinguish sharply between functional meaning and lexical meaning."[18] In some uses of function words, lexical meaning is very weak:

> Consider *to* in *I want to go.* The elements *I, want,* and *go* are referable, through the intermediary of English content structure, to aspects of human experience. But it is impossible to find a specific factor in the situation which can be considered as the "meaning" of *to.* Nevertheless, *to* does have a function, since without it *I want go.* means nothing.[19]

In other uses of function words, lexical meaning is very strong:

> The *to* of *what nature hasn't done to us will be done by our fellow man,* for example, is semantically of major importance to its sentence, so that if *for* is substituted there is a very considerable change in meaning.[20]

Whatever our decision here, we can now sort out the remaining words into classes: The **nouns** are words like *climber, girl, wart, class.* They may be inflected for the plural, and this turns out to be a basic characteristic of most of the words traditionally included in this class. They appear after such noun markers as *the, a, this, my.* If we expanded our sample sufficiently, we would find that many nouns show characteristic **derivational,** noun-forming suffixes like *–hood, –ness, –acy, –dom: womanhood, tallness, democracy, kingdom.* Whereas function words belong to "closed" classes, like prepositions, whose membership is relatively stable and slow to change, nouns, like the other major form classes we are going to set up, belong to an "open" class. New nouns are coined with relative ease as the occasion arises: *television, transistor, highbrow.* These new nouns then conform to prevailing patterns of inflection and position characteristic of established members of the class.

Adjectives are words like *young* and *pretty.* They may be inflected for comparison: *young, younger, youngest.* They fit in after the intensifier *very* or *rather,* whereas *mountain* and *freshman,* though also modifying nouns, do not. Recurrent adjective-forming suffixes would include *–y, –able, –ful, –ous: rainy, predictable, wonderful, porous.*

---

[18] Sturtevant, *An Introduction to Linguistic Science,* p. 61.
[19] H. A. Gleason, Jr., *An Introduction to Descriptive Linguistics,* rev. ed. (New York: Holt, Rinehart & Winston, Inc., 1961), p. 55.
[20] Ralph B. Long, *The Sentence and Its Parts: A Grammar of Contemporary English* (Chicago: The University of Chicago Press, 1961), p. 5.

Leaving the noun clusters behind, we proceed to analyze other strings, in which the headworks are **verbs:**

> was hitting
> has been hitting
> only rarely hits the target
> invariably hits the nail on the head
> would have been hit by a train
> could not have hit him the first time

Again we note the limited role of inflection (*hit, hits, hitting*). On the basis of a more complete sample, we could set up a typical inflectional scheme, or paradigm: *ask, asks, asked, asking* for regular verbs; *take, takes, took, taken, taking* for irregular verbs. Typical verb-forming derivational suffixes would be *–ize* and *–en: organize, redden*. Rigidity of sequence, of obligatory word order, is especially obvious in the auxiliaries that expand the simple verb forms. *Been has* and *could been have* are obviously impossible.

We note a fourth major class of words: **adverbs,** words like *rarely* and *invariably*. They frequently, but by no means always, show the derivational suffix *–ly*. Adverbs are not inflected for comparison; we find *prettier* but not *rarelier*. Contrasted with other word classes, adverbs enjoy a relative freedom of movement:

> *invariably* hit the nail on the head
> hit the nail *invariably* on the head
> hit the nail on the head *invariably*

Leaving aside some of the other elements in our verb clusters, and postponing investigation of other typical combinations, we are now ready to examine the recurrent sequence of noun cluster followed by verb cluster. We have arrived at the basic model for the unit whose better understanding is the final aim of our inductive labors—the **sentence:**

The very young mountain climber with warts invariably hits the nail on the head.

We note the very limited extent to which the subject-predicate relationship between noun cluster and verb cluster is reflected in agreement, that is, in the choice of *hits* (singular) or *hit* (plural). Relying on purely formal characteristics, we would have to define the **subject** of a sentence as the word or group of words that the verb would agree with in number if it were in the present tense.

From a sampling of relatively simple sentences we can now form some idea of the most common **sentence patterns.** Given the possibilities of expansion in both noun cluster and verb cluster, the great majority of our sentences will be found to be variations of a few recurrent patterns. We may profitably sort out our simple sentences according to the absence or presence of different kinds of **complements** after the verb. The verbs in the following sentences differ in their relations to the sentence elements, if any, required for completion of the predicate:

> 1) Birds sing.
> 2) The dog chased the cat.
> 3) The salary is inadequate.
> 4) The decision seemed a mistake.
> 5) Fred lends John a bicycle.
> 6) Fred made John his friend.

Different kinds of complements are often quite similar in position and form, as in patterns 2 and 4, or 5 and 6. One way of distinguishing the complements, and thus the different sentence patterns, is to contrast their passive equivalents:

> 2) The cat was chased by the dog.
> *but not* 4) A mistake was seemed by the decision.
>
> 5) A bicycle was lent John by Fred.
> *but not* 6) His friend was made John by Fred.

In addition to the most common basic patterns, we may wish to list minor patterns that in characteristic ways vary the normal subject-predicate relationship. The most common of these is the subjectless request or command:

> Sing.
> Sing a song.
> Be a man.
> Give him the money.
> Elect Newsome alderman.

Another common type is the *there is* or *there are* sentence with its postponed subject:

> There is *no time*.
> There are *many unresolved questions*.

To get from our set of simple recurrent patterns to the analysis of more complicated sentences, we need above all an inventory of different kinds of **connectives.** We will study the way they link one subject-predicate group to another:

> My brother liked Elvira, *who* ignored him.
> My brother liked Elvira, *though* she ignored him.
> My brother liked Elvira, *but* she ignored him.
> My brother liked Elvira; *however,* she ignored him.

In sorting these out, we will be reminded of the role of word order as a means of establishing grammatical categories. One striking illustration of how structural analysis can give concrete substance to traditional terms is the distinction to be made among co-ordinating conjunction, conjunctive adverb, and subordinating conjunction. Meaning alone gives very little help in grasping these distinctions. If one says "I shall go home soon, for I am very tired," or "I am very tired; therefore I shall go home soon," or "Because I am very tired, I shall go home soon," the meanings of the statements seem indistinguishable. The grammatical differences emerge only as we consider the ways in which the various connectives pattern: *for* can appear only between the parts it joins; *therefore* is movable: "I am very tired; I shall, therefore, go home soon." Subordinators like *because* must appear at the beginning of a clause, but the clause itself is movable: "Because I am very tired, I shall go home soon," or "I shall go home soon, because I am very tired."[21]

In other words, if a student asks, "Why is *but* a co-ordinating connective and *however* a conjunctive adverb?" the answer is that *but* is stationary, whereas *however* shares with adverbs a relative freedom of movement. We do not say, "The location is good, the pay *but* is terrible"; but we do say,

The location is good; *however,* the pay is terrible.
The location is good; the pay, *however,* is terrible.
The location is good; the pay is terrible, *however.*

In addition to investigating ways of joining subject-predicate groups, we will be concerned with the possible substitutions within them. For instance, pronouns, verbals, or noun clauses may take the place of nouns:

The salesman missed the train.
He missed the train.

The statement made me furious.
To hear him say that made me furious.

The reason is unknown.
What made him leave us is unknown.

As linguists point out, what distinguishes true language activity is not the ability to repeat a sentence previously heard, but to use it as a "substitution frame" in which appropriate alternative elements take the place of the original items. What distinguishes the child's talk from that of the parrot is that the child can go from "Michael is a bad boy" to "John is a bad boy," "Michael is a good boy," and "Martha is a pretty girl." What makes language complex rather than simple is that the child can go, further, from "Michael is a bad boy" to "Listening to him is great fun" and "What you told me last night is a big story." In performing the operations involved here, the user of language engages in a "kind of 'creativity' that leaves the language totally unchanged."[22]

Awareness of the more common possibilities of expansion, connection, and substitution allows us to analyze most sentences as variants and

---

21 John R. Searles, "New Wine in Old Bottles," *The English Journal,* L (November, 1961), 516.
22 Chomsky, "Logical Basis," *Preprints,* p. 512.

combinations of a limited number of subject-predicate sentence patterns. Again and again we find confirmation of the principle that "English syntax is a many-layered organization of relatively few types of basic units."[23] Of course, we find complete utterances that depart entirely from the subject-predicate scheme:

> So much for Grimsby.
> The less distinguished the speaker, the longer the talk.
> Let us keep this firmly in mind.

However, for the teacher eager to proceed from the spoken language to writing, the subject-predicate sentence is obviously the major subject matter of grammar. As Harold Whitehall says in *Structural Essentials of English:*

> The subject-predicate sentence is *the* sentence of written English. Its grammatical structure accounts for almost all the English grammar that is practically useful to a writer of the language. Understand this structure, this grammar, and you will have the grammatical dynamics of the language well within your grasp.[24]

If we patiently follow a book building up the structure of English in the manner here briefly sketched, we shall profit in a number of ways. We will have the comforting feeling that the grammarian is not so much defending his preconceptions as cautiously exploring difficult territory. We will take a new look at much that we took for granted and in the process gain a more authentic appreciation of the workings of language. Whatever our quarrel with a linguist over specific points of analysis, we will feel that he is indeed dealing with the phonological, morphological, and syntactic "stuff" of language, and doing so in a rigorous, systematic, and often instructive manner.

For the classroom teacher, the study of typical sentence patterns is likely to prove the most immediately fruitful part of the new grammar we have developed. The section of our school grammar that presents such patterns can *display* typical relationships rather than catalogue related items. It can thus reinforce the intuitive sense of "what goes with what" that is basic in language learning. Generally, the teacher discussing syntax is more likely to take his class with him if he starts from a display of patterns than if he starts from an inventory of parts of speech. Most teachers are Gestalt psychologists to the extent of realizing that recurrent configurations are more easily grasped and remembered than separate, disconnected items.

The most useful of the analytic tools provided by the structural linguist is his account of the major grammatical devices. By pointing out changes in word order, inflection, and use of function words, we can

---

23 Francis, *Structure*, p. 293.
24 *Structural Essentials of English* (New York: Harcourt, Brace & World, Inc., 1956), p. 37.

identify the distinctive structural features of the sentences in a set like the following:

> The boy follows the dog.
> Dogs followed the boy.
> Follow the boy's dogs.
> Dog the following boys.
> Follow the boy with the dog.
> Follow the dog to the boy.

By adding punctuation marks signaling characteristic intonation patterns we produce further variations like

> Dogs followed the boy?
> Follow the dog, boys.
> The boy had followed the *dog?*

Such sets of contrasting patterns enable the teacher to demonstrate the workings of grammar without labeling each word and relationship, as required in the traditional parsing of sentences. The most effective demonstration of the workings of grammar is a pair of sentences clearly differing in meaning but contrasting only in one or two specific grammatical features:

> I *had repaired* the faucet.
> I *had* the faucet *repaired.*
>
> Watch his *handshake.*
> Watch his *hands shake.*
>
> He set *a* poor example.
> He set *the* poor *an* example.

In these and other ways, teacher and student can learn a great deal about English from the structural grammarian. On the other hand, there is no immediate prospect of structural grammar replacing other alternatives the way Copernican astronomy replaced Ptolemaic, or the way Harvey's account of the circulation of the blood replaced earlier physiological assumptions. In practice, the decision to teach a "modern" grammar brings the teacher face to face with a number of difficult choices.

In the first place, contrary perhaps to the teacher's original expectations, *a commitment to inductive procedures will produce authoritative information but not uniformity of description.* The inductive approach in itself does not generate criteria for choice when complex phenomena present equally legitimate alternative possibilities of classification. Language being as complex as it is, two equally competent observers, two equally expert "listeners," will bring back two different descriptive systems. Let us return, for instance, to the problem of setting up major word classes, or parts of speech. We will eventually have to decide whether to pigeonhole a word like *boy* with others fitting into the same general inflectional scheme (*boy, boy's, boys, boys'; child, child's, children, children's*), or with these *and others* occupying the same position in sentences:

> *Boys* broke loose.
> *Cats* broke loose.
> *Chaos* broke loose.

It is reasonable and consistent to make allowance for the difference between the inflectibility of *rain* and the noninflectibility of *chaos*. It is equally consistent to adopt a system that does justice to the obvious parallel between "Rain threatens" and "Chaos threatens." In other words, we will have to decide whether to adopt a two-track classification or a one-track classification of parts of speech; whether to rely on one criterion —that is, *either* inflection *or* position—or whether to mix the two:

> One main distinction among modern grammarians lies in their willingness or unwillingness to establish such mixed classes. A grammarian who uses mixed classes may define the noun by saying that nouns are inflected for plural and for possessive, that they take [certain] derivational suffixes . . . , and that they occur in frames like *The* (   ) *was good;* if a particular noun does not have all these characteristics, at least it occurs in the given syntactic frames. A grammarian who does not employ mixed classes may also define the noun by saying that nouns are inflected for plural and for possessive; but he will use the syntactic frame for defining a different class, the nominal. The first grammarian will have a smaller number of classes with more complicated definitions; the second will have a larger number of classes with simpler definitions; but if both have done their work well, their statements should ultimately come to much the same thing.[25]

The same question arises in regard to the adjective: a "morphological" or inflectional class of adjectives would include words like *pretty*, which have the *er–est* inflection. A "syntactic" or positional class of "adjectivals" would include all adjectives *and* words like *beautiful* that are not inflected but fit into a frame like "The _____ house was very _____." The importance we attach to inflection in setting up parts of speech would at the same time help determine whether or not we would regard pronouns as a subclass of nouns, or auxiliaries as a subclass of verbs. Obviously, nouns and pronouns, and similarly verbs and auxiliaries, differ drastically in their inflectional schemes, with pronouns and verbs being much more fully inflected than nouns and auxiliaries.

Two grammarians employing two different systems, if they have done their work well, can take comfort in the knowledge that they are dealing with the same phenomena. Two teachers teaching two different systems cannot help being worried by the knowledge that, in successive

---

[25] James H. Sledd, *A Short Introduction to English Grammar* (Chicago: Scott, Foresman & Company, 1959), p. 235. Copyright © 1959 by Scott, Foresman & Company, Chicago.

years, they may be dealing with the same students. Such teachers should not expect differences of this kind to be settled on purely theoretical grounds, or, as one linguist put it, "to come out in the wash." To make one of these systems generally acceptable, we would have to recognize frankly the element of convention and, if necessary, of arbitrary choice, that a scientific approach rules out only if naively interpreted.

Other disagreements arise over methods of subdividing the major syntactic units, such as the noun clusters and the verb clusters, into their major constituents. Much such analysis proceeds on the assumption that "every structure may be divided into its immediate constituents (often abbreviated IC's by linguists), almost always two, each of which may in turn be divided and subdivided until the ultimate constituents (in grammar, the words) are reached."[26] Here is an example of such successive cuts into **immediate constituents:**

> While we were waiting, the dogs in the kennel barked loudly.
> While we were waiting/the dogs in the kennel barked loudly.

> While/we were waiting
>   we/were waiting
>   were/waiting

>   the dogs in the kennel/barked loudly
>   the dogs/in the kennel
>   the/dogs

>   in/the kennel
>   the/kennel
>   barked/loudly[27]

To a large extent, analysis of this kind separates familiar subunits of sentences: subordinate clause from main clause, subject from predicate, verb from adverb, preposition from its object. Some adjustment is required for the traditionally trained teacher when the major cut shifts to reflect the difference between *often* as a **sentence modifier,** set apart by a characteristic intonation pattern, and *often* as an ordinary adverb:

> Often/we walked together.
> We/walked together often.

More serious puzzles result when *the little girl* is divided *the/little girl* rather than into *the girl* and *little,* or when *did John come* is divided *did John/come* rather than into *John* and *did come.* Some linguists recognize "discontinuous constituents." Thus, H. A. Gleason, Jr. indicates that *did the man come* "is clearly to be cut *did . . . come/the man.*"[28] Hill, after cutting *did John buy* into *did John* and *buy* "reassembles" the

26 Francis, *Structure,* p. 293.
27 Paul Roberts, *Patterns of English* (New York: Harcourt, Brace & World, Inc., 1956), p. 149.
28 *Introduction to Descriptive Linguistics,* p. 142.

parts of the verb here separated in a later discussion of "sentence elements."[29]

As a result of these and similar questions, the scope and usefulness of immediate-constituent analysis is a matter of dispute, and teachers and textbook authors are wise to approach it with caution. In the words of James Sledd,

> An analysis by twos works very well on some sentences and sentence parts, but it quickly encounters difficulties, even with familiar sentences like *It's a shame the way he loafs* or *Actually, I don't have the least idea what he is talking about.* In addition, there is the problem of the pitch patterns and stress patterns . . . which must appear as constituents at some point but which many analyses of constituents quietly ignore . . . . the analyses which have so far been proposed differ widely among themselves and are often quite arbitrary.[30]

On questions of alternative analysis, the teacher necessarily depends to a large extent on the verdict of the experts. On other matters, he is likely to have strong opinions of his own. One of these concerns a basic matter of pedagogical emphasis and convenience. The teacher of rhetoric or of literature, concerned mainly with written English, finds that the detour through the sound-system is not justified by results directly relevant to his interests, such as the limited use of intonational clues in the teaching of punctuation. The traditionally inclined teacher is likely to feel strongly that

> like the Wife of Bath's Prologue, a fully worked out phonology would be an excessively long preamble to our tale, and coming first it would tend to get the most thorough teaching, at the expense of grammar proper.[31]

One major obstacle to the adoption of a school grammar on the inductive model is that the teacher of composition, eager to tell his students what is wrong with their writing, chafes at the bit while working his way through a one-hundred-page analysis of phonetics and phonemics.

One final difficulty concerns the relation of structural grammar to other closely related areas of the discipline of English. Strict adherence to inductive procedures rules out concessions to historical perspective in the description of current speech. As Leonard Bloomfield said, the observer who allows historical knowledge "to affect his description, is bound to distort his data."[32] To the traditionally oriented philologist, "understanding" a linguistic item means "seeing it in its historical relations"— a definition of "understanding" widely applicable, and most fruitful, in the humanities and social sciences. To the structural linguist, interested in the "mathematics" of language, understanding a linguistic item means

---

29 *Introduction*, pp. 350–351.
30 Sledd, *Short Introduction*, pp. 216–17.
31 Ralph B. Long, "Grammar by Breakthrough?" *College English*, XXIV (November, 1962), 104.
32 Bloomfield, *Language*, pp. 19–20.

placing it in a "synchronic," that is, strictly current and to that extent ahistorical, system of the greatest possible descriptive economy and consistency.

For instance, a historical approach makes us understand English personal pronouns as a partial survival of a system of inflections that has disappeared in other areas of the language, leaving such other remnants as the possessive form of nouns. This approach throws light on the relative lack of system, of clear-cut formal correspondences, by pointing out such developments as the importation from the speech of Scandinavian settlers

> of the pronominal forms *they, them* and *their,* which entered readily into the system of English pronouns beginning with the same sound (*the, that, this*) and were felt to be more distinct than the old native forms which they supplanted. Indeed these were liable to constant confusion with some forms of the singular number (*he, him, her*) after the vowels had become obscured, so that *he* and *hie, him* and *heom, her* (*hire*) and *heora* could no longer be kept easily apart . . . . although the *th*–forms must consequently be reckoned a great advantage to the language, it took a long time before the old forms were finally displaced, nay, the dative *hem* still survives in the form *'em* ("take 'em"), which is now by people ignorant of the history of the language taken to be a shortened *them;* her "their" is the only form for the possessive of the plural found in Chaucer (who says *they* in the nominative) and there are two or three instances in Shakespeare.[33]

A strictly synchronic approach would treat *they* simply as a present member of the system. It would note, perhaps, that like *we* and *she* it consists of initial consonant, invariant vowel, and, in the subject-form, a final glide that appears in phonemic transcription as *y. They* might then be seen as part of a system in which "the initial consonant carries the person, number, and gender distinctions," and in which the final *m* of *him* and *them* is the "morphemic norm" of the suffix for the object-forms. In such a system, we could then construct a sequence for deriving *us,* for instance, from a "normal" form of *we* + final *m.*[34] As in much other linguistic literature "X becomes Y" would not mean "X historically developed into Y" but "Y may be produced from X if we so choose for purposes of analysis."

The nonlinguist's objection to such analysis stems from the use of terms like *becomes, derives, basic, primary,* and *normal* in their nonhistorical sense: "A form called a variant may, in point of fact, be older than the norm, so that in a historical sense the term 'departure' would be more applicable to the norm than to the variant." To the historically oriented teacher, *us* is more basic a form in the English system of pronouns than the historical latecomer *them* that helps the linguist set up the *–m* forms as a "norm" from which *us* would have to be derived.

---

[33] Jespersen, *Growth and Structure,* pp. 73–74.
[34] Hill, *Introduction,* pp. 145–50.

Rigorously synchronic analysis here obscures the point that high-frequency forms (e.g. forms of *to be,* personal pronouns, etc.) survive as vestigial, nonsystematic elements, learned as individual, "irregular" items.[35]

The interests of the historian and the descriptive grammarian are not mutually exclusive; they are merely different. In theory, the historical and the synchronic approaches are two different but complementary ways of "understanding English." If we had world enough and time, each future teacher could take solid coursework in the present structure of English, solid coursework in the history of English, and then learn to convert historical into synchronic terms and vice-versa. In his practice as a student and teacher of literary texts, however, the classroom teacher typically engages in constant cross reference between the current and the historical. Since he will often be giving descriptive and historical information in the same breath, he will be hostile to terms whose descriptive meanings are the opposite of the historical meanings with which he is familiar. He will welcome a descriptive system that enables him to pass from the descriptive to the historical and vice-versa with as few methodological and terminological barriers as possible.

In the words of Albert C. Baugh, "without the historical perspective the teacher's attempt to explain the text of much earlier literature will be but a form of groping." Any teacher of English must be prepared to comment on forms and constructions like the following:

> Today we would not say *they runs,* but when Shakespeare says *Whose own hard dealings teaches them suspect the thoughts of others* modern editions often change the text to *dealing.* But *dealings teaches* is the reading of the First Folio and is neither a misprint nor a solecism. It represents a plural form of the verb quite common in London English at the end of the sixteenth century. There are differences of idiom which turn upon the use of the verb. Instead of *Is execution done on Cawdor?* we would say *has been. Goes the king hence today?* would be *Does the king go?* or *Is the king leaving?* . . . Perhaps the greatest variety of differences is in the idiomatic use of prepositions. Chaucer provides an abundance of examples, but Shakespeare offers just as many: *I'll rent the fairest house in it after* (at) *threepence a day, one that I brought up of* (from) *a puppy, the pity of* (about) *him, I am provided of* (with) *a torchbearer, that did but show thee of* (as) *a fool.*[36]

A meaningful program of instruction in language must present its current structure and its past history, not as two separate worlds, but as two intimately related branches of study that illuminate one another.

To sum up, the teacher investigating inductively oriented structural grammar finds it offers him a fresh perspective and sharpens his perception of many basic features of English grammar. It offers him a choice of materials broadly similar in their general rationale though differing to

35 *Ibid.,* p. 454.
36 Albert C. Baugh, "Historical Linguistics and the Teacher of English," *College English,* XXIV (November, 1962), 107.

some extent in procedure and in details of analysis. Its premises and methods often make it unnecessarily difficult for him to function as a teacher of English, considered a diverse but basically unified discipline, rather than as an exponent of a more narrowly limited specialty. Its successful use in the classroom requires, not discipleship, but careful and diversified preparatory study and imaginative and resourceful adaptation.

Transformational Grammar

The teacher exploring possible approaches to modern grammar soon finds that neither "descriptive" nor "scientific" is synonymous with "inductive." Linguists like Noam Chomsky and R. B. Lees have in recent years initiated a vigorous reaction against linguists who, "to render grammatical analysis scientific," advocated "a description based on directly observable physical properties of utterances." They have traced "the notion that a linguistic description be based exclusively upon the phonemic shape of expressions" at least in part to "a mistaken idea that success in the physical sciences arises from strictly empirical induction out of observables." They have rejected as inadequate a grammar limited to segmentation and classification rigidly tied to the "overt shape of sentences" and recognizing "only those syntactic features of sentences which are clearly and overtly mirrored in the physical shape of the utterance."[37]

If we are deductively oriented, we may want to model our school grammar instead on an analysis that derives more elaborate structures from a few simple patterns. This is the kind of procedure that would be applicable to the coding of an electronic speech machine. We would want a system by which the machine, through successive operations, could construct complicated patterns from relatively few simple elements. Our interest would center on how grammatical utterances could be most economically and reliably generated or produced.

Instead of trying to formulate a rigorously prescribed inductive method, we would proceed on the assumption that "one may arrive at a grammar by intuition, guess-work, all sorts of partial methodological hints, reliance on past experience, etc." The real test of such a grammar would lie not in its investigative origins but in its descriptive consequences. In much scientific work, more important than the formulation of a foolproof "discovery procedure" is verification, that is, the test of whether or not a given hypothesis works. From this point of view, "there is little motivation . . . for the feeling that syntactic work is premature until all problems of phonemics or morphology are solved."[38]

[37] R. B. Lees, "A Multiply Ambiguous Adjectival Construction in English," *Language,* XXXVI (April–June, 1960), 207–09.
[38] Chomsky, *Syntactic Structures,* pp. 56, 106.

Though thus differing sharply from the structural grammarian in his assumptions about method, the advocate of a **generative grammar** would pursue in even more deliberate and single-minded fashion the same basic aim: to explore language as a system. Convertibility of complicated structures into simpler ones makes for emphasis on the internal coherence both of the descriptive system and the underlying system of language:

> We can greatly simplify the description of English and gain new and important insight into its formal structure if we limit the direct description in terms of phrase structure to a kernel of basic sentences (simple, declarative, active, with no complex verb or noun phrases), deriving all other sentences from these . . . by transformation, possibly repeated.[39]

The resulting "transformational" grammar gives students and teachers a strong feeling that things make sense, that the complex phenomena of grammar are being reduced to a simple rationale.

The operations to be performed in such a generative or transformational grammar appeal to the teacher looking for concrete manipulations that students can engage in. In traditional approaches, the "rules" are often a labyrinth of *ad hoc* regulations outlawing more or less unrelated usages. In transformational grammar, the rules are formulas for building sentences. They are designed to provide a theoretical model of how native speakers "construct quickly during conversation a never-ending succession of novel sentences each of which conforms perfectly to the requirements of well-formedness of his language."[40]

Transformational rules show us how to construct from a **kernel sentence** like

John ate the apple

such **transformations** as

John was eating the apple
did John eat the apple
John didn't eat the apple
the apple was eaten by John
who ate the apple
what did John eat

The kernel sentences would be the familiar basic sentence patterns we encountered earlier. The three or four most common of these can be reduced to a general formula something like the following:

First noun phrase + (possible auxiliary) + verb + (possible second noun phrase)

The rule for forming the passive from a sentence like "John ate the apple," where "verb" means "transitive verb," could then be spelled out somewhat as follows:

---

[39] *Ibid.*, pp. 106–07.
[40] Robert B. Lees, "The Promise of Transformational Grammar," *The English Journal*, LII (May, 1963), 327.

Passive = Second noun phrase + (possible auxiliary) + appropriate form of
be + past participle of verb + (by + first noun phrase)

Such transformation is not a one-way procedure; rather, the possibility of this transformation is what, in this system of analysis, defines the category of "transitive verb." Obviously, the transcription of such rules can be greatly simplified by an appropriate system of notation, such as perhaps

Passive = NP_2 + (aux) + be + V-en + (by + NP_1)

A completely developed transformational grammar would provide formulas for modification, co-ordination, subordination, and substitution that would allow us to derive the most complex sentence by successive transformations from building blocks of the "The man did such and such" and "The man seemed so and so" type.

Transformational rules provide methods for demonstrating differences between certain superficially alike structures. These methods are parallel to such devices, encountered earlier, as the attempted substitution of passive equivalents for "John becomes a man" and "John shoots a man." The linking verb here is the one that does not allow a passive transform on the model of "A man was shot by John." If we try to find a similar test to explain the felt difference between "the doctor's arrival" and "the doctor's house," we can start from the observation that the one is in some way related to the subject-predicate relationship in "The doctor arrives," whereas the other seems akin to the subject-verb-object relationship in "The doctor has a house." In "John is easy to please," *John* is related to *please* in a manner akin to the verb-object relationship in "Someone pleases John"; in "John is eager to please," they are related in a manner akin to the subject-verb relationship in "John pleases someone."

A transformational grammar would make an account of such relationships a basic ingredient in much grammatical classification. It thus would get at "deeper structural relations" than are revealed by traditional sentence diagrams or by immediate-constituent analysis. For instance, there seems to be no formal or structural difference between "the growling of lions" and "the raising of flowers." It is true that we recognize the different *logical* relationship between verbal and noun in each case. According to the premises of descriptive linguistics, however, "we have no right to ascribe to any language a logical distinction which it leaves unexpressed."[41] The distinction *is* expressed, not in the phrases themselves, but in the **source sentences** from which they are derived. In other words, their transformational history is different. The first is a transform of "The lions growl"; the second is a transform of a sentence like "John raises flowers."

If a purely structural grammar has no way of formulating the felt

41 Sturtevant, *Introduction*, p. 54.

grammatical difference between the two versions of "gerund + *of* + noun," then a transformational grammar is more "powerful" to the extent that it does. Assuming for the moment that transformational analysis in syntax would prove compatible with our previous findings on other levels, it would in effect add another level of analysis to our previous levels of phonemic, morphemic, and syntactic investigation. At the same time, transformational analysis lifts us to a level of abstraction where verification no longer takes the form of reference to immediately observable data. As an account of how grammar works, it postulates mental operations in a manner not compatible with a strictly behavioristic point of view.

Addition of the transformational dimension introduces an additional criterion for such problems as the definition of parts of speech. We have seen, for instance, that "adjective" may be defined according to inflection ("a word that takes *er–est* for comparison") and according to position ("a word that fits a frame like *The* _____ *house is very* _____"). It is also possible, however, to use the term *adjective* for a group of modifiers that have the same transformational history. Thus, Noam Chomsky calls *sleeping* in "the sleeping child" an adjective, since it derives from a sentence parallel to the source sentences of "the tall boy" and "the little girl":

> The boy is tall.
> The girl is little.
> The child is sleeping.

At the same time, whereas "The boy is tall," is a kernel sentence, "The child is sleeping," is a transformation of "The child sleeps." *Sleeping* is restricted from entering such adjective positions as "the very sleeping child" because there are no sentences like "The child very sleeps." This kind of analysis does justice to the peculiar hybrid status, between verb and adjective, of verbals like the present and past participle.[42]

Adding a transformational dimension to grammar provides a solution to some of the puzzles mentioned earlier in immediate-constituent analysis. Instead of cutting "the kind man" into "The/kind man," we can now point to the source sentence, where the basic elements appear separated as "*The man* is *kind.*" Instead of cutting "bring/the criminal in," we can now analyze it as a transformation of "*bring in* the criminal." Analysis of phrases and clauses into their major elements is thus no longer tied to mere accidents of contiguity. Transformational analysis makes it possible to emphasize the often close relationships between elements separated from each other in a sentence.

The appeal of a transformational grammar lies in its being, in several senses of the word, a "constructive" approach. It makes possible

---

42 Chomsky, *Syntactic Structures*, pp. 72–75.

cumulative progression from the basic and simple to the complicated; more obviously so than in other possible approaches, one sentence leads to another. It allows the teacher to concentrate on essentials, to explore fundamental relationships. In more than isolated instances, it makes the teacher feel that he is dealing with a "deeper underlying regularity" not always sufficiently focused on in other grammatical systems.[43]

At the same time, the classroom teacher must be careful not to misinterpret the claims made by the transformational grammarians. He is likely to agree with Paul Roberts that the grammarian's task should be "to be always trying to describe languages in the shortest and simplest way possible."[44] He will further agree that we obtain a relatively neat and systematic description of English if we assume the existence of a small set of kernel sentences and then derive more complicated patterns from the kernels. On the other hand, he will soon find that the transformational formulas themselves, to be accurate and workable, must be elaborate and complex rather than short and simple. A transformational grammar is "simple" in the sense of being more unified, more highly abstract and systematic, than more miscellaneous and "atomistic" alternatives.

For example, the traditional analysis of *kind* in "the kind man" as a modifier that modifies by juxtaposition is short and simple, however hard it may prove to limit in a satisfactory way the concept of modification. To analyze "the kind man" as a transformation of "the man is kind" is an elaborate but effective technical device. In effect, it sets up a test pattern as the "derivation" of the adjective-noun relationship. That this relationship "derives" from the test pattern here means "analyzing it thus makes for an efficient and coherent over-all system"; it does not mean "it is so learned" or "teaching it thus will illuminate the felt relationship between headword and modifier." From the point of view of language learning, the simple juxtaposition of *kind* and *man* is more "basic" than the predication using the linking verb. In transformational grammar, the term "basic" refers to patterns that may be so manipulated as to produce all other patterns; it does not cover all the basic relationships intuitively grasped by the native speaker as recurrent configurations. In language learning, "There's milk on the table" contains as basic a pattern as "I drank my milk"; in transformational grammar it is possible to produce "there-is" sentences from the subject-verb sequence. In other words, *there is/there are* is *learned* as a basic pattern, though it may be *analyzed* as a transformation. When transformational analysis is presented as a literal account of how we construct sentences (rather than as an analytical device), it invites the criticism that "constructions are not produced one from

43 Chomsky, *Syntactic Structures*, p. 68.
44 *English Sentences* (New York: Harcourt, Brace & World, Inc., 1962), p. 59.

another . . . but filed side by side" and that the users of a language
do not "produce" constructions but instead " 'reach for' them, from a
pre-established inventory."[45]

The most immediate question for the teacher interested in transformational grammar is that of its compatibility with previous linguistic
work. As sketched by Chomsky, the full description of a grammatical
utterance would involve the identification of one or more kernels from
which it is derived, the application of one or more syntactic transformations, and the application of "morphophonemic" rules that would translate the syntactic sequence thus worked out into its actual phonetic
form. This analytic model differs from that of the structural or "anthropological" linguist in a number of ways. The first difference is of course
the addition of the transformational dimension in syntax, with a resulting
shift from "surface" grammar to "deep" grammar. The most characteristic contribution of the generative grammarian is his insistence that
"part of the syntactic structure of a sentence is the set of underlying, sometimes very abstract, representations of the simpler sentences from which
it may be said to be derived by explicit grammatical rules called 'grammatical transformations.' "[46]

The second, and perhaps crucial, difference between structuralist
and transformationalist is the latter's denial of the importance and
priority of phonemic transcription, since many matters of sound, for
instance, the distribution of stresses, "are exactly predictable from the
syntactic structure of the sentence."[47] The generative grammarian concerns himself with structural and transformational analysis *first* and
then shows how the results of such analysis "play a role in determining
the details of phonetic shape." Seen from this point of view, "much of
the perceived phonetic shape of an utterance . . . is a reflection of its
syntactic structure."[48] Here we have a significant departure from the
empirical, inductive linguist's program of "from sound to syntax to
sense." In working from syntax to phonetic shape, transformational
grammars on the Chomsky model would apparently eliminate the level
of phonemics, considered independent of syntactic structure, as a major
significant level of analysis. Because of the dependence of phonetic shape
on syntactic structure, the transformationalist finds "little motivation
for the objection to mixing levels" of analysis, which had been one of
the major caveats observed by the structural linguist.[49]

A transformational grammar will be an extremely tightly organized
and interrelated grammar. It will place great stress on the *order* in which

---

[45] D. L. Bolinger, "Syntactic Blends and Other Matters," *Language,* XXXVII
(1961), 381.
[46] Lees, "Promise of Transformational Grammar," p. 330.
[47] *Ibid.,* p. 329.
[48] Chomsky, "Logical Basis," *Preprints,* pp. 531, 556.
[49] Chomsky, *Syntactic Structures,* p. 106.

successive transformations and morphophonemic rules have to be applied
in order to produce correct results. In requiring ability to think several
moves ahead, structural grammar is to transformational grammar as check-
ers is to chess. Though transformational analysis frequently discovers
"underlying regularities" tying together diverse data, it will have to be
complex enough to make allowance for its own exceptions and irregularities. For instance, a passive sentence like "He was taken ill" does not have
a corresponding active "Someone took him ill." Though transformational
analysis frequently gets at distinctions that cannot be formulated in
purely structural terms, it often does so in formidably elaborate ways.
For instance, suggested transformational solutions for distinguishing
"I don't approve of [the manner of] his dancing" and "I don't approve
of [the fact of] his dancing" reach a level of complication and subtlety
that will frighten away all but the most cerebral of teachers.

There is no easily predictable outcome of conflicts between competing systems of modern grammar. The years ahead will see new developments in research and linguistic theory. At the same time, textbook
authors will be exploring the possibilities of compromise between different
systems. The teacher will be wise to concentrate on that part of the
linguist's contribution that sharpens his, and the students', perception
of specific constructions and relationships. He will focus his teaching not
on how the linguist works, but on how the language works. Such a pragmatic approach will protect the teacher against repeatedly having to
climb back after having gone out on theoretical and methodological
limbs.

Traditional Grammar

Regardless of the particular position he adopts, the advocate of a
modern grammar is confronted with the continued widespread influence
of a system that owes its authority less to a cogent methodology than to the
power of custom. And yet more than custom is involved. The teacher
trained in, or working with, one or more of the more commonly taught
foreign languages will continue to be attracted toward some sort of
proto-Indo-European grammar. That is, he will prefer a system whose
terms and categories are easily transferable from one Indo-European
language to another. He would rather not be required to remember that
chaos is a nominal in English but a noun in Greek, or that *competent* is
an adjectival in English but an adjective in German. He will feel that
there is ample historical justification for calling *cat's* a genitive in *the cat's
meow* and for preserving similar Latinizing terminology. Languages are
not "unique" any more than they are approximations of "universal
grammar." They typically exist in dialect clusters and language families
exhibiting various patterns of similarity and contrast. The teacher with

strong interlingual interests will naturally prefer a grammar that emphasizes the similarities to one that emphasizes the contrasts.

Historically, an improvised proto-Indo-European grammar was widely
adopted when schoolmasters in the different European countries began
to line up the grammar of the vernacular in a system parallel to that of
the Latin grammar then primarily taught:

> The chief language taught was Latin; the first and in many cases the only
> grammar with which scholars came into contact was Latin grammar. No
> wonder therefore that grammar and Latin grammar came in the minds of
> most people to be synonyms. Latin grammar played an enormous role in the
> schools, to the exclusion of many subjects (the pupil's own native language,
> science, history, etc.) which we are now beginning to think more essential for
> the education of the young. The traditional term for "secondary school" was
> in England "grammar school" and in Denmark *latinskole,* and the reason
> for both expressions was obviously the same.[50]

When the business of the schools was to teach the classical languages, the
adoption of a Latinizing grammar for the student's native language was
a simple matter of pedagogical expediency. Even today, as Harold Whitehall once observed, the resulting "traditional" grammar "does something
to allow the student to move smoothly into the study of such morphological languages" as Latin, Greek, or German.[51]

The weaknesses of the traditional Latinizing grammar have been
widely publicized:

> Latin was a language with a wealth of flexional forms, and in describing
> other languages the same categories as were found in Latin were applied as
> a matter of course, even where there was nothing in these other languages
> which really corresponded to what was found in Latin. In English and
> Danish grammars paradigms of noun declension were given with such cases
> as accusative, dative and ablative, in spite of the fact that no separate forms
> for these cases had existed for centuries. All languages were indiscriminately
> saddled with the elaborate Latin system of tenses and moods in the verbs,
> and by means of such Procrustean methods the actual facts of many
> languages were distorted and misrepresented.[52]

Some European languages have remained closer to the Latin mold
than others. By the same token, traditional grammar provides a much
better fit for highly inflected Old English than for its relatively uninflected
modern offspring. A verb paradigm beginning

I say	we say
you say	you say
he (she, it) says	they say

[50] Jespersen, *Language,* pp. 22–23.
[51] Walter G. Friedrich, ed., "A Modern-Grammar Chrestomathy" (Valparaiso, Indiana, mimeo., 1961), p. 12.
[52] Jespersen, *Language,* p. 23.

is an exercise in contrastive Indo-European grammar, since the items are filled in in accordance with the formal distinctions exhibited in the *amo—amas—amat* pattern of Latin. Such translated paradigms raise obvious questions of completeness and consistency. If "I *shall (will)* leave" is declared the English future tense, parallel to Latin *amabo*, it may be objected that "I *am going to* leave" has just as good a claim to the future-tense label. If "I *should (would)* leave" is included in the paradigm of the English verb, so should "I *may* leave," "I *must* leave," and "I *ought to* leave" be. If "of the boy" and "to the boy" are listed as English cases, why not "with the boy" and "without the boy"? Studying the conjugations and declensions of a full-fledged traditional grammar, the alert schoolboy used to discover the difference between the highly systematic inflections of **synthetic** Latin and the reliance on function words of **analytic** English, even though his teachers did not formulate such a distinction.

Apart from the question of its descriptive accuracy, the traditional grammar suffered from a basic weakness that handicapped its adherents in scholarly debate. Being originally a pedagogical improvisation, it lacked a clear and cogent methodology. Typically, the future teacher learned it without examining its origins and assumptions. He learned definitions and categories without having to formulate the principles underlying the system of classification, the procedures used in constructing it, or the criteria applied to determine its adequacy:

> Even the most careful and complete traditional grammar relies in an essential way on the intuition and intelligence of the user, who is expected to draw the correct inferences from the many examples and hints (and explicit lists of irregularities) presented by the grammar. If the grammar is a good one, the user may succeed, but the deep-seated regularities of the language that he somehow discovers escape explicit formulation.[53]

Nevertheless, the traditional grammar has a staying power that its adversaries tend to underestimate. Like our similarly archaic spelling system it has become a more or less ingrained part of our cultural tradition. Many a classroom teacher shares the feeling that the traditional grammar is "quite adequate for my personal needs."[54] He feels that the traditional system of classification allows him to identify adequately enough those matters of usage and style with which he is most directly concerned. When turning to linguistics for new information and new ideas, he has not always succeeded in identifying the linguist's concrete contribution to the analysis of English and its bearing on classroom work. When examining proposed new analyses, the teacher has at times felt that the linguist was shifting the grammatical blanket so as to cover the shoulders while at the same time uncovering the feet.

[53] Chomsky, "Logical Basis," *Preprints*, p. 512.
[54] William R. Bowden, ". . . The Way They Say It," *College English*, XXII (April, 1961), 479.

For instance, the traditional grammar sets up a general category of verbs and then distinguishes a subclass of auxiliary verbs, including the modal auxiliaries (*can, may,* etc.) as well as *have* and *be*. A modern grammarian, for the sake of accurate distinctions, may exclude auxiliaries from the category of verbs and further, exclude *have* and *be* from the category of auxiliaries, calling the latter, for instance, simply "a *be.*" Obviously, *can* and *be* differ greatly not only in inflectional scheme but in the roles they play in verb phrases like *can ask, was asked, can be asked,* and *could have been asked*. On the other hand, there are certain elementary statements about English structure that apply to modals, *have,* and *be* taken together. Deprived of the common category, the teacher has to enumerate its individual members. For instance, he may want to describe the change in word order when statements are transformed into questions beginning with interrogatives like *where* and *what*. Here is the generalization suggested by a set of examples like "Where can John go? Where is John going? Where does John go?":

> In the sentences with a modal, a *have,* or a *be,* the modal, *have,* or *be* plus the tense reverses with the subject. But when there is no modal, *have,* or *be,* only the tense reverses, and then a *do* is put in to carry it.[55]

Since students will find this statement hard to read, let alone remember, the teacher will be strongly tempted to convert it into traditional terms:

> In the sentences with an auxiliary verb, the auxiliary, in the appropriate tense form, changes position with the subject. But when there is no auxiliary, an appropriate tense form of *do* takes the place the auxiliary would otherwise occupy.

The pedagogical justification for setting up inclusive general categories is the limited number of discrete ideas the student can keep in mind at one time. There is truth in the linguist's charge that traditional categories lump together items quite different in grammatical behavior. But this does not mean that the distinctions between such subclasses cannot be formulated in traditional terms. For instance, *brown* in *the brown house* is obviously an "adjective" in a different sense from *brick* in *the brick wall*. The traditionalist might say that brick is "a noun used as an adjective" or, somewhat less ambiguously, a noun serving what is typically an adjective function. Pointing out that the distinction is ambiguously formulated by the traditional grammarian is a quite different matter from claiming that he is unaware of it. Similarly, the traditional grammarian may call *home* in *The man came home* a "noun used as an adverb." The formula may be ambiguous, but it does show recognition of the special status of this use of *home* and of the possible parallel it offers to such Latin "adverbial" accusatives of direction as *Romam,* "to" or "toward Rome."

55 Roberts, *English Sentences,* p. 225.

Stripped of its pretensions to completeness and finality, the traditional framework provides many teachers of language and literature with a rough and ready means of communicating about language. In recent decades, the adaptation of the traditional grammar for this purpose has taken a characteristic form. The teacher's interest is often limited to a **functional grammar,** adequate to identify usages that have social or stylistic significance. In such an approach, the concept of the sentence, for instance, is studied for its bearing on sentence fragments and run-on sentences rather than for its own sake. The inflectional scheme of personal pronouns is studied to help the student avoid "Me and my friends like it" and "between you and I." Ironically, this approach is finding wide acceptance in the secondary schools at a time when there is a massive countermovement to include the structure of the English language as "basic subject-matter for its own sake" throughout the student's high school training.[56] From the linguist's point of view, functional grammars promote a lopsided or distorted view of the language because "they overemphasize those elements of English structure where usage is divided, and underemphasize those elements where divided usage is impossible for native speakers and writers."[57]

The functional approach appeals to the teacher because it allows him to do without the clanking machinery of conventional grammatical instruction, with its endless reviews and drills for the benefit of unreceptive students. In the more extreme version of functionalism, the decision to "take up the students' problems as they come up" has an attractively businesslike air about it. However, the bits and snatches of grammar thus accumulated do not necessarily lead to a grasp of essential principles. Recognizing a sentence fragment finally requires an understanding of the English sentence with all its major characteristics and variations. Among other things, it requires the ability to distinguish finite verbs from verbals, subordinating from co-ordinating conjunctions (and more generally dependent from independent clauses), subjectless sentences from mere unattached verb phrases. Consider for instance the following pairs:

> We intend to go on fighting. For all is lost if liberty is lost.
> We intend to go on fighting. Because all is lost if liberty is lost.
>
> His comment was the same as usual. What money the youngsters make!
> He asked his usual question. What money the youngsters make.

To distinguish between the fragment and the complete sentence in each pair, the teacher has to provide explanations he cannot effectively improvise "to help you with this point that came up on your theme."

---

[56] Harold B. Allen, "With New Endeavor," *The English Journal,* LI (February, 1962), 75.

[57] James H. Sledd, "Grammar or Gramarye," *The English Journal,* XLIX (May, 1960), 300.

Carried to an extreme, the functional approach thwarts the teacher's desire "to build effectively upon preceding materials."[58]

Grammars and the Teacher

What, in retrospect, will the teacher gain from his examination of current developments in the teaching of English grammar? Above all, he will become aware of some of the criteria that an adequate grammatical system must meet. On the most elementary level, we would expect a grammar to give a fairly comprehensive inventory of the actual grammatical features of the language. We would expect it to report on such complications as the different plural forms of *horses* and *oxen,* the limitations on the uses of *ought,* the fact that words like *poor* may be used in both "He was extremely *poor*" and "The *poor* will always be with us." We say "fairly comprehensive," since anything like a complete inventory would be of staggering bulk. For instance, the native speaker automatically uses, or omits, definite and indefinite articles in accordance with a subtle set of grammatical conventions. He competently manages the distinctions that make for such contrasting pairs as

Let's have *pork chops* for dinner.
Let's have *the pork chops* for dinner.

Desertion is *grounds* for divorce.
Desertion is *a basis* for legal action.

Most school grammars wisely do not attempt to formalize these distinctions, since most students would get entangled in the grammatical machinery if they tried to do consciously and according to rule what they now do unconsciously and according to habit. On the other hand, instruction in English as a second language must be able to get at such distinctions—unless the student's first language happens to follow patterns closely related to those of English. Thus, whether or not our grammar covers the uses of the articles, or the complete system of modal auxiliaries, or the different kinds of juncture, must depend on what we consider most essential and instructive.

At the same time, the grammarian is typically interested not merely in taking inventory but in ordering his data. He is concerned with the internal logic, the consistency, the efficiency and economy of the descriptive system. The ideal system would be simple and orderly; it would move on a high level of abstraction and yet account fully for the phenomena observed. Language being as complex as it is, we look for major principles that make it work. We look for the sort of orderly and consistent descrip-

---

[58] Owen Thomas, "Generative Grammar: Toward Unification and Simplification," *The English Journal,* LI (February, 1962), 113.

tion that facilitates orientation, that makes complicated relationships intelligible.

In looking for such a description, we must remember that consistency is itself one of Bacon's idols of the theater, causing us to make intellectual systems "more compact and elegant" than the phenomena of nature. Simplicity and elegance are subjective expectations imported by the human mind into a world of raw data. Language, for instance, shows fossilized and vestigial features. Consider the irregular plural forms of *oxen* and *geese* and the absence of a distinctive plural form in *sheep* and *deer*. Hence the long lists of irregularities, exceptions, and unclassified items characteristic of many grammars. Just as the child's language in such cases shows the tendency toward analogy (forming a "regular" analogical plural *sheeps,* for example), the grammarian may look for "bookkeeping devices" that will fit recalcitrant items into an over-all system. Such a bookkeeping device in recent grammars is the concept of the **zero-form.** Postulating a "zero-suffix" allows us to fit *sheep* into a general pattern of the plural as "noun-plus-suffix."[59] In traditional grammar, the corresponding bookkeeping device is the concept of the **elliptical construction.** It allows the grammarian to fit "the man I love" into the same category as "the man *whom* I love" by postulating an omitted or "understood" relative pronoun.

From one point of view, such normalizing and systematizing devices are simply a matter of descriptive convenience. From another point of view, they frustrate the desire for the map that most accurately reflects the territory, the blueprint that most faithfully reflects the relation of parts. The desire for symmetry thus takes precedence over the search for the system that most faithfully rationalizes the speaker's intuitive feeling of similarity and difference in language.

To merit our full confidence, a grammar must make it one of its aims to recognize, to render "visible," the basic *asymmetries* of the language. Some of these asymmetries are illustrated in the grammatical behavior of *poor* and *beautiful.* Though the one is inflectible and the other is not, they share many uses as modifiers. Their characteristics overlap with those of the noun when they occur in noun positions: *"The poor* will always be with us."[60] Ingenuity in devising a scheme of analysis is misdirected if it is employed in glossing over, rather than faithfully reflecting, the complexities and overlappings here revealed.

The inevitable qualifications of the original commitment to consistency occur in some grammars sooner, in others later. As we have seen, our grammar, for the sake of consistency, may refuse to mix inflectional

59 Robert A. Hall, Jr., *Linguistics and Your Language* (New York: Doubleday & Company, Inc., 1960), p. 104.
60 Sumner Ives, "Grammar and Style," *The English Journal,* LII (May, 1963), 364–66.

and positional criteria in defining parts of speech. *Noun, verb,* and *adjective* would be defined strictly on the basis of inflection. Thus, the term *noun* would be limited to words showing the possessive or plural *s;* the term *adjective* to words fitting into the *er–est* series. The concession to inconsistency may come when we set up the adverb as a fourth major form class, but define it on the basis of the derivational suffix–*ly* rather than of inflection. It is exactly at such points that the grammarian exercises more or less arbitrary choice, basing his decision on what seems to make for the greatest possible plausibility and efficiency of his system.

It is also exactly at such points, where equally competent and accurate alternative analyses are possible, that the classroom teacher feels justified in bringing nonlinguistic criteria to bear. One of these is the need for a minimum of continuity in language teaching. The teacher cannot afford to imitate the specialist who says "the reader is urged to forget all he has ever learned about parts of speech and to follow the ensuing demonstration as if it were in some area of study wholly new to him, like molecular physics or symbolic logic."[61] Of two equally competent analyses, the teacher will have to choose, however reluctantly, the more conventional one. In the long run, he cannot contribute to a situation where *beautiful,* lacking the *er–est* inflection, would be an adjective in the eleventh grade but not in the twelfth, in the first but not in the second semester of college English. He will have to find a way of combining openness to new developments with willingness to work toward a reasonably effective consensus.

In its most elementary form, this problem confronts the teacher in connection with terminology. One of the major drawbacks of traditional grammar as a teaching tool has been the opaqueness of its Latinizing terms. Only the exceptional student was ever at ease with *subjective complement* and *objective complement, participle* and *gerund.* As a result, the teacher will welcome attempts to make grammatical terminology more native and more nearly self-explanatory. *Subordinator* is preferable to *subordinating conjunction* simply because it is less of a mouthful. *Headword, intensifier, determiner, cluster,* and *pattern* are terms English and meaningful enough to have a genuine chance to make themselves at home in the student's vocabulary. Often, however, a plain and familiar conventional term will serve once it has been more sharply defined. For instance, the teacher may be ready to admit that the term *present tense* is open to question, since the forms labeled *present* often imply future ("The bus *leaves* at eight"), habitual action involving both future and past ("He *drinks* heavily"), or simple past ("While we are marching along, I suddenly *notice* this round metallic object in the middle of the road"). However, he will not feel that he has gained anything if he adopts, with some grammarians, the term *nonpast* for the plain form of the verb. He

---

61 Francis, *Structure,* p. 235.

would trade a present tense that does not always point to present time for a nonpast form that, as in the historical present of "Suddenly I notice . . ." sometimes *does* point to the past.

The teacher or textbook author thus exercising his independent judgment will inevitably be using an "eclectic" grammar, bringing together what seems plausible and workable from different sources. The common denominator of such eclectic grammars will be *an account of the inflections and positions of the four major word classes and various minor categories, an account of basic sentence patterns, and an account of the ways in which these basic sentences may be modified, expanded, and transformed.* The linguist is likely to warn us that excessive stress on such a common denominator may lead to an eclecticism "undistinguished and even inconsistent."[62] It may well be that in the long run a complete and consistent new grammar of clearly superior plausibility will emerge from the present ferment. In the meantime, an incomplete and inconsistent but workable and informative one will have to do. The books of most urgent interest to the teacher of English are those that set out to demonstrate that various kinds and degrees of correlation between different approaches to grammar are possible. Such books are, on the high school level, Paul Roberts' *English Sentences;* on the undergraduate level, Brown, Brown, and Bailey, *Form in Modern English;* and on the undergraduate and graduate level, James Sledd's *Short Introduction to English Grammar.* Such books are contributing directly to the transition from a mere routine teaching of traditional grammar to a vigorous and well-informed teaching of the workings of language.

Not only in its eclecticism will the grammar taught in the schools differ from the work of the specialist. Constructing a school grammar is a different matter from simply following the descriptive procedures of the linguist. For instance, Robert A. Hall, in *Linguistics and Your Language,* discusses the descriptive efficiency of covering the less frequent plural forms (e.g., *oxen, sheep*) first and then concluding the description with the more general principle, introduced by "elsewhere" or "all others."[63] Teaching strategy, by contrast, puts the most frequent first, with the degree of later elaboration varying with the level of instruction and the purposes of the course. Beyond such questions of descriptive strategy, the teacher must be able to separate the substance of the grammarian's contribution not only from accidents of terminology but also from entirely optional graphic or illustrative devices. Whether to use Jabberwocky sentences to illustrate the workings of grammar, or what if any system of diagraming to employ—these are entirely secondary matters. The teacher rather than the specialist must make the necessary decisions regarding

---

[62] James H. Sledd, "Syntactic Strictures," *The English Leaflet,* LXI (Midwinter, 1962), 17.

[63] Hall, *Linguistics and Your Language,* pp. 104–05.

level of difficulty and method of presentation. The teacher who carries materials from a seminar in linguistics unchanged into his own classroom is merely sowing the seeds of disillusionment and confusion.

Grammar and Meaning

Among the considerations the teacher may bring to bear on the problem of constructing a school grammar, we have so far avoided the most controversial one. The traditionally trained teacher will ask of the school grammar that it reflect the relationship between grammar and logic, language and thought. In taking this question up last, we have already made a crucial concession to the linguist's point of view. Linguists have stressed the danger in allowing preconceptions about meaning to distract from accurate analysis of tangible grammatical signals.

The linguist usually has occasion to state his attitude toward meaning when rejecting the **notional,** that is, meaning-based definitions of traditional grammar. One such definition is that of the sentence as expressing "a complete thought." "Complete thought" is an elastic concept. Often a thought does not become reasonably complete until elaborated in a complete paragraph. On the other hand, a complex sentence may contain several distinct notions that could be called complete thoughts. Thus, the traditional definition is too vague for practical purposes. It provides no concrete clue for sorting out the sentences and nonsentences in a list like

1) He won't.
2) Because I'm not hungry.
3) For the lights were low.
4) Until next Wednesday then.
5) That does it.
6) A remarkable recovery!
7) Who has always helped us in our hour of need.
8) Who has always helped us in our hour of need?

If we decide to call 1, 3, 5, and 8 complete sentences, it is not because the thoughts they express are any more or less complete than those in the remaining examples. Instead, we apply such criteria as the presence of a subject-predicate skeleton and the absence of a subordinator (like *because* in 2) or relative pronoun (like *who* in 7). Whether we call 4 and 6 "nonsentences" or "permissible fragments" or "predicationless sentences" is a matter of terminological convenience little affected by the fact that the thoughts they express are for all practical purposes "complete."

Similarly, the formula "the verb expresses action or state of being" suffers from a fatal ambiguity. It does not enable the student to distinguish between *thieve* and *theft, evict* and *eviction, descend* and *descent*. It does not make allowance for the many grammatical devices by which some sort of action may be in some way or other "expressed." The linguist's reaction has typically been to leave the vague notional formula behind and describe grammatical phenomena concretely in terms of form, word order, and intonational contour. The resulting reorientation allows us to remove from our grammar many purely verbal definitions.

At the same time, another reaction to the vagueness of conventional meaning-based definitions is possible. We can attempt a more accurate account of the meaning relationships that the traditional definitions are groping for. As Edward Sapir says in *Language:*

> It is well to remember that speech consists of a series of propositions. There must be something to talk about and something must be said about this subject of discourse once it is selected. This distinction is of such fundamental importance that the vast majority of languages have emphasized it by creating some sort of formal barrier between the two terms of the proposition. The subject of discourse is a noun. As the most common subject of discourse is either a person or a thing, the noun clusters about concrete concepts of that order. As the thing predicated of a subject is generally an activity in the widest sense of the word, a passage from one moment of existence to another, the form which has been set aside for the business of predicating, in other words, the verb, clusters about concepts of activity. No language wholly fails to distinguish noun and verb, though in particular cases the nature of the distinction may be an elusive one.[64]

Such an attempt to formulate the semantic implications of grammatical devices appeals to the teacher whose overriding interest is in the relationship between language and experience, in the role of language in human life. Only a grammar that deals with both the signal *and* its semantic implications will strike such a teacher as complete.

The role of meaning even in the linguist's analysis and description is often more extensive than theoretical formulations would lead one to expect. Charles C. Fries formulated a prevailing view:

> Structures do signal meanings, it is true, and these meanings must be described. But the meanings cannot serve successfully to identify and distinguish the structures.

Again:

> In describing the results of the analysis, only verifiable physical terms of form, of arrangement, and of distribution are necessary. Whenever descriptive statements must depart from such formal matters, the fact is evidence of unsolved problems.

However, Fries went on to say that "I can see no merit in denying ourselves access to any sources of suggestions concerning the nature of the materials that are significant," specifying that "any use of meaning is unscientific whenever the fact of our knowing the meaning leads us to

[64] Sapir, *Language*, p. 119.

stop short of finding the precise formal signals that operate to convey that meaning."[65]

In practice, much of the linguist's work consists in finding "precise formal signals" and reliable objective formulas to pin down categories and relationships suggested by meaning. As W. Nelson Francis says, for instance, of his eleven "substitute-groups" for English nouns:

> This classification, though formal in operation, is based chiefly on meaning. Each of the groups could, in fact, be more or less accurately described in terms of the common denominator of meaning of the words it includes.[66]

Of transformational grammar, Archibald A. Hill says, "Transformational study requires that meaning be previously identified, and then states relationships between meaningful utterances."[67] Obviously, the active version of a sentence and its passive transformation are dissimilar in structure, and it is primarily their close relationship in meaning that makes us look for their grammatical connection. Conversely,

> the grammatical difference between the two following sentences, for instance, is apparent only because meanings of the words are different:
>> He wanted time to study.
>> He wanted Harry to study.
> Order, function words, forms of the words, and intonation are alike in the two sentences, but from our knowledge of the meanings of *time* and *Harry* we assume different structures.

When the generative grammarian distinguishes the two as transformations of different kernel sentences, "recognition of the difference depends on the words as semantic symbols."[68] Generally, transformational grammar will have to recognize categories conventionally considered lexical rather than grammatical: some rules may apply to nouns standing for persons but not objects, to nouns of place but not of time.

For the teacher, it is of great importance to what extent the school grammar will allow grammatical matters "to be more or less accurately described in terms of the common denominator of meaning." For instance, a formal definition of the subject-predicate relationship only partially makes explicit the felt relationship between a subject and its verb. The most tangible signal is agreement between subject and verb in that minority of instances where the verb form to be selected shows a singular-plural contrast: *asks—ask, is—are, was—were,* etc. Word order is a rough guide, but mere preverbal position does not reliably identify a noun or pronoun as subject: "On the dresser lay *an envelope.*" " 'Hello!'

---

[65] "Meaning and Linguistic Analysis," *Language,* XXX (January–March, 1954), 57–68; in Allen, *Readings,* pp 105, 112–13.
[66] Francis, *Structure,* pp. 250–51.
[67] "Linguistic Principles for Interpreting Meaning," *College English,* XXII (April, 1961), 473.
[68] Robert M. Gorrell, "Structure in Thought," *College English* XXIV, (May, 1963), 593.

said *John*." A merely formal definition of *subject* remains opaque unless it is supplemented by reference to the common "agent–action," "object–condition" relationship between subject and verb, as well as such variations of it as "receiver of action–action" and "result of performance–performance."

Similarly, we know that "John shot a man" and "John became a man" illustrate different grammatical patterns because only the first allows the passive transform: "A man was shot by John." In practice, however, we tell the patterns apart because two nouns linked by *became* point to the same referent. We can use such semantic correlations to describe the first pattern as "subject–action verb–target of action" and the second as "subject–linking verb–description of subject."

The deliberate avoidance of semantic correlations makes grammatical explanations forbiddingly technical and laborious. An example is the decision to do without the semantic definition that "an indirect object and a direct object refer to different things but a direct object and an object complement refer to the same thing." Instead, we would identify different complements on the basis of their pronoun substitutes, number correlation, and passive equivalents. Instead of saying that *teacher* and *apple* in "John brought the teacher an apple" refer to different things, we would say that they "have different personal substitutes"—which applies only when the two objects, as in this instance, differ in gender or number, so that one would be replaced by *he* and the other by *it*, for instance. We might define

> as a direct object any single object of an active verbal [here: verb or verb substitute], the second of two objects in an active sentence for which there are two passive equivalents, and the first of two objects in an active sentence for which there is only one passive equivalent.[69]

Many a teacher and student will be able to remember such a definition only if he mentally uses meaning as a guide. In other words, he will bootleg in the very semantic distinctions that a rigorously objective grammar would abandon.

The more obvious the relation between grammar and meaning, the more irresistible the temptation will be for the teacher to make grammatical categories "meaningful" by reference to typical or recurrent meanings. In rigorously technical terms, a personal pronoun is distinguished by such criteria as the absence of determiners like *a, the, this,* or *that,* a feature pronouns share with proper nouns. For the student, on the other hand, recognizing a pronoun involves a combined awareness of how pronouns typically pattern and how they typically mean. The school grammar will have to start its discussion of personal pronouns by showing them to be an economical way of renaming elements already previously identified.

[69] Sledd, *Short Introduction*, p. 131.

Thus, the school grammar will to some extent restore the interplay of grammar and meaning that the linguist, for the sake of accurate analysis, temporarily separates into its two major parts. We recognize *Kleenex* as a noun because of the way it is used in a sentence; but we use it as a noun because we know it is something we can buy at the store. However, in moving beyond a too rigid linguistic formalism, we must observe important cautions. Our grammatical categories slice experience in ways that derive from the prehistoric past:

> In English . . . all action must be conceived of in reference to three standard times. If, therefore, we desire to state a proposition that is as true to-morrow as it was yesterday, we have to pretend that the present moment may be elongated fore and aft so as to take in all eternity. In French we know once for all that an object is masculine or feminine, whether it be living or not; just as in many American and East Asiatic languages it must be understood to belong to a certain form-category (say, ring-round, ball-round, long and slender, cylindrical, sheet-like, in mass like sugar) before it can be enumerated (e.g. "two ball-class potatoes," "three sheet-class carpets"). . . . It is almost as though at some period in the past the unconscious mind of the race had made a hasty inventory of experience, committed itself to a premature classification that allowed of no revision.[70]

Furthermore,

> in actual usage most structures—including the subject-verb-object structure—gather in to themselves many different meanings. Multiplicity of meaning is unavoidable, since the nature of language makes it impossible to have a sufficient number of grammatical devices to accommodate all the different meanings that the speakers of the language wish to express by grammatical means.[71]

Our term *possessive,* for instance, emphasizes one common meaning-relationship at the expense of many others expressed by the same grammatical form: *the boy's friends* (association); *the child's innocence* (quality); *the children's capers* (agent); *the general's dismissal* (object of action); *a week's notice* (duration). In many cases, semantic descriptions will therefore supplement formal definitions, not by giving *the* meaning of a form or structure, but by pointing out the more typical meanings with which it is associated.

The general answer to the teacher's question concerning the relationship between grammar and meaning is perhaps best summed up in the words of Noam Chomsky: "Undeniable, though only imperfect correspondences hold between formal and semantic features in language." On the one hand, "meaning will be relatively useless as a basis for grammatical description" and, in fact, "important insights and generalizations about linguistic structure may be missed if vague semantic clues are fol-

---

[70] Sapir, *Language,* pp. 99–100.
[71] Dona Worrall Brown, "Does Language Structure Influence Thought?" *ETC.: A Review of General Semantics,* XVII (Spring, 1960), 341.

lowed too closely." On the other hand, "we should like the syntactic framework of the language that is isolated and exhibited by the grammar to be able to support semantic description."[72]

Later, we shall turn to the question of what would be the linguist's requirements for an acceptable semantics. In the meantime, we should point out that in investigating the semantic implications of grammatical features we are taking the step from grammar to stylistics and rhetoric. Consider the following pairs:

The ship *kept* on its course.
The ship *was kept* on its course.

The car *moved*.
The car *was in motion*.

He started the car and swung *her* around.
He started the car and swung *it* around.

In each pair, the change in grammatical structure has semantic and stylistic implications. More exactly, though the import of both statements in each pair is roughly the same, the grammatical devices carry a different residual meaning. Whereas "the ship *was kept*" implies human control, "the ship *kept*" has connotations deriving from the frequent actor-action meaning of its noun-verb sequence. The active version has possible metaphorical implications of quasi-independent movement or volition ruled out in the passive. In the second pair, both versions "express" movement. "The car *was in motion*," however, has more static connotations than "the car *moved*," justifying the editorial rule of thumb calling for action verbs that make a sentence "go." *Be* + prepositional phrase, regardless of specific lexical content, may carry suggestions of condition rather than of activity because of recurrent typical uses. The *her* in the third pair is not a purely formal contrast with the alternative *it* but has a flavor of male dominance and condescension derived from men's half-affectionate, half-superior attitudes toward machines. This use of the feminine pronoun is stylistically quite different from its grammatically parallel use in reference to personified abstractions such as *Duty* and *Freedom*.

Grammar Today and Tomorrow

What, to sum up, are the likely effects of current developments in linguistics on the grammar taught in the schools? Obviously, the road away from the full-fledged traditional grammar is a one-way street. The inherent interest of the new grammars, the impressive competence of some of the new grammarians, and the premium that new materials put on the resourcefulness and imagination of the adapter—all these attract the

[72] Chomsky, *Syntactic Structures*, pp. 101–02.

intellectually alert and professionally responsible teacher to the linguist's camp.

At the same time, linguistics is a rapidly developing discipline. Research continues in many related fields, and controversies are being conducted by men with impressive polemical talents. There is no immediate prospect that one predominant, generally accepted modern grammar will establish itself. In the meantime, the school grammar will increasingly become not necessarily a more scientific but a more English grammar. It will be freer of features read into the grammar to reflect logical distinctions or to parallel features of other Indo-European languages. It will focus more clearly than the traditional grammar on formal and structural devices. It will make the student work with tangible signals and concrete formal and structural tests. It will increasingly import some of the more apt terms and some of the more teachable concepts of applied English linguistics.

To participate responsibly in such developments, the teacher of English must know enough about relevant current work to make informed choices. He should have had at least one course in the history of the language, to acquaint him with the methods and findings of traditional philology. He should have had at least one course in applied English linguistics, if possible containing a contrastive analysis of the most important proposed grammatical systems. If he discovers his inadequate grounding in these areas in mid-career, there is no alternative to some fairly extended adult education. There will be increasing opportunities for teacher institutes and summer study. The independent teacher will find that the only essentials are an annotated bibliography and a small allowance for books.

Such a program for achieving minimum competence in an area crucial to English as a discipline is not an unfair or one-sided imposition. The linguistically trained teacher, on his part, becomes a full-fledged member of a department of English only to the extent that he takes a lively interest in those areas of English that lie outside his specialty. The teacher of literature with archaic ideas about language is no more paradoxical than the teacher of language who is tone-deaf in matters of style. Literature cannot be divorced from its linguistic medium any more than language can be divorced from its human significance.

A PROGRAM FOR FURTHER STUDY

ROBERT A. HALL, Jr., *Linguistics and Your Language*. New York: Doubleday & Company, Inc., 1960. An Anchor Book.

The second, revised edition of *Leave Your Language Alone!* A lively and concrete introduction to the assumptions, procedures, and findings of linguistic science. Written for the layman by a Cornell University Professor of Linguistics with extensive first-hand acquaintance with language teaching and language learning.

PAUL ROBERTS, *English Sentences*. New York: Harcourt, Brace & World, Inc., 1962. Like the author's earlier *Patterns of English* (1956), a workable and eminently readable school grammar written from the point of view of linguistics. Intended for high school students but relevant on all levels. Incorporates transformational grammar.

JAMES H. SLEDD, *A Short Introduction to English Grammar*. Chicago: Scott, Foresman & Company, 1959.

An impressively scholarly and nonpolemical modern grammar, valuable to teachers of English because of its continued critical analysis of and comparison with the grammatical tradition. Eminently suited for courses in Modern English Grammar for prospective teachers.

ALBERT C. BAUGH, *A History of the English Language* (2nd ed.). New York: Appleton-Century-Crofts, Inc., 1957.

The revised edition of a standard textbook in the history of the language, for future teachers of English. A comprehensive view of the development of English and of changing attitudes toward language during its history.

HAROLD B. ALLEN, ed., *Readings in Applied English Linguistics*. New York: Appleton-Century-Crofts, Inc., 1958.

An anthology reprinting key articles by pioneers in the application of linguistics to the study and teaching of English. Part II centers on the assumptions of linguistics, Part V on its application to classroom instruction. An excellent introduction to the linguist's position in current controversies. A second edition with much new material was published in 1963.

MATERIALS FOR ANALYSIS

A. Compare and contrast the following passages, illustrating the treatment of nouns in five modern grammars. Point out similarities and differences in substance and approach. Write your own composite definition of *noun*, ordering characteristic signals and functions in what you consider the most plausible or effective way. Without consulting printed sources, write a similar composite definition of *verb*.

The name *noun* is an arbitrary label for a class of words, a name we use only because it links us to tradition and is easier to remember than the letter A or the number 1. A word is a noun not because of any meaning or assumed meaning; it is a noun because it displays the signals of a noun and enters into patterns where nouns are used. We have defined the noun as a word that enters as N into the patterns N V men work, V N make trouble, and Prep N at home. It serves as headword in the noun-group D A N this old house and in the noun-cluster D A N AP AC that clean sheet of paper that you gave me. It modifies the headword in the pattern D N N the glass house.

—Donald J. Lloyd and Harry R. Warfel, *American English in Its Cultural Setting* (New York: Alfred A. Knopf, 1957), p. 233.

Nouns are identified by five criteria, some more important than others. In the following, the most important will be taken up first.

1. The most common and most clear-cut noun-marking signal is a group of function words called **noun-determiners**. These precede the nouns they mark, either immediately or with certain types of words between. . . .

2. Nouns have two inflections, the plural {—es} and the possessive (sometimes called the genitive) {—'s}. . . .

3. Many nouns may be identified as such by various noun-marking derivational suffixes, added either to stems or to other words, usually belonging to other parts of speech. . . .

4. Nouns fill certain characteristic positions in relation to other identified parts of speech in phrases and utterances. The most obvious of these is the position just before a verb . . .

5. Certain superfixes occasionally distinguish nouns from otherwise identical words that belong to other parts of speech. Thus in pairs like /ímprìnt: imprínt/ . . . we identify the word with the / ′ ˋ / stress pattern as a noun and the other as a verb. . . .

> —W. Nelson Francis, *The Structure of American English* (New York: The Ronald Press Company, 1958), pp. 237–42.

Nouns have special permanent forms which suggest strongly that they are nouns [formed with permanent noun suffixes like *–acy, –age, –ance, –ard, –dom, –hood*]. Second, the modern English noun in the written language also has three inflectional forms: the *–s* ending (and its variants) to express the idea of plural number; and the *–'s* and the *–s'* endings to express the idea of genitive case. Finally, there is the very important function word called the "indicator," [*the, a, an; my, our,* and others] and the "indicator test" may be used to identify many nouns.

> —Dona Worrall Brown, Wallace C. Brown, and Dudley Bailey, *Form in Modern English* (New York: Oxford University Press, 1958), p. 59.

We have defined a noun as a word inflected like *man* or *boy*—any word that fits into an inflectional series which is built, like *man, man's, men, men's* or *boy, boy's, boys, boys'*, on either or both of the contrasts between singular and plural numbers and between common and possessive or genitive cases, and on no other contrasts. This definition is narrower than the traditional statement that a noun is the name of a person, place, or thing; for the traditional noun would include both words inflected for plural, for possessive, or for both, and other words that occupy the same positions as these inflected words. That is, the traditional noun would include many of our nominals as well as our nouns.

> —James H. Sledd, *A Short Introduction to English Grammar* (Chicago: Scott, Foresman & Company, 1959), p. 231.

A noun is a word like *birds, snakes, building, John, mother*, as used in the sentences above. [Birds sing. Snakes crawl. The building might crumble. John left. His mother washed the car.] Other examples of words commonly used as nouns are *man, child, lawyer, chairman, beetle, grass, house, fire, time, danger, courage, resentment, Sally, Angela, Ambrose, Reginald, Harrison, Fielding*. Some of these words occur in other word classes too. Thus *man* is a noun in "The man went away" but a verb in "They manned the boat." On the other hand, *child* occurs only as a noun. Nobody ever says anything like "They childed" or "They will child it."

> —Paul Roberts, *English Sentences* (New York: Harcourt, Brace & World, Inc., 1962), p. 20.

B. Study the following inventory of basic sentence patterns, adapted from *American English in Its Cultural Setting,* by Donald J. Lloyd and Harry R. Warfel, pp. 137–44. Comment on the sequence and number of basic patterns. For each pattern, write two sample sentences—the first using only the basic sentence elements; the second an expanded version exploiting as fully as possible the resources of modification and substitution, without however introducing additional subject-predicate groups. Example:

> *This affects that.*
>
> 1) The sergeant asked the lady.
>
> 2) The incredibly naive young master sergeant from Toledo haltingly, in his miserable French, asked the charming but unresponsive young lady in the trenchcoat for directions to the city's world-famous zoo.

Basic Patterns:

I	N V N	*This affects that.*	The puppy bit Aunt Emma.
IIA	N V N N	*This calls that that.*	We nominated her secretary.
	N V N Adj		I consider that man foolish.
IIB	N V N N	*This gives that that.*	Hawaii ships us pineapples.
IIIA	N V	*This acts.*	Bees sting.
IIIB	N V Adv	*This acts thus, there, or then.*	Bees sting hard.
IIIC	N V Adj	*This acts so or such.*	Our well ran dry.
IVA	N LV N	*This is that.*	My brother is an engineer.
IVB	N LV Adj	*This is so or such.*	He seems busy.
IVC	N LV Adv	*This is thus, there, or then.*	The books are here.
VA	N PassV	*This is affected.*	The walls were washed.
VB	N PassV Prep N	*This is affected by that.*	The books were donated by a rich alumnus.
VIA	N PassV N Prep N	*He is given that by that.*	We were given a prize by the committee.
VIB	N PassV N Prep N	*That is given him by that.*	A prize was given us by the committee.

C. Take five groups of three or four words each (for example, *boy—follow—dog*). Arrange each group in five different patterns, employing variations in inflection, word order, and the use of function words. Example: *The boy follows the dog. Dogs followed the boy. Follow the boy's dogs. Follow the dog, boys. Dog the following boys.*

D. Analyze the following two sentences as fully as you can. Point out difficult or unusual grammatical features. To judge from your acquaintance with alternative grammatical systems, which features would be treated differently by different grammarians?

1. The story had held us, round the fire, sufficiently breathless, but except the obvious remark that it was gruesome, as, on Christmas eve in an old house, a strange tale should essentially be, I remember no comment uttered till somebody happened to say that it was the only case he had met in which such a visitation had fallen on a child.

—Henry James, *The Turn of the Screw*

2. We don't know what it's like to try to accommodate the swarming multitudes of new school kids, and keep them off the streets and off the labor market, and raise money for the new buildings we need, and find new teachers, and ward off the cranks who poke at the schools, and satisfy school boards and politicians, and protect the public-school system from the few who really don't believe in it, and show that the schools aren't "Godless" without offending the atheists, and fit together Puerto Ricans and old Yankees and Negroes and Southerners and cultured and uncultured and Jews and Catholics and rich and poor and bright kids and dopes into one school system, and keep all hell from breaking loose with the delinquents, and perform myriad health and civic functions that the country thrusts onto the schools, and then find these blamed intellectuals pounding on us to teach more history and English.

—William Lee Miller, "The Wastelands Revisited," *The Reporter*

E. Study, and comment on, the application of linguistic materials to specific teaching problems in the following passages:

1. The descriptions above have pointed out that the distinctive signal to separate certain structures consisted of an intonation contrast. In most of these instances, graphic marks of punctuation provide a substitute for the intonation signal.

Those three men *who are always grumbling* . . .

There is no question about the fact that the italicized word group is a unit of a structure of modification, and that *those three men* constitute the other unit, the head. In this type of modification the structural meaning is that of "identification" only if there is no change of pitch level between the Class I word *men* and the function word *who*. The meaning is that of "description" if there is at this spot a change of pitch level with a possible pause. In this expression the use of commas provides a substitute for the change of pitch level.

The three men, who are always grumbling, . . .

—Charles Carpenter Fries, *The Structure of English* (New York: Harcourt, Brace & World, Inc., 1952), p. 283.

2. Errors of this type—in fact, nearly all errors in sentence structure—can be eliminated only if the writer looks through the complicated structures to the basic patterns. What do our complicated sentences boil down to? What are the basic patterns? Are the underlying patterns grammatical? If they are not, the structures derived from them will not be grammatical either. . . .

. . . if the subject and predicate are expanded through modification, we can too easily lose track and write something like this:

His chief reason for worry about his son feared that he would fail in school

The intended idea here can be expressed grammatically in several ways. All of the following boil down to a grammatical kernel:

He was chiefly worried about his son's possible failure in school. ("He was worried.")

His chief worry was that his son would fail in school. ("The worry was this.")

His chief reason for worry was his fear that his son would fail in school. ("The reason was the fear.")

—Paul Roberts, *English Sentences* (New York: Harcourt, Brace & World, Inc., 1962), pp. 207–208.

3. Like the fixed 1, 2, 3, 4 order of the standard English sentence, the fixed order of modification tends to limit emphatic variation. Yet even here, especially in writing of a frankly literary quality, English is by no means lacking in resources. The language possesses a number of fossil constructions, chiefly drawn from medieval and legal French, in which single word modifiers occurring *after* the word they modify carry the principal stress of the word-group:

> heirs *male*
> the body *politic*
> God *Almighty*
> devil *incarnate*
> chapter *ten*

Similarly:

> Edward the *First*
> John the *Baptist*
> William the *Conqueror*
> St. John the *Martyr*

By analogy with these, we can reverse many other modifiers to bring them under the principal stress and hence make them emphatic:

> soldiers *three*
> water *enough*
> the day *following*
> the journey *inland*

A skillful writer can make use of such reversed modifiers to great stylistic advantage, particularly when he places them under emphatic stress:

> The clown *absolute* differs from the actor *droll*. . . .

Because overuse spoils their effectiveness, the various devices for securing variations of sentence emphasis should be sparingly and carefully employed. They are not, as teachers often intimate, inherently weaker than the usual constructions. Proper use of the "passive," the *it is, there is* formulae, and the reversed modifiers can be a valuable aid in writing. On the other hand, too frequent use of these devices is to be avoided because it robs them of their emphatic function. Where everything is emphatic, nothing is emphatic.

> —Harold Whitehall, *Structural Essentials of English* (New York: Harcourt, Brace & World, Inc., 1956), pp. 51–52.

F. Study one of the following books or, if applicable, those sections of it directly concerned with grammar. Report its distinctive features and evaluate its attempt to construct a grammar for school use. Pay special attention to attempts at a synthesis of traditional and linguistic materials. Present detailed evidence in support of your findings.

1. David A. Conlin, *Grammar for Written English*. Boston: Houghton Mifflin Company, 1961.

2. Dona Worrall Brown, Wallace C. Brown, and Dudley Bailey, *Form in Modern English*. New York: Oxford University Press, 1958.

3. Sumner Ives, *A New Handbook for Writers*. New York: Alfred A. Knopf, 1960.

4. Ralph B. Long, *The Sentence and Its Parts: A Grammar of Contemporary English*. Chicago: The University of Chicago Press, 1961.

5. Albert T. Anderson and Thurston Womack, *Processes in Writing: A Guide to Effective Communication* (2nd ed.). Belmont, Calif: Wadsworth Publishing Company, Inc., 1960.

Linguists have conventionally divided a language into its grammar and its lexicon. Grammar deals with the framework of recurrent patterns and relationships. The **lexicon** contains the vocabulary items that fill it out. As the grammatical patterns of a language are subtle and complex, so its lexicon, as recorded in an unabridged dictionary, is of tremendous bulk. We would thus expect competence in the use of language to be judged mainly by a speaker's or writer's command of the grammatical and lexical resources. In practice, however, his competence is often judged by how he manages his choices in areas where the language offers roughly synonymous alternatives in pronunciation, word choice, phrasing, or construction. A listener sitting somnolently through a lecture may suddenly become attentive when the speaker puts the stress in *formidable* on the "wrong" syllable; when he uses a quaint, folksy term for some object of daily use; or when he says "blamed the accident on him" rather than "blamed him for the accident." Such differences appear in the study of language under the heading of **usage.**

two

Usage

The disproportionate attention teachers and textbook authors pay to usage is a faithful reflection of the layman's tendency to pounce on and marvel at even minor variations from his own habits of speech.

In the more limited technical sense in which the modern linguist uses the term *grammar,* "blame on" is not "ungrammatical." Both "blame something on . . ." and "blame somebody for . . ." illustrate basic grammatical principles of English. For instance, they illustrate the verb-object relationship, or the association of certain idiomatic prepositions with a given verb (*concur with* or *in,* but not *to; confide in* or *to,* but not *with*). Both "blame on" and "blame for" are English in the sense that they are used spontaneously, "naturally," by native speakers of the language. They communicate equally well, both being readily understood by the native listener. The difference, if any, is in the social and cultural associations of the two phrases. To some listeners and readers, "blame on" suggests speech rather than writing, informality rather than formality. To others, it suggests a certain lack of education, "carelessness" rather than precision. The difference is not so much in the message as in the overtones—the inferences we make concerning the speaker's or writer's intentions and frame of mind, his social and educational status.

Such inferences may be shrewd or superficial, accurate or mistaken. They easily become complacently ignorant, since the first impulse of the unsophisticated user of the language is to ridicule whatever departs from his own linguistic habits. To respond accurately to the stylistic nuances of usage and to interpret correctly its social and cultural implications, the student needs a rich and varied acquaintance with language. He must learn to *listen* before he judges, let alone rejects. What is above all needed for an understanding and command of the varieties of usage is a trained ear.

For such trained discrimination, right-or-wrong rules are a poor substitute. The English teacher parodies education if he teaches future business executives to judge applicants for a position by whether they split their infinitives. Teachers of English must learn to apply to usage the same standards they apply in other areas of their discipline: they must formulate balanced conclusions on the basis of evidence carefully weighed rather than make large judgments on the basis of isolated symptoms. They must emulate the patient, receptive attitude of the scholar rather than the smug exclusiveness of the snob. They must counteract the universal misinterpretation of their responsibilities that is the penalty the profession pays for its past preoccupation with usage half-understood and illiberally taught.

Historical Attitudes Toward Usage

Historically, linguistic change and diversity of usage have attracted more attention and occasioned more controversy than any other feature of language. A number of major historical positions on the question of usage influence discussion of debated usages to this day. The most apparently modern of these positions actually has a distinguished ancestry. In various periods and places, writers have echoed Horace's view of the *norma loquendi,* his setting up of current use as "the sole arbiter and norm of speech." Whoever wants to speak good English must first of all have an ear for current usage. Whoever wants to write good English must first of all be sensitive to how English is written. To this extent, we must with Robert C. Pooley define good English as what is "true to the language."[1] From this point of view, the important question to ask about a debated usage is not whether it is "grammatical" but whether it is English.

1 "Dare Schools Set a Standard in English Usage?" *The English Journal,* XLIX (March, 1960), 179.

As Stuart Robertson says in *The Development of Modern English,* "how feeble, how grotesque would *I* have been" in Shelley's

> Be thou, spirit fierce,
> My spirit! Be thou *me,* impetuous one![2]

Or as one of the respondents in the Leonard study of attitudes toward current usage said, "I sounds quite mad in certain cases: e.g., point to a photo: 'Which is I?' ! ! ! 'Oh, I see, that's I' ! ! ! Absolutely non-English, hang all the grammarians."[3]

The **doctrine of usage,** that is, of reliance on current common use, has found its strongest support when writers asserted the adequacy of their current native language against the authority of models from a different time and region. Thus, Castiglione in the early sixteenth century felt that "use and custom" governed the Latin writers when theirs was a living language and should now equally govern the use of the current tongue. Asserting that "all good writers of olde times blamed such wordes as were refused of custome," he advised his ideal courtier to speak and write not in a language modeled on the Tuscan of Dante and Petrarch but above all in words "in use also among the people."[4] With a similar lack of uncritical conservatism, English Renaissance humanists like Sir Philip Sidney and Samuel Daniel found their current native English "capable of any excellent exercising of it" and equal in its capacity for "uttering sweetly and properly the conceits of the mind" to Latin and Greek, in fact, to "any other tongue in the world." Like Castiglione, Sidney aimed at a style marked by clarity and ease. His preference for the "fit and natural" made him warn the writer against "farfetched words," and generally against pedantry and extravagance. Thus, his affirmative attitude toward the current language combined with emphasis on discrimination and polish in matters of style.[5] Similarly, Ben Jonson's often quoted belief that "custom is the most certain mistress of language" did not keep him from warning the writer to avoid the "faint, obscure, obscene, sordid, humble, improper, or effeminate phrase."[6] Thus, many Renaissance humanists held an essentially modern view: *Though a writer must make discriminating use of his linguistic resources, what these resources are is ultimately determined by current usage.*

Two centuries later, a native American idiom and a native literature

---

[2] *The Development of Modern English* (2nd ed.), rev. by Frederick G. Cassidy (Englewood Cliffs, N.J.: Prentice-Hall, Inc., 1954), p. 295.

[3] Albert H. Marckwardt and Fred G. Walcott, *Facts About Current Usage* (New York: Appleton-Century-Crofts, Inc., 1938), p. 78.

[4] Baldassare Castiglione, *The Book of the Courtier,* trans. Sir Thomas Hoby (New York: E. P. Dutton & Co., Inc., 1928), pp. 56–60.

[5] *An Apology for Poetry,* in *English Critical Essays (Sixteenth, Seventeenth and Eighteenth Centuries),* ed. Edmund D. Jones (New York: Oxford University Press, Inc., 1947), pp. 49–51.

[6] *Ibid.,* p. 94.

began to assert their independence from a British English that, from an upstart vernacular, had in turn become a stronghold of precedent and tradition. Noah Webster, in his *An American Dictionary of the English Language* (1828), recognized and championed distinct features of American usage that throughout the nineteenth century were the target of British attacks on "Americanisms." Though generally opposed to innovations, anomalies, and "corruptions" making the language less regular and consistent than it could be, he nevertheless felt called upon in his preface to explain the need for an *American* dictionary of the English language:

> Although the body of the language is the same as in England, and it is desirable to perpetuate that sameness, yet some differences must exist. . . . the institutions in this country which are new and peculiar, give rise to new terms or to new applications of old terms, unknown to the people of England. . . . A great number of words in our language require to be defined in a phraseology accommodated to the condition and institutions of the people in these states.[7]

In the twentieth century, linguistic self-reliance was advocated by H. L. Mencken, who in *The American Language* (1919) and other writings championed a vigorous American language and literature, independent of European traditions. Mencken relished and cultivated in his own style the "delight in devastating opprobriums, and the acute feeling for the succinct and savory," of a popular American speech hospitable to pungent rhetoric, tall talk, and grotesque humor. He found in the current American use of the language a "superior imaginativeness and resourcefulness" parallel to the "expansive gusto which made for its pliancy and resilience in the days of Shakespeare." He welcomed the absence of the "suffocating formalization" that he saw in standard British English and that, through the efforts of anglophile pedagogues, had left in the upper regions even of American English lingering vestiges of "Eighteenth-century tightness." Mencken called "barbaric" such neologisms as *go-getter, he-man, go-aheadativeness, goof, semi-occasional,* and *to doxologize.* Yet he saw even in them that "yielding to natural impulses" that "is at the heart of all healthy language-making":

> The history of English, like the history of American and of every other living tongue, is a history of vulgarisms that, by their accurate meeting of real needs, have forced their way into sound usage, and even into the lifeless catalogues of the grammarians. The purist performs a useful office in enforcing a certain logical regularity upon the process, and in our own case the omnipresent example of the greater conservatism of the English restrains, to some extent, our native tendency to go too fast, but the process itself is as inexorable in its workings as the procession of the equinoxes, and if we yield to it more eagerly than the English, it is only a proof, perhaps, that the future of what was once the Anglo-Saxon tongue lies on this side of the water.

[7] James H. Sledd and Wilma R. Ebbitt, eds., *Dictionaries and That Dictionary* (Chicago: Scott, Foresman & Company, 1962), pp. 32–33.

Mencken quoted with approval a nineteenth-century linguist describing language as not an artificial product "governed by the strict rules of impersonal grammarians" but "the living expression of the mind and spirit of a people, ever changing and shifting, whose sole standard of correctness is custom and the common usage of the community."[8]

Just as persistent as the view that common usage is the sole standard of correctness has been the opposing view that mere majority use does not make an expression acceptable and right. Spokesmen of conservatism and tradition have often endeavored to establish a standard of usage transcending narrow regional, social, or temporal limitations. What sounds natural and therefore right in language is what through constant and widespread use has lost whatever traces of affectation, facetiousness, aggressiveness, exclusiveness, or harshness make the unusual and the new grate on our ears. According to this view, the writer's and teacher's primary loyalty is to language as a common medium. However much he responds to individual or regional coloring, a teacher's function is a **normative** one, retarding both change and diversification.

Historically, this normalizing tendency has found its major expression in attempts to "ascertain," that is, to fix, the language in a form closer than current usage to hypothetical standards of clarity, efficiency, and consistency. In practice, such attempts usually meant trying to bring the language closer to a rational ideal believed to be embodied in the language and literature of ancient Greece and Rome. The triumph of neoclassical standards in literature in seventeenth-century France had led to the establishment of the French Academy. It became the official arbiter of correct usage, making it its special concern, for instance, to bar neologisms and unnecessary loan words. Inspired by the example of the French Academy, English neoclassicists like John Dryden and Jonathan Swift advocated setting up similar machinery for polishing and refining the language and for giving it greater stability and permanence. Eighteenth-century grammarians adopting this general perspective established a tradition of language instruction that centered on the elimination from the student's speech and writing of deviations from a "correct" norm. Teachers and textbook authors made it their business to teach rules designed to free the student's language of "common errors."

The major theoretical shortcoming of this prevailing tradition was the absence of a clear standard of what made one usage "correct" and another erroneous, "illiterate," or "vulgar." Thus, Samuel Johnson shared the eighteenth-century preference for "the durable materials of a language" as against the "tyranny of time and fashion," "the corruptions of ignorance," and "caprices of innovation." However, when, in his

---

[8] H. L. Mencken, *The American Language*, 4th ed. (New York: Alfred A. Knopf, Inc., 1937), pp. 92–97.

Dictionary of the English Language (1765), he set out to make his contribution toward regulating the confusion of English usage, he found that

> choice was to be made out of boundless variety, without any established principle of selection; adulterations were to be detected, without a settled test of purity; and modes of expression to be rejected or received, without the suffrages of any writers of classical reputation or acknowledged authority.

Like other early lexicographers and grammarians, Dr. Johnson then improvised his own standards of correctness and "tests of purity": the practice of the great writers of the past (but admitting "no testimony of living authors"); conformity to "the genius of our tongue"; authenticity of derivation from the original languages; freedom from latter-day French influence in "structure and phraseology"; absence of the merely temporary, local, and technical.[9]

Other writers were less respectful of the practice of the best authors and the "genius of the language." Thus, Bishop Lowth, in *A Short Introduction to English Grammar* (second edition, 1764) denounced as a "very great corruption" the use of the identical form for the past and the past participle in *have spoke, has wrote,* and *was took.* He insisted on the distinct past participle, in spite of his explicit recognition that "the general bent and turn of the language is towards the other form" and that this other form "is too much authorised by the example of some of our best writers." According to his own citations, these writers included Milton, Dryden, Addison, Pope, and Swift.[10] Thus depriving themselves of authoritative use as the major test of correctness, grammarians relied on various arguments from precedent and analogy. Often they simply appealed to analogy with the rules of Latin grammar. Many such arguments merely rationalized personal preference or quite arbitrary choice. It became a minority view to hold, with Joseph Priestley, that "the custom of speaking is the original and only just standard of any language" and "is sufficient to establish a rule, even contrary to the strongest analogies of the language with itself"; or with George Campbell, that "it is not the business of grammar . . . to give law to the fashions which regulate our speech."[11]

Up to modern times, English instruction in the schools perpetuated, often almost unchanged, the rules and prescriptions of eighteenth-century grammarians whose aim had been to purify the language and arrest its "natural tendency to degeneration." In the meantime, however, scholars investigating language came to question the feasibility of influencing by

---

9 Samuel Johnson, *Dictionary of the English Language,* in *English as Language: Backgrounds, Development, Usage,* eds. Charlton Laird and Robert M. Gorrell (New York: Harcourt, Brace & World, Inc., 1961), pp. 136–42.

10 *Ibid.,* pp. 205–06.

11 Albert C. Baugh, *A History of the English Language,* 2nd ed. (New York: Appleton-Century-Crofts, Inc., 1957), pp. 341–42.

rule and prescription the slow, long-range changes they found in all stages of all languages they studied. Dr. Johnson himself had reluctantly concluded that the most the lexicographer and grammarian could do was to "retard" and "palliate" the processes of linguistic change:

> Those who have been persuaded to think well of my design, will require that it should fix our language, and put a stop to those alterations which time and chance have hitherto been suffered to make in it without opposition. With this consequence I will confess that I flattered myself for a while; but now begin to fear that I have indulged expectation which neither reason nor experience can justify. When we see men grow old and die at a certain time one after another, from century to century, we laugh at the elixir that promises to prolong life to a thousand years; and with equal justice may the lexicographer be derided, who being able to produce no example of a nation that has preserved their words and phrases from mutability, shall imagine that his dictionary can embalm his language, and secure it from corruption and decay, that it is in his power to change sublunary nature, and clear the world at once from folly, vanity and affectation.[12]

After Johnson, scholars ceased to look upon change as a deplorable but inevitable tendency of language and instead accepted it as one of the basic features of language considered as a living, dynamic, growing thing. The central subject matter of nineteenth-century **historical linguistics** was the account of the long-range changes that led from the earliest known Indo-European documents to contemporary speech. Scholars saw a continuous development from the Latin of imperial Rome through Old French and Provençal to the dialects of Renaissance and Modern French. They traced Modern High German to Middle and Old High German, Modern Low German to dialects close to the Germanic dialects that became Old English, Middle English, and English in its modern form. As heir to this tradition of linguistic scholarship, the modern linguist has stressed the point that "language doesn't stay the same":

> There are the forces of internal organic change, in phonemic, morphological, and syntactic matters; of internal borrowing (analogy); and of external borrowing, from related dialects, related languages, and non-related languages. All these kinds of change are going on all the time. Their work is like that of geological forces, in erosion and building up: at one place, the structure of the language may be wearing away through phonemic and morphological reduction, while at another place it may be building up through phonemic splitting, analogical new-formation, change of meaning, and borrowing. And, like the work of geological forces, linguistic change is, in the present state of human technology, irresistible. We may try to dam it up at one point, but it's sure to burst forth at another, and where we are least expecting it.[13]

[12] In Laird and Gorrell, *English as Language*, p. 140.
[13] Robert A. Hall, Jr., *Linguistics and Your Language* (New York: Doubleday & Company, Inc., 1960), p. 189.

Instead of resisting linguistic change, the linguist feels that

> we should accept linguistic change and its results as something entirely nat-
> ural and normal, and something which we expect to happen as surely as we
> expect everything else in the world to change, whether it suits our personal
> tastes or not.[14]

For today's teacher of English, the conflict between the modernist's
affirmative attitude toward linguistic change and diversity and the conservative's search for an ideal and stable standard continues. If the
teacher sees the shaky intellectual foundation of the traditional view of
correctness, he will feel the need for some thorough rethinking of his own
standards and preferences. The teacher who tries to arrive at a meaningful
rationale of usage does so at the cost of a painful re-examination of his
personal intellectual habits and of his responsibilities as a teacher. An
informed and responsible attitude toward usage must be based on a
careful, and if possible dispassionate, consideration of the role of diversity
and uniformity in contemporary American English, and of the arguments
and controversies concerning it.

Diversity and Uniformity

Teacher and student of language and literature are fatally handicapped unless they delight in the variety and range of language. Ideally,
they should take pleasure both in the extravagant periods of Lyly and the
terse aphorisms of Bacon. They should be able to enjoy the colloquial,
mock-naive idiom of Ring Lardner, the rhapsodic style of Thomas Wolfe,
and the strongly spiced stylistic goulash of H. L. Mencken. Nobody can be
expected to enjoy everything; and yet it would be sad if a certified English
teacher could not respond to the dialect features of Alan Sillitoe's
Saturday Night and Sunday Morning or the adolescent slang of J. D.
Salinger's *The Catcher in the Rye.* The English teacher should take a
collector's interest in such linguistic fauna as the puns of *Time* and the
malapropisms found in student papers. ("Librarians should see to it that
immortal books are removed from high-school libraries." "Chaucer understood courtly love so well because he himself had been a *courtesan.*")
Among the most successful assignments for student writing are investigations of current high school or college slang, of advertising jargon, of a
columnist's or society editor's lingo. Instruction in language is a failure
if it does not help to develop in the student a sense of the richness of our
linguistic resources.

Nor is a receptive attitude toward the riches of language exclusively
a source of aesthetic and intellectual delight. One of the oldest cultural
problems is the use of variation in language as a cause for "out-grouping,"

[14] *Ibid.,* p. 190.

ridicule, distrust. This tendency is seen not only in ignorant fifth-graders who ridicule the newcomer of different speech habits; it is equally characteristic of members of an English department who indulge in feelings of complacent superiority at the expense of a colleague of cultured Southern speech. The crudely illiberal extremes of such attitudes are illustrated in political cartoons that show the rulers of a hostile foreign country speaking among themselves not their richly idiomatic native tongue but a cruel caricature of untutored immigrant's English. The relation between language snobbery and racial prejudice or chauvinistic nationalism the reader may ponder for himself. Instruction in language must do its share to counteract the smugly ignorant assumption of superiority that is the popular reaction to language difference.

In this area, recent linguistic scholarship can make a considerable contribution. The linguist's emphasis on linguistic change and his interest in dialectal variants can help promote an open-minded interest in one's own language in all its copious variety. Similarly, linguists have been at pains to show "that our own language is nothing special in comparison to other languages, nothing particularly God-given or superior or peculiarly fitted for higher intelectual activity."[15] They have labored to show that the languages of so-called primitive peoples are as complex grammatically as those of peoples who consider themselves civilized. They have thus taught us to approach alien linguistic phenomena without preconceived value judgments.

Above all, linguists have worked to restore the native speaker's confidence in his own command of the language. Like Castiglione's courtier, they have discouraged the excessive scrupulosity of those who

> bring . . . many gentlemen and learned men in such awe, that they dare not open their mouth: and confesse plainely, that they can not speake the tongue which they have learned of their nourses, even from their cradle.[16]

As one studies successive editions of conservative handbooks of English, it becomes clear that the linguist's injunction of "Leave your language alone!" is being partially, if reluctantly, obeyed. Some rules of correctness widely taught a generation ago are now lingering on only in the uneasy consciences of middle-aged former students. As Paul Roberts says in *English Sentences,*

> many points of usage, formerly much belabored, are ceasing to be objects of concern. Probably few copy editors nowadays are bothered by such distinctions as *shall/will, further/farther, provided/providing.* Few object on principle to prepositions at the end of sentences. Some eliminate split infinitives (*to even look*); others don't mind or don't notice.[17]

Other rules of correctness now seldom mentioned are those that require

---

15 Hall, *Linguistics and Your Language,* p. 250.
16 Castiglione, *The Book of the Courtier,* p. 63.
17 *English Sentences* (New York: Harcourt, Brace & World, Inc., 1962), p. 244.

that rather than *which* in restrictive relative clauses ("the object *that* you now observe on the screen") or *of which* rather than *whose* in reference to an inanimate noun ("a theory, the validity *of which* remains to be tested").

Other debated usages, however, continue to serve as touchstones of correct writing. To many people, "good English" still means English with the negative virtue of being free from usages like *these kind, "who* are you waiting for," "looks *like* it will rain," *different than,* and *reason is because.* Surveying teachers' attitudes on such debatable usages, Thurston Womack concluded in 1959 "that in general the majority of the teachers still reject most usages that published information tends to support as acceptable."[18] That, in Womack's words, "the battle of usage has not been entirely won" is further confirmed by the prevailing editorial position in the magazines teachers of English most typically read and support: *The New Yorker, Saturday Review, Harper's, The Atlantic,* or *The Reporter.* To judge from the tone of editorials and major articles in these publications, the battle of usage has in fact developed into a sort of trench warfare in which no significant breakthrough is to be expected on either side. This stalemate is at least in part a result of overstatements and misinterpretations to which the linguist's position lends itself.

First, teachers of rhetoric and literature have been wary of the statement that "language is basically speech." No one will quarrel with it if *basically* here means "historically" or "as far as sheer quantity is concerned." But many a teacher discerns in this statement something more—a claim, however indirect, to priority in study and teaching. Trying, as he must, to develop the student's respect for the written word, he does not find this implication helpful. He will see little need for the quibble that "there is no such thing as 'written language.' "[19] When the linguist substitutes for "written language" the phrase "the written record of speech," the teacher of rhetoric and literature will protest that "the written record of speech" is always more than a mere written record.[20] It is, among other things, the primary medium of coherent, considered, responsible, edited thought. Though a brilliant or even profound idea may be first suggested in improvised speech, it is typically tested, developed, and modified in writing. Higher education and scholarship, as well as imaginative literature, work primarily with "written language." Even the grammarian who says that "grammar studies primarily the spoken language" admits that

practically, of course, grammarians work mostly with written records, since it is the nature of our minds to be more efficient when dealing with the

18 "Teachers' Attitudes Toward Current Usage," *The English Journal,* XLVIII (April, 1959), 188.
19 Hall, *Linguistics and Your Language,* p. 6.
20 W. Nelson Francis, *The Structure of American English* (New York: The Ronald Press Company, 1958), p. 225.

visible than with the audible, and since some way is needed of fixing the
fleeting sounds of speech so that they may be studied.[21]

While the linguist treats writing as a secondary reflection of speech, the
teacher often, and quite legitimately, aims mainly at a sound rationale for
written English.

Statements such as "linguistic change is irresistible" and "all dialects
have equal merit" need similar qualifications. The first does not make
allowance for the effects of sustained conditioning, deliberate choice, and
conscious imitation. Social and educational forces in various ways complicate the long-range unconscious changes investigated by the historical
linguist. To use isolated but prominent examples, the available evidence
suggests that *ain't* for *am not,* and *don't* for *doesn't,* have, under the influence of mass education, become less prominent in informal speech
during the last half-century. Of the efforts of prescriptive grammarians
in the eighteenth-century tradition, Albert C. Baugh says generally that

> though we may recognize that the grounds on which decisions were reached
> were often faulty, and the decisions themselves were often arbitrary, we
> must admit that a considerable number of disputed points, rightly or
> wrongly, were settled and have since become established.[22]

What the teacher must realize is that linguistic change can be reversed or
modified only through sustained and concentrated effort, and that the
time and energy thus spent often result in improvements of dubious value.

"All dialects have equal merit" is valid in technical linguistic terms.
Within a homogeneous speech community, an established dialect cannot
objectively be shown to be any less flexible, efficient, or elegant than the
dialect of some other speech community. However, as soon as we go beyond a relatively unified group of people speaking the same dialect, we
must recognize the problem of dialectal splintering as a barrier to communication.

> And for there is so gret diversite
> In Englissh and in writyng of oure tonge,
> So prey I God that non myswrite the,
> Ne the mysmetre for defaute of tonge

said Chaucer in concluding his *Troilus and Criseyde* (V. 1793–96). Historically, only the emerging dominance of prestige dialects has provided
the answer to Chaucer's cry: "That thow be understonde, God I beseche!"
(V. 1798). The spread of a **prestige dialect** as the medium of education and
literature means a loss in color and variety. Since the prestige dialect is
often secondary, acquired through schooling rather than absorbed from
early childhood, its adoption means a loss in ease and naturalness. At the
same time, it means a tremendous gain in effectiveness and range of com-

21 *Ibid.*
22 Baugh, *History,* p. 344.

munication. It becomes our major means of participating in a culture that goes beyond narrow regional and temporal boundaries.

In his dealings with language, *the teacher must reconcile a receptive attitude toward dialectal variety with loyalty to the common medium.* In Thomas Hardy's *The Mayor of Casterbridge,* Michael Henchard's remarks to Elizabeth-Jane illustrate well some of the implications of the use of dialect words—"those terrible marks of the beast to the truly genteel":

> " 'Bide where you be,' " he echoed sharply. "Good God, are you only fit to carry wash to a pig-trough, that ye use words such as those?" [ch. 20]

Readers of this passage would probably agree on a number of points: first, Elizabeth-Jane's use of dialect words is pleasing and natural, and social intercourse would be the poorer for their loss. Second, Michael's reaction reveals the insecurity of a man who has only recently risen fom the lower social ranks and who sees in telltale dialect features a challenge to hard-won social status. At the same time, however, the reader is grateful that Hardy himself writes in a prestige dialect without obvious geographical, social, or temporal limitations.

Ironically, statements like "all dialects have equal merit" are gaining currency at a time when dialects as a communication barrier have practically disappeared in American English, and when the languages of ethnic subgroups have all but ceased to play a role in business, culture, and education. Most Americans have never experienced the bafflement of the European who cannot follow the dialect of the rural district surrounding his own native city, let alone of a rural district a few hundred miles away. Nor have they had to face the political problems threatening the survival of multilingual states, such as Hapsburg Austria, modern India, or former colonial territories in Africa. Against such a backgound, a relatively uniform language of maximum temporal stability and geographical scope becomes highly desirable. The history of France and other European countries shows that political, cultural, and social forces can effectively retard, or even reverse, the linguistic Balkanization of a country. Language education, for political and cultural reasons, then becomes legitimately conservative and normative.

In the United States, the problem of dialectal splintering has been solved by linguistic uniformity unparalleled in history. Current research into regional varieties of American English is being recorded in the *Linguistic Atlas of the United States and Canada,* a project that has occupied American dialectologists for over thirty years and may continue for decades before present plans reach completion. According to one study of linguistic-atlas findings,

> typical intonation patterns, customary subject-verb-object word order, the inflectional –s which signals plural number or third person singular of the present tense, and the vast majority of vocabulary items belong without

distinction to all dialects of American English. Consequently no functional block in communication normally obtrudes between native users of English.[23]

In the United States, the normalized standard thus comes much closer to being a genuine common denominator than the national standard superimposed on the often sharply divergent regional dialects of many European countries. One obvious reason is the intermingling of people from different dialect areas, through early migrations and later through mobility unparalleled in more static societies. Other factors are the establishment of political unity at an early stage in the nation's history, the fact that many immigrant's children learned English not at home but at school, the unprecedented development of standardized mass media of entertainment and communication. The linguist is in fact hampered in his effort "to collect a body of valid and reliable information on American dialects" because

> The wide spread of education, the virtual extinction of illiteracy, the extreme mobility of the population—both geographically and from one social class to another—and the tremendous development of a number of media of mass communication have all contributed to the recession of local speech forms.[24]

An American teen-ager in California may have friends who grew up in Ohio, Oregon, or New Jersey; he may have teachers from New York, Michigan, or Alabama; and he may spend much of his time listening to motion picture and television actors heard at the same time by teen-agers in Minnesota, Florida, and Maine.

In practice, of course, standardized American English serves the American user of the language as an effective means of communication far beyond national borders. In view of the processes of linguistic change and differentiation that have dominated much of linguistic history, it is a minor miracle that an Englishman from Yorkshire can communicate with an American from Hamtramck. In addition to other forces that stabilize and level language, one major element in the miracle is the existence of a relatively stable and uniform written standard as carrier of a common culture and literature. Written language is typically more deliberate and self-supporting than speech. Spoken utterances not only are often reinforced by situation and gesture but can typically be immediately challenged and amplified. Written language must rely on the context it itself establishes and on words and structures that carry meaning without ambiguity and beyond a narrow regional or temporal setting. It typically deals with concerns more permanent and of more general interest than

---

[23] Jean Malmstrom, "Linguistic Atlas Findings versus Textbook Pronouncements on Current American Usage," *The English Journal*, XLVIII (April, 1959), 197.
[24] Albert H. Marckwardt, *American English* (New York: Oxford University Press, Inc., 1958), p. 133.

speech and is thus more easily hampered by personal and regional peculiarities. Thus,

> to gain command of serious written English is to acquire, quite deliberately, an abstract and generalized variety of the language differing by nature and purpose from any social or regional variety whatsoever. It is to sacrifice the local for the general, the spontaneous for the permanent. . . . It is to master a set of grammatical and vocabulary patterns not because they are "correct" but because experience has proved them efficient in the communicative activity of writing.[25]

To the writer, scholar, or scientist, the existence of serious written English as a world-wide medium of communication is a tremendous asset. It is well worth concentrating on and promoting in high school and college courses dealing with language and composition. To promote it effectively, the teacher needs a realistic estimate of its nature and its relation to other major varieties of English usage.

Major Varieties of Usage

When we begin to identify varieties of usage and give advice concerning their use, we necessarily move beyond a rigorously descriptive approach to language. We no longer simply ask whether a form occurs, but whether, under the circumstances, it is the right or appropriate one. We go beyond registering and correlating facts to express preference and make judgments concerning effectiveness. From a rigorously objective point of view, even the effects of erroneous views upon language habits are simply phenomena to be studied and analyzed. Well-established features of a language may be the result of mistaken notions, as with a spelling pronunciation like that of *author* or a "learned" spelling like that of *debt*. Both the *th* in *author* and the *b* in *debt* were inserted by Renaissance scholars mistaken in their etymological derivation of these words, adopting a pseudo-Greek or pseudo-Latin spelling for words that had actually come into English by way of Old French *autor* and *dette*. The resulting forms, however, are as much part of the raw linguistic data as a folk etymology like *carryall*, from *cariole*. A rigorously descriptive approach will simply register these and similar facts. A normative approach may lead us to deplore them as a needless complication, irrelevant to the communicative efficiency of the language. Thus, a linguist is applying normative criteria when he tells us that "spelling-pronunciation serves no good purpose, and only introduces confusion and misunderstanding into otherwise clear situations."[26] Similarly, the linguist is applying normative criteria when he calls the *I* in *between you and I* and the *whom* in *whom*

---

25 Harold Whitehall, *Structural Essentials of English* (New York: Harcourt, Brace & World, Inc., 1956), p. 5.
26 Hall, *Linguistics and Your Language,* p. 45.

did you say is coming "linguistic gargoyles." He may explain these forms as the result of **overcorrection,** used by the "superficially educated" who have heard *me* and *who* criticized in *it's me* and *who did you ask* and have come to consider them "intrinsically inelegant."[27] On the other hand, *between you and I* is mentioned in the eighteenth century as "almost universally used in familiar conversation."[28] The rigorously descriptive linguist would simply note its continued use without seeing its motivation "partly in fear and partly in snobbishness" and without describing its users as "socially insecure."[29]

In dealing with usage, in other words, we cannot simply pit our own "descriptive" against other "prescriptive" approaches. *The really significant difference is between soundly based, carefully qualified prescription and prescription that is arbitrary and dogmatic.* Modern authorities on usage have typically based their prescriptions on the principle of **appropriateness.** Choices in pronunciation, words, phrasing, and construction should be in keeping with the variety of usage appropriate to the context or situation. They should be adapted to the purposes a speaker or writer is trying to accomplish. Thus, the user of the language must distinguish "between those forms which are appropriate for serious exposition and those which are fit for laughing talk." The "writer's or speaker's task is precisely such choice among the available resources of his language."[30]

What makes such choices more than a simple either-or matter is that the context and purposes of an utterance tend to be complex rather than simple. Varieties of usage in various ways overlap and shade over into each other. As a result, they resist reliable scientific classification. Differences in usage are interesting to the teacher of English because of the different reactions they produce, the associations they suggest, the situations (or localities) to which they are felt to be appropriate. From the point of view of the scientific linguist, however,

> ideas, notions, feelings, and the like may be observed and studied only by the person in whose mind they occur. This means that they cannot be "verified by any competent observer," a requirement that we set up as essential to scientific method.[31]

Typically, the linguist will set out to neutralize the subjective "ideas, notions, feelings" that make the results of introspection variable and unpredictable. One possible avenue is to make the study of variations in usage "thoroughly statistical in its requirements."[32] On the most elemen-

---

[27] Whitehall, *Structural Essentials of English,* p. 117.

[28] Sterling Andrus Leonard, *The Doctrine of Correctness in English Usage 1700–1800,* in Laird and Gorrell, *English as Language,* p. 192.

[29] Whitehall, *Structural Essentials of English,* pp. 116–17.

[30] James H. Sledd, "Grammar or Gramarye?" *The English Journal,* XLIX (May, 1960), 295.

[31] Francis, *Structure,* p. 32.

[32] H. A. Gleason, Jr., *An Introduction to Descriptive Linguistics,* rev. ed. (New York: Holt, Rinehart & Winston, Inc., 1961), p. 393.

tary level, the investigator who finds ordinary discussions of style "too intuitive and impressionistic to carry much weight" can tabulate such indicators of complexity as word length, using a representative sampling of text. He may thus establish that an oral style, as in the dialogue of plays and novels, has a low frequency of long words, as contrasted with their high frequency in the style of argumentative prose. He would thus confirm our suspicion that long words are more characteristic of formal written English than of a more conversational style. "Mere impressions are replaced in the process by statements of data, which we can now use with confidence." Though "one may justly label such an approach crude," only "by being so unsophisticated we could hope that anybody setting out to check our results would arrive at exactly the same figures we had obtained."[33]

In a famous investigation, Charles C. Fries used statistical methods to show a difference "in the fullness of the use that is made of the resources of our language" by users of educated ("Standard") and uneducated ("Vulgar") English. Uneducated usage showed a tendency toward very long sentences in which constituents "are added in loose succession," with frequent use of the connectives *and* and *so*. In a large sample of written material, *and* was one and a half times as frequent, *so* more than six times as frequent in uneducated as in educated English.[34] Fries's findings bear out the impression of the teacher of composition that the sentence structure of inexperienced writers commonly suffers from two defects: very brief sentences offering no opportunity for the expression of complex relationships; very long sentences showing no grasp of the possible relationships between different layers of grammatical structure.

Apart from these and similar studies, however, the most prominent area for the application of objective linguistic techniques has been **dialect geography.** The dialectologist spends his time "eliciting from socially classifiable speakers of American English the linguistic forms which they habitually use" and "classifying such forms according to regional and social patterns of distribution."[35] Here, the question is typically not one of elusive degrees of complexity, formality, or appropriateness but more simply and reliably one of use or nonuse. Typically it is a question of whether an informant pronounces the *s* in *grease* like the *s* in *cease* or the *s* in *please;* of whether he calls an object a *pail* or a *bucket,* a *spider* or a *skillet.* Thus, when linguists establish in the eastern United States such major dialect areas as "North" (including New England), "Midland"

---

33 Werner Winter, "Styles as Dialects," *Preprints of Papers for the Ninth International Congress of Linguists* (Cambridge, Mass., 1962), pp. 214–19.

34 *The Structure of English: An Introduction to the Construction of English Sentences* (New York: Harcourt, Brace & World, Inc., 1952), pp. 290–92. For a more detailed account see Fries's *American English Grammar.*

35 Raven I. McDavid, Jr., "Dialectology and the Classroom Teacher," *College English,* XXIV (November, 1962), 111.

(including most of Pennsylvania, Ohio, West Virginia), and "South," the boundaries rest to a large extent upon vocabulary evidence:

> Characteristic Northern expressions . . . include *pail, swill, whiffletree* or *whippletree, comforter* or *comfortable* for a thick quilt, *brook, co-boss* or *come-boss* as a cow call, *johnnycake, salt pork,* and *darning needle* for a dragonfly. In the Midland area we find *blinds* for roller shades, *skillet, spouting* or *spouts* for eaves, a *piece* for food taken between meals, *snake feeder* for a dragonfly . . . The South has *lightwood* as the term for kindling, a *turn* of wood for an armful; string beans are generally *snap beans; hasslet* is the term for the edible inner organs of a pig, *chittlins* for the small intestine; and in this area cows are said to *low* at feeding time.[36]

What has attracted a fair share of linguistically trained manpower to the study of American dialects is that, compared with the study of other areas of language use, it yields positive, objective, and reliable results. Teachers often fail to find the results of dialect study urgently significant because of its heavy emphasis on the speech of culturally and socially peripheral nonurban areas and its relatively limited concern with the speech "of the heavily urbanized areas in which most Americans now live." On the other hand, awareness of dialectal differences helps the teacher understand or anticipate the usage problems of students from a given regional background:

> The American Negro, especially one recently arrived from the South or reared in a black ghetto, may not use in his speech the conventional inflectional suffixes on nouns or verbs, so that he may omit them in writing where they belong or write them in the wrong places. . . .
>
> . . . an educated Southerner may use such combinations of auxiliaries as *might could, used to could,* or *ought to could,* reflecting the familiar cultivated usage of his own region. . . . The Northerner, on the other hand, may say *sick to the stomach* or *hadn't ought.* . . . The Eastern Kentuckian may convert *used to* into an adverb, as previous generations converted *maybe,* and transfer it to the beginning of the sentence, as in *"Used to,* everybody around here would bake their own bread."

The teacher who is responsive to expressions with a regional flavor will agree with the dialectologist that

> For such students the remedy is not to decry their native dialect or to attempt to alienate them from their habitual linguistic behavior, but to recognize that in their situations the problem of fit between speech and writing, never a simple matter for any speaker of English, has special complications.[37]

In going beyond geographical variants, that is, dialects in the more limited sense, linguists have usually been prepared to make a "social" differentiation between informants "with a minimum of formal schooling, travel, and reading" and "cultured" informants.[38] Such a distinction,

---

36 Marckwardt, *American English,* p. 138.
37 McDavid, *College English, XXIV,* 113–15.
38 Raven I. McDavid, Jr., "The Dialects of American English" in Francis, *Structure,* p. 492.

though necessarily relative, has enabled them to distinguish between **nonstandard** and **standard** English. None of the terms used to indicate this distinction are completely satisfactory: *nonstandard* might suggest minority usage or even willful disregard of standard practice, whereas actually the usages described are part of the solid bedrock of popular speech, sometimes more conservative in its preservation of older forms than the language of the educated. "Substandard" has implications of the subnormal. "Illiterate" and "vulgar" similarly have pejorative connotations that are revealed in their presumptuous illiberality when we apply them to the individual user of nonstandard speech: a skilled mechanic, a shrewdly articulate neighbor, a wise and warmly humorous elderly relative. The crucial difference between nonstandard and standard English is that the latter enjoys social and cultural prestige. Competent use of it is a condition of advancement in many prestige occupations. It is the accepted medium of education, journalism, literature.

Nonstandard usage is no more arbitrary than standard. In other words, nonstandard forms are not errors but are selected in accordance with the characteristic conventions of nonstandard speech. The language of nonstandard speakers

> observes its own laws—not those of Standard English—in a thoroughly rigorous manner. *Hisn,* for example, is the absolute, not the secondary or adjectival form, and the two are never confused. Most speakers of the substandard language might be expected to say *the book is hisn;* no speaker of substandard English would ever say *hisn book*.[39]

Here is a brief list of distinctive features of nonstandard English, not taking into account regional variations in the status of some items:

VERB FORMS:	he *don't,* you *was,* I *says; knowed, growed;* I *seen* him
PRONOUN FORMS:	*hisself, theirself; this here* book, *that there* animal; *them* potatoes
CONNECTIVES:	*without* you pay the rent; *on account of* he was sick; *being as* she couldn't come
DOUBLE NEGATIVES:	we *don't* have *no* time; a little rain *never* hurt *no one*
VOCABULARY:	*irregardless, nohow, anywheres*

Typically, modern writers on usage have first established a rough distinction between standard and nonstandard and have then proceeded to investigate variations *within* standard English. In other words, they have tried to classify the kinds of standard English educated users of the language use on different occasions and for different purposes. In distinguishing standard and nonstandard, the investigator can apply variable but fairly concrete criteria relating to social level and educational background. In distinguishing different varieties of standard English, he must

---

[39] Marckwardt, *American English,* p. 148.

rely on more complex and elusive criteria relating to convention and style. Rather than telling people apart by their language, he is telling apart the different kinds of speech and writing a single educated user of the language has occasion to employ.

The influence of recent linguistic study on attempts to establish major varieties within standard English has been paradoxically two-sided. On the one hand, linguists have stressed the difference between speech and writing. They have discouraged people from trying to substitute artificial, bookish speech for natural conversational English:

> The failure to see and to understand the distinction between standard colloquial speech and the literary language and the failure to understand the relationship between speech and writing has been, I am convinced, the chief obstacle in imparting to our students both real literacy and a confident competence in speaking. Traditional grammar has been based, understandably enough, on the literary language, but far too often the prescriptive rules which must be followed if we are to *write* acceptably have been used as a basis for how we should *talk*.[40]

On the other hand, the scientifically oriented grammarian or lexicographer may decide that the subtle degrees of informality in language, and the manifold variables of context and intention, make the objective application of a term like *colloquial* difficult or impossible. Much of the furor that greeted the publication of *Webster's Third New International Dictionary* resulted from just such a decision. Defending the policy of "not using at all the status label *colloquial*," the editor-in-chief, Dr. Philip B. Gove, stated that "it is impossible to know whether a word out of context is colloquial or not." Furthermore, the editors used great caution in identifying slang, the more distinctly informal subspecies of colloquial that, in the words of Robert Hall, is "on the margin of the standard language":

> There is no completely satisfactory objective test for slang, especially in application to a word out of context. No word is invariably slang, and many standard words can be given slang connotations or used so inappropriately as to become slang.[41]

It is of course true that "a word out of context" does not have social or stylistic status, any more than a word out of context has meaning. But dictionaries list the meanings words commonly have in typical contexts. Similarly, the purpose of a status label is that it "provides a degree of usage orientation by identifying the character of the context in which a word ordinarily occurs."[42] The crux of the matter is the rigor with

---

[40] Henry Lee Smith, Jr., "The Teacher and the World of English," *The English Journal*, XLVII (April, 1958), 183.

[41] By permission. From *Webster's Third New International Dictionary of the English Language, Unabridged* (Springfield, Mass.: G. & C. Merriam Company, 1961), pp. 6a, col. 2; 19a, col. 1. Copyright 1961 by G. & C. Merriam Company, Publishers of the Merriam-Webster Dictionaries.

[42] *Ibid.*, p. 18a, col. 3.

which we require that such a label be established by a "satisfactory objective test." Colloquial language is normally identified not by objective test but by the trained ear of the experienced and sensitive observer. In the words of James Sledd, awareness of the colloquial character of a word like *shindig* exists "in the linguistic consciousness of the educated." In refusing to apply the label, the lexicographer acts "as though some notion of scientific objectivity should require the scientist to deny that he knows what he knows because he may not know how he knows it."[43] To be truly informative, an authoritative account of usage must include statements such as that *ain't* when used by standard speakers is often "homey or is written or uttered with tongue in cheek," that "chatty columns sometimes use *ain't* to achieve a 'plain folks' effect."[44] Such judgments concerning the speaker's or writer's intention are essential to the correct interpretation of an utterance, but they cannot be verified by objective tests.

To the person with an ear for nuance, the difference between "Come shake a leg" and "You are invited to a party" is as real and concrete as anything about language. When a dictionary lists *shake a leg* without a usage label, the student must check his own hunches concerning its status against single fragmentary citations rather than against conclusions drawn by highly qualified observers on the basis of much more comprehensive evidence. Such conclusions would have to be no more dogmatic than the evidence justifies. That a word is "not invariably slang" can be indicated as efficiently and clearly as that it is not invariably capitalized.

If a handbook or a dictionary is intended as a tool in the teaching of English, it can ill afford to brush off as "prescientific folklore" whatever defies rigorous verification. **Slang,** for instance, has a tendency toward drastically graphic metaphor, which in terms like *rubberneck, sawbones,* and *eyewash* has a characteristic humorous effect. As Mencken says, "such a term as *rubberneck* is almost a complete treatise on American psychology," showing along with "boldness and contempt for ordered forms" a delight in pungent epithets and grotesque humor.[45] There is no reliable "objective" measure of whether such a metaphor is drastic and irreverent enough to be classified as slang. Thus, the term *eyewash* in the sense of something "designed to distract attention from or conceal ulterior motives or actual conditions" is listed in *Webster's Third International* without a usage label. However, as used for instance by former President Truman, it had a quality of half-humorous, colorful exaggeration characteristic of the informal statements of the former President. For the teacher of composition, it is more important that his students be able to verify their hunches concerning such usages than that they be able to find out

---

[43] James H. Sledd, "The Lexicographer's Uneasy Chair," *College English, XXIII* (May, 1962), 685.
[44] Margaret M. Bryant, ed., *Current American Usage* (New York: Funk & Wagnalls Co., 1962), p. 16.
[45] Mencken, *The American Language,* p. 92.

the dialectal distribution of *flannel cake* as "chiefly East and Midland."

Different users of dictionaries turn to them for different things. The teacher of English necessarily judges dictionaries in part on whether they help his students make stylistic discriminations. Even so, he must not expect the lexicographer to solve miraculously the real difficulties involved in providing such help. As Albert Marckwardt has pointed out, dictionary-makers never succeeded in making the general public interpret the label *colloquial*

> in the way in which dictionary editors intended. It was not meant as a condemnation either in the Webster Second or in the various abridged dictionaries based upon it. The editors took great pains to say so, both in the prefatory material and in the definition of the word itself, but this went unheeded.[46]

Rather than recognize colloquial as the informal variety of spoken standard English, popular authorities on language continue to equate it with the "speech forms of the lower classes"; a widely used series of textbooks for high school English sets "colloquial" over against "standard" English.

Furthermore, dictionaries that do use the label are likely to apply it to numerous words that other authoritative dictionaries label slang and vice versa. Such evidence of the inherent relativity of usage labels gives the literal-minded ammunition with which to attack the lexicographer's claim to authority. If a dictionary-maker in view of these difficulties decides to drop the label *colloquial,* fair-minded teachers will regret but respect his decision. They will respect it particularly if it represents the considered judgment of the publisher of the Merriam-Webster dictionaries, whose citation files are, in the words of Priscilla Tyler, "the national archives of the language."[47]

Typically, the teacher's task is not to give a rigorously scientific description of usage but to alert his students to some of the more obvious and more important distinctions. For this purpose. Leonard Bloomfield's classification of the three most significant types of usage is still serviceable: the "literary standard" (most typically represented in formal written English); the "colloquial standard" (most typically represented in informal educated speech); and the "substandard," or, better, nonstandard, "differing topographically, without intense local difference."[48] **Colloquial standard** is the natural, informal speech of the educated. It is the most clearly conversational, "chatty" variety of standard English. If it is good enough for the faculty club or the executive dining room, it is of course

---

[46] "Dictionaries and the English Language," *The English Journal,* LII (May, 1963), 342.

[47] "An English Teacher Looks at Webster's Seventh New Collegiate Dictionary," *Word Study,* XXXVIII (April, 1963), 1. By permission. From *Word Study,* copyright 1963 by G. & C. Merriam Company, Publishers of the Merriam-Webster Dictionaries.

[48] Leonard Bloomfield, *Language* (New York: Holt, Rinehart & Winston, Inc., 1933), p. 52.

good enough for the informal speech of our students. In informed use, the term *colloquial* has nothing to do with "localisms" or with "speech forms of the lower classes." The reason teachers have come to call it a "variety" rather than a "level" of usage is that the term *level* might suggest unjustified social distinctions and moral judgments.

Here are some characteristic features of colloquial English:

CONTRACTIONS:	*don't, doesn't, isn't, won't, can't; I'm, you've, they're*
CONVERSATIONAL TAGS:	*Well,* . . . ; *why,* . . . ; *now,* . . .
PRONOUN FORMS:	it's *me,* that's *him; who* did you invite
PRONOUN REFERENCE:	everybody took *theirs;* somebody left *their* gloves
INTENSIFIERS:	*so* glad; *such* a surprise; *real* miserable; *awful* fast
CONNECTIVES:	*because you say so* doesn't make it right; a rebate *is when* . . .
ABBREVIATIONS:	*ad, gym, phone, exam, bike*
IDIOMS:	*chip in; check up on; come up with; blame* (something) *on* (somebody)
VOCABULARY:	*folks, job, boss; mean, skimpy; snoop, snooze*

The **literary standard,** or **formal written English,** can be negatively defined by its avoidance of these and similar features that have acquired associations of informality. If "good English" is that "which is customary and familiar in a given context and in the pursuit of a given objective," good formal English is that which is customary and familiar in the serious treatment of matters of general cultural significance.[49] The literary standard only reluctantly accepts common contractions and abbreviations. It typically observes such distinctions as use of the subject form of personal pronouns after *be* (it was *she* who first brought up the subject); *whom* in object positions (*whom* do you expect to win?); subjunctive in conditions highly hypothetical or contrary to fact (the bird looked as if it *were* a plane). The vocabulary of formal English tends to be more objective, learned, and technical than that of informal English, with fewer overtones of the intimate and familiar.

What determines whether a usage conforms to the conventions of formal written English is authoritative use by the best modern writers. Though not inhospitable to the rhythms of current speech, serious modern prose shows the continued influence of a rich literary tradition. Such writers as George Orwell and James Baldwin combine an ear for modern idiom with an ear for the echoes in our language of a tradition that

---

49 Sumner Ives, "A Review of Webster's Third New International Dictionary," *Word Study,* XXXVII (December, 1961), 5. By permission. From *Word Study,* copyright 1961 by G. & C. Merriam Company, Publishers of the Merriam-Webster Dictionaries.

makes the dialogues of John Dryden and David Hume models of "modern" prose. Writers such as these write "by a certaine naturall judgement, and not by art or any manner rule." No dictionary, however scientific, and no quantitative study, however statistically sound, can be as sure a guide as the cultivated taste developed in the reader's and writer's constant contact with the living language, "commune, plentifull, and variable, and (as it were) like a delicious garden full of sundrie flowers and fruites."[50] To develop in our students a confident ease in the use of the literary standard, we must expose them to a wide range of past and current writing.

Formal and informal English are not two clearly distinct and separate types, making possible neat either-or choices. Rather, we must recognize a range of variation from the extreme formality of ceremonial occasions to the chatty intimacy of a conversation among friends. Though our first task is to make our students recognize the general distinction between formal and informal, ultimately our aim is to make them sensitive to nuances of tone. Lacking such sensitivity, they will look in their reading only for the grossest kind of "plain sense," missing important clues to the attitude and intention of the writer.

Distinctive tone lends color and variety to language in proportion as it limits its versatility and scope. In the same way, a distinctive costume lends color to one's appearance while at the same time it limits the general usefulness of one's clothes. This limiting effect of distinctive tone is clearest with such extremes of colloquial usage as adolescent slang or advertising jargon. A word like *enthused,* common to both, carries like a distinct flavor the breeziness of people subject to enthusiasms too shallow or insincere to be appropriate in serious discussion. Less distinctive but equally important are the suggestions of casual ease that distinguish less colloquial language from more formal alternatives.

In many ways, educated speech and writing has over the decades moved in the direction of greater informality. Nevertheless, the degree of informality a skillful writer permits himself is clearly limited by the effect he is trying to achieve, by the tone he is trying to set. Generally, the degree of formality in word choice is closely correlated with the degree of deliberate patterning in sentence structure, the range of allusion and reference, and similar stylistic factors. Here are some sample analyses of prose passages, moving from a relatively formal to a relatively informal style:

1) Of escapes from the pressure of an increasingly mechanized life to occasional outbursts of excitement or triviality there is much to be said. At least it may be said for them that they are natural, perhaps needful, refuges from a world whose tightly woven days would otherwise be unbearable. It is perhaps a sad commentary on the angular and constricted lives we lead that we should have to seek such lurid or futile ways to peace. But it is not to be

50 Castiglione, *The Book of the Courtier,* pp. 58–59.

wondered at that, living in such a world of routine, we should plunge ever so often into the loud nonsense of inane parties, wallow in the absurd pathos and comedy of the screen, or fall enraptured victims to successive crazes of bootless puzzles and dull games. We may be forgiven our excursions to musical comedies without wit or music, and conversational evenings without humanity or ideas. The contemporary citizen is vexed beyond his own realization by the humdrum unthrilling pressure of his days; he craves naturally now and then an opportunity to be trivial, irresponsible, and absurd.—Irwin Edman, *Adam, the Baby and the Man from Mars*

This selection, while concerned with trivial amusements, is scholarly and formal in style. Its vocabulary, though not pretentious or bookish, departs enough from the level of everyday language to be reserved and dignified: *needful, enraptured, excursion, vexed.* Its metaphors are fresh and expressive rather than familiar or amusing: "tightly woven days," "angular and contricted lives." Sentence structure departs from the ordinary by inversion ("Of escapes . . . there is much to be said") and by frequent use of parallelism ("plunge . . . of inane parties, wallow . . . of the screen, or fall . . . of bootless puzzles and dull games"; "excursions . . . without wit or music, . . . evenings without humanity or ideas"). Throughout, the use of the impersonal passive reinforces the tone of dignified detachment ("it may be said," "it is not to be wondered at," "may be forgiven").

2) It happens to be a fact that all classic works without exception deal directly or indirectly with problems of conduct. That is their great virtue for school use. Not that they teach a plain goody-goody morality, but that they show and discuss and solve dilemmas that a shipping clerk or an athlete can be made to understand. For this understanding, the discussion of any classic *must be superficial.* If you dive below the surface with your pupil you drown him. Certain teachers are always terrified of superficiality; they seem to think other teachers will scoff or that the dead author will scold. Let them remind themselves that their colleagues' profundity would strike the great author as either surface scratching or pendantry; and let them remember that for every reader there is a time when a given book is being read for the first time.—Jacques Barzun, *Teacher in America*

This selection illustrates an urbane and discriminating kind of informality. It uses the conversational phrase ("it happens to be a fact that . . ."), the occasional colloquialism ("goody-goody morality"), the informal *you.* Its metaphors have a homely, familiar quality ("if you dive . . . you drown him"; "surface scratching"). Its sentences, on the whole, are shorter, more abrupt, and more emphatic than those in the preceding selection ("That is their great virtue for school use"). However, the author does not *limit* himself to the familiar, the simple. His vocabulary ranges beyond the conversational: *terrified of superficiality, scoff, colleagues' profundity, pedantry.* His sentences are deliberate and effective; they repeatedly become insistent ("show and discuss and solve"; "let them remind themselves . . . let them remember . . .").

3) If television is ever to amount to anything of cultural importance, it should rid itself of the idea that it's the motion picture industry, the book business or the stage. It's a big, new art form of its own. It was radio's lack of standards that led to that dizzy lunacy known as the giveaway program. Radio programs gave away washing machines, Cadillacs, $1,000 bills, houses —everything, in fact, except women. I could never quite understand that lone omission. If Bert Parks had thrown a beautiful 18-year-old babe into the jackpot of *Stop the Music,* even I would have stayed home and listened for the telephone. But he wouldn't. Some faint moral scruple—or con-

ceivably fear of the Federal Communications Commission—stayed the broadcaster from this final depravity. The Roman emperors who gave the populace bread and circuses—which is what radio was imitating with its giveaway programs—also threw in sexual orgies, and it always seemed to me inconsistent of the broadcasters not to follow through with the thing. I brought this to the attention of several vice presidents, but they failed to see any humor in the suggestion. They also failed to see anything wrong with the giveaway program, which shows where a lack of moral standards leads.—John Crosby, "Seven Deadly Sins of the Air," *Life*

This selection illustrates the kind of distinct informality that would be inappropriate in a more serious, more objective, less personal context. There is no doubt about the literacy and skill of the writer, suggested by such phrases as "faint moral scruple" or "stayed . . . from this final depravity." However, his style is in keeping with his brash, no-holds-barred attack on his subject. The tone of the passage is set by the colloquial phrases ("amount to anything," "follow through with the thing"), the slang expressions ("babe," "jackpot," "threw in"), the informal contractions ("it's," "wouldn't"). Overstatement runs wild ("dizzy lunacy," "sexual orgies"). Sentence structure ranges from the short half sentence ("But he wouldn't.") to the overloaded last sentence, with its parenthetical *which*-clause reaching half-heartedly for an antecedent in a manner frowned upon by guardians of correct usage. On the one hand, serious students of the mass media might object to the writer's flippancy; on the other hand, readers who would not otherwise interest themselves in the subject might be attracted by the writer's treatment of it.[51]

If distinctive informality can restrict the versatility and effectiveness of an author's style, so can an overzealous and self-conscious formality. Indiscriminate criticism of informal touches in the writing of our students leads too many of them to believe that their English teacher is happy only with the most stilted and unidiomatic kind of language. They write a tortured pseudoformal style that reflects, not their command of the resources of formal written English, but a desperate attempt to avoid anything that sounds natural or familiar. Nothing is gained if we cure our students of an indiscriminate and inarticulate informality only to have them adopt an opaque and inarticulate pseudoformal jargon. The teacher who defines formal written English as "English generally appropriate to the discussion of topics of some consequence" needs to warn his students as often against what is stilted or precious as against what is excessively informal.

Instruction in composition usually centers on a relatively formal expository style. This fact should not be allowed to make our students feel that any stigma attaches to informality that is appropriate and effective. Here for instance is a distinctly informal passage in which Robert Graves, in *Goodbye to All That,* refers to Siegfried Sassoon:

Five poems of his had appeared in *The Cambridge Magazine* (one of the few aggressively pacifist journals published in England at the time, the

[51] Hans P. Guth, *Words and Ideas: A Handbook for College Writing* (San Francisco: Wadsworth Publishing Company, Inc., 1959), pp. 179–82.

offices of which were later sacked by Flying Corps cadets). None of them, he admitted, was much good except as a dig at the complacent and perfectly unspeakable people who thought the war ought to go on indefinitely until everyone got killed but themselves. The pacifists were now urging him to produce something red hot in the style of Barbusse's *Under Fire,* but he couldn't do it.[52]

The tone of this passage would seem aggressively flippant if it were part, say, of a scholarly biography by Graves of his fellow poet. In fact, it is an autobiographical reference to an intimate personal friend, sharing intensely personal and private frustrations and resentments. It ranges from the conversational ("none of them . . . much good," "perfectly unspeakable people") to the slangy ("dig," "got killed," "red hot"). Its intimate tone is appropriate to the personal relationship; its understated, almost casual sarcasm is in keeping with the general tone of this gallant and sobering book on the nightmare that World War I was to the more perceptive among its victims. The reader who on the basis of Graves's use of language in this passage sets himself up as his superior in social status, intelligence, sensitivity, or moral stamina would be fatuous indeed.

Correctness and Logic

In teaching "good English," the teacher is hampered as in perhaps no other area of his work by inherited popular attitudes and preconceptions. Though his main task is to develop sound attitudes toward language in his students, he must be prepared to deal effectively with rationalizations that give a façade of intellectual respectability to attitudes that are less than well informed. For instance, no sooner have we set up "the practice of the best writers" as a standard of good English than we have to admit that in the past it has often been used as a misleading label for standards arrived at in a quite different fashion. The best writers employ usages like the following:

> The impertinence of *these kind* of scrutinies, moreover, was generally concluded with a compliment. (Jane Austen)

> The practical *reason why* . . . a majority are permitted . . . to rule is not *because* they are most likely to be in the right . . . but *because* they are physically the strongest. (Henry David Thoreau)

> They felt that they would sooner have had *less* figures and more food. (George Orwell)

> The Utopians do not believe that any civilized man *can* omit any of the subjects that are included in the course of study. (Robert M. Hutchins)

One familiar reaction is to identify these usages as mistakes made by a nodding Homer: "Even the best go wrong." More likely, the person nod-

[52] *Goodbye to All That* (Harmondsworth, Middlesex: Penguin Books, Ltd., 1960), p. 212.

ding was the editor, who let slip through authentic examples of the author's idiomatic use of the language. If they *are* mistakes, however, we have established that in order to label them incorrect we must appeal to some standard beyond what first-rate writers actually use. This standard is not likely to be quantitative. Statistical analysis often does not support familiar preconceptions concerning correct usage. One investigator found that in a national magazine uses of the *s* genitive, for instance, were "about equally divided between living beings and inanimate objects."[53] Another investigator said in concluding a survey of the widespread use of locutions like "the play's structure" in violation of traditional rules:

> A large portion of my data is from writers who cannot exactly be classed as "skimmed milk." Such novelists as Faulkner, Hemingway, Evelyn Eaton, and Sherwood Anderson, such literary figures as Louis Untermeyer and Archibald MacLeish, such scholars and critics as David Daiches, Howard M. Jones, O. J. Campbell, John Mason Brown, and the *New York Times*—to mention a few sources for my materials—presumably know something about style.[54]

Extending such inquiries into the past, modern investigators commanded the vast resources of the *New English Dictionary on Historical Principles,* reissued in 1933 as the *Oxford English Dictionary.* There they found extensive quotations showing for instance that, contrary to the traditional rule, *myself* had from Middle English down been commonly preferred to *me* in combinations like "my friend and *myself.*"[55] They found other debated usages supported by quotations from authors ranging from Bacon and Shakespeare through Addison and Goldsmith to George Meredith and William Morris. Study of the extensive word histories in the *Oxford English Dictionary* confirmed the teacher's suspicion "that a good many of the more puristic strictures on usage are of relatively recent origin."[56]

In practice, the person defending traditional preconceptions soon has to fall back on a standard of correctness other than the "best writers." If he is candid, he will describe his disapproval of certain debatable usages as a habitual, almost instinctive reaction. John Ciardi, "never having been taught to use 'like' as a conjunction," describes himself as

[53] Archibald A. Hill, "Correctness and Style in English Composition," *College English,* XII (February, 1951), 280–85; in *Readings in Applied English Linguistics,* ed. Harold B. Allen (New York: Appleton-Century-Crofts, Inc., 1958), p. 317.

[54] Russell Thomas, "Notes on the Inflected Genitive in Modern American Prose," *College English,* XIV January, 1953); in *Introductory Readings on Language,* eds. Wallace L. Anderson and Norman C. Stageberg (New York: Holt, Rinehart & Winston, Inc., 1962), p. 311.

[55] Marckwardt and Walcott, *Facts About Current Usage,* p. 38.

[56] Porter G. Perrin, *Writer's Guide and Index to English* (3rd ed.), rev. with the assistance of Karl W. Dykema (Chicago: Scott, Foresman & Company, 1959), p. 752.

"growling, 'as, damn it!'" every time the radio announcer employs *like* the way it is used by Presidents and janitors, professors and college freshmen alike.[57] The kind of conditioning that here bears fruit is in no way limited to English. The German schoolboy, for instance, early learns to recite, with appropriate finger-pointing: *"Wer brauchen ohne zu gebraucht, braucht brauchen überhaupt nicht zu gebrauchen."* (He who uses *brauchen* without the *zu* had better not use it at all.) He then finds *brauchen* without the *zu* as much a feature of the speech of his philology professor as of his own.

The arguments used to make the corrector's instinct intellectually respectable are various and formidable. Yet they prove hard to establish. First, the appeal to efficient communication is too often futile. As Harold Whitehall says in discussing the *it is me—it is I* quandary, "clarity of statement has nothing to do with these matters; one form is as clear as the other."[58] The most damaging feature of traditional language instruction is the teacher's pretending not to understand, or to misunderstand, usages that are perfectly clear to him and to the student. For instance, there is no doubt in either the teacher's or the student's mind that *"Can* I leave the room?" is a request for permission. There is no point in pretending to the student that "tie it *tightly"* means "tie it as if you were drunk."

Teachers must take care to apply the criterion of ambiguity only where it is clearly relevant, as with problems of pronoun reference or of modification. If a national news service reports that "The prisoner's hands were manacled, but *they* were removed at the door," many readers will be caught up short by the gory ambiguity of *they*. Similarly, misplaced modifiers on the model of "We have chairs for secretaries *with built-in padding"* make for distracting double-takes and raise a laugh at the expense of the writer. Genuine ambiguity results when both possible meanings are plausible. But warning students of such constructions is a quite different matter from using charges of ambiguity to justify objections to usages considered undesirable on other grounds.

Attempts to develop a fully thought-out standard of efficiency in language are rare. Among them is Hugh Sykes Davies' account of "Good Grammar and Bad Grammar" in *Grammar Without Tears*. "Good grammar" would use the "smallest possible amount of grammatical machinery"; it would thus prefer "I like he," analogous to "I like tea," to the use of the "unnecessary" object form *him*.[59] Such considerations could easily influence the makers of an Orwellian *newspeak*. Under present conditions, language does not seem to move in the direction of such

---

[57] "Manner of Speaking," *Saturday Review*, November 4, 1961, p. 30.
[58] Whitehall, *Structural Essentials*, p. 91.
[59] *Grammar Without Tears* (New York: The John Day Company, Inc., 1953), pp. 25–26.

apparent simplifications without sprouting unsuspected new complexities. Traditionally, however, criteria of "usefulness" and "redundancy" have been applied in a much more haphazard manner. Distinctions between *fewer—less, further—farther, each other—one another* are thus said to be useful; to use these forms interchangeably would presumably be a waste of our linguistic resources. However, language quite typically has several roughly synonymous ways of expressing the same meaning. Whatever distinction is involved is signaled by other means than our choice of *fewer* or *less:* Teachers identify without difficulty student sentences that, according to the conventional rule, require one form rather than the other.

The teacher here often pays the price for allowing the richly meaningful terms *authority* and *authoritative* to shrink to the meaning of "someone who gives right-or-wrong, true-or-false answers." Such an authority cannot afford the blurring of his image that would result if he replied to a right-or-wrong question about usage,

> in so trifling a matter the goodnesse and perfection of a tongue doth not consist, as Demosthenes answered Eschines well, that had taken him up, demaunding him of certaine wordes which he had used and yet were not auncient, what monsters, or woondrous matters they were? whereat Demosthenes laughed, and answered him, that the fortunes of Greece dependeth not upon them.[60]

Lacking the sense of proportion of Castiglione's courtier, many a teacher has felt obliged to advise the laity on whether to break their eggs at the bigger or at the smaller end. As Thurston Womack reports, "Some teachers feel that teaching that more than one usage is acceptable further confuses an already confused student."[61] However, there is no reason why students should be confused by the simple fact of **divided usage:** Languages typically have more than one way of saying the same thing; and in many instances the one is as good as the other.

The damaging effect of emphasizing peripheral distinctions is that again the student is prejudiced against an essential function of the teacher of English. Just as the teacher must alert his students to the possibilities of ambiguity, so he must train them to make finer verbal distinctions than they normally do. He must change their reactions from "I got the general idea" to "I tried to pin down the exact implications." The teacher weakens his authority in these matters if too often he stresses distinctions that are at best trivial and at worst un-English.

Like usefulness, **redundancy** is often applied in too random a manner as a criterion of usage. *The reason is because,* for instance, is no more redundant than the double genitive signal in "a friend *of* my brother's." We must distinguish between the built-in redundancy of the linguistic sys-

60 Castiglione, *The Book of the Courtier,* p. 65.
61 Womack, "Teachers' Attitudes," p. 188.

tem and the stylistic redundancy that results from padding and ineffectual repetition. As Paul Roberts says in the Teacher's Guide to *Patterns of English:*

> One of the important characteristics of any working language is a very high degree of redundancy. The meanings of a message will be signaled not once but many times in the course of an utterance. Consider such a sentence as "There were several children in the room," and notice how often the plural meaning is signaled. We get it in the *were,* in the vowel of *child-,* in the *r* of *children,* and the *en* of *children,* and in the word *several.* We need hear only one of these signals to know that more than one child is meant.
>
> Redundancy is what makes language work as well as it does. If there were no redundancy, then communication could not go on in the presence of any kind of noise, since it would be necessary to hear every particle of the message.[62]

Other traditional arguments are similarly at odds with characteristic features of the language. We are often told that *like* or *due to* "is not" one part of speech but another, as though a word might not, like the word *light,* belong to different grammatical categories in different contexts:

> Turn off the *light.* (noun)
> Let's *light* a candle. (verb)
> She had *light* hair. (adjective)
> The water was *light* blue. (adverb)

There is little support in English grammar for a belief in the integrity and mutual exclusiveness of major grammatical classes. Nouns are often transformed into verbs: *ape, house, knight,* and *lock* are typical examples. We have idioms like *"bell* the cat" and *"lord* it over somebody." Shakespeare carries this tendency even further in lines like "I shall see some squeaking Cleopatra *boy* [that is, give a boyish imitation of] my greatness." Not only the often criticized *like,* but also *after, before,* and *until* serve as both prepositions and conjunctions, giving us both *"after* dinner" and *"after* we finished dinner."

The basic weakness of many traditional arguments concerning usage is that they treat as a matter of logic what is a matter of convention, of customary use. As a result, they often serve neither the cause of good usage nor of sound logic. The double negative (to express a negative) is no more illogical than the use of an etymological positive to express a negative in *personne* or *rien.* As has often been pointed out, *it's me* is no more illogical than *c'est moi,* or, for that matter, the archaic *methinks* and *methought.* It is no more illogical that *me* should replace the *I* after a linking verb than that the *I* did in fact replace a historical dative in *"I was given the book"*—derived from an Old English construction parallel to German *"Mir wurde das Buch gegeben"*—"*Me* was given the book."

---

[62] Paul Roberts, Teacher's Guide to *Patterns of English* (New York: Harcourt, Brace & World, Inc., 1956), p. 19.

If these are "mistakes," then it is indeed true that "seen from the perspective of history, language consists almost exclusively of errors."[63]

No narrow conception of logic will long survive examination of the complexities and apparent irrationalities of language. The teacher with some linguistic sophistication knows that in Latin, for instance, nouns like *agricola,* feminine in form, are masculine in concord. Certain German words for *girl* and *woman (das Mädchen, das Weib)* take the neuter article and select neuter pronouns. English verbs like *wash,* active in form, acquire passive meanings: "This material *washes* well." The essential point is that such complexities mark the speech of logical and illogical persons alike and do not keep the former from using them in admirably logical communication.

The relationship between idiom and logic is one of the most complicated and intriguing things about language. Otto Jespersen went so far as to say that

> in most cases where, so to speak, the logic of facts or of the exterior world is at war with the logic of grammar, English is free from the narrow-minded pedantry which in most languages sacrifices the former to the latter or makes people shy of saying or writing things which are not "strictly grammatical." This is particularly clear with regard to number. *Family* and *clergy* are, grammatically speaking, of the singular number; but in reality they indicate a plurality. . . . in English one is free to add a verb in the singular if the idea of unity is essential, and then to refer to this unit as *it,* or else to put the verb in the plural and use the pronoun *they,* if the idea of plurality is predominant. . . . Inversely, there is in English a freedom paralleled nowhere else of expressing grammatically a unity consisting of several parts, of saying, for instance, "I do not think I ever spent a more delightful three weeks" (Darwin) . . . "Three years is but short" (Shakespeare) . . . "ten minutes is heaps of time" (E. F. Benson).[64]

Generally, the logic of facts and the logic of grammar adjust to one another in complicated ways. When they conflict, no simple logical formula can help us predict how the adjustment will work itself out in actual usage. Thus, in spite of traditional rules of agreement, the singular in "I am not one of those who *believes*" is common in informal educated speech. The dominating singular meaning of the whole utterance here attracts to it the singular form of the verb in the relative clause. In contemporary German, according to one indignant observer, the same construction is "every day spoken, written and printed, heard and read without attracting notice," in fact, "day after day slapped in one's face." In both cases, the logic of facts apparently overrides the logic of grammar. It does so even with conservative teachers of English, who may be ob-

---

[63] E. Standop, *"Was ist Grammatik?" Praxis des Neusprachlichen Unterrichts,* IX (1962), 131.

[64] Otto Jespersen, *Growth and Structure of the English Language,* 9th ed. (New York: Doubleday & Company, Inc., 1956), pp. 14–15.

served consciously insisting on theoretical agreement but unconsciously using the debated form.

Nevertheless, traditional rules and their logical rationalizations do in fact influence the reactions of many a reader and listener. Since they thus reflect actual preferences about language, they deserve careful attention. The reader's reaction of *"as,* damn it!" is an effective barrier to communication, regardless of the foundations on which it rests. The teacher has a double function in regard to such attitudes. He must lay the foundations for more enlightened attitudes in the young. At the same time, he must alert them to the prejudices of their elders. He will thus agree with Sumner Ives that it is "the duty of the school teacher to point out the current shibboleths . . . and to advise how much they are observed and by which people."[65] He will thus tell his students, "the careful writer avoids *like* as a conjunction because conservative readers consider it ungrammatical; he avoids *reason is because* because conservative readers reject it as redundant." In advising his students concerning their habits of speech, the teacher will tell them that *these kind* and *one of those who believes* are common in everyday conversation but invite the avoidable criticism of conservative listeners.

Generally, the need for observing the shibboleths of correctness is becoming less pressing. Their defenders have for decades been weakened by reluctant concessions to current usage. Increasingly, even stout defenders of correct English show a tendency toward a token liberalism on selected issues. Thus, a writer who feels that *like* as a conjunction, though used by "many writers of repute," from Shakespeare to Shaw, "still sounds terrible," will say about *ain't:*

> The aura of horror that surrounds this word is a classic instance of the damage done by genteelism. For centuries, *ain't* for *am not* was perfectly good English, as any pre-1850 novel shows, but the Victorian schoolmarms, worried by its use for *is not* and *are not* as well, proscribed it so effectively that it became a mark of ignorance and vulgarity to use *ain't* at all. Yet there is no other workable contraction, for *amn't* is unpronounceable and *aren't* is ungrammatical.[66]

Increasingly, even emphatic spokesmen for a traditional point of view are aware of a formidable body of opinion on the other side. Thus, teachers will more and more feel free to play down or pass over instruction in such problems of usage as Robert C. Pooley listed in 1960, collecting items "tolerated at least, and in some instances . . . in very general use":

1. Any distinction between *shall* and *will*.
2. Any reference to the split infinitive.
3. Elimination of *like* as a conjunction.

[65] "Linguistics in the Classroom," *College English*, XVII (December, 1955), 165–72; in Allen, *Readings*, p. 303.
[66] Dwight Macdonald, "Sweet Are the Uses of Usage," *The New Yorker*, May 17, 1958, p. 144.

4. Objection to the phrase "different than."
5. Objection to He is one of those boys who *is*.
6. Objection to the reason . . . is because.
7. Objection to *myself* as a polite substitute for *I* as in "I understand you will meet Mrs. Jones and myself at the station."
8. Insistence upon the possessive case standing before a gerund.

As Pooley observed,

> These items and many others like them will still remain cautionary matters left to the teacher's discretion. In evaluating the writing of a superior student I would certainly call these distinctions to his attention and point out to him the value of observing them. But this is a very different matter from setting a basic usage standard to be maintained.[67]

Usage and Style

Many matters formerly treated as problems of correct usage are best treated, from a different perspective, under the heading of effective and ineffective style. Often, the effectiveness of our stylistic choices depends on the context and the intended audience. For instance, we must distinguish between the technical and popular uses of terms that have exact meanings in philosophy, criticism, or science and have more general extended meanings in everyday language. Much of the steam can be taken out of debates over *imply—infer* and *disinterested—uninterested* by the simple observation that they tend to be synonymous in popular use, whereas the distinctions between them are clearly relevant in much college-level reading and writing. Similarly, *unique* has moved from its etymological meaning of "single" or "sole" to the extended meaning of "rare" or "exceptional." This extension, universally accepted in popular use, goes against the grain of many people vividly aware of the original Latin meaning. By the same token, scholars and scientists with some background in Latin or Greek, and using Latin and Greek terminology as a matter of daily routine, will find the original plural forms in *formulae, memoranda,* and *media* more "natural" than their Anglicized popular alternatives.

Many words are felt to be objectionable because of the company they keep; they are associated in the listener's or reader's mind with certain attitudes of the people who most typically use them. Thus, the objection to *unique* in the sense of "exceptional" is often based on its common use in glib journalistic or commercial overstatement as an all-purpose word of emphasis or praise. Similarly, expressions like "language-wise" or "in terms of language" suggest to many readers the glib insincerity of the hard sell or the self-importance of a pompously "professional" style. The negative reaction of many teachers to slang derives from its frequent association with attitudes of adolescent rebellion: the deliberate choice of a slang expression or a nonstandard form by an adolescent (where

67 Pooley, "Dare Schools Set a Standard?" p. 180.

he knows a standard or "polite" form to be expected and appropriate) may signal disrespect for adult authority, refusal to assume responsibility. Associations such as these are inherently relative; an expression that will show its user to be one of the crowd in one situation will identify him as an outsider in another.

Many traditional handbook rules become more meaningful and less rigid when clearly presented as stylistic advice. For instance, handbooks conventionally warn against upside-down subordination. As critics have pointed out, however, the "main idea" of a sentence often quite legitimately appears in what is technically the subordinate part of a sentence: "It is true *that receipts have fallen steadily during the past few years.*" The warning applies to the unintended ironic effect of essential information placed in a deceptively unemphatic position. The ironic effect of such de-emphasis may be quite deliberate:

I would advise you not to pet that dog, *because it is rabid.*

He had a perfect safety record until the last day of his employment—*when he fell from a ladder and broke both legs.*

When the ironic effect is unintentional, it makes for confusing double-takes. Generally, dependent clauses are harder to focus on, to remember, and to quote than independent ones. A reader may lose the trend of an argument if too many essential points appear in unobtrusive dependent clauses.

Reconsideration of familiar injunctions from a stylistic point of view shifts the emphasis from simple right or wrong to questions of emphasis, economy, balance, ease. To a degree, this approach was adopted by some of the more enlightened modern advocates of traditional standards in language. Thus, H. W. Fowler, in his widely influential *Modern English Usage* (1926), undertook not simply to "condemn" or "approve" but to "distinguish." He was as ready to object to pedantry and artificiality in misguided attempts at correctness as to triteness, ambiguity, false emphasis, faddishness, pretentiousness, or verbosity. He decided to "split infinitives sooner than be ambiguous or artificial." Maintaining the legitimacy of the preposition at the end of a sentence, he advised that "in respect of elegance or inelegance" every example "be judged not by any arbitrary rule, but on its own merits."[68]

When more widely and consistently applied, such an approach helps convince the student that good English requires more than mere unthinking conformity to blanket rulings. To speak and write effectively, the student needs more than the ability to find the right page in the rulebook. He must develop a sensitivity to stylistic effects that can guide him in his own stylistic choices.

[68] Margaret Nicholson, *A Dictionary of American-English Usage, Based on Fowler's Modern English Usage* (New York: The New American Library of World Literature, Inc., 1958), pp. 541, 445.

Usage and the Classroom Teacher

What, to sum up, is the general perspective toward usage that the classroom teacher will adopt? His first responsibility will be to interest himself in some of the factors that make for diversity in language. Rather than lump together all deviations from his own linguistic habits and preferences as symptoms of mass illiteracy, he will develop an ear for the dialectal variations and the nuances of tone that give color and tang to language. His knowledge of our linguistic past will convince him that many alleged errors and illiteracies have been part of the language for centuries. The student, encountering them everywhere in speech and writing, absorbs them on the same terms as countless other linguistic features. As in all other spontaneous language use, the "rules" that guide his linguistic choices are the built-in, unconscious patterns that his mind has abstracted from his daily encounters with language. Instruction designed to change his language habits, and to make his linguistic choices more deliberate, must be based on more than arbitrary and unexamined preference. It must be based on a realistic knowledge of the language, both its history and its current state. It must be sustained enough to be effectual. It must be constantly reinforced by the student's listening and reading ouside the classroom.

Caught between arguments and counterarguments, insults and counterinsults, the teacher will have to formulate a fairly explicit set of criteria for his treatment of acceptable and desirable usage. The first of these ought to be the criterion of common use. To decide whether an expression is standard English, the teacher will ask whether it is in current common use among educated people. To decide whether an expression is characteristic of serious written English, he will ask whether it is in current common use by serious contemporary writers. Serious writing here of course includes imaginative literature but is not limited to it. The teacher will be aware of the use of English by accomplished and effective writers in philosophy, science, politics, and similar fields. Thus, his standard of written English will reflect his acquaintance with writers like Bertrand Russell, Rachel Carson, Arthur C. Clarke, Adlai E. Stevenson, and Walter Lippmann. Nor will this standard be narrowly and provincially American. It will reflect the teacher's concern for the continuity and community of English prose as written, for instance, by Canadian writers like Stephen Leacock and South African writers like Alan Paton and Dan Jacobson. The criterion of common use will make the teacher suspicious of attacks on a debated usage that begin by referring to an "error now found everywhere" or "an abusage common among educated people."

The second criterion of acceptable usage should be appropriateness of tone. The objection to most slang expressions in student writing is not that they are slang but that they are too slangy for serious discussion. The objection to breezy colloquialisms borrowed from a cigarette commercial is not that they are colloquial but that, in a serious paper, they suggest glib insincerity. Appropriate tone ranges all the way from the highly conventional tenor of a stylized social note through the more flexible but dignified formal tone of serious discussion to the informality of polite conversation and the more frankly colloquial tone of a chat among friends. The English teacher's job is not to outlaw variations in tone but to alert the student to their characteristic effects and to the incongruities resulting from their indiscriminate use. To use good English means to use with confident ease language appropriate to the context and to the user's intention.

The third criterion of acceptable usage should be a decent regard for the preferences of one's readers. If the reader is offended by the split infinitive, there is no point in bringing out the worst in him by splitting an infinitive that can be just as easily left unsplit. Avoidance of the more commonly denounced alleged illiteracies is to some extent a matter of courtesy toward the reader. However, it is also a matter of the writer's self-interest. Part of every writer's task is to protect himself against the bad manners of those who, in Donald J. Lloyd's phrase, "are ready to tangle the thread of any discussion by pouncing on a point of grammar."[69]

In teaching usage from this general point of view, the instructor will avoid textbooks and manuals of style that arbitrarily label incorrect many expressions found daily in the language of people of true distinction. He will look for handbooks and dictionaries that knowledgeably help the student distinguish not only standard and nonstandard, but also formal and informal usage. He will try very hard not to let miscellaneous peripheral matters of debated usage monopolize class time. He will emphasize instead those matters of usage and style that are basic to effective speech and writing. He will make the student see language as a supple instrument of communication rather than as a crude device for separating the goats from the sheep. At the same time, he will alert the student to the many nonlinguistic factors and attitudes that complicate the use of language.

With these and similar problems, traditional rules and scientific techniques alike deal, in James Joyce's phrase, "as a cleaver deals with meat." The student who wants to know what good English is will not be helped by an authority who tells him that *due to* used as a preposition is an "abomination."[70] Neither will the student be helped by studies and dictionaries that refuse to employ such necessarily subjective and unsci-

[69] "Snobs, Slobs, and the English Language," *The American Scholar*, XX (Summer, 1951), 279

[70] Wilson Follett, "Sabotage in Springfield," *The Atlantic*, January, 1962, p. 75.

entific terms as *colloquial* and *informal*. In the end, the student has to learn, not "by the book," but "by ear," with such assistance as an experienced and sensitive teacher can furnish. In matters of usage neither rules nor statistics are a substitute for discrimination developed through much listening, reading, and writing.

A PROGRAM FOR FURTHER STUDY

CHARLTON LAIRD AND ROBERT M. GORRELL, eds. *English as Language: Backgrounds, Development, Usage.* New York: Harcourt, Brace & World, Inc., 1961. A Harbrace Sourcebook.

> Brings together examples of and observations on English usage from Old English to modern times. Discussions of varieties of English usage by writers ranging from early lexicographers and grammarians to prominent modern linguists. Excellent as an introduction to the problem of usage seen in its full historical context.

MARGARET M. BRYANT, ed., *Current American Usage.* New York: Funk & Wagnalls Company, 1962.

> Based on the work of a committee of the National Council of Teachers of English and completed with the co-operation of eminent linguistic authorities. Full discussion of disputed points of usage, with rulings based on the principle that "any expression is standard English if it is used by many cultivated people to communicate in speech or in writing." Includes a short bibliography after each item listed.

CHARLES CARPENTER FRIES, *American English Grammar.* New York: Appleton-Century-Crofts, Inc., 1940.

> A study of language forms and constructions that have "distinct social class connotations." Based on an examination of large samples of informal handwritten correspondence classified according to social and educational status. A comprehensive and carefully designed study of current usage.

BERGEN EVANS AND CORNELIA EVANS, *A Dictionary of Contemporary American Usage.* New York: Random House, Inc., 1957.

> A scholarly, comprehensive, and eminently readable modern dictionary of usage. Combines acceptance of the modern linguist's view of correctness with the authors' preference for "the forms used by the great writers of English." Decides many questions of debated usage in favor of expressions condemned by conservative authorities.

MARGARET NICHOLSON, *A Dictionary of American-English Usage.* New York: The New American Library of World Literature, Inc., 1958. A Signet Paperback.

> An American adaptation of H. W. Fowler's *A Dictionary of Modern English Usage.* A guide to attitudes and preferences shared by many conservative teachers and editors. Masterly on such matters of style as triteness, pretentiousness, and verbosity.

MATERIALS FOR ANALYSIS

A. To judge from your own experience, what is the status—social, regional, or any other—of the pronunciations roughly transcribed in the following spellings: *formidable, illústrate, labóratory; fella* (fellow), *Ameriky* (America), *eye-ther* (either), *fishin'* (fishing), *jist* (just), *git out* (get out), *forrid* (forehead). If possible, compare your findings informally with friends or colleagues with some professional interest in language. Formulate and evaluate the criteria applied by you and others during this investigation.

B. Study John Braine's account of the role of dialect in his part of England. Then prepare a comparable account of your own experience with regional variations of *American* English:

. . . what makes Yorkshire unique among English counties is that its regional accent is the only one which is halfway acceptable. There are appreciable variations from place to place; the accent of Cleveland in the East is, for instance, very much softer than that of Skipton in the West. And despite the supposed standardizing influence of the BBC, the dialect proper still flourishes. What is generally known as the Yorkshire accent, however, is the accent of the industrial West Riding with its flat *a*'s, warm, full vowels, and slightly blurred *t*'s. The second person is still in common usage, as are words like "doy" and "laike" ("darling" and "play").

There is no question, of course, of the Yorkshire dialect's being a language in its own right like Lollans or Welsh or Erse, or even of words like those I've mentioned receiving their naturalization papers. This is a terrible weakness of English at present; we admit "blitz" and "kaput" but not "doy" and "laike," which are wonderfully good and rich words because they have very specific applications. "Doy" is a term of endearment especially for children; it's much more tender than "darling," with its Noel Coward connotations of silk sheets and champagne. And "laike" means the play of children—not the highly organized adult playing of team games like football but the spontaneous tribal games of cowboys and Indians or cops and robbers or, quite simply, any physical activity which children indulge in when left to their own devices. But these, and thousands equally good, remain unused in literary English. There is a Yorkshire dialect literature, but it is, for want of a better word, amateur.

I said that the Yorkshire accent was halfway acceptable; the emphasis is on the "halfway." It's an enormous asset on radio and TV and does no harm at all as far as the independent businessman is concerned. But any lawyer or teacher or junior executive in a large concern is best advised to learn, as our phrase goes, "to talk well-off."

And many of the younger generation of Yorkshire businessmen speak much as their counterparts in the South do. In the case of those who haven't been to public schools the results can be so dreadful as to be embarrassing. For one mispronunciation in Standard English—a broad *u* in "but" or a narrow *u* in "butcher," for instance—ruins the whole effect. It's possible to have a good deal of quiet fun sitting in hotel bars and roadhouses in expensive residential districts of Ilkley and Burley listening to accents wearing thinner with each drink, until at the fourth pint "beer" turns to "ale" and "old boy" to "lad" and "darling" to "love." The convention is that it's a deliberate democratic unbending; the fact is that Standard English is torn off like a tight collar and everyone breathes naturally again.

—John Braine, "Yorkshire," *The Atlantic*, September, 1961, pp. 71–72.

C. Writing about the British class system in 1956, Alan S. C. Ross claimed that "it is solely by its language that the upper class is clearly marked off from the others." He then proceeded to contrast usages "which serve to demarcate the upper class," abbreviated *U*, from those which are not upper class, abbreviated *non-U*. As he said, "The line of demarcation relevant to this study is, often, a line between, on the one hand, gentlemen and, on the other, persons who, though not gentlemen, might at first sight appear, or would wish to appear, as such." After studying the following excerpts from Mr. Ross's observations, prepare a brief discussion of variations in American usage that have similar implications concerning the speaker's social status.

U-speakers do not sound the *l* in *golf, Ralph* (which rhymes with *safe*), *solder;* some old-fashioned U-speakers do not sound it on *falcon, Malvern,* either, but it is doubtful how far this last survives.

In *Berkeley, Berkshire, clerk, Derby,* U-speakers rhyme the first syllable with *dark* (or *bar*), non-U speakers with *mirk* (or *burr*).

Civil: this word is used by U-speakers to approve the behavior of a non-U person in that the latter has appreciated the difference between U and non-U, e.g. *The guard was certainly very civil.*

Cultivated in *They're cultivated people* is non-U and so also is *cultured.* There is really no U-equivalent (some U-speakers use *civilized* in this sense).

Cup. How is your cup? is a non-U equivalent of *Have some more tea?* or the like. Possible negative non-U answers are *I'm doing nicely, thank you* and (Quite) *sufficient, thank you.* There is a well-known non-U affirmative answer: *I don't mind if I do* (but this was U about a century ago).

Dinner. U-speakers eat *lunch* in the middle of the day (*luncheon* is old-fashioned U) and *dinner* in the evening; if a U-speaker feels that what he is eating is a travesty of his dinner, he may appropriately call it *supper.* Non-U-speakers (also U-children and U-dogs), on the other hand, have their *dinner* in the middle of the day. *Evening meal* is non-U.

La-di-da is an expression with which the non-U stigmatize a U habit, speech-habit, or person.

Mirror (save in compounds such as *driving-, shaving-mirror*) is non-U against U *looking-glass.*

Pardon! is used by non-U in three main ways: (1) if the hearer does not hear the speaker properly; (2) as an apology (e.g. on brushing by someone in a passage); (3) after hiccupping or belching. The normal U-correspondences are very curt, viz. (1) *What?* (2) *Sorry!* (3) [Silence], though, in the first two cases, U-parents and U-governesses are always trying to make children say something "politer"—*What did you say?* and *I'm frightfully sorry* are certainly possible. For Case 3 there are other non-U possibilities, e.g. *Manners! Beg Pardon! Pardon me!*

Please to meet you! This is a very frequent non-U response to the greeting *How d'you do?* U-speakers normally just repeat the greeting; to reply to the greeting (e.g. with *Quite well, thank you*) is non-U.

non-U *radio*/U *wireless* (but *radio* technically as in aircraft).

non-U *serviette*/U *table-napkin;* perhaps the best known of all the linguistic class-indicators of English.

Teacher is essentially non-U, though *school-teacher* is used by the U to indicate a non-U teacher. The U equivalent is *master, mistress* with prefixed attribute (as *maths-mistress*). Non-U children often refer to their teachers without article (as, *Teacher says* . . .).

non-U *toilet-paper*/U *lavatory-paper.*

non-U *wealthy*/U *rich.*

> —"U and Non-U: An Essay in Sociological Linguistics" in *Noblesse Oblige* ed. Nancy Mitford (London: Hamish Hamilton Ltd., 1956).

D. Report on a variety of everyday language spoken by people associated with a profession, institution, or avocation. For instance, investigate Army slang, educators' jargon, or fashionable small talk as practiced by hostesses or officers of women's clubs. Point out any characteristic or recurrent features.

E. Study the following excerpts from discussions of debated usages by five modern authorities. Formulate the assumptions that underlie their approach and evaluate their conclusions.

The verbs *will* and *shall* have in many contexts come to be auxiliaries serving to express pure futurity, the original meaning of volition and obligation being more or less effaced; but owing partly to the fact that to express the three distinct ideas of obligation, volition, and simple futurity we have only those two verbs as against German *sollen, wollen* and *werden,* the actual rules for the employment of the two verbs are somewhat complicated, and where strict grammarians require *shall* (I shall, shall you; he thinks that he shall die, he = shifted first person), the verb *will* (and the shortened form 'll) is now more and more used, even in the South of England. In Scotland, Ireland and North America, *will* has long been almost exclusively used as auxiliary. The present rules may be stated roughly thus: To indicate pure, colourless future, *will* is used everywhere, except in those cases in which it might be misunderstood as implying actual will. Often the unambiguous *is going to* is used, and in many cases the simple present suffices: *I start to-morrow if it is fine.* To express obligation or necessity we have the unambiguous expressions *must, has to,* and to express volition *want, intend, mean, choose* are often preferred where *will* was formerly used.

> —Otto Jespersen, *Growth and Structure of the English Language,* 9th ed. (New York: Doubleday & Company, Inc., 1956), p. 217.

In Group I, the letters of Standard English, *this, these, that, those* as attributives usually agree in form with the form of the noun following. . . . With two words, however, *kind* and *sort* . . . the plural forms *these* and *those* very frequently appear in those cases in which a plural noun follows the *of,* as in "These kind of letters." The use of *these* and *those* with *kind of* and *sort of* appears here in Group I, the letters of Standard English, but *not once* in Group III, the letters of Vulgar English. . . .

The distinct Vulgar English plural demonstrative form, which, however, appears only four times in the letters, is *them* as in "*them* nice little boys." . . . Paralleling the Standard English use of *these* and *those* it

also is used with the words *kind of* and *sort of,* as in *"them* kind of books."
> —Charles Carpenter Fries, *American English Grammar* (New York: Appleton-Century-Crofts, Inc., 1940), p. 51.

Any simple grammatical role for the placing of the preposition is liable to lead to trouble. It is wrong to say that it never ought to appear at the end of a sentence; but it would be just as wrong to say that it ought always to be placed there . . . if a rule should be needed, it must be sought by means of a consideration of English grammar, and its special, non-Latin use of meaning and word-order. A rule of this kind might perhaps be derived from the fact that in the average English sentence, one of the positions of greatest emphasis is the ending. The reasons for this are not quite clear; perhaps the ending remains especially clear in the reader's mind because he has heard it more recently than the rest of the sentence; or it may be that the usual intonation of English speech, which affects the 'inner voice' of the reader, gives a kind of climax at the end of the sentence. But whatever the reason may be, the fact itself is clear enough. And it would suggest this much guidance for the placing of prepositions: when the meaning of the sentence demands that weight and emphasis should fall upon them, they are well placed at the end, but when the meaning demands no such weight, they are best placed elsewhere, in a less conspicuous position that befits their less emphatic role.
> —Hugh Sykes Davies, *Grammar Without Tears* (New York: The John Day Company, Inc., 1953), pp. 116–17.

Another feature of literary language is the manipulation of word order. As an example, we may cite the split infinitive, which is sometimes almost forced on writers because English spelling does not represent intonation. In talk, intonation would make the following sentences perfectly clear:

1. Such writers have not failed heartily to abet the leaders.
2. Her ill-fitting clothes failed altogether to conceal her figure.
3. The gentlemen were determined deliberately to spread subtle propaganda. . . .

Hearing the second of these sentences, we would know immediately whether the young lady's embarrassment was slight or grave. A terminal after *failed* would make the situation no great matter, but a terminal after *altogether* would mean that the disaster was complete. The other sentences would be similarly clarified by intonation, but when they are written, the intonation is not shown and the writer must recast them. One possible revision is to split the infinitives, replacing the ambiguous *altogether to conceal,* for example, by *to altogether conceal,* which is unmistakable. The familiar taboo might be weakened if it were generally realized that split infinitives are sometimes a stylistic device to remedy the deficiencies of our writing system.
> —James H. Sledd, *A Short Introduction to English Grammar* (Chicago: Scott, Foresman & Company, 1959), pp. 270–71.

The word *reason* is often followed by the word *why,* as in *I know the reason why he didn't stay.* This use of *why* is sometimes condemned as redundant or pleonastic, but the phrase *the reason why* is a standard English idiom, and has been for many centuries. Anyone who wants to can always omit words that are not strictly necessary to his meaning, but if this is done consistently the result is a stiff, unnatural English. As a rule, it is better to be natural than to be correct according to theories that other people have never heard of.
> —Bergen Evans and Cornelia Evans, *A Dictionary of Contemporary American Usage* (New York: Random House, 1957), p. 557.

F. Formulate as fully as you can the differences in attitudes toward usage reflected in the following sampling of handbook rulings on *one of those who*. Then define and defend your own position.

The relative pronouns—*who, which,* and *that*—take singular or plural verbs depending on whether their antecedents are singular or plural. Be sure you have identified the antecedent correctly. . . .
    Correct. Bryan is one of those men who always think before they act. (The antecedent of *who* is *men.*)

> —Edwin C. Woolley, Franklin W. Scott, and Frederick Bracher, *College Handbook of Composition,* 6th ed. (Boston: D. C. Heath & Company, 1958), p. 206.

Ordinarily make a verb plural in a relative clause following *one of.*
    Daniel Webster was one of those statesmen who stand by their principles at all costs (*Statesmen,* not *one,* is the antecedent of *who.*)

> —J. C. Tressler, Henry I. Christ, and Margaret M. Starkey, *English in Action: Course Four,* 7th ed. (Boston: D. C. Heath & Company, 1960), p. 239.

In written English the clause following *one of those who* and similar locutions is usually plural:
    He is one of those people who believe in the perfectibility of man. (*Who* refers to *people.*) . . .
    In Informal speech and writing and sometimes in General writing the second verb is attracted to the singular by the emphatic main subject:
    He is one of those people who believes in the perfectibility of man.

> —Porter G. Perrin, *Writer's Guide and Index to English,* 3rd ed. (Chicago: Scott, Foresman & Company, 1959), p. 612.

Expressions like "one of the best baseball players that" commonly take a singular verb in informal usage. Although the antecedent of *that* is the plural noun *players,* the writer or speaker is influenced in his choice of a verb by the fact that *one* is singular.
    FORMAL   He is one of those people who *are* afraid to act.
    INFORMAL He is one of those people who *is* afraid to act.

> —Glenn Leggett, C. David Mead, and William Charvat, *Prentice-Hall Handbook for Writers,* 3rd ed. (Englewood Cliffs, N. J.: Prentice-Hall, Inc., 1960), p. 85.

He is one of those *men who* always *know* what to do. It is often said that *knows* would be wrong here, because there are a number of men who know. However, the meaning of the statement is that he, among others, *knows* what to do; and the temptation to use the singular form is hardly worth resisting.

> —L. M. Myers, *Guide to American English,* 2nd ed. (Englewood Cliffs, N.J.: Prentice-Hall, Inc., 1959), p. 306.

G. Study the treatment of three of the following items of debated usage in sources including the *Oxford English Dictionary* (Unabridged), *Webster's Second* and *Third International* (Unabridged), *Webster's New World* (College Edition), the Evans and Nicholson dictionaries of usage, and Margaret M. Bryant's *Current American Usage: ain't, being that, cannot help but, different than, due to* (preposition), *everybody* (with plural pronoun), *like* (conjunction), and *whom.* Report and evaluate your findings.

H. Report on the treatment of slang in the major unabridged and collegiate dictionaries. Study their treatment of the following: *dough, long green, mazuma, moola, rhino; big boy, big cheese, big shot, big wheel, big wig; on the lam, on the bum, on the blink, on the fritz, on the q.t., on the ball.*

I. Find discussions of specific usage items in several issues of one of the following periodicals: *American Speech, College English, The English Journal, Language, Language Learning, Quarterly Journal of Speech.* Formulate the rationale of usage underlying the discussions.

J. Over the years, a number of important articles representing opposing camps in the battle of usage have appeared in national magazines: Donald J. Lloyd, "Our National Mania for Correctness," *The American Scholar,* Summer, 1952; Jacques Barzun, "English as She's Not Taught," *The Atlantic,* December, 1953; Dwight Macdonald, "Sweet Are the Uses of Usage," *The New Yorker,* May 17, 1958; Wilson Follett, "Grammar Is Obsolete," *The Atlantic,* February, 1960; Bergen Evans, "Grammar for Today," *The Atlantic,* March, 1960; Wilson Follett, "Sabotage in Springfield," *The Atlantic,* January, 1962; Dwight MacDonald, "The String Untuned," *The New Yorker,* March 10, 1962; Bergen Evans, "But What's a Dictionary For?" *The Atlantic,* May, 1962; Mario Pei, "The Dictionary as a Battlefront," *Saturday Review,* July 21, 1962; Jacques Barzun, "What Is a Dictionary?" *The American Scholar,* Spring, 1963. Study and evaluate one of these or a comparable, more recent article. Discuss the author's general perspective and examine the validity of his arguments.

One unfortunate result of our preoccupation with grammar and usage is that a disproportionate amount of energy is now, as in the past, channeled into these limited areas within the general discipline of English. Compared with the vast amount of admonition, instruction, and debate currently available to the profession on the more concrete subjects of grammar and usage, a somewhat uneasy silence has descended on the core of the teacher's concern with language—the relation between language and what it stands for, and between language and the uses to which it is put.

three

Though the instructor's own interests may be focused on the structure of language or on its uses in imaginative literature, part of his central responsibility as a teacher of English is to serve as an expert on the role language plays in ordinary life. A central aim of his teaching at all levels is to promote the art of talking sense, and of speaking and writing responsibly. To work toward this aim effectively, the teacher must concern himself with the nature and conditions of meaning. In the words of W. Nelson Francis, "the teacher of English is derelict in his duty if he does not give his students at least a basic understanding of the relationship between the world of language and the outside world. This means above all an insight into the relationship between the word and the referent, into the processes of abstraction, metaphor, and analogy, and into the way language controls thought even more powerfully than thought can control language."[1]

Meaning

The Meaning of Meaning

The branch of the discipline of English that concerns itself with the study of meaning is **semantics**. Semantics deals with words as **symbols**, that is, "signs which men use to communicate one with another and

[1] *The Structure of American English* (New York: The Ronald Press Company, 1958), p. 568.

as instruments of thought."[2] In the words of C. K. Ogden and I. A. Richards, the semanticist investigates "the nature of the correspondence between word and fact, to use these terms in the widest sense." More exactly, he investigates the connection of "words with things through the ideas, if any, which they symbolize." He thus needs to analyze both "the relations of words to ideas and of ideas to things." Since much language is not concerned with ideas in the narrower sense, the study of meaning must include "the ways in which speech, besides conveying ideas, also expresses attitudes, desires and intentions." Many problems arising through the actual behavior of words cannot be accounted for unless we recognize, beyond "strict statement and intellectual communication," the "emotive" or "non-symbolic" aspects of language—including the use of language, as a matter of common courtesy, "to say something when there is hardly anything to say." The student of "the part played in human affairs by language" inquires into "the ways in which symbols help us and hinder us in reflecting on things." He alerts us both to "the ways in which words deceive us" and to the ways "of saying clearly what one wishes to say."[3]

It has become customary to begin a discussion of meaning by pointing out that words are **arbitrary** signs, that there is no necessary connection between the sounds we utter and the things and relations for which they stand. Only to a very limited extent does the sound of a word mirror its sense. Thus, we are aware of the **onomatopoeic**, or sound-imitating, element in the child's language (*bow-wow, choo-choo train*) or in slang (*whiz-bang* in the army slang of World War I). Beyond these, there may seem to be something appropriate to meaning in the sound of words like *spurt* or *snivel* or *roar*. Most such associations, however, are accidental or unsystematic and at any rate easily negated by other factors. There is no reason why a dog should be called *dog, chien, Hund,* or *canis* other than that in a given speech-community the word in question is the signal conventionally used to refer to such an animal.

The term *conventional* indicates why to call words "arbitrary" signs can be misleading. Except in naming children or products and inventions, we do not *assign* meaning arbitrarily. Meaning is conventional and associational; after repeatedly hearing the word *dog* used in connection with a certain kind of animal, we come to associate the word and the thing, the term and the referent. Since we acquire many meanings by random association rather than as the result of careful presentation and definition, they often remain more or less vague in our minds. Most people associate some sort of meaning with the terms *robin* and *com-*

---

[2] C. K. Ogden and I. A. Richards, *The Meaning of Meaning: A Study of the Influence of Language upon Thought and of the Science of Symbolism,* 8th ed. (New York: Harcourt, Brace & World, Inc., 1962), p. 23.
[3] *Ibid.,* pp. 2–10.

munist, but many people could not reliably pin down the characteristics of a robin or a communist; and quite a few would not recognize either if they saw one in broad daylight. Meaning is most likely to be specific when the thing named is readily pointed at, and when, like a horse, for instance, it presents a configuration of distinctive features easily recognized. Meaning tends to become vague when things of one name look like things of another name, and when distinctive features become hard to pin down.

Meaning necessarily involves a degree of **abstraction.** Even a proper name comes to mean what it stands for through repeated association with it. From the experience of hearing the same term applied several times to one person and not to another, we abstract the relatively exclusive relation between proper name and its referent. Terms more inclusive than proper names and less concrete than the generic names of tangible objects acquire their meaning through association with a variety of situations from which we must abstract the common element. We acquire the term *big* through recognizing in combinations like *big boy* and *big truck* the common element of large size. Since their referents can no longer simply be pointed at, abstract terms easily become elusive. An art teacher may show a series of slides to demonstrate what he means by *texture, coloration,* or *chiaroscuro.* He must rely on the students' performing inductive operations that ideally lead to the desired common element but in practice more often take the form of uncertain groping. Confusion, as Ogden and Richards point out, is "the penalty we pay for our power of abstraction."[4]

Pragmatists and anthropologists have stressed the functional element in our early acquisition of language. As Malinowski observed, the child influences its environment mainly by verbal appeal:

> To the child, words are therefore not only means of expression but efficient modes of action. The name of a person uttered aloud in a piteous voice possesses the power of materializing this person. Food has to be called for and it appears—in the majority of cases.[5]

At the same time, however, much of the child's use of the language is "disinterested" in the sense that it seems motivated by the pleasure of recognition. The small child delights in identifying by name objects that are of no possible use to him. He spontaneously rejoices in recognizing and verbalizing familiar recurrent elements in his environment; he takes pleasure in intellectually and verbally "finding his way around." This spontaneous delight in "understanding," that is, sorting out and identifying, in fortunate individuals survives even the most practical and literal-minded kind of education. *The child's pleasure in the power of language*

---

[4] Ogden and Richards, *The Meaning of Meaning,* p. 214.
[5] Bronislaw Malinowski, "The Problem of Meaning in Primitive Languages," in Ogden and Richards, *The Meaning of Meaning,* Supplement I, p. 320.

as an instrument for both understanding and influencing his environment is the central motivating force that the teacher of English must at all costs keep alive.

At an early stage, the child's acquisition of words and meanings ceases to come exclusively from direct experience. He learns to abstract the meanings of words from their verbal contexts. Words like *ocean* and *Africa* may thus become meaningful to the child without direct contact with relevant experience, though of course the modern child is much helped in acquiring such terms by audio-visual aids of all kinds. In either case, the associations that make such words meaningful may be both partial and indirect. The child further becomes aware of the difference between words with real referents and words with referents that are imaginary. He wonders whether Africa is a place where he himself might someday go or whether it is a pretended place in a story. The random and indirect quality of many of our associations and the difficulties in the way of sustained and accurate abstraction help to explain why meaning cannot be taken for granted.

Association of a different sort enables us to stretch the available stock of linguistic signs to cover things and relations not previously named. If we observe a new type of cloud, we seize on something that is close to it in shape, size, or the like and is already part of our vocabulary. For instance, we might call it a "mushroom cloud," and, if the phenomenon is frequent enough, simply a mushroom. Word history is mainly a record of such stretchings. Thus, the word *persona* shifted from "face mask" to "character in a play" (who, in Greek drama, wore a face mask) to "character in real life." It further shifted from "actor representing a character" to "clergyman representing the church," that is, *parson*. The associations employed in such **semantic change** may range from analogy and cause-and-effect relationships to mere proximity in place or time. The need of the language for efficient naming often compels the use of such associations without a regard for strict logic: a product is named after its creator; a Frankenstein's monster is named a *Frankenstein*. Nor does such association always observe the limits suggested by good taste: *cretin*, by way of etymological detours derives from *Christian; silly* derives from a word at one time meaning "blessed."

Experimental stretchings of the language that have not yet stood the test of time and standardization make up a large part of slang. When electricians call different kinds of stage lights "ash cans," "cracker boxes," and "dishpans," they show that the associational sign-making mechanism of the language is in good working order. In principle, there is no difference between naming a form of energy flowing through wires by comparing it to a "current" and by comparing it to "juice." Much standard language is slang that has made the grade. *Recalcitrant*, etymologists tell us, means "one who kicks."

The conveying of meaning through the shorthand of an implied comparison is what we call **metaphor**. Metaphorical naming exploits partial similarities between things and relations that may be widely different in other respects. It exploits the analogy between the sudden or even violent movement, the muscular energy we expend when using a *wrench* (tool) and the *wrench* (emotional reaction) that may attend a sudden separation or change of perspective. Obviously, metaphor is one of the major devices by which a limited stock of word roots can be used to verbalize a range of human experience that is staggering in scope and complexity. However, many other similar devices are at work, such as the extension of a term to cover a wide area associated with its original referent, or the restriction of a term to a relatively small part of its original territory. Like metaphorical extension, these devices give language an elasticity that bedevils the literal-minded. As one British wag observed, the duodecimal system is based on the number 12 and is so called "because there are 20 shillings in the pound (£1), 16 ounces in the pound (1 lb.), 14 pounds in the stone, 8 gallons in a bushel, and 1,760 yards in a mile." Extension or restriction may give a word pleasant or unpleasant implications. Thus, the word *accident* has through semantic narrowing come to refer primarily to injurious or untoward accidental happenings; just as in the slang idiom "I got news for you" the news tends to be undesirable.

Once we are aware of some of the ways in which meaning operates, the crucial question becomes: Does the same term mean "the same" for two different users? In answering this question, "we have to judge by indirect evidence derived mainly from observing the further behavior of the parties concerned." We have to see whether they apply it to similar situations and use it for similar purposes. We have to see whether they accompany it with similar emotional reactions. We have to see whether they use it in similar relations to other terms, for instance in relation to implied synonyms or antonyms. We can ask whether they recognize in the term the same logical difficulties or ambiguities, "whether doubt and certainty arise at the same points, whether both admit alternatives at the same point, and so on."[6] It is exactly these similarities, these recurrent elements in the material, verbal, and psychological context of a word that constitute its "meaning." It is these recurrent elements that the lexicographer, for instance, tries to extract from a wide sampling of relevant citations.

In practice, meaning for the individual depends on his own previous associations with the word. For each user of the language, a word like *horse* or *nightingale* brings into play a different complex of smells, sounds, and sights; of apprehension or nostalgic reminiscence, depres-

[6] Ogden and Richards, *The Meaning of Meaning*, p. 91.

sion or exaltation. The more abstract a word, the greater the possibility of individual variation. "Since the past histories of individuals differ except in certain very simple respects, it is probable that their reactions to and employment of any general word will vary."[7] The public meaning of a word is the more or less stable common denominator of such private meanings. *Part of the English teacher's work is to help his students obtain a firmer grasp of public meanings than they acquire through random association.*

A crucial part of the English teacher's task is to help the students acquire the verbal resources needed to give expression to a mature range of experience. It is further to help students manage these resources precisely and to good advantage. To this extent, the teacher's interest in meaning is an immediately practical one. Of course, each specialty in the curriculum constantly enlarges the student's vocabulary by the introduction of more or less specialized, more or less technical terms. But there is a large vocabulary of educated discussion that is common to all and that is by and large taken for granted. For instance, we hear constant admonitions that people in politics should "discuss the issues." However, we seldom hear it acknowledged that many voters cannot take part in even moderately sophisticated discussion of political issues because they do not know the words. They have at best a foggy notion of the meaning of such terms as *assent, rationalization, confrontation, inalienable, expedient, equivocation,* and *prudence,* let alone *rational inquiry* and *pluralistic society.* Few can deal competently with the difficulties in assigning specific and workable meanings to such terms as *liberty* and *justice.* It is true that we would like to rely on our colleagues in the social sciences to give the student the background in history, politics, and economics that gives meaning to such terms as *fascism, social contract,* and *laissez faire.* But beyond such terms, much of the vocabulary of social, political, and cultural life is part of the common language. The English teacher would be making a crucial and indispensable contribution to education even if he used his class time exclusively to discuss the meanings of words in such texts as a newspaper column by Walter Lippmann, an article about the schools by James B. Conant, or a chapter from a book on the city as a way of life by Lewis Mumford.

Enlightening in the study of current texts, the study of meaning becomes indispensable in the teaching of literature of earlier periods. Students must realize that words like *wit, conceit, vulgar,* and *industry* are likely to differ from their most common modern meanings when found in an essay by Addison, a letter by Lord Chesterfield, or a chapter from the autobiography of Benjamin Franklin. They must come to see how context signals unfamiliar meanings of familiar words in phrases like "my

---

[7] *Ibid.,* p. 127.

civil neighbor," "correct spelling and *pointing*," "within the *revolution* of a few months," or *"culture* of the earth." They can be alerted to how earlier meanings of a term like *wit* become meaningful when compared with such survivals as *half-wit* and *at my wit's end.*

Such matters become more crucial as the teacher takes up increasingly earlier texts. In stressing the historical study of meaning, Albert C. Baugh cites the example of the king's use of *nice* in *Henry V:* "nice customs curtsey to great kings." Whatever *nice* means here, it does definitely not have its most common modern meaning of "pleasant" or "agreeable." As Baugh says,

> It is often not difficult to get *a* meaning out of Shakespeare, but it is an-other thing to get *the* meaning. Similar instances of changed meaning exist on every page of Shakespeare. Not to be aware that such changes occur in language is not to realize the possibility of misunderstanding the text.[8]

A constant concern with the meanings of words is thus basic to the English teacher's work. A reader unaware of meanings present and past cannot respond adequately to the written text. A writer insensitive to verbal distinctions cannot write with subtlety and force.

Linguistic Approaches to Meaning

The teacher of English can easily see the central importance of mean-ing in his dealings with language. More difficult for him is deciding where to turn for approaches to the study of meaning that are both authoritative and relevant to his needs. Linguistics in the narrower sense "begins with phonemes and ends with sentences." It

> does not cover the whole of language activity, and since it covers neither the correspondence between the symbol and the object designated nor the artistic structures of literature, it does not cover those parts of language activity which have the most importance for us as members of society.[9]

However, linguists have generally looked forward with confidence to the future development of a linguistically oriented, scientific semantics that would treat meaning as rigorously and objectively as linguists have in the past treated the internal structure of language.

The obstacles to a scientific semantics are formidable. Noam Chom-sky suggests that in a semantic description of language "the condition of observational adequacy would be met by an account of situational regu-larities associated with actual discourse."[10] As has often been pointed

---

[8] "Historical Linguistics and the Teacher of English," *College English,* XXIV (November, 1962), 107.

[9] Archibald A. Hill, *Introduction to Linguistic Structures: From Sound to Sentence in English* (New York: Harcourt, Brace & World, Inc., 1958), p. 406.

[10] "The Logical Basic of Linguistic Theory," *Preprints of Papers for the Ninth International Congress of Linguists* (Cambridge, Mass., 1962), p. 524.

out, the "situational regularities" to be investigated would involve everything in personal feeling, shared common-sense observation, and scientific knowledge that is verbalized through language. In addition, discourse being a delayed rather than an immediate response to experience,
and being affected by complicated psychological factors, the situational
context of any utterance is in practice impossible to recover in its full
ramifications. A scientific semantics would be a true master science, not
only subsuming all other scientific knowledge but also imposing a scientific structure on practical, aesthetic, and literary experience not yet
scientifically structured. Presumably, without a scientific account of the
situational contexts of language in all their immense variety and complexity, the relationship between them and language itself could not be
described with anything approaching scientific rigor.

In practice, linguists have not embarked on any such encyclopedic
venture. As H. A. Gleason points out, attempting to gain access to the
structure of semantic content "requires an inferential method which has
not appealed to linguists busy with building a highly rigorous method
for the handling of more directly observed data."[11] The linguistically
oriented semanticist is likely to concentrate on those aspects of meaning
that his training and previous work have predisposed him to investigate.
This means that he will typically study relationships *within* language
rather than between language and experience. He may trace the **semantic
networks** or assemble the "semantic clusters" of synonyms and near-
synonyms held together by common-core meanings and distinguished by
subtle differences of use and implication. Through the multiple connections between related words charted in synonymies, words at least to
some degree lose their status as "arbitrary" signs to become part of a
semantic system. In exploring fully the differences in a series like *old-
ancient-antique-antiquated-elderly-aged-hoary,* the student learns something essential about the richness and flexibility of language. Another investigator may correlate common semantic features of words with syntactic
features they equally share. Thus, semantically, words like *interesting,
astonishing,* and *fascinating* share the meaning "involving human reaction or response"; syntactically, they are derived from normally transitive
verbs typically requiring human objects.

Even when linguists thus limit themselves to relations existing *within*
language, their measuring devices tend to become blunt and one-dimensional in proportion as they become rigorously objective. For instance, if
a linguist wishes to investigate meaning "in a fashion which is experimental and verifiable," he may ask a "group of native speakers acting as
experimental subjects" to make a list of possible substitutions for the *so*
in "That's so." If all put "true" first on their lists, this is "the substitute

11 *An Introduction to Descriptive Linguistics,* rev. ed. (New York: Holt, Rinehart & Winston, Inc., 1961), pp. 12–13.

of highest probability" and thus the "perfect synonym" in the particular linguistic environment of the test sentence.[12] If it can be adapted to the study of more elusive semantic items, such procedure could provide an instructive check on subjective impressions and private associations. At the same time, compared with the trained discrimination of the sensitive observer, it would be both cumbersome and unresponsive to nuance.

The lack of flexibility in methods meant to be more rigorous than reliance on the investigator's own command of the language is especially obvious when we go beyond literal to figurative meaning. Thus, Professor Hill describes his principle that

> any metaphor which is an isolated item is to be thought of as "dead," and so to be translated with maximum redundancy. Thus, if it is said that the ship "plows through the waves," it is reasonable to take "plow" isolated as it is, as only a synonym for "move."[13]

Such dead metaphors would be contrasted with the kind of live metaphor signaled by "structural correspondence," that is, by the reinforcement of the metaphorical parallel found in sustained metaphor and most clearly in an elaborate conceit. However, whether *plow* here lives up to its metaphorical potential depends in some measure on previous associations with the word on the part of user and listener. The potential could be irresistibly strong for someone who has a vivid picture in his mind of how "sheer plod makes plow down sillion shine" and of how the plow-share-like bow of certain warships cuts its furrow through the waves. The point at which such a metaphor, through sheer repetition and attrition, becomes first routine and finally dead must vary for each user of the language.

The cultural, rather than the structural, correspondences that determine the degree of vitality in a metaphor are well illustrated in John Ciardi's discussion of the term *broadcast:*

> For centuries, the word signified the act of a country-man in scattering certain kinds of seed in his fields. He marched back and forth carrying a sack of seed and cast it about him with a broad sweep of his arm—a broad cast.
>
> Such a firmly pictorial word inevitably lends itself to metaphor. . . . I suspect, however, that anyone in the past who used it in a metaphoric sense was aware of his metaphor, for every man of the past would have had in his head a picture of that unchanging sower at his work.
>
> Then, in the 1920s radio came along and it seized upon the word—as a metaphor. By repeated usage, however, the word went far toward losing its original metaphoric force. At the same time the United States became increasingly urbanized. And also at the same time, farmers were generally turning to new sorts of machinery to get their sowing done. The ancient broadcaster of the fields was no longer a common figure. His image dis-

12 Hill, *Introduction to Linguistic Structures*, pp. 411–12.
13 Archibald A. Hill, "Linguistic Principles for Interpreting Meaning," *College English*, XXII (April, 1961), 470.

appeared from both the world and the word as far as most Americans were concerned. The image they then began to see in the word was more likely that of a man with a microphone in his face, or of a great steel tower with diagrammatic lightning shooting forth in all directions.[14]

The linguist's lack of inclination to explore in this fashion the relation between "the world and the word" seriously handicaps him in dealing with the larger questions of poetic meaning and poetic effect. Obviously, the critic of poetry can profit from exact description of linguistic data. For instance, a critic might recognize in the phrase "a grief ago" a metaphorical heightening and rendering explicit of the idea of time, of duration, usually only latent in the idea of grief as a state of mind. However, we obtain a firmer grasp of what goes on in this phrase if we realize that *grief* here grammatically takes the place of nouns of time ("a while ago," "a year ago") and thus departs from conventional grammatical patterning. The phrase owes its vigor, its attention-inviting freshness, its lack of a worn-smooth routine quality to its relative ungrammaticality.[15] This partial—not at all arbitrary but poetically meaningful—violation of the restraints of grammar is especially noticeable in such poetry as that of John Donne or G. M. Hopkins. The difference between a facile poem and a poem of originality and power results in part from the high degree of predictability in the phrasing of the former. In the more original poem, word choice and grammatical construction will repeatedly "defeat expectancy." We will thus be compelled to attend to the specific linguistic form, instead of treating it merely as one of several possible embodiments of a given paraphrasable "content." Obviously, the critic who can bring "down-to-the-surface linguistics" to bear on the linguistic form will be in a favorable position to recognize the ways in which the poet's language stretches, adapts, and transforms conventional linguistic patterns.[16]

What limits linguistic approaches to poetic meaning is the difficulty the linguist encounters in going from the recognition of observable formal features to their full stylistic implications and their role in the full context of poetic experience. Suspicious of "our own subjective reactions," the linguist turns from what goes on in the mind of the reader to the work of literature as "a language act having reality in the outside world"; as he says, "we are not denying the reality of what goes on in the mind of author and reader, but merely stating that we cannot usefully study it."[17] Like other critical approaches centered on formal analysis, linguistically

---

14 John Ciardi, "Manner of Speaking," *Saturday Review*, October 27, 1962, p. 12.
15 Samuel R. Levin, "Poetry and Grammaticalness," *Preprints*, p. 207.
16 Harold Whitehall, "From Linguistics to Criticism: A Book Review," *The Kenyon Review*, XIII (1951), 710–14; in *Readings in Applied English Linguistics,* ed. Harold B. Allen (New York: Appleton-Century-Crofts, Inc., 1958), p. 401.
17 Harold Whitehall and Archibald A. Hill, "A Report on the Language-Literature Seminar," in Allen, *Readings,* p. 394.

oriented criticism is likely to study closely matters of recurrence and symmetry, such as grammatical parallelism, and analogy, or contrast, of statement patterns in propositions: "Typical stylistic relationships show themselves in the repetition of formal patterns from one sentence to the next."[18] Again, "other things being equal, the more symmetrical the arrangement, the more effective the poem."[19]

Thus, when Hill reads Pippa's Song, from Browning's *Pippa Passes,* his analysis centers on the "lexical and stylistic pattern":

> The year's at the spring
> And day's at the morn;
> Morning's at seven;
> The hill-side's dew-pearled;
> The lark's on the wing;
> The snail's on the thorn:
> God's in his heaven—
> All's right with the world!

Hill examines the recurrence and variation of the grammatical patterns "noun–linking verb–prepositional phrase" (as in lines 1–3, 5–7) and "noun–linking verb–adjective" (as in lines 4 and 8). He points out the semantic movement of individual lines from "larger unit" (year) to "contained smaller unit" (spring). The larger unit in successive lines is smaller than the contained unit in the preceding ones; thus, "the entities in the first three lines descend in a general order from larger to smaller." The prevailing semantic pattern is "X is at its best" or "X is in its best place." Such analysis leads Hill to postulate a "therefore" at the beginning of lines 4 and 8. It further leads him to point to a startling break in the "strict analogical pattern" of the propositions at line 7, with *snail* (very small unit) and *God* (very large unit) brought into immediate juxtaposition. It is this juxtaposition that to Hill suggests Pippa's childlike simplicity. As Hill points out, his "orderly critical procedure having a maximum of rigor at each step" rests on the assumption that "it is form which gives meaning." It does not merely supplement other critical approaches but may be contrasted with them on the basis of which is "more complete, more consistent, and more simple than the other."[20]

Many critics will feel that Hill's analysis suffers from the misinterpretation of formal features that results from too rigorous exclusion of complex variables. Rigorously formal analysis is misleading to the exact extent that it sidesteps connotative, logical, dramatic, and historical meaning. The childlike simplicity of Pippa's song is suggested at the very be-

---

18 Archibald A. Hill, "Pippa's Song: Two Attempts at Structural Criticism," University of Texas *Studies in English,* XXXV (1956), 51–56; in Allen, *Readings,* p. 403.

19 Hill, "Linguistics Since Bloomfield," *Quarterly Journal of Speech,* XLI (October, 1955), 253–60, in Allen, *Readings,* p. 22.

20 Hill, "Pippa's Song," in Allen, *Readings,* pp. 403–06.

ginning by a primer-prose repetition of the simple subject–verb–prepositional phrase pattern. This pattern does not *necessarily* suggest childlike
innocence; it may be used for emphasis or for a terse, aphoristic effect. In
Pippa's song, however, the possible connotation of the grammatical pattern (formal level) is reinforced by the "unphilosophical" concreteness
of reference (lexical content) and the contrast with the preceding lines in
Browning's play: "I crown you / My great white queen, my spirit's ar-
bitress, / Magnificent . . ." (dramatic context).

There is no startling juxtaposition of lines 6 and 7 but rather the
conclusion, signaled by a colon, of a cumulative inductive pattern (logical
level). The shifting of gears from the pre-inductive "inventory" of the
first six lines to the cumulative result is reinforced by emphatic trochaic
inversion: "Gód's in his heaven." (Compare Herbert's stress on the key
word in "The Pulley": "Alone of all his treasures/Rést in the bottom
lay.") The theological assertion is kept in the already established childlike
frame by the personalizing, "untheological" use of the possessive pronoun: "God's in *his* heaven" (parallel to "Grandfather's in his garden,"
rather than the more formal and impersonal "God is in heaven"). The
dramatically pregnant break, signaled by the dash, is between lines 7 and
8—"All's right with the world!" The sweeping *all,* in the blunt statement
of what is in more elaborately qualified and "explained" form a commonly accepted theological tenet, hooks us back into the drama with the
central thematic question: "But *is* it? Is *all* really right with the world?"
In response to Pope's "whatever is, is right" the "but *is* it?" is the knowing,
private reaction of the Voltairean skeptic. In response to Robert Browning, writing in 1841 (historical context), it is the anxious "but *is* it?" that
the Victorian poet answers, not with majestic scorn ("Shall gravitation
cease, if you go by?") but with elaborate, "dramatically" developed re-
assurance.

The insistent, assertive, dominant quality of the last line (signaled by
the exclamation mark) is reinforced by a formal relationship that Hill
does not mention: four of the "instances" leading up to the inductive
leap in line 7 take the form of an iambic "first-half-of-a-statement" followed by an anapestic prepositional phrase (lines 1, 2, 5, and 6: "Thĕ
yéar's/ăt thĕ spríng"). This is again the pattern of the last line, which by
the analogy in structure is cemented more firmly into the general inductive pattern than mere logic would justify. Hill instead stresses the
"formal similarity" between lines 4 and 8, which both, grammatically, use
the pattern noun–linking verb–adjective (or adjective phrase). In this
instance, the stylistic analogies differ from the grammatical.

Any complete formal analysis would of course also explore the traditional "discord-chord" pattern of the poem. The last line falls back into
the prevailing stylistic and metrical pattern, which has been disturbed by
trochaic inversion in lines 3 and 7 and by variations from the prevailing

anapestic second half-line in lines 3, 4, and 7, but which has been "affirmed" or reinforced by the ABCD/ABCD rhyme scheme. What is the "meaning" of such an interplay of symmetry and variation? How is that meaning related to the poem's other meanings? In exploring these questions, we shall profit from rigorous, and as far as possible objective, study of the poem's linguistic surface. However, we shall be handicapped if by concentrating on tangible matters of arrangement and recurrence we are led to operate with oversimplified assumptions about literary form and literary value. *Form, in the linguist's sense of tangible linguistic structure, gives meaning only when considered in the full context of semantic content, logical sequence, stylistic implications, and dramatic and historical setting.*

It is only fair to point out that present developments in the direction of a linguistically oriented semantics and stylistics are exploratory and tentative. The teacher of English will do well to follow future developments in this area with interest and an open mind. Nevertheless, he must, if he is going to continue what is most important in his work, dissent from a widely held assumption. Linguists have typically assumed that "in order to make the study of meaning as effective as possible, we must first have an objective understanding of structure."[21] They have assumed that when the objective analysis of the structure of language fully bears fruit, they will at last be "ready to tackle meaning." On the other hand, an authoritative and comprehensive account of the structure of English, acceptable to different schools of linguists, is not yet in sight. In the meantime, people all around us are using language, for better or, frequently, for worse. The teacher of English has no choice but to tackle meaning now.

The Contribution of Semantics

It is in the teaching of rhetoric, of composition, of workaday expository prose that the study of meaning is most immediately and crucially important. Whether *beautiful* should be classified as an adjective becomes insignificant compared with whether there are legitimate uses of the terms *Americanism* and *un-American,* and what such uses might be. *Like* as a conjunction is not an abuse of language, but the indiscriminate use of the term *communist* to label student demonstrators and advocates of civic rights is. The teacher of English is the one person in the curriculum whose specialty includes responsibility for the general, nonspecialized, nontechnical uses of language. Important as effective communication by and among specialists remains, even more crucial in a free society is the responsible and humane use of language by and among laymen, citizens, human beings.

21 Gleason, *An Introduction to Descriptive Linguistics,* pp. 94–95.

The current emphasis in language studies on what can be rigorously formulated and controlled should not be allowed to obscure the teacher's obligation to promote responsible linguistic behavior. To do so, he must rely on a kind of semantics that developed outside of and separate from modern linguistics. The semantics most immediately relevant to the English teacher's needs is neither a scientific semantics, rigorous but relatively uninformative, nor the highly abstract logical semantics practiced in departments of philosophy. Rather it is the kind of **applied semantics** that charts some of the most obvious recurrent relations between words, mind, and reality. It regards the study of meaning as a means of securing improved communication in a rational and humane society.

Historically, such a semantics derives from the concerns of writers like Sir Francis Bacon, Thomas Hobbes, and Jeremy Bentham, who were vividly aware of the resistance offered to their investigations by linguistic habits. Modern semanticists have tended to identify with one of two major groups. The first are the followers of C. K. Ogden and I. A. Richards, who in 1923 published their programmatic and widely influential *The Meaning of Meaning*. The second are the followers—and critics— of Korzybski, who in 1933 published *Science and Sanity* and became known as the founder of "General Semantics." Through the work of writers like S. I. Hayakawa, Stuart Chase, and Wendell Johnson, the major ideas and concerns of general semantics reached a large popular audience. Setting aside the conventional boundaries of academic disciplines, general semanticists have studied human behavior in which language and other uses of symbols play a crucial part. They have explored symbolic and linguistic factors in a wide variety of areas, notably mental therapy, economics, personnel management, and international relations.

Whatever his antecedents or affiliations, the semanticist insists from the beginning that "the most important thing about language is meaning."[22] What to the linguist is a mere truism is to the semanticist a rallying cry and a program of action: "A structured system of verbal responses would not be a language unless it has a symbolic, communicative function."[23] Focusing his interest on the symbolic function of language, the semanticist insists that "linguistic events are to be studied not in isolation, but in the full context of their nonverbal antecedents and their nonverbal consequences, interpersonal, social, or political."[24]

Since Bacon and Hobbes, it has become a commonplace that an analysis of how language means must precede meaningful discussion in science, politics, and ethics, to mention only some of the more important

[22] Albert Upton, *Design for Thinking: A First Book in Semantics* (Stanford, Calif.: Stanford University Press, 1961), p. 11.
[23] John B. Carroll, *The Study of Language: A Survey of Linguistics and Related Disciplines* (Cambridge, Mass.: Harvard University Press, 1959), p. 9.
[24] Anatol Rapoport, "Two Marxist Critiques of General Semantics," *ETC.: A Review of General Semantics*, XVIII (October, 1961), 313.

fields. Not only in psychology and the theory of knowledge, but in many major fields of inquiry, difficulties are often due "to an approach to a question through symbols without an initial investigation of their functions."[25] As Bacon observed,

> words, being commonly framed and applied according to the capacity of the vulgar, follow those lines of division which are most obvious to the vulgar understanding. And whenever an understanding of greater acuteness or a more diligent observation would alter those lines to suit the true divisions of nature, words stand in the way and resist the change. Whence it comes to pass that the high and formal discussions of learned men end oftentimes in disputes about words and names; with which (according to the use and wisdom of the mathematicians) it would be more prudent to begin, and so by means of definitions reduce them to order.[26]

Since Bacon's time, science has made considerable progress in altering the "lines of division" embedded in popular language to make them "suit the true divisions of nature." Typically, it has done so through the "rejection of everyday symbolizations and the endeavor to replace them by more accurate accounts."[27] Prescientific expressions like "the sun sets" or "the moon shines" remain as a kind of metaphorical shorthand referring to events involving the rotation of the earth and the reflection of sunlight from its satellite. Similarly, expressions like "heartfelt sympathy" are relics of a prescientific view of psychology that have long since lost their literal application. Scientific description typically substitutes more specific and technical language for the language of common-sense observation.

Semantic analysis compels similar realignments in fields not subject to scientific verification. Observing Bacon's requirements, the semanticist demands accurate verbal **definition** of large abstractions. If such definitions are to be meaningful, "it is necessary to recur to individual instances."[28] One effect of this procedure is to correct the assumption that words always imply corresponding things. The Baconian scientist found that the scholastic learning of his ancestors contained many merely verbal entities. The student of modern politics, aesthetics, and related fields similarly finds abstractions without easily identifiable referents. The purely verbal as against the referential use of an abstraction may be illustrated by different uses of the term *instinct:* Until scientists investigated the sensory mechanism that enabled bats in flight to avoid wires strung in a dark room, the layman would explain the bat's flight as guided by "instinct"—which thus became a verbal label covering ignorance. In scientific use, the term *instinct* might apply to inherited be-

---

25 Ogden and Richards, *The Meaning of Meaning*, p. 14.
26 Francis Bacon, *Novum Organum,* in *The English Philosophers from Bacon to Mill,* ed., Edwin A. Burtt (New York: Random House, 1939), p. 40.
27 Ogden and Richards, *The Meaning of Meaning*, p. 13.
28 Bacon, *Novum Organum,* in Burtt, *The English Philosophers,* p. 41.

havior patterns isolated through tests requiring rigorous verification and concrete reference.

More typically, the search for concrete reference shows us how many familiar terms cover a variety of related but by no means identical meanings. This is notoriously so for all-inclusive general terms like *beauty* or *truth:* "Any reference to human activities which are neither theoretical nor practical tends to be symbolized by the word 'aesthetic'; and derivatively anything which we are not merely concerned either to know or to change tends to be described as beautiful."[29] A literary critic must identify some of the possible meanings of *beauty, aesthetic, literary,* and similar terms and decide which of these meanings he will treat as relevant or fruitful. The student of the history of ideas must realize that the meanings of *truth* range from "what faithfully mirrors relations existing in the universe" to "what can be confirmed by pragmatic test."

Again, examination of "individual instances" shows us how variable are the referents of terms that are inherently **relative.** Bacon pointed to the sources of error in words like *heavy, light, hot,* or *expensive.* What articles a speaker calls expensive depends on his situation, his intention, his needs, his scale of values, and the state of his pocketbook. The word by itself is therefore relatively uninformative. It is the everyday counterpart of political and moral terms like *free* and *oppressive.* What we consider oppressive depends on the degree of freedom we have come to demand or expect. The terms remain uninformative unless substantiated by definition and example. Study of such words counteracts the popular assumption that words stand in stable and reliable relations to things and conditions in the outside world, that they have simple, reliable meanings self-evident to all men of good will and common sense.

The search for concrete referents thus helps us to use words with clarity and precision. It also leads to the root of controversies that stubbornly resist all efforts at solution. Many important terms show a basic **ambiguity.** As the author of a seminar paper reported,

> I asked my thirteen-year-old son, "What's honor?"
> "Trustworthiness," he replied promptly. "You know, like the school 'code of honor.' "
> "Then what about *honor* in 'honor roll'?"
> He looked perplexed and said, "Well, that's for people who make good grades."
> "Even if they cheat?"
> "If nobody finds out," he answered, stalwart but sorrowful.
> We agreed that it was a crazy, mixed-up word.

Honor may mean primarily one's private integrity; to have honor then means to be honorable, to live in accordance with one's own standard of conduct. On the other hand, *honor* may mean reputation, prestige,

29 Ogden and Richards, *The Meaning of Meaning,* p. 131.

recognition; to have honor then means to be honored and respected by the community. Often we approach such a term on the assumption that it *must have* one true or essential or basic meaning. Thus, the idealist might say that "true" honor is independent of outward recognition and is entirely a matter between the individual and his own conscience. The realist in the Hobbesian tradition might say that honor is really "only" recognition, esteem, and the power and influence that result from it. What we must recognize is that such definitions of "true honor," "true love," or "true beauty" are **stipulative** and hortatory. We specify for which of the possible meanings we are going to reserve the term, at the same time setting it up as a standard to follow or to observe.

The weakness of such "essentializing" approaches to meaning is that they obscure the complexity of human motives and human interaction that in such cases is mirrored in the ambiguities of language. "True democracy," "true freedom," and "true art" are hard to define because under each of these headings we group a number of related but not always compatible motives, values, or practices. W. B. Gallie comments on the "sheer duality" of the two opposed uses of *social justice:*

> Of these the first rests on the ideas of merit and commutation: justice consists in the institution and application of those social arrangements whereby the meritorious individual receives his commutative due. The second rests upon, in the sense of presupposing, the ideas (or ideals) of cooperation, to provide the necessities of a worthwhile human life, and of distribution of products to assure such a life to all who cooperate. It is natural to take these two descriptions as characteristic of two facets of contemporary morality, which might be labeled liberal and socialist respectively. But in fact these two facets would seem to appear in any morality or moral teaching worthy of the name: witness, e.g., the opposed lessons of the parable of the talents and the parable of the vineyard, or, on a humbler plane, contrast the encouragement one gives to children now to show their worth, now to pitch in for the sake of the family or group or side.[30]

Appeals to "justice" are likely to be unenlightening unless we are prepared to specify "the kind of justice I advocate" or "the kind of justice I believe in."

There is no support in the close study of language for the popular expectation that there should be one definite meaning for every term. When we have a term of as variable application as the adjective *good,* it is quite possible that the set of things "in connection with which we heard it pronounced in early years (a good bed, a good kick, a good baby, a good God) have no common characteristic."[31] The mature reaction to such multiplicity of meaning is not what Ogden and Richards call "linguistic nihilism." It is not the complaint that terms mean "whatever you want

---

[30] W. B. Gallie, "Essentially Contested Concepts," in *The Importance of Language,* ed. Max Black (Englewood Cliffs, N.J.: Prentice-Hall, Inc., 1962), p. 137.
[31] Ogden and Richards, *The Meaning of Meaning,* p. 125.

them to mean." To use language without deceiving ourselves and others, we have to be ready to identify several distinct and at times contradictory meanings of major terms. We have to be sensitive to crucial prevailing trends and countertrends in their use. We have to define, illustrate, and make plausible our own uses of such terms so as to avoid ambiguity and equivocation.

In thus reducing "words and names" to order "by means of definitions," we are merely meeting the most elementary requirement for successful communication. Definition is the technique necessary "to keep the parties to an argument in contact and to clear up misunderstandings." It provides the means of controlling words as symbols, "of readily discovering to what in the world on any occasion they are used to refer."[32] It makes discussion profitable, not by automatically resolving disagreements, but by giving us the necessary preliminary understanding of what our agreements and disagreements are.

For the teacher of writing, the semanticist's emphasis on concrete reference is of great immediate importance. The ability to translate the abstract into the concrete has always been a hallmark of great writing, whether in poetry or prose. Conversely, sweeping undeveloped generalizations and repetitious unsubstantiated judgments mark the faltering first steps of the beginner. The student in a composition class must learn to stop using terms like *courage, fair play,* or *freedom* as vaguely honorific terms, more often than not used in a spirit of self-congratulation. He must look for the concrete situations where the term occurs and learn to identify the common denominator that makes the term applicable. Class time is seldom more profitably spent than when students describe situations where the term *fair play* would be used and together try to hunt down their criteria of "fairness." The first requirement for informative writing or discussion is that it must be more explicit than the application of an undefined one-word label.

Generally, the tone of educated discussion has improved as the result of the semanticist's attack on undifferentiated abstractions. The student of semantics remembers not only that communist is not socialist is not liberal, but that communist$_1$ is not communist$_2$ is not communist$_3$; that Marx is not Lenin is not Tito. He knows that an argument operating for any length of time with the large, undifferentiated label is likely to become deceptive.

Insistence on specific application has strengthened our resistance to some of the more misleading kinds of persuasion. It has alerted us to the possibilities of **strategic naming**, that is, selecting of several more or less inclusive labels the one most likely to produce a desired reaction. "If one disputant talks of public opinion," he may be referring "to what others

[32] Ogden and Richards, *The Meaning of Meaning*, pp. 15–19.

would call the views of certain newspaper owners."[33] *Public service, democracy,* and *fair play* are all terms that make the person with even the least semantic sophistication insist on definition and concrete reference.

The general outlook that results from such semantic awareness has by one school of semantics been called the **extensional** orientation. The extensional orientation aims at making the user of the language "aware of things, facts, and operations in the way they are related in nature instead of the way they are talked about."[34] It thus aims at freeing men of the "tyranny of words," at making language a flexible symbolic instrument rather than a rigid system of mental one-way streets.

Obviously, a skeptical analysis of what Bacon calls "unskillful" abstractions can, in an oversimplified form, become a naive debunking of ideas and worship of "the facts." Jonathan Swift satirized attempts to reduce language to the rock-bottom factual in his account of the school of languages at Laputa:

> Since words are only names for *things,* it would be more convenient for all men to carry about them such things as were necessary to express the particular business they are to discourse on. . . . Many of the most learned and wise adhere to the new scheme . . . which hath only this inconvenience attending it, that if a man's business be very great, and of various kinds, he must be obliged in proportion to carry a greater bundle of things upon his back, unless he can afford one or two strong servants to attend him.[35]

Kenneth Burke, in his review of Stuart Chase's *The Tyranny of Words,* warned against using semantics mainly "as a new weapon for the debunker" and against an "overly empirical bias" in one's approach to meaning.[36] In a more recent discussion, Anatol Rapoport criticized Chase's equation of abstractions with fictions and set out to show "how the *extensional* orientation, naively conceived as the primacy of direct sense impressions and carried to extremes," can lead to absurd results. While the goal of semantics has been to "sharpen the average man's critical sense so as to enable him to separate reality from verbal fiction," *semantic awareness should ideally lead to greater accuracy not only in pointing to concrete referents but also in the formulation and manipulation of abstract relations.*[37] In fields like ethics, politics, or aesthetics, semantic awareness can help make discussion specific and fruitful without debunking concepts and attitudes that escape crudely behavioristic identification. Language as often refers to psychological realities as to those external realities of which the learned Laputans carried scale models upon their backs.

33 Ogden and Richards, *The Meaning of Meaning,* p. 126.
34 Anatol Rapoport, "What is Semantics?" in *The Use and Misuse of Language,* ed. S. I. Hayakawa (Greenwich, Conn.: Fawcett Publications, Inc., 1962), p. 20.
35 *Gulliver's Travels* (New York: Random House, 1950), p. 212.
36 *The Philosophy of Literary Form: Studies in Symbolic Action* (Baton Rouge: Louisiana State University Press, 1941), pp. 396–99.
37 Rapoport, "Two Marxist Critiques," pp. 300, 311–12.

Concern with precision of meaning and concreteness of reference inevitably leads to concern with the variables of **context** and intention:

> Considering the number of ways of taking a particular word, the task of speaking clearly and being understood would seem pretty hopeless if it were not for another very important fact about language. Though a word may have many senses, these senses can be controlled, up to a point, by the *context* in which the word is used. When we find the word in a particular verbal setting—that is, take it with the words that come before and after it in a discourse—we can usually decide quite definitely which of the many senses of the word is relevant.[38]

In the context of a faculty conference, in the neighborhood of terms like "standards," "subject matter," "maintain," and "improve," *academic* is likely to mean "having a degree of intellectual content and rigor." In the context of a chamber of commerce meeting, surrounded by terms like "practical," "down to earth," and "proposal," *academic* is likely to mean "theoretical, purely hypothetical, and more than likely unrealistic." Emphasis on how context shapes meaning helps weaken the hold of the "one word–one meaning" fallacy. It discourages insistence on the "essential" meaning of a word and instead makes us appreciate the manifold and unpredictable ways in which words branch out from their root meanings. Training a student to see words in context is teaching him to interpret accurately and fairly.

Failure to grasp a speaker's or writer's intention is most serious when it makes us miss facetiousness or **irony,** which can drastically modify and even reverse the surface meaning of a passage. What is signaled in speech by the knowing wink or the arch look may be signaled in writing by intentional discrepancies of style and treatment. Thus, Jonathan Swift employs an intentionally callous, mock-pedantic style in presenting his gruesomely inhuman *Modest Proposal* for alleviating poverty in Ireland. Incongruous colloquialisms or exaggerated formality, a dramatic treatment of the obvious or a casual treatment of the momentous—any of these can alert the reader to an ironic intention. ("After taking profound thought, and considering carefully the evidence that has come to his notice, Professor Ashley Montagu has come out fearlessly in favor of mother love.")

Even when no definite ironic intention is present, different degrees of deliberateness, insistence, and substantiation can greatly affect the seriousness and thus the "meaning" of a passage. A casual remark is necessarily more tentative or hypothetical than a considered judgment. A comment on a superior, made after the second glass, does not "mean" the same as the identical comment made at a public hearing.

As important as the immediate verbal context of an utterance, is the

---

[38] Monroe C. Beardsley, *Thinking Straight: Principles of Reasoning for Readers and Writers,* 2nd ed. (Englewood Cliffs, N.J.: Prentice-Hall, Inc., 1956), p. 153.

larger nonverbal context. The present level of achievement in championship swimming determines whether "John swam 100 yards in 45 seconds"
means "He just broke the world record" or "He is a poor prospect for a
championship team." Charles C. Fries well illustrates the role of historical
context in his discussion of the story of Rip Van Winkle, who proclaimed
himself "a poor quiet man, a native of the place, and a loyal subject of the
King," only to be denounced as a Tory and a spy:

> It was not the linguistic meaning of the utterance that produced the vigor-
> ous response. Twenty years before, when Rip started out on his tramp in
> the mountains, such a statement would have elicited no such reaction. It
> would have meant simply that he was a "good" citizen. But there had been
> twenty years of history, including the Revolutionary War. The linguistic
> meaning of the utterance was the same as it would have been twenty years
> earlier, but its "social" or "cultural" meaning had changed. Rip's statement
> now meant (in its social meaning) that he was an "enemy" of the newly
> established government. The reader of the story of Rip Van Winkle has
> missed its "meaning" unless he grasps at once the significance of the reaction
> of the group to Rip's words. The total meaning of our utterances consists
> not only of the linguistic meaning—the lexical meaning and the structural
> meaning—but also of the "social" meaning. To grasp only the linguistic
> meaning is "mere verbalism."[39]

Any student working on a research paper, or, for that matter, engaged in independent reading, must become aware of how context, verbal
and nonverbal, affects the meaning of an utterance. One of the most
common kinds of intellectual irresponsibility is to present to an audience
a passage written in 1934 or 1946 with the intention of provoking the
reaction it would cause if it were written today. The ludicrous extreme of
a disregard for context was shown by the Communist border guard who
passed George Orwell's anticommunist classic, *Animal Farm*, because he
took it for an agricultural treatise, and who confiscated Tucholsky's
satiric *Deutschland über Alles*, because he disapproved of its chauvinistic
title. The more serious everyday example of a similar literal-mindedness
is the investigator who solemnly quotes the "relevant excerpt" without
regard for context or intention.

Semanticists were led to emphasize the need for referents and the role
of context by their desire to make the linguistic map reflect the referential
territory. To this extent, their work was perhaps only a natural extension
of the modern search for objective, reliable description. However, in
examining the conditions of objectivity, they inevitably became aware
of the role of nonobjective, nondescriptive factors in language. Perhaps
the crucial and distinctive contribution of semantics has been its stress on
overtones, implications, and suggestions. In our concern with the practical, communicative functions of language we often overlook a more

[39] Charles C. Fries, *The Structure of English: An Introduction to the Construction
of English Sentences* (New York: Harcourt, Brace & World, Inc., 1952), p. 295.

primitive use. Language serves to express, and to some extent relieve, emotion:

> Some of the pent-up nervous energy of such basic states as fear, anger, awe, contempt, yearning, pity, joy, and sorrow is normally drawn off by the more or less rhythmic repetition of conventional syllables or common names like *oh, ah, wow, oops, pooh, hurrah,* or *oh boy, man, rats, fiddlesticks.* Upon occasion a little salutary profanity may ease an otherwise destructive mood; in Hamlet's phrase, we may "unpack our hearts with words and fall a-cursing."[40]

Though the symbols used are conventional, that is, vary from speech community to speech community, such "expressive" language does not necessarily depend upon an audience with whom we share meanings. However, when the expressive function *does* blend with the communicative function of language, it complicates communication in important ways. No study of communication can be informative unless it makes allowance for the overriding importance of **emotive language.** Thomas Hobbes said in the *Leviathan:*

> The names of such things as affect us—that is, which please and displease us—because all men be not alike affected with the same thing nor the same man at all times, are in the common discourses of men of *inconstant* signification. . . . For though the nature of that we conceive be the same, yet the diversity of our reception of it, in respect of different constitutions of body and prejudices of opinion, gives everything a tincture of our different passions. And therefore in reasoning a man must take heed of words which, besides the signification of what we imagine of their nature, have a signification also of the nature, disposition, and interest of the speaker: such as are the names of virtues and vices, for one man calls *wisdom* what another calls *fear,* and one *cruelty* what another *justice,* one *prodigality* what another *magnanimity,* and one *gravity* what another *stupidity,* etc.[41]

Much can be learned from such pairing of terms with roughly the same **denotation,** or referential meaning, but widely differing **connotations,** that is, favorable or unfavorable associations, suggested attitudes and values. The student may share the automatically favorable response to terms like *pride, faith,* and *firmness.* He is awakened to the need for responsible, independent judgment when his initial, unthinking response is neutralized by their unfavorable counterparts—*arrogance, dogmatism,* and *obstinacy.* He begins to realize how much of our language serves, not primarily to symbolize referents, but to arouse emotion, ranging from joy and sympathy to horror and disgust. He learns to recognize, with David Hume, terms that "savour more of panegyric than of philosophy," and, inversely, terms that carry more insult than information.[42] When ex-

---

40 Upton, *Design for Thinking,* p. 209.
41 Thomas Hobbes, *The Leviathan* (New York: The Liberal Arts Press, 1958), pp. 44–45.
42 David Hume, *Dialogues Concerning Natural Religion* (New York: Hafner Publishing Co., Inc., 1959), p. 71.

amined from this point of view, much language ostensibly describing things and relations in the outside world reveals the attitudes, emotions, and standards of the speaker.

Obviously, the informative and the emotive aspects of meaning are not clearly distinct, let alone mutually exclusive. When we call someone an "old fox," we may be informing our audience of his shrewd intelligence while at the same time suggesting an attitude of disapproval and distrust:

> The distinction which is important is that between utterances in which the symbolic function is subordinate to the emotive act and those of which the reverse is true. In the first case, however precise and however elaborate the references communicated may be, they can be seen to be present in an essentially instrumental capacity, as means to emotive effects. In the second case, however strong the emotive effects, these can be seen to be by-products not essentially involved in the speech transaction. The peculiarity of scientific statement, that recent new development of linguistic activity, is its restriction to the symbolic function.[43]

Science has made progress through the development of a rigorously denotative vocabulary. In our political, social, and private lives, however, the connotative element in language often seems paramount. The role of emotive language in human relations can hardly be overestimated. It is among our chief means of advancing our own interests, and of making them acceptable to ourselves and others. The investigator realizes with growing humility how many laudatory terms are "first person" nouns and adjectives: "On this point, I remain firm"; "With renewed dedication, we set forth"; "We affirm our unshakeable faith in truth and justice." By contrast, many derogatory terms are, typically used in the third person: "He is prejudiced"; "She is inconsiderate"; "They are conspirators." Vance Packard's definition of a *social clique* as "a pack of people running together" not only will not make the reader any fonder of cliques than he already is; it also demonstrates that a clique is a group of people that does *not* include ourselves. Similar distinctions lurk in the merest semantic tags: our own people "state," "affirm," "declare"; the others "admit," "allege," "assert." As used, for example, in *Time* magazine, language becomes the instrument of continuous in-grouping and out-grouping, of placing people and events in the column "with us and all the other knowing and right-thinking people" or in the column "with those others, who, from a regrettable lack of sophistication or plain malice, have opinions and preferences different from our own."

Emotive language often implies or expresses judgments of value. It is thus closely related to the **directive** function of language. We all recognize the directive function in explicit pleas, requests, commands: "Move over"; "No Smoking"; "Please be seated." Just as frequently, however, we encounter directives that are merely implied: "Candidate X is a man of

---

43 Ogden and Richards, *The Meaning of Meaning*, p. 124.

unwavering integrity"—therefore vote for him; "A person who would do such a thing is no better than a mad dog"—therefore let's treat him like one. Even statements clearly informative in appearance may be made primarily for the sake of the directive implications: "Prices for lodgings and food in Majorca are among the lowest in Western Europe"—therefore spend your vacation there.

Emotional overtones and directive implications lend power and interest to much first-rate writing. A writer must be able to show not only that he knows but also that he cares. In much of our reading we look not only for a dispassionate understanding of a subject but for guidance concerning the attitudes and the courses of action we should adopt. Nevertheless, the close intertwining of the informative and the emotive elements in language confronts the writer with serious questions of responsibility and the reader with difficult problems of interpretation. Such questions and problems are minimized when language reaches the one or the other extreme: In a report on the distribution of stresses and strains of a projected bridge, we expect a treatment that is as far as possible emotionally neutral. In reading a selection from the *Prejudices* of H. L. Mencken, we expect a display of inspired invective, rich in emotional appeal, though not ruling out an occasional shrewd observation. Difficulties typically result when utterances that express subjective attitudes and emotions are mistaken for objective observation.

The sources of such confusion are mainly of two kinds. A writer animated by strong conviction but linguistically naive may present, as an honest, "straightforward" accounting of how things actually are, utterances with a strong emotive slant. Such a writer is likely to be baffled by dissent, interpreting it as a sign of wrongheadedness or malice rather than of a difference in values. Less candid is the writer who deliberately gives a false air of objectivity to statements with a strong emotive and directive element. Voters and customers must learn to recognize emotional and directive implications in utterances that purport to "report the facts."

Once the student learns to look in language for elements other than hard-core information, he discovers features that are **ceremonial** rather than functional in a narrowly practical sense. He becomes aware of what S. I. Hayakawa calls the "presymbolic factors" in such superficially meaningless communications as polite conversation and cliché-laden oratory.[44] Language may, without pointing in more than the vaguest manner to referential territory, express polite interest, attitudes ranging from respect to unconditional loyalty, a feeling of communion or a desire to establish it. The polite "How are you?" is not generally a request for information; just as the perfunctory "That looks very nice" is not an at-

---

[44] *Language in Thought and Action* (New York: Harcourt, Brace & World, Inc., 1949), pp. 69–79.

tempt at candid evaluation. Apart from its practical uses in the co-ordination of purposeful activities, language has another definite social function. It reflects the human tendency "to congregate, to be together, to enjoy each other's company"; it serves to make us overcome "the strange and unpleasant tension which men feel when facing each other in silence."

> A mere phrase of politeness, in use as much among savage tribes as in a European drawing-room, fulfils a function to which the meaning of its words is almost completely irrelevant. Inquiries about health, comments on weather, affirmations of some supremely obvious state of things—all such are exchanged, not in order to inform, not in this case to connect people in action, certainly not in order to express any thought.

Malinowski called this use of language "phatic" communion, "a type of speech in which ties of union are created by a mere exchange of words."[45]

The tragicomic obstinacy of Alceste, in Molière's *The Misanthrope*, stems from his refusal to recognize this use of language as legitimate and useful:

> Be sincere; by a strict code of honor abide;
> Let in all that you say your heart be your guide.

> We should speak man to man, and strive to reveal
> In the words we pronounce the convictions we feel. (Act I, Sc. 1)

Alceste refuses to admit that language is not exclusively a vehicle for the direct communication of information, or even of attitude, but, among other things, a social instrument that makes peaceful, civilized intercourse possible by veiling our more candid responses:

> Consider, for instance, these words, which might be spoken by any departing guest to his hostess: "Thank you for a lovely party—we've had a delightful time." Sometimes the guest has had anything but a pleasant time; but he is not for that reason to be regarded as dishonest. To insist that "a really truthful person" would, if necessary, say "Good-bye, I've had a very dull and uncomfortable time" would be to repeat the mistake which occurs when poetry is treated as if it were science. A formula of polite thanks is not intended, or understood, as a factual claim. . . . Questions of truth and falsity are no more applicable to such *ceremonial* uses of language than they are to a handshake.[46]

Closely related to this social use of language is what we might call its ritual use. It is futile to look in a political speech for an objective discussion of the "issues" if the real intention of the speaker, and the real expectation of the audience, is to have the speech function as the equivalent of a war dance or of a patriotic song. The cheers that greet the speaker who knows how to address a partisan crowd reward his ability to express their common frustrations and resentments in order to confirm their feel-

[45] Ogden and Richards, *The Meaning of Meaning*, Supplement I, pp. 313–15.
[46] Max Black, *Critical Thinking*, 2nd ed. (Englewood Cliffs, N.J.: Prentice-Hall, Inc., 1952), p. 166.

ing of common purpose. We read Tom Paine's pamphlets on "The American Crisis" not as historical accounts of the War of Independence but as magnificent examples of the power of language to build morale:

> The summer soldier and the sunshine patriot will, in this crisis, shrink from the service of his country; but he that stands it NOW, deserves the love and thanks of man and woman. . . .

> Heaven knows how to put a proper price upon its good; and it would be strange indeed, if so celestial an article as FREEDOM should not be highly rated. . . .

> God Almighty will not give up a people to military destruction, or leave them unsupportedly to perish, who have so earnestly and so repeatedly sought to avoid the calamities of war, by every decent method which wisdom could invent.

In dealing with such texts, semantics focuses attention upon the ways of words and the uses of language. The resulting linguistic sophistication benefits the student in many fundamental ways. It helps him become a more perceptive listener and reader. It teaches him the art of reading between the lines and the elementary distinction between what is said and what is meant. It prepares him to look for the "precise shade that a word has in its context, the subtle hints conveyed by a metaphor or a simile."[47] Semantic analysis of persuasive techniques helps the student maintain a measure of private judgment, of independence from the manipulators of language in politics, advertising, public relations. Semantic awareness is just as relevant to making the student notice the nuances of meaning in a newspaper editorial as it is to sharpening his reactions to what is half said and what is left unsaid in a Henry James novel. It is indispensable to the literary critic, who must be ever sensitive to the penumbra of suggestion surrounding the written word and who cannot afford to be tone-deaf to the wistful ironies of Chaucer or the sardonic humor of James Joyce.

Equally important is growing semantic sophistication in the student's own use of language. A writer trained in semantics can hardly revise an article or a chapter without substituting, however reluctantly and incompletely, a direct statement for a snide implication, a substantiated charge for a derogatory label. No one trained in semantics can, without violent wrenching, write *Time*-style or *Democratic Digest*-style or any other style that exploits the potential of language for innuendo. The glib use of the term *appeasement* becomes more difficult after one studies Monroe C. Beardsley's discussion of *compromise, appeasement, conciliation, give-and-take* and other near-synonyms for "coming to terms with someone through willingness to modify one's original demands." Though "the kernel of these terms is a process that nearly everyone can recognize to be

[47] Beardsley, *Thinking Straight*, p. 229.

a part of normal democratic human and social relations," a term like
appeasement "will also, unless the context guards against it, import a
judgment about the case"—that one of the parties to the agreement

> gave in too far, or got too little in return, or was too spineless, or too hasty.
> These judgments, or some of them, may be true; the point to notice here,
> however, is that they are not stated explicitly so that they can be discussed on
> their merits; they are brought in slyly, via the connotations of the word
> selected, and they are easily overlooked by the unwary. Because the term
> "appeasement" is *roughly* apposite, its *extra* hints are accepted uncritically.
> Someone might call the agreement a "Munich," but that would be less
> subtle.[48]

We can derive a warm glow of self-righteousness from applying invidious
labels; we may experience a hot flush of gratification in delivering a
telling, if unfair, verbal blow. To do without such satisfactions requires
self-control. As Aldous Huxley says, "To learn to use words correctly is to
learn, among other things, the art of foregoing immediate excitements
and immediate personal triumphs."[49]

Students of semantics have been willing to explore areas of language
use crucial to the nature and future of our culture but outside the domain
of traditional academic disciplines. The semanticist concerns himself with
various kinds of manipulation of language that confuse if not deliberately
deceive. He may explore the role in our society of **euphemisms,** the constant attempts at verbal face lifting or wholesale verbal upgrading. Some
school districts require their teachers to use the following kinds of translations:

Cheats—	depends on others to do his work
Below average—	working at his own level
Steals—	takes without permission
Lies—	has tendency to stretch the truth

These euphemisms attempt to substitute for bluntness a more cautious
handling of the student's (and the parent's) ego. Meant to be objective,
they easily become evasive and belittling. Above all, they are vague enough
to make effective communication about teaching and student conduct
difficult. At the same time, euphemisms wear out. Once neutral or favorable terms themselves acquire the unfavorable connotations they were
supposed to neutralize. Since "unclean" is translated as "having poor
habits," and *habits* generally appears in euphemistic phrases for unpleasant traits, the word *habit* itself is becoming popularly associated with
the idea of something repulsive.

The tendency of language to be worn out by excessive stretching is
especially evident in the advertiser's constant reaching for dramatic,
promising, inviting terms. As contrasted with *house, home* connotes

[48] Beardsley, *Thinking Straight*, p. 235–36.
[49] "Words and Their Meanings," in Black, *Importance*, p. 11.

family ties, domestic comfort, childhood associations, and the like. As *home* is again and again used by the real-estate dealer for the bare, un-lived-in structure, it loses its affectionate glow and dwindles into a mere synonym for *house*. Similarly, the constant dramatizing by the journalist of unspectacular data promotes a general deafness to emphasis. Not always is the overemphasis and false glamour of headline and commercial as neatly deflated as in the newspaper story that was headlined "Ex-banker Takes Life," then identified the victim and "ex-banker" as a "career-banking official," and finally, in the last paragraph, admitted he had been an "assistant cashier." Phrases like *dramatic, exclusive, vital,* and *totally new* become mere routine:

> In the same way a rhetoric that keeps using the floodlights of emphasis finally reaches the opposite of the intended effect: beside the multitude of things flooded by glaring light nothing distinctly visible remains, and only acoustic chaos reigns in language.[50]

Many trends in modern literature are more fully understood when seen in relation to the popular culture against which they react. It is possible, for instance, to trace a relation between the modern poet's distrust of large, uplifting abstractions and the prevailing trends in our mass media. S. I. Hayakawa explained the modern poet's finding it so difficult "to say anything with enthusiasm or joy or conviction" at least in part by "the pre-emption by the venal poet of the common value-symbols of our culture, the symbols of courage, of beauty, of domesticity, of patriotism, of happiness, and even of religion, for the purposes of *selling*, that is, of advantaging the speaker at the expense of the hearer."[51] Similarly, the terse, monosyllabic style of Hemingway's fiction was at least in part a reaction against the flood of mercenary patriotic oratory of World War I. His heroes were tactiturn because, like Krebs in "Soldier's Home," they "did not want to tell any more lies."

Equipped with a detailed understanding of the symbol-manipulating ways of our culture, the semanticist can undertake to refute the arguments of apologists for the "encouragement of irrational and impulsive choice." He can effectively protest against the "drowning out of all serious messages from the educator, the clergyman, the artist, the scientist" by large-scale advertising and its control of the mass media.[52] It is perhaps not too late for the semanticist's more disengaged colleagues in other areas of language study to learn something from him about how to keep their own messages from being drowned out.

[50] Dolf Sternberger *et al., Aus dem Wöterbuch des Unmenschen* (Munich: Deutscher Taschenbuch Verlag, 1962), p. 58.

[51] "Poetry and Advertising," *Poetry: A Magazine of Verse,* LXVII (January, 1946), 204–12.

[52] S. I. Hayakawa, "Advertising vs. Proper Evaluation," *ETC.: A Review of General Semantics,* XVIII (October, 1961), 371–72.

It is of course in the political sphere that our common future is most directly affected by our uses and abuses of language. In their *From the Dictionary of Inhumanity*, published in Germany in 1957, the authors subject to semantic analysis the "masculine," quasi-military jargon prevailing in the Germany of the thirties:

> One remembers this way of using words and the time when it became popular. Only the stupid could overlook it, and only the complete conformists of the time considered it right and proper. But almost to a man we underestimated its seriousness: What we considered a playing at soldiers, naive and in bad taste, was in reality already total war, long before it was officially declared. The foreign ambassadors were still sitting in Berlin as honored representatives. They and the Germans did not yet perceive to what extent language bodes forth, and quite literally shapes, future reality.[53]

American teachers of English are fortunate to be able to conduct this kind of analysis as preventive linguistic therapy rather than as a grim postmortem.

Language and Thought

The subject matter of semantics is the relation between language, thought, and behavior. Whereas linguist and logician often go their separate ways, students of semantics have stressed the organic relationship between language and **logic.** They have helped us make the forbidding discipline of formal logic directly relevant and fruitful in the study of meaningful discourse. They have led us to emphasize from the beginning that "for the most part we do our thinking in a *medium*" and that "critical thinking involves the critical use of language."[54] They have made us spend less time on the bare bones of the syllogism and more on the ambiguous and connotative items that fill it out. Many an argument that seems superficially sound is unreliable because it shifts and stretches the meaning of such elastic terms as *conservative, radical,* and *alien.* Many an apparently logical argument employs connotative terms that, in Hobbes's phrase, "can never be true grounds of any ratiocination." Semanticists have made us realize how many logical fallacies are "verbal shifts and dodges" and involve some kind or other of "verbal misbehavior."[55]

Semantic awareness can help correct misuses of logic that affect basic attitudes. "Either-or" thinking, for instance, is facilitated where language furnishes neat pairs of verbal opposites. An accurate observer of human behavior must recognize, not a simple alternative of "courage" and

[53] Sternberger, *Aus dem Wörterbuch des Unmenschen,* p. 44.
[54] Beardsley, *Thinking Straight,* pp. xvii–xviii.
[55] *Ibid.,* pp. 175–80.

"cowardice," but different degrees of determination and fearlessness, whose appropriateness and desirability depend on the situation. A simplified alternative of "freedom" and "regimentation" may prevent us from formulating the delicate balance of freedom and order, of private initiative and social duty, that makes for a free society in the Western tradition. An all-or-nothing choice of "loyalty" or "disloyalty" does not make allowance for the open-eyed, critical commitment to the standards of one's own country that marks the loyalty of free men.

Semanticists have effectively attacked either-or thinking as the result of a **two-valued** orientation. Many people look for two clearly distinct sides to every issue while neglecting the third or fourth side that may be the most important. They look for black-and-white contrasts even in cases where the real difficulty is to distinguish between different shades of gray. Awareness of the popular tendency toward a two-valued orientation makes one suspicious of such forms of discussion as the formal debate. As Stuart Chase says, the debate is "a two-valued verbal combat with the effect of over-simplifying and distorting questions" that are usually "many-valued."[56] The competitive spirit of the debate discourages one from acknowledging complications he has overlooked and conceding elements of truth unexpectedly discovered in the opponent's position. It is hard for the debater to say: "Now for the first time I really see what you mean. I admit I never looked at it from this point of view before." Part of growing up is shifting from polar verbal opposites to modes of expression that allow one to express differences of degree and to reflect such changes in one's position as might become necessary.

Much of the power and danger of words derives from their relative distinctness and permanence. Words help us divide the changing continuum of experience into manageable portions. They identify points of rest and recurrent configurations that make it possible for us to orient ourselves in the world around us. They make it possible to map out the territory of experience not only for our own use, but for the use of future generations, who can build on the knowledge that their predecessors have formulated and recorded in words.

However, it is not only knowledge that thus gains permanence through verbal formulation. Words serve to give distinctness, clarity, and permanence to our purposes and motives. They permit "human beings to behave with a degree of purposefulness, perseverance and consistency unknown among the other mammals":

> The consistency of human behavior, such as it is, is due entirely to the fact that men have formulated their desires, and subsequently rationalized them, in terms of words. The verbal formulation of a desire will cause a man to go on pressing forward towards his goal, even when the desire itself lies dormant. Similarly, the rationalization of his desire in terms of some theo-

56 *Power of Words* (New York: Harcourt, Brace & World, Inc., 1954), p. 188.

logical or philosophical system will convince him that he does well to persevere in this way. It is thanks to words and to words alone that, as the poet says:

> Tasks in hours of insight willed
> May be in hours of gloom fulfilled.

If we do not follow every whim or sudden impulse, if we pursue remote long-range goals, it is at least in part because of the "descriptive and justificatory words with which we bind our days together."[57]

While this purposefulness makes us human and makes possible all distinctly human achievements, it also makes possible distinctly human failings. Not only may a system of ideas rest on a hasty and oversimplified interpretation of experience, but the definiteness and permanence of its verbal formulations may make the system survive until even the circumstances to which it was partly relevant have changed. Writers like Carlyle, Ibsen, and Shaw derive their polemical impetus from their attack on the resulting rigidities of thought and purpose. Such writers try to counteract the hardening of our moral arteries that results from our relying on words that have lost their living, dynamic relationship to experience. What these writers do by means of satiric exposure and dramatic demonstration, the semanticist tries to accomplish by semantic analysis. He tries to keep our words from becoming ossified; he helps us to restore their flexibility and suppleness as instruments for the formulation of living ideas.

This overriding concern with the relationship between words and ideas can easily lead the semanticist onto treacherous ground. He must resist the constant temptation to take short cuts from specific observations of language to sweeping psychological, philosophical, and political implications. Many suggested relationships between language and thought remain unconvincing. For example, Stuart Chase comments on the way the vocabulary of Chinese counteracts the tendency toward a "two-valued" orientation and concludes that "as a result Chinese thought has been traditionally tolerant, not given to the fanatical ideologies of the West."[58] Another writer refers to the "democratic habits of speech" characteristic of "analytic" tongues, including Chinese, in which "a word is relatively free to do as it pleases, provided it takes a cooperative attitude towards its fellows."[59] The ways in which such impressions may lead one to misjudge political developments in a country such as China are obvious.

In such instances, followers of semantics have accepted, with Benjamin Lee Whorf, too sweeping a version of the thesis that the linguistic system "is itself the shaper of ideas, the program and the guide for the individual's mental activity."[60] With Stuart Chase, they have taken too

---

57 Huxley, in Black, *Importance,* pp. 4–5.
58 Chase, *Power of Words,* p. 106.
59 Upton, *Design for Thinking,* p. 26.
60 "Science and Linguistics," in Allen, *Readings,* p. 33.

literally the idea that "thinking follows the tracks laid down in one's own language."[61]

It is possible to underestimate the plasticity of language, the multiple and constantly changing meanings of grammatical features and lexical items. As Dona Worrall Brown observes,

> Associations between structures and meanings are not rigidly set, but are always subject to change without notice, just as the meanings connected with the lexical elements of the language may be changed at any time if enough speakers of the language choose to do so.[62]

It is true that "I see the tree" uses the same construction as "I cut the tree," but it is doubtful that this construction, often signaling an actor–action pattern, "makes it appear as if the *I* was the *subject* from which issued the seeing, and as if the seeing was a sort of action directed at the tree." It is doubtful that "a whole world picture is wedded to the use of the transitive verb and the actor–action scheme that goes with it."[63] Language does not seem to interfere with the common-sense view that the tree is entirely unaffected by our "act" of seeing it; nor has language noticeably facilitated acceptance of the philosophical view that the existence of the tree depends on its being perceived by a beholder; nor does language seem to interfere with the scientific view that takes "I see the tree" to mean "light waves reflected from the tree are registered on my retina." Similarly, "it rains," though modeled on the subject–verb, actor–action pattern, does not make us imagine a possible performer for the action of "raining." If a language renders our "I hear" by linguistic elements roughly translatable as "to me is a sound," this does not mean that our own linguistic framework tends to emphasize action. Many verbs express concepts of condition, rest, relation, or permanence with quite static connotations.

Considerations such as these lend support to the skeptical view expressed for example by Joshua Whatmough:

> Some linguists in the past, Max Müller for example, have held that we are bound hand and foot by linguistic habit, that our model of the universe is merely our language, English or Navaho as the case may be. . . . There is a specious half-truth, but no more, in the view that meaning is controlled by the very grammatical structure of a particular language. It seems more likely that in standard average European the structure of language has been made to correspond with what the speakers of it have discovered about their universe, and that what they believe about it depends not only upon the structure of the universe itself but on free inquiry.[64]

61 Chase, *Power of Words*, p. 101.
62 "Does Language Structure Influence Thought?" *ETC.: A Review of General Semantics*, XVII (Spring, 1960), 339–45.
63 Friedrich Waismann, "The Resources of Language," in Black, *Importance*, p. 108.
64 *Language: A Modern Synthesis* (New York: The New American Library of World Literature, Inc., 1956), p. 84.

Vocabulary, with its resources of metaphorical extension, adapts with amazing flexibility to different environments, specialized trades, complicated technical subject matter, new scientific discoveries, new systems of thought, and new avenues of sensibility. On the most elementary level, the Eskimo's language distinguishes without difficulty between several different kinds of snow, just as the fashion designer's language distinguishes easily between many different shades of green. H. A. Gleason describes the botanist's regrouping of the usual division of the spectrum into major colors:

> Yellows, oranges, and many reds are found to constitute one series. Blues, purples, and purplish reds constitute another. These two exhibit fundamental differences that must be treated as basic to any botanical description. In order to state the facts succinctly it has been necessary to coin two new and more general color terms, *xanthic* and *cyanic,* for these two groups.[65]

Typically, technical terminology serves to pin down concepts and distinctions that are inadequately, or not at all, recognized in ordinary speech. The important point is that language easily lends itself to a labeling of these distinctions once they become relevant.

Language seems to be similarly elastic in making the established grammatical machinery serve in the expression of new concepts and attitudes. This is the more remarkable since typically the grammar of a language preserves in fossilized form concepts that at some earlier stage may have been relevant enough to be explicitly noted in routine utterances. Languages differ widely in how they make the speaker choose between alternative grammatical features more or less exactly correlated with concepts like "male, female, or sexless," "singular, dual, or plural," "unilateral, reflexive, or reciprocal," "animate or inanimate," "in vicinity of or at distance from the speaker," "continuous or discontinuous," "factual or hypothetical," "isolated or habitual," "past and done or past but affecting the present," "active, passive, or instrumental." What is difficult to show, however, is that the routine, in fact, quite automatic observance of these grammatical conventions effectively guides or limits the speaker's awareness of sex, process, probability, regularity, continuity or any other aspect of experience. English, for instance, enables us to indicate temporal relationships with whatever subtlety and flexibility we may desire, regardless of the way our limited system of distinctive grammatical tenses would seem to hem us in in talking about time.

Recurrent grammatical relationships are often said to favor one perspective toward external events over another. They would thus tend to channel observation. Again, however, the typical flexibility of language makes it hard to identify such obligatory perspectives reliably. Compare, for instance, "Socrates is wise," "Socrates speaks wisely," and "Wisdom is

[65] Gleason, *An Introduction to Descriptive Linguistics,* p. 5.

a characteristic of Socrates." If the language had only the first possibility at its disposal, it might be said to favor a view dividing reality into substances and qualities. If only the second, it might be said to encourage emphasis on action or process. If only the third, it might be said to favor the setting up of qualities and attributes as independent entities. In fact, of course, the grammatical resources of English allow us to choose among all these as well as numerous other possible perspectives toward the same fact or event. The variety and flexibility of these resources makes it difficult to accept the view that "so far from a grammar—the structure of a symbol system—being a reflection of the structure of the world, any supposed structure of the world is more probably a reflection of the grammar used."[66]

Whorf, in defending such a view, showed how, in various languages, "different isolates of meaning" are put together to describe identical events. Such comparisons, however, illuminate some of the very processes that account for the adaptability and flexibility of language. The same event may be described as "The father slapped his son" or "The teenager received a box on the ear from his elderly relative." Here different names for the same thing identify it by pointing to different selected aspects or qualities. The contrast between the two versions illustrates how various ways of referring to the same event may emphasize action or result, process or product. What makes non-Indo-European languages seem alien to us is that they exploit the possibilities of alternative reference in new and unsuspected ways.

A balanced view of the relationship between language and thought must recognize both the possible rigidities and the compensating flexibility of our linguistic medium. The teacher of literature, more than anyone else, is in a position to appreciate the resources, as well as the constraints, of language. Heine's travel pieces, Schiller's *Ode to Joy*, Mann's *Magic Mountain*, Hitler's *Mein Kampf*, Kafka's *Amerika*, and Rilke's *Elegies* were all written in the same standard dialect of German. To study English literary history since about 1500 is to study the ways in which the same basic inventory of structure and vocabulary can be used to project a world picture as different from that of Milton as that of Blake, as different from that of Tennyson as that of Ezra Pound. Part of every poet's task is to refute the grim conclusion that man "is a prisoner of his language."[67]

If thought and attitude are influenced and controlled by language only within limits, it follows that there are obvious limits to what semantic analysis can accomplish. Many a disagreement we hopefully identify as a "question of semantics" is in reality a question of conflicting interests obscured by the similarity of the terms and slogans through

66 Ogden and Richards, *The Meaning of Meaning*, p. 96.
67 Chase, *Power of Words*, p. 104.

which they find expression. For example, a merciful fog of phrases such as "increase in productivity" and "wage-price spiral" usually veils the underlying economic motives in conflicts between wage-earner and management. Brutal clarity in the statement of these motives might merely aggravate the underlying clash of interests.

Expectations of what semantic therapy can do easily become over-optimistic. Many of our most fundamental interests, resentments, apprehensions, and rationalizations, though they often operate *through* language, are subject to verbal manipulation and qualification only to a limited extent. For instance, it is true that the critic of ideological fanaticism will remain naive and ineffectual without an awareness of its linguistic rigidities and verbal fallacies. He will have to be aware of its exploitation of the directive and ceremonial dimensions of language. But ultimately, he will have to concern himself with the psychological and political factors behind arguments and slogans. Regardless of language, people tend to compensate for humiliation and defeat by doctrines of inherent moral, national, or racial superiority; they tend to blame multifarious shortcomings and frustrations on a clearly identifiable scapegoat; they respond to leaders who counteract confusion and hopelessness by working up a powerful feeling of common purpose. Such factors provide a formula for political success that operates to a large extent independently of the language—clumsy or sophisticated, "ideological" or popular—through which it finds expression.

No one can long study the role of language in human life without confronting basic philosophical, moral, and political problems. In dealing with such problems, popular exponents of semantics have often relied on assumptions that many teachers cannot, and need not, share. Semanticists have often echoed the convictions of those who consider it our most urgent need to extend the "scientific attitude" beyond the sphere of the natural sciences to such areas as politics and ethics. The popular semanticist is likely to speak of "the scientific method conceived as a way of life"; he is likely to believe that "if you would build a world of social justice, you must model it after the world of science."[68] When first propounded by such nineteenth-century scientists as T. H. Huxley, such faith in the ethical potential of science reflected a generous vision of man's more rational and more humane future. Modern students of the role of science in human life have inevitably had sobering second thoughts. Kenneth Burke, in "Semantic and Poetic Meaning," concerned himself with the incompleteness of a semantic ideal devoted to "the programmatic elimination of a weighted vocabulary" and the search for a "vocabulary that does not *judge*, but *describes* or *places*." He pointed out that such "neutral" or "non-moral" ideals of meaning, when

[68] Upton, *Design for Thinking*, p. 26.

attained, would make it necessary to "let moral purposes creep in as contraband."[69] Like any other orientation emulating the objectivity of physical science, such a semantic ideal shares the limitations of science described by William James:

> A moral question is a question not of what sensibly exists, but of what is good, or would be good if it did exist. Science can tell us what exists; but to compare the *worths*, both of what exists and of what does not exist, we must consult not science, but what Pascal calls our heart. Science herself consults her heart when she lays it down that the infinite ascertainment of fact and correction of false belief are the supreme goods for man. Challenge the statement, and science can only repeat it oracularly, or else prove it by showing that such ascertainment and correction bring man all sorts of other goods which man's heart in turn declares.[70]

In practice, nevertheless, the impulse behind the semanticist's approach is not likely to be far removed from what motivates many a teacher's work. Faith in the humanizing effect of communication is part of the convictions of any teacher of language and literature. He will recognize objectivity as the condition of knowledge and at the same time recognize understanding as its end. With its characteristic ambiguity, the term *understanding* has overtones of sympathy and human interest that qualify it, more than any other synonym of *truth,* to express the necessary reconciliation of disinterested curiosity and humane commitment. It is in this sense that the study of semantics helps us "understand" language and promote its humane and civilizing use.

Semantics and the Teacher of English

What, to sum up, is the place of semantics in the English teacher's work with language? Students of semantics have sharpened and reinforced our concern with meaning in a number of crucial ways. They have identified as the central problem in responsible language use the "fit" of language—the adequacy of its relation to the outside world. They have stressed the need for identifying and limiting the referents that our words symbolize. They have thus reinforced the English teacher's traditional concern with adequate definition. In stressing the need for definition, they have emphasized the difficulties inherent in words on a high level of abstraction. They have taught us to be suspicious of sweepingly general terms without visible means of referential support. They have shown us how language ossifies—how verbal labels prejudge our responses, how catchwords and slogans produce stock reactions. By constantly asking "What do you mean?" semanticists prod us into using language flexibly, with clarity and precision. More emphatically and more insistently than any other group of scholars or critics, they have

[69] Burke, *Philosophy*, pp. 146–51.
[70] *Essays on Faith and Morals* (Toronto: Longmans, Green & Co., Inc., 1947), p. 53.

reminded teachers of their task to teach students "so to control language that experience, reality as it is given us to know it, is not mutilated in its precarious passage through words."[71]

Teaching the student to use language meaningfully and responsibly, semantics can at the same time teach him to interpret language knowingly and maturely. It stresses the importance of context. It thus alerts him to the multiple meanings of words, with the selection of the appropriate meaning guided both by the physical context of an utterance and the verbal environment of the individual word or phrase. It makes the student look for clues to the speaker's intention or mood, since a facetious or ironic tone can fundamentally alter or even reverse apparent meaning. It makes the student distinguish between remarks made in casual conversation and those expressing a considered judgment.

Finally, the study of semantics alerts the student to the different uses and purposes of language. It shows him that, in popular use, the distinction between "liberty" and "license" is not in the referent, which is roughly "absence of restrictions," but in the judgment made by the speaker on the desirability of that absence. It shows him that a statement like "business is business" is not a description of business but a directive that recommends or justifies certain courses of action when business is confronted with social or human demands. The student of semantics becomes aware of the resources of language for presenting judgment as fact, for presenting opinion indirectly so that the need to defend it is obscured.

The relations and techniques the semanticist investigates are of the greatest interest to organizations and institutions whose business it is to exploit the irrational responses of customer, citizen, and voter. One defense of a free society against the merchants of irrationality is the linguistic sophistication that enables readers, listeners, and viewers to maintain their independent judgment. The teacher of English here has a tremendous responsibility, and an unequaled opportunity, to work "in defense of reason." The specialist who neglects to make his contribution to this work enjoys the privileges of academic life without having paid the price of admission.

BOOKS FOR STUDY

s. i. HAYAKAWA, *Language in Thought and Action.* New York: Harcourt, Brace & World, Inc., 1949.

The revised edition of *Language in Action.* Deservedly the most popular and influential book on the role language plays in human life. Devoted to the

[71] Louis Zahner, "What Kinds of Language Teaching?" in *Essays on the Teaching of English,* eds. Edward J. Gordon and Edward S. Noyes (New York: Appleton-Century-Crofts, Inc., 1960), p. 17.

theme that improved cooperation among human beings depends on the improved understanding of human interaction through language. Good on the different purposes and effects of different uses of words.

MONROE C. BEARDSLEY, *Thinking Straight: Principles of Reasoning for Readers and Writers,* (2nd ed.) Englewood Cliffs, N.J.: Prentice-Hall, Inc., 1956.

A thorough and systematic introduction to applied logic as it concerns the critical reader and writer. Throughout pays special attention to the relationship between critical thinking and the critical use of language.

S. I. HAYAKAWA, ed., *The Use and Misuse of Language.* Greenwich, Conn.: Fawcett Publications, Inc., 1962. A Premier Paperback.

Selected essays from *ETC.: A Review of General Semantics.* Includes essays by such pioneers in general semantics as Anatol Rapoport, Irving J. Lee, and Wendell Johnson.

MAX BLACK, ed., *The Importance of Language.* Englewood Cliffs, N.J.: Prentice-Hall, Inc., 1962. A Spectrum Book.

A collection of substantial and illuminating essays on the importance of language as both object of study and medium of inquiry and expression for critic, scientist, anthropologist, and philosopher.

MATERIALS FOR ANALYSIS

A. Study the following semantic cluster, which traces the network of synonyms and near-synonyms of *give up.* Give some indication of their mutual relations and idiomatic uses. Assisted by your dictionary, construct a similar semantic cluster for another everyday word rich in synonyms and related terms.

```
give up
  abandon
    resign
    submit
    yield
    abdicate
      —a throne
      —a position of power
    renounce
      repudiate
      cast off
      disclaim
    relinquish
      withdraw from
      desist from
      cede
      waive
      forego
    quit
        discontinue
        discharge an obligation
        have done with
```

<pre>
      leave
          depart from
          desert
          allow to remain
          cease from
   surrender
      yield
          —payment
          give up to superior
          —argument
          —power
      submit
          —in compliance with
          —in obedience to
          —to treatment for
          —to something to be undergone
             succumb
             relent
             defer
                —to opinion
                —to authority
                —to wishes
             —as a prisoner
          capitulate
          release
          turn loose
</pre>

    —Sumner Ives, *A New Handbook for Writers* (New York: Alfred A. Knopf, Inc., 1960), pp. 339–40.

B. After studying the following passage from Stuart Chase's *Power of Words,* write a similar paragraph in which you take up a term covering a large and vaguely defined territory and then proceed "down the abstraction ladder to the solid earth":

I sit here at my desk, thinking about the term "welfare state" . . . as a verbal tent to cover a large and active circus. I take up one of the sharp pencils and, in the first paragraph which I write, assert that no such thing as a "welfare state" exists anywhere but in our heads. No camera can find it, no radar screen pick it up; it is an abstraction with very limited usefulness.

After thus locating the term in the stratosphere, I proceed down the abstraction ladder to the solid earth. What are the referents for "welfare state"; what tangible administrative bodies and government organizations can legitimately be called welfare agencies? The American Constitution aims to provide for the "general welfare," and a great deal of legislation in the last 150 years falls under the welfare clause. How far down the ladder must I go before finding something I can take a picture of?

I jot down a few notes from memory, then swing around to the reference shelves beside my desk and consult the Congressional Directory, the World Almanac, and various other sources. After a period of fact-finding I come up with a list of nearly 100 activities which are clearly concerned with welfare and supply at collective expense needs which individuals cannot, or do not, meet for themslves. It turns out to be quite a comprehensive and interesting list, including:

The public school system	Land grant colleges
The Homestead Act	The GI Bill of Rights

The Public Health Service   Unemployment insurance
Pure food and drug inspection   The W.P.A. of the 1930's
The Red Cross   Public housing
The child labor law   Subsidy to the merchant marine
Community chests   Subsidy to potato farmers
Taft-Hartley labor law   Federal insurance of bank deposits
School lunch programs   Soil Conservation Service
Old-age pensions   Public credit agencies

This is only a sample, but enough to show what is going on under the label of "welfare state."

> —Stuart Chase, *Power of Words* (New York: Harcourt, Brace & World, Inc., 1954), pp. 188–89.

C. After studying the inherent ambiguities of the terms *honor* and *justice,* discuss fully three other important abstract terms with similarly contradictory possible meanings. Can such contradictions be resolved? How should such terms be treated?

D. Study the differences in connotation among the following synonyms of *plan:*

Plan refers to any detailed method, formulated beforehand, for doing or making something (vacation *plans*); **design** stresses the final outcome of a plan and implies the use of skill or craft, sometimes in an unfavorable sense, in executing or arranging this (it was his *design* to separate us); **project** implies the use of enterprise or imagination in formulating an ambitious or extensive plan (they've begun work on the housing *project*); **scheme,** a less definite term than the preceding, often connotes either an impractical, visionary plan or an underhand intrigue (a *scheme* to embezzle the funds).

> —*Webster's New World Dictionary of the American Language,* College Edition (Cleveland: The World Publishing Company, 1956).

Then trace in editorials in newspapers and newsmagazines representing varying shades of opinion the role of these and other related connotative terms in references to some recent governmental, institutional, or individual plan, project, or proposal.

E. George Orwell says in his essay on Dickens:

Everyone remembers the revolutionary scenes in *A Tale of Two Cities;* they have the quality of nightmare, and it is Dickens's own nightmare. Again and again he insists upon the meaningless horrors of revolution. . . .
. . . the bloody knives and the tumbrils rolling to and fro create in his mind a special, sinister vision which he has succeeded in passing on to generations of readers. Thanks to Dickens, the very word "tumbril" has a murderous sound; one forgets that a tumbril is only a sort of farm-cart.

> —*Dickens, Dali and Others: Studies in Popular Culture* (New York: Reynal and Hitchcock, 1946), pp. 14–16.

Find three other terms with connotations that can be traced more or less definitely to a specific historical event, literary source, or the like.

F. Study D. H. Lawrence's discussion of the individual meanings and associations of *bread.* Then write a paragraph each on three other fairly common and concrete words, developing their full range of "individual meaning."

When it comes to the meaning of anything, even the simplest word, then you must pause. Because there are two great categories of meaning, forever separate. There is mob-meaning, and there is individual meaning. Take even the word *bread*. The mob-meaning is merely: stuff made with white flour into loaves that you eat. But take the individual meaning of the word bread: the white, the brown, the corn-pone, the homemade, the smell of bread just out of the oven, the crust, the crumb, the unleavened bread, . . . French bread, Viennese bread, black bread, a yesterday's loaf, rye, Graham, barley, rolls, Bretzeln, Kringeln, scones, damper, matsen—there is no end to it all, and the word bread will take you to the ends of time and space, and far-off down avenues of memory. But this is individual. The word bread will take the individual off on his own journey, and its meaning will be his own meaning, based on his own genuine imaginative reactions.

> —*Sex, Literature and Censorship,* ed. Harry T. Moore (New York: Twayne Publishers, 1953), pp. 70–71.

G. Study the following model of a fairly ordinary conversation. Show what it reveals about possible or typical uses of language and about elements that would have to be considered in definitions of the terms "meaning" and "communication."

JEAN: *(coming in)* Hi, Honey.
GEORGE: Hi.
JEAN: Brrr. It's chilly in here. Maybe we better close that window.
GEORGE: *(Silence)*
JEAN: George, would you please close that window for me?
GEORGE: Wait till I finish this page.
JEAN: Yes, dear.
GEORGE: You don't have to be sarcastic.
JEAN: Well, is it too much to ask to have you do one little thing for me once in a while?
GEORGE: I have to study for my exams, don't I? Used to be, wives were taught to respect their husbands' work.
JEAN: What about the husband respecting the wife for a change? You and your ideas about wives! This isn't the nineteenth century!
GEORGE: *(gets up)*
JEAN: Where are you going?
GEORGE: I have an important meeting at three o'clock.

H. Select one of the following terms: "human nature," "science," "national honor," "society," "fair play." Review its most typical uses: phrases in which it frequently occurs, situations where it is typically applied. Then discuss its full range of meaning, paying attention to denotative meaning, emotional overtones, typical associations, directive implications, and ceremonial uses.

I. Study one of the following books. Concentrate on those sections most directly concerned with semantics rather than with formal logic or literary analysis. Report on the book's success in making the concerns of semantics relevant to the English teacher's work with language. Use detailed illustrations.

1. Doris B. Garey, *Putting Words in Their Places*. Chicago: Scott, Foresman & Company, 1957.
2. Bernard F. Huppé and Jack Kaminsky, *Logic and Language*. New York: Alfred A. Knopf, Inc., 1956.
3. John C. Sherwood, *Discourse of Reason: A Brief Handbook of Semantics and Logic*. New York: Harper & Row, Publishers, 1960.

The discipline of English derives its unity from its concern with the nature and uses of language. It ranges from the code of linguistic signals to the use made of it by the poet. In practice, however, English is often subdivided into language and literature. Though convenient enough for many purposes, this division tends to produce an artificial simplification of interest —as though language could be studied apart from its functions, or as though literature could be studied apart from its linguistic medium. The most serious effect of this twofold division is that it leaves no logical place for a major area that provides a bridge between the linguistic and the literary. This third major area is **rhetoric**—the art of prose composition, concerned with language as a medium of ordinary self-expression and communication.

four

Rhetoric

Rhetoric is the art of writing effectively and responsibly. *The first requirement for the teacher of rhetoric is that he must treat writing as a creative process.* The art of writing well is the art of making up one's mind. It is the art of establishing clarity where there was confusion, of working out one's conclusions and commitments. Ideally, at least, it is *not* the skill of presenting a preconceived point of view to advantage. Nor is it skill in filling in a preconceived pattern, say, one of three ways of writing an argumentative theme.

The process of composition is first of all a process of exploration. There is the essential preliminary stage of investigation and woolgathering and false starts. There is a gradual collecting of notes—mental and written, concrete and abstract, peripheral and to the point. This stage is followed by an important intermediate one: the sorting out and ordering of first impressions, the seeking out of missing information, the reviewing of evidence in order to test and confirm tentative conclusions. The final result is the statement and support not merely of an honest opinion but of a *considered* opinion. It is the formulation of judgments more balanced and responsible than we are likely to formulate in the heat of discussion.

In writing considered as a creative process, organization is not imposed from without. Instead, it becomes a matter of doing justice to the subject. The writer explores his subject in order to discover its inherent structure. He examines his assumptions in order to determine the necessary steps in his argument. Though in some ways the final outline of a composition is like the architect's blueprint for a house, it is also in important ways like the map that does justice to the terrain. If teacher and student are to take composition seriously, the teacher must believe that

> The compelling job in all teaching of language . . . is to get at truth, reality, the world as we know it and believe it to be, through words. It is the specific and special job of language teaching to establish the methods by which this can be done, and the conviction that it is worth doing.[1]

Rhetoric Old and New

The student of rhetoric explores the conditions of coherent discourse, the structure of argument, and the dynamics of persuasion. Though he pays close attention to words and sentences, he is typically concerned with their role in a larger context. While he focuses on the study of actual discourse, he aims at elucidating the intentions of the author and the probable reactions of his audience. To make a rhetorical approach to a text means to examine its structure in order to discover the purposes and strategy of the writer.

The concerns of rhetoric are central to the teaching of English at all levels, even in instruction not directly devoted to composition. Whether we teach grammar or literary theory, the student must be an articulate participant, formulating his observations and judgments in orderly and responsible fashion. Whatever our subject in a given class, we are concerned with developing the student's ability to express himself and to hold his own in discussion and debate. Nevertheless, the teaching of rhetoric requires a special kind of commitment, a special kind of perseverance. Instruction in rhetoric is less predictable, and its results more uncertain, than instruction in more tangible fields. The rhetorician must deal with the hypothetical intentions of an author, the imponderable psychological effects of style, and the complex variables of audience expectation. He must develop in his students an awareness of motives, an interest in ideas. He must develop their ability to think critically and

---

1 Louis Zahner, "What Kinds of Language Teaching?" in *Essays on the Teaching of English: Reports of the Yale Conferences on the Teaching of English*, eds. Edward J. Gordon and Edward S. Noyes (New York: Appleton-Century-Crofts, Inc., 1960), p. 14.

responsibly. All these are elusive, long-range goals. Of the various major areas within the discipline of English, rhetoric is the one least likely to satisfy teachers who

> want some core content—something to give a feeling of measurable accomplishment, and something which they can teach as information with some sense of security.[2]

Inevitably, today's emphasis in language studies on what is objective and observable will have its effect on programs in rhetoric and composition. Generally, such programs will tend to give more time to what we concretely know about language than they now do. Increasingly, there will be research into such tangible matters as linkage patterns, recurrence of synonyms, and similar aspects of the structure of prose. Linguists interested in both grammar and style will continue to develop methods for analyzing an author's "habits of structure." They will make us observe

> such matters as the density of adjectives and adverbs, the transitional devices, the distances between such pivotal words as simple subjects, main verbs, and simple objects, the type and amount of material preceding subject constructions, notional continuity in the subjects.

They will encourage us

> to discover how often an author uses inverted order, how much he relies on grammatical continuity for coherence, how he varies the density of, say, constructions built on nonfinite verb forms as he moves from one kind of expression to another, as from description to narrative, and how he varies the syntactic tempo for different tones.[3]

Such inquiries will necessarily be of interest to the rhetorician, since "anyone who writes is constantly selecting certain grammatical patterns from among those provided by his language," and since it is likely that "his ability to make felicitous selections . . . can be increased through appropriate training."[4]

What is essential, however, is that the teacher of composition be able to establish the connection between form and substance. He must make sure that his charting of concrete matters of structure is organically related to the larger questions of purpose and effect. He must treat sentence style and patterns of semantic continuity in a paragraph as merely the most concrete among the resources of disciplined expression. The student must come to see how structure and pattern *function* when our purposes and commitments are formulated and revealed through language.

In exploring such questions, teacher and student find that they can

---

[2] "Report of the Interpretation Committee," *College Composition and Communication*, XIII (October, 1962), 37–38.
[3] Sumner Ives, "Grammar and Style," *The English Journal*, LII (May, 1963), 367.
[4] *Ibid.*, p. 364.

rely much less on published theory and research than in other major areas of English. One reason is that for the aspiring young scholar the study of writing has long been synonymous with the study of imaginative literature. As a result, serious scholarly studies of the principles of rhetoric are few and little read. But another reason is that in rhetoric, even more so than in other areas of English, theory is thin and unsatisfying unless it is firmly anchored to practice. The instructive articles and books in this area are those that again and again return to the study of actual sentences and paragraphs and essays. As teachers, we should

> know rhetoric and logic, not as a set of rules or topics which we deliver to the students, but as principles which direct the strategy and structure of individual texts. . . .
> . . . if we work inductively, as we should, using a variety of samples as laboratory materials, we can develop in students a degree of capability in reading, thinking, and writing.

It is in working with examples of good prose that we develop the skill of

> recognizing at once the program statements in a text, of discovering whether it is laid out in blocks or organically developed, of discovering and following the writer's signals and knowing their implications, of discovering and testing his hypotheses and his evidence and his assumptions, of discovering his definitions or the lack of them and recognizing and testing his abstractions, of discovering his devices of persuasion and his analogies and metaphors—in general, of discovering through the ways he uses language what it is he communicates.[5]

Many teachers will look for a larger conceptual framework than that offered by such an inductive approach. Recently, there have been calls for a "new rhetoric," as for instance by Albert R. Kitzhaber in *College English:*

> We need to know a great deal more about the writing process and the teaching of writing. We need fifteen or twenty years of the same kind of intense activity by bright minds that has recently benefited the study of language and the study of literature. We need, in short, a comprehensive modern theory of discourse.[6]

However, while work in this direction progresses, we should realize that some of the apparent limitations of rhetoric may well be its basic strengths. In the teaching of writing, our premises and procedures are tested by direct contact with young minds. Our influence, if any, must overcome ingrained habits and well-developed interests and preconceptions. The public lecturer in a large hall can respond graciously to warm applause without inquiring too closely into how much of what he said

5 Gordon Wilson, "College Freshman Composition: How Can We Improve It?" *College Composition and Communication,* XII (February, 1961), 30.
6 "New Perspectives on Teaching Composition," *College English,* XXIII (March, 1962), 444.

made an impression. The teacher who reads, rather than corrects, the writing of his students is constantly reminded of how difficult it is to *teach* rather than merely to lecture, to theorize, to publish, and to grade. Some of our colleagues in other fields may be able to equate learning with the student's retaining information long enough for it to be registered by a machine scoring objective examinations. Writing is too complex, that is, too human an accomplishment to lend itself to that kind of test. By the same token, however, writing registers much more fully and permanently what impact, if any, education has had on the student.

If we employ the label *rhetoric* for the branch of English devoted to the teaching of purposeful and effective student writing, we must clear up a number of ambiguities resulting from other uses of the term. Historically, the term referred to the art of oratory, and rhetoricians concentrated on the conditions of effective public speech. If we limit the term *rhetoric* to written composition, and if we separate instruction in composition from instruction in speech, such a division is to some extent arbitrary. Much of what needs to be said about the structure of argument and about problems of intention and responsibility applies to oral and written discourse alike. Courses in oral and in written composition reinforce each other in many significant ways. If teachers of English in practice often concentrate on the *written* word, they do so because such a division of interest allows them a clearer focus on what they consider most important. Writing is typically more permanent and more deliberately structured than speech. It is more self-contained than speech, less dependent on external circumstance. As E. B. White observed after commenting on the "spoken word, which in heated moments moves great masses of people to noble or ignoble action": "The written word, unlike the spoken word, is something which every person examines privately and judges calmly by his own intellectual standards, not by what the man standing next to him thinks."[7] While courses in writing can focus on the structure of discourse, courses in speech must pay attention to numerous complicating factors, ranging from the personal impression made by the speaker to the psychology of crowds.

But even when focused on written rather than oral composition, the term *rhetoric* may remain ambiguous. Broadly concerned with the effective communication of ideas, rhetoric tends towards two extremes. The first is the *rhetoric of inquiry,* in which writer and reader share in the discovery of truth. The second is the *rhetoric of persuasion,* in which the goal of persuading one's audience justifies the means. The first is dynamic; it requires an open mind and a commitment to rational procedure. The second is static in that it is devoted to the promotion of

[7] *One Man's Meat* (New York: Harper & Row, Publishers, 1944), p. 170.

foregone conclusions. The first is disinterested and to a large extent its own reward. The second proceeds from ulterior motive to often impressive practical results. The first is rhetoric as modeled on a **dialectic** process; the second is rhetoric in its more popular and often pejorative sense:

> The method of dialectics is to confront ideas with opposing ideas in order that the pro and con of the dispute will lead to true ideas. But the dispute must not be treated as a trial of strength. It must be a means of elucidation. In a Socratic dialogue the disputants are arguing cooperatively in order to acquire more wisdom than either of them had when he began. In a sophistical argument the sophist is out to win a case, using rhetoric and not dialectic. "Both alike," says Aristotle, "are concerned with such things as come, more or less, within the general ken of all men and belong to no definite science." But while "dialectic is a process of criticism wherein lies the path to the principle of all inquiries," "rhetoric is concerned with the modes of persuasion."[8]

When the teacher of English concerns himself with the responsible communication of ideas, he is concerned with rhetoric in the first sense. He is concerned with purposeful and effective expression as practiced by someone who, in arguing with others, has not lost the ability to argue with himself.

Thus defined, rhetoric is central to a liberal education. It deals with writing as "a way of coming to know as well as a way of communicating what is known"; it starts from the premise that writing "is no less than the principal means by which the educated man tries to discover and transmit the truth about himself and about the world as he understands it."[9] Considered from this point of view, composition

> is not just a practical skill, not a mere bag of tricks, but instead an important way to order experience, to discover ideas and render them more precise, and to give them effective utterance. It is intimately related to thought itself. Considered in this light, composition is a liberal study, lying at the heart of any rounded scheme of education.[10]

The choice of an unambiguous label for the kind of writing that rhetoric investigates similarly presents some difficulty. **Expository prose** has connotations of the prosaic and dryly technical. "Essay" traditionally suggests "informal" essay and consequently informality of manner, lack of method, openness to whimsey:

> That irascible genius who won a part of his mid-eighteenth-century bread and butter both by writing essays and by compiling a dictionary, defined the essay as "a loose sally of the mind; an irregular indigested piece; not a regular and orderly composition." Dr. Johnson here apparently harked

---

8 Walter Lippmann, *The Public Philosophy* (New York: New American Library of World Literature, 1956), p. 97.
9 Harold C. Martin, *The Logic and Rhetoric of Exposition* (New York: Holt, Rinehart & Winston, Inc., 1958), p. 4.
10 Kitzhaber, *College English*, XXIII, 441.

back some forty years to Addison's opening paragraph of the 249th *Spectator:* "When I make Choice of a Subject that has not been treated on by others, I throw together my Reflections on it without any Order or Method, so that they may appear rather in the Looseness and Freedom of an Essay, than in the Regularity of a Set Discourse.[11]

Nevertheless, as used by most teachers of composition, the term *essay* has come to cover the full range of styles, from formal and systematic to informal and improvised, with emphasis more often than not on the more serious and methodical.

In subject matter and in range of interest, if not always in tone, the informal **familiar essay** is the legitimate ancestor of the kind of serious prose that the teacher of rhetoric most typically explores. Joseph Wood Krutch once deplored the tendency of magazines to give the reader a choice between the ominous treatment of current crises and desperately trivial amusement. He deplored the relative scarcity of "non-fiction which is to some extent personal and reflective as opposed to the factual and bleakly expository" and said

> the familiar essay affords what is probably the best method of discussing those subjects which are neither obviously momentous nor merely silly. And since no really good life is composed exclusively of problems and farce either the reading of most people today does not actually concern itself with some of the most important aspects of their lives or those lives are impoverished to a degree which the members of any really civilized society would find it difficult to understand.[12]

"Non-fiction to some extent personal and reflective" and concerning itself with "some of the most important aspects" of our lives may well serve us as a preliminary description of the subject matter rhetoric investigates. The essay, as the most typical representative of this kind of prose, is

> personal not because it is necessarily *about* the self, but because it is an expression of the self thinking. The beauty of the form is that it allows the writer, as himself, the freedom to discover and to develop his individual statement on things. This is the freedom to find out what one really wants to say and *has* to say. In a novel or play, even in a "personal" and lyric poem, an imagined individual speaks; but it is in the name that is signed to an essay, the name of the author himself, that the essayist speaks. He starts from the fact that is himself, and there is nothing that he can say about himself that is more personal than what he thinks.[13]

The study of such self-expression cannot be reduced to the scope of a rigorously limited specialty. The humane use of language is the most

[11] Charles B. Shaw, ed., *American Essays* (New York: The New American Library of World Literature, Inc., 1955), p. ix.
[12] "No Essays—Please!" in *Saturday Review Reader* (New York: Bantam Books, Inc., 1951), pp. 151–52.
[13] Alfred Kazin, *The Open Form: Essays for Our Time* (New York: Harcourt, Brace & World, Inc., 1961), p. x.

necessarily general of academic subjects. In the words of William Stein-hoff, "writing and reading are closely associated with ideas, attitudes, values, persons, with thinking and feeling—in short, with being a human being."[14] Even so, within the discipline of English the opposition of expert and generalist is to some extent a false dilemma. Our choice is not be-tween narrow specialization and taking all knowledge for our province. An expert must be knowledgeable about fields beyond his immediate professional competence. Even the most ardent generalist tends to return to the topics that his experience equips him to discuss with confidence and authority. The choice for the composition teacher is not whether to be an expert on grammar and usage or an amateurish popularizer of psychoanalysis, sociology, and nuclear physics. The choice is whether to interpret his responsibility as an expert on language in a narrowly technical or a broadly humane way. As Aldous Huxley says,

> A great deal of attention has been paid . . . to the technical languages in which men of science do their specialized thinking, particularly, of course, to mathematics. But the colloquial usages of everyday speech, the literary and philosophical dialects in which men do their thinking about the problems of morals, politics, religion and psychology—these have been strangely neglected.[15]

Serious expository prose is one of the dialects in which we do our thinking about our role as human beings. It cannot be studied and taught as information. It must be studied and taught by a person open to experience, sensitive to the personal and emotional dimensions of life.

Rhetoric, then, is a major branch of the discipline of English, central to its contribution to the student's general education. It borders on the one side on those branches of applied linguistics that go up to but not beyond the sentence, and on the other side on the study of imaginative literature. Ideally, the teacher will be competent both in applied linguistics and in literature, to prevent the kind of lopsidedness that re-sults when either the linguistic or the imaginative elements in rhetoric are treated out of context. Rhetoric concerns itself with purposeful, effective, and responsible expository or nonfiction prose. The specialist in this area is someone who gives concentrated attention and a major share of his time to the study and practice of effective writing.

The Materials of Rhetoric

The first business of instruction in rhetoric is to expose the student to the written word. By and large, the effective writer is the one who has first been a voracious reader. Alfred Kazin says,

14 "Some Remarks on the Future of the Required Course in Freshman Composi-tion," *College Composition and Communication,* XII (February, 1961), 24.
15 "Words and Their Meanings," in *The Importance of Language,* ed. Max Black (Englewood Cliffs, N.J.: Prentice-Hall, Inc., 1962), p. 1.

I read walking in the street, to and from the Children's Library on Stone Avenue; on the fire escape and the roof; at every meal when they would let me; read even when I dressed in the morning, propping my book up against the drawers of the bureau as I pulled on my long black stockings.[16]

W. Somerset Maugham says,

I read everything that came my way. My curiosity was such that I was as willing to read a history of Peru or the reminiscences of a cowboy as a treatise on Provençal poetry or the *Confessions* of St. Augustine. . . . I made lists of what I read and one of these lists by some accident I still have. It is my reading for two months and, but that I made it only for myself, I could not believe that it was veracious. It shows that I read three of Shakespeare's plays, two volumes of Mommsen's *History of Rome*, a large part of Lanson's *Littérature Française*, two or three novels, some of the French classics, a couple of scientific works and a play of Ibsen's. . . . During the time I was at St. Thomas's Hospital I went systematically through English, French, Italian and Latin literature. I read a lot of history, a little philosophy and a good deal of science. My curiosity was too great to allow me to give much time to reflect upon what I read; I could hardly wait to finish one book, so eager was I to begin another.[17]

Many a successful writer has shared the experience of H. L. Mencken, who says, after an account of boyhood reading ranging from Chambers' *Encyclopedia* through Tennyson's poems to scientific papers by Herbert Spencer: "I read them all, sometimes with shivers of puzzlement and sometimes with delight, but always calling for more. . . . to this day I am still what might be called a reader, and have a high regard for authors."[18] If the student cannot develop the reading habit, much of what his English teachers tell him will fail to carry conviction. If instruction in rhetoric is to bear fruit, the student must see the strategies and devices of good prose at work in a wide variety of reading, assigned and unassigned.

In the reading program designed for the student of writing, the writing of the expert as expert plays a respectable but minor role. His presentation of factual material and systematic analysis of relationships provide the model for **technical writing** ranging from the theme on "How My Refrigerator Works" to the research paper on the variations of sentence structure in Jonathan Swift's prose. Students must learn to respect the expert's regard for facts, and his ability to distinguish them from inference and hearsay. They must learn to emulate his patience when confronted with knotty problems of classification, his skill in marshaling complex materials.

[16] *A Walker in the City* (New York: Harcourt, Brace & World, Inc., 1951), p. 22–23.
[17] *The Summing Up* (New York: Doubleday & Company, Inc., 1938), p. 88–89.
[18] *Happy Days, 1800–1892* (New York: Alfred A. Knopf, Inc., 1940), p. 175.

At the same time, the teacher knows how often the expert's writing about his own field remains uncommunicative. The expert's writing *outside* his own field may become naive polemics. The teacher of rhetoric therefore distinguishes between the expert, who may or may not communicate, and the writer who is a writer first and a specialist, if at all, second. Thus, in philosophy, William James seems more relevant to the concerns of rhetoric than John Dewey. In politics, George Orwell is more of a writer than Richard Nixon.

It is therefore not the function of a reading program for rhetoric to provide a representative sampling of materials from various academic specialties. Rather, it assembles readings of high quality and great significance that the various academic specialties tend to leave unclaimed. Though teachers of composition disagree on theory and method, they tend to agree remarkably on what is first-rate prose of general significance. We agree that a senior in high school or a freshman in college would do well to read books like Thoreau's *Walden,* Loren Eiseley's *The Immense Journey,* or James Baldwin's *Notes of a Native Son.* The essential common element in this kind of nonfiction prose is the one that Thomas De Quincey identified as the one essential element in *all* literature—"some relation to a general and common interest of man."

The source of such writing, and the source of its authority, is the author's observation and experience and reading. As James Baldwin says, "One writes out of one thing only—one's own experience. Everything depends on how relentlessly one forces from this experience the last drop, sweet or bitter, it can possibly give."[19] Such writing is personal because all forceful and purposeful and authentic writing is ultimately the expression of someone's personality. Authentic style is not an external manner adopted to suit a particular publisher or audience. It is a clue to the quality of a writer's mind. This point of view rules out all synthetic prose. It rules out the anonymous and uncommitted "writing up" of materials gathered by a "researcher" who is part of a staff operating according to formula rather than according to conviction.

Just as the source of authentic writing is ultimately the experience of the author, so its validity lies in its appeal to the experience of the reader. As Joseph Wood Krutch said about humane letters in general, what makes such writing effective is the "shock of recognition." For the writer as for the artist,

> there is no objective test for the truth or falsity of his assumptions. For his success or failure he depends upon one thing only—the extent to which he can carry conviction, and he convinces just to the extent that our own experience confirms his.[20]

[19] *Notes of a Native Son* (Boston: The Beacon Press, 1957), p. 7.
[20] "If You Don't Mind My Saying So." *The American Scholar,* XXXI (Autumn, 1962), 518.

Such writing may move on the level of elementary but authentic observation; it may move on a high level of abstraction and sophistication. What matters is that it should engage our attention as readers concerned with the scene of which we find ourselves a part, the relationships between ourselves and others, and the purposes that give our lives shape and direction.

Certain writers, certain subjects are exceptionally well suited to furnish materials for the study of rhetoric. A competent writer is first of all a competent observer. He has kept alive powers of **observation** too often blunted by habit and routine. He knows how to do justice to the concreteness, the sensory texture of life. The teacher of rhetoric is not an enemy of abstraction, but he is an enemy of *premature* abstraction. He is wary of abstraction cut loose from its moorings. He will typically look for authors whose abstractions are rooted in full and accurate first-hand observation.

One rich source of such writing is the work of authors who show a spontaneous interest and satisfaction in exploring our natural environment. The student can see his own partial and inarticulate perception of the natural world deepened and made eloquent and explicit in the work of nature writers from Henry Thoreau and John Burroughs to Loren Eiseley and Joseph Wood Krutch. Such writing may remain as graphically descriptive as Rachel Carson's *The Sea Around Us,* well within the reach of the capable high school junior. It may become as philosophical as some of the essays by Mr. Krutch, more appropriate fare for the sophomore in college. Such writers have the patience of the receptive observer, a more essential condition of substantial writing than a life crowded with incident. They have an eye for the significant detail—the characteristic, meaningful part that helps us visualize the whole. They have the gift of expressive language, of finding the word that graphically projects their impressions and emotions. They have the lively sense of wonder that makes us conscious of what before we merely took for granted.

When the student compares the work of such naturalists with the treatment of nature in the natural sciences, he learns something essential about the difference between knowledge that is abstract and operational and knowledge that is, in Keats' phrase, "proved upon our pulses." The writer's knowledge remains three-dimensional: it sharpens our sensory perceptions; it makes us more than usually responsive to nature's sights and sounds. It involves our feelings; it appeals to our capacity for sympathy, and fear, and awe. It appeals to our understanding; it discovers in an experience the characteristic pattern, the clue to its human significance.

Equally instructive for the student, because equally close to what he can compare with his own experience and observation, is the work of writers who write about the urbanized, mechanized scene that is the setting of most of our lives. The attention-reviving, thought-provoking quality of such writing is best illustrated by selections that take an entirely new look at something familiar, that assume a naive, unspoiled perspective. Such a perspective may be pretended, as in Montesquieu's *Lettres Persanes* or Goldsmith's *Citizen of the World,* or real, as in impressions of American life recorded by an Englishman like Alistair Cooke, a South African like Dan Jacobson, or a Frenchman like Jean-Paul Sartre. The writer who sees a new environment for the first time may notice what is significant or characteristic yet is overlooked by the person who takes it for granted. At the same time, such writing dramatically confronts the student with questions of accuracy and responsibility. While the comments of the outside observer may be fresh and provocative, they may also strike us as superficial and one-sided. We then come face to face with the central role that **selection** plays in all attempts to record and interpret what we observe. We begin to define standards of objectivity and fairness. We become aware of the role of preconceptions and stereotypes, of latent sympathies and dislikes.

For similar reasons, autobiography lends itself exceptionally well to study in a rhetoric program. Ordinary experience is miscellaneous, one-thing-after-another. In the study of autobiography, the student learns something essential about how writing not merely records but *organizes* experience. He sees how mere sequence is transformed into **structure.** He sees how the essential is distinguished from the peripheral, the meaningful from the trivial. The effective autobiographical writer does not merely present the passive record of nostalgic memory. He is looking in his experience for its characteristic pattern, for the clues to what he is or hopes to become.

By the same token, the study of autobiographical writing counteracts the student's tendency to fall back on the stereotyped and secondhand. Writing concerned with personal experience broadens our sympathies and helps correct the limitations of a self-satisfied or provincial outlook. It can convince us of the inadequacy of the categories we often use when we label and judge other people. It can demonstrate the thinness of psychological and sociological abstractions when not tested against three-dimensional human experience. Writing that explores this territory contrasts with the issue- and problem-mongering of much popular journalism. As Alfred Kazin says about James Baldwin's title essay in *Notes of a Native Son,*

> This is not an essay on "the Negro problem," but a report of what it means to be James Baldwin. The power and brilliance of this essay come from Baldwin's ability to confront his own experience, to make us see the incidents, associations, loyalties, anguish, doubts, of a life like James Baldwin's. "Notes of a Native Son" should encourage the student to see his own and perhaps vastly different experience *as* an experience; it should

help to break up the generalities and abstractions, the empty repetitions and the resounding slogans that are constantly offered to us as "reality" by the newspapers, television, movies and advertising.[21]

To deal meaningfully with abstractions, the student writer must be able to relate them to his own observation and experience. Here lies the difficulty in leading him from the more personal to the more general topics that are his concern as a citizen and educated human being. There is something self-defeating about the essay topic that forces the student into halfhearted generalizations about issues on which he has little information and no convictions. The teacher will therefore look for readings that help the student become aware of the more general implications of his own relations to his society and his culture. Such readings may lead him to take stock of his many years as a participant, however reluctant, in the educational process. They may lead him to formulate some of his thinking about the terms on which he and others live together in civilized society. They may confront him with some of the ethical and philosophical questions on which he must begin to make up his mind.

It is only in materials realistically related to his own perspective and sense of the world that the student can study the workings of logic—not as a self-contained discipline but as a means of co-ordinating and interpreting experience. He learns to judge the author's justification in taking the inductive leap—from a thin sampling of slanted evidence to a vast generalization, or from a solid array of relevant detail to cautious inference. He learns to formulate the implied assumptions that help an author proceed toward apparently unmotivated conclusions. He learns to distinguish reiteration, designed to hammer home a crudely oversimplified message, from the kind of systematic discussion that patiently examines arguments for and against, carefully refutes objections. The author's avoidance of common kinds of short-cut thinking—the either-or approach, the *post hoc* fallacy—becomes a measure of his respect for the truth and for the reader.

Even at an advanced level, much writing otherwise to the point will prove too complex or too sophisticated for our purposes. The teacher of rhetoric is forever hunting for writers who can make serious matters intelligible to adolescent minds. There are educators like Jacques Barzun and Robert M. Hutchins, who talk not about education but about schools and teaching and students. Among writers on political questions, authors like Walter Lippmann and George Orwell can make politics appear a personal responsibility. Among philosophers, authors like William James and Bertrand Russell know how to make the abstract concrete. The basic criterion for the inclusion of an author in a reading

21 Kazin, *The Open Form*, p. ix.

program for rhetoric in his ability to make a serious subject come to life.

There are of course strong arguments for choosing readings with emphasis on the topical on the one hand and the student's interests on the other. Computers, jet planes, sputniks, spacecraft going to the moon— such subjects provide, for a time, the interest of novelty and at the same time appeal to the technical interests of our students. Essays—casually chatty or ponderously sociological—on dating and football pay flattering attention to the immediate concerns of the student reader. Such reading offers welcome help to the teacher confronted with lethargy or hostility. When carefully selected and restricted, it can help him lead his charges from the extracurricular to the curricular without pain.

In the long run, nevertheless, readings selected for their immediate appeal work against the teacher rather than for him. They feed the student's prejudice that English as such is not of interest, that it needs to be boosted by extraneous appeals and ulterior motives. This is the opposite of the impression that, from the first day of class, the English teacher should strive to create. Rather than dwell on his own current excitements and discomforts, the student must learn to broaden his view of himself and of the world around him. The interest and excitement offered by the discipline of English is, to use Arthur Miller's phrase, the fascination of the "truly written word." In trying to make his students share this fascination, the teacher must guard against blurring the focus of his course by yielding to peripheral attractions.

The borderline between what is of general and permanent significance and what is not may not always be obvious, but it is not impossible to draw. The details of recent technological advances are not the English teacher's concern, but their impact on our way of life may become the theme of an article or a book that *is*. The scientific work of scientists belongs in science courses, but teachers of English follow the scientist attentively when he writes about his motives, his struggle for recognition, the vicissitudes of inspiration, the problems of validity and verification, the relation between science and ethics and politics. Civil War strategy belongs in a history class, but personal experience of war and an attempt to comprehend it as a moral disaster and a challenge to civilized ideals makes for accounts like those of Robert Graves in *Goodbye to All That* and George Orwell in *Homage to Catalonia*.

Obviously, the teacher of rhetoric will be strongly attracted to authors who, in addition to being first-rate writers, show a thoughtful awareness of problems of language and of the conditions of their craft. Somerset Maugham in *The Summing Up* and Joseph Wood Krutch in many of his essays and columns wrestle with what it means to be a writer. Shaw and Mencken have shrewd things to say about the relation between writing and intelligence and conviction. Obviously, the teacher of composition will welcome examples of good prose by a writer who both elucidates his practice and practices what he preaches. However, this is a quite different thing from devoting work in composition exclusively, or even largely, to language about language and writing about writing. When most of his reading is drawn from what other writers have said about writing, the student is twice removed from writing as a means of actively interpreting and ordering experience.

In recent years, numerous readers for the college course in composition have assembled essays on language written not primarily by writers but by linguists, anthropologists, historians. Often such collections concentrate on grammar, usage, lexicography, or the history of the language, with merely a nod in the direction of semantics and style. Even when such books are better balanced and thus more likely to fulfill their promise of giving the student "real insight into the workings of language," they fail to provide the "good writing in a variety of styles and on a variety of topics" that the teacher needs if he is to demonstrate the workings of first-rate prose of general interest.[22]

A review of subjects suitable for the study of significant prose should not suggest undue preoccupation with the *what* rather than the *how* of what a writer says. A persistent criticism of instruction in rhetoric has been that teachers tend to become absorbed in the subject matter of an essay, rather than in what the author *does* with the subject matter. It is important that the teacher should in this respect strike the right balance. The divorce of content from form is as undesirable in rhetoric as it is in literary criticism.

Rhetoric is concerned not with ideas and attitudes but with ideas and attitudes as revealed through language. Conversely, a discussion of descriptive writing can no more treat structure and form without reference to what is being described than a literature course can treat Romantic nature poetry without reference to nature:

> Teachers of writing concern themselves not with "subject matter" but with subject matter as organized, interpreted, evaluated by the first-rate writer. They deal not with "issues" but with issues as reflected in the personal commitments of a perceptive and responsible observer.[23]

As Alfred Kazin says, "it is not the 'subject' that counts with us, for this subject might have been arrived at by anyone—it is the subject as arrived at by the writer, as it has grown in his thought, as it has been done justice to by himself alone."[24]

Even the most incompletely rationalized composition program can provide the setting for the crucial contact between the accomplished

[22] Wallace L. Anderson and Norman C. Stageberg, eds., *Introductory Readings on Language* (New York: Holt, Rinehart & Winston, Inc., 1962), pp. v–vi.

[23] Hans P. Guth, *Essay* (Belmont, Calif.: Wadsworth Publishing Company, Inc., 1962), p. iii.

[24] Kazin, *The Open Form*, p. xi.

writer and the student reader. It is sometimes said that a feeling for style, critical thinking, and sensitivity to values cannot be taught, that they are "catching." This would seem to be an excellent argument for exposing the student to the work of writers who are known to be carriers of infection. The teaching of writing at its least methodical can work with what the student derives from substantial and significant reading. When the teacher takes the demand for concrete subject matter too literally, he is often in the position of asking the students for good writing without ever having shown them any. His first task in a composition program is to convince the student that good writing exists—and that it matters.

Criteria of Good Writing

Once the instructor has appropriate materials to work with, he can proceed to work out some of the criteria that *make for* forceful and significant prose. These criteria need not be announced at the beginning, nor should the student be required to pay them lip service. What matters is that they be implied in what happens in the classroom, that they be reiterated in various guises in the discussion of actual writing, whether the student's or the author's in an anthology.

An obvious but often slighted preliminary requirement is **fluency**. This requirement does not imply a marvelous substitution of ease for the more usual toil of composition. It merely reminds us that the effective writer is typically one who has done much previous writing. The student must cease to regard writing as a special task, to be accomplished only with the most strenuous contortions. The teacher will encourage anything that promotes the students' familiarity with composition. He will institute free writing in student journals, to be sampled but not systematically criticized and graded by the instructor. He will urge copious note-taking in all the student's courses. He will use what influence he has with colleagues in other areas to fight the substitution of objective tests for written work as subacademic and antieducational. He will encourage the student to formulate, while walking along or taking a shower, sentences and paragraphs to be put down on paper before prolonged staring at a blank sheet produces mental paralysis.

Moving on from the prerequisites, we can formulate some more specific criteria. The first such criterion is that good writing carries **conviction**. This requirement may sound too vaguely inspirational to be relevant on the first Monday of a new course. However, it is basic to even elementary progress and can be concretely applied to every piece of prose the student produces. Even on the most elementary level, and in the most poorly prepared class, the instructor can establish that whatever good writing is, it is *not* the docile repetition of a few thin generalities about the American way of life. The student's writing must be something that he himself is willing to stand up for, something to which in some way he is personally committed. Conviction is slighted in the subject-matter course that teaches the student to work with information whose origins and implications he must not question. It is equally slighted when a course centered on style teaches the student to weave second-hand opinions and thirdhand facts into a graceful pattern. The student must learn that writing means recording one's own observations, pinning down one's own reactions, interpreting one's own experience, formulating one's own judgments, questioning one's own premises, and making one's own mistakes. No one can write intelligibly, let alone responsibly, "unless he lets his own mind do the writing."[25]

A second criterion of good writing is **concreteness.** The natural instinct of the first-rate writer is to anchor what he says to concrete reference. Similarly, the search of the philosophically or semantically trained for specific reference in definition gives substance to otherwise largely verbal controversies. The ability to translate abstract idea into vivid image makes writing graspable, intelligible, and readable. It is this feature of good writing that the instructor can most graphically illustrate by reference to models, that is, simply, to first-rate prose. It is this feature that the instructor, as editor, can most persistently encourage in the work of the student as writer. In the average class, the phrases most frequently needed in the teacher's marginal commentary on the students' writing are "develop," "give an example," "illustrate," "be specific," "evidence?" "who said?" and "say when and where."

A third crucial quality of good writing is that it has **focus,** or coherence. It is true that many of our students need to learn first of all to write with some degree of spontaneity and conviction. We have to be wise enough to realize, with Holden Caulfield, that it is often the "relevant" comment that is faked or perfunctory and the "digression" that is revealing and worth reading. But at some stage every writer must learn to follow up one point at a time. By encouraging sustained and focused discussion, the teacher counteracts the student's tendency toward hasty sampling, superficial induction, one-sided or slanted evidence, and logical *non sequiturs.* The student must learn that a point important enough to be made is important enough to be supported. Though the average student theme is necessarily too short and tentative to do full justice to a topic, the student can begin to become aware of the skimpiness of the two-sentence paragraph and the one-sentence judgment. He can begin to see why a varied display of opinionated comment may entertain or even impress but fail to produce conviction. In his own writing, he can begin to develop the habit of making clear where he stands and backing up what he has to say.

25 Valborg Anderson, "My Students Wear a Mask," *The Atlantic,* June, 1961, p. 68.

A fourth quality of good writing that the teacher of rhetoric works on from the very beginning of a course is **expressiveness,** that is, resourcefulness and flexibility of idiom. A writer must be able to express himself—if possible aptly and precisely and vigorously. He needs a feeling for words. He must be in control of the resources of language and take pleasure in their richness and variety. He must develop a love and respect for language that is the result neither of following arbitrary rules nor of studying usage statistics. By alerting the student to distinctions and implications and overtones, the instructor can train the student's eye and ear. A writer of contemporary American prose is the poorer for not having explored the inflammatory rhetoric of Thomas Paine, the satirical marksmanship of Samuel Clemens, the wistful ironies of James Thurber. No one can be a forceful writer unless language means something more to him than a prosaic vehicle for communication.

Finally, good writing involves **responsibility.** In developing the student's ability to express himself, it is not our aim to make him follow wherever his preconceptions and indignations will lead. It is not our aim to have him give eloquent expression to unexamined preferences and dislikes. The first obligation of a writer is not to his reader but to his own standards of fairness and of truth. He must learn to resist the tendency to favor evidence that supports a familiar thesis. He must guard against proving uncritically receptive to observations that can be made to fit a favorable pattern. He must resist the inclination to discredit unwelcome arguments by exploiting irrelevant associations or appealing to extraneous motives. In this as in other respects, the writer least vulnerable to hostile criticism is the one who has learned to be his own critic.

The Structure of Prose

In teaching effective and responsible writing, the rhetorician draws on material from several closely related fields. He will need to work out a coherent rationale of usage, reinforced by detailed study and exploration. He will spend part of his time on word study, ranging from etymology and the study of synonyms to the kind of semantics focused on verbal resources, on levels and kinds of meaning. Specifically, however, he will explore the structure of discourse, the dynamics of persuasion, and the resources of style. He will concern himself with the *logic of rhetoric,* that is, the kind of logic at work in the selection, interpretation, and organization of the writer's materials. He will study the *strategy of rhetoric,* the requirements for securing the reader's attention and consent. He will investigate the elements of *prose style,* paying attention to such matters as clarity, emphasis, balance, effective use of figurative language.

The structure of discourse and the resources of style can be treated in the most concrete, down-to-earth fashion, satisfying the perennial demand for specific "things to teach." They can be dealt with on various levels of complexity and sophistication. On the most elementary level, rhetorical devices can easily seem artificial. One may well grant, for instance, that no one will produce immortal prose by filling in paragraphs starting with a predetermined topic sentence. However, in much powerful writing key phrases and **key sentences** paraphrase and echo a major theme. Often a crucial sentence sums up a key point. The student who traces in a well-organized essay the network of **synonyms** and near-synonyms that keep pointing to the topic at hand learns something important about the difference between rambling and structured prose. The student who notices the key sentence that holds a crucial paragraph together is learning how to read.

Obviously, the teacher will guard against having his students approach every piece of prose as something to be marked up and diagrammed and charted. Rather, he will watch out for passages that lend themselves to exceptionally graphic demonstration of the features that make for coherence, for well-planned, systematic forward movement. Notice how in the following excerpt each paragraph begins with a topic sentence that clearly maps out the point to be developed, illustrated, supported. The repetition of key terms like *work, toil,* or *labor* identifies each paragraph as a subsection of the discussion that starts with the initial question and with the thesis sentence, about the American habit of work, that provides its answer:

> What elements of the national character are attributable to this long-time agrarian environment? First and foremost is *the habit of work.* For the colonial farmer ceaseless striving constituted the price of survival. . . .
>
> The *tradition of toil* so begun found new sustenance as settlers opened up the boundless stretches of the interior. "In the free States," wrote Harriet Martineau in 1837, *"labour* is more really and heartily honoured. . . ."
>
> One source of Northern antagonism to the system of human bondage was the fear that it was jeopardizing this basic tenet of the American creed. "Wherever *labor* is mainly performed by slaves," Daniel Webster told the United States Senate, "it is regarded as. . . ."
>
> Probably no legacy from our farmer forebears has entered more deeply into the national psychology. If an American has no *purposeful work* on hand. . . .
>
> This *worship of work* has made it difficult for Americans to learn how to play. As Poor Richard saw it, "Leisure is. . . ."
>
> The first mitigations of the daily grind took the form of hunting, fishing, barn-raisings and logrollings—*activities that* had no social stigma because they *contributed to the basic needs of living.* . . .

The importance attached to *useful work* had the further effect of helping to make "this new man" indifferent to aesthetic considerations. . . .[26]

The internal structure of individual paragraphs may be demonstrated in similar ways. When systematically catalogued, the rhetorician's blueprints for successful paragraphs may easily seem too restrictive. They may make us feel that no actual living paragraph ever behaves the way composition teachers say it should. But if we examine in a national magazine an article by a truly effective writer, we will again and again find familiar basic patterns like the following:

1) Topic sentence substantiated by examples:

> In the long catalogue of human folly *an endless series of propositions which afterwards turned out to be false have been thought so indubitable as to justify persecution of skeptics.* Witchcraft, sorcery, black magic, though wicked, were firmly believed to be practised; innumerable victims died in agony because they were supposed guilty of these sins. A Spanish lady was tortured on the rack because she put on clean underclothes on Saturday and said that pork gave her indigestion, which caused the Inquisition to suspect her of being a Jewess. . . .

2) Topic sentence followed by elaboration and detailed application:

> *Power is sweet; it is a drug, the desire for which increases with habit.* Those who have seized power, even for the noblest of motives, soon persuade themselves that there are good reasons for not relinquishing it. This is particularly likely to happen if they believe themselves to represent some immensely important cause. They will feel that their opponents are ignorant and perverse; before long they will come to hate them. What right have these wretches to oppose the coming of the millennium? If they have to be persecuted, no doubt that is regrettable, but, after all, you can't make an omelette without breaking eggs. . . .

3) Topic sentence developed by chronological account:

> *During the dark days of the First World War the Russian Revolution seemed like a sudden golden dawn in the East.* The British alliance with Czarist tyranny since 1907 had oppressed the hearts of all humane and progressive people in the West; now at last it seemed that the immense weight of Russia was to be thrown in favor of the thing that we desired. The blind and mendacious hatred that reactionaries displayed towards the Soviet regime made it easy to regard all criticism as mere propaganda. When I decided, in 1920, that the aims and methods of the Soviet Government were abhorrent to me almost all my friends of the Left were horrified and condemned me as a renegade. Gradually, with the years, the number of those who have recanted has increased.[27]

The teacher of rhetoric cannot be content with taking inventory of such patterns and relationships; he must show them at work in co-

---

[26] Arthur M. Schlesinger, *Paths to the Present* (New York: The Macmillan Company, 1949), pp. 7–10.
[27] Bertrand Russell, "Came the Revolution . . .", in *Saturday Review Reader*, pp. 125–29.

herent and significant prose. Writers vary greatly in the degree to which their work clearly exhibits, or elegantly disguises, its structural skeleton. The more sophisticated the writer, the more likely his work is to show a complex interplay of various kinds of structural and stylistic pattern. For the purposes of instruction, on the other hand, the teacher is likely to look for examples of prose that show a given structural or stylistic feature in a relatively pure form.

For instance, the student of rhetoric can learn much from nineteenth-century essayists like Macaulay, Ruskin, Arnold, or T. H. Huxley. These writers shared Bernard Shaw's assumption that "effectiveness of assertion" is the final test of style:

> For Macaulay, the "first law of writing, the law to which all other laws are subordinate, is this, that the words employed shall be such as convey to the reader the meaning of the writer." The written page, says Newman, is "the lucid mirror" of its author's "mind and life"; and on it he tries "to give forth what he has within him; and from his earnestness it comes to pass that, whatever be the splendour of his diction or the harmony of his periods, he has with him the charm of an incommunicable simplicity. Whatever be his subject, high or low, he treats it suitably and for its own sake." Arnold is more abrupt: "Have something to say, and say it as clearly as you can. That is the only secret of style."[28]

Making no fetish of profundity or sophistication, these writers aimed at the effective communication of ideas of some consequence to an educated audience. As a result, their writings continue to be instructive models of substantial and effective prose. Their very mannerisms, such as Macaulay's antitheses or Arnold's insistent repetition of key ideas, illustrate for the student basic rhetorical devices.

What distinguishes these nineteenth-century writers is their deliberateness in constructing an argument, their competence in marshaling relevant material. Notice the typically systematic presentation of major points and refutation of objections that is mirrored in the **transitional phrases** of one of Ruskin's lectures:

> *And now I pass to* the arts with which I have special concern, in which, though the facts are exactly the same . . .
>
> *And, first,* they are a perfect exponent of the mind of the workman . . .
>
> *It is, of course, true that* many of the strong masters had deep faults of character . . .
>
> *It is true, however, also* . . . *that* the strong masters fall into two great divisions . . .
>
> *Finally, you must remember that* great obscurity has been brought upon the truth in this matter by . . .
>
> *Let me assure you once for all, that* . . .

28 William E. Buckler, ed., *Prose of the Victorian Period* (Boston: Houghton Mifflin Company, 1958), p. xiv.

I pass to the second, and for us the more practically important question . . .

Respecting which phenomena, observe first, that . . .

Secondly, the virtues of the inhabitants of many . . .

But you will observe also that *absolute* artlessness, to men in any kind of moral health . . .

Again, I need not repeat . . .

But the truly great nations nearly always begin . . .

It is true that mere **enumeration**, moving systematically from "in the first place" to "fourthly and lastly," is the most mechanical of transitional devices. And yet it effectively demonstrates to the student the need for subdividing a process into its major steps, for reducing a confused debate to order by identifying the major arguments. Even writing that proceeds by simple enumeration helps the teacher make the point that competent exposition requires two basic skills: resourcefulness in gathering relevant materials, and competence in sorting them out.

Many of Matthew Arnold's essays illustrate the processes of **classification and division.** They illustrate the process of examining relations and establishing connections between the ideas thus isolated and classified. In the first few paragraphs of "Sweetness and Light," Arnold with characteristic deliberateness identifies three possible motives of culture:

(The first possible motive of culture—exclusiveness—is identified and rejected.)

The disparagers of culture make its motive curiosity; sometimes, indeed, they make its motive mere exclusiveness and vanity. . . . No serious man would call this *culture,* or attach any value to it, as culture, at all. To find the real ground for the very different estimate which serious people will set upon culture, we must find some motive for culture in the terms of which may lie a real ambiguity; and such a motive the word *curiosity* gives us.

(The second possible motive—curiosity—is identified and the ambiguity of the term examined.)

I have before now pointed out that we English do not, like the foreigners, use this word in a good sense as well as in a bad sense. With us the word is always used in a somewhat disapproving sense. A liberal and intelligent eagerness about the things of the mind may be meant by a foreigner when he speaks of curiosity, . . . Montesquieu says: "The first motive which ought to impel us to study is the desire to augment the excellence of our nature, and to render an intelligent being yet more intelligent." This is the true ground to assign for the genuine scientific passion, however manifested, and for culture, viewed simply as a fruit of this passion; and

(The third possible motive—humanitarian impulse—is presented as an alternative.)

(A comprehensive definition of culture is derived from a synthesis of the second and third alternatives.)

it is a worthy ground, even though we let the term *curiosity* stand to describe it.

But there is of culture another view, in which not solely the scientific passion, the sheer desire to things as they are, natural and proper in an intelligent being, appears as the ground of it. There is a view in which all the love of our neighbor, the impulses towards action, help, and beneficence . . . come in as parts of the grounds of culture, and the main and preeminent part. Culture is then properly described not as having its origin in curiosity, but as having its origin in the love of perfection; it is *a study of perfection.* . . .

Only, whereas the passion for doing good is apt to be over-hasty in determining what reason and the will of God say, because its turn is for acting rather than thinking and it wants to be beginning to act . . . what distinguishes culture is that it is possessed by the scientific passion as well as by the passion of doing good; that it demands worthy notions of reason and the will of God, and does not readily suffer its own crude conceptions to substitute themselves for them.

One need not go far in the analysis of cogently developed prose to show that what makes such an essay move are basic logical processes. At the same time, *an effective pattern of organization is not applied from the outside but seems inherent in the material.* It seems to organize the material by discovering its internal relations. Thus, an essay pleading the cause of pure research may start from identifying

1) the basic *motive* of the true scientist as disinterested curiosity, proceed to describing

2) the typical *method* of science as the cumulative development of knowledge through the efforts of many investigators, and conclude by pointing to

3) possible *applications* of scientific findings to welfare or warfare.

When we say that a student has not learned to think, we mean that he lacks experience in working out relationships from cause to effect, from specific instances to a general pattern and from a general principle to specific instances. We mean that he has not learned to sort out doubts and objections according to their degree of seriousness, and to marshal the evidence that will modify or refute them. He lacks competence in the basic processes of classifying, examining for relevance, establishing connections, and drawing conclusions that go into the writing of cogently organized expository prose.

Study of the logical structure of discourse, rather than being an optional pursuit for instructors with a strong logical bent, is thus an elementary requirement in any study of rhetoric. Students are often told to state and develop a key idea, whether in a paragraph or in a theme. This is an empty, if not harmful requirement if it does not imply attention to the observing and thinking out that *lead up* to the stating of an idea. The student who "has nothing to say" is often the one whose experience and reading have been woefully limited. But just as often he is the one who is slow to compare, distinguish, establish connections, generalize.

Some patterns of organization mirror the processes of observation and thought that lead to the formulation of ideas worthy of the name. Such is the **inductive** pattern that through a detailed inspection of relevant observations leads the reader towards answers to questions of a more general kind. Thus, an essay on the characteristic quality of American life may examine a number of things acknowledged to be typically American and attempt to determine their common quality. Other patterns are **deductive:** the "Socratic" pattern modifies and elaborates initial assumptions in the light of possible objections and difficulties. It formulates a final point of view through the successive examination of questions and complications. The "Hegelian" pattern more dramatically than the Socratic method confronts two major opposed ideas and leads the reader from thesis to antithesis to synthesis:

I. *Thesis:* Modern industrial society makes for unprecedented interdependence among its citizens.

II. *Antithesis:* However, such interdependence is an essential condition of mass production and mass consumption.

III. *Synthesis:* Interdependence is the price modern society pays for its high standard of living.

Writing so organized has a persuasive effect on the thoughtful reader because it allows him to participate in the process of inquiry. Such a reader is likely to suspect ideas presented too abruptly and unconditionally as the only possible answers.

On the other hand, not even such inductive or deductive patterns of organization *directly* reflect logical processes. They rather represent these processes in a refined, ideal state. In the course of writing and revision, false starts and tentative conclusions have been eliminated. The evidence has been sifted, with some of it first tentatively admitted but then excluded as not really relevant or not telling enough. The paper that defends an **initial thesis,** though simpler in appearance, actually represents a more advanced stage of the same process of sifting and rearranging. In such a paper, the writer starts by giving the *results* of his inquiry. On the basis of the material then presented in support of the thesis, his readers must form what partial impression they can of the processes of observation and inference that led him to his conclusions. In this sense, the sequence "initial thesis—detailed development and support" is less spontaneous and more artificial than the apparently more complicated logical patterns. By the same token, it is more easily cut loose from its moorings. It tempts the writer to support as best he can the thesis he is "stuck with," and to avoid considerations that might lead to its revision. Whether in a five-hundred-word theme or in a doctoral dissertation, *the writer must resist the temptation to commit himself to a thesis before he has finished making up his mind.*

The advantage of the "thesis paper" is that it tends to be clear-cut, unified, easy to follow. Evidence can be checked for relevance to the central point; digressions can be easily identified. The beginning writer especially learns to achieve continuity by focusing on a central point to be explained and proved. By contrast, the advantage of the think piece is that it discourages faking. It is harder to follow but easier to believe. Once it engages the reader's attention, it can carry him along by a kind of interest not aroused by the support of a fully formulated position.

Though competence in writing cannot be developed without serious attention to logic, more than logic is obviously involved. Organization is to a large extent a matter of doing justice to the inherent logical structure of the subject, but it is also a matter of working out an advantageous strategy for presenting it to the reader. The writer must develop a sense for what needs to be emphasized and what played down, what needs to be led up to and what assures a propitious start. In dealing with a complex subject, the writer must know how to proceed from the simple to the more complicated. In dealing with what is new or debatable, he must know how to build on what can be most easily understood or accepted. T. H. Huxley, in his essay "On the Advisableness of Improving Natural Knowledge," invites our agreement by first confirming the familiar impression of science as a "fairy godmother," as a magician's wand producing health and comfort. Having put the reader in an assenting mood, Huxley then goes on to the less familiar but to him crucial moral and philosophical implications of nineteenth-century science.

The teacher looking for sturdy, clearly structured prose of a later date than that of Matthew Arnold or T. H. Huxley must avoid certain pitfalls. Much newspaper prose is written on the concertina principle, with salient points made in the first few paragraphs and miscellaneous elaboration provided later, to be added or cut off as required by the available space. Some magazine prose, such as that of *The New Yorker* "Profiles," avoids coming to the point as studiously as certain forms of modern jazz avoid lapsing into rhythm or tune. Nevertheless, many an article in the more serious national magazines illustrates the drive, the cogency of clearly organized writing. Here is an outline of an article exceptionally deliberate in its logical structure and therefore exceptionally well suited for demonstrating the clarifying effect of a clear-cut organizational scheme:

> *What are the students like?* They come from all sorts of backgrounds. . . .
> Only one thing they are certain to have in common: they are roughly in the same age group. . . .
>
> *Why do they come to college?* . . .
> (1) They come because it is assumed that they will come, because almost everyone they know does. . . .
> (2) A second and related reason why students come is to make good contacts. . . .
> (3) Then there is sheer laziness. . . .
> (4) There is another group of students who have come to college to bide their time. . . .
> (5) To escape or at least postpone military service is another reason. . . .
> (6) Many come simply to learn to make a living. . . .
> (7) To have fun is still another motive. . . .
> (8) To obtain an education. There are students who actually come because they want to learn. . . .
>
> *What happens to students in college?* . . .
> It is the students' first meeting, most likely, with a national and perhaps international group of men and women of their own age. . . .
> Even the shift in the kind of curriculum is upsetting. . . .
> Furthermore, college is the students' first encounter with live intellectuals. . . .
> Students are surprised, too, at their first meeting with really violent political opinion of all possible varieties. . . .
> It is in college, too, that the sharp bitter sting of failure is first experienced to any appreciable extent. . . .
>
> *What does the student learn?* . . .
> On the simplest level he has acquired a considerable amount of information. . . .
> He will also have learned to question. . . .
> This is what the educational system has given him. It is also worth seeing what the system has not given him. . . .
> There is no course in college designed to prepare the student for what he will encounter in the way of brute facts. . . .[29]

In filling in such an over-all design, the writer relies on techniques that, in their various adaptations and disguises, make the difference between purposeful exposition and improvised thinking out loud. Repeti-

[29] James K. Feibleman, "What Happens in College," *Saturday Review,* October 20, 1962, pp. 74–76.

tion, which in the beginning writer is often a symptom of inability to start thinking, is for the competent writer a means of maintaining focus, of keeping before the reader the thesis that is being developed in the course of an extended argument. In a key chapter of Robert M. Hutchins' *The University of Utopia*, the author's general perspective on education is repeated and paraphrased in a number of passages:

> The Utopians believe that education is a conversation aimed at truth. Their object is to get everybody to take part in this conversation. . . .

> Almost all the teaching in Utopia is conducted through discussion. The educational system is a paradigm of the conversation through which learning is advanced and through which a democracy works. . . .

> The Utopians have the conviction that intellectual activity and the discussion of the most important theoretical and practical problems is indispensable to a happy life and to the progress, and even the safety, of the state. . . .

> Thus the educational system of Utopia is a paradigm, or prototype, or model of the republic of learning and the world political republic for which the Utopians yearn. The civilization that the Utopians have established is one in which discussion takes the place of force, and consensus is the basis of action. . . .[30]

In dealing with a reasonably complex and abstract subject, the writer is helped by programmatic **definitions**. They help him set apart major trends, fix major categories, identify major objects of attack. Thus, Hutchins sets up an opposition between "custodial" education, in which the content of education is left to choice and chance, and a "liberal" education based on the assumption that there are subjects that no one can afford not to study. Matthew Arnold, in *Culture and Anarchy*, sets up the terms *Hebraism* and *Hellenism* to help him in tracing the "Hebraic," Puritan, moralistic and the "Hellenic," humanistic, rational elements in the Western tradition.

Such setting up of alternatives at the same time illustrates the resources of **comparison and contrast**. It shows the effectiveness of explaining the unknown by stressing its partial similarity with what is familiar, of explaining what something is by showing what it is not. Macaulay's essay on Bacon is an extreme example of how contrast dramatizes and clarifies. It shows on the one hand the effectiveness of a terse, antithetical statement of conflicting ideas; as one editor observed, whatever one may think of Macaulay's views, there is no denying his power as a writer. At the same time, Macaulay's essay illustrates the constant temptation to overstatement that inheres in a habitually antithetical style:

---

[30] Robert M. Hutchins, *The University of Utopia* (Chicago: The University of Chicago Press, 1953), pp. 56–68.

> To make men perfect was no part of Bacon's plan. His humble aim was to make imperfect men comfortable.
>
> The aim of the Platonic philosophy was to exalt man into a god. The aim of the Baconian philosophy was to provide man with what he requires while he continues to be man. The aim of the Platonic philosophy was to raise us far above vulgar wants. The aim of the Baconian philosophy was to supply our vulgar wants. The former aim was noble; but the latter was attainable.
>
> The philosophy of Plato began in words and ended in words,—noble words indeed,—words such as were to be expected from the finest of human intellects exercising boundless dominion over the finest of human languages. The philosophy of Bacon began in observations and ended in arts.

In writing such as Macaulay's, the structure of prose, determined by the inherent logic of the subject, seems to find its suitable reflection in the **style,** defined as the texture of sentence and paragraph, determined by details of phrasing and construction. Often, the relationship between structure and style is less easy to formulate. Nevertheless, we should always keep in mind the role of style in its larger context when for the purposes of analysis we give it separate attention.

The Elements of Style

Apart from differences in point of view, what to some extent alienates the modern reader from writers like Macaulay, Ruskin, or Arnold is their firm, authoritative air. They tend to adopt towards the reader the benevolent condescension of teacher towards pupil. On the positive side, this didactic manner leaves no doubt about the writer's seriousness, about his concern with communicating his message. On the negative side, their seriousness is a "high seriousness" that a modern reader tends to find too rigidly dignified. They tend to lack the ease that prevents fatigue; they lack the **urbanity** that is for the writer what the relaxed, spontaneous smile is on the face of the speaker.

Somerset Maugham once said of Dryden that his prose "has a springtime gaiety, a conversational ease, a blithe spontaneousness," that it recalls "an English river winding its cheerful way round hills, through quietly busy towns and by nestling villages, pausing now in a noble reach and then running powerfully through a woodland country. It is alive, varied, windswept; and it has the pleasant open-air smell of England."[31] Lucidity, ease, variety, and wit—these are the qualities that make prose readable as well as substantial, that make reading pleasurable as well as instructive. Perhaps only the first of these qualities can be directly taught, though all of them can be effectively demonstrated in the work of accomplished writers.

Lucidity is not normally the result of happy inspiration. It is a

[31] Maugham, *The Summing Up,* pp. 27–28.

familiar paradox that simplicity and directness are as often the result of conscious discipline as of spontaneous ease. The student who writes "naturally" and "exactly as he speaks" may reproduce the natural woolliness of half-thought-out ideas. As Maugham says, one of the causes of obscurity is that the writer

> has a vague impression of what he wants to say, but has not . . . exactly formulated it in his mind and it is natural enough that he should not find a precise expression for a confused idea. This is due largely to the fact that many writers think, not before, but as they write. The pen originates the thought. The disadvantage of this, and indeed it is a danger against which the author must always be on his guard, is that there is a sort of magic in the written word. The idea acquires substance by taking on a visible nature, and then stands in the way of its own clarification.[32]

George Orwell, another writer himself noted for lucidity, for simple and direct expression, said

> What is above all needed is to let the meaning choose the word, and not the other way about. In prose, the worst thing one can do with words is to surrender to them. When you think of a concrete object, you think wordlessly, and then, when you want to describe the thing you have been visualizing you probably hunt about till you find the exact words that seem to fit it. When you think of something abstract you are more inclined to use words from the start, and unless you make a conscious effort to prevent it, the existing dialect will come rushing in and do the job for you, at the expense of blurring or even changing your meaning.[33]

Thought clarifies itself through the trial and rejection of an approximate but not quite exact word, through the tentative phrasing of an idea:

> If we begin to describe an experience by testing one series of words after another, rejecting or altering as we do so, gradually the vagueness of our understanding diminishes as "wrong" words are eliminated and as "right" or "nearly right" words are accepted as proper symbols of the experience. We are directed by a vague understanding of the experience to words roughly suitable for its expression; by testing a variety of words which are roughly suitable we refine our understanding of the experience. Thus we come to know the shape of experience through the process of using words to describe it.[34]

The importance of revision lies in the opportunity it offers the writer to clarify and strengthen his thinking. It gives him a chance to rephrase what in the first draft remained opaque, to realign major steps in an argument in a more logical sequence. It gives him a chance to look at his writing no longer mainly from the point of view of the writer, trying to formulate what is on his mind, but of the reader, trying to follow someone else's trend of thought.

[32] *Ibid.*
[33] *Shooting an Elephant and Other Essays* (New York: Harcourt, Brace & World, Inc., 1950), p. 91.
[34] Martin, *The Logic and Rhetoric of Exposition*, pp. 1–2.

Every teacher of English must be concerned with the most common obstacles to clarity and precision. One basic obstacle is **triteness,** the tendency to rely on the fashionable word, the prefabricated phrase. As one critic said, "great," second only to "beautiful," is the most overworked word in the English language. But more serious than the use of such vogue words is reliance on the ready-made string, the series of words that provides a ready-made channel for thought. When the appropriate button is pushed, a certain kind of speaker or writer inevitably produces phrases like "eternal vigilance," "undying faith in the principles," and "the solemn realization of the awful responsibility that rests upon us in this hour of unprecedented national stress."[35] George Orwell said of modern writing that at its worst it

> does not consist in picking out words for the sake of their meaning and inventing images in order to make the meaning clearer. It consists in gumming together long strips of words which have already been set in order by someone else.[36]

The difficulty in dealing with triteness is that not every common phrase is to be avoided as a cliché. There is a not always clearly distinct borderline between the hackneyed and the idiomatic. **Idiom** is the familiar and at the same time apt and expressive phrase whose deliberate avoidance produces opaqueness and circumlocution. **Clichés** are often phrases that owed their original aptness to a touch of color that has since faded, to an imaginative flavor that has gone stale. They may have a solemn implication or a dramatic twist that has become routine. Fowler said of such phrases

> Each of them comes to each of us at some moment in life with, for him, the freshness of novelty upon it; on that occasion it is a delight, & the wish to pass on that delight is amiable. But we forget that of any hundred persons for whom we attempt this good office, though there may be one to whom our phrase is new & bright, it is a stable offense to the ninety & nine.[37]

Such phrases are, to excerpt Fowler's list, "conspicuous by his absence," "a consummation devoutly to be wished," "more sinned against than sinning," and "to throw the baby out with the bath."

The test of the cliché is that it retains an element of the elegant, the figurative, the dramatic, or the facetious that has become too familiar to be appreciated. *Iron curtain* is a familiar term whose figurative element serves the purpose of apt naming; *acid test* is a cliché that typically over-dramatizes the situation described and calls attention to itself. It is therefore a mistake for the teacher to attack indiscriminately all common

---

[35] Frank Sullivan, *A Rock in Every Snowball* (Boston: Little, Brown & Company, Inc., 1946).

[36] Orwell, *Shooting an Elephant,* p. 85.

[37] Margaret Nicholson, *A Dictionary of American-English Usage* (New York: The New American Library of World Literature, Inc., 1958), p. 225.

phrases. As Jacques Barzun said in a review of the Evans *Dictionary of Contemporary American Usage,* "to mark with equal reprobation *wear and tear, tilting at windmills,* and *more in sorrow than in anger* because all three are 'hackneyed' is to be blind to distinctions upon which good writing depends." *Wear and tear* is an apt, common phrase with a homey, colloquial touch. *Tilting at windmills* is a literary allusion that, though overworked, is still striking enough to serve as literary shorthand where it clearly fits the situation. *More in sorrow than in anger* has the faded elegance of the true cliché. Many familiar phrases have *become* familiar because they aptly and efficiently convey a fairly complicated idea. They are useful "if one is to be brief and unmistakable at the same time, e.g.: *sour grapes, cold blood, high and dry, good Samaritan, . . . cry wolf or cold shoulder.*"[38]

Indiscriminate criticism of familiar phrases may lead the student to the opposite extreme. The too officious avoidance of the commonplace leads to the pretentiousness and obscurity of professional and bureaucratic **jargon.** Jargon borrows the prestige of science and scholarship by treating the commonplace in unnecessarily abstract and technical language. To the jargon addict, every idea is a "hypothesis," every relation is an "interrelationship," every method is a "methodology." Programs are not simply planned but "preplanned"; changes are not effected but "effectuated"; decisions are not carried out but always "implemented." Simple everyday situations are described in terms of "factors," "strata," "criteria," "aspects," "phases," and "data."

The objection to jargon is not to abstraction as such. A sentence like the following moves on the highest level of abstraction and is yet a model of clear and vigorous writing: "The truth may lie between two extremes, but it assuredly does not lie halfway between right and wrong" (Edmund S. Morgan). Nor is the objection to technical terminology. A physician or a psychologist must use terms of more exact application than everyday language and free from irrelevant emotional associations. *The objection to jargon is that it uses abstract and technical language to make the trivial seem important.*

The mark of a first-rate writer is that he can discuss technical subject matter with admirable clarity without diluting it. Here is a distinguished anthropologist describing the finding of a fossil skull:

There were marks of generalized primitiveness in that low, pinched brain case and grinning jaw that marked it as lying far back along those converging roads where cat and man and weasel must leap into a single shape. It was the face of a creature who had spent his days following his nose, who was led by instinct rather than memory, and whose power of choice was very small. Though he was not a man, nor a direct human ancestor, there

[38] Jacques Barzun, "A Chance to Tinker to Evans," *The American Scholar,* XXVII (Winter, 1957–58), 45.

was yet about him, even in the bone, some trace of that low, snuffling world out of which our forebears had so recently emerged.[39]

To be effective, teachers and textbook authors must learn to translate technical information and abstract principles into this kind of vivid, graphic, vigorously idiomatic language. Somerset Maugham says of his reading of the English philosophers,

> I found that besides being philosophers they were uncommonly good writers. . . . I should think that few could read Hobbes' *Leviathan* without being taken by the gruff, downright John Bullishness of his personality and surely no one could read Berkeley's *Dialogues* without being ravished by the charm of that delightful bishop. And though it may be true that Kant made hay of Hume's theories it would be impossible, I think, to write philosophy with more elegance, urbanity and clearness. They all, and Locke too for the matter of that, wrote English that the student of style could do much worse than study.[40]

As Maugham says, when experts deal with matters "that are of pressing concern to all reflective persons," one can only regret "that they cannot make their meaning so plain that all who read may understand."

In admiring the simplicity and directness of the intelligible writer, we must remember that it involves a degree of deliberate simplification for impact, for clarity. On the one hand, the composition teacher must encourage his students to use the differentiated vocabulary and the complex, elaborate sentences that are appropriate for detailed explanation and argument. At the same time, students must learn to use the graphic, familiar word and the short, incisive sentence—to summarize key ideas, to make an important statement memorable and emphatic, to introduce variety into a paragraph that moves at too predictable a pace. Notice the gain in clarity and emphasis through the short sentences italicized in the following passage:

> Bennett was always facing the wonder of the actualities of living. It was wonderful to him that we live as we do, that time will pass and change us, that we will die and perhaps die painfully, that life is what it is. *He never decorates or embroiders. He is wholly materialistic. Common sense is the salt of his plate.* We are never swept away, but we are curiously won over, and we, too, are filled with wonder at the slow unspinning of life.[41]

Much apparent simplicity and directness is in reality achieved by shifting from the literal to the figurative. The shorthand comparison of simile or metaphor is often a more graphic and forceful means of expression than the "direct" literal account. The bracing effect of figurative language is most obvious in the discussion of a fairly abstract subject: "Unnecessary precision is pedantic and fussy, *like honing a razor to cut*

39 Loren Eiseley, *The Immense Journey* (New York: Random House, Inc., 1957), p. 5.
40 Maugham, *The Summing Up*, p. 240–41.
41 John Van Druten, "My Debt to Arnold Bennett," *Saturday Review Reader 3* (New York: Bantam Books, Inc., 1954), p. 114.

butter." (Monroe C. Beardsley) "One can write nothing readable unless one constantly struggles to efface one's own personality. Good prose is *like a window pane."* (George Orwell)

The pitfalls in the use of figurative language are familiar. There is the trite metaphor, already noted in our discussion of clichés. Equally common is the **mixed metaphor:** "In this great state, where we *forge the sinews* of freedom . . ." (shift from the metallurgical to the physiological); "In this poem, the poet seems to be coming out of a dream-world and *stepping into the face* of reality" (mixture of two anatomical metaphors). Often, the blurring of images is less obvious, as in the following sentence: "As the sectional tension increased, the sense of irrepressible differences, long buried in the national consciousness, began to burst into the clear." As an observant reader pointed out, the four parts of this sentence create four different effects:

> The first gives us the sense of *pulling,* the second of energy contained under *pressure,* like steam in a kettle, the third *buries* this steam kettle, the fourth allows it to "burst into the clear" which seems superficially to fit with the idea of "irrepressible differences," but is vaguely disconcerting until we realize that the stress is on "into the clear," which is a hunting term.[42]

Finally, the **extravagant metaphor,** by calling too much attention to itself, becomes distracting rather than illuminating: "In such ripe discourse as this the syllables literally crawl with maggots of meaning for the epicure with a stomach for poetic Gorgonzola" (this might turn even the cheese-lover's stomach).

Again, however, it is possible for the critic to approach figurative language in a spirit that is too literal-minded and destructive. Metaphors may be familiar, they may be technically mixed, they may be strong enough to offend the squeamish—and yet make for powerful and effective writing. When on the death of Eleanor Roosevelt, Adlai Stevenson said that "she would rather light candles than curse the darkness," his tribute owed its power to the appropriateness of a familiar metaphor, for once living up to its full potential. When Shakespeare has Hamlet debate whether "to take arms against a sea of troubles," not only does his mixed metaphor pit the heroic protagonist against an opponent of vastness and dim grandeur, it also by its very incongruity hints at a futility parallel to that of the king who ordered his followers to lash the waves.

A strong, or even violent metaphor is one of the most effective ways of securing emphasis, of assuring emotional impact. Alfred Kazin describes the anguish of a stammering child in a school where his speech defect meets with incomprehension and ridicule:

> The word was my agony. The word that for others was so effortless and so neutral, so unburdened, so simple, so exact, I had first to meditate in ad-

---

[42] Geoffrey Moore, "American Prose Today," *New World Writing 8* (New York: The New American Library of World Literature, Inc., 1955), p. 53.

vance, to see if I could make it, like a plumber fitting together odd lengths and shapes of pipe. I was always preparing words I could speak, storing them away, choosing between them. And often, when the word did come from my mouth in its great and terrible birth, quailing and bleeding as if forced through a thornbush, I would not be able to look the others in the face, and would walk out in silence, the infinitely echoing silence behind my back, to say it all cleanly back to myself as I walked in the streets.[43]

The matter-of-fact circumspection of the plumbing metaphor sets up a powerful contrast with the violence of the birth metaphor, itself violently mixed through the tied-in simile of the thorns. The violent, figurative language used here powerfully communicates the point that from a child's perspective nothing is more immediate, nothing more desperately serious than emotional crises of this kind.

The same selection illustrates other stylistic resources that make for emphasis. Notice the different kinds of **repetition**. There is the insistent piling up of near-synonyms: "so neutral, so unburdened, so simple, so exact . . ."; the repetition of a phrase for elaboration: *"the word* was my agony. *The word* . . ." "*the silence, the* infinitely echoing *silence* . . ."; the balanced pairs of related terms: "great and terrible," "quailing and bleeding." These devices are at the opposite extreme from the kind of repetition shown in thoughtless redundancy and deliberate padding.

Repetition skillfully handled makes for emphasis, coherence, and balance in much effective prose. Typically, parallel sentence structure goes hand in hand with repetition for an insistent effect or for antithetical contrast of meaning:

> The general principles of any study you may learn by books at home; but *the detail, the color, the tone, the air, the life* which makes it live in us, you must catch all these from those in whom it already lives. (John Henry Newman)

> No awards for gallantry had come, or were to come, my way; but I was entitled to certain medals and ribbons. *I never applied for them; I was never sent them; I have never had them.* (J. B. Priestley)

> Lord Chesterfield was right when he wrote to his son that the power of attention was the mark of a civilized man. *The baby cannot attend; the savage and the boor will not.* (Jacques Barzun)

It is in the author's handling of such elements as repetition and parallelism that the difference between ease and weightiness of style becomes most readily apparent. A mannered, **ornate** style and a more **urbane** style differ in the degree of obtrusiveness with which metaphor, allusion, repetition, parallelism, and similar elements of style do their work. Notice the rapid succession of figures of speech and allusions in paragraphs from Robert Louis Stevenson's "Aes Triplex":

---

43 Kazin, *A Walker in the City*, p. 23.

The changes wrought by death are in themselves *so sharp* and final, and so terrible and melancholy in their consequences, that the thing stands alone in man's experience, and has no parallel upon earth. . . . Sometimes it *leaps suddenly upon its victims, like a Thug;* sometimes it *lays a regular siege and creeps upon their citadel* during a score of years. And when *the business is done,* there is *sore havoc made* in other people's lives, and *a pin knocked out* by which many subsidiary friendships *hung together.*

Indeed, it is a memorable subject for consideration, with what unconcern and gaiety mankind *pricks on* along *the Valley of the Shadow of Death.* The *whole way* is *one wilderness of snares,* and the end of it, for those who fear the *last pinch,* is irrevocable ruin. And yet we go *spinning* through it all, like *a party for the Derby.*

Notice the sustained parallelism in sentences by Samuel Johnson:

We are *all prompted by the same motives, all deceived by the same fallacies,* all *animated by hope, obstructed by danger, entangled by desire,* and *seduced by pleasure.*

If a life be delayed till *interest and envy* are at an end, we *may hope for impartiality,* but *must expect little intelligence;* for the incidents which give excellence to biography are of a *volatile and evanescent* kind.

A definition of urbanity must be in part negative: it is marked by the absence of patterns so regular as to attract our attention, of devices so habitual as to become mannerisms. Johnson himself said of some examples of Dryden's prose, "They have not the formality of a settled style, in which the first half of the sentence betrays the other. The clauses are never balanced, nor the periods modelled; every word seems to drop by chance though it falls into its proper place."[44]

However, some features of an urbane style can be more positively identified. It has a lightness of touch that is most obvious in the way it employs humor and irony. Here is a representative passage:

Twenty miles east of New York City as the New Haven Railroad flies sits a village I shall call Spruce Manor. The Boston Post Road, there, for the length of two blocks, becomes Main Street, and on one side of that thundering thoroughfare are the grocery stores and the drug stores and the Village Spa where teen-agers gather of an afternoon to drink their cokes and speak their curious confidences.[45]

This passage illustrates a casual, understated kind of wit. The first sentence ironically varies the familiar "as *the crow* flies"—ironically, since commuter trains are *not* noted for the effortless speed of birds. **Irony** is more obvious when a two-block village street is called a "thundering thoroughfare" but again more subtle in the formal, old-fashioned phrasing of the reference to the slangy, up-to-date teen-age crowd: "gather of an

[44] Bertrand H. Bronson, ed., *Rasselas, Poems, and Selected Prose* (New York: Rinehart & Co., Inc., 1958), p. 478.
[45] Phyllis McGinley, *A Short Walk from the Station* (New York: The Viking Press, Inc. 1951), p. 9.

afternoon," "speak their curious confidences." Irony here effectively mirrors the ironic gulf between the teen-ager and the adult, the benevolent and yet somewhat baffled attitude of the middle-aged and young at heart toward the young in fact.

A writer must become sensitive to the ironies and subtle cross references of words as words. He must overcome the painful seriousness of the writer to whom words are a mere vehicle. Unobtrusive touches of **verbal humor** have a leavening effect. Such are verbal echoes and twists on familiar phrases: A teacher refers to students who "sing in the glee club, *act* in plays, and *act up* on college weekends"; a scholar refers to colleagues more interested in prestigious assignments than in teaching as "campus followers"; a publisher, speaking of books returned from bookstores, says that his stock "is gone today and here tomorrow."

Obviously, verbal humor plays a different role when instead of leavening pleasantly understated prose it becomes a major weapon in polemical and satirical writing. Occasional rhetorical exaggeration, offered tongue in cheek, may become drastic **overstatement:** "Ickes was so fantastically vain and ambitious that he saw the world as a conspiracy designed to deprive him of his rights; he would scarcely have been content with anything less *than the perpetual presidency of the entire solar system.*" (Gilbert Highet) Subtle play on words may give way to deliberate **puns:** "The old saw says, 'Let a sleeping dog lie.' Right. Still, when there is much at stake it is better to get a newspaper to do it." (Mark Twain) Irony may become broad **sarcasm:** "The good qualities of this so-called Anglo-Saxon are many, and I am certainly not disposed to question them, but I here pass them over without apology, for he devotes practically the whole of his literature and fully a half of his oral discourse to celebrating them himself, and so there is no danger that they will ever be disregarded." (H. L. Mencken) The subtle twist on a familiar phrase may become deliberate **paradox:** "Do not do unto others as you would that they should do unto you. Their tastes may not be the same." (G. B. Shaw) Occasional antithetical heightening may become the deliberately balanced playing off against each other of verbal opposites: "Democracy substitutes selection by the incompetent many for appointment by the corrupt few." (G. B. Shaw)

Such devices give polemical writing its emotional impact and persuasive effect. Nevertheless, its persuasiveness is limited by factors that the polemicist tends to overlook. It tends to be too obviously partisan, as when Dr. Johnson, in his *Dictionary,* defines *Whig* as "the name of a faction" and *patron* as "commonly a wretch who supports with insolence, and is paid with flattery." The more emphatic polemical writing becomes, the more likely it is to appeal mainly to those already more than half-convinced and to alienate the fair-minded reader. Further, the satirist may reach the point where his habitual overstatement is discounted by the audience and enjoyed for its humorous effect. A writer who was first disliked as a critic may come to be tolerated as a jester. Thus, Shaw so well succeeded in entertaining the bourgeois whom he set out to bait that he saw himself "defrauded" of his "just martyrdom":

> In vain do I redouble the violence of the language in which I proclaim my heterodoxies. I rail at the theistic credulity of Voltaire, the amoristic super- stition of Shelley, the revival of tribal soothsaying and idolatrous rites which Huxley called Science and mistook for an advance on the Pentateuch, no less than at the welter of ecclesiastical and professional humbug which saves the face of the stupid system of violence and robbery which we call Law and Industry. . . . And yet, instead of exclaiming "Send this incon- ceivable Satanist to the stake," the respectable newspapers pith me by an- nouncing "another book by this brilliant and thoughtful writer."[46]

Twain, Shaw, and Mencken all had the kind of humorous self-detach- ment, the twinkle in the eye, that put even their most cruel barbs in the context of a fallible humanity shared with the reader. With more single- minded controversialists, emphasis tends to defeat itself because where all is emphatic, nothing is emphatic. Where everything is a crusade, nothing is a crusade. Where every human undertaking is only a new example of human folly, folly becomes normal, predictable, and acceptable.

The best modern prose is distinguished by its tendency toward under- statement, by its economy of stylistic effects. The difficulty in teaching style is that awareness of stylistic resources may introduce a self-conscious- ness, a deliberateness that distracts from the writer's meaning. As Somer- set Maugham says, "a good style should show no sign of effort." A too de- liberate style loses its persuasiveness; "you would not believe a man was very intent on plowing a furrow if he carried a hoop with him and jumped through it at every other step."[47]

Some of the features that make for a lack of affectation, for an un- forced, natural effect, are pointed out in Geoffrey Moore's analysis of the following passage:

> *My purpose was to sketch the genesis and set in some crude historical perspective the present troubled world scene, and then to attempt to defrost a tiny segment of the opaque window through which we see others and others see us. . . .*

> Two things are immediately noticeable: first, the modest tone, and, second, the use of an original figure of speech which has been drawn naturally and unaffectedly from American experience. Almost all Americans . . . find it necessary at some time during the winter to "defrost," either manually or by aid of a device built into their cars, a driving window which has been made opaque by frost or frozen snow. The style might be described as "literary" (e.g., "genesis," "present troubled world scene"), yet it gives an impression of ease. It has the ring of sincerity and makes us feel that we

46 *Man and Superman* (Baltimore: Penguin Books, Inc., 1952), p. xxxiv.
47 Maugham, *The Summing Up,* p. 43.

can trust a man who is at once so unpretentious and yet so quietly convinced that he can clarify our vision of world affairs.[48]

As Moore said in connection with another passage, we say that writing has style if "the language is both elegant and precise, the manner judicious but not portentous, flavored by just the right amount of everyday reference." Such writing uses the resources of language for emphasis to underline what deserves attention, not to dramatize the insignificant. It neither hides nor shows off the writer's education. It shows that the writer, while able to think seriously and systematically, has an eye for the color of everyday life, an ear for the sounds of living speech.

Rhetoric and the Reader

The critic examining the structure and style of an essay can guard against capricious impressions by staying close to what he can point to in the actual text. At the same time, textual analysis remains artificial and incomplete unless it concerns itself with the effect of the text on a reader. Students of **communication theory** have stressed the need for paying attention not only to the nature of one's message but also to the condition of the receiver. They have stressed the futility of broadcasting on a wave length that the audience is unable or unmotivated to tune in.

Obviously, one of the difficulties in the teaching of composition is that the student may come to regard writing as busywork rather than as a process in which he shares ideas, impressions, and information with an audience. Papers returned to the student should carry comments like "good point," "makes a good story," "well observed," "well put," "I agree" and, on the other hand, "why?" "not clear," "I don't follow," "I doubt it," and "How do we know?" The student must learn to anticipate the reactions of someone trying to follow him from point to point. *Regard for the reader makes the writer aim at clarity and precision. It makes him try to convince as well as to assert.* It makes him attempt to make controversy fruitful by mapping out areas of agreement and avoiding the shrill and the snide.

At the same time, emphasis on the role of the reader can easily be carried too far. Producing a desired effect on the audience may become the writer's chief preoccupation. Such a writer is likely to make a fetish of intelligibility. He will do without terms that require a knowledge of history, literature, or the arts; he will avoid words that require subtle discriminations, or ironies and allusions that might be missed. He is likely to avoid sustained argument and play up those elements of his subject that make for humor, drama, entertainment. He will assume the role of the friend, the expert, the fellow common man. In short, the writer may

---

48 Moore, "American Prose Today," p. 50.

come to employ style, in Kenneth Burke's phrase, as "ingratiation"—as a means of placating, in order to influence, his audience.

Such writing, designed to please its audience, leaves undeveloped whatever capacity for discrimination that audience might have. By its habit-forming effect on the reader, it tends to perpetuate itself and promotes what Clifton Fadiman has called "the decline of attention," the "attrition of the ability to read prose and poetry of meaning and substance." Any teacher interested in serious prose must be aware of its competition from the kind of writing marked by

> brevity, superficiality, simplification, the emphasis on timeliness (with its corollary, the conscious neglect or unconscious ignorance of the past), planned non-literary English, the avoidance of abstract ideas, . . . the emphasis on "personalities" as well as the avoidance of *personality*, the exploitation of the "column" as against the discursive essay, the preference of the wisecrack to wit, . . . an almost religious veneration for the "fact" (to be "well informed" is our substitute for the capacity to reflect), the rapid alternation of appeals (known as "balance," or something for everybody), and the careful exploitation of certain not highly cerebral interests, mainly in the areas of vicarious sex, criminality, violence, "inspiration," gadget-worship, and the idolization of contemporary gods, such as cinema stars, sports heroes, and clean-faced high-school girl graduates.[49]

To balance the arguments in favor of adapting the message to the capacity of the audience, the teacher of English is likely to stress another basic function of style: "incantation," in Burke's phrase—the power of style to make the reader over in its own image. Somerset Maugham describes his youthful admiration for Walter Pater and George Meredith, in spite of Maugham's lack of congeniality—felt even then by a carping, unconvinced part of his mind—with these authors. As Walker Gibson has pointed out,

> The fact is that every time we open the pages of another piece of writing, we are embarked on a new adventure in which we become a new person—a person as controlled and definable and as remote from the chaotic self of daily life as the lover in the sonnet. Subject to the degree of our literary sensibility, we are re-created by the language. We assume, for the sake of the experience, that set of attitudes and qualities which the language asks us to assume, and, if we cannot assume them, we throw the book away.[50]

Truly powerful writing does not merely confirm expectation. It compels us to broaden our perspective; it opens new channels of thought and feeling. It becomes significant to the exact extent that it refuses to take us as we are.

Needless to say, little of the writing we supervise in our classes will be significant in this sense. In practice, we will have to work toward a less

---

49 Clifton Fadiman, "The Decline of Attention," *Saturday Review Reader*, pp. 25–29.
50 "Authors, Speakers, Readers, and Mock Readers," *College English*, XI (February, 1950), 265.

ambitious but nevertheless closely related objective. Writing should broaden the perspective and clarify the thought, if not of the reader, at least of the writer. Before we can participate in the writer's thought and feeling, we must be able to feel that his honest aim was to record and interpret his experience. We must see evidence of his lonely pleasure in working out a problem to his own satisfaction. If we cannot respect a writer's sincerity, we will resist his persuasive devices as mere manipulation.

Once the writer achieves this kind of sincerity, concern with his audience becomes a salutary discipline rather than a temptation or a distraction. As Edmund S. Morgan says of the writing of the scholar:

> Communication is not merely the desire and the responsibility of the scholar; it is his discipline, the proving ground where he tests his findings against criticism. Without communication his pursuit of truth withers into eccentricity. He necessarily spends much of his time alone, in the library or the laboratory, looking for the answers to his questions. But he needs to be rubbing constantly against other minds. He needs to be tested, probed, and pushed around. He needs to be made to explain himself. Only when he has expressed himself, only when he has communicated his thoughts, can he be sure that he is thinking clearly.[51]

In such communication, the relation between writer and reader becomes a partnership with mutual responsibilities. The reader is no longer a passive object. He endeavors to be open to new ideas, new information, new avenues of feeling. He reads in context, is alert to clues, keeps out irrelevant associations. He determines to look for meaning and coherence even where it may not be immediately apparent. He determines not to oversimplify or distort a position to which he objects.

Communication defined as a partnership serves the purposes of inquiry and is for both writer and reader a method of education. Like other methods of education, it differs from techniques of indoctrination and propaganda in that it "demands from the subject some effort, especially some effort of attention." Both parties to such an exchange know that "no one can learn anything worth knowing unless he is willing to learn, as well as willing to be taught."[52]

Communication is something that writer and reader must work at. This view of communication as a co-operative enterprise helps both writer and reader confront their tasks with a businesslike attitude. It reassures the writer who despairs of reaching across the barriers between isolated individuals, "each in his prison"; who feels with Prufrock that "It is impossible to say just what I mean!" Since Walter Pater, modern critics

---

51 "What Every Yale Freshman Should Know," *Saturday Review,* January 23, 1960, p. 14.
52 Joseph Wood Krutch, "If You Don't Mind My Saying So," *The American Scholar,* XXIV (Summer, 1955), 349.

have stressed the "final and irreconcilable lapse, gap, between actual experience in its flux and flow and mystery on the one hand and our verbal, highly artificial, highly contrived effort to control it on the other"; they have been "constantly aware, constantly conscious, of the gap between word and thing, the gap between the blur of experience and the very artificial order of language."[53]

Emphasis on the necessary cooperation of the reader shifts our attention from the limitations of language as a man-made contrivance to its potential as a common medium. At the same time, it counteracts the superciliousness of the reader who defies an author to please and convince him. If understanding is something the reader must work at, the Olympian aloofness of the more fastidious reader is as much an obstacle to successful communication as the disabilities, if any, of the writer.

Part of the English teacher's credo is that, after all the necessary qualifications and reservations have been made, communication *is* possible. As teachers of literature, we try to make our students hear and understand voices coming to them across gulfs of time and convention. As teachers of rhetoric, we try to make them communicate with contemporaries sharing a common culture.

Rhetoric and the Teaching of English

What, to sum up, is the role of rhetoric in the teaching of English? In its concern with mature and responsible writing, rhetoric serves something more than a "service" function. We sometimes hear it said that the English teacher should aim at making his students "competent at simple expository writing, the practical kind that goes into a business letter, a committee report, an office memorandum, a set of instructions." Certainly, teachers of English are more directly responsible for their students' ability to spell, to punctuate, and to write a straightforward utilitarian paragraph than their colleagues in other areas. But the more substantial goals of instruction in rhetoric and composition differ from these utilitarian ones by the same margin that the goals of liberal education differ from those of a secretarial college.

Instruction in rhetoric aims at developing the students' confidence and skill in writing something that is worth reading. To do so, it must sharpen their powers of observation and develop their ability to select and order information and ideas. The average human observer suffers from limited vision and distracted attention. His observations are channeled by preconceptions, colored by preference, and censored by private interest. Before we give our students a mistaken impression of the value of their

---

[53] Walker Gibson, "The Voice of the Writer," *College Composition and Communication*, XIII (October, 1962), 13.

improvised opinions, we should encourage them to make more accurate and reliable the observations on which their opinions are based.

As our students learn to profit from accurate observation, they must develop the habit of open-mindedness. Like juror, historian, biographer, and scientist, they must learn to suspend judgment. They must be prepared to adjust tentative hypotheses in the light of new evidence. As our students begin to write papers calling for an expression of opinion, they must learn to reverse an almost universal procedure: to start with one's present view of the matter and then confirm it with whatever evidence and arguments can be marshaled in its support. They must learn to weigh conflicting evidence in order to reach a balanced but not necessarily final conclusion.

Generally, the students must be made to see that between the asking of a question and the giving of an answer there must be a process of finding out. They must learn to apply inductive procedures: The best and most productive writing practice for the student in school and college deals with topics that call for a stock-taking of previous experience and observation. The student thus learns to correlate what may have seemed random impressions. Such writing trains the student to be cautious in taking the inductive leap: he must learn to shun the initial *all* or *none* of generalizations so sweeping as to be out of all reasonable proportion with the handful of instances actually observed.

In arguing out questions of some complexity, the student writer learns to examine the origin and scope of his premises. He begins to pay attention to the difference between "All Marxists read Hegel," Only Marxists read Hegel," "Some Marxists read Hegel," and "No Marxists read Hegel." He learns to combat the tendency to filter out the complications that interfere with the simple, decisive answers we find most manageable, most workable, most reassuring. He becomes suspicious of arguments that start with the question "Now what does all this boil down to?" and conclude with a triumphant "It's as simple as that." A gain in reasonableness typically means increased willingness to make, and accept, the necessary qualifications of sweeping charges, theories, and generalizations.

The teacher of English cannot teach reasonableness in a series of lessons. He can, however, call the students' attention to problems of clear thinking in both their reading and writing. Sometimes the writer's strategy of presentation directly mirrors logical processes. An inductive paper may lead up to a generalization by surveying a number of relevant instances. A deductive paper may elaborate the implications of accepted general principles for a specific situation. However, even when the organization of a paper does not mirror the process of inquiry, it owes its cogency to the relevance of supporting material, the coherence of its argument, its avoidance of common temptations to illogicality.

Obviously, a concern with logic may be carried to extremes. Teachers of English need not be warned that neither external fact nor human desires and emotions conform to logical patterns of order, coherence, or symmetry. As a means of interpreting and ordering experience, logic interacts with feelings and commitments hard to formulate, let alone to prove, in logical terms. In the words of Brooks and Warren, "Thought shades off into feeling, and feeling shades off into thought." A considerable part of "our use of language involves an attempt to clarify our feelings, to come to grips with them. . . . In other words, the talking-out process not only helps us make up our minds but helps us 'make up our feelings,' too."[54]

Like the study of imaginative literature, rhetoric is concerned with language as a vehicle for the expression not merely of ideas but of sensations, feelings, and attitudes. The student writer must learn to make prose graphic and tangible rather than thin and abstract. He must learn to recognize and control tone, ranging from casual ease to insistent seriousness and hot indignation. He must begin to see how metaphor and sentence structure convey or modify emotion. He must become sensitive to nuances and overtones that are lost in literal translation.

Because of its concern with the student's ability to observe and think and feel, the teaching of rhetoric cannot be modeled on the teaching of subjects that can be conveyed as "information," as "content." The teacher of rhetoric cannot be content with conveying factual knowledge about language; he must help students translate this knowledge into an informed awareness of language at work. He cannot be content with charting patterns of organization and logic; he must cultivate in his students habits of responsible and informed critical thought. He cannot treat style as an inventory of devices but must treat it instead as the expression of the writer's commitment and experience and skill. Instruction in writing cannot miraculously widen and enrich the student's experience. But neither can it teach skill in a vacuum. What it can at least start to do is to teach disciplined self-expression, responsible interpretation of experience, articulate participation in the public dialogue.

Good writing requires personal involvement. It thus reflects the influence of complex psychological factors. The teacher of rhetoric can set these aside only at the risk of drastically narrowing and distorting his subject. Composition, which at its least inspiring dwindles into a service course, can be a crucial part of the student's liberal education. The most pressing need in the teaching of composition is not for a more rigid definition of its content but for an improvement of the teacher's self-confidence and self-respect.

[54] Cleanth Brooks and Robert Penn Warren, *Modern Rhetoric: Shorter Edition* (New York: Harcourt, Brace & World, Inc., 1961), pp. 3–4.

A PROGRAM FOR FURTHER STUDY

CLEANTH BROOKS AND ROBERT PENN WARREN, *Modern Rhetoric: Shorter Edition.* New York: Harcourt, Brace & World, Inc., 1961.

A shortened paperback version of the most authoritative modern rhetoric. Contains a detailed and well-illustrated discussion of the traditional four forms of discourse: exposition, argument, description, and narration. Good on stylistic resources and their relation to meaning and purpose.

HAROLD C. MARTIN AND RICHARD M. OHMANN, *The Logic and Rhetoric of Exposition* (rev. ed.) New York: Holt, Rinehart & Winston, Inc., 1963.

A rhetoric concentrating on the resources and conditions of disciplined expression. Based on the assumption that "a book which proposes to help people to write well must concern itself with ways of knowing experience as well as with ways of expressing it."

ALFRED KAZIN, *The Open Form: Essays for Our Time.* New York: Harcourt, Brace & World, Inc., 1961.

A collection devoted to "the essay as a modern form," drawing on articles and books by current writers. Eminently successful in its attempt "to present the possibilities of the essay as a form for our time."

WILLIAM E. BUCKLER, ed., *Prose of the Victorian Period.* Boston: Houghton Mifflin Company, 1958. A Riverside Edition.

A substantial selection from the writing of major British nineteenth-century essayists, from Macaulay and Carlyle to Huxley and Pater.

CHARLES B. SHAW, ed., *American Essays.* New York: The New American Library of World Literature, Inc., 1955. A Mentor Book.

A convenient and inexpensive collection of essays by American writers from Franklin and Paine to Thurber and E. B. White.

MATERIALS FOR ANALYSIS

A. Study the leads of major articles in a magazine like *Harper's, The Atlantic,* or *The New Yorker.* Classify them and report to what extent your investigation bears out the following observations:

Suppose that you have drawn a subject out of your mental box and you find that it is "Fish." Now if you were living in the time of Henry Van Dyke and Thomas Bailey Aldrich your best lead would be: "Many of my friends are ardent disciples of Izaak Walton." That would have had the appropriate personal touch and the requisite, not too recondite literary allusion. But today of course no live-wire editor would read any further, not because this sounds like a dull familiar essay but simply because it sounds like a familiar essay. But "Fish" is still a perfectly usable subject provided you remember that salable non-fiction "pieces" almost invariably fall into one of three categories: the factual, the polemic, and what we now call—though I don't know why we have to deviate into French—*reportage*.

If you decide to be factual a good beginning would be: "Four million trout flies were manufactured last year by the three leading sports-supply houses." That is the sort of thing which makes almost any editor sit up and take notice. But it is no better than certain other possible beginnings. The polemic article ought to start: "Despite all the efforts of our department of wild life conservation, the number of game fish in American lakes and streams continues to decline steadily." Probably this kind of beginning to this kind of article is best of all because it sounds alarming and because nowadays (and for understandable reasons) whatever sounds alarming is generally taken to be true. However, if you want to go in for the trickier *reportage* start off with a sentence something like this: " 'Cap' Bill Hanks, a lean, silent, wryly humorous down-Easterner probably knows more about the strange habits of the American fisherman than any man alive."

> —Joseph Wood Krutch, "No Essays—Please!" *Saturday Review Reader* (New York: Bantam Books, Inc., 1951), pp. 148–49.

B. Outline a recent magazine article that you considered an example of exceptionally cogent, well-organized prose.

C. Study the following examples of English prose from the sixteenth to the nineteenth century. Examine the characteristic style and tone of each passage. To what extent could it serve as a model of modern prose? What stylistic features tend to identify it with its period or with its author?

1) When the right virtuous Edward Wotton and I were at the Emperor's Court together, we gave ourselves to learn horsemanship of John Pietro Pugliano, one that with great commendation had the place of an esquire in his stable. And he, according to the fertileness of the Italian wit, did not only afford us the demonstration of his practice, but sought to enrich our minds with the contemplations therein which he thought most precious. But with none I remember mine ears were at any time more loaden, than when (either angered with slow payment, or moved with our learner-like admiration) he exercised his speech in the praise of his faculty. He said, soldiers were the noblest estate of mankind, and horsemen the noblest of soldiers. He said they were the masters of war and ornaments of peace; speedy goers and strong abiders; triumphers both in camps and courts. Nay, to so unbelieved a point he proceeded, as that no earthly thing bred such wonder to a prince as to be a good horseman. Skill of government was but a *pedanteria* in comparison. Then would he add certain praises, by telling what a peerless beast a horse was, the only serviceable courtier without flattery, the beast of most beauty, faithfulness, courage, and such more, that, if I had not been a piece of a logician before I came to him, I think he would have persuaded me to have wished myself a horse. But thus much at least with his no few words he drove into me, that self-love is better than any gilding to make that seem gorgeous wherein ourselves are parties.

> —Sir Philip Sidney, *An Apology for Poetry* (1595)

2) To begin, then, with Shakespeare. He was the man who of all modern, and perhaps ancient poets, had the largest and most comprehensive soul. All the images of nature were still present to him, and he drew them, not laboriously, but luckily; when he describes anything, you more than see it, you feel it too. Those who accuse him to have wanted learning,

give him the greater commendation: he was naturally learned; he needed not the spectacles of books to read nature; he looked inwards, and found her there. I cannot say he is everywhere alike; were he so, I should do him injury to compare him with the greatest of mankind. He is many times flat, insipid; his comic wit degenerating into clenches, his serious swelling into bombast. But he is always great, when some great occasion is presented to him; no man can say he ever had a fit subject for his wit; and did not then raise himself as high above the rest of poets,

Quantum lenta solent inter viburna cupressi.
[As the cypresses among the bending viburnums.]
—John Dryden, *An Essay of Dramatic Poesy* (1668)

3) Having pursued the history of a pun, from its original to its downfall, I shall here define it to be a conceit arising from the use of two words that agree in the sound, but differ in the sense. The only way therefore to try a piece of wit, is to translate it into a different language: If it bears the test you may pronounce it true, but if it vanishes in the experiment you may conclude it to have been a pun. In short, one may say of a pun as the countryman described his nightingale, that it is *vox & praeterea nihil,* a sound, and nothing but a sound. On the contrary, one may represent true wit by the description which Aristinetus makes of a fine woman, when she is *dressed* she is beautiful, when she is *undressed* she is beautiful.

—Joseph Addison, *The Spectator* (1711)

4) I continued this method some few years, but gradually left it, retaining only the habit of expressing myself in terms of modest diffidence; never using, when I advanced anything that may possibly be disputed, the words *certainly, undoubtedly,* or any others that give the air of positiveness to an opinion; but rather say, *I conceive or apprehend a thing to be so and so; it appears to me;* or *I should think it so or so, for such and such reasons;* or *I imagine it to be so;* or *it is so, if I am not mistaken.* This habit, I believe, has been of great advantage to me when I have had occasion to inculcate my opinions, and persuade men into measures that I have been from time to time engaged in promoting; and, as the chief ends of conversation are to *inform* or to *be informed,* to *please* or to *persuade,* I wish well-meaning, sensible men would not lessen their power of doing good by a positive, assuming manner, that seldom fails to disgust, tends to create opposition, and to defeat every one of those purposes for which speech was given to us, to wit, giving or receiving information or pleasure. For, if you would inform, a positive and dogmatical manner in advancing your sentiments may provoke contradiction and prevent a candid attention. If you wish information and improvement from the knowledge of others, and yet at the same time express yourself as firmly fixed in your present opinions, modest, senisble men, who do not love disputation, will probably leave you undisturbed in the possession of your error. And by such a manner, you can seldom hope to recommend yourself in *pleasing* your hearers, or to persuade those whose concurrence you desire.

—Benjamin Franklin, *Autobiography* (1771)

5) The human species, according to the best theory I can form of it, is composed of two distinct races, *the men who borrow,* and *the men who lend.* To these two original diversities may be reduced all those impertinent classifications of Gothic and Celtic tribes, white men, black men, red men. All the dwellers upon earth, "Parthians, and Medes, and Elamites," flock hither, and do naturally fall in with one or other of these primary distinctions. The infinite superiority of the former, which I

choose to designate as the *great race,* is discernible in their figure, port, and a certain instinctive sovereignty. The latter are born degraded. "He shall serve his brethren." There is something in the air of one of this cast, lean and suspicious; contrasting with the open, trusting, generous manner of the other.

—Charles Lamb, *Essays of Elia* (1820)

6) Critics give themselves great labor to draw out what in the abstract constitutes the characters of a high quality of poetry. It is much better simply to have recourse to concrete examples;—to take specimens of poetry of the high, the very highest quality, and to say: The characters of a high quality poetry are what is expressed *there.* They are far better recognized by being felt in the verse of the master, than by being perused in the prose of the critic. Nevertheless, if we are urgently pressed to give some critical account of them, we may safely, perhaps, venture on laying down, not indeed how and why the characters arise, but where and in what they arise. They are in the matter and substance of the poetry, and they are in its manner and style. Both of these, the substance and matter on the one hand, the style and manner on the other, have a mark, an accent of high beauty, worth, and power. But if we are asked to define this mark and accent in the abstract, our answer must be: No, for we should thereby be darkening the question, not clearing it. The mark and accent are given by the substance and matter of that poetry, by the style and manner of that poetry, and of all other poetry which is akin to it in quality.

—Matthew Arnold, *The Study of Poetry* (1880)

D. Examine the following examples of modern English prose. Distinguish the kinds of writing represented by the different passages. Discuss fully each author's use of stylistic resources.

1) Sometimes, sitting there in the mountain sunshine above prairie-dog town, I could imagine the attraction of that open world after the fern forest damp or the croaking gloom of carboniferous swamps. There by a tree root I could almost make him out, that shabby little Paleocene rat, eternal tramp and world wanderer, father of all mankind. He ruffed his coat in the sun and hopped forward for a seed. It was to be a long time before he would be seen on the grass again, but he was trying to make up his mind. For good or ill there was to be one more chance, but that chance was fifty million years away.

Here in the Paleocene occurred the first great radiation of the placental mammals, and among them were the earliest primates—the zoological order to which man himself belongs. Today, with a few unimportant exceptions, the primates are all aboreal in habit except man. For this reason we have tended to visualize all of our remote relatives as tree dwellers. Recent discoveries, however, have begun to alter this one-sided picture. Before the rise of the true rodents, the highly successful order to which present-day prairie dogs and chipmunks belong, the environment which they occupy had remained peculiarly open to exploitation. Into this zone crowded a varied assemblage of our early relatives.

"In habitat," comments one scholar, "many of these early primates may be thought of as the rats of the Paleocene. With the later appearance of true rodents, the primate habitat was markedly restricted." The bone hunters, in other words, have succeeded in demonstrating that numerous primates reveal a remarkable development of rodent-like characteristics in the teeth and skull during this early period of mammalian evolution. The movement is progressive and distributed in several different groups.

One form, although that of a true primate, shows similarities to the modern kangaroo rat, which is, of course, a rodent. There is little doubt that it was a burrower.

—Loren Eiseley, *The Immense Journey* (New York: Random House, Inc., 1957), pp. 8–9.

2) Intelligence must necessarily be regarded as a central powerhouse that sends out current into any performance. The very nature of intelligence is adaptability, and it is this general quality which modern schools, modern tests, and modern life systematically neglect in favor of robot "aptitudes."

The excuse for doing so is slight but real. In the first place, an industrial world thinks it wants only a pinch of intelligence to season a great plateful of mechanical aptitudes. In the second place, though intelligence is and always will exist as a general power, it appears nowhere in full perfection. The man who can solve differential equations probably hits his thumb with the hammer at every stroke. Physical and emotional barriers keep intellect from shining like a bright light in all directions. Hence psychologists, noting the dark bands of interference, imagine separate entities which they name aptitudes. They ought perhaps to remember how widely "gifted" most children are, both physically and mentally, and although observers may later find versatility reduced, they should still assume a center of unspecialized mental force.

Teachers should not only assume it but work on it, for it atrophies if unused. Darwin has told us how his taste for poetry passed away as he specialized, and everyone can note in himself the loss of comparable powers. We may be reconciled to it as a sacrifice for greater ends, but we must not forget that they are *powers,* no less than sources of pleasure. Every college should therefore be dedicated to Intellect—not in the sense of pedantry, or verbalism, or highbrow superiority, but in the sense of Mind, free and restless in its desire to experience, comprehend, and use reality.

—Jacques Barzun, *Teacher in America* (New York: Doubleday & Company, Inc., 1955), pp. 186–87.

3) The British Army never saw itself as a citizens' army. It behaved as if a small gentlemanly officer class still had to make soldiers out of undergardeners' runaway sons and slum lads known to the police. These fellows had to be kept up to scratch. Let 'em get slack, they'd soon be a rabble again. So where the Germans and French would hold a bad front line with the minimum of men, allowing the majority to get some rest, the British command would pack men into rotten trenches, start something to keep up their morale, pile up casualties, and drive the survivors to despair. This was not done to win a battle, not even to gain a few yards of ground, but simply because it was supposed to be the thing to do. All the armies in that idiot war shoveled divisions into attacks, often as boneheaded as ours were, just as if healthy young men had begun to seem hateful in the sight of Europe, but the British command specialized in throwing men away for nothing. The tradition of an officer class, defying both imagination and common sense, killed most of my friends as surely as if those cavalry generals had come out of the château with polo mallets and beaten their brains out. Call this class prejudice if you like. I went into that war without any such prejudice, free of any class feeling. No doubt I came out of it with a chip on my shoulder; a big heavy chip, probably some friend's thighbone.

—J. B. Priestley, "Carry on, Carry on!" *The Atlantic,* February, 1963, p. 70.

E. In Margaret Nicholson's, *A Dictionary of American-English Usage,* look up Fowler's discussions of such stylistic defects as Elegant Variation, Genteelisms, Battered Ornaments, Pedantic Humor, Polysyllabic Humor, Pomposities, Stock Pathos, and Facetious Formations. Select one of these and discuss its role in current writing, giving a full range of examples from your own reading.

F. After defining the "mock reader" as the fictitious reader that a writer's language "invites us to become," Walker Gibson, in "Authors, Speakers, Readers, and Mock Readers" (*College English,* XI, [February, 1950], 265–69), says that the job of the editor of a periodical is largely the definition of his magazine's mock reader, conceived as its "ideal audience." Study Gibson's account of the mock reader of sample passages from *Partisan Review* and *The New Yorker.* Then prepare a similar analysis of a passage of nonfiction from another periodical aimed at an audience with at least some intellectual and cultural interests.

G. A speech teacher said about his subject:

> A public speaking class deals mainly with the art of persuasion. It also stresses critical listening—or the art of "knowing when to shut the damn thing off." This involves some semantics, plus practice in recognizing orderly, logical presentation and analysis of supportive evidence. Now, any student worth his salt learns quickly that there are certain primitive devices of persuasion, such as noisy repetition ("Sieg Heil! . . . Sieg Heil! . . . Sieg Heil!"), name-calling, the plain-folks gambit, the appeal to status, etc. When students overwork these old gimmicks, their class-mates become embarrassed and wish they were somewhere else—that is, if we have done our job properly. We like to think these students are equally sensitive outside the classroom; that they react in similar fashion to an absurd detergent commercial on television, or to a full page featuring the Big New Look in something or other.
>
> —Charles L. Todd, " 'Anti-Advertising' Educators?" *Saturday Review,* November 10, 1962, p. 74.

What devices of persuasion call for the attention of the teacher who wants to stress "critical reading" as well as "critical listening"? Use detailed examples from your recent or current reading.

H. Read a collection of essays written by a master of modern expository prose. Some outstanding collections to choose from are E. B. White, *One Man's Meat* (New York: Harper & Row, Publishers, 1940); Lewis Mumford, *The Human Prospect* (Boston: The Beacon Press, 1955); George Orwell, *A Collection of Essays* (New York: Doubleday & Company, Inc., 1957); Loren Eiseley, *The Immense Journey* (New York: Random House, Inc., 1957); James Baldwin, *Notes of a Native Son* (Boston: The Beacon Press, 1957). Select the essay that seems to illustrate best the author's use of the essay form. Write a full critique of it, concentrating on those matters that you consider most important for the teacher and student of rhetoric.

I. Select and contrast two essays on a common or related subject, one by a nineteenth-century and the other by a twentieth-century writer. Prepare a detailed comparative analysis of approach, structure, and style.

J. Study a discussion of expository prose, and of teaching students how to write it, by someone other than a teacher of English. For instance, read Jacques Barzun, "How to Write and Be Read," in *Teacher in America* (New York: Doubleday & Company, Inc., 1955), pp. 46–58; or Wendell Johnson, "You Can't Write Writing," in S. I. Hayakawa, ed., *The Use and Misuse of Language* (Greenwich, Conn.: Fawcett Publications, Inc., 1962), pp. 101–11. Present and argue in detail that part of the author's discussion you consider most important for the teacher of composition.

K. Discuss the following student papers. Pay full attention to such matters as the nature of the topic, the type of writing, the purpose of the author, organization, adequacy of development, appropriateness of tone, use of stylistic resources, and suitability for different kinds of readers. What did these student writers know about writing that other students would do well to emulate? What shortcomings do these papers show that could be corrected in revision and avoided in subsequent work?

THEME 1

Ceramics—My Hobby

Have you ever picked up a piece of free-form earthenware and thought how very satisfying and enjoyable it must have been for the person who worked it up from mere earth and water? By "free form," I mean the potter's own creative idea modeled in clay. Such free-form modeling is rather an involved process—many times, it is true, heartbreaking, but nevertheless an enjoyable and thoroughly gratifying experience.

It is possible to dig one's own clay from the earth. By moistening it with water and adding certain chemicals, one can make the clay mass more elastic, more workable, and stronger. Then follows the mixing of a glaze which, according to a specialized formula, will have an affinity to the original clay body. This in itself can become a long and tedious procedure. So, unless one has a pioneering spirit, it is better to find a standard clay body and glazes which have already been processed according to the manufacturer's own formula.

Cutting, shaping and molding the clay mass into the desired form with one's own hands is one of the biggest thrills imaginable. It is surprising what can be done with moist clay! A creative spirit can really go "wild" and still come up with something both beautiful and practical— say a flower vase or planter in the exaggerated form of some sea shell.

When the piece is thoroughly dry, it is known as "greenware" and is very fragile, but it becomes hardened through firing in a kiln. The firing is done slowly. The heat goes up to about 2000°F. It is measured by a cone-shaped pin set in a clay base and made to melt at the desired temperature. This is known as the pyrometric cone. The entire firing period takes about eight hours. Then the kiln is cooled slowly. It should not be opened or disturbed during the cooling time, which may take twelve hours or more. The greenware is now referred to as "bisque."

Bisque may be painted in a variety of colors, called underglaze, and then dipped in a transparent glaze. It may be sprayed or brushed with or dipped in any of the colored glazes. A second firing to bring out the glaze effect is now necessary. Usually, this firing is slow too, with the temperature not as intense as before—about 1800°F. However, the pyrometric cone must be watched more closely than in the bisque firing, especially with certain glaze formulas.

Glazes are extremely difficult to control, and many unexpected effects are obtained—probably caused by moisture in the air, uneven firing elements, firing time, dirt particles, or some chemical reaction. Many unique and unusual effects can be obtained through experimentation with underglazes, overglazes, colored clay bodies, sifted sands, crushed colored glass and even salt! I remember my first experiment. I used the sifted sand which I found in my backyard. I dusted the sand over the glaze coating and, after firing, found there were bright red and black raised granules throughout the glaze.

One can look at this hobby from a practical point of view. Gifts alone, especially at Christmas time, make it worth while. But it is the ideas and experiments that make it a truly fascinating and worthwhile hobby.

THEME 2

"Brains" Wanted

One of the most serious problems existing in the educational system of America is that of "anti-intellectualism." The existence of this problem is particularly noticeable on the high school level, while obviously not so prominent among college students.

I believe that this problem is serious because its existence could possibly destroy the whole idea behind our educational system. Our educators endeavor to give our students the will to educate and improve themselves; transmitting the idea of self-improvement to the students is, in my opinion, the backbone of our educational system. If the students of the nation continue to belittle intellectual achievement, and if they keep scorning those who do have the will for self-improvement, how, then, can our educational system survive?

Every high school has its honor students, who strive to further their educational standing by means of conscientious study and outstanding class participation. It would be in an exceptional school that these honor students would be encouraged and admired by their peers. Unfortunately, these intellectually outstanding students are often ridiculed and scorned by their fellow students, sometimes to such an extent that they jeopardize their grades in order to be accepted by their classmates. This conflict between the desire for intellectual improvement and the desire for social acceptance creates an uncomfortable position for these students.

In order to illustrate the seriousness of this problem, I turn to an experience which I witnessed during my junior year in high school. John, a serious student who had performed exceptionally well in grammar school and during his first years in high school, was publicly commended for his achievements at a student assembly. It was a proud and happy boy who walked across the stage to receive his award. His happiness turned to a feeling of embarrassment and shame, however, when after the assembly some of the other boys followed him to class, deliberately ridiculing him in front of the entire student body. Despite warning from faculty members, these boys continued to make fun of John for the remainder of the term. Their scorn was evidently more than he could take, for an entirely different boy returned to school in the fall. The boy who had been so proud of his intellectual achievements such a short time before was now just "one of the gang." The troublemakers who had ridiculed him before were now his friends, and *his* name, too, was in the "guest book" at the juvenile hall.

In a land so full of educational opportunities, it seems ironic that students should take such a stand against intellectual achievement. If, for some reason, a teen-ager decides that a student's life is not for him, he should keep his decision to himself instead of ridiculing those who do take an interest in their studies. I cannot but see a bit of jealousy in the person who calls a serious student "the brain," "bookworm," or "professor" in an attempt to embarrass him before his friends.

There is little that the teachers can do to correct this problem. The ability to come to a solution rests with the students themselves. The serious sudents should take their achievements in their stride and under no condition brag about their grades to the poorer students. This would undoubtedly eliminate most of the feelings of jealousy. Perhaps if the poor students didn't begrudge the high grades of their classmates the problem of "anti-intellectualism" would not exist.

THEME 3

Teen-Agers and Matrimony

Teen-age marriages long ago were a common occurrence. Girls were raised to be homemakers, and they were taught the arts of cooking, sewing, and raising children. Boys were brought up to do the work and to support a family. It was only logical that early marriages were common; however, times have changed. Girls now have the same opportunities and the same rights that boys do. Girls can select a career and further it to make something of themselves. In education almost all the subjects taught are open to girls as well as boys. Today a girl deprives herself of many opportunities if she marries young.

There are many reasons for teen-age marriages. Among them is the feeling of wanting to "get away from everything," "everything" usually meaning dominating parents. As an example I would like to use the case of two of my friends. The girl, sixteen, was ruled by the law of her parents. They made her conform to their every wish. The boy, eighteen, had almost the same problem; however, his main trouble was his mother always treating him as her little boy. The boy joined the service to get away from his mother, and the girl married him to get away from her folks. The marriage is now breaking up because the girl feels she has missed out on several years of fun and because the boy hates the service. He feels his wife pushed him into it. They are raising a little girl. As they go along, each one blames the other for the hasty marriage and the child.

A feeling of insecurity is another cause of early marriages. The feeling of not being wanted can often drive a boy and girl to marry to find the security that they didn't have at home. They don't stop to realize that even if marriage brings them security, it also brings other and larger problems.

Sometimes a teen-age marriage breaks up because the woman wants a career. I met such a couple three years ago. When I met them, they seemed well suited to each other. The man held a well-paying job; the woman was working part time as a beauty operator. They had a five-year-old little girl. Then the woman was offered a full-time job with a substantial increase in salary. This job brought her into contact with things she had never had or done. She is now suing for divorce; her husband left her. She cared more for her work than for her husband and her home. This couple was married when she was seventeen and he was nineteen.

Sometimes early marriages result from a strong physical attraction. A girl meets a tall, dark, and handsome boy, and right away she thinks she is madly in love. Rush marriages sometimes fail because the couple finds it wasn't love but physical attraction that brought them together. Girls and boys have to be able to get along mentally as well as physically to be happy.

With all the social life that a girl has now I don't feel that she is able to settle down to a life of raising a family and taking care of a home. With a boy it might be different, but I doubt that it is. To hold a good job now a boy almost has to have a college diploma, and then there is the service that may enter his life either before or after college. That is why I don't think that teen-age boys are any more ready for marriage than girls are.

Of course I'm not saying that all teen-age marriages don't work. If the girl is mature emotionally and mentally, and if the boy besides being mature has some type of support, the marriage has a good chance of working. I'm not even saying that the majority of teen-age marriages fail, but there are more strikes against them than for them. If a boy and girl wait until they are very sure of themselves, they will have a better chance for a successful marriage.

Any brief discussion of literature is likely to raise more questions than it answers. Literature, like language, is rich and complex. Few of the major issues in the history of literary criticism can be settled once and for all.

five

Even more so than other major areas in the discipline of English, literature baffles the person looking for neat categories, efficient approaches, and simple answers.

Indeed, the first point to be made about the teaching of literature is that the teacher must be willing to entertain conflicting theories and to explore works widely different in nature and scope. Literature is a mansion with many rooms. As in the teaching of language, the teacher needs first of all an open-minded, receptive attitude. He will find it hard to develop in his students a lasting relationship to literature if his interests are narrow, his tastes fastidious, his standards one-sided and exclusive. He must first of all learn to regard literature as a source of rich and varied insight, inspiration, and enjoyment.

Literature

Nevertheless, the second point to be made about the teaching of literature is that it must reflect something more than uncritical appreciation. Certainly, the teacher must make his students feel he cares about literature; he must communicate to them his sense of its significance and excitement. But he cannot do so by teaching that is an extended variation on the theme of "I like what I like." He needs a workmanlike grasp of what makes literature what it is. He must be able to talk about literary significance and value, not in vaguely inspirational terms, but with specific reference to the work before the class. In the words of W. K. Wimsatt, Jr., though our discussion of a poem "will almost inevitably be charged with intimations of its value," the staple commitments of the teacher are

Explanation . . . —of the explicit and clearly ascertainable but perhaps obscure or disguised meaning of words; *description*—of the poem's structure and parts, its shape and colors, and its historical relations; *explication*—the turning of such description as far as possible into meaning.[1]

[1] "What to Say About a Poem," *College English*, XXIV (February, 1963), 381.

Linguists have insisted that language cannot be meaningfully taught by the amateur relying for guidance on his prejudices. Similarly, modern critics have required of the teacher something more than subjective preferences, tempered by good intentions. Modern literary criticism has thus helped to demolish the assumption that "anyone can teach English."

As in his teaching of language, the teacher aiming at workmanlike competence in his teaching of literature will do well to steer clear of dogmatism and discipleship. He should recognize, with R. S. Crane, the existence of a number of significant critical approaches, "each of which exhibits the literary object in a different light, and each of which has its characteristic powers and limitations."[2] There is no one tome that will furnish all the important answers, complete with lesson plans. There is instead a vigorous growth of different critical tendencies, some of them more relevant to the teacher's task than others. Here as elsewhere, the teacher must learn to distinguish between the solid and the merely fashionable. If he approaches modern literary criticism in such a discriminating frame of mind, his sensitivity will be sharpened by an awareness of the more crucial problems that critics and teachers of literature before him have had to face.

Approaches to Literary Study

The modern linguist has typically concentrated on the relations existing *within* language. Similarly, the modern critic has typically concentrated on the relations *within* the literary text. He has focused attention on the internal structure and texture of the individual poem, novel, or play. More traditional approaches had concentrated on *preparing* the reader for a fuller appreciation—by study of background, setting, authorship, sources, currents of which the individual work was a part. At times, what had been intended as preparation became a substitute for *the careful reading of the work itself.* Reacting against such extremes, modern criticism has recommended from the beginning a frontal assault on the text. It has put a premium on **explication,** on close formal analysis. It has assumed, in the words of R. P. Blackmur, that "criticism must be concerned, first and last—whatever comes between—with the poem as it is read and as what it represents is felt." Once we adopt this point of view, we will judge the critic first of all by whether his speculations too early and too fast leave the actual work behind or whether he succeeds in maintaining throughout "a sense of continuous relationship, of sustained contact" with the work under discussion.[3]

The crucial gain in adopting this general approach lies in the au-

2 *Critics and Criticism: Essays in Method,* abridged ed. (Chicago: University of Chicago Press, 1957), p. iv.
3 *Language as Gesture: Essays in Poetry* (New York: Harcourt, Brace & World, Inc., 1952), pp. 390, 385.

thenticity it can give to literary study. The student reading *Oedipus Rex* will feel the horror of incest more powerfully when he is led to respond to it in the text than when he encounters it, with all its edges blunted, in the background lecture. The student asked to read and reread Shakespeare, rather than the critics, can feel that he is dealing with what is, first and last, important about literature. He can early be weaned from reliance on thirdhand categories and secondhand judgments. He will early learn to co-operate with the writer—to follow the pattern of a work with little interference from preconceptions and stock responses. He will learn, as it were, to yield the author's right of way, to become, in Virginia Woolf's phrase, his "fellow-worker and accomplice."

The second benefit to be derived from stress on close study of the text is intimately related to the first. By keeping the actual work in mind at all times, the student has a better than usual chance of establishing an over-all view. He has a chance of developing that sensitivity to the whole, without slighting the parts, that we mean by his "understanding" a poem or a story. We come to understand a work by responding to the clues that reinforce each other and direct our attention in appropriate channels. We follow the lines converging toward points of major emphasis. We see how one passage echoes or qualifies another. An interpretation tracing such clues and patterns explains the sense of "rightness," of coherence and purpose, that we experience when reading the work in a less analytical frame of mind.

In our reading of a novel, for instance,

> there is a stage beyond comprehending the plain sense of the text, a stage beyond participating imaginatively within the world of the novel; there is a stage where we contemplate the book, see it as a whole, and recognize in its structure some kind of "meaning."[4]

An interpretation aiming at such a sense of the whole must consider, in their mutual relations, the elements of which the novel is made. Thus, we take stock of the most significant relations and contrasts among the characters. We examine the way in which the author, whether through revealing ironies or overt commentary, guides our emotional involvement with them. We trace the pattern that emerges as the events of the plot are played off against the characters' expectations, their intentions, their standards. We examine the role of crucial incidents, of recurrent symbols, of insistent questions concerning a character's motives or view of life. We relate the action of the plot to the setting, which may be more than an incidental backdrop. We try to pinpoint features of imagery or of tone that significantly affect a prevailing mood, an emerging emotional

---

[4] Paul Pickrel, "Teaching the Novel: *Great Expectations*," in *Essays on the Teaching of English: Reports of the Yale Conferences on the Teaching of English*, eds. Edward J. Gordon and Edward S. Noyes (New York: Appleton-Century-Crofts, Inc., 1960), p. 218.

quality. In short, we examine the structure and texture of the work with
an eye toward its total significance. In doing so, we may hope to formulate, without intolerable simplification, the way the novel as a whole
shapes experience.

While a text-centered approach thus ideally makes us more receptive
toward literature, in practice it brings with it preconceptions of its own.
It can easily make us pay disproportionate attention to the way the author
shaped his materials, and not enough attention to the broader significance
of the materials so shaped. Modern studies of fiction, for instance, have
paid much attention to the problem of **point of view.** They have investigated the perspective adopted by the author, the vantage point from
which he surveys people and events. Point of view often affects not only
the tone but the substance of a work: Stephen Crane, in a story like "The
Blue Hotel," assumes the stance of the businesslike, unsentimental reporter. Crane thus achieves an effect of immediacy, of the "facts" hitting
the reader with their full original impact, that is denied to the author
using one of his characters as a narrator or stepping in himself as a com-
mentator on the action. Mark Twain, in *Huckleberry Finn,* uses Huck as
the assumedly naive spectator in the tradition of Voltaire's *Candide.*
Huck's unspoiled receptivity gives added impact to the violence, squalor,
and treachery he observes. More effective than condemnation in so many
words is Huck's simple and open-eyed registering of what men are
capable of. As T. S. Eliot has observed, Huck does not judge the world;
he allows it to judge itself. In our reading of Henry James's *The Am-
bassadors* or Faulkner's *The Sound and the Fury,* we can hardly miss the
crucial role of the **reflector** or reflectors through whose consciousness the
action is filtered. The reflector's preconceptions and limitations in crucial
ways limit the reader's view of events.

On the other hand, concern with perspective, as with other matters of
technique, can easily become overanxious. A critic's insistence on the conditions imposed by a narrator's limited point of view can become as
literal-minded as the neoclassicist's protest that stretching the span of a
tragedy from a day to a day and a half would violate common sense and
destroy the unity of time. Modern critics have typically censured in novelists like Thackeray and Hardy the mingling of objective narration, narration through the eyes of a character, and commentary by the **intruding
author.** Such considerations can prejudice the student against a rich and
vital tradition. The intrusion of the chatty, self-disparaging author is as
much a convention in the novel since Fielding as the self-conscious self-
effacement of the author is in the novel since James. The reader would
hardly want to miss such passages as Thackeray's presentation, at the
beginning of *Vanity Fair,* of the characters on his imaginary puppet stage,
or Hardy's comment, at the end of *The Mayor of Casterbridge,* on the sad
wisdom of Elizabeth-Jane, whose

experience had been of a kind to teach her, rightly or wrongly, that the doubtful honor of a brief transit through a sorry world hardly called for effusiveness, even when the path was suddenly irradiated at some half-way point by daybeams rich as hers. (Ch. 45)

We should take care not to inhibit the student's response to novels such as these by purely theoretical considerations.

Similar problems for the classroom teacher are caused by the preference of text-centered literary study for stylistic subtlety. With Cleanth Brooks, advocates of intensive reading have typically looked for "the requisite closeness of grain, the fineness of texture, the attention to the detail of the pattern that go with the arrangement of more subtle effects."[5] They have looked for a network of parallels and correspondences within the work—often discovering unsuspected coherence in an apparently episodic novel or loosely structured poem. Thus, Brooks, in reading *Huckleberry Finn*, does not respond to the rehearsal by the duke and king of a scene from *Romeo and Juliet* merely for its grotesque, farcical appeal. Rather, he is reminded of the earlier feud between the Grangerfords and the Sheperdsons, and the parallel it offers to Shakespeare's account of the Capulets and the Montagues, the feuding clans to which Romeo and Juliet belong. When Huck watches the drunken spectator at the circus who finally reveals himself as an accomplished performer, Brooks is reminded of Huck's insanely drunk father, of the fatal bragging of the drunken Boggs, and of other figures in the novel who are drunk with pride and honor, if not literally with corn whiskey.

The skeptical reader will often demand of such a critic: Which of these parallels are significant or intentional, and which are merely fanciful? Emphasis on such correspondences can make literary creation seem overly deliberate and "artificial." It makes it seem as if adequate response is something for the deep reader. This is an impression the teacher must try to counteract. He must guard against making his students feel more obtuse than they really are. Carrying his predilection for complexity to an extreme, the text-centered critic has often made a virtue of obscurity, real or imagined:

> The more possible relationships, the more explication will have to say. It has thus concerned itself more with the difficult and obscure poem. Worse, it has upon occasion produced a kind of ingeniousness and obfuscation in approaching poems that have little difficulty, producing the kind of explication burlesqued in a treatment of "Thirty Days Hath September" by Theodore Spencer in "How to Criticize a Poem (In the Manner of Certain Contemporary Critics)," *The New Republic* (1943), where it is discovered that "February is 'alone,' is cut off from communication with his fellows . . .

[5] "The Teaching of the Novel: *Huckleberry Finn*," Gordon and Noyes, *Essays*, p. 203.

the solitary and maladjusted individual who is obviously the hero and the crucial figure of the poem."[6]

Text-centered study may thus have undesirable side effects when its preferences become unquestioned values. However, cultivated less dogmatically, it has had a pervasive leavening effect on more conventional approaches to literary study. The biographical approach to literature, for instance, had long suffered from the lack of a clear rationale. The student who wanted to read Wordsworth's "Tintern Abbey" was first taken to Cumberland, to Cambridge, to France, to Germany, and to the Lake Country. He was acquainted with the poet's parents, his sister, his friends, his wife. Often the biographical account proved so extensive that the student was trusted to read "Tintern Abbey" for himself, between classes. Even when biographical material was clearly treated as a prelude to the poems, its relevance and significance were not always clearly thought through. Often it was simply assumed that the student would find reading *about* the poet as pleasant as the teacher, and that such reading could not fail to enhance the student's appreciation of the literature itself.

Some of the ways in which **literary biography** *does* enhance our response to the work are obvious. It is not only that in order to grasp the plain sense of a work we may have to understand allusions to the author's private history. The occasion and biographical context of a work are often in a true sense part of its meaning. Milton's *Areopagitica* owes its drive and power to its being not merely a theoretical discussion of censorship but the personal plea of someone deeply involved in the controversies of his time. Byron's references to freedom in *Childe Harold* and in *Don Juan* acquire an additional dimension, of authenticity and personal commitment, in the context of his life: his rebellion against respectability, his support of libertarian revolutionaries in Italy and Greece. It is impossible to read James Joyce or Sean O'Casey without being reminded at every turn of their having reached manhood in early twentieth-century Ireland, with its traumatic legacy of divided loyalties, of love and hate.

However, in dealing with such relations, literary biography in textbook and classroom often did justice neither to the complexities of personality, nor to the thorny problem of the relationship between life and literature. Even the most obvious pitfalls were not always avoided: In times past, biographical material was often sifted to extract edifying details considered suitable for schoolroom use. To the skeptical student, literary biography thus became another of the devices by which adults pass themselves off as better than they are. At the other extreme, writers with private lives considered unfortunate, such as Shelley or Poe or Wilde, were occasionally deprived of a fair hearing for their literary efforts.

[6] George Arms, "Poetry," in *Contemporary Literary Scholarship: A Critical Review*, ed. Lewis Leary (New York: Appleton-Century-Crofts, Inc., 1958), p. 246.

On a more sophisticated level, many a biographer seemed to accept a variation of Ruskin's view that "great art is produced by men who feel acutely and nobly"; that true artistic perfection is not consistent "with any viciousness of soul, with any mean anxiety, any gnawing lust, any wretchedness of spite or remorse, any consciousness of rebellion against law of God or man." Much scholarly labor was expended to make the powerfully idiosyncratic personality of an Alexander Pope or an Emily Dickinson conform to a hypothetical ideal of psychological normalcy—of kindness, of tolerance, of an ordinary concern for ordinary things. Such efforts, loyal and well meant, make less rather than more intelligible the brilliant spite that animates the satires of Pope, the savage indignation that in the writings of Swift forces us to qualify our stereotypes about the coolly intellectual "age of reason." Generally, literary biographers have not been sufficiently mindful of the elementary warning that

> nothing can so quickly blur and distort the facts as desire—the wish to use the facts for some purpose of your own—and nothing can so surely destroy the truth. As soon as the witness wants to prove something he is no longer impartial and his evidence is no longer to be trusted.[7]

The biographer truly worth listening to is the one who has an overriding interest in the ascertainable and yet never fully revealing facts. He makes no pretense to a full knowledge of the private sphere of thought and motive, nor does he apply one-dimensional moral standards to complex, contradictory personalities. Such a biographer can furnish an authoritative account of matters in which readers of literature have a legitimate interest: Milton's role in church and state, Wordsworth's acquaintance with the realities of the French Revolution, O'Neill's relations with his family.

Modern critics have typically avoided the incompleteness and partiality of much conventional literary biography by concentrating on the artifact rather than its creator. T. S. Eliot set the direction for many followers when he said

> the poet has, not a "personality" to express, but a particular medium, . . . in which impressions and experiences combine in peculiar and unexpected ways. Impressions and experiences which are important for the man may take no place in the poetry, and those which become important in the poetry may play quite a negligible part in the man, the personality.

Indeed, Eliot asserted that although the mind of the poet "may partly or exclusively operate upon the experience of the man himself . . . the more perfect the artist, the more completely separate in him will be the man who suffers and the mind which creates; the more perfectly will the mind digest and transmute the passions which are its material."[8]

[7] Marchette Chute, "Getting at the Truth," *Saturday Review*, September 19, 1953, p. 12.
[8] "Tradition and the Individual Talent," in *Selected Essays: 1917–1932* (New York: Harcourt, Brace & World, Inc., 1932), pp. 7–9.

To many readers, this view of the autonomy of the creative impulse will seem to slight the intense personal commitment they sense in the literature they respond to most deeply. They will object to too dogmatic a rejection of "personality" in favor of "medium." But even critics taking a more moderate view have concentrated on the identity the writer assumes *as writer*. They have set out to discuss the *persona* rather than the person:

> It is now common in the classroom as well as in criticism to distinguish carefully between the *author* of a literary work of art and the fictitious *speaker* within the work of art. Most teachers agree that the attitudes expressed by the "lover" in the love sonnet are not to be crudely confused with whatever attitudes the sonneteer himself may or may not have manifested in real life. Historical techniques are available for a description of the sonneteer, but the literary teacher's final concern must be with the speaker, that voice or disguise through which someone (whom we may as well call "the poet") communicates with us. It is this speaker who is "real" in the sense most useful to the study of literature, for the speaker is made of language alone, and his entire self lies on the page before us in evidence.[9]

It is true that in some sense all literature, as Goethe said, is confession. But it is also true that it communicates by exploiting elements common to human experience, by dramatizing common human possibility. By focusing on the personality of the writer as writer, we to some extent sidestep the thorny and never conclusive task of disentangling the private and public elements in his work. Thus defining our interest in literary "personality," we can and should proceed beyond the individual work to develop our response to the personal vision, the personal **idiom,** of the writer. Henry James said of the novel that it is "in its broadest definition a personal, a direct impression of life: that, to begin with, constitutes its value." He said more generally that

> the deepest quality of a work of art will always be the quality of the mind of the producer. In proportion as that intelligence is fine will the novel, the picture, the statue partake of the substance of beauty and truth.[10]

The writer, indeed, is likely to protest against "the delusion that books are not produced by authors, that authors are less deserving of critical concern than their characters are." He is likely to insist that "criticism by *writers* is always sensitive to the individual mind and personality behind a book."[11]

We present literature to our students under false pretenses if we give them an isolated poem, which then turns out to be by Wordsworth or

9 Walker Gibson, "Authors, Speakers, Readers, and Mock Readers," *College English,* XI (February, 1950), 265.
10 "The Art of Fiction," in *Criticism: The Foundations of Modern Literary Judgment* (rev. ed.), eds. Mark Schorer, *et al.* (New York: Harcourt, Brace & World, Inc., 1958), pp. 47, 54.
11 Alfred Kazin, "Writers as Characters," *The Reporter,* October 11, 1962, p. 62.

Coleridge or Keats. The teacher himself typically does not read literature anonymously; as everyday usage has it, he reads "Keats," or "Milton," or "Joyce." Learning to read literature means at least in part learning to recognize an author's characteristic voice, his recurrent concerns, his way of looking at experience. Like the modern linguist, the modern critic prides himself on the objectivity achieved through concentrating on the medium rather than on the message. At its extreme, modern criticism "isolates the poem from biographical considerations, not regarding it as a message from author to reader but rather as an object that once produced by the author has an existence of its own."[12] Such a procedure may prove fruitful as a strategy for rigorous investigation. The classroom teacher, however, can never afford to forget that language is first and last a means of interaction among human beings.

Proceeding beyond the private history of the author, traditional literary instruction typically placed his life and work in their **milieu,** their full historical setting. Literary history "cannot be fully understood unless its relationships to other kinds of history are discovered and defined at every point."[13] The history of imaginative literature is intertwined with political, military, economic, religious, and intellectual history. Much English literature remains obscure to the student unaware of the historical role of the Anglican state church, of the historical relations between England and occupied Ireland. Not only Sir Thomas Browne's *Religio Medici* and Milton's *Paradise Lost* but also Swift's *Gulliver's Travels* requires of the reader some knowledge of the religious controversies of the seventeenth century. In reading the poetry of Tennyson and Browning we must grasp its references, direct and indirect, to contemporary religious and scientific thought.

Today more than ever, our students are handicapped in their reading of literature because they lack a knowledge of Western cultural history. Rather than being studied as one of the most basic elements in civilized man's understanding of himself, history in the schools has for decades been more or less optional, a subject to be "coordinated" with more glamorous or immediately interesting subject matter. But even today the English teacher must resist the temptation to do the historian's job rather than his own. As one eminent literary historian has said, "the tendency of historical scholarship was dangerously centrifugal and it was possible to lecture eloquently on an author without reading a word of his own writings." Today's teacher of literature has learned to use historical knowledge "from the inside out rather than from the outside in."[14] He has learned that "history is as much *in* our literary texts as our texts are

---

12 Arms, in Leary, *Scholarship,* p. 238.
13 Robert E. Spiller, "Is Literary History Obsolete?" *College English,* XXIV (February, 1963), 346.
14 *Ibid.,* pp. 348–51.

in our history."[15] Wherever possible, he lets the play, the novel, re-establish its own context. To strengthen the student's weak historical sense, he relies on selections that have a strong intrinsic interest and at the same time illuminate important elements of our cultural heritage.

Turning to literature itself, traditional scholarship focused attention on major trends in the history of style, on the literary currents of a **period.** Writers do not write in isolation. Whether or not they join literary movements and issue literary manifestoes, they react in complicated ways to the literature of their time and to the literary tradition as a whole. As Lionel Trilling has said, "a culture is not a flow, nor even a confluence; the form of its existence is struggle, or at least debate—it is nothing if not a dialectic."[16] Part of Richardson's aim in *Clarissa* was to give the *coup de grâce* to the Dorimants, Harcourts, and Mirabells of Restoration comedy. He set out to show that a polished manner, a ready wit, and all the advantages of birth and education might be but a façade for gross perfidy and heinous crimes. Fielding in turn was moved to write *Joseph Andrews* by way of protest against the oppressively self-important virtue of Richardson's heroines. He set out to show that lust and promiscuity might have their petty and comic as well as their melodramatic side; that even Virtue, when naive or misdirected, could on occasion be laughable—and as a result be more human than the relentless casting up of moral accounts by the middle-class prude. Jane Austen was writing at the height of the Romantic vogue when in *Sense and Sensibility* she pitted solid common sense against enthusiasm and impetuous desire.

Tracing similar patterns of action and reaction can help the student make sense of the history of style. Familiar patterns through excessive repetition become insipid; they are superseded by a more complex, more forceful style. Reaching its extreme, this "new" style is felt to be too strained, too artificial, with a resulting reaction toward deliberate smoothness and simplicity. Donne was not alone in abandoning the conventions of the Petrarchan sonnet; Dryden in turn was not alone in rejecting a tortured metaphysical style. Ezra Pound was not the only early twentieth-century poet laboring to restore a genuine poetic texture to what had become too facile a medium for versified sentiment.

Part of the meaning of every literary work resides in its relationship to established **patterns of expectation.** These the writer satisfies or disappoints, making them serve his own purposes. Extending such a perspective to include the literary tradition as a whole, T. S. Eliot in "Tradition and the Individual Talent" said that no poet "has his complete meaning alone." The continued growth of the literary tradition is a "development which abandons nothing en route," which is perhaps refinement and

15 Roy Harvey Pearce, "Literature, History, and Humanism: An Americanist's Dilemma," *College English, XXIV* (February, 1963), 364.
16 *The Liberal Imagination: Essays on Literature and Society* (New York: Doubleday and Company, Inc., 1953), p. 20.

certainly complication. The historical sense is "nearly indispensable to anyone who would continue to be a poet beyond his twenty-fifth year." That historical sense "involves a perception, not only of the pastness of the past, but of its presence."[17] Eliot thus combined his "impersonal" theory of poetry with one that was the opposite of ahistorical.

However significant in principle, in practice literary history suffered from familiar defects. Influenced by late nineteenth-century positivism, many literary historians aimed above all at rigor and reliability. Too often, as Jacques Barzun has said, they did so by "applying the literal part of the historical method—the part that stops short of intuition and imagination. . . . Whatever was not factual and 'shown,' whatever was imaginative and readable, was unscholarly."[18] To many a frustrated student, the scholar's prized discoveries—controverted dates of composition, obscure sources, variant texts—came to seem mere dust and ashes.

At the same time, paradoxically in a climate of worship for the facts, textbooks and classroom practice encouraged excessive reliance on secondhand generalization. Students were allowed to repeat stereotyped labels that they had not earned the right to use. Too often such labels—the "artificiality" of courtly love, the "decadence" of the Jacobean playwrights, the "immorality" of the Restoration stage—kept the student from coming to grips with the complex patterns of feeling and form in the actual works. Textbooks glibly and superficially labeled eighteenth-century "optimism" glib and superficial—without facing up to, let alone solving, the age-old paradox of vindicating to man the ways of a good God in creating a world in some respects evil. We defeat the whole purpose of historical instruction if we seem to dismiss Pope's deism merely because it is out of fashion. The first thing the student must understand is that in its time deism was taken *seriously,* that it affected in significant ways the intellectual, emotional, and imaginative orientation of important writers. If we want to criticize it meaningfully, we must do it the courtesy of engaging it on the level of its own assumptions.

Finally, conventional literary history encouraged excessive compartmentalization. In the colleges and universities, literature was chopped up into periods firmly separated by the conflicting interest and prejudices of their respective specialists. As a result, the student often failed to gain a feeling for the basic and continuing concerns of literature, for some of the basic and recurrent problems in literary theory. The teacher trained in traditional programs often went out into the schools with a mass of detail but with a dimly felt lack of a clear rationale, of a clear sense of what literature is all about.

Often the most illuminating relationships cut across the arbitrary limits of the period course. Certain major **themes** in human experience,

17 Eliot, *Selected Essays,* pp. 4, 6.
18 "The Scholar-Critic," in Leary, *Scholarship,* pp. 4–5.

certain major avenues of approach to central problems of life and art, furnish constants in literary history that the period course tends to obscure. Great literature tends to return to such questions as the relationship between desire and reality, between impulse and duty, between individual and society, between human hopes for a meaningful, ordered universe and blind coincidence. The student develops a historical rather than merely an antiquarian perspective when he sees how such major themes are treated by authors of different temperaments and influenced by different contemporary assumptions.

One such theme is the conception of cosmic order that Arthur O. Lovejoy, in *The Great Chain of Being* (1936), traced from the ancients to Pope's *Essay on Man*. In his reading of Spenser, of Shakespeare, or of Pope, the student must respond to the powerful appeal of the concept of a cosmic hierarchy, of all things in their infinite diversity yet being in their appointed place:

> The heavens themselves, the planets and this center,
> Observe degree, priority, and place,
> Insisture, course, proportion, season, form,
> Office, and custom, in all line of order.
> (Shakespeare, *Troilus and Cressida,* Act I, Sc. 3)

The student must learn to see the persuasive force of this concept when applied as a rationalization of a hierarchic society, based on inherited privilege:

> How could communities,
> Degrees in schools and brotherhoods in cities,
> Peaceful commerce from dividable shores,
> The primogenitive and due of birth,
> Prerogative of age, crowns, scepters, laurels,
> But by degree, stand in authentic place?
> (Act I, Sc. 3)

Another such theme is the idealization of love, which C. S. Lewis in *The Allegory of Love* (1936) traced from the troubadours through the *Roman de la Rose* and Chaucer's *Troilus* to Spenser. The tradition of courtly love is more than a historical curiosity, affording the student at best some condescending chuckles at the endless sighs and scruples of the lover. It is a living part of the paradoxically idealized and belittled role of the second sex in the Western tradition. It furnishes one side of the paradox that Ibsen's Nora rebels against in *The Doll's House,* that tortures and lacerates Sue Bridehead in Hardy's *Jude the Obscure,* that D. H. Lawrence attacks with fanatical insistence. As C. S. Lewis said, "humanity does not pass through phases as a train passes through stations":

> French poets, in the eleventh century, discovered or invented, or were the
> first to express, that romantic species of passion which English poets were

still writing about in the nineteenth. They effected a change which has left no corner of our ethics, our imagination, or our daily life untouched, and they erected impassable barriers between us and the classical past or the Oriental present.[19]

In adopting a thematic approach, the teacher in high school or in college can give a much-needed sense of continuity to literary study. In doing so, however, he must be aware of a basic problem. Lovejoy's approach became identified as the study of the **history of ideas**. When taken literally, this term leads to a lopsided philosophical and ideological emphasis. Such a bias may make the scholar concentrate on the common denominator of current thought as reflected in the writings of second- and third-rate authors. It may make him trace paraphrasable and quotable concepts from one obscure source to another. To make thematic study literary rather than philosophical, the teacher will have to explore a central theme as given form and meaning by major writers. His interest will not be in a bare idea but in an author's wrestling with it, his coming to terms with it:

> Loneliness, for example, considered merely as an idea, is indifferent. It becomes great, trivial, or vulgar only because it has been handled by Alan Paton or Edgar Guest or a deodorant company. It is technique, craftsmanship, use of the means of concentrating ideas into words, style—call it what you will—which makes literature a great communication of experience.[20]

A generation of modern critics has warned the teacher against using a work as a mere vehicle for the author's thought. They have warned against the dangers of paraphrasing and message-hunting, insisting that "poetry is idiom, a special and fresh saying, and cannot for its life be said otherwise."[21]

A writer's treatment of a major theme is of interest to us not as a system of abstract ideas but as a configuration of attitudes, a pattern of sensibility. It can serve as a possible clue to a work's structure, its mood, its emotional impact. The themes that are of major interest to the literary historian are not abstractly logical: the theme of cosmic order is crucial in English literary history because it has an imaginative as well as a theological and philosophical dimension. A poet's treatment of love reflects not so much a system of ideas as a characteristic pattern of thought and feeling.

Thus qualified, emphasis on major literary themes has an illuminating and integrating effect. Adapted to the adolescent's level of sophistication, it can make the high school student's first introduction to literary history seem more than history for the sake of the historical record. Adapted to the level of a senior seminar or graduate colloquium in

[19] *The Allegory of Love: A Study in Medieval Tradition* (New York: Oxford University Press, 1958), pp. 1, 4.
[20] Rev. William J. O'Malley, S.J., "Literary Craftsmanship: The Integration of Literature and Composition," *The English Journal*, LII (April, 1963), 268.
[21] Blackmur, *Language as Gesture*, p. 381.

college, it can help unify and render fruitful the English major's perhaps extensive but often fragmented previous training in literature. *The most meaningful course in literary history is one that concentrates on major works, presents them in a sequence reflecting major lines of development, and stresses a number of major themes in the history of literary sensibility.*

One way of combining close attention to the individual work with awareness of its historical context is study of literature by **genre,** or major literary type. Often the history of a genre helps to explain otherwise strange features. For instance, the English novel in the eighteenth century betrays its indebtedness to the **picaresque** tradition. Many early novels were accounts of the adventures of the *picaro,* or vagrant rogue, making his living by his wits in an often hostile or sordid environment. This background helps explain the episodic plot of many early novels, stringing together the miscellaneous incidents of a journey. It helps explain the low-life perspective, the openness to the farcical, the sordid, the grotesque. It helps explain why in a novel like Defoe's *Moll Flanders* the elevating moral sentiments seem tacked on to a story of exuberant rascality.

Study of genre thus calls attention to the role of **convention.** It alerts the reader to procedures and assumptions that have become accepted by writer and audience as part of their willing suspension of disbelief. Before we construct an elaborate explanation for a puzzling detail, we should ask to what extent it reflects the conventions of the genre. Sometimes, such questions have a bearing on crucial matters of interpretation. For instance, is Hamlet, as Coleridge claims, "endlessly reasoning and hesitating," indecisive, irresolute—or is he, as the minority view has it, a forceful, even impetuous Renaissance prince? Here it *is* relevant that *Hamlet* was not the first tragedy of revenge ever written. Certain features of such a play had become more or less familiar to playwright and audience. First, the play, and thus the revenge, had to occupy a certain length of time. By killing the king in the first act, Hamlet would have defeated the play's most elementary purpose, namely to keep the spectators of a "large, cheap, and popular" commercial theater occupied for a conventional period.[22] More seriously, however, a number of steps in such a tragedy could be expected: first, the guilty party had to be discovered and his guilt confirmed, perhaps by roundabout and ingenious methods. Second, the difficulties in the way of the revenge had to be overcome. Third, refinements of the revenge had to be worked out to make sure the punishment would adequately pay for the crime. In *Hamlet,* we have the hero proceed from his initial bitterness and disillusionment to the first hints of foul play with the appearance of the dead king's ghost ("I'll speak to it though Hell itself should gape/And bid me hold my peace"). However, like Hieronimo in Kyd's *Spanish Tragedy,* Hamlet distrusts the first identification of the murderer. He decides to act mentally deranged so as to be better able to

---

22 G. E. Bentley, "Shakespeare and His Times," in Leary, *Scholarship,* p. 58.

confirm or prove unfounded the ghost's charges ("The Devil hath power / to assume a pleasing shape. . . . I'll have grounds / More relative than this"). Hamlet plots the ingenious play scene as a means of testing the king's conscience, taking Horatio into his confidence and arranging with him to compare their interpretations of the king's reactions. The king's guilt confirmed, Hamlet lets pass his first opportunity when he sees the king at prayer:

> Up, sword, and know thou a more horrid hent.
> When he is drunk asleep, or in his rage,
> Or in the incestuous pleasure of his bed—
> At gaming, swearing, or about some act
> That has no relish of salvation in 't—
> Then trip him, that his heels may kick at Heaven
> And that his soul may be as damned and black
> As Hell, whereto it goes.
>
> (Act III, Sc. 3)

Hamlet makes use of his second opportunity, but finds that the person hiding behind the curtain in his mother's room is not the king but Polonius ("I took thee for thy better"). In the meantime, the difficulties of the revenge are compounded by the king's counterplotting—his planning of the trip to England, his inciting Laertes against Hamlet as guilty of the deaths of Polonius and Ophelia. Almost, but not quite, outmaneuvered by the king, Hamlet finally succeeds in consummating his revenge. His rhetorical self-denunciations by which he spurs himself to action can be taken as the conventional expression of an impetuous, passionate temperament rather than as the literal record of sober self-realization. Observations such as these are not designed to make the reader forget the grim reluctance with which Hamlet enters upon his appointed task. They merely make it harder to make that reluctance the clue to an inherently indecisive temperament.

Taking into account the limitations and conventions of a genre is often a cautionary step. More central in a balanced, over-all view is our awareness of characteristic appeals and concerns. For instance, it is illuminating to approach drama with emphasis on the role of **conflict** in a serious play. Whether the conflict involves persons, institutions, or psychological forces, we often profit from studying closely its conditions, its development, its resolution. This line of inquiry may lead us to set up a distinction between **melodrama** and a mature play: Melodrama uses a black-and-white conflict, pitting the hero against the villain. A mature play, as A. C. Bradley pointed out in a famous discussion of Hegel's theory of tragedy, pits the protagonist against an antagonist of often considerable stature. In the framework of Hegel's theory, indeed,

> the essentially tragic fact is the self-division and intestinal warfare of the ethical substance, not so much the war of good with evil as the war of good

> with good. Two of these isolated powers face each other, making incompatible demands. The family claims what the state refuses, love requires what honour forbids.[23]

Thus, Antigone's loyalty to her dead brother conflicts with Creon's demand for loyalty to the state. The conflict is more than a stage conflict in which we complacently identify with those representing purity, motherhood, and the flag. Instead, it brings into play conflicting parts of our own being.

Generally, dramatic conflict is the more real the closer the antagonist comes to presenting a believable and powerful alternative to whatever is represented by the hero. For instance, in an early play by Arthur Miller, *All My Sons,* an idealistic younger generation is opposed to the narrow dedication to business and family of the generation represented by Joe Keller. During the war, Joe has shipped out defective airplane engines for fear of losing the defense contract on which his factory depends. Twenty fighter pilots have died in plane crashes as a result; Joe's own eldest son failed to return from a mission after learning what had happened. After we know these facts, every comment the play makes about life in a capitalistic society is loaded; every moral question is prejudged. There can be no real conflict but only atonement, achieved when Keller puts a bullet through his head in the final scene. In a later play, by contrast, Miller deals with a subject that would seem to invite a black-and-white treatment: the Salem witch trials of *The Crucible.* However, the greater power of this play derives at least in part from Miller's resisting the temptation to make the Puritan ministers and judges into beady-eyed grotesques. Instead, they are men of varied and believable temperaments. They are animated by such motives as pride of scholarship, belief in authority, horror of heresy, and consciousness of injured merit. In this play, the issue—the limits of justified compromise with oppressive and misguided authority—is in doubt until the last scene.

If conflict turns out to be a fruitful central idea for a discussion of drama, the teacher will naturally look for similar central ideas in the treatment of other genres. For instance, the novel, in the most mature of its traditional forms, typically *develops* character, whereas drama *presents* it. This effect of drama is most obvious in plays devoted to satirical exposure: In Ben Jonson's play, Volpone remains Volpone, and the only thing we can do at the end of the play is to hand him over to the magistrates. But a similar effect may be shown in the most serious drama: Antigone's defiant nonconformity is fully revealed in her conversation with her sister in the first scene of the play. Othello's fatal irascibility is shown on the occasion of the drunken brawl among his officers after the landing in Cyprus.

[23] A. C. Bradley, *Oxford Lectures on Poetry* (New York: St. Martin's Press, 1959), pp. 71–72.

By contrast, novelists like George Eliot and Thomas Hardy set out not to show but to transform character. In George Eliot's *Adam Bede,* the central character becomes more tolerant, more understanding toward other people. Change here does not mean the sudden repentances and conversions of melodrama. It means the cumulative effect of years filled with painful experience, useless regrets, diffident and sober renewed hope. Change means the gradual broadening of human understanding, the slow and painful cultivation of human susceptibilities. Cardinal Newman, in rendering account of the gradual changes in outlook leading to his conversion to the Catholic Church, says,

> it was not logic that carried me on; as well might one say that the quicksilver in the barometer changes the weather. It is the concrete being that reasons; pass a number of years, and I find my mind in a new place; how? the whole man moves.[24]

The novel, of the different literary genres, comes closest to the autobiography in its power to convey the authentic feeling of how "the whole man moves."

On the debit side, the dangers in excessive reliance on classification by genre are obvious. To the critic with a systematic mind, genres soon cease to be a convenience of classification and instead become prescribed forms. Thus, we find Sir Philip Sidney attacking the "mongrel tragicomedy" of the Elizabethan stage; we find later neoclassicists adopting similar assumptions concerning purity of genre. However, as Walter Pater said in his essay on "Style," efforts "to limit art *a priori* . . . are always liable to be discredited by the facts of artistic production."[25] The critic taking a balanced view will let a work make its appeal on its own terms. He will not allow a notion of the inherent distinctness of genres to prejudge the unconventional, to rule out new ways of feeling or experiments in form. Some of the most enduringly interesting works do not fit easily into established categories. Is Spenser's *Faerie Queene* an epic or a romance? Is James Joyce's *Ulysses* a novel? As Robert B. Heilman has said,

> we have to acknowledge the right of any work to escape from the traditional guide-lines of its apparent genre and to disturb the peace with all sorts of generic novelties, some of which we may be tardy in placing. But we can suspend the rules in this way and still believe that there are persisting patterns of form and function that provide a partial basis for assessing the individual work, viewing it comparatively, and thus, by reducing its singularity, defining its uniqueness more intelligently.[26]

Literary biography, literary history, the study of genres—all these profit from periodically having to prove their relevance to the teacher

[24] *Apologia Pro Vita Sua,* ed. A. Dwight Culler (Boston: Houghton Mifflin Company, 1956), p. 169.
[25] In *Prose of the Victorian Period,* ed. William E. Buckler (Boston: Houghton Mifflin Company, 1958), p. 554.
[26] "Genre and Curriculum," *College English,* XXIV (February, 1963), 361.

who above all wants to read and discuss with his classes important individual works. Biographers and historians profit from periodically
being reminded that "scaffoldings of date or incident or ideology need
not be erected in such pattern that they obscure or even blur the outlines of a work of literary art."[27] In turn, these auxiliary disciplines keep
our interpretation of the individual work from becoming arbitrary. By
reminding us of relevant facts, they discourage mere capricious speculation. They counteract the modern preoccupation with technique, discouraging the kind of teaching that "divorces technical analysis in the
student's mind from content."[28] They keep our concern with the tools
of the writer's craft from becoming a barren cult of technical virtuosity.
*In a balanced literature program, biography and history serve—rather than
crowd out—our close study of the work itself.*

The skillful teacher will adapt from various conventional approaches
those elements that help him toward a balanced treatment of content
and form, of meaning *and* technique. He knows that on the one hand
meaning is accessible only *through* form, and that on the other hand
form divorced from meaning becomes sterile. With R. P. Blackmur, he
will thus be looking for "approaches to criticism wherein these two
problems—of form and value—will appear inextricable but not confused—like the stones in an arch or the timbers in a building."[29] The
teacher of literature must ask both *what* a work means and *how* it means.
He must ask how the author, drawing on and adapting the forms and
conventions of a rich literary tradition, has shaped a work that is at
once one of a kind and an instance of continuing developments in the
history of literary sensibility.

The Meaning of Literature

Whatever the teacher's approach, and whatever the nature of his
scholarly apparatus, his teaching will be based on assumptions concerning
the sources of literary significance. It will reflect assumptions, clearly
formulated or not, concerning what gives literature its meaning, its
relevance. There are several major sources of literary significance, and
the teacher in the classroom should draw on them all, including those that
may be temporarily out of favor in the critical journals.

*Considered in its most elementary function, literature is an extension
and enrichment of experience.* The most elementary motive in reading is

[27] Lewis Leary, "Literary Scholarship and the Teaching of English," in Leary,
Scholarship, p. 10.
[28] Report of the Literature Committee of the School and College Conference on
English, in *Issues, Problems, and Approaches in the Teaching of English*, ed.
George Winchester Stone, Jr. (New York: Holt, Rinehart & Winston, Inc., 1961),
p. 45.
[29] Blackmur, *Language as Gesture*, p. 372.

curiosity—in the sense of a yearning for experience, a hunger for life. Carl Van Doren describes himself in his early reading as "inquisitive as a village gossip, feverish as an eavesdropper," accepting "all I learned as evidence that the world was as rich as I demanded."[30] The basic motive for reading that we must keep alive in our students is "our own insatiable curiosity about other human beings, and about ourselves."[31]

Whatever else his qualifications, the imaginative writer must first of all be more receptive, more observant, more fully alive than his fellows. As Wordsworth said, he must be "endowed with more lively sensibility, more enthusiasm and tenderness"; he must have "a more comprehensive soul than are supposed to be common among mankind."[32] He must be capable, in the words of Coleridge, of

> awakening the mind's attention from the lethargy of custom and directing it to the loveliness and the wonders of the world before us; an inexhaustible treasure, but for which, in consequence of the film of familiarity and selfish solicitude, we have eyes, yet see not, ears that hear not, and hearts that neither feel nor understand.[33]

In much of ordinary life, our attention is limited to matters of some practical concern. Our observation is channeled by habit; our emotions are blunted by routine. Literature, like the other arts, revives our power of attention. It extends our sphere of observation; it exercises our capacity for emotion. Like paintings and tapestries, the poet's imagery can satisfy what John Dewey calls the "hunger of the eyes for light and color." Like music, the rhythms of literary language can give us "the dropping down and the exalted rising, the surging and retreating, the acceleration and retardation, the tightening and loosening, the sudden thrust and the gradual insinuation of things." By taking us beyond the familiar and routine, the writer can satisfy our yearning for settings and situations whose novelty has not yet worn off, which have not yet lost their emotional interest through repetition: "Demand for variety is the manifestation of the fact that being alive we seek to live, until we are cowed by fear or dulled by routine. The need of life itself pushes us out into the unknown." Such **aesthetic experience** is cut short in ordinary, nonaesthetic perception. It is "cut short when there is recognition . . . For such recognition suffices to enable us to employ the object for customary purposes. It is enough to know that those objects are rain-clouds to induce us to carry an umbrella."[34]

---

[30] *Three Worlds* (New York: Harper & Row, Publishers, 1936), p. 79.
[31] Louis L. Martz, "The Teaching of Poetry," Gordon and Noyes, *Essays*, p. 246.
[32] Mark Van Doren, ed., *Selected Poetry* (New York: Random House, Inc., 1950), p. 684.
[33] Elizabeth Schneider, ed., *Selected Poetry and Prose* (New York: Holt, Rinehart & Winston, Inc., 1951), p. 269.
[34] John Dewey, *Art as Experience* (New York: G. P. Putnam's Sons, 1934), pp. 124, 207, 168–69, 177.

Literature satisfies our yearning for experience most obviously when it takes us to distant periods and exotic settings. It may feast our eyes on the feudal pageantry of the Middle Ages, or the at once luxurious and threatening life of tropical jungles. To enhance our interest in man, literature may present everyman to us writ large, in the myths and tragedies of kings, heroes, and demigods; in what Keats called in *Endymion*

> the grandeur of the dooms
> We have imagined for the mighty dead.

In a way more specifically literary, however, because relying less on its subject matter and more on the creative potential of language, is a different kind of literature. It follows Wordsworth's program for treating "incidents and situations from common life" and "the essential passions of the heart" and yet transforming them by the poetic imagination so that "ordinary things should be presented to the mind in an unusual aspect."[35] *Presentiment,* for instance, is an ordinary enough term for an ordinary feeling. A dictionary definition rates barely a nod of recognition: "a feeling that something, especially of an unfortunate or evil nature, is about to take place." The most striking thing about a poem on the same theme is the completely different manner in which it engages our attention:

> Presentiment is that long shadow on the lawn
> Indicative that suns go down;
> The notice to the startled grass
> That darkness is about to pass.
>
> (Emily Dickinson)

The dictionary definition is abstract. We intellectually take note of it; we check it off, as it were. The poem is visualized and felt, that is, experienced. It illustrates several of the devices by which the poet restores ideas to their full life in three-dimensional experience: The first of these is **metaphor.** The revealing, significant image—the shadow on the lawn—by a metaphorical equation becomes the concrete representative of impending darkness. Another such device is **personification.** The "startled grass" projects human feelings into the inanimate world. It thus illustrates Wordsworth's description of the poet as "pleased with his own passions and volitions . . . delighting to contemplate similar volitions and passions as manifested in the goings-on of the Universe, and habitually impelled to create them where he does not find them."[36]

More extended literary forms can with similar effectiveness involve us in more extended, yet similarly familiar patterns of experience. They may direct our attention to life in our town, to the assistant of a Jewish

---

[35] Van Doren, ed., *Selected Poetry*, p. 677.
[36] *Ibid.*, p. 684.

neighborhood grocer, to the junior executive who has reached the point of no return, to the death of a salesman. The characters and events treated may not be earth-shaking. As Linda says about her husband in Arthur Miller's play,

> I don't say he's a great man. Willy Loman never made a lot of money. His name was never in the paper. He's not the finest character that ever lived. But he's a human being, and a terrible thing is happening to him. So attention must be paid. He's not to be allowed to fall into his grave like an old dog. Attention, attention must be finally paid to such a person.[37]

Even when a writer takes us to exotic settings, he may do so not to pursue the strange and new but to explore the range of common human possibility. Joseph Conrad takes characters to distant, savage surroundings to show how, deprived of the props offered by civilized routines, their essential nature reveals itself under stress. Shakespeare may ostensibly take his audiences to ancient Rome or Renaissance Venice, but the real setting of his plays is the more familiar topography of human motives, of our ideas, ideals, and passions. As Samuel Johnson said, "his characters are not modified by the customs of particular places . . . they are the genuine progeny of common humanity, such as the world will always supply, and observation will always find."[38]

Literature broadens and deepens our experience, but not necessarily by exploring the bizarre byways. It typically makes us respond to the stuff of our common humanity as embodied in different attitudes toward life, as shaped by different conventions of thought, feeling, and form. Literature thus helps us break out of perspectives that are rigidly local and provincial. This function of literature explains the futility of trying to use selected literary works to instill in our students narrowly conceived "desirable attitudes." If we assemble a unit on the theme of war, we are likely to find few selections that project the socially approved attitude of Auden's "Unknown Citizen":

> When there was peace, he was for peace; when there was war, he went.[39]

Instead, we are likely to find selections that discover in war the inhumanity of its irrevocable disasters; the bootless defiance and anguish of its victims; the intoxication and mad pounding of the heart when "worth's won and the swords clash"; the grim determination of the man who has decided that some people are easier to fight with than to live with. Such reading may not make the student a better soldier or patriot, but it will make him a better educated one. One aim of every class in literature is to broaden the student's imaginative sympathy:

---

[37] *Death of a Salesman: Certain Private Conversations in Two Acts and a Requiem* (New York: The Viking Press, 1958), p. 56.

[38] Bertrand H. Bronson, ed., *Rasselas, Poems, and Selected Prose* (New York: Holt, Rinehart & Winston, Inc., 1958), p. 241.

[39] *Collected Poetry of W. H. Auden* (New York: Random House, Inc., 1945), p. 143.

Within broad limits, students can be taught to use their imagination and enter with appreciation into a universe of sensibility and conviction that may not be theirs. Thomas Hardy will teach the Christian what it feels like to live and move in a world whose only God wears a face of blank indifference or sly malice. *The Four Quartets* can give the skeptic the taste of Christian mysticism. In each instance, the reader is like the theater-goer swept along by the inner logic of the events upon the stage. The good citizen who waits hopefully for Hamlet's just vengeance, though in private life he would regard blood revenge as worth life imprisonment, should have no difficulty in entering the internal logic of any good poem that presents a system of ideas and emotions far removed from his own particular constellation of attitudes.[40]

Imaginative literature is tied neither to a particular kind of subject matter, nor to a particular atttiude *toward* subject matter. However, there are certain perspectives to which the imaginative writer is likely to be particularly attracted. Poets and novelists have frequently turned to childhood as a period when we respond to experience more fully and unconditionally than in later life. Wordsworth saw it as

> a time when meadow, grove, and stream
> The earth, and every common sight,
> To me did seem
> Appareled in celestial light,
> The glory and the freshness of a dream.[41]

To Dylan Thomas,

> it was all
> Shining, it was Adam and maiden . . .
> So it must have been after the birth of the simple light
> In the first, spinning place, the spellbound horses walking warm
> Out of the whinnying green stable
> On to the fields of praise.[42]

In many biographical novels, the magic, spellbinding passages are those dealing with childhood and adolescence. The child's observations are more acute and unchanneled, his joy and grief more elementary, more spontaneous, than that of the adult world. Above all, the child is more *imaginative* than the adult: He is a ceaseless teller of stories and babbler of verses. His clapping and skipping and reciting of jingles reflect a sense of rhythm, a rejoicing in being alive. Every teacher of literature must nourish or, if necessary, revive this interest in story and rhythm and put it to his own uses.

Similarly, the imaginative writer is likely to be attracted to man in a state of nature, or at least in a state less fully regulated, mechanized, and hemmed in than that of highly interdependent modern society. In

---

[40] Chad Walsh, "When a Poem Confronts an Undergraduate," *College English,* XXIV (February, 1963), 387–88.
[41] Van Doren, ed., *Selected Poetry,* p. 541.
[42] *Collected Poems of Dylan Thomas* (New York: New Directions, 1953), p. 179.

such a state, man is more dependent than the servant of routine on his keen observation of his environment, on the alertness of his response to threat and challenge. Writers like Ernest Hemingway substitute for the blunted and dispersed attention of uneventful, everyday living, situations in which a character is intensely alive, taut with controlled energy, in John Dewey's phrase, "active through his whole being."[43]

Though the search for experience is openly acknowledged as a basic motive by many readers, it has typically found less favor with the critics. To many modern critics, "vicarious" experience has implied a kind of self-indulgent substitute experience, deficient in philosophical or pragmatic sanctions. They have typically required that imaginative sympathy must be qualified, indeed transformed, by a specifically aesthetic response. Insisting on the difference between life and art, they have required the mature reader to maintain the proper **aesthetic distance.** Thus, Eliseo Vivas in his discussion of D. H. Lawrence insists on the "unique" function of art, on the "intransitive" quality of aesthetic experience. In art, sex, though involved, "does not function as sex functions outside art, it does not elicit either our moral or our erotic response."[44]

Sooner or later, every teacher has to tackle the question of art's specifically aesthetic functions. By and large, however, in its effect on our teaching, the modern emphasis on detachment, the modern fear of being carried away, tends to be wrong. The literature most truly meaningful to us we do not read with detachment—we are *absorbed* in it and by it. We find it difficult to lift our eyes off the page; we *live,* imaginatively, in the world created for us by the author. The true teacher of literature is the one who, when hurriedly trying to look up a quotation in *Hamlet* or *Othello,* finds himself irresistibly drawn into a full rereading of the play. The most frustrating kind of student to have in a literature class is the conscientious reader who nevertheless fails to get involved.

To respond fully to *Othello,* we must do more than contemplate its characters, we must in some sense identify with them. We must in some sense share not only in Othello's terrifying passion but also in Iago's exuberant, exulting rascality, his glorying in the power his brilliantly evil wit gives him to manipulate people less shrewd, less nimble, less cynical. The answer to the familiar question about Iago's motives will not be found by the properly detached critic, puzzling over the conflicting evidence on his note cards. It will be found by the reader who projects himself into Iago the way an actor must if he is to realize the tremendous vitality of Iago's role.

In studying our response to a play like *Othello,* we become strongly aware of the second major function of literature: it not only extends but

---

[43] Dewey, *Art as Experience,* p. 19.
[44] *D. H. Lawrence: The Failure and the Triumph of Art* (Evanston, Ill.: Northwestern University Press, 1960), p. 144.

intensifies experience. *We feel in our reading of great literature a characteristic heightening, a sense of something* more *vital than ordinary life.* Keats, in making us respond to the sensuous texture of experience, takes us into a world richer than ordinary sensation. He creates a world almost painfully intense in sights, sounds, and smells—whether of civilized artifacts, such as in "The Eve of St. Agnes" the casement "all garlanded with carven imag'ries," or of nature in a summer night that makes him

> in embalméd darkness, guess each sweet
> Wherewith the seasonable month endows
> The grass, the thicket, and the fruit-tree wild;
> White hawthorn, and the pastoral eglantine;
> Fast-fading violets covered up in leaves;
> And mid-May's eldest child,
> The coming musk-rose, full of dewy wine,
> The murmurous haunt of flies on summer eves.[45]

Aristotle began his definition of tragedy in the *Poetics* by describing it as an "imitation," through language, of life, of "men in action"; he traced one of its root motives to our pleasure "in things imitated." However, he explored in detail the conditions that make a work "true to life and yet more beautiful," that achieve a "concentrated effect" more pleasurable than one that is diluted.[46] Henry James said in "The Art of Fiction," that "the only reason for the existence of a novel is that it does attempt to represent life"; he called the "air of reality," the "illusion of life," the "supreme virtue of a novel," the merit on which all its other merits "helplessly and submissively depend." Yet he made the test of value the *intensity* of the artist's impression of life, emphasizing the need for sensitivity to implication and nuance, telling the writer "Try to be one of the people on whom nothing is lost!"[47]

Apparently, what we need is a concept of **ideal imitation,** of experience not merely copied but transformed—to make it satisfy our needs, our wishes, our expectations. Our wish may be quite frankly for a world of experience more congenial, more deeply and consistently satisfying than ordinary life. Much great literature owes its powerful attraction to the fact that in some way or other it satisfies the heart's desire. Sir Philip Sidney said,

> nature never set forth the earth in so rich tapestry as divers poets have done—neither with pleasant rivers, fruitful trees, sweet-smelling flowers, nor whatsoever else may make the too much loved earth more lovely. Her world is brazen, the poets only deliver a golden.[48]

---

[45] Richard Harter Fogle, ed., *Selected Poetry and Letters* (New York: Holt, Rinehart & Winston, Inc., 1951), p. 245.

[46] S. H. Butcher, trans., in Schorer, *Criticism,* pp. 199–200, 217.

[47] In Schorer, *Criticism,* pp. 45–49.

[48] In *English Critical Essays (Sixteenth, Seventeenth, and Eighteenth Centuries),* ed., Edmund D. Jones (London: Oxford University Press, 1956), p. 7.

Both Sidney and Fielding found the true appeal of comedy not in our laughter at deformity and misfortune but in our delight in what is agreeable to our nature—our joy in a beautiful face, in "fair chances" and lucky coincidences, in the happiness of others.

It is obvious, however, what keeps literature from being simply **wish-fulfillment.** The more experienced the reader, the more likely he is to find the sweet bird song of continual May mornings and the unexcelled beauty of the poet's lady too good to be true. Here we recognize a basic tension in literature: *We yearn for experience that is heightened, concentrated, intense. But at the same time we insist that it should ring true.* On the one hand, we require of literature wonder, excitement, elation. On the other hand, we require cogency, **verisimilitude,** "realism," truth. Aldous Huxley, in "Tragedy and the Whole Truth," discusses Homer's account of how Odysseus saw Scylla lift from the ship and devour six of his companions, "still screaming, still stretching out their hands to me in the frightful struggle." Later, the danger passed, Odysseus and his men went ashore for the night and "expertly" prepared their supper. "When they had satisfied their thirst and hunger, they thought of their dear companions and wept, and in the midst of their tears sleep came gently upon them." As Huxley says, in many another great poem the survivors would not have been allowed to cook and eat their supper; "they would simply have wept, lamenting their own misfortunes and the horrible fate of their companions, and the canto would have ended tragically on their tears." Homer, however,

> knew that even the most cruelly bereaved must eat; that hunger is stronger than sorrow and that its satisfaction takes precedence even of tears. He knew that experts continue to act expertly and to find satisfaction in their accomplishment, even when friends have just been eaten, even when the accomplishment is only cooking the supper. He knew . . . that, even as hunger takes precedence of grief, so fatigue, supervening, cuts short its career and drowns it in a sleep all the sweeter for bringing forgetfulness of bereavement. In a word, Homer refused to treat the theme tragically. He preferred to tell the Whole Truth.

At one extreme, Huxley sees literature that filters out the trivialities and irrelevancies of life. In great tragedy, the pattern of events has a coherence that satisfies our yearning for significance, thwarted by the miscellaneous quality of everyday existence. Such literature "acts quickly and intensely on our feelings"; in it, "the elements of our being fall, for the moment at any rate, into an ordered and beautiful pattern."[49] At the other extreme is literature that implies, if not actually establishes, the wider context, the vast, majestic, irresistible river of life. Such literature is likely to be less exalted or apocalyptic, but its effect may be the more profound and lasting.

[49] Aldous Huxley, *Music at Night and Other Essays* (New York: Doubleday & Company, Inc., 1931), pp. 7–10.

Though the greatest literature heightens our sensitivity and deeply engages our emotions, it also gives us a sense of **recognition.** In concentrating our attention it seems to clarify; in heightening and intensifying our perception it seems to seize on the essential. As Henry James said, "Art is essentially selection, but it is a selection whose main care is to be typical, to be inclusive."[50] Here we have the third major function of literature: It reorders experience, not to distort it, but to bring it into focus. It seems to express clearly and powerfully what before we had dimly felt. In the words of Thornton Wilder:

> The response we make when we "believe" a work of the imagination is that of saying: "This is the way things are. I have always known it without being fully aware that I knew it. Now in the presence of this play or novel or poem . . . I know that I know it."[51]

Readers have always felt that literature expresses a kind of truth more deeply and significantly human than the truth-of-facts of history and the abstract truths of science. Aristotle said that poetry "is a more philosophical and a higher thing than history: for poetry tends to express the universal, history the particular."[52] Taking their clue from this statement, neoclassicists through the ages have ascribed to the poet a superior grasp of the underlying nature of things. They have seen in the poet's "true lively knowledge" a superior sense of the fitting, the natural, the probable. Romantic critics have ascribed to the poet a kind of knowledge different from that of science because literature preserves the full context of sensation and emotion. It thus gives us a true living knowledge not artificially limited to the sphere of the abstracting, analytical intellect. The poet's thought is passionate, imaginative thought, "not standing upon external testimony, but carried alive into the heart by passion."[53] John Dewey said of art generally that its function is to elicit the characteristic reality, the intrinsic qualities of things:

> Through art, meanings of objects that are otherwise dumb, inchoate, restricted, and resisted are clarified and concentrated, and not by thought working laboriously upon them, nor by escape into a world of mere sense, but by creation of a new experience.[54]

Whatever our view of how the poet's insight operates, we experience in great literature the feeling that things are falling into place, that things have meaning. In great literature, life has significance, pattern—if only, as in Camus' *The Stranger,* the pattern imposed by an all-pervading sense of the ultimate absurdity of life, of the *insignificance* of our indignations and rationalizations. The book as a whole dramatizes a

50 Schorer, *Criticism,* p. 51.
51 *Three Plays* (New York: Bantam Books, Inc., 1961), p. vii.
52 Schorer, *Criticism,* p. 204.
53 Wordsworth, *Selected Poetry,* ed. Van Doren, p. 686.
54 Dewey, *Art as Experience,* pp. 132–33.

philosophy of life, even though the theme of that philosophy is "anti-philosophy"—an insistence on the rock-bottom reality of elementary perception and sensation: "I perceive; therefore, I am."

Similarly, meaning, general significance, may be discovered even in poetry that seems to cater most directly to our appetite for the strange, the new, the supernatural, the unique. W. K. Wimsatt, Jr., says of Keats's "La Belle Dame Sans Merci" that literally it is

> about a knight, by profession a man of action, but sensitive, like the lily and the rose, and about a faery lady with wild, wild eyes. At a more abstract level, it is about the loss of self in the mysterious lure of beauty—whether woman, poetry, or poppy. It sings the irretrievable departure from practical normality (the squirrel's granary is full), the wan isolation after ecstasy.[55]

In Byron's *Don Juan,* we seem farthest from common human life, and closest to the never-never land of wish-fulfillment, when we see Juan and Haidée, "half naked, loving, natural, and Greek," on a wild, moonlit Mediterranean beach where

> on the lone shore were plighted
> Their hearts; the stars, their nuptial torches, shed
> Beauty upon the beautiful they lighted:
> Ocean their witness, and the cave their bed,
> By their own feelings hallow'd and united,
> Their priest was Solitude, and they were wed:
> And they were happy, for to their young eyes
> Each was an angel, and earth paradise.[56]

Yet the whole scene is at the same time a comment on the ignorance and trustfulness of youth; on our hard-bought prudential wisdom, "ever on the watch to rob joy of its alchemy"; on the perennial clash between our dreams and the forms and laws that establish society.

One basic motive in our reading of literature is our interest in what Edmund Wilson once called the writer's "scrutiny of life," his "view of the world and his conception of the powers that move it."[57] How far we can trust a writer to state his view of the world explicitly is a moot point. The relation between the felt truth of a literary work and general, intellectually graspable truths formulated by the writer has long been a thorny problem in literary theory. Modern critics have typically shown a distrust for abstract statement. They have been impatient with the writer who in the poem or story itself proceeds to interpret, to translate its meaning into logical terms. Many modern critics have adopted from

---

[55] "The Structure of the 'Concrete Universal' in Literature," *PMLA,* LXII (March, 1947); reprinted in Schorer, *Criticism,* p. 400.
[56] Edward E. Bostetter, ed., *Selected Poetry and Letters* (New York: Holt, Rinehart & Winston, Inc., 1951), p. 308.
[57] *Classics and Commercials* (New York: Farrar, Straus and Company, 1950), pp. 43–45.

Coleridge and the Romantics a view of the imagination as a superior and integral form of insight, to be clearly distinguished from the laborious and pedestrian processes of the logical intellect. As a result, they have often seemed to discount or belittle the role in literature of "doctrine," idea, generalization.

T. S. Eliot set the tone for much later comment when he said that the function of poetry is not intellectual but emotional, that the poet who "thinks" is merely able to express the emotional equivalent of thought and not necessarily interested in the thought itself. So considered, the greatness and coherence of the Thomistic philosophy behind Dante is an irrelevant accident from the point of view of poetry. Neither Dante nor Shakespeare did any real thinking in the ordinary sense; each used current thought as a vehicle for his feeling.[58] In a similar vein, R. P. Blackmur said,

> The vital or fatal nexus is in interest and emotion and is established when the terms can be represented dramatically, almost, as it were for their own sakes alone and with only a pious or ritualistic regard for the doctrines in which they are clothed. . . . We either discount, absorb, or dominate the doctrine for the sake of the life that goes with it, for the sake of what is *formed* in the progressive act of thinking.

One may indeed agree with Blackmur that Dante (like some other great poets) had a habit of imagination that "enabled him to dramatize with equal ardour and effect what his doctrine blessed, what it assailed, and what, at heart, it was indifferent to."[59] Milton's Satan has an imaginative force and persuasive power that makes the reader forget that in the scheme of doctrine dramatized in *Paradise Lost* Satan is irretrievably and for all eternity in the wrong. With Shakespeare, indeed, the attempt to formulate a coherent world view leads in a myriad different directions. Stoic, nihilist, Aristotelian, hedonist, Christian, cynic —all speak in the plays with compelling eloquence. The critic who looks for more than confirmation of his own philosophical bias will ultimately admit his bafflement. As A. C. Bradley said in *Shakespearean Tragedy,*

> We find a few references to gods or God, to the influence of the stars, to another life: some of them certainly, all of them perhaps, merely dramatic —appropriate to the person from whose lips they fall. . . . Sometimes from the very furnace of affliction a conviction seems borne to us that somehow, if we could see it, this agony counts as nothing against the heroism and love which appear in it and thrill our hearts. Sometimes we are driven to cry out that these mighty or heavenly spirits who perish are too great for the little space in which they move, and that they vanish not into nothingness but into freedom. . . . But these faint and scattered intimations that the tragic world, being but a fragment of a whole beyond our vision, must needs be a contradiction and no ultimate truth, avail nothing to interpret

58 "Shakespeare and the Stoicism of Seneca," Eliot, *Selected Essays,* pp. 115–16.
59 Blackmur, *Language as Gesture,* pp. 374–76.

the mystery. We remain confronted with the inexplicable fact, or the no less inexplicable appearance, of a world travailing for perfection, but bringing to birth, together with glorious good, an evil which it is able to overcome only by self-torture and self-waste.[60]

Critics writing after Bradley have often found themselves in a paradoxical position. On the one hand, following Eliot and Blackmur, they have had no difficulty accepting the merely "dramatic" and provisional quality of ideas being played off against each other in a complex literary work. On the other hand, they have aimed at recovering in great literature an ultimately philosophical and moral meaning more definite than the one found by Bradley in Shakespeare's plays. They have tried to formulate in intellectual terms a "world view" conveyed in a work by recurrent patterns of imagery, by the notation of its metaphors, by the dynamic principles determining its structure. Thus, we have the typical effect of much current academic criticism: paraphrase introduced by elaborate warnings against paraphrase, highly intellectualized renderings of the poet's intent introduced by orthodox warnings against looking in poetry for mere acted-out intellectual content. As Wimsatt has observed,

> Today there is nothing that the literary theorist . . . will be more eager to repudiate than any hint of moral or religious didacticism, any least intimation that the poem is to measure its meaning or get its sanction from any kind of authority more abstract or more overtly legislative than itself. But on the other hand there has probably never been a generation of teachers of literature less willing to admit any lack of high seriousness, of implicit and embodied ethical content, even of normative vision in the object of their study.

Despite "our reiterated denials of didacticism," we make for poetry "claims the most momentous conceivable, as they advance more and more under the sanction of an absolutely creative and autonomous visionary imagination."[61]

To the extent that this orientation has influenced classroom procedure, it has had one important beneficial effect. It discourages the teacher from reducing a work *too hastily* to its intellectual skeleton. It forces him to pay full attention to the role of image, structure, emotion. Many a teacher has found in the orthodox critical opposition of the intellectual and the imaginative a plausible rationale for his rejection of the kind of writer who clothes his sentiments in verse the way a proud mother dresses her boy in a Sunday suit.

On the other hand, this orientation has tended to prejudge our treatment of literature in equally important ways. It has often kept the teacher from doing justice to the **didactic** drive as a powerful basic

[60] *Shakespearean Tragedy* (New York: Meridian Books, Inc., 1955), p. 40.
[61] *College English*, XXIV, 382.

motive in much literary creation. Milton and Bunyan, Pope and Swift, Wordsworth and Shelley, Jane Austen and George Eliot, Browning and Shaw—all wrote to *teach* as well as to delight, to move, to create. What they, and writers like them, tried to teach they more or less successfully formulated in intellectual terms. There may never be a one-to-one correlation between such an intellectual system and its imaginative embodiment, just as there may never be a perfect correspondence between a man's purposes and the verbalizations and rationalizations into which he projects them. But we cannot do justice to such a writer if we are unable to take his ideas seriously, if these ideas have become so much discarded intellectual furniture. Teachers need not be told that one of the most elementary motives for taking pen in hand is the need to explain oneself, to show to others how confusion should be reduced to order, how bewildering detail should be made to fall into place.

By emphasizing the gulf between prose logic and imaginative insight, much modern criticism serves to obscure an important kinship between the intellectual and the artistic ordering of experience. Both are rooted in the fact that mere inchoate experience, mere "life-in-the-raw," fails to satisfy. We have an elementary need for organizing the flux of multifarious impressions in such a way as to make possible meaningful response. We have an elementary need for order: for structuring experience so as to make it intelligible and manageable. We prefer clarity to confusion; we prefer feeling oriented to feeling lost. This preference is an equally powerful motive in the work of the scientist and the artist.

If we contrast the Square of St. Peter's in Rome with a comparable area elsewhere in the city, one difference is that the square magnificently facilitates orientation, enables one to find one's bearings. It is reduced to an over-all simplicity by a "beautiful" symmetry; it is made comprehensible by its beautiful regularity. Our feeling of satisfaction here is related to what the scientist feels when he sees a cogent pattern emerge from at-first miscellaneous data. There is nothing "coldly intellectual" about this experience of order. There can be the intense gratification we feel when jarring details are submerged in profound calm, when intricate details mesh in a finely attuned system.

Both artist and thinker sooner or later confront the question of rigor. They must decide whether and to what extent they will allow their "rage for order" to overrule their respect for recalcitrant fact. They must ask to what extent they *discover* a pattern inherent in reality, and to what extent they *impose* a pattern upon it. There is an artistic integrity that keeps the artist from satisfying those for whom, in Henry James's phrase, "art means rose-colored window-panes."[62] There is a thinker's integrity that makes philosopher, critic, and scientist resist the pull toward a system more elegant, more simple than the facts allow.

[62] Schorer, *Criticism*, p. 51.

To the scientist, the artist tends to appear as self-indulgent, forever willing to mistake beauty for truth. To the artist, the scientist tends to appear as someone satisfied with that small section of the truth that can be rigorously controlled, as someone forever afraid to venture beyond the mere material facts. This difference in temperaments does not mean that the respect for fact and the pursuit of order may not to some extent merge in the great writer. Keats said that "with a great poet the sense of beauty overcomes every other consideration," but he also said,

> An extensive knowledge is needful to thinking people—it takes away the heat and fever; and helps, by widening speculation, to ease the burden of the mystery: a thing I begin to understand a little, . . . The difference of high sensations with and without knowledge appears to me this—in the latter case we are falling continually ten thousand fathoms deep and being blown up again without wings and with all the horror of a bare-shouldered creature—in the former case, our shoulders are fledge, and we go through the same air and space without fear.[63]

The kind of literature that plays an essential and basic role in the student's liberal education is, in the largest sense of that term, a learning about life. It is the kind of literature whose beauty and power are difficult to separate from the insight it offers into human life.

What the teacher must guard against is defining the insights to be sought in literature in a narrow **moralistic** sense. Because of its immediacy and emotional impact, literature has an obvious power to move men to action, to make them embrace standards of desirable (or undesirable) conduct. Newspaper statistics concerning disasters and injustices are often too impersonal to move us. But a striking detail, a graphic account of a single incident, may produce a hot flush of indignation. In the neoclassical tradition, such considerations long provided the rationale for the "defense" of poetry: Sidney declared the epic the highest form of literature, demonstrating perfect patterns of courage, liberality, wisdom, friendship. He said that "poetry ever setteth virtue so out in her best colours, making Fortune her well-waiting handmaid, that one must needs be enamoured of her."[64] Samuel Johnson required the novelist to avoid mingling good and bad qualities in their principal characters, for vice

> should always disgust; nor should the graces of gaiety, or the dignity of courage, be so united with it, as to reconcile it to the mind. Wherever it appears, it should raise hatred by the malignity of its practices, and contempt by the meanness of its stratagems; for while it is supported by either parts or spirit, it will be seldom heartily abhorred.[65]

For obvious reasons, it is this tradition that of all literary approaches was deemed most directly suitable for the teaching of literature in the

[63] Fogle, ed., *Selected Poetry and Letters,* pp. 305, 314–15.
[64] Jones, *Critical Essays,* p. 19.
[65] Bronson, *Rasselas, Poems, and Selected Prose,* p. 65.

schools. Whether from his own inclination, or to placate the pillars of morality on school boards and boards of regents, the teacher for decades seemed to assume with Ruskin that "poetry is the suggestion by the imagination of noble grounds for the noble emotions," to wit, "Love, Veneration, Admiration, and Joy (this latter especially, if unselfish)."

In one sense, the teacher can take the community's anxious awareness of the moral dimensions of literature as a flattering and realistic recognition of the importance of his subject. Semanticists have made us aware of the directive implications of what appear to be mere statements of fact. Critics like Kenneth Burke have labored to show similar directives in what appear to be works read merely for aesthetic enjoyment. Charles Lamb said that in watching Restoration comedy we are taking a "moral holiday"; but most theatergoers do not keep their aesthetic and their moral responses in such watertight compartments. The spectator who laughs uproariously at a scene by Wycherley or Congreve is likely to be predisposed to a somewhat different moral outlook from that of the critic who primly explains that he really finds Restoration comedy insufferably dull. Just as the literature we read may affect our moral values, so our moral values may affect our response to literature: In defining the ideal tragic hero, Aristotle points out that we are not likely to feel the appropriate compassion for a character we detest; at the other extreme, we are likely to feel merely shocked by the unmerited downfall of a man of outstanding virtue.

However, though the teacher of literature must be aware of moral implications at every turn, any

> directly moralistic attitude toward literature is a constant danger in teaching, not a help. To use literature as a text for moral lessons is certain to destroy it in the pupil's eyes as an art to be enjoyed, and may also destroy the very end the teacher has in view. . . . If a student has inclinations toward stealing automobiles, it is at least problematic whether reading about Macbeth, who stole a kingdom, will act as a very powerful deterrent. . . . Literature, taken as a whole and in its infinite variety, does not indoctrinate its readers in any one set of values; it provides a record of the many different values by which men have lived and died, suffered or found satisfaction. The books are never closed and the audit never final on these primary questions of value. The record begins in the past and is still active in the present. It is a continuous record of moral struggle, not a closed record of moral dogma.[66]

It is not only that the moralistic requirements made of literature by the layman are often naive. When an editorial in *Life* complains that American novelists do not properly sing the praises of prosperity, one need only point out that the serious writer, of all Americans, is least likely to have any prosperity to sing about. However, even a more sophisticated moralistic approach creates basic problems for both writer and critic. If

[66] Report of the Literature Committee, Stone, *Issues*, p. 49.

the writer follows Dr. Johnson's prescription for showing virtue, if not angelical, at least "the highest and purest that humanity can reach,"[67] his heroes may cease to be believable. This is the difficulty with such patterns of ideal conduct as Spenser's Redcross Knight or Sir Guyon. They remain a blur in our minds; they never acquire the vitality and interest of crafty, hypocritical Archimago; of Spenser's fiery and defiant pagan knights; of the luxurious temptresses that populate his pages. Conversely, if a writer succeeds in making virtue believable, as Richardson does with the overpowering Clarissa, he may have difficulty with his villains. Richardson's Lovelace, though occasionally showing sparks of genuine mischief, too often does not carry conviction. Too often, his character is twisted to enforce the author's moral: A man who dares snatch a kiss from his fiancée is capable of the most unspeakable crimes.

The main difficulty is that teacher or critic may try to impose a pattern borrowed from the moral allegory of Spenser or the didactic melodrama of Richardson to works that it simply does not fit. He then typically has two choices: He may, with Matthew Arnold, deny a poet like Chaucer true greatness because he lacks the "high seriousness" the moralist requires. Or the critic may read *into* a poem moral lessons that are either not there at all, or at least are not there in the simple, uncomplicated form that conventional morality tends to take. As Wimsatt says of Shakespeare's *Antony and Cleopatra,*

> By any ethical standard at all what Antony does to Fulvia, to Octavia especially, to his political allegiance, to himself, to Cleopatra even, must be bad. Yet the death of Antony and of Cleopatra is in the high Roman fashion, what's brave, what's noble. "For it is great To do that thing that ends all other deeds, Which shackles accidents, and bolts up change." We are called upon to admire Antony and Cleopatra. In short, the play is immoral. The play, however, is great poetry because of the complexity of its immorality— if one may venture the phrase, its mature immorality. The death of Antony and Cleopatra is the climax of a subtle blend of human richness—of imperial extravagance and the opulence of burnished thrones, of drink and surfeits that rot themselves with motion, of the versatility, perverseness and charm of a woman, the infatuation, gallantry and bravery of a grizzled warrior.[68]

Every teacher must learn to make some such distinction between moral and aesthetic value as is here implied, the better to trace their subtle interaction in the actual literary work.

It is perversion of our literary heritage to use it, as it has typically been used by the totalitarianisms of the left and the right, to teach any one set of moral values. It is a mutilation of literature to censor it, starve it, or suppress it whenever it fails to elevate in the manner prescribed by those temporarily in charge. *The ethical effect of literature generally is*

[67] Bronson, *Rasselas, Poems and Selected Prose,* p. 65.
[68] "The Concrete Universial," Schorer, *Criticism,* p. 402.

that it extends our awareness of moral possibility, that it broadens our understanding of human motives. The teaching of literature contributes to the development of the student's moral character in the sense and to the extent that understanding and imaginative sympathy are conditions of any mature moral judgment.

Even a preliminary survey of the sources of literary significance thus reveals a number of essential points to which instruction in literature must do justice. First, imaginative literature heightens our perception; it restores freshness and vigor to our jaded observation of the world in which we live. Second, literature requires our emotional involvement; what the student feels in reading a work is as important as what he learns to say about it. Third, literature focuses and orders experience. We shall shortly return to some of the questions that arise concerning the nature and source of the order it creates. So far, we can say that this order is not identical with the intellectual and moral structure we impose upon life, but that it can to some extent be formulated in intellectual and moral terms. As a result, unlike other more fragmented or more exclusive ways of dealing with experience, literature as a whole deals with life in its full sensory, emotional, moral, and intellectual dimensions.

Modern Approaches to Literary Significance

The teacher's dealing with literature is likely to be most fruitful when he operates with a view of literary significance as tentative and open-ended as the one that has just been sketched. However, in his reading of critical studies and of editorial material in textbooks, he must be aware of more definite and more ambitious attempts to establish the relationship between literature and life.

In the past, the critic looking for a direct correlation between aesthetic and philosophical or moral significance found powerful support in a **Neo-Platonic** view of art. The Platonic tradition brought the true, the good, and the beautiful into relation as merely different reflections of the same divine essence. Truth, goodness, and beauty, diverse in appearance, when seen from the vantage point of the philosopher merged in the Platonic vision of ultimate reality. Our insights into human life, our observation of deeds of kindness, our contemplation of beautiful objects—all these move us in essentially similar ways. They appeal to the best in us; they remind us of the ideal homeland of the soul. To Coleridge, to Keats, to Shelley, the task of the artist was to recover in the distractions and confusions of experience an underlying ideal order, partaking equally of beauty and of truth. In this framework, beauty is never merely decorative; our immediate pleasure in literary form is far from a passing entertainment. Its creation, as Wordsworth said, is "an acknowledgment of the beauty of the universe" and "a task light and easy to him who looks at the world in the spirit of love."[69] Even a work of literature having no overt moral or philosophical implications could thus be seen as indirect homage to a universal moral order. The artist was provided with a unified, integral rationale for his work, making of him the high priest or at least the interpreter of divine essence.

The modern critic, convinced like the Romantic that literature is in the service "of the most integral purposes of life," had to find a new foundation for his conviction in an age that has largely lost Wordsworth's view of "man and nature as essentially adapted to each other." With Matthew Arnold in "Dover Beach," the contemporary writer has often seen himself as an alien in a world that has really neither love, nor light, nor certitude. He has, with Stephen Crane, seen the Universe as a power in which the fact of man's existence had not created a sense of obligation.

In a universe more or less definitely deprived of its metaphysical dimension, modern literary theory has in various ways attempted to relate beauty to a view of behavior as adaptive adjustment. In this framework, literary creation, literary form, must somehow be related to biological utility. As John Dewey has said, with the adoption of an evolutionary perspective, the "primary fact, the basic category," becomes the "interaction of organism and environment resulting in some adaptation which secures utilization of the latter." Human behavior, including the pursuit of knowledge and beauty, must be interpreted as "involved in the process by which life is sustained and evolved."[70]

Such a **pragmatic** perspective is bound to be fruitful at least to some extent; as Lionel Trilling has observed, "emotions and ideas are the sparks that fly when the mind meets difficulties."[71] When this point of view is rigorously and consistently applied, literature becomes, in Kenneth Burke's phrase, part of our "equipment for living." Like other apparently irrational, nonpurposive behavior, literary creation can then be explained as a matter of unconscious or intuitive "strategies," aiming at ulterior benefit or at any rate having an ulterior significance. The critic will be interested primarily in the poem's "function," assuming "that the poem is designed to 'do something' for the poet and his readers."[72]

One way of establishing the pragmatic relevance of literature is to study closely the writer's relation to society. Predictably, Marxist sociology focused attention on the writer's possible economic and social motives, raising questions concerning his identification with or rejection of a social class. In the study of earlier American literature, spokesmen of a liberal tradition, such as V. L. Parrington, examined the writer's role in

---

[69] Van Doren, ed., *Selected Poetry*, p. 686.
[70] *Reconstruction in Philosophy*, enlarged ed. (Boston: The Beacon Press, 1948), pp. 84–87.
[71] Trilling, *The Liberal Imagination*, p. 16.
[72] *The Philosophy of Literary Form: Studies in Symbolic Action* (Baton Rouge: Louisiana State University Press, 1941), p. 89.

the struggle of social forces and competing ideologies. Critics like J. W. Beach examined modern American writers for their treatment of social problems, their program for the revision of the existing social structure.

Obviously, the question of an **engaged literature** as against an uncommitted one tends to seem urgent in times of great stress; it seems more remote in times of economic stability or political stalemate. As Kenneth Burke said in speaking of Remy de Gourmont's espousal of the Allied cause in World War I, "ironic detachment is a difficult position to uphold when men are being copiously slaughtered."[73] Predictably, the economic and political disasters of the thirties led Burke and others to an urgent reconsideration of the artist's social responsibilities.

Whatever our final estimate of the topical significance of imaginative literature, this significance can play a definite role in the teacher's strategy. In using literature with definite current relevance, the teacher can rely on the intrinsic interest of content to reinforce the student's as yet precarious interest in the more specifically literary. To understand the power of literature, the student must have the experience of being carried away by an author's eloquence, of being moved to indignation or compassion. This is more likely to happen with works of some direct contemporary significance than with those the student must approach through a thicket of historical footnotes.

Certainly, every student in our affluent society should at some time encounter the literature of **social protest** of the thirties, as represented for instance by John Steinbeck's *The Grapes of Wrath*. He should ponder Steinbeck's picture of an economic system out of control, no longer either understood or mastered by its prophets, unable to distribute the fruits of skill and labor and choking on its own plenty. He should live through Steinbeck's account of a system brutally impersonal in its operation and brutalizing those that make their terms with it; frustrating the need for meaningful, productive work; baffling the impulse toward kindness. He should remember that even in the best of all possible economic and political worlds there was a time, not very long ago, when it could be said that "in the eyes of the people there is the failure; and in the eyes of the hungry there is a growing wrath."[74]

Similarly, a student should not grow up in our time without reading some of the antitotalitarian literature of the thirties and forties. He should imaginatively participate in the pattern, repeated in the experience of writers like André Gide, Stephen Spender, and Richard Wright, of ideal aspirations betrayed, of humanitarian impulse exploited and perverted by crude force and low cunning. He should share George Orwell's scorn, in *Animal Farm*, for a black-and-white mentality stifling all criticism, branding all dissent as treason, making impossible all fair

---

[73] *Counter-Statement* (Los Altos, Calif.: Hermes Publications, 1957), p. 65.
[74] *The Grapes of Wrath* (New York: The Viking Press, Inc., 1939), p. 477.

judgment of the relative merits of conflicting policies, drowning all thought in the mindless chant of "Four legs good—two legs bad." Orwell gives voice to a generation of long-since silenced victims when he castigates the obscene vilification of former heroes of the revolution, the abject glorification of the all-wise leader, the paranoid search for a capitalist under every bed, the squealing of meretricious hacks rationalizing the zigzags of the party line. He writes the epitaph of all made-to-order literature when he mimics the court poet's anthem:

> Friend of the fatherless!
> Fountain of happiness!
> Lord of the swill-bucket! O how my soul is on
> Fire when I gaze at thy
> Calm and commanding eye,
> Like the sun in the sky,
> Comrade Napoleon![75]

In the American literature of the fifties and sixties the impetus of social criticism is most powerful in the Negro writer's attempt to come to terms with his role in American society. Thus, Ralph Ellison's *Invisible Man* reflects the young Negro's turning away from an older generation of leaders that had preached patience and humility, that had insisted on the need for presenting to the complacent white the flattering façade of the humbly grateful liberated slave. There is in the book a black anger at the white man's thoughtless, lazy assumption of superiority. ("So I was not so highly developed as they! What did he mean? Were they all Ph.D.'s?")[76] There is a blazing consciousness of the Negro's centuries-old record as a victim of callousness, injustice, and condescension. However, there is at the same time a brilliant scorn for the educated Negro's attempt to avoid identification with his own culture—the humor and magic of the Negro's folklore, the earthy harmonies of his spirituals, the wild emotion of popular preachers. The more mature student will find in this book an inescapable treatment of the theme of invisibility—our failure to *see* the Negro as an individual, as a person; the futility of expecting responsibility without granting recognition.

The pitfalls in using books with direct social or historical significance are familiar. First, they may seem to date more rapidly than the "timeless" literature with which scholar and critic are more at ease. It may seem difficult, for instance, to recreate for our students the feelings of disillusionment and baffled anger that animated the response of a generation of writers to the senseless carnage of World War I. And yet, one mark of a truly "documentary" work is that it has a meaning beyond its immediate setting. Orwell's beast fable, like those of earlier times, speaks eloquently to people in societies whose political and ideological history is radically

---

[75] *Animal Farm* (New York: Harcourt, Brace & World, Inc., 1946), p. 78.
[76] *Invisible Man* (New York: Random House, Inc., 1952), p. 169.

different from that of Stalinist Russia. Squealer and Comrade Napoleon may be observed, in quite different political and ideological guise, in societies where they have by luck, tradition, or vigilance been to some extent hampered in the exercise of their talents.

Besides, in all earlier literature the literary historian must be ready to reconstruct a possible social meaning that may be an integral part of the work's dynamics. The problem of dynastic succession, the yearning for stability, the threat of constant civil war, the hope for the emergence of a strong and if possible benevolent ruler—such political considerations are latent in much of the literature of feudal and late-feudal Europe. Unless seen in this context, Shakespeare's history plays, for instance, lose much of their topical significance.

The second major objection is that the teacher may mistake his agreement with the author's political commitments for an unbiased appreciation of the author's eloquence. Effective propaganda is not necessarily significant documentary literature. Actually, however, it is likely to be the other way around: Significant literature tends to transcend the narrow bounds of propaganda. Arthur Koestler's *Darkness at Noon* is a powerful tract for the times, but it does not make a good textbook for an anti-communist crusade. Part of its central theme is that there is a solidarity that goes beyond solidarity with class, with party, with historical purposes and great causes: man's solidarity with man.

Even when an author is ostensibly committed to a definite ideology, to a definite philosophy of action, in proportion as he is a true artist his work is likely to transcend his official philosophy. In Bertolt Brecht's *Galileo,* there is a sense of irony, an openness to the variety of human possibilities, that is at odds with the one-track political message the play preaches. As is often the case with Brecht, the work itself is too big for its ideological frame. Somewhere Brecht says, "When those in charge talk of peace, the little man knows that war is coming." This makes a poor motto for a huge government-sponsored peace rally in Red Square.

Part of our interest in a book like Dos Passos' *U.S.A.* derives in fact from a paradoxical and revealing tension between its ideological assumptions and its human appeal. Like Dreiser and others, Dos Passos had overtly embraced a tough-minded historical determinism, and he proceeded to show how the lives of individuals are conditioned, and often thwarted by prevailing social conditions. Yet the implied message is throughout an appeal for compassion, a plea that man can by a tremendous effort of moral regeneration lift himself out of the deterministic framework that is the theoretical foundation for the author's view of history.

There was a time when stress on the social dimension especially of contemporary American literature would have seemed merely a fashionable cliché. Today, our critical clichés tend to run in the opposite direction. Here as elsewhere, however, the teacher must do more than merely follow the current trend. By drawing to some extent on works of urgent contemporary significance, he can keep his students from ever entertaining the suspicion that to the literary critic metaphors matter more than people.

If one way of relating literature to life is to stress its social significance, another way is to treat it as an expression of man's private self. The same decades earlier in the century that saw a growing concern with the sociology of literature saw a growing influence of a kind of psychology designed to plumb the depths below the social surface. There is a large share in imaginative literature of what to the narrowly practical person seems idle, fantastic, irrational. The literary artist is someone more sensitive than his fellows. Often he seems profoundly disturbed or even possessed, seized by what Plato called a kind of divine madness. It therefore seemed logical to apply to literature the kind of **depth psychology** developed by Freud and his followers, which had resulted in the rediscovery of the repressed chaotic forces lurking behind the façade of respectability, hiding under the thin veneer of civilization. As Lionel Trilling said in his essay on "Freud and Literature,"

> The Freudian psychology is the only systematic account of the human mind which, in point of subtlety and complexity, of interest and tragic power, deserves to stand beside the chaotic mass of psychological insights which literature has accumulated through the centuries. . . . the human nature of the Freudian psychology is exactly the stuff upon which the poet has always exercised his art.[77]

As Trilling pointed out, the Romantic-Rousseauistic tradition in literature had always been "passionately devoted to a research into the self." To Blake, to Shelley, the affective, emotional forces in man were the source of truth and beauty; the analytical understanding, the "false secondary power," was the enemy that narrowed and distorted our vision of life. The Romantic rebellion against the practical, the conventional, the merely rational can be formulated in Freudian terms: "Again and again we see the effective, utilitarian ego being relegated to an inferior position and a plea being made on behalf of the anarchic and self-indulgent id."[78]

In the literature of our century, an almost obsessive theme has been that of the emotional aridity of contemporary life. In T. S. Eliot's *The Waste Land* as in James Joyce's *Ulysses,* the basic quest is the search for the healing waters in the land where "the dead tree gives no shelter," the land of "empty cisterns and exhausted wells." With a writer like D. H. Lawrence, the key problem of modern man becomes that of coming to terms with his instinctual self. The ideal becomes a new integration of

[77] Trilling, *The Liberal Imagination*, p. 44.
[78] *Ibid.*, pp. 44, 47.

personality, a life in harmony with the "dark forces" of the soul that our cerebral and mechanistic civilization attempts to proscribe and destroy. In the fiction of Sherwood Anderson, of Truman Capote or Carson McCullers, a recurrent underlying theme is the search for love. That search has little in common with the reassuring clichés of popular entertainment. As Carson McCullers has it, the heart is a lonely hunter.

In the hands of the simple-minded, Freudian categories can lead to a fatal narrowing of interest. The doctrinaire Freudian critic is forever trying to impose upon literature his poverty-stricken inventory of a few sexual symbols and familial relations. In more expert hands, Freudian insights become one way of giving substance to our impression that literature engages us at levels deeper than that of literal action. In great literary art, we have a sense of something that matters more deeply than a mere tale, more lastingly than mere entertainment. One way of substantiating this feeling is to trace in literature the **symbolic action** by which the writer attempts to deal with his psychological "burdens." We will then look in literature for patterns of alienation and rejection, of attraction and repulsion, of a new identity emerging from the integration of warring psychological elements. With a critic like Kenneth Burke, we will look in literature for strategies for rationalizing or disguising guilt or weakness, for rituals of self-acceptance and self-justification.

The first thing an interest in Freudian approaches does for the teacher is to reopen the question of the relationship between the writer's life and his work. Conventional literary biography often left untouched those areas of the poet's sensibility likely to color most profoundly the consciousness revealed in his poetry. A biography of a poet like Whitman is worse than misleading if it merely accepts at face value the public image of himself created by the poet, the result of his attempt "To prepare a face to meet the faces that you meet." As Mark Van Doren said of Whitman, his poetry is personal "in the best sense" because it was written by a "disturbed spirit attempting to understand, disguise and magnify itself."[79]

But even where biography is less directly relevant, modern depth psychology may furnish hints concerning the possible psychological dynamics of a major work. There is an intensity of sexual revulsion in *Hamlet* and *King Lear* that is often ignored by Shakespeare's explicators. There is an obsessive quality in the "ferocious indignation" of a satirist like Jonathan Swift, a paradoxical mixture of horror and fascination. With such problems, the critic will be the better equipped to deal if he recognizes in literature what Rilke in his *Duino Elegies* has called "inner history's luxuriant growth," the "older terrors," the "rising ancestral tides."

[79] "Walt Whitman, Stranger," *The American Mercury*, XXXV (July, 1935), 277–85.

Both the strength and the weakness of critical approaches indebted to psychoanalysis is "the injunction to read the work of literature with a lively sense of its latent and ambiguous meanings, as if it were, as indeed it is, a being no less alive and contradictory than the man who created it."[80] On the one hand, this perspective alerts the critic to overtones and suggestions. It alerts him to the particular emotional aura of a work; it warns him not to force a work of literature into too superficially "rational" categories. On the other hand, such a perspective can easily lead the critic to discount the "surface" level of theme and form. He will become preoccupied with the crucial contradictions and revealing ambiguities that allow him to reach a work's deeper meaning. He will start looking for them not only in works that by their paradoxical and unfinished quality reflect underlying psychological tensions but also in those where a greater degree of stability, of control, has been achieved. Such a critic may approach the overt structure and texture of a work not as the full embodiment, the "objective correlative," of fully integrated aesthetic experience but rather as a disguise, which the critic must interpret the way the psychoanalyst must interpret the dream. Seen from such a point of view, minor weaknesses and inconsistencies may assume an importance quite out of proportion with their role in the work as a whole. Thus, criticism indebted to Freudian psychoanalysis has on the one hand made us more sensitive to the ambivalence and depth of the literature that most deeply engages our emotions. It has on the other hand reinforced the modern critic's general distrust for the obvious, the tendency to prefer any esoteric explanation, however willful, to common-sense observation.

An alternative, and currently more influential, way of making the critic "sensitive to the tap-roots below"[81] is to adopt the **analytical psychology** of C. G. Jung. The resulting critical perspective sees the underlying significance of literature not so much in the expression of the individual subconscious and the psychological adjustment of the individual as in a preconscious level of experience common to the race. Poetic intuition then becomes an avenue to a deep-seated preconscious, prerational knowledge. To the Freudian view of poetry as intensely personal and subjective, Jung opposed a view of the poet as "objective and impersonal— even inhuman":

> the specifically artistic disposition involves an overweight of collective psychic life as against the personal. Art is a kind of innate drive that seizes a human being and makes him its instrument. . . . As a human being he may have moods and a will and personal aims, but as an artist he is "man" in a higher sense—he is "collective man"—one who carries and shapes the unconscious, psychic life of mankind.[82]

80 Trilling, *The Liberal Imagination*, p. 48.
81 Blackmur, *Language as Gesture*, p. 398.
82 *Modern Man in Search of a Soul* (New York: Harcourt, Brace & World, Inc., 1933), p. 194–95.

Jung distinguished between literature clarifying or heightening materials from conscious human experience and literature that draws on "a strange something that derives its existence from the hinterland of man's mind," rising in its enormity or grotesque foreignness from timeless depths, giving expression to primordial experiences "that rend from top to bottom the curtain upon which is painted the picture of an ordered world." With the conscious ego swept along as on a subterranean current, such literature expresses something "not clearly known and yet profoundly alive." It expresses the **myths** of the race, the **archetypes** that live in the collective unconscious as Jung felt Faust lived as a primordial image in the German soul:

> The archetypal image of the wise man, the saviour or redeemer, lies buried and dormant in man's unconscious since the dawn of culture; it is awakened whenever the times are out of joint and a human society is committed to a serious error. When people go astray they feel the need of a guide or teacher or even of the physician. These primordial images are numerous, but do not appear in the dreams of individuals or in works of art until they are called into being by the waywardness of the general outlook. When conscious life is characterized by one-sidedness and by a false attitude, then they are activated—one might say, "instinctively"—and come to light in the dreams of individuals and the visions of artists and seers, thus restoring the psychic equilibrium of the epoch.[83]

Literature, like all art, thus meets the deep-seated spiritual needs of society or of the age; it draws on the "healing and redeeming forces of the collective psyche that underlies consciousness."[84]

Jung thus furnished a powerful new rationale for those who follow Coleridge and the Romantic tradition in opposing the poetic imagination, representing a primordial, beneficent, all-integrating intuition, to the restricted and isolated analytical understanding, forever mistaking its own narrow categories for the final truth, forever entangling itself in insoluble logical dilemmas. A Jungian perspective provided a powerful alternative to what Keats had called the "irritable reaching after fact and reason"; it furnished a new explanation why, as Keats once said, "what the imagination seizes as beauty must be truth." In the words of R. P. Blackmur,

> By intuition we adventure in the pre-conscious; and there, where the adventure is, there is no need or suspicion of certainty or meaning; there is the living, expanding *prescient* substance without the tags and handles of conscious form. Art is the looking-glass of the pre-conscious, and when it is deepest seems to participate in it sensibly.[85]

Many critics thus found in the Jungian analysis of mythical significance a new way of relating literature to "the momentum of the whole

83 *Ibid.*, pp. 180–81, 197.
84 *Ibid.*, p. 198.
85 Blackmur, *Language as Gesture*, p. 398.

human enterprise." They set out to demonstrate that underlying the technical and conceptual aspects of a work there is a level of symbolical action through which forces greater than ourselves press into and transform our experience. Thus, we see a critic like Francis Fergusson, in *The Idea of a Theater*, accept Jung's view of myth "as a way of ordering human experience" and as a way of "understanding and representing human experience . . . prior to the arts and sciences and philosophies of modern times." We see him search for dramatic art "popular, traditional, and ritualistic," and "based upon a uniquely direct sense of life." We see him find such art in the plays of Sophocles and Shakespeare, written for a theater "which had been formed at the center of the culture of its time, and at the center of the life and awareness of the community," there focusing "the complementary insights of the whole culture."[86]

The difficulty with criticism focused on archetype and myth is that like the Freudian approach it tends to treat much of the actual structure and texture of a work as mere surface, as "rationalization," as disguise. It exploits hints and ambiguities that to the naked eye seem merely incidental. Thus, Fergusson, in discussing *Oedipus Rex*, characteristically states that "no one who sees or reads the play can rest content with its literal coherence." The "suggestive mystery of the Oedipus myth" is not to be solved by a literal acceptance of Sophocles' theological and didactic purpose; rather, it will slowly come into focus, "like repressed material under psychoanalysis," as we respond to the deeper "rhythm" of the play. The true action of the play, we are made to feel, is not the attempt by Oedipus to solve a fateful challenge to his wisdom, authority, and self-reliance. It is rather the consummation of his "quest" for his true nature and destiny. In trying to find the slayer of Laius, he "finds himself." This element in the play links it with rites and ceremonies circling around individual growth and development, initiation, passage from one stage of life to another. At the same time, by a not fully explained coincidence in the economy of the myth-making preconscious, the play presents the "tragic but perennial, even normal, quest of the whole city for its well-being." The "over-all aim" which "informs" the play is "to find the culprit in order to purify human life":

> The figure of Oedipus himself fulfills all the requirements of the scapegoat, the dismembered king or god-figure. The situation in which Thebes is presented at the beginning of the play—in peril of its life; its crops, its herds, its women mysteriously infertile, signs of a mortal disease of the City, and the disfavor of the gods—is like the withering which winter brings, and calls, in the same way, for struggle, dismemberment, death, and renewal. And this tragic sequence is the substance of the play.[87]

[86] *The Idea of a Theater* (New York: Doubleday & Company, Inc., n.d.), pp. 26, 14–17.
[87] Fergusson, *The Idea of a Theater*, pp. 27–52.

From the overt theological import of the play, with its drama centered on the relationship between man and god, the critic thus takes us to the pretheological, ritualistic past, where our interest is in the perennial rites of the tribe. We thus presumably reach a "deeper" level than that reached by the Chorus in the concluding lines of the play:

> Men of Thebes: look upon Oedipus.
>
> This is the king who solved the famous riddle
> And towered up, most powerful of men.
> No mortal eyes but looked on him with envy,
> Yet in the end ruin swept over him.
>
> Let every man in mankind's frailty
> Consider his last day; and let none
> Presume on his good fortune until he find
> Life, at his death, a memory without pain.[88]

A whole school of cultural anthropology has assumed that in the myths and rituals of "primitive" tribes we can catch a glimpse of something more profound, something in an obscure way more meaningful, than we find in the consciousness of rationalistic, conceptual Western man. Insofar as this tradition has furnished to the literary critic an inventory of mythical archetypes, it seems doubtful that truly meaningful material has been disentangled from the arbitrary accretions of centuries-old convention, tradition, and ceremony. We *can* hear in *Oedipus Rex* a strong echo of the tribal past, in which the community tried to restore fertility to its women or its crops by cleansing itself of whatever "pollution" might have angered the gods. But we can also see how in an urban, commercial society, like the Athens of Sophocles, crop failure is ceasing to be an overriding, primordial fear. In the play, we see it rapidly receding into the background as Sophocles focuses on his true theme: the relation between religious reverence and secular pride, between obedience and insubordination. To guard against reading too much into a work, we should focus on the way the poet reflects and transforms the myths, taboos, and rituals *of his own contemporary culture*. In these, we are likely to find, in their particular local and historical guise, recurrent patterns of human experience, universal tendencies of the human mind. We do not really need a hypothetical common substratum of mythical lore to explain the human tendency toward scapegoating, leader-worship, or propitiatory sacrifice. Often, indeed, the mythical lore of the anthropologist seems to obscure rather than illuminate psychological processes that may be studied more revealingly in our relatively susceptible, ideologically and culturally volatile modern societies than in the ossified cultural structure of the tribe.

---

[88] Sophocles, *The Oedipus Cycle: An English Version*, trans. Dudley Fitts and Robert Fitzgerald (New York: Harcourt, Brace & World, Inc., 1949), p. 78.

Jungian criticism has a strong appeal for many a teacher of English, since "the prerational image of human nature and destiny" found in myth and ritual is a fascinating study in itself. Nevertheless, the teacher must be aware of the problems caused for him by the current vogue of interpretations in the Jungian vein. In the first place, it has reinforced the current critical prejudice against literature of a realistic or naturalistic bent. Fergusson for instance finds that, among the ancients, Euripides as contrasted with Sophocles deals with the human psyche "cut off from the deepest levels of experience." If we can accept Jung's estimate of the preponderance of literature fully concerned with conscious human experience, much of the literature most fruitful in the classroom will turn out to be similarly cut off.

Second, concern with mythical significance tends to make critic and teacher move too fast and too vaguely from the actual work to abstractions about life cycles and prehistoric patterns of existence. This is true even when a critic like Northrop Frye subscribes to the view that every poem "is a unity," when he makes myth the key to a poem's unified structure, calling it "the shaping principle of a work of literature." This is what Frye says early in his discussion of *Lycidas,* Milton's elegy on the death of Edward King, his fellow poet "unfortunately drowned in his passage from Chester on the Irish Seas":

> King is given the pastoral name of Lycidas, which is equivalent to Adonis, and is associated with the cyclical rhythms of nature. Of these three are of particular importance: the daily cycle of the sun across the sky, the yearly cycle of the seasons, and the cycle of water, flowing from wells and fountains through rivers to the sea. Sunset, winter and the sea are emblems of Lycidas' death; sunrise and spring, of his resurrection. . . . The imagery of the opening lines, "Shatter your leaves before the mellowing year," suggests the frosts of autumn killing the flowers, and in the great roll-call of flowers towards the end, most of them early blooming flowers like the "rathe primrose," the spring returns.[89]

However, the *overt,* as against the alleged mythical meaning of Milton's opening lines is that the poet is *disturbing* the "season due" of the plants mentioned, plucking berries and leaves contrary to their usual life cycle, *"before the mellowing year,"* for a special ceremonial purpose: Regardless of the cyclical rhythms of nature, the laurels, myrtle, and ivy are needed for the symbolic crowning of the dead poet. Similarly, the profusion of flowers with which the speaker in the poem strews the imaginary hearse help to "interpose a little ease"; they serve their familiar paradoxical ceremonial function that cuts short their usual, natural cycle of life. The plant-and-flower symbolism, as interpreted by the speaker in the

---

[89] Northrop Frye, "Literature as Context: Milton's *Lycidas," University of North Carolina Studies in Comparative Literature,* XXIII (1959), 44–55; in *Milton's* Lycidas: *The Tradition and the Poem,* ed. C. A. Patrides (New York: Holt, Rinehart & Winston, Inc., 1961), pp. 200–11.

poem, is thus not dimly and primordially vital but richly and conventionally ceremonial.

Similarly, Frye finds a major principle of unity in the poem's "water
imagery": the Muses are invoked as the "Sisters of the sacred well"; the
references to Arethuse and Alpheus deal with Arcadian water spirits;
references to Orpheus and Peter are linked "in imagery" with Lycidas:

> Orpheus was also an "enchanting son" or spirit of nature; he died young
> in much the same role as Adonis, and was flung into the water. Peter would
> have drowned too without the help of Christ; hence Peter is not named
> directly, but only as "The Pilot of the Galilean Lake," just as Christ is not
> named directly, but only as "Him that walked the waves." When Orpheus
> was torn to pieces by the Maenads, his head went floating "Down the swift
> Hebrus to the Lesbian shore." The theme of salvation out of water is con-
> nected with the image of the dolphin, a conventional type of Christ, and
> dolphins are called upon to "waft the hapless youth" just before the perora-
> tion begins.[90]

The skeptical reader will feel that in the poem several of the references
collected here are too peripheral to carry through an essential underlying
pattern. The periphrastic reference to Peter as "pilot" is a small part of
a long passage in which the dominant symbols are the conventional ones
of Peter as keeper of the keys and master shepherd; the association of the
Muses with the "sacred well" is as conventional as their association,
followed up in detail, with poetry.

In *Oedipus Rex,* Sophocles' use of references to the gods is theological
in the sense of having a fully developed intellectual dimension that is
intimately a part of a complex pattern of thought *and* feeling. In *Lycidas,*
Milton's use of Greek myths is not mythic but *mythological:* The employment of each mythical reference, as of each topical and historical reference
in the poem, is guided by the full range of its intellectual *and* imaginative
implications. Ultimately, the unity of the poem must be sought not in a
pattern of affinities among its images but in its peculiar blend of a richly
ceremonial tone with a powerful polemical, didactic drive. If there is a
unifying image in the poem, it is that of the shepherd as the type of the
poet-priest. If there is a unifying theme in the poem, it is the reply of
Phoebus to the poet's question about the wisdom of serving "the thankless
Muse":

> Fame is no plant that grows on mortal soil, . . .
> But lives and spreads aloft by those pure eyes
> And perfect witness of all-judging Jove;
> As he pronounces lastly on each deed,
> Of so much fame in heaven expect they meed.

It is true that water is everywhere in the poem, but this very ubiquity
makes it symbolically neutral. In the poem, water takes the form of both

[90] Patrides, *Milton's* Lycidas, p. 202.

"fresh dews" and "rank mist," of "gushing brooks" and the "remorseless deep," of a "sacred well" and the "whelming tide." "Fountain, shade, and rill" are as much part of the earthly shepherd's life as "other groves and streams" are part of the "blest kingdoms meek of joy and love." This symbolical ambivalence of nature is not surprising in pre-Rousseauistic, pre-Romantic English Renaissance literature, where, as in Spenser's *Faerie Queene,* nature is just as likely to spew forth savage monsters and blatant beasts as to exert a beneficent, healing influence on those entrusting themselves to her tutelage.

Here, as elsewhere in criticism focused on the poet's use of myth, the reader finds it hard to reconcile suggested analyses of mythical significance with what exactly a poem or a play seems to say. On occasion, the teacher will find the probings of critics practicing literary depth psychology, whether inspired by Freud or Jung, provocative and illuminating. Nevertheless, as a whole, their performance does not measure up to their pretensions. The term *myth* is perhaps most meaningful when applied to a major theme clearly shaping the concerns of a literary tradition. Such a central theme may be found for instance in the struggle of nineteenth-century American writers to establish an American identity somehow reconciling the conflicting strands of nature and civilization, wilderness and gentility, Puritan concepts of sin and Romantic concepts of man's innate goodness, Rousseauistic idealization of nature and the rawness of pioneer reality. Leslie A. Fiedler has called attention to how D. H. Lawrence's *Studies in Classic American Literature,* for all its capriciousness, points to some of the "obsessive and recurring themes" that make the great literature of the American past unmistakably American.[91] As an example, one could hardly read Lawrence's attack on Benjamin Franklin without becoming more fully aware of on the one hand the particularly American mastery of common sense, efficiency, practicality, and on the other hand the narrowing and distorting effect that a worship of the practical can have on life as a whole. However, investigations of such underlying themes are most convincing when they are firmly anchored to psychological forces and cultural trends that can be cogently documented in the available texts. They are least convincing when they invoke the term *myth* as an indiscriminately honorific term for *motifs* dimly perceived.

The greatest literature, such as the tragedies of Shakespeare, can be discussed in illuminating fashion in terms of generally accessible, rather than obscure and disguised, human motives. Criticism that examines their overt role in the play can be relatively objective; it can stay close to what the characters actually say and do. Such "objective" criticism, in the words of W. K. Wimsatt,

<hr>

[91] "American Literature," in Leary, *Scholarship,* p. 165.

rests on facts of human psychology (as that a man may love a woman so well as to give up empires), facts, which though psychological, yet are so well acknowledged as to lie in the realm of what may be called public psychology—a realm which one should distinguish from the private realm of the author's psychology and from the equally private realm of the individual reader's psychology (the vivid pictures which poetry or stories are supposed to create in the imagination, or the venerable action of catharsis—all that poetry is said to *do* rather than to *be*).[92]

The teacher investigating the possible deeper meanings and ulterior purposes of literature will finally reach a two-sided conclusion: On the one hand, they can help him explain both the immediate significance and some of the more lasting echoes of a work. On the other hand, they can and should be distinguished from some of the more basic and indispensable ingredients of literary art. The teacher who fits literature into the framework provided by a definite political, religious, or psychological doctrine runs the risk of shutting his students off from much of what literature has to offer.

A balanced survey of the claims made for the significance of literature leads inevitably to an eclectic point of view. The teacher must make allowance for a number of major elements: sensation, emotion, idea, attitude, form. He must recognize a number of central motives: a hunger for experience, a need for meaning, a yearning for order. He should be prepared to study the interplay of these factors in the works he is going to teach. In some of these works, considerations will be paramount that will be peripheral in others. The teacher should not allow too narrow a definition of literary significance to deflect his attention from whatever kinds of meaning prove to be central in a given work.

Form and Value

Though study of the ulterior significance of a work may prove illuminating, it may not answer our question about the value of the work as literature. A work may be of great interest as a historical or psychological document and yet be of dubious literary quality. The philosophical currents of a period may appear more clearly in the work of a merely fashionable writer than in the intensely personal synthesis of a great literary artist. A novel of social protest that is uneven and cliché-ridden may yet reveal a great deal about class structure, class consciousness, major ideological developments. The psychologist may find compulsive, rhapsodic fragments more revealing than a fully integrated, finished poem.

Modern criticism, insofar as it continues the tradition of the New Criticism of Richards and Brooks and Warren, has typically endeavored to provide criteria of value that can be directly applied to the structure

[92] Schorer, *Criticism*, p. 402.

and texture of a given work. It has made us focus on **form** as the "unique structural means" without which the elements that go into art "would remain nothing but experience, neither beauty nor esthetic truth." Literary form "has been the great contemporary concern, and contemporary criticism has taught us that if we neglect art in its technical actualities, we are not talking about art at all, but about something else—life as the artist has lived it, or life as the critic would like it to be."[93] Characteristically, the tradition of the New Criticism has tried not to separate considerations of form and value. It has tried to make formal analysis the direct avenue to our final questions about the value and greatness of a work.

The criteria of value furnished by this tradition will often provide the teacher with a rationale for his intuitive feeling of what is great and powerful in literature. Even when they seem inappropriate or insufficient, they will help the teacher understand some of the prevailing standards of critics, reviewers, and textbook authors. Most important, a study of these criteria will help him see how in much modern criticism discussion of apparently technical matters can turn out to be concerned by implication with a work's essential literary value.

The most important of the prevailing modern standards have already been touched on in various ways in the preceding discussion. *Typically, a modern critic requires in a literary work of the first rank concreteness, complexity, inclusiveness, and wholeness.* Each of these requirements deserves detailed explanation and illustration.

The modern insistence on **concreteness** was in part a reaction against a tradition of versified abstraction and facile rhetoric. As the poet explains that life is real, life is earnest, and the grave is not its goal, we long for a kind of poetry that will somehow get its teeth more firmly into actual experience. As the Memorial Day speaker eulogizes the happy dead assured of their country's gratitude, we long for something more real, if only, as in MacLeish's "Memorial Rain," the rasp of the wind, the minutely shifting sand, the first thin spurts of the relaxing, loosening rain. With MacLeish in "Ars Poetica," we will be ready to ask for images rather than ideas, for things rather than meanings:

> A poem should be palpable and mute
> As a globed fruit
>
> Dumb
> As old medallions to the thumb
>
> Silent as the sleeve-worn stone
> Of casement ledges where the moss has grown—
>
> A poem should be wordless
> As the flight of birds. . . .

[93] Schorer, *Criticism,* p. ix.

A poem should be equal to:
Not true

For all the history of grief
An empty doorway and a maple leaf

For love
The leaning grasses and two lights above the sea—

A poem should not mean
But be.[94]

One of the most persistent themes in modern criticism has been that a poem should deal not in abstractions but in sights, sounds, textures, feelings. A novel should not *tell* us things, it should involve us in them, make us participate. As John Ciardi says, one of the basic principles of good writing

> is to let the action speak for itself. A good novelist does not tell us that a given character is good or bad (at least not since the passing of the Dickens tradition): he shows us the character in action and then, watching him, we know. Poetry, too, has fictional obligations: even when the characters are ideas and metaphors rather than people, they must be *characterized in action*. A poem does not *talk about* ideas; it *enacts* them.[95]

In this respect, as in many others, the modern critic adopted principles laid down over a century earlier by Coleridge, who included among the essential requirements for poetry "that it be sensuous, and by its imagery elicit truth at a flash; that it be impassioned, and be able to move our feelings and awaken our affections." In its modern application, this view has at times taken an extreme form. As I. A. Richards pointed out in *The Philosophy of Rhetoric,* it may lead the critic to a "fear of the abstract"; it may lead the writer to "anxious, over-careful attempts to *copy* perceptions and feelings *in words,* to 'hand over sensations bodily.' " What *is* essential in literature is that we should fully apprehend and realize, that we should "really take in and become fully aware" of its meaning. Reliance on the visual, the concrete, the physical, is one possible way of promoting that fully realized attention and response. But, as Richards points out, it is not the only and indispensable way; "the language of the greatest poetry is frequently abstract in the extreme." In much of Shakespeare's poetry, something powerfully compels our attention in spite of the abstract or generic terms used:

> Let me not to the marriage of true minds
> Admit impediments. Love is not love
> Which alters when it alteration finds, . . .

[94] Archibald MacLeish, *Collected Poems: 1917–1952* (Boston: Houghton Mifflin Company, 1954), pp. 40–41.
[95] "Robert Frost: The Way to the Poem," *Saturday Review,* April 12, 1958, pp. 13–15.

Or, to use Richards' example:

> If thou didst ever hold me in thy heart
> Absent thee from felicity awhile
> And in this harsh world draw thy breath in pain
> To tell my story.[96]

Avoiding an extreme formulation, we may set up as the first condition of literary value that a writer's abstractions be firmly anchored in three-dimensional experience. They should not be mere second-hand counters but be borne in on us in a medium making full use of the perceptual and emotional dimensions of language. Such a requirement will encourage the teacher to direct the student's attention to those features of literary language that give it a more immediate, more compelling reality than ordinary talk.

Next to the requirement for concreteness, the most pervasive characteristic of modern criticism has been its insistence on **complexity**. Modern readers of serious literature have generally preferred the demanding and difficult to the smooth and predictable. Many former terms of critical praise have come to acquire derogatory connotations: "regularity" and "symmetry" have come to suggest the facile; "elegance" suggests superficiality. The slow and steady movement of Tennyson's verse has come to seem simple-minded; Poe's breathless rhythms and multiple rhymes, once admired as a mark of technical virtuosity, have earned him his modern reputation as the "jingle-poet." Much more to the modern taste proved the tense convolutions and syncopations of a poet like G. M. Hopkins, who preferred

> All things counter, original, spare, strange;
> Whatever is fickle, freckled (who knows how?)
> With swift, slow; sweet, sour; adazzle, dim.[97]

This general trend may be part of another great swing of the stylistic pendulum from the relatively simple to the relatively involved. However, the requirement for complexity in great art is at least to some extent independent of stylistic fashions. To be truly and lastingly satisfying, order must not be static. It should be *achieved* order; it will be the more gratifying if it has been imposed upon resistant materials. The most deeply gratifying art does not simply project a calm serenity; rather it involves us in struggle and diversity. Its unity is unity enforced upon variety. Its order is that of richly, even chaotically vital experience brought under control. As Robert Penn Warren said, a poem "is a motion toward a point of rest, but if it is not a resisted motion, it is motion of no consequence."[98]

96 I. A. Richards, *The Philosophy of Rhetoric* (New York: Oxford University Press, 1936), pp. 129–30, 133.
97 W. H. Gardner, ed., *Poems of Gerard Manley Hopkins*, 3rd ed. (New York: Oxford University Press, 1948), p. 74.
98 "Pure and Impure Poetry," *The Kenyon Review*, V (Spring, 1943), 251.

When a beautifully simple theme emerges late in a Beethoven or Brahms symphony, it owes its triumphant power to its being the climax of a complex development. The arranger who takes the melody out of context to include it in a medley of tunes by great composers shows that he has missed the point. Coleridge came close to the secret of truly powerful art when he described as one effect of the poetic imagination its combining "a more than usual state of emotion with more than usual order," its paradoxical combination of a "steady self-possession" with feelings "profound or vehement."[99]

A Coleridgean recognition of the element of *variety* as well as unity in art is reflected in modern discussions of such technical features of poetry as **meter**. Rhythm in a poem does not mean imposing the monotonous regularity of a "tedum-tedum-tedum" pattern. The more regular the meter becomes, the more likely it is to put us to sleep. The interest of meter lies in the tension between the actual rhythms of speech and the underlying regularity of the pattern to which they are partly made to conform. To today's teacher of poetry, rhythm means

> that continuous excitement that always occurs in a good poem when we feel the tension between the basic pattern of the verse and our actual timing, accent, and tone of voice as we read it. Our natural emphases, our natural pauses, guided by meaning, are continually straining away from the strict pattern, but never far away.[100]

To the modern critic, complexity of style is merely the most external manifestation of the **inclusiveness** of literary art. Henry James had insisted that "the province of art is all life, all feeling, all observation, all vision. . . . it is all experience." He had ridiculed those who would fence in the artist by putting up little signs warning him not to step on the grass or not to bring dogs into the public gardens. To him, it was "the essence of moral energy" to "survey the whole field."[101] To the modern critic, the virtue of such openness to experience has been the opportunity it offers for imaginative control. I. A. Richards made the reconciliation of disparate elements one of the chief virtues of poetry. He saw the greatest difference between the artist and the ordinary person in "the range, delicacy, and freedom of the connections he is able to make between different elements of his experience."[102] Robert Penn Warren said that "other things being equal, the greatness of a poet depends upon the extent of the area of experience which he can master poetically."[103] Combining the requirement for concreteness with the requirement for unified, mastered com-

---

[99] Schneider, ed., *Selected Poetry and Prose*, p. 275.
[100] Louis L. Martz, "The Teaching of Poetry," in Gordon and Noyes, *Essays*, pp. 248–49.
[101] Schorer, *Criticism*, pp. 52, 54.
[102] *Principles of Literary Criticism* (New York: Harcourt, Brace & World, Inc., 1952), p. 181.
[103] *Kenyon Review*, V, 250.

plexity, W. K. Wimsatt concluded that "unified concrete complexity" is "the structural specific difference between art and other forms of knowledge." To him as to others, complexity of form was merely the external manifestation of a work's "maturity or sophistication or richness or depth, and hence its value."[104]

For the classroom teacher, the most direct effect of this stress on inconclusiveness has been to confirm his belief "that fine poetry can derive from the roots of common life—that poetry does not dwell apart in some rarefied realm called Beauty."[105] Most teachers were ready to surrender the view that poetry should achieve beauty by limiting itself to subject matter inherently "poetic": flowers, May mornings, young love. The great literature of the past, and certainly the literature of our century, show that the true artist goes beyond the conventionally beautiful. No preconception about the purely poetic can keep him from treating the prosaic, the ugly, the taboo and transforming it into art. By presenting to our students a poem like "Auto Wreck" by Karl Shapiro, we can show that the poet does not *have* to write about flowers. He may write about the pulsing red light of the ambulance, the policemen hosing off the pavement spattered with blood, the tightened throats and sickly smiles of the passers-by. As Cleanth Brooks once said, as far as poetry is concerned, it is the public, and not the poet, that inhabits the Ivory Tower; since it insists in poetry on certain conventional emotional responses uncontaminated by contact with the complexities of the real world.

A second effect of the emphasis on inclusiveness has been more indirect but nevertheless all-pervading. Critic and teacher have concentrated on those features of literary language by which, according to the tenets of the New Criticism, the poetic integration of an enriched and widened experience is achieved. *The requirement for inclusiveness provides the rationale for the modern critic's treatment of metaphor, symbol, irony, and ambiguity.* To the modern critic, these have not been merely optional poetic devices. They have seemed the key to what poetry essentially is and does.

For instance, modern critics have insisted that **metaphor** is not merely illustrative. It is not merely a more vivid, a more pictorial way of saying what could be said more abstractly. Even if it were, it would make language that much more concrete and complex, giving it more bite. However, beyond translating idea into image, metaphor brings into play emotions and attitudes. When Hamlet says, "What should such fellows as I do crawling between earth and heaven?" the word *crawl*, associated as it is with insects or vermin, projects Hamlet's feelings of disillusionment and disgust. It is often fruitful to approach metaphorical language first of all as a notation of emotions. As W. K. Wimsatt says,

[104] Schorer, *Criticism*, pp. 400–01.
[105] Martz, "Poetry," in Gordon and Noyes, p. 244.

272 THE DISCIPLINE OF ENGLISH

Keats discovering Homer is like a traveler in the realms of gold, like an astronomer who discovers a planet, like Cortez gazing at the Pacific. The title of the sonnet, "On First Looking into Chapman's Homer," seems to furnish not so much the subject of the poem as a fourth member of a central metaphor, the real subject of the poem being an abstraction, a certain kind of thrill in discovering, for which there is no name and no other description, only the four members of the metaphor pointing, as to the center of their pattern.[106]

To critics like I. A. Richards, the interesting metaphor is the one that not only puts together things "from very different orders of experience" but makes us establish previously unnoticed connections between them. Metaphor thus becomes a manifestation of the "mind's endless endeavor to order itself."[107] It is

the supreme agent by which disparate and hitherto unconnected things are brought together in poetry for the sake of the effects upon attitude and impulse which spring from their collocation and from the combinations which the mind then establishes between them. . . . Metaphor is a semisurreptitious method by which a greater variety of elements can be wrought into the fabric of experience. . . . what is needed for the wholeness of an experience is not always naturally present, and metaphor supplies an excuse by which what is needed may be smuggled in.[108]

As Richards points out, this conception goes counter to the neoclassical view, which stresses the need for the logical fitness of the resemblances between two different things that the metaphor exploits. The modern critic indeed turned to the "farfetched" and "extravagant" conceits that critics like Dryden and Johnson had rejected. In "The Ecstasy," Donne says of the two lovers

Our eye-beams twisted, and did thread
Our eyes upon a double string.

To the logical mind, the picture of eyes threaded like buttons on a string is at once too prosaic and too grotesque to furnish an appropriate metaphorical expression for the close communion of the lovers looking as in a trance into each other's eyes. To the orthodox modern critic, however, the metaphor would merely illustrate T. S. Eliot's description of Donne as constantly amalgamating disparate experience, constantly forming new wholes of what in the ordinary man's experience is chaotic and fragmentary. As Eliot said, what to us seems disconnected and irrelevant—love, Spinoza, the smell of cooking—is absorbed by the poetic sensibility into a previously unperceived order.[109]

What is of course difficult to show is in what sense the individual metaphor brings about any real "reconciliation" or "ordering" of ex-

[106] Schorer, *Criticism*, p. 399.
[107] Richards, *Philosophy of Rhetoric*, p. 131.
[108] Richards, *Principles*, p. 240.
[109] "The Metaphysical Poets," in *Selected Essays*, p. 247.

perience. When Donne discusses love in terms borrowed from astronomy, geography, and theology, we respond to a richly blended paradoxical effect. We are jolted into paying attention; we are braced by a mixture more tonic than the sugary elegance of the conventional love lyric. But we may still feel that in any real sense the worlds of love and science or of love and theology are as far apart as ever. Brooks, in *The Well-Wrought Urn* (1947), uses Donne's "Canonization" as a crucial example of the "welding together" of the discordant and contradictory. In the poem, the lover rejects secular fame and wealth for earthly love the way the saint rejects them for divine love. But throughout the poem, the religious metaphors *serve* the earthly theme; the central paradox is that the lovers reject the world not for the spirit but for the flesh. It is doubtful that the poem in any valid sense brings the world of the saint and that of the lover closer together. After decades in which Donne was considered the type of a unified poetic sensibility, this more skeptical view seems to be gaining ground:

> Even among Donne's friendliest critics in recent years there has been a growing perception that (to use Douglas Bush's words in *English Literature in the Earlier Seventeenth Century*) whereas "the greatest artists dominate and unify experience. . . . Donne's fragments of experience remain fragments," and "his sensibility is not unified but multiple."[110]

In Donne's religious poems, by contrast, we find paradoxical metaphors we can resolve. They give figurative expression to concepts and feelings that can be more or less perfectly reconciled on the level of prose logic. These metaphors are the "fit" embodiment of familiar paradoxes of Christian doctrine, which can be expressed at least in part in intellectual terms. Thus, when Donne calls Death "slave to fate, chance, kings, and desperate men," when he exclaims "Death, thou shalt die," he is projecting imaginatively an orthodox view of how the power, and the fear, of death shrink with the certainty of immortality. In the sonnet, "Batter My Heart, Three-Personed God," Donne concludes,

> Yet dearly I love you, and would be loved fain,
> But am betrothed unto your enemy:
> Divorce me, untie or break that knot again;
> Take me to you, imprison me, for I
> Except you enthrall me, never shall be free,
> Nor ever chaste, except you ravish me.[111]

Bold and paradoxical as is the metaphorical *ravish* in the concluding line, it can be analyzed in conventional terms as a cogent figurative embodiment of the yearning for an overpowering experience of God, putting an end to backslidings and uncertainties. At the same time, it carries to a

110 Merritt Y. Hughes, "The Seventeenth Century," in Leary, *Scholarship*, p. 73.
111 J. William Hebel and Hoyt H. Hudson, eds., *Poetry of the English Renaissance: 1509–1660* (New York: Appleton-Century-Crofts, Inc., 1929), p. 489.

startling extreme conventional poetic imagery applying the vocabulary of human love to religious experience. In this sense, the metaphor is indeed a clue to the poet's ordering of experience, his characteristic pattern of sensibility.

The safe conclusion seems to be that poetic metaphors range widely from such truly revealing, existential metaphors to those that merely vivify perception. The classroom teacher will be fully justified in approaching a metaphor in the conventional fashion as a figure of speech in which one thing is illuminated by a compressed comparison with another. He can then proceed to demonstrate the difference between the familiar metaphors of ordinary speech and the bolder, more complex, more connotative metaphors of imaginative literature. In a much analyzed passage, Shakespeare uses the familiar analogy between the approach of age and the tree in autumn:

> That time of year thou mayst in me behold
> When yellow leaves, or none, or few, do hang
> Upon those boughs which shake against the cold,
> Bare ruined choirs, where late the sweet birds sang.
> (Sonnet 73)

In the last line, the comparison is complicated and enriched by a further analogy between the defoliated tree and the choirs of abandoned churches, now in ruins, where the choristers used to sing as sweet birds used to sing in the foliage of the tree. The prevailing emotion of sadness and regret is thus reinforced by an image evoking a special kind of nostalgia, of beauty, of awe. If the average student pursues the metaphor this far, he has learned a great deal about literature without having to lean excessively upon the mere say-so of his instructor.

Similar questions about how far to follow the contemporary critic confront the teacher in dealing with the role of **symbol.** It is obvious how symbolic analysis helps satisfy the modern requirement for fullness or richness of the imaginative experience. To the literal meaning of a work—"the meaning accessible to everyday practical habits of thought"—it adds the level of symbolic meaning, with symbols taken to "constitute a richer, fuller affective language than the language of rational discourse."[112]

As modern criticism has been uninterested in the merely illustrative metaphor, so it has shown little interest for the kind of clearly defined, clearly instrumental symbol that the student can be most easily made to understand. Such are the symbolic props in the tradition of realistic drama: In Ibsen's *Hedda Gabler,* Hedda's pistols throughout symbolize the explosive, destructive potential of her rebellion against upper-middle

---

[112] Frederick A. Pottle, "Modern Criticism of *The Ancient Mariner,*" Gordon and Noyes, *Essays,* p. 265.

class society, the fatal impossibility of her fitting into the mold. In Arthur Miller's *Death of a Salesman,* there is an ironic poignancy in our hearing that Willy, coming rapidly to the end of his rope, is blundering about in his dark back yard trying to plant seed: He engages in a gesture symbolic of hopeful preparation for the future (where there is no future nor hope); he clings to something that suggests open space and freedom (when he is actually being ground down by a jostling, competitive society). Here the symbol plays a clear dramatic role and is clearly related to the theme of the play.

In looking for symbols offering more of a challenge to the interpreter, the critic has often turned to writers like Yeats or Joyce, who use a symbolic language to some extent private and obscure. Here the critic must "read" the symbol by studying its recurrence in typical contexts, or by tracing it to sources in the author's reading and experience. In several of the best known poems by the later Yeats, "the blood-dimmed tide," the "dolphin-torn" and "gong-tormented sea," the "salmon-falls" and "mackerel-crowded seas," are opposed to the world of art and intellect. The sea thus becomes symbolic of formless and anarchic sensual existence. The question that the teacher must ask is at what point a work like Pound's *Cantos* is removed from the public domain by the author's indulgence in purely private reference, recoverable only by the most persevering as well as lucky investigator. For obvious pedagogical reasons, the teacher can make only limited use of literary artists who need too large a retinue of soothsayers and private etymologists. More fundamentally, the teacher is likely to agree with Saul Bellow that

> a true symbol is substantial, not accidental. You cannot avoid it, you cannot remove it. You can't take the handkerchief from "Othello," or the sea from "The Nigger of the Narcissus," or the disfigured feet from "Oedipus Rex." You can, however, read "Ulysses" without suspecting that wood shavings have to do with the Crucifixion or that the name Simon refers to the sin of Simony or that the hunger of the Dubliners at noon parallels that of the Lestrygonians. These are purely peripheral matters; fringe benefits, if you like. The beauty of the book cannot escape you if you are any sort of reader, and it is better to approach it from the side of naïveté than from that of culture-idolatry, sophistication and snobbery.[113]

In their study of the more substantial symbol, critics have often used symbolic analysis to ascribe to a work a meaning more profound than its overt message or theme. For instance, modern critics have typically found Coleridge's "The Ancient Mariner" too pat in its overt moralistic message. The stated moral of the poem is that redemption for the parched soul lies in the capacity for spontaneous love of one's fellow creatures:

---

[113] "Deep Readers of the World, Beware!" *New York Times Book Review,* February 15, 1959, p. 1, col. 4.

> He prayeth well, who loveth well
> Both man and bird and beast.

This theme is certainly close to the heart of the Romantic's message generally. It is also potentially most profoundly relevant to the deliberate brutalities and casual callousness of our own time, to a world haunted by the specter of silent springs and gutted cities. Repeatedly, nevertheless, critics have tried to explain the poem's power by a symbolic surcharge more or less directly felt.

As is often the case with symbolical analysis, it has proved difficult for critics to agree on the meaning of the central symbols. Depending on a critic's major interests, the underlying symbolic pattern of a work is likely to emerge anthropological, Freudian, theological, or aesthetic. "The Ancient Mariner," for example, has been viewed as following an archetypal pattern of regeneration and rebirth; a theological pattern in which the shooting of the albatross is parallel to Original Sin; a philosophical pattern in which the sun is symbolic of the dryly analytical understanding, the moon of the beneficent, all-integrating imagination; a therapeutic pattern in which the poem becomes a ritual for the redemption of the drug to which Coleridge was addicted. What has indeed to a large extent discredited symbolical analysis is the absence of procedural controls, the lack of restraints on a critic's perception of parallels and associations. To one critic, the opening lines of Milton's *Lycidas* suggest "the frosts of autumn killing the flowers"; another points out that the branches the poet is gathering are those of laurel, myrtle, and ivy, all "symbols of immortality." To one critic, the sea in *Lycidas* is an emblem of death; to another reader of the same poem, water is the "principle of life."[114]

When symbolical analysis reaches its extreme, as in the writings of Kenneth Burke, "even the most concrete of imageries" can be considered as "symbolic" or "representative." Burke's concept of **synecdoche** allows him to make an object stand for anything associated with it in one of a great number of ways; if no such association can be discovered, the symbol points up the thing to be symbolized by its "polar otherness." Thus, Burke identifies the mariner's albatross with Sarah Coleridge, because Coleridge associates both with the idea of Christianity. The shooting of the albatross then turns out to be parallel to the mariner's interference with the wedding feast, symbolic of the institution of Christian marriage.[115] Not surprisingly, critics like Elder Olson have attacked the uncontrolled associationism of such interpretations. As Olson said in discussing Robert Penn Warren's symbolic interpretation of "The Ancient Mariner," "all such interpretation is really uncontrolled analogy; the

---

114 Richard P. Adams, "The Archetypal Pattern of Death and Rebirth in *Lycidas*," *PMLA*, LXIV (1949), 183–88, in Patrides, *Milton's* Lycidas, pp. 122–23.
115 Burke, *Philosophy of Literary Form*, pp. 83, 71.

double themes, their fusions, and the multivalent symbols permit anyone to make of the poem whatever he may choose."[116]

Thus warned, the teacher will take care not to impose on his students symbolical interpretations that an attentive reading of the poem fails to verify. What he *can* do with symbolical interpretation may be illustrated by a discussion of one of Robert Frost's most frequently anthologized poems:

> Whose woods these are I think I know.
> His house is in the village though;
> He will not see me stopping here
> To watch his woods fill up with snow.
>
> My little horse must think it queer
> To stop without a farmhouse near
> Between the woods and frozen lake
> The darkest evening of the year.
>
> He gives his harness bells a shake
> To ask if there is some mistake.
> The only other sound's the sweep
> Of easy wind and downy flake.
>
> The woods are lovely, dark and deep.
> But I have promises to keep,
> And miles to go before I sleep,
> And miles to go before I sleep.[117]

Here the critic may discover in the dark loveliness of the woods a symbolic hint of the peacefulness and dark tempting beauty of death. This interpretation is supported by many details *in the poem:* the woods are associated with darkness, hostile to activity, and with snow, hostile to life. They are remote from farmhouses, villages, and other centers of human life and endeavor. They are associated with the ceasing of motion, of purposeful forward movement. Their attraction is represented as an alternative to the keeping of promises and an implied commitment to the future. The silence, the "easy wind," the "downy flake," the dark depth of the woods—all point toward rest, sleep. At the same time, the reader is hearing echoes of a literary tradition. Before Frost, Keats had been "half in love with easeful death/Called him soft names in many a mused rhyme." Whitman had heard whispered in the darkness "the low and delicious word death. . . . laving me softly all over,/Death, death, death, death, death."

The clear antithesis of a life of activity and obligation and of the loveliness of rest is made possible by the relative simplicity of Frost's

[116] "A Symbolic Reading of the *Ancient Mariner,"* in *Critics and Criticism Ancient and Modern,* ed. R. S. Crane (Chicago: The University of Chicago Press, 1952), p. 144.

[117] *Complete Poems of Robert Frost* (New York: Holt, Rinehart & Winston, Inc., 1949), p. 275.

poem. As a work of literature becomes more complex, the broad antitheses and dichotomies of the symbol-seeker may lead us to oversimplify
rather than enrich our response. It is true, for instance, that in Hawthorne's "Young Goodman Brown" the nocturnal forest lives up to its
familiar associations with uncontrolled wilderness, lurking Indians, and
threatening Satanic forces. But it is misleading to stipulate in the story
too sharp an antithesis of day and night, and of town and forest, to
correspond to a sharp dualism of Good and Evil. We gather from the
story that Quaker women are whipped through the streets in broad daylight; while the night may be starlit and calm. The night could have
been devoted to calm sleep, pure and sweet, in the arms of Goodman
Brown's wife, but he chose to pursue his "present evil purpose." The
point of the story is Young Goodman Brown's discovery of evil, not in
places where it is conventionally reputed to exist, but in "church, bed-
chamber, street, field or forest"—in the early morning sunshine as much
as in the secrecy of the night. The pervading irony of the story is that
the devil is "not as black as he is painted." On the contrary, he is a
master of all the urban civilities; indeed, clad in grave and decent at-
tire, he "had an indescribable air of one who knew the world, and who
would not have felt abashed at the governor's dinner table or in King
William's court, were it possible that his affairs should call him thither."
Young Goodman Brown discovers that what the orthodox call Good and
Evil are paradoxically intermingled everywhere in human life. He finds
himself united with the pious and the dissolute alike in "a loathful
brotherhood" by "the sympathy of all that was wicked in his heart."
Unable to accept this discovery, he allows it to become an obsession—an
obsession that makes him shrink from his fellows, making him "a stern,
a sad, a darkly meditative, a distrustful, if not a desperate man." Here
as elsewhere, the teacher must make sure that he sees how the symbol
serves the story. He must take care not to make the story serve the symbol.

The critic following the tradition of Richards and Brooks often makes
metaphor and symbol serve too directly the integrating function of art, its
function of co-ordinating disparate experience. Often the teacher will
feel that more freight is being put upon these devices than they are
equipped to carry. The way literature brings together apparent opposites
can usually be more successfully demonstrated when the critic deals with
his third major preoccupation: **irony.** In the conventional view, irony
makes for a wry comical effect by pointing to the practice that belies
the preaching, to the bare, ugly rear of the motion-picture palace with
the profusely ornamented façade. To critics like Cleanth Brooks, by contrast, irony is one of the principal ways by which the poet reconciles the
apparently warring elements of experience. In a complex and mature attitude, there may be a mingling of tenderness with intellectual awareness,
or of pity with laughter:

Very many, and, indeed, nearly all mature attitudes represent some sort of mingling of the approbative and the satirical. Frequently, the more complex attitudes are expressed, and necessarily expressed in varying degrees of irony.[118]

Such attitudes are less "vulnerable" than more single-minded attitudes. They disarm, by anticipating and absorbing, the barbs of the skeptic, the gibes of the cynic. While **sentimentality** takes short-cuts to intensity by oversimplifying experience, **wit** does justice to experience by reflecting its complexity.

That irony as here defined does indeed play a central role in much great literature may be demonstrated by reference to many of Shakespeare's plays. Lear has his fool; Antony has his Enobarbus; Hotspur, who sets out to "pluck bright honor from the pale-face moon," is answered by Falstaff:

> Honor pricks me on. Yea, but how if honor prick me off when I come on? How then? Can honor set to a leg? No. Or an arm? No. Or take away the grief of a wound? No. Honor hath no skill in surgery, then? No. What is honor? A word. What is in that word honor? What is that honor? Air. A trim reckoning! Who hath it? He that died o' Wednesday. Doth he feel it? No. Doth he hear it? No. 'Tis insensible, then? Yea, to the dead. But will it not live with the living? No. Why? Detraction will not suffer it. Therefore I'll none of it.
>
> *(Henry VI, Part I; Act V, Sc. 1)*

However, the shrewd comments of Enobarbus do not simply invalidate the greatness of Antony; just as Falstaff does not simply and conclusively have the last word. In *Romeo and Juliet,* we have in the lovers all the hyperbole of a centuries-old tradition of idealized love:

> Oh, she doth teach the torches to burn bright!
> It seems she hangs upon the cheek of night
> Like a rich jewel in an Ethiop's ear—
> Beauty too rich for use, for earth too dear!
>
> *(Act I, Sc. 5)*

If this were all, we would soon be rudely brought back to earth by the knowing leer of the cynic who mutters to himself: "*I* know what he climbed up to the balcony for!" But at this point we have, in the play itself, already heard all the obscene jokes; what is more, we have already seen glimpses of that violent, unheeding world that hems in and cuts short young love. Thus, when we hear the "Haw, haw!" of the sophomoric reader, we can only say, "We know all that! We know that souls inhabit bodies; we know that the same relationship that inspires Romeo's lyrical raptures furnishes to Mercutio the materials for endless bawdy jests. But will you not treasure both the tenderness of Juliet

[118] *Modern Poetry and the Tradition* (Chapel Hill: The University of North Carolina Press, 1939), pp. 28–29, 39–45.

and the exuberance of Mercutio—will you not treasure the beauty and gallantry that flower forth in this grim and violent and earthy world?"

Consequently, it is futile to present this play to high school students in an expurgated version, with all the exuberant jests of Mercutio and the obscene chuckles of Juliet's nurse trimmed away. Half a Shakespeare is *not* better than none. We do not serve the cause of great literature by reducing it to a manageable conventionality. If our students (or our school boards) are not yet ready for Shakespeare, he will still be there a few years later when they have grown up. The teacher loyal to literature will refuse to imitate the eighteenth-century practice of presenting "Shakespeare Improved." Shakespeare's work predisposes us to accept with Robert Penn Warren "a scale of excellence based, in part at least, on degree of complication." The good poem "must, in some way, involve the resistances"; it must "come to terms with Mercutio."[119]

If we thus make irony one possible clue to the greatness of complex literary art, we must make sure that the student does not mistake it for a simple debunking irony, an irony that impoverishes rather than enriches. The deadliness of many an influential blockhead results from his lack of humor: He is unable to see that one may at times indulgently smile at a superior and yet respect his authority; one may relish Mencken's barbs at the *boobus Americanus* and yet be proud of his country. The unsatisfying, immature kind of irony reflects the author's discovery that people are all too human and that idols have feet of clay—but it also reflects the author's feeling that this discovery puts him one up on his fellows. It reflects the complacency of an author who considers himself less fallibly human than his readers.

If irony proves one of the more fruitful contemporary critical preoccupations, perhaps the least fruitful for the classroom teacher is the fourth: **ambiguity.** Modern criticism has typically been attracted by the sense of richness afforded by language pregnant with ambiguities and multiple meanings. Again, the teacher must recognize the role of ambiguity in its more conventional sense. In Hawthorne's short stories, for instance, there is often a characteristic refusal of the author to commit himself, a raising of questions that remain unanswered. Hawthorne thus effectively reinforces the impression that he is dealing not with those regions of the mind where everything can be catalogued and classified but with those whence rise questions that disturb and perplex. Is Young Goodman Brown's vision a hallucinatory distortion of reality, or is it the symbolic expression of a true insight into human nature? Are the good people of Salem ensnared by the devil's wiles as Goodman Brown thinks they are? The story does not say. It's something for the reader to

[119] *Kenyon Review*, V, 251.

think about, something to test his own view of human motives. Was Faith, the pure and sweet young wife, in the forest on that fateful night, or is Goodman Brown obsessed by a Calvinist suspicion of sin? Hawthorne won't tell. Perhaps Calvinism is an evil dream that like other evil dreams contains a large share of human truth. The ambiguity of the story teases the reader, but it is by no means gratuitous mystification.

Again, however, the modern critic's interest in ambiguity is not limited to its specific stylistic or thematic role. Like other modern critical preferences, the search for literature exploiting freely the resources of ambiguity leads him to the first half of the seventeenth century, to the language of Shakespeare and of the metaphysical poets like Donne and Marvell. William Empson, for instance, labors to show that the puns and paradoxes we find there are more than examples of ingenious verbal humor, that often they are the poet's way of hinting at his central intentions. A **pun** may be the poet's way of pointing to a crucial relationship. It may be his way of "reconciling" or "uniting" two ideas that in the normal use of language are contradictory but that to a more profound insight are in an essential way connected. Thus, when the clown in *As You Like It* puns on the *faining* (desiring) and *feigning* (pretending, deceiving) of lovers and poets, Empson feels that Shakespeare in getting at an underlying truth. The lover pretends with a purpose, that is, motivated by desire. Similarly, the poet's craft involves a paradoxical mixture of desire, purpose, serious intention on the one hand and detachment, make-believe, pretense on the other.

It is of course true that to be effective pun and paradox must get at an underlying relation between apparently disparate things. In some of the more serious passages of Shakespeare and Donne paradox is truly functional. But we must also recognize the poet's pleasure in verbal ingenuity, his ability to be at times only half-profound. Criticism like that of Empson makes us take every joke seriously; it drastically narrows the sphere of the playful and of incidental virtuosity in literature.

Once we develop the habit of searching too earnestly in the "fantastic treasure chest of the poet's thought," we are likely to prefer as a matter of principle the strained association to the plain sense of a passage. For instance, Empson finds in Marvell's "Garden" a typical example of the way richly ambiguous language unifies widely disparate ways of thinking and feeling. Ascribing to Marvell a "Puritan ambivalence" about pleasure, Empson finds the "Alpha and Omega" of the following stanza in "the Apple and the Fall," thus discovering in it "a rich and intuitive use of Christian imagery":

> What wond'rous life in this I lead!
> Ripe Apples drop about my head;
> The Luscious Clusters of the Vine

> Upon my Mouth do crush their Wine;
> The Nectaren, and curious Peach,
> Into my hands themselves do reach;
> Stumbling on Melons, as I pass,
> Insnar'd with Flow'rs, I fall on Grass.[120]

This giving of a sinister moral overtone to the literal "ensnaring" and "falling" of the stanza contradicts the plain sense of the poem, which insists earlier that the poet has found in this garden "innocence," sister dear of "fair quiet." A later stanza clearly places the garden in a prelapsarian context, *before* the Fall:

> Such was that happy garden-state
> While man there walked without a mate;
> After a place so pure and sweet,
> What other help could yet be meet!

Like I. A. Richards, Empson is vaguest and least convincing on how contradictory ideas are mysteriously fused, rather than merely juxtaposed, in the poet's use of language. The literature of the early seventeenth century, more so than that of other periods, shows that a poet may be *genuinely* ambivalent in his attitude toward sensual pleasure or the natural world, without any real psychological integration. We may find the strong pull of sensual attraction side by side with a capacity for intellectual detachment, or with moral restrictions and a superstructure of more or less coherent rationalization. The literature of the English Renaissance owes its fascination to this presence of many contradictory impulses and ideas, allowing critics of widely different taste and outlook to emphasize what they find most congenial.

In the study of ambiguity, as elsewhere, the New Critic is trying to find in the specific technical devices of literature the means by which the writer achieves an insight superior to that of the reasoning intellect. Much as the teacher of literature will sympathize with this aim, he must be aware of the arbitrary and centrifugal effects of the resulting critical method. One task of the teacher is to make the student more responsive, to alert him to overtones and associations. But another task is to provide criteria of relevance. Classroom discussion cannot be an exercise in uncontrolled associationism, with the prize going to the most ingenious interpretation.

Fortunately, the tradition of modern criticism furnishes its own corrective to the extremes of arbitrary association. It has typically insisted on the **wholeness** of a work. Rather than exhibit, with Matthew Arnold, beautiful passages as "touchstones" of great poetry, the modern critic has stressed the structural, architectonic relations that determine the

---

[120] *English Pastoral Poetry* (New York: W. W. Norton & Company, Inc., 1938), p. 131.

impact of the work as a whole. Literary taste in this respect reflects the general modern suspicion of mere ornament, of decorative details stuck onto a building *after* the completion of its design, of embellishments added to the basic structure as frosting is to the cake. Our interest should be not so much in the separate appeal of each detail of a work as in what these details show by their arrangement, in what emerges from their mutual relations. Today's teacher is likely to accept the view that just as in drama "the central point of view emerges from the total inter-action of every aspect of the play," so in a poem "the meaning resides in the interaction of every element—image, statement, rhythm, rhyme—every element which goes to make up the whole poem."[121]

On the most elementary level, such a perspective reminds us of the importance of **context**. Simple insistence on context can serve to correct many of the extravagances of the more ingenious critic. Here for in-stance is what Cleanth Brooks says about the opening lines of Words-worth's sonnet,

> It is a beauteous evening, calm and free,
> The holy time is quiet as a Nun, . . .

> The comparison of the evening to the nun actually has more than one dimension. The calm of the evening obviously means "worship," even to the dull-witted and insensitive. It corresponds to the trappings of the nun, visible to everyone. Thus, it suggests not merely holiness, but, in the total poem, even a hint of pharisaical holiness, . . .[122]

This observation sets up a contrast with the unconscious, spontaneous sympathy for nature of the girl addressed later in the poem:

> Dear Child! dear Girl! that walkest with me here,
> If thou appear untouched by solemn thought,
> Thy nature is not therefore less divine. . . .

But notice the phrase immediately following the word *Nun* in the poem, a phrase emphasized both by trochaic inversion at the beginning (*Bréath-less*) and the heavy caesura at the end:

> The holy time is quiet as a Nun,
> *Bréathless with adoration:* ‖ the broad sun
> Is sinking down in its tranquillity; . . .

Whatever preconceptions about pharisaical holiness the reader brings to the poem would have to be stubbornly willful to survive the powerful countersuggestion of that phrase.

On the more ambitious level, concern with the interrelation of parts makes us try to grasp the work in its totality. Obviously, a concern with the artistic unity of a work is as old as criticism. Aristotle had insisted that the beauty of a tragedy depends on unity and the "sense of the

---

121 Martz, "Poetry," Gordon and Noyes, *Essays*, p. 256.
122 "The Language of Paradox," in Schorer, *Criticism*, pp. 358–59.

whole." The neoclassical tradition, however, often emphasized unity in the more external aspects of a work: unity of plot, unity of place, unity of time. Coleridge anticipated the modern view when he described the imagination as the supreme integrating and synthesizing power, "blending materials and fusing the parts together" in a "more striking whole" than would conform to the classical canons of symmetry and formal perfection. Following Coleridge, modern critics have looked in a work for an organic rather than a merely formal unity; they have looked for an informing principle to which details may be related.

Emphasis on the organic whole can serve to focus discussion on the essential rather than the peripheral, on features embodying the dynamic principle of a work rather than on what Saul Bellow calls the "fringe benefits." Thus, we will be interested less in the local and limited than in the **structural metaphor** that helps organize a whole poem. One way of making students see a principle of coherence in a work is to have them chart in a Petrarchan or Shakespearean sonnet the terms carrying out the central metaphor:

> My love is as a fever, longing still
> For that which longer nurseth the disease,
> Feeding on that which doth preserve the ill,
> The uncertain sickly appetite to please.
> My reason, the physician to my love,
> Angry that his prescriptions are not kept,
> Hath left me, and I desperate now approve
> Desire is death, which physic did except.
> Past cure I am, now reason is past care,
> And frantic-mad with evermore unrest.
> My thoughts and my discourse as madmen's are,
> At random from the truth vainly expressed,
> For I have sworn thee fair, and thought thee bright,
> Who art as black as Hell, as dark as night.

1.		fever. longing	
2.		nurseth	disease
3.	Feeding		ill
4.		sickly appetite	
5.		physician	
6.		prescriptions	
7.		desperate	
8.	death	physic	
9.	cure		care
10.	frantic-mad		
11.		madmen's	
12.		vainly	
13.			
14.			[123]

---

[123] "Analysis of Shakespearean Sonnet CXLVII," Gordon and Noyes, *Essays*, p. 307.

In the Petrarchan tradition, such a metaphor merely traces in its full implications a basic analogy: The lover is like a ship lost at sea; the wind is his sighs, the rain his tears; the clouds are the dark disdain of his beloved; the drowned pilot is the lover's reason, overruled by a cruel, desperate passion. A metaphysical poet like Donne or Marvell often proceeds by giving to the same metaphor new and paradoxical applications, using it as it were as a catalyst to thought. Donne's "The Anniversary," for instance, explores the relationship between love and the passing of time. The anniversary of a king's reign, though conventionally an occasion for rejoicing, is paradoxically also a reminder that "all other things to their destruction draw"—but "our love hath no decay." In some respects, however, the lovers are *like* princes—in one another's eyes, for instance; they are also like princes—in that eventually their bodies must go to their graves. In the afterlife, their souls will be blessed like all the others, but on earth the lovers are like kings—standing out from all the rest by their love. They are *more* kingly than kings—since treason can come only from themselves. Their first anniversary, like that of a king, is an occasion for looking forward to years and years of a continued reign.

As the clue to the structure of a poem may be an extended metaphor, so the clue to the unifying theme of a novel may be a **central symbol**. In Hawthorne's *The Scarlet Letter,* the scarlet *A* embroidered on the gown of the adulteress becomes symbolic of the burden of sin carried by others less obviously stigmatized. In Melville's *Moby Dick,* the white whale is at times, like the sea, serene and peaceful, of sublime beauty. At times, like the sea, it is wrathful and destructive, marked by overpowering and heedless violence. The whale thus becomes symbolic of the basic ambivalence of life, its two-faced quality of mingled beauty and ugliness, serenity and violence, good and evil. Students often ask which of the many conflicting interpretations of *Moby Dick* is the "right" one. No interpretation *can* be right that, like Captain Ahab, sets out to destroy one of the complementary principles, that is unable to accept, with William Blake, both the tiger and the lamb.

Even a central metaphor or symbol must be seen in its full interaction with theme, tone, setting, plot, or other relevant features. In teaching students to interpret metaphor and symbol, the teacher must early lead them to distinguish suggestions that "fit in" and those that don't. Stephen Crane's often anthologized "The Open Boat" is an example of a short story exceptionally tightly unified around a **central theme**. There are several thematic passages suggesting the idea that, contrary to man's confident expectations, "nature does not regard him as important," that she is serenely indifferent amid the struggles of the individual. This ironic discrepancy between man's hopes for himself and the indifference of nature is throughout developed and echoed in characteristic incongruities and *non sequiturs*. The shipwreck, like the accident that is always expected to happen to other people, was "apropos of nothing." The boat the four shipwrecked men find themselves in is absurdly small contrasted with the "wrongfully and barbarously" tall waves. The sea is wildly picturesque, but the men are hardly in the mood to appreciate its savage splendor. The comfortable safety of the water birds enrages the men threatened with extinction by elements that to the birds are home. The call, on the men rowing the boat, for sheer raw physical exertion is beyond all that is reasonable. The surf keeping the boat from reaching the shore already clearly within sight seems a preposterous and abominably unjust obstacle to offer to the men's revived hopes. And so on. In the end, the injured captain, who seemed the most likely candidate for drowning, makes it to the shore. The oiler, the strongest swimmer and at first "ahead in the race" after the boat is swamped, drowns. The correspondent is at first immobilized by a current but then by sheer luck able to swim on and swept by a lucky large wave clear of the dangerous overturned boat.

The point here, in keeping with the theme and the prevailing mood, is the ironic survival, not of the virtuous, nor even of the fittest, but merely of those who happen to survive. Thus, we must be suspicious if a reader stresses the point that "the oiler, who strikes out alone, is drowned; the three others survive *together*."[124] The oiler does not really strike out alone; he is merely temporarily "ahead in the race." He had all along done his share and more; he was a full member of the gallant brotherhood of the victimized that to the correspondent is the chief compensation for the unheeding cruelty of nature. An interpretation that makes the survival of the remaining three an affirmation of the value of "sticking together" must be rejected as out of keeping with the story read as a whole.

If we finally summarize the criteria of literary value here surveyed, we will arrive at a conclusion by no means revolutionary. *Imaginative literature should be concretely embodied and yet have general significance; it should present to us compelling images that are yet meaningful beyond their immediate impact. Imaginative literature should be rich and complex and yet unified; it should achieve order without an arbitrary narrowing of our vision. Imaginative literature should not be a mere vehicle, whether of thought or emotion; its texture and structure should compel our full attention.* Literature so defined is not for rapid reading. It tests the student's command of language; it stretches his mind; it exercises his moral and emotional being.

---

[124] Thomas J. Wertenbaker, Jr., "A Surfeit of Surveys: Thoughts on Chronology and Theme in American Literature," *The English Journal*, LII (January, 1963), 11.

Criticism and the Classroom Teacher

The difficulty the classroom teacher has with literary criticism is that the critic tells him more than he wants to know. At times, there seems to be a great gulf between the Jamesian sentences of a critic like Blackmur or the hypersensitivity to nuance of a critic like Empson and the interests and capacities of our students. As compared with the critic, the teacher must pursue limited objectives. Wherever he is headed, he must be able to take his students along with him.

In their determination to show the greatness and fullness of literary art, modern critics have generally been guilty of the fallacy of **overinterpretation**. It is a counsel of perfection to say with John Ciardi, "poetry cannot be discussed meaningfully unless one can assume that everything in the poem—every last comma and variant spelling—is in it by the poet's specific act of choice."[125] It puts a strain on the common reader's capacities to say with Wimsatt, "a good story poem is like a stone thrown into a pond, into our minds, where ever widening concentric circles of meaning go out."[126]

The teacher should take comfort in the knowledge that even the greatest literary art is much less fully and deeply "controlled" in every detail than the critics would have us believe. Even in a play like *Hamlet* or *King Lear* there is room for the conventional, the perfunctory, and the incidental. The teacher need not be forever anxiously explanatory about every minor puzzle, every apparent contradiction. Even the greatest writers tend to fall into certain mannerisms and predictable attitudes. If this were not so, literary parody would be a much less fruitful field than it is.

Taking even the greatest writer with a grain of salt will protect the teacher against mistaking literature for the sacred mysteries. It will keep him from taking extreme positions on such matters as for instance the relation between sound and sense. There is bound to be something strained about an interpretation of a poem that makes every rhyme functional, every variation in meter significant. As with all other matters of literary interpretation, the teacher must take a vow to show meaning only when he is convinced it is truly there. For instance, sound *does* seem related to sense in G. M. Hopkins' plodding repetition of a phrase in

Generations have trod, have trod, have trod.

Similarly, in his "the dearest freshness deep down things," the insistent equal stress on "déep dówn" seems to reinforce the word *deep*, getting

[125] "Robert Frost: The Way to the Poem," *Saturday Review*, April 12, 1958, pp. 13–15.
[126] Schorer, *Criticism*, p. 400.

us *deeper down* into things than we would in a more normal iambic meter. However, the teacher who wishes to retain his students' confidence will not press this sort of analysis too far.

Even when the writer definitely controls, unifies, or orders his materials, the resulting order may not be meaningful or functional in any ordinary sense. In the poet's world of symbols, form is itself to some extent symbolic. It is at least to some extent a symbolic celebration of the principle of coherence that makes the universe inhabitable. In its purest state, artistic form can be interpreted as a ceremonial in praise of life. Critics of the most diverse hue have agreed that we derive from literature a feeling of being in control of experience, of being reconciled to life, of a superior balance of our faculties—often in contradiction of what the work actually seems to say. One way of solving this paradox is to hold that, apart from any specific or thematic meaning, form is a symbolic affirmation that life is ordered and meaningful, that life makes sense. It is thus that, in the words of W. H. Auden, poets

> In the prison of his days
> Teach the free man how to praise.[127]

Obviously, writers, like artists generally, vary greatly in the intensity of their pursuit of order. In the Byzantium poems of Yeats, for instance, there is a vision of a pure art, a "golden handiwork," taking us beyond "the unpurged images of day," "the fury and the mire of human veins." In Yeats's poems, "ceremony," "artifice," far from being derogatory terms, describe a kind of art releasing us from the "bitter furies of complexity" of an anarchic sensual world. On the other hand, a too single-minded pursuit of the ideal order of art may lead us to feel a lack of relevance. We may react in favor of writers like Theodore Dreiser, whose very clumsiness then seems a measure of their commitment. As Robert E. Spiller said of Dreiser, "he wrote what he knew—what he was."[128] However, in much of the literature we read, there seems to be a balance between the two extremes. The unity achieved by the writer's intense personal vision of the world, and the unity due to his sense of order, blend in what seems an organic whole.

What course, then, to sum up, will the teacher steer in his teaching of literature? His major problem will be to maintain a general perspective. Confronted with the vast output of contemporary literary scholarship, he must maintain some elementary criteria of relevance and significance. He must on the one hand quicken and diversify the students' response to literature. He must on the other hand prevent the students' interest from being dissipated in the pursuit of a myriad contradictory and highly cerebral theories and interpretations.

[127] "In Memory of W. B. Yeats," *Collected Poetry*, p. 51.
[128] *Literary History of the United States*, rev. ed. (New York: The Macmillan Company, 1953), p. 1206.

The less sophisticated the student, the wiser the teacher will be to concentrate first of all on literature as experience. He will focus on the way imaginative literature sharpens our observation, develops our emotional sensitivity, extends our acquaintance with life. The basic educational function of literature is that it broadens our horizons. It makes us realize that our own little parochial framework of ideas and expectations was not made for everyone and for all time. Like other educational experiences, the student's reading of literature cannot be guided forever by what he likes: His resistance to what he considers weird or wrongheaded is a sign that he is taking his reading seriously. His indignation can spark the kind of classroom exchange that leads to a fuller understanding.

A second step in the teacher's strategy will be to exploit the relations between literature and other ways of dealing with experience. It is true that teacher and student must be able to distinguish life and art, that they must where necessary discuss literary matters in specifically literary terms. But the student learns something essential about literature when he realizes it is of absorbing interest not only to the critic but to the philosopher, the psychologist, the psychiatrist, the anthropologist, the sociologist, the historian. Even the backhanded compliment paid literature by the vigilance of political and religious censors attests in its own way to the basic fact: We cannot rigidly separate the images we contemplate in literature from those we try to live up to in life. We cannot sort out into neat compartments illusion and aspiration, make-believe and make-belief. Much of our discussion in the classroom will be concerned with the ideas and ideals embodied in literature—provided we treat these as projected imaginatively in the whole of the literary work, as rooted in the full three-dimensional context of perception, emotion, and thought.

Third, the teacher will try to give pattern to the student's reading by emphasizing the recurrence in great literature of major themes. This does not mean that literature has to be presented in thematic units. It merely means that a course gains in continuity if major preoccupations recur, successively treated from different points of view. Depending on the level of a class or focus of a course, such a recurrent theme may be as elementary as man's dependence on nature, or as complex as the relation between the artistic and scientific temperaments. Whatever the organization of a course, we can early give our students the feeling that literature tends to return to some of the most basic questions about our common humanity.

Finally, and especially on the more advanced level, we will focus on the ways in which literature is not only an exploration but an *ordering* of experience. We will try to make our students respond to the particular pattern of consciousness embodied in a work. We will develop a sense of how a unifying theme may emerge from the way different passages in a poem qualify each other, from the way different characters in a play or in a novel interact. We will study those features of language that give literature its characteristic texture; and we will explore the relations between form and meaning. We will try to make our students see how a work as a whole offers for our contemplation a world of its own, with its own characteristic relations and principle of coherence.

In thus teaching literature, the teacher of English has to do what he must always do: He must concern himself with technical detail without losing sight of the whole. He must deal with language as concrete structure while at the same time doing justice to its role in human experience. He must look at language with critical detachment and yet be passionately involved in its humane purposes.

A PROGRAM FOR FURTHER STUDY

MARK SCHORER, JOSEPHINE MILES, AND GORDON MCKENZIE, eds., *Criticism: The Foundations of Modern Literary Judgment* (rev. ed.). New York: Harcourt, Brace & World, Inc., 1958.

An authoritative collection of major documents in the theory and practice of literary criticism. Makes available in one volume crucial contributions by important critics from Aristotle and Longinus to I. A. Richards and Edmund Wilson.

LEWIS LEARY, ed., *Contemporary Literary Scholarship: A Critical Review*. New York: Appleton-Century-Crofts, Inc., 1958.

A survey sponsored by the Committee on Literary Scholarship and the Teaching of English of the National Council of Teachers of English. Provides a study, by periods and genres, "of trends and specific achievements in the study of literature during the past thirty years." Written by eminently qualified contributors, individual articles help put current critical approaches to important authors and works in perspective.

LAURENCE PERRINE, *Sound and Sense: An Introduction to Poetry* (2nd ed.). New York: Harcourt, Brace & World, Inc., 1963.

A concrete and eminently sensible introduction to the careful reading of the individual poem. Systematic and well-illustrated coverage of the major elements of poetry. Fresh and varied in its selection of poems.

MAURICE BEEBE, ed., *Literary Symbolism: An Introduction to the Interpretation of Literature*. Belmont, Calif.: Wadsworth Publishing Company, Inc., 1960.

Prints a number of often taught short stories and poems, each followed by critical discussions illustrating a range of modern interpretations and approaches.

HANS P. GUTH, ed., *Literature*. Belmont, Calif.: Wadsworth Publishing Company, Inc., 1962.

A selection of imaginative literature ranging from the historically significant to the fresh and contemporary, grouped thematically within the major types. Introductory essays on fiction, drama, and poetry.

MATERIALS FOR ANALYSIS

A. The extent to which a relatively limited set of recurrent terms has become the small change of critical discussion is well illustrated in Fred H. Marcus, *"The Scarlet Letter:* The Power of Ambiguity," *The English Journal,* LI (October, 1962), 449–458. All the following terms and phrases occur: *structure, explication of text, complexity, point of view, theme and form, symbol, irony, allegory, ambiguity, paradox, pluralism, hierarchy, omniscient author, myth, alienation, tension.* Define and illustrate each of these as used by the author of the article. Comment on his success in making each term relevant and meaningful in his discussion of Hawthorne's work.

B. Study the following definition of image, metaphor, and symbol. Then write a similarly concise but well-illustrated definition of another set of closely related critical terms, such as *meter—rhythm; comedy—farce; irony—paradox—satire; epic—romance; symbol—allegory.*

Image, metaphor, and symbol shade into each other and are sometimes difficult to distinguish. In general, however, an image means only what it is, a metaphor means something other than what it is; and a symbol means what it is and something more too. If I say that a shaggy brown dog was rubbing its back against a white picket fence, I am talking about nothing but a dog and am therefore presenting an image; if I say, "Some dirty dog stole my wallet at the party," I am not talking about a dog at all, and am therefore using a metaphor; but if I say, "You can't teach an old dog new tricks," I am talking not only about dogs but about living creatures of any species, and am therefore speaking symbolically.

—Laurence Perrine, *Sound and Sense: An Introduction to Poetry,* 2nd ed. (New York: Harcourt, Brace & World, Inc.), pp. 69–70.

C. Study the following account of the relationship between theme and symbol in James Joyce's short story "The Dead." Then write a similar brief interpretation (no more than five hundred words) of your own favorite short story, or of a story chosen by your instructor.

The device of the muted symbol is superbly used in "The Dead." The events of the story have already long taken place, and were never very significant. A tubercular young man who sang a song called "The Lass of Aughrin" fell in love with a West of Ireland girl called Gretta. One night, she found him outside her window, wet and shivering, and soon after, he died. The story proper opens years later with the arrival of Gretta and her husband at a musical party given by two old music teachers in Dublin. As Gabriel Conroy, the husband, enters, he scrapes snow from his galoshes and cracks a joke with the maid about getting married. She retorts bitterly that "the men that does be there nowadays are nothing but old palaver and all they can get out of you." These two things—the snow and the maid's retort—form the theme of the story, and they are repeated in varied and more menacing forms until the climax.

"The men that does be there nowadays" cannot be great lovers; it is only the dead who can be perfect. The young Gaelic League girl with whom Gabriel chats about the West of Ireland—the subject, like the dead themselves, rising—may be charming, but she cannot have the courtesy and grace of the old music teachers who are passing into the shadow; Caruso—a subtle touch, this—may, for all we know, be a good singer, but he cannot be as great as Parkinson, the obscure English tenor, whom one of the old ladies once heard. And in the tremendous cadenza we realize that Gabriel, good husband though he may be, can never mean to his wife what the dead boy who once stood shivering beneath her window means—till he too has been buried under the snow which is Death's symbol.

> —Frank O'Connor, "And It's a Lonely, Personal Art," in
> *Highlights of Modern Literature: Essays from* The New
> York Times Book Review (New York: The New American
> Library of World Literature, Inc., 1954), p. 78.

D. Frank O'Connor said that "in any novel the principal character is Time"; "the chronological ordering of events establishes a rhythm, which is the rhythm of life itself":

> But what to the novelist is the most precious element in his work is a nightmare to the short-story writer. He is all the while trying to get round the necessity for describing events in sequence; the rhythm is too slow, . . . Every great short story represents a struggle with Time—the novelist's Time—a refusal to allow it to establish its majestic rhythms ("Chapter I, A Walk on the Heath"). It attempts to reach some point of vantage, some glowing center of action from which past and future will be equally visible. The crisis of a short story *is* the short story, and not, as in the novel, the logical, inescapable result of everything preceding it, the mere flowering of events.
>
> —O'Connor, *Highlights*, p. 77.

Drawing for illustrations on novels and short stories you know well, write an essay (no more than two thousand words) in which you discuss *one* major contrast between these two forms of fiction.

E. In his essay on "The Tragic Fallacy," Joseph Wood Krutch said, "Tragedy arises . . . when, as in Periclean Greece or Elizabethan England, a people fully aware of the calamities of life is nevertheless serenely confident of the greatness of man, whose mighty passions and supreme fortitude are revealed when one of these calamities overtakes him." Since modern man has lost the belief in his own importance and potential greatness, true tragedy is beyond his reach: "The best that we can achieve is pathos and the most that we can do is to feel sorry for ourselves." (*The Modern Temper: A Study and a Confession* [New York: Harcourt, Brace & World, Inc., 1929], pp. 122, 137). Select a nineteenth- or twentieth-century play that might be called a "modern tragedy" and show why or why not it lives up to this title. Limit yourself to the one feature or quality that you consider most essential in a tragic play.

F. Write a poetic description of a landscape in the style of a neoclassical poet like Dryden, Pope, or Johnson. Then describe the same landscape in the style of a Romantic poet like Wordsworth, Coleridge, or Keats. *Or,* write several versions of a love poem addressed to the same person. For example, you might write one version in the style of John Donne, another in the style of Elizabeth Barrett Browning, a third in the style of E. E. Cummings.

G. In a campus literary magazine or a national publication like *New Campus Writing,* find a short story or a group of poems by a student author. Describe and evaluate his work. First give a factual account of his handling of genre, convention, form, theme. Deprived of the guide to judgment offered by a writer's reputation, how would you estimate the value of the student's work? Be prepared to explain and defend your criteria. *Or,* be prepared to answer the same questions concerning mimeographed copies of student work provided for class discussion by your instructor.

H. The following analysis of a poem by George Herbert attempts to relate sound to sense, detail to theme, technique to larger significance. Prepare a similar analysis of a poem you know well, or of a poem chosen by your instructor.

The Pulley

When God at first made man,
Having a glass of blessings standing by,
Let us, said he, pour on him all we can:
Let the world's riches, which dispersèd lie,
Contract into a span.

So strength first made a way,
Then beauty flowed, then wisdom, honor, pleasure;
When almost all was out, God made a stay,
Perceiving that alone of all his treasure
Rest in the bottom lay.

For if I should, said he,
Bestow this jewel also on my creature,
He would adore my gifts instead of me,
And rest in nature, not the God of nature;
So both should losers be.

Yet let him keep the rest,
But keep them with repining restlessness;
Let him be rich and weary, that at least,
If goodness lead him not, yet weariness
May toss him to my breast.

Herbert's poem is dramatic and allegorical. It is **dramatic** because it makes us watch God act and speak, as if we were watching a short scene from a play. It is **allegorical** because a number of symbols ("the glass of blessings," the one "jewel" God withholds, etc.) are worked into a meaningful whole. What in a nonpoetic treatment would be a study in the psychology of faith becomes a concrete, graphic "acting out" of the theme of "What brings men to God?"

Another obvious feature of this poem is the formal discipline imposed by the division of the poem into four stanzas. Each stanza follows the rhyme scheme *a b a b a;* in each stanza the first and last lines are trimeter (six syllables each); the other three lines are pentameter (ten or eleven syllables each). The division into stanzas corresponds to four stages in a logical progression, signaled by the transitional phrases "So . . ." (second stanza), "For . . ." (third stanza), and "Yet . . ." (fourth stanza). Within each stanza, expression is brief and direct. Notice, for instance, the economy with which the basic situation is established (and the underlying symbolic parallel introduced) in the first three lines of the first stanza. Brevity of presentation and clear logical progression join with dramatic vividness and the concreteness of allegory.

What is the jewel withheld by God? "Rest"—which thus becomes a key word in the poem, with "restlessness" finally compelling man to find in God's love the contentment he has looked for in vain in "the world's riches." When these riches are enumerated in the second stanza, the poem follows a regular, predictable iambic pattern:

> So stréngth first máde a wáy,
> Then beáuty flowéd, then wísdom, hónor, pleásure;

But the unexpected key term is emphasized by trochaic inversion:

> Rést in the bóttom láy

(rather than, for instance, the iambic "Contract into a span"). It is further emphasized by the reshuffling of the usual sentence pattern, which would have been "Rest lay in the bottom." Further emphasis derives from the later **pun** on the key word ("Yet let him keep the *rest*"), where the same word is repeated in the quite different sense of "remainder." Thus, both what God grants and what he withholds are paradoxically called "rest."

As the word play here is paradoxical and unexpected, so is the meaning. Not faith, not good works, not love for one's neighbor, not the avoidance of sin lead man to God but restlessness, weariness, frustration. There is another example in the poem of "sound" mirroring "sense." As the dispersed riches of the world "contract into a span," the pentameter contracts to a trimeter line. The poem is more than a prose paraphrase of it would be, because the poet's language is more expressive, more concentrated, more subtle than that of ordinary prose.

Of the concentration of the poet's language, and its richness of implication and association, a fairly conventional example is Herbert's use of the word "jewel." It calls forth the idea of something precious and hard to come by, surrounded by manifold visual associations, echoes of literary phrases, and memories of symbolic uses. A more revealing example of richness of implication is Herbert's title. Designed to lift a heavy object (man), the pulley (restlessness) is an ingenious contrivance constructed by the craftsman (God). At first the difficulty of moving the object may seem insuperable (the poet has no facile optimism about man's nature). But once the principle of the pulley is discovered and applied, the contrivance will perform its work with startling efficiency and ease. Of course, the reader may be used to thinking of religious matters with vague reverence and half-formed images. He may then find the concrete material quality and the everyday associations of the pulley irreverent, or lacking in due solemnity. But it is exactly by dealing with religion in the vocabulary of concrete everyday reality that Herbert succeeds in bringing it to our attention.

—Hans P. Guth, *Literature* (Belmont, Calif.: Wadsworth Publishing Company, Inc., 1962), pp. 636–38.

part two

The Teaching
of English

The teacher of English does not teach his subject in isolation. Especially in high school, and to a lesser extent in college, what he does in the classroom is influenced by conditions affecting the schools in general. In making fruitful in the classroom the work of scholars in his discipline, he must take into account the expectations of his administrators and his community.

The same years that have produced important developments in the discipline of English have seen equally important developments affecting the nation's schools. Some work in favor of the teacher committed to serious, solid work in his subject. Others work against the teacher who as a fully qualified professional claims responsibility for the substance and method of his teaching. Whether he finds them welcome or not, however, the teacher must understand some of the premises and likely effects of current trends. He must make his influence felt in the evaluation of programs and procedures that can profoundly alter the nature of his work. He must soberly estimate how compatible prevailing directions in education are with the basic requirements for the successful teaching of his subject.

A Preliminary View

The most important development affecting our schools in recent years has been a renewed emphasis on subject matter and intellectual achievement. A general swing of the pendulum is moving our schools toward "content," as the orthodoxy of earlier decades is suffering the penalties of its own partial success. As parents compared the training of their children with their own subject-centered schooling, as educators contrasted the American high school and college with their counterparts in more traditional educational systems, a general reaction set in against what was loosely identified as "progressive education." Rarely heard today are the prevailing slogans of earlier years: "teach the whole child," "teach children, not subjects." Present discussions of education center on "the need for trained manpower," "the return to fundamentals," "the structure of knowledge," "the cultivation of excellence," the ways of providing "enrichment" and programs for the gifted.

The rediscovery of subject matter has had its most immediate effect in the re-examination of offerings in mathematics and natural science. These areas have seen a massive cooperative effort to develop, even at the earlier stages of instruction, courses that offer genuine intellectual challenge and are fully in harmony with current scholarship. In the humanities, the impact of this trend has been most dramatic in the teaching of foreign languages. Long the stepchild of modern American education, it has turned out to be a true Cinderella, rapidly regaining lost ground as a required subject in school and college.

In less dramatically visible fashion, the teacher of English stands to gain from the same general trend. More basic than any concrete advance is the renewed respect he can claim for his field. He is likely to be less handicapped than in years past by administrative preoccupation with more glamorous curricular and extracurricular offerings. He can hopefully devote less time to making his subject attractive, or at least acceptable, to prejudiced students. Taking advantage of the renewed prestige of scholarship and intellectual attainment, he can act on his conviction that "interest in the material to be learned is the best stimulus to learning."[1] He can concentrate on bringing out the intrinsic interest of his discipline, relying more than in years past on public and administrative support and on academic competition among students to provide a measure of additional, external motivation.

Generally, those concerned with improving instruction in English have found the re-evaluation and strengthening of subject matter a congenial theme. In the words of George Winchester Stone, Jr.,

> the primary need for English teachers, at this point of time, is mastery of the subject, i.e., a rich and resourceful knowledge of the literature, an understanding of the nature and structure of the language, and skill in the writing of it.[2]

Nevertheless, the current emphasis on solid content in school offerings is not an unmixed blessing. Often, the English teacher working in this direction will find himself allied with forces aiming at goals different from his. Some currently fashionable terms suffer from a serious ambiguity. For instance, what is promoted as a return to **fundamentals** is often merely a return to rote learning. It often means a return to "item" learning rather than "pattern" learning. In some private schools advertised as championing solid content, students again memorize the isolated names of capitals rather than study factors that explain the location of cities. They again memorize obsolescent words from spelling books first copyrighted in the previous century. In the name of stressing fundamentals,

---

[1] Jerome S. Bruner, *The Process of Education* (Cambridge, Mass.: Harvard University Press, 1962), p. 14.
[2] "Cooperative English Program Notes," *PMLA*, LXXVII (September, 1962), Part 2, vii.

we may thus lose sight of a hard-won basic principle of modern education: knowledge must be *meaningful*. We should heed the findings of psychologists who in studying the process of learning have concluded

> Perhaps the most basic thing that can be said about human memory, after a century of intensive research, is that unless detail is placed into a structured pattern, it is rapidly forgotten.[3]

What is truly fundamental in education is developing the student's ability to grasp underlying principles and essential relations: "What is meant by 'fundamental' in this sense is precisely that an idea has wide as well as powerful applicability."[4] *What is fundamental for the teacher of English is to develop in his students habits of responsible inquiry and straight thinking, of systematic development and forceful expression, of perceptive reading.* Fundamental is creating a perspective toward language and literature that encourages the exploration of recurrent problems, of central patterns. Fundamental is the teacher's ability to focus on such central problems as the relationship between system and diversity, between form and content, between structure and meaning and to find in his concern with these the unity of our discipline.

Another powerfully evocative term that must be carefully defined is **excellence.** Stress on excellence must not become an excuse for the teacher's pursuing his own scholarly interests—without concerning himself with how his knowledge may be communicated and how students may be led to develop scholarly interests of their own. Stress on "standards" must not become an excuse for ignoring all students but the docile, the eager, and the well-prepared. *The pursuit of excellence should mean the aim of developing the full potential of each student,* whether gifted or handicapped. The professor in a prestige college or the high school teacher working with superior students can easily lose sight of the problems implied in an ideal of education for all. In the words of John W. Gardner,

> The problem is to achieve some measure of excellence *in this society,* with all its beloved and exasperating clutter, with all its exciting and debilitating confusion of standards, with all the stubborn problems that won't be solved and the equally stubborn ones that might be.[5]

Finally, stress on subject matter and intellectual achievement should not lead us to neglect more intangible but crucially important goals. If in recent years we have seen "a widespread renewal of concern for the quality and intellectual aims of education," we should make sure that this concern bears fruit "without abandonment of the ideal that edu-

---

[3] Bruner, *The Process of Education,* p. 24.
[4] *Ibid.,* p. 18.
[5] *Excellence: Can We Be Equal and Excellent Too?* (New York: Harper & Row, Publishers, 1962), p. xiii.

cation should serve as a means of training well-balanced citizens for a democracy."[6] At least part of the present criticism of our schools is aimed not at what they are doing poorly but at what they are doing well. Typically, our schools counteract the cruder forms of prejudice; they keep alive an elementary sense of social responsibility in a complacent society; they give students a sense of identity with humanity beyond narrow political and ideological borders. They teach students to accept as a matter of course conflicting interests and points of view, introducing them to ways of at least partly reconciling such conflicts. In cultivating these attitudes, the schools provoke the opposition of powerful illiberal forces in our society. The teacher gives aid and comfort to these forces if he neglects the moral and social goals of education for the sake of academic achievement narrowly defined.

In spite of such reservations, the teacher of English clearly stands to gain as a result of the current stress on quality in our schools. Less welcome and more disturbing is the second major trend—a growing preoccupation with quantity and numbers. Responding to the pressure of rising enrollments, administrators and educational foundations are everywhere supporting studies that, whatever their other announced goals, are directly concerned with more efficient use of staff and facilities. Often, proposals for "improving" education are aimed at efficiency in "turning out the educational product" rather than at promoting the student's intellectual and moral growth. As Norman Cousins has warned in the *Saturday Review:*

> If we are to help Johnny to think—which is to say, if we are to help him become truly educated—it becomes necessary to respect the natural requirements of thought. Somewhere along the line in recent years, a speed-up has taken place in large areas of education. Johnny is expected to read faster, study faster, write faster, and think faster. . . . But the problems posed by an Age of Speed are not met by snap judgments, one-page memos on complex subjects, lightning-fast reading techniques, or rapid writing. We meet our problems only as we comprehend them and give them sustained and sequential thought.[7]

One symptom of a confusion of quality and quantity is a continuing emphasis on concretely measurable results. As much as ever, teacher, students, and parents are made to worry over tests and norms, medians and percentiles. In the teaching of English, reliance on **objective measurement** of the student's achievement creates as many problems as it solves. Ability to identify misspelled words and "incorrect" usages is measured more easily than articulateness, conviction, sensitivity, capacity for sustained critical thought. Stress on concrete results shifts the emphasis in an English course from the primary to the secondary. It shifts attention from

[6] Bruner, *The Process of Education,* p. 1.
[7] "Not So Fast," *Saturday Review,* July 6, 1963, p. 14.

substance to mechanics, from an understanding of relationships to a mastery of terminology, from mature response to literature to the memorization of dates and names, from independent criticism to the repetition of approved commonplaces.

As a result, collaboration between English teachers and testing experts has in the past been fitful and unsatisfactory. English teachers tend to view the advocate of objective testing with suspicion and hostility. They "know there is a tremendous difference between *recognizing* a correct answer and *formulating* a sound answer in one's own words"; they "understand the difference between, on the one hand, the ability to think something out in a coherent pattern of sentences and paragraphs, and, on the other hand, the ability to outsmart the clever fellow who concocts these five multiple choices, one of which is dead wrong, one of which looks right but isn't, one of which really is right, and the other two of which are silly."[8] Testing experts, for their part, are eager to return the compliment. They are likely to charge that the essay tests preferred by teachers of English "are neither reliable nor valid," pointing to studies showing "how inconsistent, shaky, and unreliable even the most careful essay reader is." They may feel that the English teacher puts the premium on "verbal glibness" rather than on "sound reasoning and through comprehension."[9]

Whatever the teacher's solution to the problems here suggested, he must remember the difficulty of constructing simple and workable measuring devices for what is elusive and complex, of devising objective tests for what necessarily brings into play the student's personality and private history. This does not mean that achievement in English is impossible to estimate. After a few weeks' work with a class, the teacher knows which student is likely to participate independently and critically in discussion, which student needs to be nudged into participating, which student is likely to wander far from the point at issue, and which student is eager to tell his teachers what he thinks they want to hear. After the fourth or fifth week of a course, the teacher taking home a stack of papers can predict fairly well which papers are likely to be substantial and readable, which honest but plodding, and which glib or insincere. He will even know who among his superior students are the conscientious and diligent ones who do best on objective tests and who are the independent ones who resent having their responses channeled by a test-maker whose assumptions they are not given an opportunity to challenge.

If the teacher is resourceful and persevering, and if the conditions are right, he will know that even after one semester's work the superficial student will be somewhat less glib, the callow student will be somewhat

---

[8] Fred H. Stocking, "The Two Jobs of English Teachers," *The English Journal*, L (March, 1961), 163.

[9] Orville Palmer, "Sense or Nonsense? The Objective Testing of English Composition," *The English Journal*, L (May, 1961), 314–20.

less ignorant, the plodding student's papers will be somewhat less painfully awkward. The diffident student may speak up in class with a little more assurance. The willful and imaginative student may or may not have become less impatient with the academic decencies and conventions. None of this knowledge on the part of the teacher can be substantiated by the kind of evidence that can be expressed in rigorously objective terms and forwarded to the dean's office for statistical evaluation. *At the most, the teacher will use the results of objective tests as rough indicators that corroborate, or else alert him to re-examine, judgments based on his firsthand acquaintance with the students' work.*

Similar considerations, inherent in the nature of his discipline, restrict the usefulness to the English teacher of conventional educational research and experiment. Techniques of statistical measurement, for instance, are more applicable to the concrete than to the intangible aspects of English. Some results of such statistical investigation are highly instructive. For example, every teacher of English should be aware of the large number of repeated exposures necessary to affect permanently the student's language habits: to make automatic the correct spelling of a difficult word, to make a new word firmly a part of the student's recognition vocabulary, to change a phonetic habit that contributes to the foreign accent of an adult speaker. Very soon, however, the investigator has to deal with a complex interplay of factors that are difficult to isolate and to measure in any reliable way: the extent and ease of the student's control of the sentence-producing mechanisms of English grammar; the extent and nature of his previous experience with words and things; his semantic sophistication; his willingness to search out and respond to nuance; his reactions to the philosophical, aesthetic, and emotional dimensions of language and literature. As one investigator concluded after studying ninety items of research related to the teaching of high school English:

> Chief among the reasons for the dearth of rigorously controlled experimental studies in the English language arts is the difficulty of identifying or defining, and thus controlling, the variety of variables involved in such a complex process as developing growth in the power to use the English language and in the ability to appreciate the subtleties of literary genre.[10]

Even English teachers actively participating in the planning of research in the teaching of English are likely to wonder out loud "whether all aspects of it are testable" and to call for "continued submission of teaching problems to reason, common sense, and imagination, as well as to controlled experimentation."[11]

[10] Ingrid M. Strom, "Summary of Investigations Relating to the English Language Arts in Secondary Education: 1960–1961," *The English Journal*, LI (February, 1962), 123.

[11] Erwin R. Steinberg, "Needed Research in the Teaching of College English," *College English*, XXIV (November, 1962), 152.

Whatever the unfortunate effects of an increasing preoccupation with quantitative measurement, they are likely to prove far less drastic than those of other far-reaching developments, aimed at stepping up the quantitative output of education. More revolutionary in its implications than our increasing faith in the IBM machine is the increasing experimental use of teaching resources and devices that make it possible to teach larger numbers of students without a corresponding massive effort to train and recruit teachers. Current experiments could prove the beginning of a technological revolution that would profoundly alter the character of our schools. In the words of one of the pioneers in this field,

> education has been, for a century or more, one of the areas of American society which has walled itself off from technological advances and, consequently, has created a technological vacuum. That vacuum is now rapidly being filled.[12]

Current experimental programs move in two major directions. On the one hand, there will be more instruction in **large classes,** lectures over school- or district-wide closed-circuit television, courses recorded on film or tape. Often such instruction will be prepared by teaching teams and followed up by assistants. Whatever the misgivings of classroom teachers, administrators and foundation officials have long since learned to make a virtue of necessity by enthusiastically presenting as improvements changes dictated by shortages of teachers and funds:

> . . . the most capable and experienced teachers *in specific fields* will teach large classes. Every teacher, inevitably, is more experienced in one subject or one phase of a subject than in another. So the students can be better motivated by contact with the very best teacher available for that phase of the subject. . . . For students, large classes will offer another particularly important advantage: They will serve as transitional experiences for college classes and for many other occasions of adult life. Students can learn to take notes, hold back questions until an appropriate time, and develop more responsibility for planning their own learning. . . . Discussions among teachers and counselors in the setting of the teaching team will provide coordination of learning experiences provided for students.[13]

The second and complementary direction these projects take is toward what is euphemistically called **independent study**—increased time for independent reading, for self-teaching by various automated devices, for individual use of instructional films and records:

> Independent study will involve many types of activities: reading, viewing, listening, writing, working on automated learning devices, and doing a variety of things under supervision in different kinds of laboratories. In-

---

12 James D. Finn, "A New Theory for Instructional Technology," in *Programmed Learning: Theory and Research*, eds. Wendell I. Smith and J. William Moore (Princeton, N.J.: D. Van Nostrand Company, Inc.), p. 4.
13 J. Lloyd Trump and Dorsey Baynham, *Focus on Change: Guide to Better Schools* (Chicago: Rand McNally & Company, 1961), pp. 30–32.

dividual differences among students will be recognized in these activities in ways that are impossible in today's schools. . . . Students will gradually increase their responsibility for reaching individual goals. They will learn to select and carry through projects and to show initiative in seeking study materials and aids. They will experience satisfaction in an environment that stimulates creative efforts.[14]

The sponsors of such programs envision schools in which television, having "made the standard lecture obsolete," provides "the medium for mass instruction," while programmed learning provides "the ultimate in individualized instruction." In this educational Brave New World,

> Each student progresses at his own rate. Much of the time he studies on his own, or with fellow students, but always with instant access to the complete range of learning resources: taped lectures, programmed course materials, language audio-tapes, bibliographies, and original documents on microfilm.[15]

If teachers remain skeptical of such proposals, it is not for lack of skilled persuasion by their proponents. While one member of a teaching team teaches a large class, "other teachers of the team . . . find the time to prepare for their own, future large-class presentations or to perform other professional tasks that today's school arrangements seldom permit." Teacher's aides "will perform those clerical and routine duties which now take much of a teacher's day"; instruction assistants "will read and evaluate some parts of English themes" and confer with students.[16] In the colleges, "the senior faculty members, having been spared the drudgery of repeating over and over the basic substance of their fields, are in fresher mind to work with students on advanced topics."[17]

All such promises and rationalizations skirt the basic difficulty: the teacher's view of his relationship with his students. Teachers overwhelmingly see as their ideal a limited number of classes under their full personal supervision, small enough to permit personal knowledge of each student and personal guidance of his work. Under ideal circumstances, instruction in such a setting can have an immediacy and coherence impossible to duplicate in a scrambled schedule of large lecture, small discussion group, and individual study. The advantage of the conventional classroom is that it makes possible a feeling of shared endeavor. Over the weeks, the instructor develops a sense of his class—he begins to anticipate the reactions of individuals, learning how to channel them in productive directions; he relates their written work to his image of their personalities; he becomes aware of emotional complications while it is still not too late to deal with them. He finds his reward for such personal instruction

[14] *Ibid.*, pp. 27–29.
[15] Alvin C. Eurich, "Higher Education in the 21st Century," *Atlantic*, June, 1963, p. 53.
[16] Trump and Baynham, *Focus on Change*, pp. 31–34.
[17] *Atlantic*, June, 1963, p. 53.

in the student's equally personal response. Whatever the merits of team teaching, instructional television, or programmed learning, their common danger lies in their tendency to narrow the sphere of this personal element. In the humanities, at any rate, they thus endanger what is most precious in the teacher's work and in the student's education.

At least some of the specialists in the new instructional media are well aware of the possibility that "the medium governs the image." In education as elsewhere, the means to some extent affect the ends. The teacher is likely to find that technology, offering itself as a servant, inevitably to some extent becomes a master. *To judge from current statistics concerning teacher training and future enrollments, some movement in the direction of educational mass production and instructional automation is inevitable. It is essential that teachers as a profession learn to control this movement instead of being controlled by it.*

What is the alternative to the increasing use of an elaborate teaching technology? Reduced to its simplest terms, it is success in attracting to a teaching career a proportionate share of the growing number of students in our schools and colleges. Such success depends greatly on current efforts by the profession to have the American teacher become more prestigious, more independent, and better paid. It depends on the willingness of teachers already in the profession to carry on vigorously the struggle for improved professional status. One test of such status will be the extent to which the experienced judgment of the classroom teacher—rather than the fiat of administrator, school-board member, or legislator—will determine the use to be made of new technical resources.

In addition to such major trends as the renewed emphasis on intellectual substance and the development of new technical aids, a number of less widely publicized developments are having an effect on the English teacher's work. In recent years there has been some weakening of the artificial barriers that have long separated teachers at different levels and in different areas from each other. Curriculum studies in the sciences, and increasingly in the humanities, have brought together high school teachers, professors from college departments of education, and scholars from appropriate subjects. Increasingly, college teachers are taking an active interest in the work of the public schools. In English, as in other related fields, it may be said that "despite a good deal of grumbling and suspicion, professional education and liberal-arts education are moving closer together, to their mutual advantage."[18]

If such developments become a general trend, they can go far toward unifying the present split professional image of the teacher of English. We should resist use of the term *professional* to label training in departments of education as distinct from training in subject matter. A true teacher of

[18] Donald D. Walsh, "The MLA FL Program in 1962," *PMLA*, LXXVIII (May, 1963), 21.

English does not study English as an academic discipline and then turn to a department of education to be trained for his profession. If he is to be a true professional, the relationship between his academic major and his future vocation must be more organic. To participate effectively in the training of teachers, the scholar must be able to convey to his students a rounded view of the teacher's craft; the professor of education must be able to anchor his discussion of method and motivation firmly to specific subject matter.

The teacher who welcomes increased cooperation between those representing different parts of the educational enterprise need not be guilty of a naive faith in groupthink, in the work of conferences and committees. In our conference discussions and curriculum studies, there is inevitably an element of repetition and waste motion. Nevertheless, every teacher profits from thinking through his premises and problems, and from arguing them out with others whose experience can supplement his own. If only in order to hold his own in educational planning and debate, he stands to gain from a sober, balanced appraisal of his objectives, his methods, his resources.

The story goes that when Pestalozzi was asked to explain his experimental educational program he told the questioner to go and see for himself. Looking back on our own schooling, we realize that our own best teachers were successful because of a combination of personal gifts hard to state in terms of a coherent theory or to check off on an inventory of aptitudes. As teachers of English, furthermore, we are painfully aware of how irrelevant our resounding statements about educational objectives may seem when we look at a piece of prose produced by one of our less successful students.

six

Nevertheless, every teacher must sooner or later think through some of the assumptions underlying his classroom work. In selecting the materials he teaches, he must apply criteria of relevance and significance other than his own current interests. He must be able to trace his successes and failures in the classroom to causes other than his native talent or the lack thereof in his students.

Objectives

Even when the teacher is content to guide his work largely by his own intuitive judgment, he must realize that teaching is a co-operative enterprise. Legislators, school boards, and trustees make their decisions at least in part on the basis of assumptions about the nature and purposes of education. If teachers are reluctant to formulate such assumptions, those who determine the conditions of the teacher's work will turn to theorists and administrators who do not share that reluctance.

Teachers have during recent decades frequently deplored the influence of current educational theories on their schools. However, they cannot counteract such theories simply by denying the competence of their proponents. They must have some understanding of prevailing trends in educational philosophy, and they must have a coherent rationale of the contribution their own subject makes to the student's schooling. As teachers of English, we must be equipped to argue the objectives of education generally and of education in English in particular.

Educational Philosophy

Modern American education is exceedingly articulate on questions of educational philosophy and method. The professional success of the public-school teacher depends not only on his ability to teach but also on his ability to verbalize the premises, methods, and objectives of his teaching. This state of affairs results in part from a reaction against an era when too much about education was taken for granted.

When the imparting of subject matter was tacitly assumed to be the end of schoolroom activity, learning often meant rote learning. It meant the passive acceptance and memorization of material imperfectly understood. When carried to extremes, this kind of schooling became the mindless drudgery described in the autobiographies of men like Winston Churchill, Robert Graves, and Lincoln Steffens. Here is Winston Churchill describing his first experience with this type of education:

> Behold me then on a gloomy evening, with an aching heart, seated in front of the First Declension.

Mensa	a table
Mensa	O table
Mensam	a table
Mensae	of a table
Mensae	to or for a table
Mensa	by, with or from a table

> What on earth did it mean? Where was the sense of it? It seemed absolute rigmarole to me. However, there was one thing I could always do: I could learn by heart. And I thereupon proceeded, as far as my private sorrows would allow, to memorize the acrostic-looking task which had been set me.
> In due course the Master returned.
> "Have you learnt it?" he asked.
> "I think I can *say* it, sir," I replied; and I gabbled it off.
> He seemed so satisfied with this that I was emboldened to ask a question.
> "What does it mean, sir?"
> "It means what it says. Mensa, a table. Mensa is a noun of the First Declension. There are five declensions. You have learnt the singular of the First Declension."
> "But," I repeated, "what does it mean?"
> "Mensa means a table," he answered.
> "Then why does mensa also mean O table," I enquired, "and what does O table mean?"
> "Mensa, O table, is the vocative case," he replied.
> "But why O table?" I persisted in genuine curiosity.
> "O table,—you would use that in addressing a table, in invoking a table." And then seeing he was not carrying me with him, "You would use it in speaking to a table."

"But I never do," I blurted out in honest amazement.

"If you are impertinent, you will be punished, and punished, let me tell you, very severely," was his conclusive rejoinder.

Such was my first introduction to the classics from which, I have been told, many of our cleverest men have derived so much solace and profit.[1]

Here is George Orwell's description of instruction in another area of the traditional curriculum:

History was a series of unrelated unintelligible but—in some way that was never explained to us—important facts with resounding phrases tied to them. Disraeli brought peace with honour. Clive was astonished at his moderation. Pitt called in the New World to redress the balance of the Old. And the dates, and the mnemonic devices! . . . I recall positive orgies of dates, with the keener boys leaping up and down in their places in their eagerness to shout out the right answers, and at the same time not feeling the faintest interest in the meaning of the mysterious events they were naming.

"1587?"

"Massacre of St. Bartholomew!"

"1707?"

"Death of Aurangzeeb!"

"1713?"

"Treaty of Utrecht!"

"1773?"

"The Boston Tea Party!"

"1520?"

"Oh, Mum, please, Mum—"

"Please, Mum, please, Mum! Let me tell him, Mum!"

"Well; 1520?"

"Field of the Cloth of Gold!"[2]

In recent years, critics of our schools have increasingly set up traditional European methods of education as an ideal for the American teacher to emulate. Often such critics have had little firsthand experience with the traditional European system. They are often unaware of the extent to which this system has encouraged learning without understanding and mere outward conformity on the part of students to patterns established by their teachers.

Modern education rests on the premise that the teacher's handing on of ready-made subject matter is not enough. It accepts as basic the point that A. N. Whitehead identified as the main idea of his *The Aims of Education:* "The students are alive, and the purpose of education is to stimulate and guide their self-development." As Whitehead said,

Culture is activity of thought, and receptiveness to beauty and humane feeling. Scraps of information have nothing to do with it. A merely well-informed man is the most useless bore on God's earth. . . . In training a

---

[1] Winston Churchill, *A Roving Commission* (New York: Charles Scribner's Sons, 1930), pp. 9–13.

[2] George Orwell, *Such, Such Were the Joys* (New York: Harcourt, Brace & World, Inc., 1953), pp. 20–21.

child to activity of thought, above all things we must beware of what I will call "inert ideas"—that is to say, ideas that are merely received into the mind without being utilised, or tested, or thrown into fresh combinations.[3]

In the words of another educator, the process of education is not to be compared to the filling up of an empty pot but rather to the lighting of a fire. When we look for "solid subject matter," our real problem is to find information and ideas that our students can think about, make their own, adapt and modify according to their own tentative standards. Our problem is to present material that will kindle the student's permanent interest, leading him to read, explore, and discover on his own.

Many of the assumptions underlying modern educational practice appear as early as Jean-Jacques Rousseau's *Émile, or On Education* (1762), a complete account of the upbringing and schooling of an imaginary child. Rousseau insisted that childhood has its own ways of seeing, thinking, and feeling. In prematurely imposing adult standards of understanding, taste, and responsibility, the adult teaches the child to dissemble in order to be rewarded or escape punishment. *To be effective, a teacher must to some extent be able to look at the world, and at the material being taught, through the eyes of the student.* He must have an understanding of the student's interests and motives.

In this respect, as wherever else the human dimension of teaching is concerned, the teacher of English ought to have an advantage over his colleagues in more practical fields. It is difficult to teach short stories like Willa Cather's "Paul's Case," Nelson Algren's "A Bottle of Milk for Mother," or Eudora Welty's "A Visit of Charity" without acquiring a fuller appreciation of the adolescent's vision of the world. It is difficult to read autobiographical novels like *David Copperfield* and *The Way of All Flesh* without thinking hard and long about what cuts off communication between adolescents and adults. Generally, the teacher of English has less excuse than his colleagues for lacking the imaginative sympathy that helps a teacher communicate with his students.

Once having through an act of imaginative sympathy come down to the level of his pupil, Rousseau decided that true learning is what the student learns for himself rather than what he is told. He wanted the teacher to exploit to the full the motive-power of the child's native curiosity, without killing curiosity by excessive hurry. As far as possible, he wanted the child to **learn by doing**—by questioning, experimenting, exploring. *True learning requires the student's active participation.* This requirement the English teacher is again in a favorable position to appreciate: The writing that expresses the student's own views and personality, and the reading that is truly a personal experience, are necessarily activities that the student must perform for himself. More specifically, much

[3] *The Aims of Education* (New York: The Macmillan Company, 1929), pp. v, 1–2.

classroom work in English will involve the student in active exploration: Instruction in language remains barren unless the student becomes a perceptive observer of how people around him use language. He must learn to pay attention to how speakers and teachers handle debated points of usage, to how accomplished writers develop a passage.

A third major point in Rousseau's educational program requires careful qualification. While Rousseau recognized the motive power of disinterested curiosity and the satisfaction to be derived from discovery, he also urged teachers and parents to motivate the student's learning by an appeal to **immediate interest.** As he observed, a child resisting his reading lessons might become eager to read upon receiving a party invitation that an adult would refuse to decipher for him. Within limits, every teacher will welcome the added impetus learning can get from being related to the immediate concerns of the students. But the teacher must be careful not to reinforce these short-range interests at the expense of developing interests more lasting and significant. In the teaching of literature, especially, he is trying to develop interests and tastes and standards different from the norms of popular prejudice and popular taste. The teacher of English will appeal to those existing interests of the student that are most helpful to him in his work: the child's delight in patterned sound, his fondness for rhythm and word play and rhyme; the child's curiosity about new settings and periods and people; the adolescent's readiness to question existing standards and authority. Typically, the teacher will appeal to these interests in order to lead the students beyond them. Thus, he will exploit an existing interest in plot and theme in leading his students to an understanding of structure and form.

Educational principles derived from Rousseau and other early theorists found widespread acceptance in the twenties and thirties of this century. They were reflected in trends often grouped together under the label **progressive education** and identified with John Dewey and his followers. In theory, what today most clearly separates the tradition of progressive education from its opponents is John Dewey's insistence on the responsibility of the schools for the development of **the whole child.** Dewey envisioned "Utopian schools" in which "the whole concept of acquiring and storing away" subject matter would be "displaced by the concept of creating attitudes by shaping desires and developing the needs that are significant in the process of living." Emphasis was to be put not on inert knowledge but on the full human potential of each child.[4] As against such emphasis on the student's whole personality, educators like Robert M. Hutchins have defined the purpose of the educational system as promoting "the intellectual development of the people."[5] They have argued that home and church have their role to play in the personal and

---

[4] *The New York Times,* April 23, 1933, Sec. E, p. 7, col. 4.
[5] *The University of Utopia* (Chicago: The University of Chicago Press, 1953), p. 55.

emotional maturing of the student, and that the school is the one place primarily responsible for training the student's mind.

For the teacher of English, the opposition of intellectual training and personality development is to a large extent artificial. English is a discipline as demanding in intellectual substance as any other in the curriculum. However, few English teachers would or could teach language and literature exclusively as a matter of intellectual development. If we cannot get our students to be *moved* by literature, we do more harm than good in furnishing them with the tools for its intellectual analysis. Every teacher of literature must make sure that analysis is not carried beyond the point where it ceases to deepen and strengthen our full imaginative response and begins to become coldly intellectual dissection. Coleridge said that poetry brings the whole soul of man into activity. In our fragmented culture, with its countless specialized pursuits, literature appeals to man's whole intellectual, emotional, and moral being. The study of literature not only broadens the student's perspective but contributes in manifold ways to his growth in emotional maturity and human sympathy.

Through the students' writing, the English teacher has a more intimate and comprehensive view of his students' personalities than can be gained through the psychologist's and sociologist's questionnaires. Autobiographical writing traditionally has been a way for men to come to terms with their desires and hopes and frustrations. Argumentative writing, through its drive, its direction, its characteristic preoccupations, in a more indirect way reveals personality. Nothing more surely kills the student's willingness to write than the feeling that the reader is not interested in him as a human being.

If our subject matter cannot be defined in exclusively intellectual terms, neither can our influence as teachers. Everyone has known teachers competent in their subject matter who nevertheless took the joy out of life—and out of their subject. In English even more than in other academic fields, it is essential that the teacher be able to help students enjoy their work. Enjoyment here does not mean fun-loving good fellowship. It does not require of the teacher the kind of chumminess that breeds contempt. It requires pride in accomplishment, appreciation of work well done. It means purposeful and satisfying work under a teacher who basically respects and likes people, who has at least a rudimentary sense of humor and the minimum of emotional balance needed to come to terms with life.

Probably in no other field is joyless learning, or learning against the grain, as self-defeating as in language and literature. At the same time, every teacher has responsibilities beyond his own field. Intellectual development is a barren virtue if it is not joined to the emotional maturity and moral sensitivity that enable men to live sanely and humanely with their fellows. As was shown by the recent history of Germany and Japan, an educational system may stress intellectual accomplishment and yet, measured by other standards, be a disastrous failure.

Even if teachers could escape their share of responsibility for the larger catastrophes, their work intimately affects, for better or for worse, the outlook of individuals still in an indeterminate and susceptible stage. Every teacher remembers a student for whom a few minutes of respectful listening, a cautious word of encouragement, or a casual smile served as a significant break in the familiar patterns of a to him hostile or meaningless world. As J. N. Hook says in *The Teaching of High School English,* it may well be a teacher's interest or lack of it that decides whether a problem student grows up to become a good auto mechanic or whether the reform school gets him first.[6] What rightly attracts idealistic young people to teaching is the opportunity to be a good influence, to make a living by helping people rather than by exploiting their weaknesses and limitations. This kind of influence exerted by a good teacher cannot be defined in terms of subject-matter competence narrowly interpreted.

Though schools have always professed to develop personality, to shape attitudes, American public schools have gone much further than their European counterparts in trying to tackle this responsibility in earnest. In the words of the authors of *Education for College,*

> More and more the schools have assumed—or had thrust upon them—dozens of responsibilities formerly accepted elsewhere; in many ways the high school has been substituted for the church, apprenticeship programs, the reform school, the vacant lot playground, and the home.[7]

The question is not really whether American schools and colleges can divest themselves of these responsibilities. The question is how we can meet these responsibilities without diluting the intellectual training that is our schools' most specific duty. The answer lies in stress on those subjects that combine solid intellectual content with broad relevance to human concerns.

It is this combination of intellectual substance and humane significance that marks the subjects we group together as the **humanities**—language, literature, history, philosophy, the fine arts. It is this combination that accounts for the basic role of the humanities in any meaningful definition of **liberal education.** The liberally educated person is not a walking encyclopedia. Nor is he the model pupil who through constant exhortation by his teachers has been made to strive for tolerance, enthusiasm, and constructive thinking. *In the liberally educated person, knowledge, thought, and attitude exist in meaningful relations.* A liberally

---

6 *The Teaching of High School English,* 2nd ed. (New York: The Ronald Press Company, 1959), p. 16.
7 Albert R. Kitzhaber, Robert M. Gorrell, and Paul Roberts, *Education for College: Improving the High School Curriculum* (New York: The Ronald Press Company, 1961), p. 4. Copyright © 1961 The Ronald Press Company.

educated person has learned how to secure relevant knowledge, how to think through his data in a balanced fashion, and how to define and reconcile his purposes and commitments. His values do not come to him ready-made; they are a reflection of his knowledge and his experience.

Such a definition implies that teachers should resist their inclination to teach attitudes directly, by admonition. One weakness of modern American education has been the growth of formless general subjects giving the student an opportunity to absorb desirable attitudes toward the family, the country, the world. English itself, in some schools and some textbooks, has become a mere label for such generalized instruction. The following is the conclusion of a case history providing the basis for discussion in an "experience unit" from a text for high school juniors. In the first such unit, the student has been asked to study his own personality for "admirable" and not so admirable traits. Now, later in the text, he hears the story of Art, who at first was going to pocket the change for five dollars, given to him by mistake by an absent-minded drugstore owner in return for a one-dollar bill. Only the frowns and pregnant hints of his classmates have finally made him return the money:

> "Do you know what makes him that way?" wondered Virginia.
> "Yes, partly," Joe answered. "I lived next door to him when we were little. His dad was always tough with him, cuffing him around. When Art was fifteen, he started to cuff back. Now the only one he's really nice to is his mother. He would do anything for her, but his dad made him believe you have to be tough."
> "Gosh," said Virginia, "my parents have given me so much love all my life. They just never let me down."
> "Well," Joe commented, "I take human nature as it comes. I guess I'm ready for the worst, but I'm always hoping for the best. Let's ask Art to ask Margie to the dance, and we'll all go together. What do you say?"
> "Sure," said Virginia enthusiastically. "Maybe he will believe in us yet."[8]

If the editors were not English teachers, one might be able to forgive them for thus reinforcing soap-opera stereotypes. (Tough fathers breed delinquents; if a boy loves his mother he can't be all bad; all will turn out for the best if you're "nice" to people.) What is basically wrong here is that the "story," anonymous and *ad hoc*, lacks the authenticity and substance to illuminate the kind of question the editors have in mind. ("Is a boy like Art evil or good when he is born, or was Art's disposition shaped by his environment?") Furthermore, the student is ostensibly asked for his honest reactions, even though the story and the questions and exercises that follow it are clearly slanted in favor of the editors' own *Reader's Digest* morality. ("'But you're just kidding, aren't you, Art?' asked Virginia, her brown eyes soft and calm.")

[8] Don M. Wolfe, Ellen M. Geyer, *et al., Enjoying English 11,* 3rd ed. (Syracuse: The L. W. Singer Company, Inc., 1960), pp. 46–47.

Such a text merely demonstrates, at the expense of our true objectives, the difference between made-to-order prose and "the truly written word": the one blurs, befogs, flatters, and reassures; the other sharpens, explores, disturbs. When the same text builds a unit around the theme that "a handicap is an opportunity for self-development," one can only hope that teachers and students alike will recognize its superficiality. When a text on one page teaches spelling and on the next "ideals of friendship," the editors need to be reminded that ethical standards cannot be furnished like recipes in a cookbook.

As Jacques Barzun says in *Teacher in America*, "it is not possible by fiddling with vague topics to insure or even to increase the dissemination of virtue."[9] No self-respecting school will offer a course in "Americanism," for instance, that is not a solid exploration of what was felt and thought and said by great Americans from Thomas Jefferson, James Madison, and Benjamin Franklin to Abraham Lincoln, Woodrow Wilson, and Franklin Roosevelt. Instead of encouraging students to talk glibly about what it means to be American, such a course will explore the religious and political configurations of colonial America, the role of European political and philosophical thought in shaping the consciousness of the new nation, the major political and moral crises of the nation's history. In short, the true course in Americanism is the kind of solid program in American history that illuminates our present institutions, ideals, commitments, and predicaments. History, if taught as the history of our ideas and our culture, is a truly humane and liberalizing discipline and therefore a cornerstone of any curriculum designed to provide education as well as mere training. Another such cornerstone is the discipline of English, provided that it is allowed to develop its full humane and liberalizing potential.

In recent years, there has been a widespread reaction against progressive education and all its works. Insofar as this reaction means insistence on solid subject-matter competence of the teacher and sustained intellectual effort by the student, it is to the good. Insofar as it encourages a sink-or-swim attitude, it is bad. As Jacques Barzun says,

> Progressive education in this country, if it has done nothing else, should forever be honored and given thanks for insisting on genuine, hand-to-hand teaching, as against the giving out of predigested hokum.[10]

At the same time, the very seriousness of the progressive educator's concern with genuine teaching, and with involving the student, has in practice led to a lack of purpose and direction. Many teachers agree that the student should actively participate in the process of learning. They do not agree, however, that the student should in any but an

9 Jacques Barzun, *Teacher in America* (New York: Doubleday & Company, Inc., 1955), p. 14.
10 *Ibid.*, p. 27.

advisory sense participate in the planning and evaluation of instruction. With Robert M. Hutchins, they "do not doubt that the educational profession is better qualified to say what children should study than the children themselves."[11] The teacher of English should realize that his students cannot assign priorities within his subject matter in any really informed way. Nor can they meaningfully discuss the objectives of a contemplated unit of study, the feasibility of a suggested approach. In evaluating work done, the student is not in a position to decide whether the difficulty he encountered was a result of his own limitations, inherent in the subject matter, or related to the method or personality of the teacher. We do not train our students in democracy by urging them to make decisions beyond their competence. The intelligent student easily recognizes the leading questions and other hints by which the "democratic" teacher steers the students' choices. In the classroom, as in the faculty conference, progressive educators have too often extolled the right to democratic decision while nudging people toward "co-operation." As a group of skeptical observers concluded:

> We have seen students allowed to go on proposing various problems until one came up that met the teacher's fancy. We have seen lists of objectives chosen after discussion by consensus of the students, which looked to be almost indistinguishable from those on the teacher's previously prepared lesson plan. . . .
>   The dull student is thus simply deluded, whereas the keen student is likely to be left with the understanding that the best way to make democracy work is to rig the elections.[12]

The teacher of English, then, will on a number of points be in sympathy with modern educational philosophy while registering some important reservations. First of all, he insists on the necessity for focus. Stress on the student's whole personality cannot be allowed to lead to a scattering of interest, to a miscellaneous schedule of unrelated activities where one thing is as important or unimportant as another. Instruction must be protected against frequent interruption by activities that are only peripherally educational. Extracurricular interests should as far as possible be pursued on extracurricular time.

As regards the clearly curricular, there must be a distinction between the essential and the optional, the indispensable and the merely desirable. There must be a clear priority for knowledge and skills that the educated citizen of a free society cannot afford to be without. Students must be able to give a number of important subjects their concentrated attention. In Whitehead's words, "The result of teaching small parts of a large number of subjects is the passive reception of disconnected ideas, not illumined with any spark of vitality."[13]

---

11 Hutchins, *The University of Utopia*, p. 58.
12 Kitzhaber, Gorrell, and Roberts, *Education for College*, pp. 101–02.
13 Whitehead, *The Aims of Education*, pp. 2–3.

Stress on focus is thus closely related to a second major point: The teacher of English will be aware of the role of **structure** in the student's learning. He will try to develop in his students a feeling for the internal coherence of his subject. He will try to develop their "eye for the whole chessboard, for the bearing of one set of ideas on another."[14] *More important than making things palatable for the student is giving him the feeling that the subject as taught by his instructor makes sense.* This feeling cannot be conveyed in a course that takes up one interesting idea today and examines a topic of current concern tomorrow. The teacher has a feeling of control over his subject because it is structured in his own mind: It is classified and subdivided according to its history, according to divisions inherent in its substance, according to the logic underlying its theoretical assumptions. Some of this feeling of control the student must begin to share. He must experience the intellectual rewards of systematic exploration. He must share the gradual illumination that results from reducing a bewildering subject to order.

Third, the teacher of English will put the emphasis on what the teacher does in the classroom rather than on what he says at a teachers' conference. He will emphasize **practice** rather than theory. What most damages modern educational philosophy in the eyes of the critically inclined is that, like other orthodoxies, it has long since become ritualistic. Certain catchwords have been repeated endlessly at meetings and in journals. Terms like *challenging, purposeful, dynamic, vitalize, unique, rewarding, insights,* and *values* have become empty through overuse. Concepts like "incremental learning," "integrated programs," "democratic participation," "process rather than product," and the demand for change in a "complex and fast-moving age" have become clichés. Generally, modern educators theorize too much and teach too little. A generation of American teachers has been conditioned to accept the view that "it is an intellectualization about method for which the teacher must strive—an intellectualization placing theoretical concerns central in his viewpoint."[15] Even beginning teachers are asked to formulate purposes and objectives, to experiment and assess and evaluate, and to reassess and re-evaluate. The implication is that to be successful the teacher must be an articulate, if not voluble theorist. Inevitably, the teacher begins to look, not for what somehow or other seems to work in his own classroom, but for what bears public inspection, rationalization, and justification. In too many schools, teachers are made to worry about formulating the "demonstrable value" and the "anticipated outcomes" of something that their training, their experience, and their schooled intelligence tell them is worth doing.

[14] *Ibid.,* p. 18.
[15] Walter Loban, Margaret Ryan, and James R. Squire, *Teaching Language and Literature: Grades 7–12* (New York: Harcourt, Brace & World, Inc., 1961), p. 6.

Though a teacher should certainly think about his work, he should not become nervously self-conscious about it. He should be able to reconsider practices that have become habit without feeling the pressure never to "teach the same course twice." Above all, he should be able to develop his own style and personality as a teacher without being made to conform to a predetermined pattern.

The teacher of English can work best in a school operated according to an educational philosophy that combines the virtues, and avoids the defects, of traditional and modern views of education. Such an outlook stresses on the one hand respect for the teacher's authority and emphasis on subject matter and intellectual achievement. It requires on the other hand the concern with the student's interest, readiness, and participation that keeps learning from becoming a mere façade. It places more emphasis on successful practice than on theory. It places less emphasis on clearly formulated objectives than on how successfully a teacher responds to his students and makes them respect his subject.

Sequence and Articulation

Many of the conditions that help determine the effectiveness of instruction in English are beyond the teacher's control. He typically has little control over the composition of his class and over their previous training in his field. In a system of quasi-universal education with often only halfhearted attempts at grouping students according to ability, the range of aptitude and competence in any given class is likely to be wide. As Joseph Mersand observes of the typical secondary school:

> Any course of study at best can interest, meet the needs, and stimulate only a fraction of the class. The slow students will never meet the "minimum essentials" despite exhortation, threat, or punishments. The bright students, on the other hand, have met them several years before in the fifth or sixth grade.[16]

Though individual schools and districts have sequential programs, there is little of the kind of statewide or nationwide co-ordination that would protect a hypothetical student from encountering a "review of grammar" and Stephen Crane's *The Red Badge of Courage* in every year from his freshman year in high school through his freshman year in college. The teacher attuned to the American system, or, as the wags have it, non-system of education soon learns to take little for granted and to treat most linguistic and literary subjects as though he were starting from the beginning.

The duplication of effort that results from this lack of system is the price American teachers pay for escaping the dead hand of bureaucratic

16 'If Articulation Succeeds—A Cautionary View," *The CEA Critic*, XXIII (December, 1961), Supplement, 11.

regulation that rests on their colleagues in more orderly societies. Nevertheless, insofar as he has a voice in the adoption of textbooks and syllabi, the teacher must exert his influence to help establish or preserve patterns that alleviate the uncertainties resulting from a general lack of sequence and articulation. In their most practical form, such efforts may result in informal consultation among the staff of a department to prevent a student from being assigned a book like Hardy's *The Mayor of Casterbridge* in three successive general-education courses in English. However, the profession will in the coming years be increasingly engaged in efforts to develop coherent and systematic curricula on a larger scale.

In participating in these efforts, the teacher of English can take advantage of a number of current trends. First, public opinion has in the last decade or so veered sharply toward favoring hard, concentrated work in "basic" or "fundamental" academic fields. *In the present climate of opinion, there need be nothing defensive or apologetic about attempts by English teachers to construct sequential curricula around solid materials clearly relevant to their discipline.* Their first step should be to "eliminate from the English program all material and activities not directly related to the study of English—such things as orientation to high school, instruction in library use, advice on choice of careers."[17]

Second, the proportion of high school graduates that go on to some form of higher education has continued to rise. This trend helps the English teacher counteract the illiberal division of the student body into vocationally oriented terminal students and intellectually oriented academic students. At its extreme, such a division leads to the false pride of the intellectual, and the smug anti-intellectualism of the "practical" man, experienced in countries where the higher levels of education are restricted to a cultural elite. Providing at least a rudimentary liberal education for the "terminal" student is at least as crucial to the success of our common cultural and political enterprise as the training of Ph.D.'s in language and literature. Besides, there is an obvious flaw in the assumption that

> students at their entrance into high school may be divided into two groups, (a) those who are going to college, and (b) those who are not. For the most part this simply is not true, and to the degree that it is, the distinction results less from the native ability of the student than from the financial standing of the parent. There are, of course, a few students who enter high school with such brilliant social and intellectual gifts that they are clearly marked for leadership; and there are others so obviously handicapped that there is little hope for their future development. But what will happen to the great majority of students who enter high school cannot be certainly predicted. Most of them can be educated. How they develop in the future will depend in significant part on the education they receive in high school.

17 Kitzhaber, Gorrell, and Roberts, *Education for College*, p. 92.

At any rate, whatever the student's future prospects,

> it is especially important to provide opportunity for intellectual and fully-human development for those students whose home environment or early schooling has denied them educational opportunities which more fortunate children have received.[18]

In assuming these responsibilities, the teacher should not deceive himself concerning the nature of his task. If English is going to be part of a liberal education for all students, he must concern himself with the problems posed by the differences in their backgrounds and abilities. He must ask himself what kind of study and practice will take them from where they are, closer to where he wants them to be. This question cannot be answered by a decision to "give them only the best." The person committed to raising standards must decide whether he aims at raising the level of the student or simply the level of a class or institution. The latter can be achieved without expenditure of teaching talent by screening out students of low previous achievement.

Our basic problem is to get the student, such as he is, to participate in solid work in materials properly representing the discipline of English. To reach this aim, we must proportion the difficulty of our materials so that the satisfaction of difficulty overcome does in itself become one of the major rewards of the student's work. When the excessive difficulty of the materials offered too often deprives the student of this satisfaction, he develops a "Teacher, tell me" attitude. This attitude is fatal to true progress. The satisfaction of difficulty successfully faced and overcome helps to make education self-motivating and self-directed. It is an essential motive in the work of the writer producing a piece of prose; it is part of the reward for the reader of a demanding or unconventional book.

In planning for progressively more substantial work in English throughout the student's schooling, teachers must for better or for worse rely on their own experienced judgment. Recent surveys of research bearing on meaningful sequence in work in language and literature have emphasized the questions that remain unanswered rather than any solid consensus based on experimental evidence. They have expressed the hope that in the future teachers of English at all levels will collaborate with their colleagues in education and psychology "to relate our English curriculum to the typical capacities of children and youth of different ages and differing abilities, so that the curriculum in English will not ignore the principles of continuity and development that are apparently

---

[18] Report of the Modern Language Association Commission on Trends in Education, "The English Language in American Education," in *Issues, Problems, & Approaches in the Teaching of English*, ed. George Winchester Stone, Jr. (New York: Holt, Rinehart & Winston, Inc., 1961), pp. 143–45.

so important to progressive learning."[19] In the meantime, teachers and administrators must to a considerable extent base their work toward continuity on their own observation of what they can do with their students.

For instance, grammar must ultimately deal with structures of considerable complexity. In the absence of conclusive experimental evidence, the teacher must empirically form an estimate of how age and intelligence affect the student's ability to distinguish consciously the structures he unconsciously uses. Obviously, students will learn to recognize the various simple sentence patterns before they learn to identify the various kinds of substitution and expansion that transform them into more complex statements. A related but separate question is how severely the student's age and intelligence limit the size and sophistication of the terminological apparatus that the teacher can profitably employ. The teacher at any level will try hard to keep **terminology** from becoming a barrier to understanding rather than an instrument of efficient communication. On the one hand, he knows how opaque many technical terms remain to his students. Yet he also knows how vague and inefficient instruction becomes when instead of *preposition* he must say, "You know, the little words we use to tie nouns to a sentence." Rather than merely take for granted a set of terms that over many years have become second nature to him, such a teacher will welcome the efforts of textbook authors to make terminology as apt and self-explanatory as possible. When a textbook author after extensive consultation with teachers and experimental use with students replaces *predicate noun* and *predicate adjective* with the more self-explanatory *linked noun* and *linked adjective,* he deserves something better in return than the incredulous indignation of the teacher who finds established routine changed in however minute detail. Generally, the teacher at the next higher level of instruction will be more grateful for a few terms and concepts, fully understood and reinforced by varied repetition and practice, than for a mass of knowledge that remains half-digested.

Similar considerations affect the teacher's strategy in teaching literature. He can establish empirically that many students respond to poetry and fiction with a strong narrative emphasis before they respond to thematic implications other than those clearly spelled out as a "moral." He can attempt to gauge the amount of analysis the average adolescent will tolerate without becoming alienated from literature altogether. On the one hand, the teacher must introduce his students to "the distinguishing features of each kind of writing and the handles by which he can get hold of the forms and talk about them." On the other hand, he must

---

[19] Erwin R. Steinberg, ed., *Needed Research in the Teaching of English* (Proceedings of a Conference Held at Carnegie Institute of Technology, May 5–7, 1962), p. 20.

keep the study of terminology from becoming mere barren classification. Generally, the student's program in English should develop purposefully over the years, "always within his capacity for understanding, but offering him the pleasures and challenges of stretching his mind."[20]

This requirement for gradual development must be weighed against the need for doing justice to the internal coherence of the subjects studied. In allocating his time, or in constructing a syllabus, the teacher must make possible the intellectual satisfaction that results when study is sustained enough to allow different aspects of a subject to reinforce and illuminate each other. Any subject of any importance remains confusing, difficult, and "uninteresting" until skillful teaching begins to disentangle some of its complexities. The reward of intellectual effort comes at the point where confusing elements begin to fall into place. It is from this point of view that linguists have in recent years objected to "the annual rehash" of **grammar** that is "common from the seventh or eighth grade through the tenth, eleventh, or even freshman year in college." They have urged teachers to experiment with making the teacher of grammar both less scattered and less repetitious:

> A consistent, accurate, and realistic grammar, aimed at studying the dynamic aspects of language structure . . . can be presented and thoroughly learned in one year—perhaps in the eighth or ninth grade. Such a grammar is of about the same order of complexity and difficulty as algebra, and bears some resemblances to it which can be capitalized upon. It can also be prepared for in the earlier grades. But once taught it should be assumed, and not re-taught or extensively reviewed each year. If continued use is made of it in the subsequent teaching of literature and composition, review will not be needed.[21]

It is true that we must keep our students aware of the relations between the various areas of language study. Nevertheless, our teaching gains in effectiveness from clear focus on one or the other of these areas. One possible sequence that has been suggested would stress the history of the language in one grade, the social and regional aspects of usage in the next. It could then move on to vocabulary and semantics, "not with the aim of artificially increasing vocabulary, but with the idea of developing an understanding of the nature of meaning, the derivational and morphological relationships of words, and the reasons for vocabulary and semantic change."[22] Teachers will want to experiment to see where, and in units of what size and scope, these various areas of language study can most profitably be taught. Regardless of their decisions in detail, they

---

[20] Members of the Conference on Basic Issues in the Teaching of English, "An Articulated English Program: A Hypothesis to Test," *PMLA,* LXXIV (September, 1959), Part 2, p. 14.

[21] W. Nelson Francis, "The Study of Language and English Teaching," Steinberg, *Needed Research,* p. 41.

[22] *Ibid.*

will profit from recognizing that each of these areas has its own coherence and rationale.

Respect for the internal coherence of subject matter should affect the teacher's view of the relationship between grammar and **composition,** between the study of language and the teaching of writing. Clearly, our programs should be balanced and integrated in such a way as to leave the student with an improved command and understanding of language in its various aspects and uses. Just as clearly, these different aspects of language cannot and should not be kept in separate compartments. For instance, the teacher will have occasion to refer to matters of punctuation in the study of grammar, of expository prose, and of imaginative litera-ture. But if they are to make sense, the conventions of punctuation must at some point be studied in orderly, coherent fashion. What we say about commas becomes meaningful by way of comparison and contrast with what we say about semicolons, colons, and dashes.

Generally, we do justice neither to grammar nor to writing if we treat grammar piecemeal in connection with courses in composition or if we treat composition as a mere adjunct to courses in grammar. Grammar earns its place in the curriculum as the most tangible part of our study of an activity central in all human experience. An educated person should have some understanding of how language works as a signaling system, how it uses the major grammatical devices, and how recurrent gram-matical patterns underlie the great variety of utterances we encounter. This understanding will shed light on problems, and prevent erroneous views, in many other areas of education. It need not be justified in shortsighted practical terms. In fact, the practical value of grammar as a means of improving student writing is harder to establish and may be considerably more limited and indirect than is often assumed.

Grammar and rhetoric obviously overlap, because no one can write effective English prose who does not have a command of the English sentence. Effective use of language requires the control of "adult sentence patterns," the ability to "incorporate the complex patterns of sophisticated prose" into one's own patterns of thinking.[23] To promote the student's control of such patterns, the teacher can use a combination of four possible approaches:

1) He can *show* the students, by systematic analysis of complex sentences, what the resources of the language are. He can demon-strate the possibilities of coordination, subordination, variety.

2) He can have the students *practice* complicated patterns by having them construct sentences according to given formulas.

3) He can have the students *read* as much adult prose as possible,

23 Charlton Laird, "Structural Linguistics: Notes for a Devil's Advocate," *College English,* XXIV (November, 1962), 96.

agreeing that "I have never had a bad student of writing who had read adult prose omnivorously."[24]

4) He can have the student *write* as much as possible, and as purposefully as possible, on the assumption that practice in the expression of increasingly mature thought and attitude will lead to increasing flexibility and resourcefulness of expression.

Of these four, the most crucial are the student's reading and writing, just as in the child's learning to speak the crucial elements are his listening and speaking. Analysis, "applied grammar," makes the student's reading more fruitful by making him respond to the grammatical variety and complexity of good prose. At the same time, it can, if overdone, make the student's writing not just conscious but self-conscious, introducing an artificial element of deliberate patterning and choice. Drill develops habits; it makes for ease and skill. At the same time, it can, if overdone, kill motivation by shifting the emphasis away from writing as a purposeful activity, as an attempt to get down on paper what one wants to say.

All this merely amounts to saying that grammar will be central in work focused on language and secondary in work focused on writing. *Much debate over the role of grammar in composition programs can be avoided if curricula and syllabi allow for both work in grammar and work in composition.* Generally, the more concrete and tangible areas of language study offer themselves as suitable subjects for students with relatively limited experience. Robert Hutchins once said that "subjects that cannot be understood without experience should not be taught to those who are without experience."[25] Though even the more tangible areas of language study become fully meaningful only as the student's range of experience broadens, there is much in these areas that can be directly taught and that can be concretely observed, even by the high school freshman, in everyday language use. On the other hand, though students should receive instruction in writing throughout their high school years, mature writing depends on a more or less adult range of experience and a sensitivity to problems of responsibility and purpose. As a rule, the freshman in college is just beginning to develop the kind of maturity that is required for a full understanding of the more serious concerns of rhetoric. When colleges attempt to delegate all instruction in composition and rhetoric to the high schools, they encourage writing that is not so much mature as precocious. Insofar as it is desirable to indicate major emphases for the study of language in high school and college, we should agree with Sumner Ives that "Ideally, matters of

24 *Ibid.*, p. 97.
25 Hutchins, *The University of Utopia,* p. 56.

structure and usage belong in the graded levels, and the primary attention in college should be on rhetoric."[26]

Generally, then, constructing a language program that is marked by both gradual development and internal coherence is not without difficulty. The same is true for programs in literature. Even more than the study of rhetoric, *the study of literature depends for its success on the student's general linguistic sophistication, range of experience, and degree of maturity.* The question is how we can best develop such sophistication and maturity through the student's reading of serious materials to which he can respond with both profit and pleasure.

In phrasing the question in this fashion, we have already ruled out the self-defeating approach to literature through nonliterary materials. We have ruled out the subliterary writers who deliver fun, uplift, and adventure. On the other hand, we have made the crucial point that literary sophistication must be *developed*. To judge from the autobiographical testimony of writers and critics, lovers of literature often pass through a period when their reading in voluminous rather than technically demanding. Typically, they pass through *Robinson Crusoe* and *Tom Sawyer* before they reach Henry James; they read *Pilgrim's Progress* before they come to appreciate *Lycidas*.

If our own experience does not lead us to make the obvious application to teaching, the history of style will: The bracing ironies, the yoking together of disparate elements, and the toughly involuted forms of Donne's poetry have their full original appeal for a reader for whom the bittersweet wistfulness and the formal perfection of the Petrarchan sonnet, through too frequent repetition, have just begun to cloy. This does not mean that the teaching of **poetry** must be chronological: A student is being prepared to appreciate Marvell's "Definition of Love" or "To His Coy Mistress" if for the present we have him dwell on E. B. Browning's "How Do I Love Thee" and Edna St. Vincent Millay's "What Lips My Lips Have Kissed." To make this kind of preparation possible, the teacher may at times have to overcome his condescension toward his own earlier favorites. It is doubtful that a teacher can effectively interest young people in poetry if he was not, during a now mercifully forgotten adolescent stage, able to luxuriate in E. A. Poe's "The Raven" or Sidney Lanier's "The Marshes of Glynn." It is doubtful that we can make the student follow the subtler rhythms of T. S. Eliot's "Prufrock" if we cannot make him respond first to the more luxuriant verse of Tennyson's "Ulysses" or Whitman's "Out of the Cradle Endlessly Rocking."

It is true that the poetry most accessible to the student in style and

26 "Grammar and the Academic Conscience," *College English,* XXIV (November, 1962), 98.

form is often remote to him in setting and theme. Schools are prone to the kind of cultural lag that made Scott's "The Lady of the Lake" and Tennyson's "Passing of Arthur" staple fare long after the fashions that had made them popular had passed. But much poetry from Burns and Blake to Housman and Hardy combines accessibility with relevance to general human experience and relative timelessness of setting. Among the moderns, E. A. Robinson, the early Yeats, Robert Frost lack the forbidding technical difficulty of many other twentieth-century poets.

Trying to translate these observations into a sequential, cumulative literature program, the teacher is hampered by obvious considerations of prestige. There is a world of difference between opening a conversation with "We were reading Wallace Stevens last week" or with "We've been on Tennyson lately." These prestige factors operate both in favor of the sophisticated moderns and the difficult classics. When they are allowed, as they traditionally have been, to operate in favor of the classics, we must guard against self-deception. Suppose that in order to expose our high school freshmen to the best and most significant we decide to make them read a Shakespeare play. After various plays have been ruled out as too adult, too difficult, too demanding, we settle on *Midsummer Night's Dream*. The question then is whether we are really offering our students the most significant or rather a minor play that makes a delightful evening's entertainment for adults steeped in Greek mythology and in the conventions of English Renaissance literature. As one teacher observed, high school freshmen "get *Midsummer Night's Dream* because it is, by pure chance, free of profanity and other taboos."[27]

Even when the play in question is more representative, as is *Julius Caesar* or *Romeo and Juliet* or *Macbeth,* the difficulties involved are often underestimated. The teacher must realize that in his own reading of Shakespeare he brings to bear everything he has ever learned as a full-time professional student of the language and its literature. Even so, there are few extended passages he can read without calling on the footnotes of Kittredge, G. B. Harrison, and other patron saints of Shakespearean scholarship for help. Just the linguistic barrier between Shakespeare's Elizabethan English and the high school student is roughly comparable to that between Chaucer's Middle English and the college English major. In ten lines chosen at random, the student must deal with *nay, dotage, musters, tawny front, reneges all temper;* he must grapple with metaphor and hyperbole in "o'erflows the measure," "glowed like plated Mars," "turned the office and devotion of their view," and "burst the buckles on his breast." All this in a passage that is both an example of casual conversation and an essential part of the exposition of the play. Shakespeare is comparable to the most difficult modern poetry

27 Daniel Albright, "An Organic Curriculum for English," *The English Journal,* LII (January, 1963), 19.

in boldness of metaphorical implication and in density, that is, frequency and difficulty, of allusion. His frame of reference is that of a familiarity with ancient history, literature, and mythology of which the high school student can take no part for granted.

Obviously, everything the student learns about the early stages of the language, about both English and ancient history, and about Greek mythology is all to the good. In an *introduction* to literature, however, *philological and historical study should not loom so large as to obscure the central purpose: to make the student respond to the power, the structure, the characteristic language of a literary work.* Teachers of the classics did neither Vergil nor poetry a service when they used the *Aeneid* as a vehicle for instruction in the rudiments of Latin.

Even where specifically literary matters are concerned, Shakespeare is bigger than the analytical and terminological frame that the teacher in the early years of high school is beginning to supply. The complexities and ambiguities of Shakespeare's work tend to upset the preliminary generalizations about literature that students in the early years of high schools should just be attempting. There may be some virtue in giving the student a first preliminary acquaintance with classics to be studied more thoroughly at a later and more mature stage. But there is also a danger that students will develop the habit of skimming blithely over passages that present knotty linguistic and critical problems. Investigators like I. A. Richards, in *Practical Criticism,* have tried to convince us of the amount of just plain misreading that superficially trained students are guilty of even when confronted with fairly conventional texts.

Our first task as teachers of literature is to convince the student that serious literature speaks not only to his teachers but to him. In the introduction to **drama,** we should look for plays taking place in an environment whose assumptions and tensions are meaningful to the student, whose characters respond to motives and standards he can understand. Depending on the level and emotional maturity of the class, we can choose among such plays as Thornton Wilder's *Our Town,* Arthur Miller's *All My Sons,* Tennessee Williams' *The Glass Menagerie,* Lorraine Hansberry's *A Raisin in the Sun.* Here the student will recognize a world in which the desire for recognition and success is a painfully nagging daily reality. He will find conflicts deriving from the tension between a younger generation and the older one by which it feels itself misunderstood. The language spoken will be idiomatic modern American, leaving language barriers to be erected *after* the student has developed the incentive and the perseverance to scale them.

Furthermore, the student, in his writing and in class, will feel free to *react*—to criticize, to object, to applaud. A genuine, living relationship with literature requires more than passive admiration. In seeing a play, we may at one point be delighted and exultant, and at another resistant, skeptical, or offended. Obviously, this kind of relationship cannot develop in a classroom where "The Bard can do no wrong" is written in large invisible letters on the blackboard. Even where Shakespeare is taught this side idolatry, it is difficult to convince the high school freshman or sophomore that his own reactions could be meaningful and to the point. A student whose father runs a pipe factory can write a substantial paper trying to argue that Arthur Miller's portrait of businessmen is in some significant way limited, or stereotyped, or one-sided. But a Jewish student cannot question the prevailing critical view of the non-antisemitism of *The Merchant of Venice* without rattling all the skeletons in the academic closet. Both student and teacher need considerable experience with dramatic conventions and Elizabethan literature before they can tackle the question of how they are supposed to react to Antonio, how to Shylock, and how to the rewarding of the virtuous and the punishment of the villains at the end of the play.

Even an introductory program need not be narrowly contemporary and provincial. Plays by John Galsworthy, Henrik Ibsen, and G. B. Shaw place the student in a world not far removed from their own world of middle-class values, while at the same time questioning its possible shortcomings and rigidities. Again, Ibsen is more teachable than, say, Chekhov, because Ibsen's milieu is often a society shaped by competition and a cult of personal success, as for instance in *The Master Builder*. By contrast, Chekhov's *The Three Sisters* evokes a world of deteriorating aristocratic values for which the student must gradually develop interest and understanding. Generally, even the student impatient with the lyricism of poetry and the elaborateness of fiction will respond to the clash of opposed purposes and values in plays from *Antigone* to *Death of a Salesman*. The teacher should make sure that remoteness of setting and difficulties of language and technique do not unduly obscure this basic dramatic appeal.

Like the teaching of poetry and drama, the teaching of **fiction** will be most profitable if it gradually builds up from the familiar to the strange, from the simple to the complex, from the plot-centered to the thematic and philosophical. Obviously, our students will be ready for the simple kinds of challenge and suspense found in the tales of Jack London before they are ready to delve into the ambiguities and digressions of Melville's pursuit of the white whale. They will be ready for John Steinbeck's "The Leader of the People" before they are ready for William Faulkner's "The Bear." They will be able to understand the conflicts of a story by Hemingway before they are able to penetrate the symbolic disguises of Franz Kafka.

By the same token, Ring Lardner's "Haircut" and Sherwood Anderson's "The Egg" will be meaningful to our students before the novels of Charles Dickens and George Eliot are. British nineteenth-century fiction is a rich source of good reading. What especially suits it for teaching purposes is that it stays close to the main-travelled roads of human experience, whereas modern novelists often explore some of its more obscure byways. Written for a large audience and often for magazine publication, Victorian and post-Victorian novels typically observe standards of intelligibility and more or less straightforward narrative development long since abandoned by the structure-conscious, experiment-prone modern writer. However, the Victorian novelist is treating a still semirural world, elaborately stratified and seen against the background of a complex political and religious history. This treatment must be presented to the student not with the attitude of "this is what fiction is" but of "this is what fiction was in nineteenth-century England."

In selecting fiction for his classes, the teacher of literature is constantly reminded of his basic problem: Great literature is written by adults for adults. Battling to interest his students in serious fiction, he will be on the lookout for books like William Golding's *Lord of the Flies,* that shape and transform the world of the adolescent the way most other novelists shape the world of the adult. There is a lesson for all English teachers in the success of Salinger's *The Catcher in the Rye,* "widely read by college students—often on an unassigned basis" and "a symbol of unrequired reading more meaningful to the high school student than the eternal verities of *Silas Marner.*"[28] *The Catcher in the Rye* runs counter to the stereotypes of gregariousness and false glamour to which experts on the teenage market kowtow. Its treatment of sex is miles apart from the keyhole sensationalism of *Peyton Place.* Its wistful irony and quixotic kindness is the opposite of the unrelenting moronic brutality of much popular entertainment. Yet for many of our students, this is the one book of "genuine literary respectability" and "legitimately within the province of the English teacher insistent on quality"[29] that they have read without prodding and "assignments." For our students, if not always for their teachers and parents, it has caught "the very note and trick, the strange irregular rhythm of life"; it has succeeded in the attempt whose strenuous force, according to Henry James, "keeps Fiction upon her feet."

In planning the students' introduction to literature, the teacher must soberly contemplate the statistical chances that his charges will grow up to join a large population of adult nonreaders. Whatever he does, his work cannot miraculously bring solvency to our vanishing bookstores and prosperity to our serious writers. However, it can at least be realistically and single-mindedly devoted to its central aim: to strengthen the

---

28 Fred H. Marcus, *"The Catcher in the Rye: A Live Circuit," The English Journal,* LII (January, 1963), 1.
29 *Ibid.*

student's interest in serious literature. If he is to be effective in pursuing this aim, the teacher must refuse to be influenced by ulterior considerations.

First, the teacher should not allow himself to be swayed by superficial considerations of prestige, by a desire to impress his colleagues. In trying to introduce his students to the true complexities of literature, he should never seem to be deliberately cultivating the esoteric, the willfully obscure. In trying to make the reading of his students balanced and meaningful, he should not be distracted by a false opposition of modern literature and the classics. The teacher is concerned with our literary heritage not as a legacy from a vanished past but as a living part of our culture. He will try to develop in his students a sense of tradition, but

> the sense of tradition will remain incomplete and may never come into active relation with the student's personal life unless he is led to see that the works produced in his own generation themselves grow from tradition, and that some of them may in the future take their own place among the classics. Then too, it is sound pedagogy to move frequently from the known to the unknown, from John Steinbeck to Dickens, from the student's own idiom and the life with which he is familiar to the idiom and the life of more remote times.[30]

Second, the teacher must resist pressures toward limiting his students' reading to the inoffensive, the "wholesome," the inspirational. He must resist the constant temptation to eliminate all **controversial** reading. Obviously, in high school and to a lesser extent in college, the teacher's selection of reading materials is complicated by the fact that much great literature is candid on subjects on which our culture is evasive. Given the ambiguities of our culture concerning sex, the teacher need not blame himself if a passage that seems honest, or tender, or moving, when read in private becomes embarrassing when discussed in the classroom. Depending on his ability to stay in control in such a situation, every teacher must in this regard write his own script. What he cannot afford to do, however, is to restrict the reading of his students to books faithfully mirroring standards of middle-class gentility. We need to be reminded that even writers like George Eliot, who now seems eminently safe, in their time took "a somewhat unorthodox view of human affairs."[31]

If the teacher simply removes from the reading list all books that in some way fail to conform to a hypothetical public norm, he confirms his students in the suspicion that literature is one of the devices by which adults try to insulate adolescents from the real world. For instance, whatever the other merits or demerits of Aldous Huxley's *Brave New World*

---

[30] School and College Conference on English, April, 1942; "Report of the Literature Committee," Stone, *Issues*, p. 52.

[31] Edwin H. Sauer, *English in the Secondary School* (New York: Holt, Rinehart & Winston, Inc., 1961), p. 161.

and George Orwell's *1984,* our students read them with the feeling that these are real books for real people. What is more, these books introduce the student to some of the crucial political and cultural problems of our time. It is a sad defeat for the English teacher when *1984* is locked up in the library's poison cabinet because with great candor and justice it traces the Puritan, kill-joy tendencies of modern totalitarianism, its hostility to what makes life livable and people human.

Similar considerations apply to books controversial on political, ideological, or religious grounds. Again, works now safely enshrined as classics are, when read and understood, as subversive of oversimplified and complacent norms as the work of any contemporary. Charles Dickens is unrelenting in his attacks on the nineteenth-century abuses of the free-enterprise system. Mark Twain's treatment of prevailing orthodoxy is as grimly disillusioned as Voltaire's *Candide* was in its time. The sharpened perception of the great writer, like the independent moral insight Thoreau describes in *Civil Disobedience,* "is essentially revolutionary, and does not consist wholly with anything which was." When reading a book, our students should not expect it to confirm them in their complacencies. They should expect it to sharpen their powers of observation, to enlarge their horizons, to broaden their sympathies.

Teachers of English do not serve their cause by stirring up avoidable controversy. It is just as true, however, that when unavoidable controversies arise, English teachers as individuals and as a profession have in the past not always spoken with the kind of emphasis and determination worthy of their aspirations and responsibilities.

Standards of Achievement

Whether in language or literature, variations in the standards of schools and in the abilities of students make it difficult to set up norms of achievement for different levels of instruction. Besides, in the past the setting up of minimum standards has often led teachers to concentrate on testable matters of language etiquette rather than to give their students a balanced program aimed at long-range objectives. Nevertheless, each teacher necessarily works with some rough standard of what, under favorable circumstances, students with neither outstanding gifts nor obvious handicaps should be able to accomplish.

1) *Study of language:* High school freshmen and sophomores should acquire a basic knowledge of the workings of grammar. They should recognize basic grammatical devices, such as word order, inflection, structure or function words, and intonation. They should be familiar with major word classes and various basic sentence types. *Emphasis should be not so much on their mastery of a definite scheme of classifi-*

cation as on their familiarity and ease with the process of defining grammatical categories according to structure, form, and meaning. In its practical application, the grammatical terminology at their command should be adequate, for instance, for an understanding of basic conventions of punctuation. These conventions should be familiar to them, not as a pedantic inventory of miscellaneous rules, but as a means of setting apart sentences and clauses, indicating different kinds of links established by different kinds of connectives, and setting off various kinds of nonrestrictive and parenthetical material.

In their study of vocabulary resources, high school students should early become aware of the role of Greek and Latin roots, and of the extensive borrowings from French and other European languages. *They should be firmly aware of the many different meanings of individual words, and of the need for selecting the meaning that fits the context.* Though they should have developed a firm sense of the distinction between standard and nonstandard English in their earlier schooling, they should now acquire an understanding of its rationale, of its social and cultural dimension. They should know, and actively explore, such major variations in usage as dialect and slang.

High school juniors and seniors should be expected to understand some of the processes that lead from elementary grammatical building blocks to a fairly complex sentence. They should come to regard grammar, not as a body of knowledge enshrined for all times, but as a field in which, as in physics or psychology, research is vigorously in progress. They should become acquainted with the history of the language, so that historical knowledge can begin to illuminate such areas as spelling, grammar, vocabulary.

Juniors or seniors in high school should recognize the distinction between denotation and connotation. They should be familiar with such elementary logical problems as the relation between fact and inference, and differences in level of abstraction. They should be developing a sense for formal and informal varieties of standard English; they should recognize the limitations both of a clearly colloquial and of a stilted style. Ideally, the graduating senior should command the terminology needed in the reading and discussion of materials from a standard dictionary and a standard grammar.

One important function the freshman course in college can fulfill is to take stock of the student's previous work in language. It can relate his previous exploration of grammar, usage, and semantics to a coherent and mature perspective. More specifically however, the college freshman or sophomore should develop competence in three major areas. In semantics, he should be aware of the relations between referent and symbol and the way this relationship varies for different kinds and uses of language. In studying the relation between language and thought, he should acquire an understanding of the processes of induction and deduction and the major logical fallacies. In studying prose style, he should come to understand the role of stylistic elements ranging from variation or parallelism of sentence structure to the techniques of the satirist.

2) *Reading of expository prose:* High school freshmen and sophomores should be able to handle material comparable in difficulty to feature articles in *Life, Look,* or *Saturday Evening Post.* Not only should they read such material with adequate comprehension, but *they should be able to correlate information and opinions from different sources.* They should early be weaned from the habit of relying on *one* textbook or *one* encyclopedia. In the last two years of high school, our students should read with comprehension those articles in magazines like *Harper's, Atlantic,* or *The Reporter* that are not unduly technical or sophisticated. They should be able to discuss with reasonable maturity ideas and issues suggested by these articles. They should distinguish writing that relies on systematic presentation of material and detailed support of major points from writing that employs various irrational means of persuasion. The freshman and sophomore in college should read with comprehension, and some appreciation of stylistic nuance, prose comparable to that found in *Saturday Review, The American Scholar,* and *The New Yorker.* He should be aware of the writer's strategy, organization, and use of stylistic resources, as well as of his short-cuts, confusions of purpose, and unsubstantiated asides.

3) *Reading of imaginative literature:* High school freshmen and sophomores should be able to read with reasonable understanding and appreciation writers like Carl Sandburg, Rudyard Kipling, and John Steinbeck. High school juniors and seniors should be able to read and understand short stories by Ring Lardner and Willa Cather, novels by Sinclair Lewis. The college freshman and sophomore should be able to read and appreciate without more than token assistance fiction by Hawthorne, Conrad, Hardy. Needless to say, our most capable students will be far ahead of the average in their ability to read material of great technical sophistication. The bright high school senior will be ready for poems by E. E. Cummings, for Joyce's *A Portrait of the Artist as a Young Man,* for Shakespeare's *Hamlet.* The slow high school senior may not get far beyond John Masefield and O. Henry. However, even for the bright high school student there will be definite limits on how truly meaningful his reading can become without a corresponding range of more or less adult experience.

College teachers have often been tempted to draw up lists of major works that all high school students should have read. There is a danger that in practice such demands may merely reinforce the tendency toward dreary repetition of a few second-rate works by first-rate authors. More to the point are demands for early development on the part of the student of certain kinds of knowledge and sensitivity that help him to read with understanding and profit. The student's maturity in reading literature depends on his ability to recognize allusions to a common body of myth and legend. It depends on his ability to respond to the forms and conventions of different literary types or genres. It depends on his ability to reconstruct the historical context of a work both as part of a literary tradition and as part of a social and cultural setting. There has been considerable agreement among teachers working toward articulated English programs that emphasis on these different aspects of literature should be distributed roughly as follows:

> folklore, legend, myth—the web of literary reference in grades 1–6; literary works making use of such materials for specific artistic and cultural purposes in grades 7–9; wide reading to introduce the role of forms and conventions in literature and what constitutes them in grades 9–12; sequential presentation of the English and American literary heritage in college.[32]

The high school teacher adopting this rationale will not slight in his teaching the role of historical context. He will merely assume that for his students more important than knowing *about* authors and periods is knowing what to look for in a short story, a play, a lyric poem.

College teachers have at times blamed the high schools for not developing in students a solid and lasting interest in literature. It is not clear, however, that they themselves have been notably more successful. Too often, the required college course in literature has been the dead end of the student's literary education. By and large, college teachers of English have done little to institute and promote the kinds of courses for nonmajors that would capitalize on the potentially more mature response of upper-division and graduate students to serious reading. English departments should realize that

> for the non-major, elective courses should be available in writers, types of literature, and periods, in hopes that the permanent interest in reading and discussing, which his previous participation in English courses should have given him, may continue to be stimulated.[33]

4) *Composition and rhetoric:* The high school junior and senior should have completed the transition from simple autobiography, simple narrative, simple chronological organization, to writing that requires the independent marshaling of ideas. He should be able to organize a paper in accordance with the logical relations between data and inference, cause and effect, objection and refutation. He should be able to argue in balanced fashion the pros and cons of a not too complicated issue. Even though much of his writing should draw on personal experience and

---

[32] "An Articulated English Program," *PMLA*, LXXIV, Part 2, 15.
[33] *Ibid.*

observation, *the emphasis should be on interpreting and correlating, rather than merely reporting, experience.*

College teachers of writing generally consider it premature for the secondary student to attempt a more ambitious kind of writing modeled on scholarly **research.** As one statewide group of college teachers concluded,

> The "research" paper is in general inappropriate in the secondary school. Genuine research requires synthesizing power and a kind of motivation which ordinarily do not develop until much later. To require such a paper, based usually upon extracts from encyclopedias, is therefore, at worst, to encourage the student to believe that he is conducting real research, and, at best, to deprive him of the time for the more fundamental kind of clear, fluent, and self-disciplined writing.[34]

Another group of college teachers made the same point in a more emphatic way:

> Where a scholar will bring enormous knowledge of a general field to bear on a small area within the field, the high school student is encouraged to invert the pyramid and to attack some mammoth question equipped with total ignorance. Thus he will write on such topics as "Labor Unions" or "Miracle Drugs" or "The Causes of the Russian Revolution." . . .
>
> Even so, the project might have some small value if it meant that the student read as widely as library facilities permitted on the Russian Revolution and reported his findings. But it almost never means this. What the student ordinarily reads is the article on Russia in the *Encyclopaedia Britannica.* And even *this* might have a dim usefulness if he reflected on the article and summarized it, but he doesn't usually. He usually just copies the paragraphs he judges to be pertinent, adds a transition here and there, prepares an ornate title page, and hands it in, enjoying the illusion that he has done research on Russia.[35]

Such observations confirm the skeptical observer in the suspicion that the so-called research paper often teaches the student little "except how to plagiarize and cut and paste."

How to introduce the student to the standards and procedures of genuine scholarship is a question that the colleges themselves have found difficult to answer. The conventional freshman research paper too often requires of a student lacking in relevant background the "manipulation of unknown quantities."[36] It makes his exploration of library resources a painfully inefficient search for material whose authoritativeness the student is often not equipped to judge. Admitting at least partial defeat, many teachers have in recent years settled for token research papers based on materials preassembled in **controlled research** texts. Thus, problems in

---

34 Representatives of English Departments in California colleges and universities, mimeographed statement on "High School Preparation in English."

35 Kitzhaber, Gorrell, and Roberts, *Education for College,* pp. 105–06.

36 Stephen O. Mitchell, "A Look at Controlled Research," *The CEA Critic,* XXIV (April, 1962), 1–3.

the correlation and evaluation of material from different sources can be demonstrated on the basis of reading shared by all students. Many a teacher will be happy neither with the aimlessness of the "free" research paper nor with the artificiality of the "controlled research" text. If so, he must take care to introduce his students to scholarship by way of topics and library materials clearly within their, and his, competence.

A Summary of Goals

What, to sum up, are the objectives of instruction in English? The teacher will know that successful work in English requires concentrated attention and sustained intellectual effort. The student must come to see that the material presented to him in English has its own rationale, its own principle of coherence. He must feel that what he learns in English, whether it is presented to him directly or worked up inductively, adds up and makes sense. Teacher and administrator must develop a respect for the integrity of subject matter, for the internal structure of what is being taught. It is thus that they can hope to motivate the students' learning at least in part not through reward and punishment but, in the words of Jerome S. Bruner, through "intrinsic rewards in the form of quickened awareness and understanding."[37]

At the same time, the goals of instruction in English cannot be defined narrowly or exclusively in intellectual terms. The study of language must make the student sensitive to the way language reflects attitude, emotion, purpose. Mature writing requires the student to examine and interpret his attitudes, to control and give disciplined expression to his feelings. Imaginative literature makes the student participate in the whole of human experience. *No instruction in English can be successful that ignores the student as a person.* More so than teachers in more conveniently limited fields, the teacher of English must try to do justice to the way in which ideas, emotions, and values interact and shade over into each other in human life.

Ultimately, the goal of all instruction in English is to make the student more mature in his understanding and use of language. He should become an alert observer of the workings of language, responsive to intention and nuance, not distracted in the attempt to communicate by irrelevent associations and preconceptions. He should learn to convey articulately and forcefully his knowledge, to formulate effectively and responsibly his thoughts and commitments. He should learn to respond fully to the power of literature to satisfy his need for imaginative participation, to impose an aesthetic order upon experience, to broaden his sympathies and develop his full potential as a human being.

[37] *The Process of Education* (Cambridge, Mass.: Harvard University Press, 1962), p. 50.

Because of the central role of language in human experience, English plays a central role in the student's general education. Teachers of English should not allow themselves to be distracted from this primary task. The high school teacher of English must resist having his work tied to the social sciences, to give it topical content, or to journalism and business English, to give it practical application. The college teacher must avoid treating his general-education classes in English as an introduction to his own scholarly specialty. From junior high school through graduate school, English teachers should provide progressively more substantial and demanding courses "valuable for *any and all* students."[38]

A PROGRAM FOR FURTHER STUDY

JOHN W. GARDNER, *Excellence: Can We Be Equal and Excellent Too?* New York: Harper & Row, Publishers, 1961. A Harper Colophon Book.

Sets up the full realization of individual promise as our educational goal and relates it fully to the assumptions that shape our society. Devoted to the theme that "it is possible to have excellence in education and at the same time to seek to educate everyone to the limit of his ability" and that "a society such as ours has no choice but to seek the development of human potentialities at all levels."

RONALD GROSS, ed., *The Teacher and the Taught: Education in Theory and Practice from Plato to James B. Conant.* New York: Dell Publishing Co., Inc., 1963. A Delta Book.

Important excerpts from the writings of educational theorists and reformers. Includes selections by Rousseau, Pestalozzi, John Dewey, Arthur Bestor, and Jerome S. Bruner. Editorial comments relate the selections to major trends and problems in education.

JAMES BRYANT CONANT, *The American High School Today: A First Report to Interested Citizens.* New York: McGraw-Hill Book Company, Inc., 1959.

Specific recommendations for the improvement of the American high school, based on a comprehensive view of the distinctive nature of American education and on the view that one major objective of the high school is to provide a general education for all future citizens. Written by a former president of Harvard University who knows both American and European education intimately, this study assumes that "American education must keep its eye on its own goals and be strong in its own terms."

ALBERT R. KITZHABER, ROBERT M. GORRELL, AND PAUL ROBERTS, *Education for College: Improving the High School Curriculum.* New York: The Ronald Press Company, 1961.

A discussion, eminently authoritative and in vigorous plain English, of the college-preparatory curriculum. Concerned with "the exact content of courses, the quality of textbooks, the preparation of teachers, the philosophies that the public schools exemplify and the influence of these philoso-

[38] "An Articulated English Program," *PMLA,* LXXIV, Part 2, 15.

phies on the curriculum." Based on the Portland (Oregon) High School Curriculum Study and written by three prominent college teachers of English.

GEORGE WINCHESTER STONE, JR., ed., *Issues, Problems, & Approaches in the Teaching of English.* New York: Holt, Rinehart & Winston, Inc., 1961.

A paperback collection, edited by the executive secretary of the Modern Language Association, of important articles on the content and teaching of English. Reprints the reports of a number of important national committees.

MATERIALS FOR ANALYSIS

A. In Ronald Gross's collection, *The Teacher and the Taught,* study the selections from Comenius, Rousseau, Pestalozzi, Dewey, and Counts. Discuss fully important common elements that would lead one to include these men among the precursors and initiators of modern education.

B. Study Plato's account of the early education of the guardians in Book III of *The Republic.* To what extent are Plato's questions about educational goals and methods relevant to today's schools? To what extent can or should the modern teacher model his answers on Plato's?

C. Study one of the following books, each in its own way representative of a major movement or countermovement in American education: 1) John Dewey, *Democracy and Education: An Introduction to the Philosophy of Education* (New York: The Macmillan Company, 1916; paperback reprint, 1961); 2) Harold Benjamin (J. Abner Peddiwell, pseud.), *The Saber-Tooth Curriculum and Other Essays* (New York: McGraw-Hill Book Company, Inc., 1939); 3) Robert M. Hutchins, *The University of Utopia* (Chicago: The University of Chicago Press, 1953); 4) H. G. Rickover, *Education and Freedom* (New York: E. P. Dutton & Co., Inc., 1960). Explain, illustrate, and discuss as fully as possible one important aspect of the author's definition of educational goals. Insofar as possible, try to discount polemical overstatement in order to form an objective estimate of the author's basic assumptions.

D. Magazines like *The Reporter, Harper's, The Atlantic,* and *Saturday Review* have in recent years published much vigorous criticism of American education. Find a recent article in this vein; identify and evaluate fully implied assumptions concerning the nature and purposes of education.

E. From your reading of literature, bring together salient accounts of schools or teachers that strongly shaped your own views of the nature and purposes of education. Discuss their implications for future teachers.

F. Write an autobiographical paper in which you discuss and evaluate the educational objectives implicit in your own early schooling and the degree to which these objectives were realized.

G. In recent years, numerous organizations and institutions have concerned themselves with the problem of developing sequential curricula in

English. Study a recently published outline of such a suggested curriculum. Discuss fully its rationale and implications.

H. Among classics that have been suggested for inclusion in basic reading lists for high school literature programs are Homer's *Odyssey*, Sophocles' *Antigone*, Euripides' *Medea*, Cervantes' *Don Quixote*, Shakespeare's *Macbeth*, Pope's *Rape of the Lock*, Coleridge's "The Rime of the Ancient Mariner," Jane Austen's *Pride and Prejudice*, and Henry James's *Daisy Miller*. Select one of these that you know exceptionally well. Discuss fully the difficulties and rewards you think it would offer the average or above-average high school student.

I. Discuss fully a recent novel that in your judgment combines high literary quality with exceptional relevance to adolescent interests and concerns.

J. Prepare an annotated list of ten standard literary selections that you found most meaningful or rewarding in your own experience as a student.

The subject matter of English is far-ranging and complex. Not infrequently, someone is assigned to teach it whose command of the subject matter is fragmentary or out-of-date. Too often, the net effect of the half-trained teacher's work is to perpetuate misconceptions about language and to prejudice the students against literature. To the extent that this is true, discussion of teaching method must remain academic. On the other hand, we cannot assume that once the teacher is competent in subject matter his teaching will take care of itself.

seven

Competent scholarship and good teaching are in many ways related, but they are not identical. The Big Name in graduate school who is too busy to teach his students is not a creation of academic folklore. Neither is the specialist who has retreated to one minor corner of literary history and cannot be bothered with what his students are thinking and reading. Neither finally is the graduate English major who finds the adjustment from advanced study to teaching at a much less advanced level a jolting and bewildering experience.

Method

What nevertheless makes it difficult to give the beginning teacher advice is that many different approaches to language and literature work in their own way for different teachers and students. People turn to literature for realism or fantasy, for insight or vicarious experience, for excitement or richly patterned sound. Any approach to literature that too early and too peremptorily suppresses the one or the other kind of interest is to be regretted. By the same token, no method, however fully endorsed by the experts, is likely to work for the teacher if it seems to cut off the sources of his own interest and satisfaction in his work. *English has to be taught with conviction.* There is no substitute for the teacher's ability to become absorbed in his subject, and to make it come to life for his students.

Even so, the prospective teacher need not feel that whim is king, that he should follow his inclinations wherever they might lead him. The beginning teacher is entitled to know the tried and true, and to profit from the mistakes of his elders. He needs some preliminary idea of what is and what is not likely to work with his students. Being warned of familiar problems and difficulties, he may be able to escape the kind of disillusionment that prematurely turns the enthusiastic first-year teacher into a routine performer of routine functions.

Lecture and Discussion

Once the teacher, the textbook author, or the curriculum committee has chosen the materials for a course, we can decide how to present them to advantage. The teacher's function is to mediate, to interpret, to translate. He must make his subject matter accessible in more than the physical sense; he must help his students absorb it in such a way that it becomes truly their own. For many a teacher of English, the model of such mediation between subject and students is an idealized composite version of some of his own experiences in college and graduate school. He would like to think of himself as a lecturer, not without prestige, addressing a receptive audience. He would like to see himself as an authority sharing his knowledge with students both well-qualified and appreciative. Some of the frustration that besets English teachers results from the contrast between this ideal and everyday reality. The answer lies in a sober appraisal of both the virtues and the limitations of the authoritative lecture as a means of instruction.

Certainly, the organized classroom presentation is one of the basic ways in which the teacher of English communicates with his students. In each major area of the discipline of English, there is a substantial body of material that is best presented in coherent segments, planned in advance, and presented without major interruption. A teacher discussing sentence structure will need opportunities to talk long and continuously enough to develop major relationships and fit them into some sort of general pattern. A teacher sketching the historical and cultural milieu of Tennyson and Browning will need leisure and scope to discuss such matters as industrialism, imperialism, the higher criticism, and Darwinian science. By concerning himself with the solidity of such presentations, the English teacher can correct the image of himself as a belletristic amateur long on opinion and short on information.

Furthermore, the lecture, whether or not it is a full hour-length talk, is the most direct way the English teacher has of demonstrating by example what he preaches about the effective use of language. It is his opportunity to show the difference between miscellaneous and perfunctory talk and organized discourse, brought to life by purpose and conviction. As Jacques Barzun says in *Teacher in America,*

> In some teachers a large class filling a sloped-up amphitheater brings out a wonderful power of emphasis, timing, and organization. The speaker projects himself and the subject. The "effects" are not laid on, they are the

meaningful stress which constitutes, most literally, the truth of the matter. This meaning—as against fact—is the one thing to be indelibly stamped on the mind, and it is this that the printed book cannot give.[1]

As in other kinds of teaching, part of the secret of successful lecturing is to know when to stop preparing. The lecture most likely to be a success is solidly structured in the form of notes without actually being written out in detail. It thus combines the cogency of systematic exposition with the spontaneity of delivery that results from thoughts being freshly phrased in front of the listener. Though perhaps based on study or research completed some time ago, it shows traces of recent re-examination and rethinking. By allusion to current trends or controversies in the field, it reassures the listener that it is in the full sense of the word a "live talk."

However, in English sooner than in other subjects, teaching reaches the point when the students' active participation becomes essential. Even in such an elementary matter as vocabulary study, what counts is whether the student learns to handle a new word competently in his own reading and writing. On a more general level, the student's control of language as a speaker and writer depends to a large extent on his ability to give substance and limits to abstract terms. For the teacher trying to help students develop such control, it is futile to provide the "right" definition of, for instance, *sportsmanship* or *fair play*. Instead, in class and in their writing, students must have a chance, first, to formulate their vague impressions and associations, and then, in the give-and-take of discussion or in the working out of a theme, to clarify and to focus them. Only thus can the teacher hope "to make definition seem important, to make it become not the process of 'looking up the word in a dictionary' but that of thinking the matter through."[2]

Here is a list of tentative definitions of *sportsmanship* that emerged from one representative class:

1. Sportsmanship is applauded by crowds at boxing events when the boxer allows his opponent to stagger to his feet before being smashed to the canvas again.

2. Sportsmanship is the quality of wanting to let another fellow have a chance. It is parallel to the ideal embodied in the Ten Commandments. Religion teaches a way of life that will always have the sportsman as a part of it.

3. Sportsmanship means playing a game according to the rules and obeying the instructions of the referee. If a player does not obey the rules, he is penalized.

1 *Teacher in America* (New York: Doubleday & Company, Inc., 1955), p. 38.
2 Harold C. Martin, "Writing and Thinking," in *Essays on the Teaching of English,* eds. Edward J. Gordon and Edward S. Noyes (New York: Appleton-Century-Crofts, Inc., 1960), p .166.

4. Sportsmanship is the ability to get along with one's fellowman and at the same time oppose him. It enables a player to congratulate an opponent who has just handed him a crushing defeat.

5. The American athlete is known for his high sense of sportsmanship. Sportmanship is hard to explain, but most people recognize it when they see it. It means being friendly, fair, just, and sincere.

6. In order to have good sportsmanship, a person must be able to mingle. For example, our fraternity is a closely knit group with everyone pitching in together to get things done.

7. Sportsmanship is a luxury. The gentleman hunter who hunts for amusement can afford to observe a sportsmanlike code in shooting animals. The hunter who has to find food for a starving family cannot afford to be particular about his methods.

8. Sportsmanship is the quality of being sportsmanlike. A sportsman, in other words, is the person who adopts a standard of sportsmanlike behavior and lives up to it.

9. Sportsmanship is the willingness to live up to the established traditions of a sport. Through the years, a certain kind of conduct has come to be expected of the players. A player is unsportsmanlike when he violates the traditions of the sport.

10. The most important ingredient in sportsmanship is courtesy. Consideration and restraint make the difference between a courteous player and a ruffian.

11. Sportsmanship means playing not in order to win but for the love of the sport. The sportsman who plays primarily for profit or for personal glory is not a sportsman in the true sense of the word.

12. Sportsmanship is a meaningless term because everybody can define it exactly as he pleases. If I call cheating on examinations a sportsmanlike act, then to me it is sportsmanlike, because I am entitled to my own definition.

As these possibilities are played off against each other in **class discussion,** the students in effect co-operate in clearing away the more vague and arbitrary elements suggested and in focusing on what can be agreed upon as substantial and clearly relevant. Students will soon eliminate the more woolly or peripheral suggestions (2, 5, and 6), the merely circular definitions (8). They are likely to agree that something more is involved than observing the rules (3). With a minimum of steering by the instructor, the discussion will come to concentrate on the crux of the matter: the element of restraint, of courtesy, of respect for the opponent; the "whatever-it-is" that imposes limits on unrestrained competitive impulse. In trying to pin down this quality, the students will realize for themselves the need for concrete and representative examples. True definitions—those that identify and illustrate a common quality—can then be distinguished from comments that suggest value judgments (1, 7). In the course of the discussion, the students learn something about the vagueness of common abstractions, the need for concrete reference, the relevance

and plausibility of examples, the difference between description and judgment—all with the crucial difference that instead of being *told* these
things they *discover* them in arguing out their own differences and confusions.

In the teaching of literature, what counts is the student's ability to
read, interpret, and judge for himself. He will never develop this ability
unless he is made to participate in the process of interpretation, and to
question interpretations offered by others. Again, *class discussion can
transform the tentative groping of the individual into a fruitful common
endeavor.* Here is a poem by Emily Dickinson with a range of reactions
that one might obtain from a class of high school seniors or college freshmen:

> Because I could not stop for Death,
> He kindly stopped for me;
> The carriage held but just ourselves
> And Immortality.
>
> We slowly drove, he knew no haste,
> And I had put away
> My labor, and my leisure too,
> For his civility.
>
> We passed the school, where children strove
> At recess, in the ring;
> We passed the fields of gazing grain,
> We passed the setting sun.
>
> Or rather, he passed us;
> The dews grew quivering and chill,
> For only gossamer my gown,
> My tippet only tulle.
>
> We paused before a house that seemed
> A swelling of the ground;
> The roof was scarcely visible,
> The cornice in the ground.
>
> Since then 'tis centuries, and yet
> Feels shorter than the day
> I first surmised the horses' heads
> Were toward eternity.

1. Emily Dickinson writes about death in a calm and uninhibited way, as
though it were just one of the occurrences of everyday life. Her presentation
of death is simple, not magnified as is quite often the case. First, death calls
whether or not one is ready. There is no hurry, though; there is time to
view life's passing incidents. Miss Dickinson talks about passing a school
where children are playing, about passing fields of gazing grain, and about
the setting sun. All of these things are part of one's everyday life, things one

remembers most vividly. In the fifth stanza, she talks about a house, conveying to us that the home is probably the most significant part of one's life.
Although death arrives, these things will be present in one's mind for an
eternity.

2. When I read the poem I get the idea that someone is near death. The
person has led a good life and has probably retired. He is waiting for death
to catch up with him. Before death arrives, the person takes an imaginary
ride in a carriage and takes in the highlights of his life. He passes a school
where children play, and this reminds him of his own youth. He also passes
a field of grain, which reminds him of his days as a farmer or of the time
when he was working to earn a living. Finally, death catches up with him, as
the setting sun indicates. The person is buried, the mound being the symbol
of a cemetery. The pause near the mound is probably the funeral service
held for him.

3. The poet regards Death as a person always present in the background of
life. Death knows "no haste," because once he has made his claim upon a
person the only goal is immortality. There is no hurry, the carriage of Death
always leads to that one goal. The carriage passes children playing happily.
Even though Death is in the background, life, carefree and gay, will continue
for them. Other things that are not disturbed by the thought of Death are
"fields of gazing grain," for they remain peaceful and serene. The setting
sun symbolizes the "twilight" or ending of life. The house that seemed a
swelling of the ground is the last sight which reminds the rider in the
carriage of life on earth. He takes a last look at these objects but still moves
slowly, though deliberately, toward eternity.

4. The poem gives an impression of calmness and serenity. After the writer
has been "kindly" picked up by death for immortality, their progress is slow
and orderly, as if there were no rush or limit on time. As soon as she enters
the chariot, her labor and her leisure—all worldly ambitions, pleasures, and
pursuits—are ended, and she is devoted entirely to death "for his civility."
The journey past the various scenes could represent her life in retrospect;
the children could represent her youth, the fields of grain could mean
maturity or the middle years of her life. The pause at the "swelling in the
ground" symbolizes to me the fact that they pause by her grave long enough
to leave her material body on earth in the customary manner. Only her spirit
accompanies the driver of the chariot on through the centuries of immortality into eternity.

5. I don't particularly like this poem by Emily Dickinson. It feels like sand
running through my toes. I'm sure I can't say why she mentions playing
children, gazing grain, and a setting sun. Perhaps these are the things she
loves best. The lightness of the poem reminds me of a woman riding home
and casually remarking about the things she sees that impress her. The last
stanza leads me to believe that she knew what it would feel like after death.
She thinks she'll know when she is approaching death, because she'll experience some sequence of emotions, or see some particular sequence of
objects. I feel as if I were running after the carriage with Emily Dickinson
in it and hollering to her to tell me what she means. But she keeps going
slowly on toward something mysterious, saying casual things that I don't
quite understand. I'm not going to guess at what she means. Maybe she
doesn't mean anything. Maybe the poem is as light as it feels.

A discussion playing off such reactions against each other can impress the student with the modern critic's first principle: *Find it in the text.* The student learns to ask "What does it say?" before he asks "What do I think of it?" However, once he has acquired a degree of confidence in interpretation, discussion gives him an opportunity to crystallize his personal response.

In dealing with the students' reactions, the teacher's task is not to *correct* them. It is to make the students strengthen, test, or modify them as the teacher repeatedly leads the discussion back to the poem. The first reaction, for instance, shows a developing sensitivity to style. The poet's treatment of her theme is indeed "simple, not magnified." The student should be led to illustrate these qualities from the poem—and also, if possible, to illustrate the conventional solemnity, grandiloquence, or unction here missing. At the same time, the first reaction shows a typical case of plain misinterpretation—the student missed or ignored significant detail. If the fifth stanza refers literally to a house, why are there four lines describing it as low, in the *ground* except for the barely visible roof? This question will be the more effective if asked not by the teacher but by the student's classmates. Here as elsewhere, the teacher must be able to restrain the corrector's instinct sufficiently to allow the students to put their own thinking machinery into gear.

The second student's reaction shows him reading *into* the poem conventional associations: retirement, waiting for death. Again the question should be: where are these in the poem? The person in the poem puts away *labor* as well as leisure for the courteous caller. A similar question arises with the third student's comment. Is there a hint in the poem of the idea of "life goes on"? If this question becomes an issue, the teacher might capitalize on the interest thus created by providing for contrast a poem like A. E. Housman's "Is My Team Plowing":

> Ay, the horses trample,
> The harness jingles now;
> No change though you lie under
> The land you used to plough.

The fifth student's reaction, though on the surface the most willful, is at the same time the most imaginative; though critical of the poem, it is in its own way in tune with the style of the poem itself. It effectively gets at the paradoxical casual quality of the poem, at its teasing lack of explicitness. This student's contribution should not be impatiently dismissed—lest there be a promising future English teacher lost.

This last student comment illustrates the kind of dissent that is more valuable than docile acceptance. Literature must become a personal experience. For instance, if published criticism is any guide, Restoration comedy produces in different readers reactions varying widely in kind and in degree of sophistication. A class treatment based on the assumption that there is only one way of looking at Congreve and Wycherley (the teacher's) is therefore futile. Similarly, Thoreau was a man of strong and unconventional opinions. Not every reader shares them all; and every reader, be he only a freshman in high school, must relate Thoreau's ideas to his own picture of man and society as best he can. If the student is considered mature enough to read Thoreau or Milton or Bertrand Russell, he is mature enough to disagree with them—unless reading means something much more passive and ceremonial than it meant to either Thoreau or Milton.

Obviously, the passive acquiescence encouraged by the lecture method does not serve to keep this kind of independent reaction alive. *When relied on excessively, the lecture approach too long and too frequently bottles up the student's responses, opinions, queries, resentments, and frustrations.* Furthermore, the student who is used to being lectured at is hardly likely to engage in a lively dialogue with the teacher when asked for a piece of writing. We are often told that students write badly because they have not learned to transfer their oral fluency from speech to writing. Unfortunately, it is often true that as far as verbal exchange with the teacher and oral discussion of academic subjects is concerned they have little to transfer.

As classwork shifts from the one-way communication of the lecture to the give-and-take of discussion, certain realities obscured by the lecture method assert themselves. Students vary greatly in aptitude, independence, maturity, and, specifically, attitude towards English. The teacher insisting on active exchange with his students will be aware of these differences, and he will be much more realistically aware than the lecturer of what he can expect and do. At first, a bright and lively class will make him feel brilliant and cause him to send glowing articles to the professional journals on "an approach that worked well with my students at Oakland High." A slow, unresponsive class will make him feel stupid and unwanted. If he perseveres, however, he will learn to garner the rewards to be had in working with students of low aptitude and perhaps initial hostility. He will learn to carry on cheerfully, regardless of the impossibility, in most of his work, of producing the dramatic surface results that stir the imagination of administrators and of journalists assigned to demonstrate a newspaper's benevolent interest in the local schools.

Regardless of the students' level and aptitude, the teacher must observe important cautions if student participation is going to be fruitful. First, *discussion must be anchored firmly to what the student has read, experienced, observed.* Few things are as antieducational as a discussion of current events in Europe by students who are ignorant of European history and culture. Few things are as antiliterary as a group of students collating their impressions of a short story by James Joyce or Henry James that they have not really read. More so than the lecturer, the teacher insisting on discussion must first insist on regular study, close reading. If necessary, he must make it a habit to administer the spot checks that tend to make even the naturally indolent student keep up with current work: brief vocabulary quizzes; tests asking for character sketches, plot outlines, summaries of major points.

Discussions, to be fruitful, must avoid two extremes. One is a one-sided dialogue, in which the teacher asks questions with predetermined answers. These are then after much prodding and hinting delivered at least in part by himself, or by the type of model student who makes a career of studying the teacher's mind. The other extreme is the aimless free-for-all, which the teacher supplements with an occasional encouraging remark and stokes, when it threatens to die down, by raising a new and more or less unmotivated question. By contrast, discussion becomes a meaningful part of English instruction when we apply to it the principles that generally make for substantial and responsible expression.

With students who are alert, and used to sustained hard thought, the teacher may stay rather firmly in control and force the students through their intellectual paces. The result is a dialogue serving as "a dramatic rehearsal of an activity of mind, an activity in which one part of the mind—the impulsive, the suggestive—is represented by the students' quick answers, and another part, the resistive and reflective—is represented by the teacher's interrogative objections and summations."[3] In the definition of terms, for instance, a student with the necessary intellectual stamina will find the disciplined arguing through of exact logical distinctions an exhilarating experience. More typically, however, the teacher will deal with students for whom exact logical distinctions easily become fruitless quibbling and with whom driving, insistent questions easily become self-defeating bullying. With such students the teacher is more likely to obtain results if he knows how to let the discussion develop its own spontaneous drive.

When a student offers a tentative generalization, the teacher must restrain the impulse to shake his head and say "I'm afraid that isn't it" or "the critics agree that isn't so." He must learn to nod in recognition of an honest attempt at contribution and, if necessary, ask "for instance?" or "what passage do you have in mind?" or "now what does that mean applied to this particular play?" As evidence or amplification is presented, other students or, if necessary, the teacher will point to examples or data that challenge or modify the tentative generalization first offered. By similar means, students will be led to state explicitly, and examine, judgments at first merely implied. The group as a whole will participate in an exercise in forming valid generalizations and responsible judgments that is an exact model of what each student must learn to do for himself

[3] Martin, in Gordon and Noyes, *Essays*, p. 166.

in his own writing. After the discussion has ranged over a variety of points, the teacher or members of the class will in the last five or ten minutes demonstrate the very skills of correlating points previously made, bringing in points overlooked, and tying up loose ends that the student must practice in marshaling ideas in his own themes.

Given his superior argumentative resources, the teacher must remind himself not to dominate and inhibit discussion. One device he can use is to assume the stance of the silent recorder at the blackboard. As various points are made, he can try to pinpoint different alternatives suggested by summing them up in a term or phrase. Merely by writing these out, he will stimulate students to question the original contributions and supply further alternatives. He will also stimulate earlier participants who feel misrepresented by his summary to clarify or amplify their points. By lining conflicting points up as alternatives or simply putting a question mark after a point just made, the teacher can steer the discussion in a productive direction without actually having to interrupt or coax the students. His efforts at the blackboard can at the same time help to make his students aware of how their minds work, and of how their thinking can become more fruitful and systematic.

What has to some extent brought the discussion method into disrepute is that some teachers have equated it with an exercise in brainstorming for which less preparation is required than for a lecture. This attitude represents a sad misinterpretation of the teacher's responsibilities. The combination of lecture and discussion that most fully involves the student in the material under study requires a command of detail and a freshness of memory greatly more demanding than those of the lecturer who can follow prepared notes. Important questions about a literary work become much more real when raised by a student in the course of authentic discussion than when raised abstractly in a systematic lecture. However, they are not likely to receive an answer that has any sort of impact unless the instructor can at the strategic moment point to a telling piece of evidence, quote a crucial line. As Barzun says of the instructor conducting a discussion, "his imagination must swarm with connecting links, factual illustrations, answers to unexpected questions."[4] He must have a sure grasp both of detail and of the larger relationships that give significance to the material being read.

Such questions as the teacher himself contributes must as far as possible be genuine and open questions. There is

> no worse professional disease for the teacher than the habit of putting questions with a half-smile that says "I know that one, and I will tell it you: come along, my pretty." Telling and questioning must not be put-up jobs designed to make the teacher feel good about himself.[5]

[4] Barzun, *Teacher in America*, p. 40.
[5] *Ibid.*, p. 22.

The teacher must avoid the very specific and peripheral question that leads the students to rack their brains for an item of information or an allusion that they obviously missed. ("What is the name of the girl introduced to the heroine at the beginning of Chapter Four?") He must use sparingly open invitations to comment on large topics without raising problems specific enough to put the student to work selecting relevant materials, marshaling evidence. The good questions are the ones that put the student to shuffling, selecting, and redistributing materials clearly within his reach. They are not the minimum questions of programmed instruction, designed to take the student by the hand and lead him one little step at a time. They are what Jerome Bruner calls the **medium questions,** questions "that can be answered and that take you somewhere."[6]

Most teachers soon find out that student response is easy to kill but hard to revive. It is true that on any level there will be students who thrive on controversy, who are stimulated by provocative questions and goaded into energetic rebuttal by a broadside attack on their views. Certainly, by the time a student reaches a senior colloquium in college or a graduate seminar he should be able to hold his own in vigorous intellectual exchange. But more typically the relationship between teacher and student is not one between intellectual peers. What people find frustrating in criticism and sarcasm they encounter from their superiors is not that they are subjected to criticism and sarcasm but that they are not free to reply in kind. Ironical or sarcastic comments by a teacher tend to kill student participation, not because at the right time and with the right student irony cannot have a bracing effect, but because often the student rightly feels that the teacher is taking unfair advantage of his own immunity to criticism.

Obviously, the problem of tone in handling student responses that seem ludicrous or inane is part of the larger question of a "positive" as against a "negative" approach. Since the positive approach is the stock in trade of many a quack, teachers rightly tend to be suspicious of it. Certainly the teacher of English must convince his students that he means business, that he will not allow them to bluff or fake their way through his classes. But if he is going to work with them rather than merely lecture at them, his relationship with them must be something more than strictly businesslike. He must offer them at least an approximation of the ideal which one student described as the "kind, patient, and mature consideration of students as individuals."

When discussion fulfills these various requirements, it becomes an essential part of the teaching process. *Fruitful discussion can convince the student that knowledge is barren until it becomes part of his system—until*

6 *The Process of Education* (Cambridge, Mass.: Harvard University Press, 1962), p. 40.

he correlates it with what he knew before, actively tests it in debate, and productively employs it in the solution of new problems. In the words of Gilbert Highet,

> a discussion of this kind, conducted with constant reference to the material the pupils have been studying, and so organized as to bring in the maximum number of suggestions and answers from the class, will not only deepen their understanding of that particular field, but teach them the invaluable lesson of organizing their thoughts. They soon learn by example. They will half-unconsciously start to arrange their own essays and plan their own work on similar logical models. They will jump the gap between memorizing and creative thinking.[7]

Strategies of Presentation

To a large extent, the sequence of material to be taught is determined by curriculum pattern, course syllabus, or textbook. However, in his day-to-day presentation of material, the teacher employs strategies that can make the difference between a fresh, resourceful approach and dull, routine work. Whatever his method in detail, the English teacher must strive to counteract a familiar application of Gresham's law to the teaching of our discipline. Some of the things we do are absorbing and rewarding, while others strain our patience and dull our minds. Both in our own work and in the work of the profession at large, the dull tends to drive out the rewarding. As Dwight Burton said editorially in *The English Journal,* we too often operate on the principle that "what doesn't work we should do more of."[8] A student after years of drill in correctness of expression is found not to have mastered the "fundamentals." The remedy, it is decided, is to give him more drill. This pattern is perpetuated by "minimum standards" and by achievement and college entrance tests that stress the external symptoms of literacy rather than the substance of competent reading and writing.

If the student is to enjoy his English classes, they must offer him not routine busywork but systematic and fruitful exploration. *The ideal unit of work makes the student feel that a hitherto confusing area is gradually being clarified, that previously miscellaneous observations are being fitted into a meaningful pattern. At the same time he feels that light is being shed at least in part as a result of his own efforts; that he is contributing rather than merely absorbing.* Whatever knowledge we present to the student must come to life for him through active participation and discovery. As the year's or the semester's work unfolds, the student must feel that current work on the one hand covers new material but on the other supplements, clarifies, or reinforces work done in the past.

[7] *The Art of Teaching* (New York: Alfred A. Knopf, Inc., 1950), p. 129.
[8] *The English Journal,* LII (March, 1963), 234.

Even when we do what we consider significant and profitable, we have to guard against falling into certain patterns that may kill interest. The most common of these is the **inventory approach.** Instruction intended to be systematic and comprehensive, designed to "cover" the subject, easily becomes mere dreary stock-taking. Some teachers list in numerical order twenty-six miscellaneous rules for the use of the comma. Others mimeograph check sheets with thirty-five numbered instructions for successful compositions. Some introductions to an author or to a work consist largely of a listing, by title, and with dates, of the author's works, early and late, significant and insignificant, famous and obscure.

Even when the emphasis is on memorization, material must be presented in graspable segments, in meaningful units. This is even more true when, as in most instruction in English, the appeal is less to the student's memory than to his understanding. To make students "understand" the comma, we need to group its uses under a few major headings—whether according to their relation to other punctuation marks, to grammatical structure, to intonation, or perhaps even to the history of printing. The important thing is not *how* our presentation of the comma is organized but *that* it is organized. The same principle applies when we want our students to recognize the name and the importance of an author. They will remember one or two titles—if the descriptions are carefully related to what they know and understand about literature. The complete bibliographical listing will be reluctantly skimmed in reading and forgotten with all possible speed.

One major area of our discipline, rhetoric, to this day struggles to free itself of the reputation for pedantry it gained when rhetoricians devoted a major share of their time to the inventory of rhetorical devices, from metonymy and synecdoche to syllepsis and zeugma. In the teaching of poetry, there is a similar temptation to start with a formal inventory of the different kinds of meter, common stanza forms, recurrent technical devices. Many a teacher who has tried this approach will agree that

a freer, more impressionistic and opportunistic approach is better, at least for the first few weeks. This is not to deny that the formal elements of poetry should be taught. They should be. But they should be taught in concrete situations, when particular poems are being examined. A Shakespearean sonnet, for instance, gives an opportunity for some wise words about iambic rhythm, the pentameter as a measure of line length, and the special impact of that fourteen-line structure called a sonnet. If a student learns the word pentameter the second week and does not encounter tetrameter until after mid-semester examinations it is no great matter. Toward the end of the course the loose ends can be systematically pulled together, and the technical gaps filled in.[9]

[9] Chad Walsh, "When a Poem Confronts an Undergraduate," *College English,* XXIV (February, 1963), 385–86.

The teacher of English will be wary of any sequence that is merely rigid rather than systematic. He will often go the opposite extreme. He will simply assign or bring to class a passage or poem, asking his students to study it for what it reveals about the nature and use of language. Many of our students respond to such an appeal to their curiosity and independent judgment. If the selections are well chosen, they bring out points that contribute to a gradual, balanced, and varied exploration of a major area. They thus make possible the combination of spontaneous participation by the student with systematic planning by the teacher. Many a teacher finds it profitable not even to mention terms like *irony* or *satire* until they are injected *by a student* into a discussion of a passage by Swift, Thurber, or Shaw. When such terms are then in the give-and-take of discussion defined, modified, and tested, they come to the student as a means of correlating his observations of language in action rather than as items in an inventory of inert knowledge.

Generally, the modern attitude toward language, with the emphasis on observation rather than precept, provides the rationale for a wealth of exploratory and inductive activities. Even the teacher who starts by demonstrating a general principle will often let the class, rather than the textbook, provide the examples and applications. For instance, he can develop the students' feeling for the major grammatical categories by having students fill in examples of words made into different parts of speech by the addition of suffixes:

	ADJ	*V*	*N*
1.	red	redden	redness
2.	_____	_____	_____
3.	_____	_____	_____

or

	N	*V*	*ADJ*
1.	organ	organize	organic
2.	_____	_____	_____

A feeling for connotation can be developed in similar ways:

We are all familiar with Russell's conjugation of value judgments:

> *I* am firm;
> *You* are obstinate;
> But *he* is a pig-headed fool.

We can repeat this technique, with some enjoyment, on many of the value words we habitually use: *loyal, obedient, slavish; famous, well-known, notorious; generous, liberal, spendthrift,* and so on. The list may be increased to five words, going from approval to neutrality to condemnation; you may present a list of five words, to be put in correct order of degree of connotation. You may ask for words which have increasingly romantic connotations: *boat, ship, frigate, galleon.*[10]

However, the student can often be led to discover, as well as merely to illustrate, a general principle. Students can discover major principles of word order by arranging in the most plausible sequence a group like *tall—many—buildings—office* or *old—a—man—rich.* They can generalize concerning the relation between word order and meaning by contrasting such pairs as "the door is open" and "is the door open" or "kites fly" and "fly kites."

On a larger scale, the **inductive approach** provides the general model for numerous writing assignments and class projects. For instance, students will expect the teacher to dislike teen-age slang. They are likely to listen to any theoretical remarks of his about slang with a firmly prejudiced ear. By contrast, an inductive exploration of slang can teach students a number of generally important things about language. Students can prepare papers or oral reports on their observation of slang; a class can compile a short glossary of slang as a co-operative venture. A number of important generalizations can emerge from such work. These will concern the difference between standard language and language whose currency is limited in area and time; between literal language and figurative; between relatively neutral language and language highly connotative, or marked by extravagant humor, or expressing an irreverently sarcastic attitude; between language that identifies those who are "in" and language that marks off those who are "out" or "square."

A similar project may adapt for class use the procedure of dialect geography. Once he has firmly established that "linguistic interest is not criticism nor ridicule," the teacher can send out "field workers" asking parents and neighbors if they remember or recognize items from a check list of dialectal forms.[11] By correlating the results with information about the areas where the "respondents" have grown up or lived most of their lives, a class may draw its own tentative and partial conclusions about dialect areas. Priscilla Tyler, in *Word Study,* reported on a planned project in "amateur lexicography," aimed at building a token "class dictionary":

> We will see what it means to collect citations, looking for stable and unstable meanings. We will compare Hemingway as a source for these citations with Hortense Calisher and Herbert Gold. Our corpus will be mainly the material which the students read in the daily course of their lives, their own papers, and some taped class sessions. We will note the growth of a class vocabulary and any expressions coined by the class. We will observe the

10 Harold H. Owen, Jr., *et al.,* "Some General Remarks on the Teaching of Poetry," Gordon and Noyes, *Essays,* p. 279.
11 Eleanor Matthew, in "English Language Study in Portland High Schools," *The English Journal,* LII (May, 1963), 361–62.

lexical stock of individuals, the "borrowing" among the class members, and the use of words in the . . . unstandard categories.[12]

For a less ambitious project, the teacher may ask his students to build a citation file on words starting with *ab* or *ad* as found in a week's or two weeks' reading. Each occurrence of such a word would be recorded, with the short phrase or sentence in which it was found, on note cards filed in alphabetical order. When several cards for the same word have accumulated, its meaning, or its several different meanings, can be formulated on the evidence the cards provide.

In the teaching of literature, the teacher will look for similar ways of forcing the students into participation and discovery. One familiar way of getting them to look at the structure and texture of literature *from the inside* is to call for stylistic **imitation** of sample passages. Presenting to the class a passage from Charles Lamb or Henry James or Ernest Hemingway, the teacher can ask each student to fill in exactly the same skeleton of sentence structure, writing on a topic of his own choice. Called the "sedulous-ape" approach by its detractors, this kind of exercise nevertheless forces the student to grapple with an author's style in a manner radically different from aloof criticism.

More generally, any device for making the student of literature less of a passive spectator is welcome. For instance, early in a course

> the students can be plunged, the more abruptly the better, into some experience in writing poetry. Not much of it will be any good, but if it is done in a devil-may-care spirit, it admirably serves to break down the wall of partition between reader and poetry, by giving the students a new respect for the technical mastery of real poets. Each instructor will have his own way of handling this. I prefer to give students some partial guidance, such as assigning a particular form or a specific subject (usually an "unpoetic" one, such as "The City Dump," so as to obviate poems that are a patchwork of half-remembered lines).[13]

One popular form for such experiments is a simplified version of the Japanese *haiku:* It encourages the student to concentrate on the mood, the image, the unified over-all impression; it does not make him lose his initial interest by a struggle with meter and rhyme. Here are some sample *haiku* that a teacher obtained from twelve-year-olds:

> A hot summer day;
> I see no children playing
> —just the butterflies.
>
> Deer go through the woods
> swift, but very noiselessly.
> Hunter strikes one down.

[12] "An English Teacher Looks at Webster's Seventh New Collegiate Dictionary," *Word Study,* XXXVIII (April, 1963), 8. By permission. From *Word Study,* copyright 1963 by G. & C. Merriam Co., Publishers of the Merriam-Webster Dictionaries.
[13] Walsh, *College English,* XXIV, 386.

> Three very small elves
> took rides on the rainbow slide,
> Now, colorful elves![14]

Activities such as these reflect the teacher's belief that imitation compels attention; that even parody is preferable to perfunctory, insincere "appreciation."

To make the student's participation as fruitful as possible, the skillful teacher finds materials that mutually illuminate each other. One of the most reliable helps in the teaching of both language and literature is well-planned **contrast**. Most of the points we need to make about sentence structure, usage, or style are best demonstrated by clearly contrasting passages, or by a series of passages showing typical variations. Whether teaching intonation, punctuation, or syntax, we do well to have ready such pairs as

> Think of the poor, child.
> Think of the poor child.
>
> She dislikes fraternity boys who are conceited.
> She dislikes fraternity boys, who are conceited.
>
> When hunting, lions stay away from wooded areas.
> When hunting lions, stay away from wooded areas.

In first alerting the students to what is distinctively poetic in a poem, the teacher may ask them to explore as fully as possible the differences between the poem and a paraphrase like the following case history based on E. A. Robinson's poem "Mr. Flood's Party":

> . . . the subject of this report, aged 74, lives in an old substandard dwelling on the outskirts of the town. Although subject-named person is reputed to have been a man of multiple social contacts in past years, his participation in community or social activities has dwindled to a minimal level. At irregular intervals, Mr. Flood visits the village, usually returning near midnight in an inebriated state. . . .[15]

Contrasting selections treating a similar theme can effectively demonstrate important points concerning a writer's attitude, tone, and style. In teaching the short story, for instance, the teacher may group together two of the most famous treatments of the theme of pursuit: John Steinbeck's "Flight" and Ernest Hemingway's "The Killers." The first is literal narrative. The author establishes the setting, then introduces the characters, foreshadowing future developments by dwelling on the boy's pride in handling his dead father's knife. Then Steinbeck sets the stage for the killing that triggers the pursuit of offender by avenger; leads us slowly, inexorably through the flight from the first businesslike preparations to its

---

14 Allaire Stuart, "Creative Writing: Japanese Haiku," *Elementary English*, XXXX (January, 1963), 36.
15 Joseph A. Rogers, "Poetry's Extra Dimension," *Exercise Exchange*, VIII (October–December, 1960), 7.

desperate final stages; and ends the story when suspense is satisfied and expectation fulfilled as the victim's body rolls down a rocky slope. The major departure from straightforward narration is that the crucial incident itself is not directly described but dramatically revealed by the boy already in flight. By contrast, Hemingway's story has none but the most sparse and incidental account of setting. Apart from a few ominous hints (the gunmen eat with their gloves on), there is little description of characters. The story is a sequence of three major portions of matter-of-fact dialogue with no overt action. We are not told what if anything is going to happen to the former prizefighter being tracked down by the gunmen with whose friends he "got in wrong." We are thus made to dwell on the presumable state of mind of the pursued who is "through" running, and on the inarticulate horror of the bystander who is unable to help.

The Steinbeck story has a solemn, almost ceremonial tone, which tends to give it a timeless quality, remote from the reader's own immediate world. It has a ritualistic quality, treating as it does the archetypal theme of the transition, fraught with danger and uncertainty, from adolescence to manhood. "The Killers" is almost aggressively trivial in setting and in tone of dialogue. The menacing wisecracks of the gunmen heighten horror, playing a role that might profitably be compared with the role of the drunken porter in *Macbeth*. In contrasting the two stories, students can be led to think about the role in fiction of actions as against states of mind, of the ceremonial as against the realistic, of the explicit as against the implied.

Contrast is especially effective in demonstrating differences between slight and more serious fiction. O. Henry's "The Gift of the Magi" and Guy de Maupassant's "The Necklace" are in many respects similar. They are examples of straightforward narration without technical complexity or esoteric appeal, suitable for an audience of little literary sophistication. Both aim at dramatizing the poignancy of expectations defeated by misunderstanding, of people at cross purposes. But, typically, O. Henry, like the children's dentist, sees to it that the operation does not really hurt. He sees to it that no illusions or complacencies are disturbed. The young wife, though poor, is slender and girlish, tender-hearted and devoted, unselfish and uncritical. The major moral and psychological problem caused by her poverty is her inability to buy her husband the platinum watch chain, for his treasured watch, that would make a Christmas gift worthy of her love for him. The sacrifice that demonstrates the extent of her love is the cutting short, and selling, of her beautifully unreal hair, falling down, when undone, below her knee, "rippling and shining like a cascade of brown waters." With equally beautiful and improbable symmetry, the impecunious husband has sold the watch to buy a set of beautiful jeweled combs for his wife's long hair. The story concludes with a moral on the superior wisdom of the heart manifested in these apparently so unwise gifts.

In "The Necklace," the wife, rather than being reconciled to genteel shabbiness the way a clerk's wife should be, yearns for a less sordid setting. She shares the futile and humiliating feelings of inferiority that beset people who have developed a feeling for beauty, for style, for luxury, for elegant leisure and stimulating companionship, beyond what their economic status allows them to satisfy. The sacrifices she and her husband are called upon to make are real: from the husband's surrendering his hopes for a long-planned vacation to enable his wife to attend a rare social occasion in a presentable dress, to the wife's accepting the scrounging drudgery of outright poverty in order to help her husband pay off a debt incurred through a cruel misunderstanding. At the end of the story, the wife discovers that she and her husband sacrificed ten years of their lives to pay off the real diamond necklace bought to replace an imitation necklace they had borrowed and lost. The devotion and futile heroism of their labor, the irrevocability of their loss, precludes a moral that would congratulate them on their superior wisdom of the heart.

Following up such possibilities of comparison and constrast, the teacher soon realizes the opportunities for demonstrating in this way the recurrence of major literary themes, the validity of major distinctions in the analysis of style and in the history of literary sensibility. Here, for instance, are some groupings of poems, with some of the topics for exploration and discussion they suggest:

1) the ballad of "Thomas Rhymer," Keats's "La Belle Dame Sans Merci," Heine's "Lorelei"—the nature of folk poetry, contrast of popular and literary ballads, the theme of the demon lover;

2) the ballad of "Lord Randal" and W. H. Auden's "The Quarry"— the appeal of the ballad style, its appropriateness to a modern theme, the poetic treatment of violence, the poem as a comment on current history;

3) Shelley's "To a Skylark," Keats's "Ode to a Nightingale," Whitman's "Out of the Cradle Endlessly Rocking"—the role in a poem of a central situation or a central symbol; the role of the bird in each poem; the poets' relationship to nature;

4) Wordsworth's "Tintern Abbey" and Arnold's "Dover Beach"—the reflective nature poem, the poem as autobiography, Romantic and Victorian attitudes toward nature;

5) Wordsworth's "Tintern Abbey" and Dylan Thomas' "Fern Hill," or Wordsworth's "Ode on Intimations" and Thomas' "Poem in October"—Romantic and modern attitudes toward nature; descriptive and evocative language; traditional and free verse;

6) Stephen Crane's "The Wayfarer" and Robert Frost's "The Road Not Taken"—the poem as parable; the limits of symbolic application; the nature of satire.

More varied groupings can illuminate characteristic effects and limitations of different literary types. Thus, a class will profit greatly from studying the tragic and the comic treatment of a similar theme by two different dramatists. It will profit from seeing the same theme treated in the narrow compass of a short story and developed more fully in a novel. When more extended groupings include works representing several major genres, the work of several weeks or months may be unified around a major recurrent theme, such as that of desire greedily over-reaching itself:

> *Radix Malorum est Cupiditas*, the theme of Chaucer's *Pardoner's Tale*, looks back to the New Testament. It is treated by Chaucer in a sermon, by Marlowe in the Tragedy of *Dr. Faustus*, by Ben Jonson in a series of comedies, *Alchemist, Volpone, The Magnetic Lady*, and by Conrad in the novel *Nostromo*, and in many modern novels and plays. How effectively in each medium? What makes each literature instead of extended pious statement? What can the sheer weight of wording do to transform a platitude into a rare insight?[16]

Here are some examples of materials for extended thematic groupings:

1) *Man and Nature*

Daniel Defoe, *The Adventures of Robinson Crusoe*
Jack London, "To Make a Fire"
Stephen Crane, "The Open Boat"
John M. Synge, *Riders to the Sea*
Robinson Jeffers, "Hurt Hawks"
D. H. Lawrence, "Snake"
Henry Thoreau, *Walden*
William Faulkner, "The Bear"
Herman Melville, *Moby Dick*

2) *Man and the Machine*

Emily Dickinson, "The Train"
Stephen Spender, "The Express"
E. M. Forster, "The Machine Stops"
Charles Dickens, *Hard Times*
Carl Sandburg, "Chicago"
Kenneth Fearing, "Travelogue in a Shooting-Gallery"
Aldous Huxley, *Brave New World*

3) *Man and Society*

Robinson Jeffers, "The Purse-Seine"
George Orwell, *Animal Farm*

[16] Members of the Conference on Basic Issues in the Teaching of English, "An Articulated English Program: A Hypothesis to Test," *PMLA*, LXXIV (September, 1959), Part 2, p. 15.

Henrik Ibsen, *The Doll's House*
Arthur Miller, *The Crucible*
Sophocles, *Antigone*
Henry Thoreau, "On Civil Disobedience"
W. H. Auden, "The Unknown Citizen"
Albert Camus, *The Stranger*

4) *The Clash of Cultures*

Joseph Conrad, "An Outpost of Progress"
Somerset Maugham, "The Outstation"
Eugene O'Neill, *The Emperor Jones*
E. M. Forster, *A Passage to India*
Bernard Shaw, *The Devil's Disciple*
Henry James, *The American*
Evelyn Waugh, *The Loved One*
W. H. Auden, "Fleet Visit"

There are certain dangers in relying too heavily or too exclusively on such thematic groupings. As critics have pointed out, the simpler works and the less outstanding writers are often easier to fit into a thematic scheme than the thematically complex works of the great. It is hard to fit *Lycidas* and *Hamlet* into a thematic unit without seeming officious. The same is true among the moderns for books like Joyce's *A Portrait of the Artist as a Young Man* or Faulkner's *The Sound and the Fury*. By the same token, emphasis on a central theme may misdirect the reader's response. In its more superficial form, the thematic approach leads to message-hunting and oversimplification.

Furthermore, the thematic unit must not be allowed to become ahistorical. Selections representing widely different styles and periods should not be treated without attention to the conventions and traditions that helped shape them. A teacher basically in sympathy with grouping selections around a major theme will therefore try to arrange them in an order that at the same time does justice to chronological sequence or to significant similarities and contrasts of genre and style. In most of the student's general-education courses in literature, the teacher will find most effective a strategy of presentation that takes into account chronology, literary type, and stylistic convention as well as theme.

Handling Written Work

Whatever our strategies in classroom instruction, an equally important part of our teaching is our handling of written work. The teacher should not develop a routine for assigning and reading student papers without thinking through its purposes and effects. The basic problem is to keep student writing from being a perfunctory exercise, identified with drudgery in the minds of both student and teacher. The student must come to feel that he is writing in order to say something, that he is writing with a purpose. The teacher must know how to be for the student first of all a *reader* rather than a taskmaster or corrector.

The teacher determined to keep his handling of student writing from becoming perfunctory is not likely to discover any revolutionary new approach. Though some experimental trends have been praised by their champions, none at present seem likely to gain a general following. One such trend is reliance on **free writing**. The assumption here is that "you learn to write by writing." The student is told to keep his pen moving— without assignments, topics, outlines, revisions—for ten or twenty or thirty minutes. This pressure to keep writing down whatever comes to mind is maintained over the weeks. At least with some students, this approach produces an important result: The wretched, halting pseudo-formal style of earlier compositions disappears, and a more fluent, more natural kind of expression takes its place. Teachers tired to the death of the ordinary student theme testify that student writing becomes more *readable*—more imaginative, more revealing.

The skeptic, on the other hand, is likely to feel that while the papers of imaginative students become more imaginative, ordinary student writing merely becomes more fluently vapid. He is likely to commend free writing as a preliminary limbering up, or as therapy after prolonged exposure to an ossified rhetoric. But he will continue to see the crux of composition teaching in how to develop the student's sense of *structure*. Thinking a subject through, developing an argument step by step, systematically supporting a major point—these processes necessarily narrow the range of a writer's spontaneity. The teacher must try to make the students' writing more deliberate without destroying spontaneity altogether. With the truly successful writer, structured, deliberate writing itself becomes second nature, itself begins to seem spontaneous. The major defect of the free-writing approach is that it tends to make a fetish of spontaneity for its own sake. It thus slights the task of helping students

> become actively aware of what goes on inside good expository prose so they may come to know a little more about the nature of the tools they themselves are using and thus perhaps learn to use them more intelligently.[17]

A second experimental way of escaping from a merely perfunctory writing program is to stress the **peer group** as the true audience of the student writer. As contrasted with free writing, this approach puts the emphasis on writing as communication, as a message from writer to reader. When students respond to what a fellow student has written, the basic nature of communication as action and *reaction* can be effectively simulated. A program in which papers are written to be read or distributed to a peer group supplies the link missing in most composition work: an

[17] Albert R. Kitzhaber, *Themes, Theories, and Therapy: The Teaching of Writing in College* (New York: McGraw-Hill Book Company, Inc., 1963), p. 139.

audience whose standards the writer can not only respect but also understand.

The difficulty here is that the standards of the peer group are not identical with those the teacher is trying to develop. Actually, the student in a composition program is writing for a mythical "educated" reader. He should think of this reader not so much as a classmate but as what his classmates might become when they are more experienced, less caught up in their current interests. The basic function of the teacher *as reader* is to interpret to the student writer the standards and expectations of a more or less idealized educated audience.

Whatever experiments the teacher will wish to try, the bulk of the students' writing is likely to follow a familiar model:

1) assignments to a large extent structured by the teacher;
2) papers read by the teacher simulating the "common reader";
3) class discussion of student writing, designed to clarify the teacher's standards and help develop the students' own independent judgment.

The first step, making the assignment, deserves more attention than it usually gets. Finding the right assignment, and wording it right, is half the battle. *A good writing assignment must do justice to three requirements: It should be meaningful, realistic, and specific.*

The assignment should be meaningful: The student will develop neither honest thought nor forceful expression by writing on topics about which neither he nor the teacher could possibly care. Obviously, some of the writing topics in the first years of high school will be trivial by graduate-school standards. But it is impossible to take composition seriously as an academic subject when a college freshman is solemnly asked to record his thoughts on the pleasures of stamp-collecting, on how to knit a sweater or design a coffee table, on the problems of keeping a pet.

Pitiful as these theme topics are, they are no worse than the opposite extreme: topics asking the student to take a stand on issues beyond his ken. The student must never feel that composition is the art of stating superficial impressions with conviction. The teacher must ask himself what kinds of generalization the students at their present stage of development can be realistically expected to formulate and support. He must make it clear to them that their generalizations must be *genuine* generalizations, formulated *by them* on the basis of their own observation, experience, and reading. The high school junior cannot honestly write on racial prejudice in the United States, but he might be able to write with conviction on the treatment of a minority group at a school he knows well. The college freshman cannot honestly write on the relative merits of communism and democracy, but he might be able to write on the conflicting claims of competition and team spirit, whether on the athletic field or in the classroom.

Here lies the strength of high school texts devoting major sections to the use of language in the **mass media**. Study of the mass media suggests many realistic writing assignments requiring the student to generalize about the language of advertising, the stereotypes of television drama, the nature of front-page "news." Such assignments can be both realistic and meaningful: the student here has a wealth of easily accessible evidence from firsthand observation; at the same time, the study of the mass media raises questions about the use of language that are of concern to every responsible listener and reader.

The need for steering the student toward generalizations anchored to concrete reference is one illustration of the need for specific, **structured assignments.** A structured assignment does not merely suggest a topic; it also furnishes hints, or outright directions, concerning appropriate strategies. The basic defect of the routine general topic is that it invites mere miscellaneous impressions, often held together by a perfunctory and basically meaningless chronological scheme: "My Summer Vacation," "Registration Day," "A Day at the Beach." To wean the student from mere chronology, the teacher will formulate topics that compel choice, that force the student to commit himself. Such a teacher will ask a question whose answer will necessarily become a unifying thesis, to be illustrated, defended, supported. One simple device is to avoid the topic that makes the student write *about* causes, functions, influences, people. Instead, a topic can ask the student to select the *one* most important cause or influence, the *one* most meaningful function of student government, the *one* most important lesson he has learned from a certain kind of experience. Similarly, a topic can force a systematic comparison and contrast of two things (rather than a rambling discussion of three or four); it can force a close analysis of one crucial argument for or against teen-age marriage or the teen-age vote (rather than a sketchy survey of several).

A structured assignment tries to anticipate the most predictable ways in which a student may fail to do justice to his topic. Often a topic offers its own characteristic temptations. The assignment can directly or indirectly remind the student to limit his scope, support his points, define his terms. As Albert R. Kitzhaber says,

> If a word of caution ahead of time from the teacher will prevent most of the students, or even a handful of them, from making useless mistakes that the teacher must only try to explain later after they have been made, he is well advised to take the trouble to explain them in the first place. Thus if the teacher decides to assign his class to write on cynicism in *Richard III,* he should expect that a considerable part of the class will need to be reminded that it is important to define terms at the outset. If he does not

remind them when he makes the assignment, he will later find himself writing on paper after paper, "You should have established at the beginning an authoritative definition of *cynicism, cynical,* and *cynic.*"[18]

Finally, the effective theme topic does not suddenly come out of nowhere. Class reading and class discussion have led up to it. The student has some idea of what there is in the topic to get excited about. He knows what there is in the subject that he can get his teeth into. He is impatient to reopen a discussion that left him dissatisfied, that by implication challenged a favorite cliché or prejudice. The effective teacher of composition knows how to stimulate in his students a certain polemical drive and yet channel it into solid, systematic exposition. The student theme should be the student's opportunity to talk back, to defend a view under attack, but also to settle for himself a perplexing question, to restore an equilibrium that has been disturbed.

Generally, it is desirable to give the student a choice among several related topics. He should not feel that for better or for worse he is saddled with a single topic that, to him at any rate, may seem to beg the question or miss the point. In reading over a choice of three or four topics, even if they merely present the same basic question in slightly different form, he is more likely to hit on the one that triggers a response. The more mature student can often be encouraged to exercise his right to some degree of choice by narrowing down a general area in his own way.

Once the student has finished his paper, a new set of questions arises. Should the teacher read every theme? If he does, should he record his reactions each time, and in how much detail? The teacher groaning under a heavy load may try reading only every second or third theme, or reading only every second theme "carefully." Such expedients are likely to satisfy neither the teacher nor the student. If a theme is not important enough to be read, the student will have difficulty considering it important enough to be written. There are some kinds of student writing that the teacher may merely sample: journals or logs designed to help develop the writing habit; written reports, only a sampling of which may be read and discussed in class. But a formal writing assignment should mean that the teacher is ready to read and evaluate a set of papers.

Elaborate analyses of the students' writing are usually not feasible, nor are they necessarily helpful to the easily overwhelmed ordinary student. But reading a set of themes should not be synonymous with "marking," let alone "correcting," them. It is true that even the conscientious teacher will use **abbreviations** for some of the most frequent comments: *dev* (develop), *trans* (transition), *agr* (agreement), *ref* (reference), and so on. If he has a thoroughly systematic mind, he may use the numerical key of the traditional handbook, sending the student to

18 Kitzhaber, *Themes, Theories, and Therapy,* p. 56.

section *51b* or *P 12a* for the appropriate information on the comma splice or the last comma in a series. However, even the teacher pressed for time must know where to draw the line in yielding to such temptations to efficiency:

> Except for a personal conference, the most effective way to show the student where a paper needs improvement and where it is satisfactory is to write comments on the theme. A student whose paper comes back to him marked only with rule numbers and cryptic abbreviations like *coh, ts, X, Z,* and *ab* sometimes feels as though the paper might as well have been run through a machine. . . . The advantages of comments over symbols and abbreviations, other than the evidence they give of the teacher's personal interest, are principally that they can be highly specific, referring not just to a type of error but to a particular error in a particular context, and that they can be used not only to point out errors and weaknesses but to commend the student for a well-turned phrase, a clear line of reasoning, an improvement in sentence structure over previous papers.[19]

The basic defect of conventional ways of treating the student theme is the preoccupation with the student's weaknesses rather than his potential. The paper returned to the student with red ink spattered over it from top to bottom is a pedagogical disaster. It is also an admission of defeat, since the student who does everything wrong cannot be expected to learn all at once how to do everything right. As Ben Jonson observed over three hundred years ago,

> No more would I tell a green writer all his faults, lest I should make him grieve and faint, and at last despair. For nothing doth more hurt than to make him so afraid of all things as he can endeavor nothing. . . . Therefore a master should temper his own powers, and descend to the other's infirmity. If you pour a glut of water upon a bottle, it receives little of it; but with a funnel, and by degrees, you shall fill many of them, and spill little of your own.[20]

There is one crucial requirement for the teacher's response to written work: *Negative criticism must be selective.* The teacher's evaluation of a student's papers must not be a weekly inventory of the student's deficiencies, real and imagined. Of each negative comment the teacher should ask soberly: Will it do any good? No matter how deficient the student's work, the teacher must convince him that, appearance to the contrary, there *is* a point in his continuing to work, in his continuing to pay attention to what the teacher has to offer. In the words of William J. Dusel, if marking papers "is a form of instruction," it should both "communicate the kinds of information which the learner needs in order to improve" and "strengthen the pupil's motive or interest in writing."[21]

[19] Kitzhaber, *Themes, Theories, and Therapy*, p. 65.
[20] Edmund D. Jones, ed., *English Critical Essays (Sixteenth, Seventeenth, and Eighteenth Centuries)*, (London: Oxford University Press, 1956), p. 97.
[21] "Some Semantic Implications of Theme Correction," *The English Journal*, XLIV (October, 1955), 391.

By necessity, the high school teacher is more aware than his colleague in college that his students have motives, aspirations, and, in short, egos of their own. As Edwin H. Sauer says in *English in the Secondary School,*

> a paper should never be returned unless the student receives some word of encouragement and praise. Remember that nothing which the student does for you or anyone else is so much a product of his own effort as a composition. It is his *creation;* no part of it existed before he sat down at a desk with a pencil. With all of the solecisms, tortuous constructions, and upside-down logic which it may contain, he is nonetheless proud of it. Don't massacre him. Of course, this determination to compliment the student may set you to scratching your head at times. You will feel that in some cases about all you can say is, "That's an interesting shade of ink you are using," or "I like the way you observe margins." Most of the time, however, something stands out —a clever use of idiom, a colorful comparison, an unexpectedly mature judgment. Show the student that you approve.[22]

Closely related to the tenor of the teacher's written comments is the atmosphere in which student writing is discussed in class. Most teachers rely too much on the practice of presenting student writing to the class in order to show what is wrong with it. Bricklayers do not train an apprentice by endlessly showing the different ways in which a wall may be built crooked; music teachers do not insist on showing the innumerable ways in which the violin may be mishandled. Instead, they demonstrate again and again how things are done right. *The teacher of composition should show his students again and again examples of effective, substantial student writing.* He should have a file, constantly enlarged and brought up to date, of dittoed or mimeographed student papers representing the students' own level of maturity and demonstrating the level of achievement they can reasonably be expected to reach. Insofar as possible, some of these papers should come from the current writing assignments in a given class.

The **model paper** should typically not be an exceptional paper so far ahead of most students in stylistic sophistication as to be clearly beyond their reach. It should be a paper that can be discussed in detail to show how examples have been used to flesh out a general point, how transitions have been established from paragraph to paragraph, how and where the key point of the paper emerges, and how adequately the paper as a whole serves to back it up. Not infrequently, such a model paper should have the kind of strategy that can be clearly formulated, and the kind of structure that can be graphically outlined by the class. When the basic question is "How effective is this as a piece of writing?" the students soon realize that there is something inadequate about answering "There is a comma missing in the second line of Paragraph Two."

[22] *English in the Secondary School* (New York: Holt, Rinehart & Winston, Inc., 1961), pp. 92–93.

The most usable sort of paper is one that represents good solid work and yet allows for discussion of how it could have been strengthened in further revision. The class should explore what could have been achieved by tighter restriction of the subject, further development of a weak paragraph, or elimination of a too superficially handled side issue. When the paper contains problems of punctuation and of usage, opaque or awkward passages, the teacher can demonstrate how these are handled in businesslike copyreading and revision.

Generally, such procedures shift the emphasis in the discussion of student writing from a mechanical inventory of "errors" to considerations of substance, structure, and style. In his comments on student papers and in class discussion, the teacher of writing must constantly make clear his first requirement: the student's writing should make sense. It is this responsibility that is neglected in much conventional teaching of composition:

> A mistaken form or order is obvious; we can see it, isolate it, prescribe directly for it. It is not so when words lose touch with reality. To be sure, when a pupil is talking about the sensory, physical world, there is no trouble, or if there is, we can spot it. . . . It is when he gets into abstractions, into generalizations, into the whole world of ideas that the rub comes; and this is the world that his school and his maturing life lead him into. And it is hard to spot this trouble, and to help him see it and prevent it. . . . in our emphasis on form and elegance, we accept with joy from a pupil something like this:

>> The cynical attitude of the common adolescent borders closely on the fatalism of Henchard. A connection may be seen if one notices that the cynic ascribes the lowest motives to an act. The fatalist says, "These things will invariably be so." In saying this, he assumes the lowest motives for man's actions, because higher motives would inevitably tend to change the evil that the fatalist says is irrevocably so. Thus I should call Hardy even more a cynic than a fatalist, because he takes cynicism for granted, but writes about fatalism. . . .

> All the skills of writing that this twelfth-grader has been so carefully taught were brought to bear in making nonsense sound convincing to himself and his reader. . . . he ignored his own experience by making statements about the relationships in this world between motives and outcomes that are just not so, and that, a conference revealed, he did not believe.[23]

Such concern with "reference to human experience in the world as we know it" does not mean that the teacher of composition will adopt a policy of "the form doesn't matter, as long as the content is all right." Rather, the teacher will be concerned with language, with form and structure and style, as the means of shaping and conveying meaning. In the words of George Winchester Stone, Jr.,

[23] Louis Zahner, "What Kinds of Language Teaching?" Gordon and Noyes, *Essays*, pp. 10–11.

Future teachers of composition, wishing to *educate* their students (and hold their jobs) will have to de-emphasize theme grading as a proofreading exercise. . . . They will have to come to grips with what the process of writing is, with what goes on in the mind before the pen takes up the tale, with the attaining of effects for which the mind strives, with the plainness, the forcefulness, and the subtleties of wielding words to shape the matter.[24]

To make such work fruitful, both teacher and student have to take a mature view of the relationship between writer and critic. It is easy to ridicule the student's pitiful present performance; it is hard to get him to do better. When having his own work evaluated by an M.A. or Ph.D. committee, by editors or reviewers, the teacher realizes how judicious, cogent, and motivated by genuine interest criticism must be if it is to have an invigorating rather than a frustrating effect. We should more often apply to the teaching of writing in general what John Ciardi says about the teaching of imaginative writing in particular:

No good teacher will insist that his word is law. He knows he is a groper. He suggests, prods, points out, and hopes to make a contact that will count. His work is pointless if the writer comes to him in a defensive fury, and just as pointless if the writer comes too submissively.[25]

If this is the sort of advice that needs to be given the teacher, the student, for his part, needs to be given the sort of advice that helps him respond to criticism in mature and relevant fashion. He has to learn the art, no easier for him than for the adult, of interpreting criticism not as a threat to his ego but as a guide to improvement. He has to realize that overt criticism, candid and in good faith, is greatly to be preferred to silent disapproval, hidden behind a smilingly noncommittal façade. It is a rare writer whose work does not profit from the criticism of a patient and perceptive editor. In being cruel to be kind, the good teacher, like the good editor, helps make the writer fit, both in substance and in spirit, to encounter that much more merciless critic that is the heedless, spoiled, unthinking general reader.

The teacher's work is successful to the extent that the student succeeds in becoming his own critic. In writing and revising, the effective writer mentally makes the notes that during his apprenticeship were contributed by teacher and critic: "This paragraph is too thin. Better look for a more plausible example." "I am using this term here in a slightly different way. Make sure it is clearly and consistently defined." "I know this isn't quite the right word for what I am trying to say. Keep hunting." "I just read something dealing with this point very effectively. Where was it? Let me find the passage." "I know what I am getting at here, but I'm not really saying it. Rephrase." "I am laboring the obvious. Let me cut this down." The best mutual compliment teacher and student can

---

[24] "The Modern Language Association and the Shape of Things to Come," *PMLA*, LXXIII (December, 1958), Part 2, p. 88.
[25] "On Writing and Bad Writing," *Saturday Review*, December 15, 1962, p. 12.

pay each other is the student's saying in reply to a critical observation: "Yes, I sort of felt that while I was writing that down."

To make instruction in writing effective, teachers of English must counteract two equally unfortunate tendencies. Work focused on composition is often too mechanical, designed to drill into the students patterns they should instead develop organically through much reading and writing. Work focused on language or literature is often considered a holiday from the grind of trying to improve the student's written work. However, some of the most effective instruction in writing takes place when quizzes, written examinations, and term papers are evaluated and discussed as examples of purposeful composition. Here is the teacher's opportunity to demonstrate that knowledge of a subject cannot be separated from the ability to present it, to argue out its inherent problems, to trace important relations. An examination on a literary subject should not be returned with subscores to be totaled up at the end; it should be returned with comments showing the student how effectively he dealt with his subject. English teachers must convince their students that effective student writing is a primary concern in everything English teachers do.

Lay Readers and Team Teaching

Establishing a clear rationale for the reading of papers is especially important when the reading is farmed out to assistants. In recent years, instructors in college and high school composition have begun to copy the common upper-division and graduate-school practice of delegating the reading of student papers. There is always a basic unfairness in such procedure, felt most strongly by the student who takes his writing seriously. Any teacher gradually establishes a climate of opinion, a set of expectations. He thus keeps his student writers from writing in a vacuum. Of the many factors that contribute to competence in writing, he will stress those that seem most basic to him, or most relevant to the students' present stage of development. He will suggest questions for the students to argue, set up perspectives for the more able students to question. He will convey to his students some idea of his tolerance for irony and whimsey, and for the polemical or strictly experimental.

There is an inevitable letdown when writing designed to meet standards thus developed in the give-and-take of the classroom is taken out of its context and assigned to an outside reader. No matter how competent the reader, his reactions will seem at least to some extent irrelevant and arbitrary. The student finds that in effect he is talking to a stranger. It is hard for the student to put urgency and conviction into what he is saying if his instructor, by appointing a deputy, has just made clear the limits of his interest in the student's writing.

Obviously, the instructor must at least attempt to reduce this feeling of irrelevance by careful consultation with his readers. In addition to providing them with fairly explicit theoretical guidelines, he should arrange for detailed discussions of typical student papers. The best corrective to capricious standards for the evaluation of student writing is the practice of holding paper-grading sessions in which the assumptions behind conflicting evaluations are brought out into the open. By whatever means, the instructor must strive to overcome the lack of continuity between classroom work and the outside reader's reactions.

In view of these difficulties, the use of reading assistants should, if necessary, reluctantly be accepted as an expedient rather than promoted as a promising innovation. In their more sober moments, advocates of the use of **lay readers** will admit that "all that we hoped to prove was that teachers could be relieved of half or more of their impossible load of paperwork without handicapping their students."[26] Clearly, a substantial writing program making partial use of lay readers is preferable to the kind of token program whose infrequent writing assignments make any real progress impossible.

Whatever values are lost when the criticism of student writing is delegated to an assistant are not the kind that can be graphically demonstrated by objective tests. The basic objection to any large-scale use of graduate assistants and lay readers for this purpose is that it constitutes another small step toward the kind of anonymous, depersonalized, homogenized mass education that most educators in theory deplore but in practice find hard to resist. The most desirable effect of a lay-reader program is that it will identify talented individuals who should be encouraged to consider English teaching as a career, to participate in the work of the profession not as part-time help but as confident professionals.

Related problems are raised by the reorganization of teaching personnel in **team teaching.** In team teaching,

> teachers, working together, both plan and carry out instruction for the same group of students, with opportunities to observe each other teach, to observe the effects of that teaching, and to hold discussions of teaching based upon common observations. The typical teacher leads a professional life that is relatively isolated from that of other teachers. When school is in session, he is busy teaching "his" students in "his" classroom. When the school day is over, he plans the lessons for "his" courses. Under team teaching, the individual teacher is able to study and benefit from the strengths of other teachers and to receive criticism and help in his own work.[27]

26 Paul B. Diederich, "Innovations in English Teaching," in *Needed Research in the Teaching of English,* ed. Erwin R. Steinberg (Proceedings of a Conference Held at the Carnegie Institute of Technology, May 5–7, 1962), p. 60.
27 Judson T. Shaplin, "Team Teaching," *Saturday Review,* May 20, 1961, p. 54.

Such arrangements, familiar to college teachers participating in group teaching of general-education courses with large enrollments, counteract tendencies toward intellectual isolation and toward routine teaching that year after year repeats itself. Working closely with alert and demanding colleagues can be an invigorating experience. Under ideal circumstances, students can witness an exciting kind of intellectual exchange and collaboration.

On the debit side, dividing the work of a course between "specialists" makes it harder to maintain the continuity and the sense of direction that are the condition of purposeful work. To the extent that it involves large numbers of students, team teaching dilutes the personal relationship between teacher and student and inhibits discussion. Large lectures and small discussion groups, where they are part of such a plan, are hard to work into a really organic sequence. It becomes more difficult than usual to maintain an organic relationship between classroom work, student writing, and evaluation of written work by the teacher. Finally, the more susceptible teacher begins to concentrate less on the reactions of his students and more on those of supervisors and colleagues.

At its extreme, team teaching presents the student with the kind of scrambled schedule in which various kinds of presentations in large lecture halls alternate with small discussion groups, activity periods, and independent reading. Such a program calls for a great deal of administrative activity and resourcefulness, requiring the services of a computer for effective scheduling on a large scale. By the same token it appeals to the teacher who is organization-oriented rather than to the one who wants to close the door behind him and start teaching. When it reaches the proportions envisioned by its more enthusiastic advocates, team teaching gets in the way of the relationship between a teacher and a group of students that is ideal for instruction in English. This is the relationship that exists when students and teacher over the months, through their common reading and writing, through their shared exploration of material, develop a sense of participation in meaningful and productive work.

On the other hand, when its possibilities are made use of in much more limited and diffident fashion, team teaching suggests ways by which teachers of English may hope to resist some of the pressures and break up some of the patterns that threaten to make their teaching routine and unproductive. In the average high school, the largest single obstacle to successful English teaching is the unrelenting pressure on the teacher to meet five oversize classes five days a week. If on each fifth day a class would participate in a large lecture or in a program of independent reading, the teacher thus freed from attendance might have a chance to think about what happened in class on the four preceding days and to prepare to meet the class on the next four days with a renewed sense of purpose. Team teaching on a small scale makes possible the kind of imaginative scheduling that can help protect a teacher against being forced, against his better intentions, to meet a class when he is only superficially prepared, to return a set of papers only hastily read.

Evaluation

In English, and in other areas in the humanities, it is notoriously difficult to assess the performance of teachers and the achievement of students in an objective way. However, this difficulty makes itself felt in less drastic form in all areas of education. Measurement psychologists are often more cautious in evaluating the measuring and testing devices they have developed than the teachers and administrators who use these devices. The experimental psychologist who is an expert in measuring changes in complex behavior patterns is likely to be well aware of the difficulties in constructing reliable and meaningful tests, whether for the evaluation of experimental programs and approaches or for the testing of ordinary student progress.

Generally, the measurement psychologist is likely to be more aware than the layman of variables in background and motivation of students and of personality, emphasis, and approach among teachers. In evaluating teaching methods, he will be aware of the kinds of questions left unanswered by ordinary statistical results:

A method which is effective for the learning of some students may be ineffective for others in the same classroom. Ordinary group comparisons between teaching methods may thus hide very important differences in the effects of the methods upon particular types of students. . . .

Because passing or excellent grades are so important to students, they may compensate for ineffective teaching by additional study in order to pass the course examination at the level to which they aspire. . . .

When significant differences in achievement are found in an experiment, the difference may simply reflect the degree to which students in differing classes were able to find out what the examination was to be and the degree to which it would determine the course grade.[28]

The psychologist knows the special impetus experimental approaches receive from the enthusiasm of their advocates and the interest created by their novelty. On the one hand, he hesitates to ascribe changes in test results to the introduction of a particular teaching technique or any other single factor. On the other hand, he knows how often comparisons set up to neutralize as many complicating factors as possible lead to results showing no statistically significant difference.

Similarly, the testing expert is likely to be aware of the difficulty of constructing tests that will in a balanced and comprehensive manner

---

[28] W. J. McKeachie, "Problems and Perils in Controlled Research in Teaching," Steinberg, *Needed Research,* pp. 53–54.

measure the concepts and skills, let alone the more intangible attitudes and perspectives, taught in a course. He knows that achievement as measured by objective tests does not necessarily correlate with achievement on essay tests designed to "measure understanding and integration of the materials."[29] Generally, "a measurement psychologist views a test with cautious distrust" and admits that

> a good teacher is well aware of the difficulties involved in relying upon tests for the evaluation of students. Most teachers feel it necessary in assigning course grades to balance examination performance with their own subjective appraisal of what the student has learned.[30]

In turning specifically to English, the testing expert will be aware both of the complexity of the factors involved in effective language use and of the variations in the values placed upon different elements in language competence by different judges. Predictably, the more concrete but less significant elements in the student's achievement in English are the ones that can be most reliably measured:

> Many phases of ability in the use of the English language have been successfully measured, i.e., measured with acceptable reliability and meaningfulness. Reading can be scored reliably and meaningfully for speed, recall, and understanding. Vocabulary may be tested by means of forced choice tests, or by graders' judgments with reasonable inter-judge agreement. Such matters as spelling and grammatical usage are readily summarized in rules. But attempts to measure meaningfully and reliably the complex abilities involved in actively using the language to convey ideas, as in composition, have met with small success. No method for evaluating abilities in composition in terms of "objectively" scored items is apparent.[31]

From the psychologist's point of view, such considerations are a spur to continued attempts to develop testing procedures that are as reliable and significant as possible. From the teacher's point of view, they are a warning never to use test results without full awareness of their limited significance. Obviously, such tasks as the screening of large numbers of high school graduates for admission to college are greatly expedited by reliance on carefully developed objective tests. In such circumstances, even teachers with a strong preference for written examinations will be reassured by the thought that "English is a combination of skills and knowledge, so intricately intertwined that a direct measurement of one is very likely to afford an indirect measure of another." A vocabulary test, for instance, is a good predictor of performance in composition if it measures "thoroughly a student's range and accuracy in the use of words. Words are, after all, the substance of all writing." Objective tests that require the student "to show some logical sense

29 *Ibid.*
30 Garlie A. Forehand, "Psychological Measurement and Research on the Teaching of English," Steinberg, *Needed Research*, p. 45.
31 *Ibid.*, p. 46.

of organization of ideas, or to exhibit a feeling for rhythm or style, have usually succeeded in identifying those who can write at least acceptably."[32]

However, what value such tests have as indicators of student ability must be balanced against their negative effects on both the teacher's and the students' view of their subject. In the words of a teacher for many decades closely connected with the preparation of examinations for the College Entrance Examination Board,

> If the secondary schools begin to concentrate on training candidates to put the right marks on an answer sheet, I fear that they will stray far from the major aims of all English teaching: the complementary aims of helping students to read with understanding and delight, and to write with accuracy and clarity. I still think that a student well trained in these aims will do better, even on purely objective tests, than one whose teachers have drilled him on finding the "right" answers to multiple choice items.[33]

To the extent that objective examinations have been allowed to play a central role in our schools, they have given students and administrators a badly distorted mechanistic and quantitative view of education. However well designed the individual test, in the aggregate, objective tests make the student aim, not at developing an authoritative command of live relationships, complex and interdependent, but at looking for the individual "items" that can be simplified to the point of becoming "objective." Rather than make the student explore connections, the routine test item cuts off all connections but one. In the words of Gilbert Highet,

> the sense which teachers must strive hardest to develop in their students is the sense of structure: the power of grasping a broad historical process, a large geographical nexus, the plot and purpose of a great book. As students become more inured to this type of examination, their attention is shifted away from these broader questions to the atomic facts which can be learnt almost entirely without real knowledge and real education.[34]

Generally, English teachers tend to deplore the widespread use of objective tests, "believing that it encourages reading only for the purpose of finding answers, that it leads students to assume that content is always separate from form, and that it inhibits students from developing independent power of thought and expression."[35]

Wherever the pressure of numbers permits, the teacher should use quizzes and examinations that more adequately reflect the purposes of his course. For instance, a vocabulary test should require the student to write a brief definition and provide two or three illustrations of the word used in context. It thus provides much-needed practice in the writ-

---

[32] Edward S. Noyes, "Teaching and Testing of English," *College Composition and Communication*, XII (February, 1961), 37.
[33] *Ibid.*
[34] Highet, *Art of Teaching*, p. 120.
[35] Representatives of English Departments in California colleges and universities, mimeographed statement on "High School Preparation in English."

ing of miniature paragraphs. Quizzes on literary selections should not require the mechanical matching of names and events but instead ask for brief character sketches or short accounts of significant plot developments. *In English, as in the humanities generally, examinations should wherever possible be synonymous with written examinations. They should be an organic part of a course, not a homogenized set of questions prepared by anonymous experts.* Ideally, "every question directly asked of a pupil at any examination is either framed or modified by the actual teacher of that pupil in that subject."[36]

If English teachers stress the limited scope of objective measures of achievement, they are correspondingly obligated to keep more subjective measures from being merely capricious. The apprentice teacher profits greatly from detailed discussion and evaluation of representative student papers. Often what seems an arbitrary difference in grading standards reflects a genuine problem of evaluation. An exceptional paper may be well phrased but illogical; another competently written except for a dozen misspellings. No objective formula can simplify the difficult decision of how to balance off against each other factors not really commensurate. One instructor will fail a paper because, in spite of other virtues, it fails to meet minimum standards in one crucial area. Another may assign split grades to avoid a succession of colorless, unmotivating, averaged-out C's. A third may put fluency above logic, or substance above form, or originality above soundness. A departmental consensus on some of these alternatives can assure reasonable continuity of grading standards as the student proceeds from one class to the other.

More arbitrary are other kinds of variations. At one extreme is the teacher who never gives an A because only God is perfect. At the other extreme is the teacher who deprives grades of their role as indicators of performance, making a B stand for effort and co-operation rather than for achievement. One of the most common complaints of college students who used to receive high grades in their high school English classes is that grades were not employed more effectively as an incentive to more serious work.

The experienced teacher develops his standards by reading compositions and examination papers by numerous students, on different levels, over a long period of time. He grades examinations, not on a curve, but by way of comparison with the achievement of other students in a similar class, at a similar institution. He hesitates in assigning some of the grades, less from his failure to recognize the merits and defects of a paper than from the difficulty of balancing them off against each other. Aware of such difficulties, he tries to provide his classes with a reasonably plausible and consistent explanation of his standards. He makes sure that students

[36] A. N. Whitehead, *The Aims of Education* (New York: The Macmillan Company, Inc., 1929), p. 7.

do not come to regard examinations they write in English as shots fired in the dark.

For the teacher of English, the value of objective examinations, apart from their efficiency as a screening device, is that they provide a check on more subjective, but also potentially more searching methods of evaluation. They provide a counterweight to the irrelevant associations and unconscious favoritism that even the most fair-minded teacher cannot entirely escape. Whatever his sources of evidence, the responsible teacher will never assign a grade in a cavalier or highhanded manner. As John W. Gardner has said,

> The sorting out of individuals in a society is an exceedingly serious business —and a potentially explosive one. No stone should be left unturned to insure that decisions are based on a wide range of evidence, carefully gathered and sifted. And precisely because the consequences for the individual are so serious, the final weighing of evidence, the final judgment that puts it all together, must be made by a qualified and responsible human being rather than by a machine.[37]

The Art of Teaching

What, to sum up, should the teacher know about methods of instruction in English? Every teacher sooner or later realizes there are no sure-fire methods for transforming an apathetic or hostile student into an eager and appreciative one. Every teacher must learn through trial and error how he can best establish contact with his students. As for his training in effective approaches and devices, he will receive some "consciously and some subconsciously. By the time he rates a B.A. degree he will have observed a fair number of teachers, and will remember as excellent some from high school and some from college. Teaching is in large part imitative."[38]

Nevertheless, a number of important principles are more effectively observed when the teacher explicitly recognizes them. First, teaching is not simply presentation but mediation. The teacher is not a mere guardian of knowledge but a translator, an interpreter, a guide. His first duty is not to cajole and denounce but to explain and show and demonstrate. He must keep in mind the kind of advice given by Gilbert Highet in *The Art of Teaching:*

> You must think, not what you know, but what they do not know; not what you find hard, but what they will find hard; then, after putting yourself inside their minds, obstinate or puzzled, groping or mistaken as they are, explain what they need to learn. And you must be sure they understand

---

[37] *Excellence: Can We Be Equal and Excellent Too?* (New York: Harper & Row, Publishers, 1961), pp. 52–53.
[38] George Sherburn, "Perspectives on the Profession," *The CEA Critic,* XXIII (December, 1961), 1.

your words. A strange name, a phrase only vaguely understood, will blur an explanation badly. Abstract words mean little on first hearing. Illustrate them. Give pictures and examples.[39]

The second principle to be remembered is the need for time and patience. A teacher must learn to persevere, to pursue limited objectives, to do the same thing over again in different ways until it has a chance to sink in:

> Real teaching is not simply handing out packages of information. It culminates in a conversion, an actual change of the pupil's mind. An important change takes a long time to carry through, and should therefore be planned carefully and approached in slow stages with plenty of repetition disguised by variation.[40]

The third principle is that of student participation. The final end of teaching must be to equip the student to learn on his own. In the teaching of English, "the ultimately important things to teach boys and girls are the processes of examination of language and literature rather than a sequence of factual conclusions arrived at by others who have examined them."[41] The teacher is successful to the extent that the student ceases to be a passive recipient of knowledge, to the extent that the student learns to explore and use language with growing confidence and skill.

The fourth principle is that of the personal relationship between teacher and student. In a subject that requires the human involvement of the student, teaching can take place only through personal contact with a teacher equally involved as a human being. Such human involvement is not shown through discussions of motivation or through periods devoted to establishing a friendly atmosphere. It is demonstrated through the teacher's handling of the material to be studied and of the student's work. It finds its expression in a working relationship between teacher and student that is at once respectful and friendly, demanding and relaxed, businesslike and humane.

A PROGRAM FOR FURTHER STUDY

JACQUES BARZUN, *Teacher in America.* New York: Doubleday & Company, Inc., 1955. An Anchor Book.

> An invigorating book on "the nature of subject-matter and the practice of teaching," by the eminent historian and publicist. Effective warnings against the foibles of educators.

[39] Highet, *The Art of Teaching*, p. 248.
[40] *Ibid.*, p. 249.
[41] G. Robert Carlsen, "The Way of the Spirit and the Way of the Mind," *The English Journal*, LII (February, 1963), 78.

GILBERT HIGHET, *The Art of Teaching.* New York: Alfred A. Knopf, Inc., 1950. A Vintage Book.

A wise and painfully honest book on the ingredients of successful teaching. Written by a Columbia University teacher of Greek and Latin who was born and educated in Great Britain.

EDWIN H. SAUER, *English in the Secondary School.* New York: Holt, Rinehart & Winston, Inc., 1961.

A lively and outspoken discussion of the purposes and problems of teaching high school English. Good balance of theoretical considerations and concrete observations on classroom practice.

J. N. HOOK, *The Teaching of High School English* (2nd ed.). New York: The Ronald Press Company, 1959.

Stressing "application more than theory," this book is a good introduction to the task confronting the high school teacher in the classroom. Contains many useful suggestions for classroom work, many references to discussions of teaching problems in professional magazines.

EDWARD J. GORDON AND EDWARD S. NOYES, eds., *Essays on the Teaching of English: Reports of the Yale Conferences on the Teaching of English.* New York: Appleton-Century-Crofts, Inc., 1960.

"A book for the high school teacher of English," this volume has been eminently successful in getting good teachers to "say in concrete language how they have handled problems relevant to any English classrooom: in the teaching of language, writing, and literature." Useful bibliographies accompany each section.

COMMISSION ON ENGLISH OF THE COLLEGE ENTRANCE EXAMINATION BOARD, *End-of-Year Examinations in English for College-Bound Students: Grades 9–12* (Princeton, N.J., 1963).

Sets of sample examination questions with a full range of representative student responses, followed by illuminating analysis and evaluation. Imaginative and demanding, these model examinations stress accuracy and sensitivity in the student's response to language, articulateness and responsibility in his use of it. An important part of the Commission's continuing effort to define "what English is and what it ought to be."

MATERIALS FOR ANALYSIS

A. Read several treatments of the principles of fruitful group discussion. Are there any assumptions or observations the authors share? How applicable are their conclusions to the effective use of the discussion method in the teaching of English?

B. Study a number of recent articles describing inductive procedures in the study of language that can be adapted for classroom work. Examples are Dennis R. Dean, "Slang is Language Too!" *The English Journal,* LI (May, 1962), 323–26; Norman V. McCullough, "The Lexical Method as a Significant Factor in Vocabulary Fixation," *College English,* XXIV

(November, 1962), 144–46. On the basis of the articles and your own experience, discuss the scope and limitations of the inductive method. Formulate concrete suggestions for its use in the classroom.

C. Study the exercises in one of your favorite high school or college texts. How successfully do they appeal to the student's understanding? How successfully do they promote his participation in active discovery? Cite detailed examples.

D. Examine the treatment of the comma and the semicolon in a number of high school or college texts. Then write an outline of a lesson (or series of lessons) designed to teach or review the most essential uses of these two marks. Include a statement of your over-all strategy, a summary of the major principles to be taught, and a sampling of the illustrative material to be used. (Unless your instructor specifies otherwise, this outline should run about 1000–1200 words.)

E. To judge from published statistics, the most popular arrangement of work in literature in selected high schools of above-average academic quality was by literary types, the second was by chronological sequence. On the basis of your own experience in study or teaching, discuss in detail the characteristic strengths and weaknesses of one of these approaches.

F. Read and evaluate accounts of units of study grouped around a major theme, as described for instance in the September, 1960, and March, 1963, issues of *The English Journal*. Discuss the rationale and plausibility of the suggested units, the relevance of the material suggested to the concerns of the teacher of English, and its appropriateness at the level for which it is intended.

G. The following questions are raised for the consideration of future English teachers in J. N. Hook's *The Teaching of High School English*, 2nd ed. (New York: The Ronald Press Company, 1959). Select one of these and develop your answer as fully as you can on the basis of your own observation and experience:

  1) What is your present opinion concerning the relative amounts of classics and contemporary literature that should be taught in high schools? (p. 47.)

  2) How would you yourself draw the line between "mere reading" and "literature"? (p. 153.)

  3) Choose a fairly difficult modern poem which you enjoy and which you believe would be suitable for high school seniors. Decide what traps in vocabulary, allusions, and sentence structure might catch students unless you help to spring them. (p. 236.)

H. In a book on the teaching of English, find the section that deals with instruction in writing. Report and discuss what you consider concrete and practical suggestions for the teacher's work. Some possible books to choose from are Edwin H. Sauer, *English in the Secondary School* (New York: Holt, Rinehart & Winston, Inc., 1961), Chapter Six; J. N. Hook, *The Teaching of High School English*, 2nd ed. (New York: The Ronald Press Company, 1959), Chapter Nine; Walter Loban *et al.*, *Teaching Language and Literature: Grades 7–12* (New York: Harcourt, Brace & World, Inc., 1961), Chapter Ten.

I. Study a copy of an objective test widely used to measure the student's command of the elements of written expression. Which of these elements are measured by the test, and how effectively or comprehensively? How valid does the test seem as an indicator of what it is designed to measure? Use detailed evidence in supporting your answers.

J. The following articles of more than usual interest discuss often taught selections from the point of view of the classroom teacher. Report fully on one of these, concentrating on what solid advice you think the article might offer an inexperienced instructor.

    1) Kellogg W. Hunt, "Getting into the Novel," *The English Journal,* L (December, 1961), 601–06.

    2) Sherwood Cummings, "What's in *Huckleberry Finn?*" *The English Journal,* L (January, 1961), 1–8.

    3) Janet M. Cotter, *"The Old Man and the Sea:* An 'Open' Literary Experience," *The English Journal LI* (October 1962), 459–63.

    4) Louis Josephs, "One Approach to the Puritans," *The English Journal,* L (March, 1961), 183–87.

    5) Leonard F. Dean, *"Julius Caesar* and Modern Criticism," *The English Journal,* XLVIII (May, 1959), 254–61.

    6) Charles Calitri, *"Macbeth* and the Reluctant Reader," *The English Journal, XLVIII* (May, 1959), 254–61.

    7) Michael Yatron, "Carl Sandburg: the Poet as Nonconformist," *The English Journal,* XLVIII (December, 1959), 524–27, 539.

    8) Georgia Christopher, "Literature and the Beginning Teacher," *The English Journal,* XLVIII (September, 1959), 321–25.

K. For each of the following student themes, write comments and a final evaluation that you think would prove meaningful and helpful to the student writer.

    1)   *Discipline is Needed*

    I think that most parents are not strict enough with their children. If parents were not so lax with their discipline, there wouldn't be as much delinquency as there is today. Most parents want there children to have everything they didn't have when they were young. The problem today is that children are spoiled.

    An excellent example of how children are spoiled is my niece. My sister and her husband give Kathy (my niece) every thing her heart desires. The results are clearly visable. Kathy is a spoiled brat. If my niece doesn't get whatever she wants, she cries. My sister wasn't going to give Kathy any ice cream before dinner the other night. Well, Kathy became very upset. My sister said, "Let her cry." Then two seconds later she said, "Oh, a little ice cream won't hurt her." This is a clear example of what a parent should not do. A parent should stand firm and not be pushed over by their child.

    If a child has too easy of a life, he has nothing to work for. Children need to work for what they get. If something is given to them, they will not respect it as much as they would if they earned it themselves. A child will not take as much care of an article that was given to him as he would an article which he earned himself. How can a child respect something that is easy to come by? The answer is, he can't.

    I think a child wants to be controlled by his parents. He will try to get away with as much as he can, but he actually wants his parents to tell him he can't do something. If his parents are strict, he soon learns what he can and can't do. By knowing that his parents care about what he does, he has a sense of security. All children want their parents to control them. They want to be guided and not turned loose to do as they please. It's the children who get to do everything they want that turn out to be delinquents.

When raising children it's better to be a little strict than too easy. No child was ever hurt because he didn't get what he wanted, but many children are hurt for life because they did get everything they wanted. A child is lucky if his parents are strict. In the long run, it will pay many dividends.

2)   *Sports*

Here has always seemed to be a great interest from the American people, towards sports. But lets ask ourselves, what is this interest focused on? Is this interest basically from the view point of the spectator or from the participant? There are many different types of sports and they all seem to be focused toward the spectator. One sees sports such as baseball, basketball, football, boxing, hockey, and tennis, to name just a few, that are definately sports for the spectator.

In high school, one find that a great deal of importants is put on football, baseball, and basketball, encouraging the student body to "come out and support the team." There are, of course, many that go try-out, in an attempt to make the team, but the majority of the time is spent in prompting the student body to come out to the games.

The same thing is true as far as colleges are concerned. The main difference between high school and college is it is on a much wider scale in college. Where in high school, the team would play in their own little valley league, in college it becomes more nation wide.

Take football, a sport that is one of the best attended of all spectator sports. The stands are usually jam packed when there is a good game going on. When in my senior year in high school, every football game was well attended. In fact, one couldn't even get in the gates a half hour before the games were to start.

I remember one of the last games of the season was played at our stadium. The weather had been bad all day and it looked as if it was about to pour any minute. Well, about 8:30 pm it did start to pour, only a half hour from the starting of the game. It happen to be the biggest turn out of the hole season. There was a crowd of about 6,000 that came out. This did not stop the rain from coming down in bucket fulls, however. But do you think they would stop the game and cancel it; do you think the crowd would go home because of the rain? No! For another hour and a half, the spectators stayed and the football players continued playing.

How can one even dare to say, sports today are not primarily just for the spectator. It is impossible to call it anything but a spectator sport.

3)   *Animal Farm*

One of the most important points of the "Animal Farm" is that the pigs controlled the whole farm once the owner was ousted in the Animal Rebelion.

Once on thier own, the pigs used their shrewdness in convincing the other animals on the farm that they were the smartest. The pigs could read and write and since no other animal could do both, they were made the leaders of the animals.

Throughout the whole book, the shrewdness of the pigs was brought out. For example, they didn't like the idea of sleeping in the barn with the rest of the animals so they convinced the animals that if they lived in the house; they could think better and come up with better ideas on how to improve the farm.

A certain number of rules, which were made up mainly by the pigs, were being broken by them but they made the animals think differently by adding on certain clauses to the commandments they already had. One such rule was not to drink alcoholic beverages but the pigs extended it to "to excess" since they were the only ones to have alcohol present.

Eventually the whole animal farm was a dictatorship government held by the pigs but somehow the animals didn't understand this. They were happy to do what they were told because of; mainly, their independence (what they thought was independence) Some of the animals did try to revolt but the pigs had ways of dealing with them. One way was that the leader, Napoleon, had trained six dogs to be mad fighters since they were born and this scared the animals into doing what they were told to do.

The pigs used their authority to great means. Aside from ordering the animals on the farm, they handled business with the other farms in order to bring themselves luxury. Dealing with human beings was also another one of the commandments they broke.

In conclusion, I would like to add that if the animals weren't so foolish and stupid, they would have seen what the pigs had done to them. But they weren't and they fell into the coniving hands of their leaders

Teaching in recent decades has shown the influence of three major kinds of change. The first, originating in the twenties and thirties, was a fundamental change in educational philosophy. In varying degrees, and with varying degrees of success, teaching has moved away from an authoritarian imparting of knowledge to procedures requiring the student's active participation. The second wave of change, originating in the forties and fifties but just now making its full influence felt in the schools, resulted from a basic re-examination of content in the fundamental academic subjects: mathematics, science, English. Efforts on a large scale are underway to re-establish harmony between these subjects as taught in the schools and contemporary scholarship and research in each field. The third kind of change, which has gained its impetus in the current decade, is affecting the technology of teaching, the technical resources at the teacher's disposal. The teacher trying to come to terms with recent developments in subject matter may find that at the same time the conditions of his work are being radically altered by new instructional materials and techniques.

eight

Resources

Even when the teacher's major resource is an assigned textbook, conformity to the pattern established by the book can basically affect, for better or for worse, what happens in the classroom. When schools employ instructional television and programmed instruction, the teacher is in danger of being no longer the master but the servant of the technical resources being employed. Such innovations are often effectively promoted by persons specializing in their development and use. *If teachers of English are going to be effective in determining the conditions and objectives of their work, they must realistically evaluate new developments in teaching technology.* They must be aware of their implications for the teaching of language and literature.

Textbooks

The selection of textbooks was once a matter of choosing among a few well-established books by a small number of textbook publishers. It has become a matter of choosing from a wide variety of offerings by numerous publishers competing for a share of the rapidly growing text-book market. Increasingly, texts are available to represent every major emphasis or shade of opinion in the discipline of English. For committees charged with the selection of texts, surveying even the more important possibilities is becoming a large task.

Inevitably, the teacher will to some extent find his own approach at odds with that adopted in the textbook he is using. The competent and alert teacher has worked out his own rationale of the subject matter; he has developed his own approaches to specific problems. Through trial and error, he has discovered materials and selections his training and temperament equip him to present to students with special success. By such a teacher, even a good textbook will to some extent be felt as a constraint. He will use it selectively, supplementing it in his own way. He may well decide to rely on the publishers of paperbacks and on the departmental ditto machine to provide him with his own set of text materials.

By thus in effect compiling his own textbook, the teacher learns to form a realistic judgment not only of the convenience but also of the other possible virtues of available texts. Unlike someone making assignments from day to day, the textbook author has to think through and structure a course or a sequence of study as a whole. Many textbooks result from a sharing of experience. Many an author starts with highly personal ideas and approaches. After years of buffeting by editors, publishers' readers, reviewers and critics, after extended reconsideration and testing of sample materials, he often emerges a more knowledgeable, if not a wiser man. In successful collaborations, authors engage in a process of arguing out and reconciling differences that is considerably more thorough than casual conversation among colleagues. By and large, the textbook author has worked harder at the job of making teaching a going concern, and knows more about it in a practical sort of way, than many of his colleagues.

Nevertheless, the preparation of text materials for English presents special problems, not easily solved. What we teach our students about language and literature is not simply a body of knowledge; it involves attitudes, preferences, values. Thus, the textbook author who departs from the trodden path often provokes negative reactions that seem out of proportion to the importance of individual items criticized. Often, the book that is widely adopted is not one that enjoys vigorous and outspoken support but one that has managed not to step on anyone's toes. Discouraged by such observations, the more independent author must resist the temptation to make his writing unprofitably polemical, belaboring his more apathetic colleagues rather than enlightening the students. It is hard to convince the student of the central importance in his own education of a subject expounded by authorities who spend much of their time refuting and belittling each other. Furthermore, one of the major ways in which teachers keep abreast of new developments is by exploring textbooks incorporating new materials and points of view. *Author, reviewer, and user, apart from immediate needs and problems, must recognize their common professional aim to work responsibly toward an informed consensus.* Such work requires on the part of the teacher willingness to explore the new, and on the part of the textbook author the ability to present the new on its merits, without erecting gratuitous barriers in its path.

Apart from such general problems of perspective and of tone, the textbook author in English faces special problems in the selection and presentation of his materials. For decades, the major text dealing with language and composition was a **handbook** for the correction of student themes. In a well-established pattern, the typical handbook presented perhaps one hundred fifty or two hundred numbered and labeled rules, whose conscientious application was to rid the student's writing of error. Instructions were deliberately emphatic and concise, encouraging memorization by the more diligent users. A well-developed reference system typically made possible considerable efficiency in the marking and revision of student papers.

The major shortcoming of these linguistic etiquette books was that they gave both teacher and student a distorted view of what English is all about. They presented little information about language beyond what was meant to be narrowly utilitarian in its application to writing. They stressed the mechanics and bare bones of writing, obscuring factors and processes that make for authentic, substantial, effective prose. In their treatment of grammar and usage, they shut off intelligent inquiry by requiring unreasoning acceptance of authority, by failing to give a responsible accounting of their various rulings and prescriptions. Whatever the compensating virtues of the individual book, as a group the traditional handbooks were narrow in scope, dogmatic in tone, and negative in approach.

The inevitable reaction to the traditional handbooks took the form implied in this account of their defects. Texts have increasingly recognized that the student should have an informed understanding of language, both as an educated person and as a writer who must make intelligent choices rather than apply mindless rules. More and more, texts are reflecting the view that

> the student of writing or speaking makes real progress only as he learns more and more about the language he is using. He needs to know what sort of thing language is, how it developed and thereby what it has become. He needs to know as much as he can both of its possibilities and of its limitations for thinking and communication. He must be able to sense what is

appropriate and what is likely to be effective. He must gain the kind of familiarity with his tools that comes only from intimate acquaintance.[1]

To the extent that they reflect this point of view, handbooks for student writing have become more comprehensive in scope and more liberal in perspective. They show a recognition that man writing is a reflection of man thinking. They show a recognition that there is more to writing than a command of grammar and usage, but also that a treatment of grammar and usage, to be acceptable from a scholarly point of view, must do without gross simplifications. The grammarian cannot hope, any more than any other representative of an academic discipline, to be exempt from the requirement for a reasoned explanation for generalizations and advice he wishes to present. Even where textbooks in language and composition preserve the handbook format, they have as a group become more discursive and humble, and, as a result, more instructive. Increasingly, they are putting stress on developing positive skills rather than on correcting mistakes already made.

Obviously, discursiveness can be carried too far. The textbook author must resist a number of familiar temptations. In trying to establish an attitude conducive to learning, he does not really gain by talking *about* motivation, by announcing his *intention* to be friendly and informal. It is much more important that he hit the right tone in treating his subject, that he show his respect for the students in his phrasing of questions and advice. Similarly, he will want to establish a rationale for his organization and procedures. However, he gets in his own way by being always anxiously self-explanatory about everything the book requires the students to do. In the present state of the discipline, there is the added danger that the student will be used as a pawn in professional controversies, that he will be asked to mark "wrong" tenets he clearly remembers as dear to the heart of last year's teacher. Again, the author gains by deciding to refute alchemy in professional articles or books and to use the text to teach the students in objective and nonpolemical fashion. Quite apart from these various temptations to loquaciousness, there remains the basic question of how much of the "talking" in a course the teacher will allow the textbook to do. Every teacher looks for the textbook that is competent, businesslike, and articulate—without usurping the teacher's role.

In college, the traditional handbook is usually presented as a reference guide for college writing. One would thus expect students to keep and use it during their college years. In practice, such books are usually resold by the student along with his other textbooks at the end of one or two semesters—a period perhaps too short to allow the book to do much good or harm. In high school, however, a series like the widely

---

[1] Albert R. Kitzhaber, *et al.*, *Education for College: Improving the High School Curriculum* (New York: The Ronald Press Company, 1961), p. 83.

used Warriner's *English Grammar and Composition* provides a volume of traditional handbook format for each year from the seventh through the twelfth grade. In the very first book, the student is introduced to the familiar pattern of rule—illustration—exercise, with the traditional definitions and categories. The latter are put to work in the familiar injunctions against sentence fragments, run-on sentences, faulty agreement, confusion of *lie-lay*, faulty pronoun case. Traditional diagramming is employed throughout, as allegedly "for many pupils" an "important means to the understanding of the relationships between sentence parts."[2] In each successive book, this material is repeated, or rather "reviewed," with increasing attention to ramifications and refinements, but with continuing focus on the elimination of real and imagined faults from the student's writing.

Throughout the series, "good usage" is illustrated by contrasting forms simply labeled "right" and "wrong." Throughout, the occasion for discussing usage is the need to avoid **common errors**. In Books 11 and 12, however, the student is introduced to the concept of "levels of usage." In theory, at least, colloquial English is here recognized as appropriate to informal situations, though it is set over against "standard" English, described as "always correct." *It's me,* invariable interrogative *who,* and *like* as a conjunction are recognized as colloquial usages. The basic distinction, however, remains that between correct English and English "incorrect grammatically, poor in vocabulary, and mispronounced."[3] The latter kind, variously labeled "poor English" and "illiterate," is described as "never correct" and "not to be used at all."

It is not surprising that after six years' acquaintance with such a series even a superior student will have come to feel that good writing is primarily a matter of avoiding "mistakes." It is not surprising that the novice teacher compelled to use such books finds it hard to come to grips with the true fundamentals of his subject. He cannot be blamed for falling into the old trap of making English synonymous with "grammar": In the traditional text, there are ninety pages on "correctness" for every ten pages on writing, with five of the latter devoted to the outline, the précis, the business letter, and the social note. The traditional text thus perpetuates the image of the English teacher as the person who teaches the juvenile delinquent to say *"Whom* did you see at the rumble?"

However, the most damaging effect of the traditional book is the way it prejudges the relationship between teacher and student. One can only wonder how a student from a minority group or of foreign-born parents reacts when the textbook sorts out students into those the speech of whose "parents, brothers and sisters, and friends has been that of educated

---

2 John E. Warriner *et al., English Grammar and Composition 8* (New York: Harcourt, Brace, & World, Inc., 1963), p. iv.
3 Warriner, *English Grammar and Composition 11,* p. 72.

people" and those whose families are presumably "illiterate." One teacher, daughter of Irish immigrants, tells the story of how at a private academy she finally discovered in an old prayer book a sin she could meaningfully confess to the priest: Her schooling had made her ashamed of her parents. She was then, she says, "a sophomore, not without the connotations attaching to that term."

In the high schools, the attempt to escape from the strait jacket of the traditional handbook has typically taken the form of adopting a definition of English as devoted to the **language arts**. Even the most traditional books have come to devote perhaps thirty pages out of six hundred to speaking and listening, supplementing the familiar concern with writing and reading. In many other series, the treatment of grammar and usage has been shifted to the back of each volume, with material devoted to various language activities filling the earlier pages. However, as William R. Slothower found in a recent study, the typical commitment in the preface to comprehensive coverage of the language arts has not seriously affected either the bulk or the repetitiousness of the grammar materials:

> The English teacher who directs his class to "take out your grammar books" is speaking realistically, if not entirely accurately. . . . despite the authors' and publishers' claims that books in series are cumulative and that material is "developmental" or "sequential" and not merely repetitive, the treatment of grammar is, in fact, highly repetitive from year to year and book to book.[4]

Equally discouraging is the nature of the materials often introduced in the name of more balanced and more comprehensive language study:

> Much is offered as material for serious study that has little or nothing to do with the development of precision and responsibility in the use of English; much is offered as material for serious study that can hardly be regarded as intellectually respectable, either by the teacher or the student. . . . the books show a tendency, especially for but not restricted to the lower high-school years, to approach language through the "natural" medium of conversation, coupled with a kind of How-To-Win-Friends-And-Influence-People philosophy, complete with detailed techniques. As a result, typically we find introductory units on "getting acquainted with classmates," "making introductions," "talking it over with others," and "telephone etiquette."[5]

The well-meant inanity of some of the sample conversations and conversational "problems" has to be seen to be believed. As one observer noted,

> A persuasive case could in fact be made for teaching not how to phone but not to phone. . . . Many teachers . . . preferring some other oral exercise or written syntax, elect to skip the telephoning unit and trust to luck that

4 "School Textbooks in the Language Arts," *San Jose State College Institute Record*, I (June, 1963), 2.
5 *Ibid.*, p. 8.

their pupils will be able to break an appointment with the hairdresser without offending her.[6]

In spite of these generally discouraging findings, it is possible to find especially in recent high school texts a trend toward inclusion of substantial materials clearly relevant to the English teacher's fundamental concerns. Slothower reports that

> With reference to the treatment of the role of language in thinking processes, the situation in current textbooks is encouraging. Most of them include at least a chapter in which elementary logical concepts and principles are introduced. . . . An ambitious treatment of language and thinking appears in Book 6 of the McGraw-Hill series [*Your Language*]. Skills developed in the chapter on critical thinking include recognizing ambiguity and shifts in meaning, recognizing assumptions, drawing conclusions, deductive reasoning, inductive reasoning, and the nature of evidence and processes of generalization. Scott-Foresman's *Guide to Modern English* series offers an extended treatment of thinking processes, more than that in any of the other texts examined, in their books for Grades IX and X.

Many texts successfully adapt material from semantics, often, as in the Harcourt-Brace *The English Language* series, in an effectively graphic presentation:

> Scott-Foresman's series does a particularly good job in Books 10 and 11 with such concepts as concrete and abstract words, connotative words, and such principles as the symbol-referent relationship and "slanting" by selection and distortion of facts.[7]

As regards the grammatical structure and the history of our language, books are beginning to appear that give more than lip service to the need for adapting material from modern linguistics for serious study in the schools. The sections contributed by Donald Bird to Books 5 and 6 of the McGraw-Hill *Your Language* series are notable examples. As regards usage, the Corbin-Perrin *Guide to Modern English* series has for years made available an approach to "good English" that compared with the tone of the traditional handbook is like a breath of fresh air.

If critics were justified in approaching the traditional handbook with a jaundiced eye, they were similarly justified in scrutinizing its traditional companion, the **anthology**. For many decades, the major defect of literature collections, whether in high school or in college, was their practice of bringing together little pieces of great writers. These were further obscured by being put on the same footing with equally fragmentary selections from numerous minor authors. To many users, the word *anthology* became synonymous with a miscellaneous collection of unrelated snippets. A recent study of representative anthologies for the last two years of high school found that

---

[6] Elizabeth Toohy, "The English Plank in a Conservative Platform," *Elementary English*, XXXX (February, 1963), 149.
[7] *San Jose State College Institute Record*, I, 2.

too many authors are represented and the snippet editing is exasperating. "We ask the whole," Emerson wrote in "Gifts"; "nothing less will content us." But this essay is followed (editors have not been notable for their humor) in the eleventh-grade anthology by one column from "Nature," one from "Manners," etc., etc. A virtue is solemnly made of this mayhem. "Since the whole poem," the reader is told of the Intimations Ode, "is long and difficult, only the core of it is given here."[8]

The editorial matter in such an anthology too often presents the established platitudes of literary history and criticism, which the fragmentary selections prove inadequate to illustrate and substantiate. Not being comprehensive enough, the selections do not enable the student to test, and where necessary modify, the complacent generalizations of the editor. The student is thus trained to talk about literature at second hand.

As the result of these defects, the conventional survey anthology became one of the chief targets of those who in the forties and fifties attacked the mere perfunctory teaching of literary history as staple fare in high school and college:

> Some teachers of literature concentrate their efforts almost exclusively on the historical side of their subject. Their students learn the succession of recognized periods in literary history, the dates of birth and death of the principal authors, the titles of their chief works, and the stereotyped catalogue of influences supposed to obtain among them. They are told that the great literary periods are characterized by certain general traits as, for example, that the Romantic Period is marked by a love of the common man, a nostalgic return to the past, and so on. They often learn these generalizations without any direct acquaintance with the authors or works to which they are supposed to apply, or with only the scantiest acquaintance gained through fragments in anthologies.[9]

One obvious remedy, adopted in many **masterpieces** or **major writers** collections, is to limit the number of authors covered and to print as far as possible complete poems and short stories and plays. One of the basic assumptions of modern criticism is that the literary work functions as a structured whole; it follows that to excerpt a poem or short story is to truncate it. Another assumption of modern criticism is that to read one selection thoroughly and well tells us more about the writer than a cursory sampling of many miscellaneous pieces. Even where excerpting is defensible, as in presenting a selection from an epic poem or in abridging a long chapter from a book of nonfiction prose, the selection should be fully representative and as far as possible preserve intact extended sequences of uncut material.

[8] Kitzhaber, *Education for College*, p. 62.
[9] Report of the Literature Committee of the School and College Conference on English, April 1942, in *Issues, Problems, and Approaches in the Teaching of English,* ed. George Winchester Stone, Jr. (New York: Holt, Rinehart & Winston, Inc., 1961), p. 43.

None of this is meant to imply that the basic aim of the old-style anthology is unsound: to develop in the student a knowledge and appreciation of his literary heritage, of significant writers *in context.* Up to a point, a student can read Coleridge without being aware of the aesthetic theories and poetic practices of one William Wordsworth. But only up to a point. Similarly, T. H. Huxley can be studied for what he says directly to the modern reader. But what he says becomes more meaningful as the student becomes aware of such writers as Bacon, Hobbes, and Hume. A writer typically works in the context of a literary and cultural tradition, whether he works in it or against it, or whether, more typically, he adapts and shapes and transforms the tradition in complex ways. If the student does not develop a sense of history, the literature of the past easily comes to seem capricious in its forms and factitious in its thematic concerns. The true problem in the teaching of literary history, as of history generally, is to present what is truly significant, representative, and instructive.

The editor who takes his work seriously knows that finding instructive selections is not simply a matter of choosing material that he himself finds fresh, or satisfying, or stimulating. For good reasons, anthologies, out of the wealth of available literature, often choose a number of familiar pieces that have proved their capacity of promoting fruitful discussion and substantial student writing. Though they may be "chestnuts" to the experienced teacher, they are of course new to the student—and to the novice teacher looking for materials that will work for him rather than against him in the classroom. Often such selections are direct and accessible enough to be presented uncut and without elaborate footnotes. They may explore situations that are either close to the student's experience or such that he finds it easy to project himself into them imaginatively. At the same time they offer or imply some serious comment upon life; they offer not merely confirmation of familiar ways of feeling but add some dimension to the student's experience.

Willa Cather's "Paul's Case," for instance, takes up the theme of the adolescent's rebellion against the adult world and yet makes the student contrast his own feelings with those of a boy of a different temperament, in a different setting. It thus illustrates the kind of selection that not so much "meets the student at his own level" as meets him and *takes* him somewhere. The teacher will exploit but also try to pass beyond the student's interest in adventure, adolescence, romance. He will wish to see included in an anthology selections that provide a bridge from the student's experience to some of the great recurrent themes: the passing of time, the clash between desire and responsibility, the conflict of effort and circumstance. For instance, Eudora Welty's short story "A Visit of Charity" shows us the girl scout whose good deed for the day is to comfort old people at whom she stares with total and apprehensive incomprehension. By studying her reactions, the student can begin to examine the gulf that separates the young, and in the story, the callously efficient middle-aged, from the old.

In recent years, there has been a sharply negative reaction against the extensive **editorial apparatus** with which modern anthologies have sur-rounded the readings themselves. There is always a danger that introduc-tions to a literary work will channel and narrow the student's response rather than prepare him to respond to the work as fully and as relevantly as possible. They may tell the student things that he would more effec-tively learn by reading the work for himself. Questions for analysis may train the student to hunt for specific answers rather than to read with an open mind and an alert ear.

Nevertheless, anthologies providing such apparatus are not, as their critics claim, put together by people afraid of "just plain books." Rather, they were a reaction against the kind of textbook Gilbert Highet describes in *The Art of Teaching:*

> Well do I remember the first book of Homer I ever read. It was an ugly brown book. The scholar who produced it had written explanatory notes on every line (mainly on that fascinating subject, Homeric grammar), but he had not thought to tell me
> —who Homer was, if anybody
> —where he lived, and when
> —what the *Iliad* was
> —what Book One of the *Iliad* was (I didn't see how a book could have Books inside it, and I didn't find out until I had learnt about individual papyrus rolls)
> —what the general plan of the poem was, and how Book One fitted into it; nor to answer a hundred other simple questions which occurred to me.[10]

The apparatus in a good literature anthology both provides the framework for a purposeful course and undertakes some of the more prosaic but nonetheless indispensable teaching tasks. It helps clear away some of the obstacles that result from the students' lack of alertness to the importance of historical setting, cultural influence, and literary conven-tion. It prevents certain predictable kinds of plain misreading. But it also directs the student's, and the teacher's, attention to some of the matters—technical, structural, and thematic—that in a well-planned course are illuminated through successively more ambitious exploration.

To avoid extremes, the editor must realize that in the preparation of editorial aids thoroughness becomes a vice rather than a virtue. Questions should be illustrative rather than exhaustive. They should steer the student's attention in profitable directions rather than channel and control his response. A student should never read a poem by Emily Dickinson with the depressing feeling that afterwards there will be two

[10] *The Art of Teaching* (New York: Alfred A. Knopf, Inc., 1950), p. 71.

pages of questions to answer, with every word and metaphor to be accounted for. He should always feel that such questions as there are serve the text rather than vice versa.

Especially in high school texts, editors tend to make their questions too predictably and prosaically didactic in intention. It is true, for instance, that O. Henry's "The Gift of the Magi" is a story about the real meaning of gifts, and that O. Henry's view of the useless sacrifices of the two young lovers, hopelessly at cross purposes in their gift-giving, is predictably rose-colored and sentimental. However, we bring the student back to reality with too much of a thud if one of our first questions about the story is: "In your opinion, what should one consider in giving and receiving gifts?" On a more serious plane, students are likely to get suspicious when editors stress the theme of free enterprise with stories on initiative rewarded and handicaps overcome, but sidestep the same theme in stories of initiative miscarried and handicaps proving insuperable.

Questions must be genuine and open questions. The editor must avoid imposing upon the students his own standards and interpretations, however worthy, instead of eliciting their honest responses, however immature. One editor, under the heading "Reading Critically to Evaluate Ideas," discusses "Paul's Case" in terms of the normal versus the abnormal, the well adjusted versus those "refusing to accept reality." Once Paul is thus set over against the "normal high school student," all the really important questions about the relations between individual and society have already been prejudged. When the student is asked how Paul might have used his longings "constructively," the dice are far too obviously loaded in favor of conventional adult standards and compromises.

Whatever the nature of required major texts, recent developments in paperback publishing have made the teacher increasingly independent of textbook limitations. Where it is possible to have students buy supplementary paperback books, the teacher can come much closer than in the past to setting up a schedule of classwork or of readings that he finds fully satisfactory. Almost every major novel or play assigned in English courses is available in one or more inexpensive soft-cover editions; collections of poems and short stories are numerous and varied. The teacher who regularly recommends a paperback "Book of the Month" or "Book of the Week" can lead students to consider books not as textbooks but as books—to be bought, read, and kept.

One area in which recent publishing activity has provided exceptionally rich resources is **translations** from other literatures. There is a fashionable prejudice against translations in general, often held by people whose acquaintance with the hard, concentrated work and the rewards of literary translation is entirely theoretical. For the cliché that literature is untranslatable, the responsible critic will substitute an awareness of the many and often conflicting demands on the translator's ability. The translator must be unusually responsive to the language of the original—not only to the plain sense, but to the grammatical, semantic, and stylistic nuances, the allusions and verbal reminiscences and overtones, the general tone and its subtle local variations. He must have the knack for finding for each of these elements the right rendering, and for adjusting their often conflicting claims in a formula that does at least partial justice to the original author. The attentive reader is aware of the many contemporary translations that magnificently meet these requirements: Cornford's Plato, Rieu's Homer, Humphries' Ovid, Coghill's Chaucer, Wilbur's Molière, Yarmolinsky's Chekhov, Magarshack's Turgenev, and the Muirs' Kafka. To all of these applies what Dryden said in introducing his version of Chaucer, proceeding from the premise that "the first end of a writer is to be understood":

> How few are there, who can read Chaucer so as to understand him perfectly? And if imperfectly, then with less profit, and no pleasure. It is not for the use of some old Saxon friends that I have taken these pains with him: let them neglect my version, because they have no need of it. I made it for their sakes who understand sense and poetry as well as they, when that poetry and sense is put into words which they understand.[11]

It is not surprising that poets from Chaucer through Dryden and Pope to Baudelaire and Rilke have been intrigued and fascinated by the translator's art. Translation provides a more intimate insight into the complex workings of language than any other approach. For the teacher and critic, "the criticism of translations provides a particularly fascinating and instructive method of language study."[12]

As the result of recent publishing developments, many critical and scholarly materials have become as conveniently and inexpensively accessible as major primary sources. The teacher's own preparation is greatly helped by the many current paperbacks assembling articles on language and literature otherwise scattered in not easily accessible sources. There is a wealth of inexpensive collections of material on major writers, major works, major issues, major literary themes. As teaching devices, some of these volumes may justify the objections of reviewers who call them "books designed to keep the students out of the library by providing them with all the material they might want for themes on a particular subject" and "bastard books that make patchwork quilts of the literature we presumably love."[13] However, for the teacher plagued by lack of time

---

[11] Edmund D. Jones, ed., *English Critical Essays (Sixteenth, Seventeenth and Eighteenth Centuries)*, (London: Oxford University Press, 1956), p. 194.
[12] C. K. Ogden and I. A. Richards, *The Meaning of Meaning* (New York: Harcourt, Brace and World, Inc., 1923), p. 230.
[13] "Book Reviews," *College English*, XXIV (February, 1963), 413.

and incomplete library resources, such collections are an excellent means of keeping his professional interests alive and up to date.

The present state of vigorous activity and competition in textbook publishing inevitably contributes to the publication of books that are routine or improvised. At the same time, this state of affairs makes it possible for teachers to obtain books up-to-date in content and knowledgeable in execution. To make use of the present opportunities, teachers of English must resist the influence of academic inertia. However, they must also overcome the attitude of the academic status-seeker who looks with condescension on the prosaic task of the textbook writer. There are few things more important for us as a profession than securing text materials in language and literature that are respectable from the point of view of the scholar and effective from the point of view of the teacher.

Generally, publishers provide the textbooks they can reasonably expect teachers to adopt. If substandard books continue to be published and used, the reason is not necessarily that publishers do not believe in quality. Rather, they have learned from sad experience that books of high quality do not always sell. To improve the quality of textbooks used, teachers of English should clearly formulate and propagate their criteria for texts they find acceptable: *Textbooks on language should help the teacher develop in his students an interest in exploring language, an understanding of its diversity, and a respect for the demands it makes on speaker and writer. Textbooks on composition must show that instruction in writing does not mean constant ill-tempered nagging concerning picayune details of linguistic etiquette. A composition text must make the student aware of the processes of exploration and of thought that he employs in distilling his observation, experience, and reading into ideas of his own. Textbooks on literature should contain representative selections of literary quality. These selections should reflect a realistic estimate of the student's preferences, prejudices, and abilities and yet furnish the means for broadening his interests.* They should reflect a recognition that the enjoyment of great literature must be carefully kindled and kept alive, that sophistication must be developed rather than bestowed.

Increasingly, textbooks are becoming available that meet these criteria. For instance, for the teacher instructing high school juniors there are books as thoughtfully prepared as the Corbin-Perrin *Guide to Modern English 11* (Scott, Foresman, 1963) or the LaBrant-Leary-Bird-Painter *Your Language 5* (McGraw-Hill, 1960); the McCarthy-Rodabaugh *Prose and Poetry of America* (L. W. Singer, 1963) or the Fuller-Kinnick *Adventures in American Literature* (Harcourt, Brace, 1963). Teachers are responsible for demonstrating, in words and actions, their support for publishers who invest in textbooks of genuine substance and quality.

Audio-Visual Aids

The evaluation of textbooks the English teacher can undertake with considerable confidence. After all, they represent a kind of writing and editing that he should be well equipped to criticize. Other resources available to him present a different kind of problem. In their attempts to demonstrate the potentialities of the written word, English teachers have often been wary of external aids. Ultimately, it is their job to show what the *word* can do—unaided by picture, diagram, and chart. At the same time, words may remain *mere* words for the student because they are lacking in visual associations, because they relate to nothing meaningful to him from personal observation and experience.

The teacher teaching an Elizabethan play visualizes characters with the dress and manners of their time, surrounded by the artifacts of their civilization, moving through cities and countryside different from ours. He further visualizes the action of the play as taking place on a certain kind of stage, before a certain kind of audience, in a certain historical and cultural context. In creating this context for his students, he will be greatly aided by a well-illustrated text and by pictorial aids in classroom, study hall, and library. He will be greatly aided by authentic staging of an Elizabethan play at a school or professional theater, by the magnificent recreation of late feudal pageantry in a motion picture like Olivier's *Henry V*.

Similarly, the teacher teaching Wordsworth and Keats must realize that most of his students are unfamiliar with the thoroughly cultivated and inhabited and yet nonurbanized rural European landscape whose peculiar charm is present in much of the poetry; that they have never heard a lark or a nightingale. The teacher reading with his students G. M. Hopkins' reference to "all trades, their gear and tackle and trim" must realize that most of his students have never been inside the workshop of a pre-machine-age shoemaker or harness-maker or potter. Students reading Dickens and Thackeray will have difficulty visualizing the streets and shops of nineteenth-century London. In meeting such difficulties, well-chosen **audio-visual aids** can give the teacher much-needed assistance.

Every teacher of poetry will draw on the numerous magnificent recordings of poetry that have become available in recent decades. The booming voice of Dylan Thomas on Caedmon Records has done more to make poetry a living thing for college students than all the earnest estimates of the poet's role published by academic critics. Obviously, reliance on the record and the motion picture easily becomes habit-forming. It encourages the students to become a mere passive audience and the teacher to shirk the arduousness of actual teaching. Just as the best motion picture of a Shakespeare play is no substitute for a play locally performed, so the best recording of poems is no substitute for the teacher who loves to recite poetry and uses every opportunity, curricular and extracurricular, to do so.

Programmed Instruction

The best illustration of how teaching aids can cease to be aids and begin to transform the substance of what is being taught is the recent development of programmed instruction. The general procedure followed in self-teaching by teaching machines or programmed textbooks is familiar:

> Auto-instruction presents a body of subject matter in a carefully prepared sequence of questions, to which the learner must respond at every step of the way. As soon as each response is completed, the learner may check his thinking against the correct response; errors are corrected immediately. Using one of the well-known, less expensive machines, the learner turns a knob or lever which brings the first "frame" into view. A frame is a short paragraph which presents an item of information and is followed by a question to be answered or a statement to be completed by the learner. He writes his answer to the question in a window of the machine. At the next turn of the knob, a transparent shield covers the learner's answer so that it cannot be changed, and a black shield disappears, revealing the correct answer. The student then compares his answer with the correct one, and, if he erred, he may reread the question, thinking through the reason(s) for his error. When he is satisfied that he understands, he turns the knob again, the second question appears, and the process is repeated.

Though many such programs consist of one continuous sequence, others arrange for detours designed to give the individual student help with special difficulties:

> A few electronic wonders, after an incorrect response, automatically shift the learner's attention to a series of questions designed to remedy the faulty reasoning which led to the incorrect response.[14]

When the principles of programmed instruction are applied to a textbook, the turning of pages and the filling in of answer spaces take the place of the switching of frames.

What makes programmed instruction intriguing is that it proceeds on the principle of taking the student along at every step. Ideally, it develops concepts cumulatively, going from the simple to the complex, from the familiar to the unknown. Each step must be small enough and logical enough to be taken successfully even by the slow student. In other words, though programmed texts may not be proof against cheating by students, they discourage cheating on the part of the instructor. The pro-

[14] Jerry E. Reed, "AID for the Teacher of English," *The English Journal*, L (February, 1961), 93–94.

grammer must think through his subject and assure successful guidance of the student with a thoroughness mercifully not expected of live teachers.

As one critic observed, the chief value of programmed instruction "lies in its capacity to impose a discipline upon the programmer."[15] Wendell Johnson once said that he found it more helpful to refer students who had trouble organizing their writing to a cookbook than to a textbook of composition. In the cookbook, order *must* be sequential and cumulative; there is no way of beating the egg whites that have already been mixed into the dough. There can be no reliance on merely verbal formulas; there is no point in standing over the stove reciting, "A good meal must have a beginning, a middle, and an end." A teacher who has studied programmed texts cannot help applying the cookbook principle to some extent in his own teaching. Whether in the classroom or as the author of text materials, he will be more wary than before about operating with terms and concepts he has not taken time to establish or define. He will take care never again to introduce three or four difficult new terms in the same crowded and opaque sentence. In the words of one reviewer, "programmed instruction will almost certainly have a sharp and lasting impact on the way textbooks are written" and "it will even have an effect on the way teachers teach when they are not using machines or programmed texts."[16]

While teachers will rightly view programmed instruction as dangerous competition, students will be attracted by its promise of a pedagogical new deal. First, the student knows he cannot progress unless he pays attention and masters each step along the way. Unlike the live teacher, the machine does not prod, nag, or penalize the student. Its only function is to convey knowledge. Furthermore, programmed instruction solves the teacher's problem in dealing with students of different capacities. Students

> will be able to move ahead at their own best rates. Bright pupils will not have to wait for group instruction to come to a point where they will again be challenged and interested; slow pupils will not give up because the group instruction is moving too fast for them to understand.[17]

The crucial advantage of a programmed text is that at every step it provides a check on comprehension. A conventional text typically presents a principle followed by examples. A programmed text may provide the examples and make the student select the principle to fit it:

[15] Kenneth S. Rothwell, "Programmed Learning," *College English,* XXIII (January, 1962), 246.
[16] Spencer Klaw, "What Can We Learn from the Teaching Machines," *The Reporter,* July 19, 1962, pp. 19–20.
[17] Reed, *The English Journal,* L, 95.

> *Her eyes shining with joy,* Judy showed me her new dress.
> Judy, *her eyes shining with joy,* showed me her new dress.
> Judy showed me her new dress, *her eyes shining with joy.*

Can a noun-participle phrase be shifted from one position to another in a sentence? *(Yes, No)*

(frame 1243)

Or the programmed text may state the principle and make the student apply it to examples:

> In line with the modern tendency to eliminate unnecessary commas, many publications omit commas in dates when *only* the month and the year are stated.
> a. In May 1961 construction of the bridge was started.
> b. On May 27 1961 construction of the bridge was started.
> Which sentence can do without commas? _____

(frame 2846)[18]

Such a procedure compels attention and participation; it eliminates much waste motion in teaching and study.

The difficulty in applying programmed instruction to English is similar to the difficulty the teacher of English encounters in his use of objective examinations. Both devices aim at the common denominator of information, of knowledge, in a subject that requires a large measure of sensitivity, judgment, and skill. Programmed instruction is more applicable to the teaching of grammar than the exploration of usage, to vocabulary building than the study of connotations and overtones. It lends itself more easily to teaching the more tangible aspects of literary history and critical terminology than to teaching literary interpretation. In the teaching of writing, it leads to emphasis on concrete patterns that become artificial when divorced from considerations of substance and purpose. In the more significant areas of the discipline of English, questions typically do not have one correct answer but a variety of possible answers deserving more or less serious attention.

Programmed instruction will appeal to the student who wants to "know exactly what I am doing wrong." It will appeal to teachers who look for a subject matter that can be systematically catalogued and labeled, and who are predisposed to reduce the manifold alternatives in effective writing and responsive reading to manageable either-or choices. Such teachers will confidently apply programming to "the mechanics of exposition, involving simple matters of right or wrong." In teaching a poem or essay, they will proceed to show that the student "can be forced by a programmed sequence of questions to wring the text dry." They will deal with literature on the assumption that "characters, situations,

[18] Joseph C. Blumenthal, *English 3200: A Scientific Program in Grammar and Usage* (New York: Harcourt, Brace & World, Inc., 1962), pp. 340–41.

motifs, modes of narration, being finite, are classifiable."[19] In other words, to the extent that programmed instruction is applied to English, it will strengthen the hand of those who look in their subject for solid matter of fact. It will reinforce tendencies toward teaching that is mainly a thorough inventory of grammatical, rhetorical, and literary devices.

Closely related to the narrowing effect that programmed instruction can have on the content of English is its effect on methods of inquiry and exploration. Programmers find it difficult to model the students' reasoning on anything like sustained induction or systematic analysis. Programming compels the author to break up larger logical operations into minute learnable sequences. It thus tempts him to institutionalize the two least stimulating of familiar teaching devices. The first of these is the nudging question that broadly hints at the right answer: "Frost spent most of his life in New England. He wrote many poems on New England subjects. Though we cannot be certain, therefore, we may guess that the speaker in the poem lives in _____ _____."[20] The second is the reassuring pat on the back for the student docile enough to take the hint. To enable each student to keep up, the clues to the right answer often become so broad as to be a mere disguise for a request for outright repetition of information just provided. Though advocates of programmed instruction claim that the student must reason his way through the typical programmed sequence, reasoning here does not mean independently tracing connections and discovering new unanswered questions in the very process of working out the answers to the original ones.

The kind of inquiry that makes progress while keeping in suspense an increasingly large number of unanswered questions is ruled out by the theory of learning that the advocates of programmed instruction have adopted from B. F. Skinner and other experimental psychologists. That theory is **behavioristic** in the sense that its advocates refuse to speculate about mental processes and aim instead at conditioning directly the overt behavior desired. As Skinner says in discussing the teaching of arithmetic,

> the techniques which are emerging from the experimental study of learning are not designed to "develop the mind" or to further some vague "understanding" of mathematical relationships. They are designed, on the contrary, to establish the very behaviors which are taken to be the evidences of such mental states or processes.[21]

To motivate desired behavior, the followers of Skinner do not rely on the rewards of discovery, the satisfactions derived from grasping the rela-

19 Rothwell, *College English*, XXIII, 246-8.
20 James M. Reid, John Ciardi, and Laurence Perrine, *Poetry: A Closer Look (Programed Instruction with Selected Poems)*, (New York: Harcourt, Brace & World, Inc., 1963), p. 6.
21 "The Science of Learning and the Art of Teaching," in *Programmed Learning: Theory and Research*, eds. Wendell I. Smith and J. William Moore (Princeton, N.J.: D. Van Nostrand Company, Inc., 1962), p. 32.

tionships within structured wholes. They do not aim to develop the student's pleasure in recognizing recurrent configurations. As they tell their students,

> as soon as you turn the page, you find out whether your reasoning was right. At this point something very important happens. The instant you find out that your answer is right, all doubt disappears and the idea "takes root," so to speak, in your brain.
> The psychologists who developed programing call this *reinforcement,* and it is a most important factor in learning. The more often reinforcement takes place and the more quickly it follows the writing of your answer, the better you learn.[22]

This kind of conditioning is least suited to those areas of English where, far from seeing to it that "all doubt disappears," the teacher aims at developing the students' capacity for independent observation, skeptical inquiry, and critical judgment. In these areas, the behavior expected of the student is too complex and self-directed to support the behaviorist's sanguine assumption that "behavior, verbal or otherwise, can be controlled with ease and precision."[23] Conditioning through instant reinforcement is best suited to drill, memorization of facts, recognition of clearly distinct concepts. Its advocates correctly point out that the modern teacher is a poor drillmaster. At best, he can check and guide the responses of the individual pupil only in intermittent and delayed fashion. He is further hampered by pedagogical scruples concerning the mindless nature of drill as such. For the teacher thus handicapped, the programmed text or the teaching machine offers an efficient substitute. As presented by its more businesslike supporters, programmed instruction "offers a very rapid and effective way of covering routine material" and "frees the teacher from incessant drill work."[24] Unlike the conventional workbook, a programmed workbook can present exposition, exercises, and review in a tightly knit, self-teaching and self-checking sequence.

Some of the shortcomings of programmed texts now available are inherent, not in the principles of programming, but in conventional subject matter. Since it spreads out every step in the learning process for inspection, a programmed text graphically reveals the defects of familiar assumptions and procedures. Thus, a "scientific" program in grammar and usage, whose preface calls on the student to think his way step by step, may begin with the familiar definition that a sentence "gives us a sense of completeness." It will then proceed to ask the student whether "The dog is barking" or "The barking dog" is a sentence (frame 2). The thinking answer to such a question is "What do you mean, *complete?*" The frames

---

[22] Blumenthal, *English 3200,* p. iv.
[23] James G. Holland, "Teaching Machines: An Application of Principles from the Laboratory," Smith and Moore, *Programmed Learning,* p. 35.
[24] M. W. Sullivan, "Teacher's Manual" for *Programmed English* (New York: The Macmillan Company, Inc., 1963), p. 2.

of the program, of course, make no allowance for this response. The unconvinced, as well as the unenlightened, student then starts on a kind of thinking not recognized by the programmer: From samples labeled "correct" the student can inductively derive certain features of the complete sentence, such as the presence of a finite verb in "The dog *is barking*." From subsequent exposition, the alert student can piece together a partial definition of "completeness": A "complete" group of words both "names" and "tells" (frame 4); the telling part "is built around" the verb (frame 11); verbs may be recognized by a possible change for past time (frame 15), etc.[25] Programming traditional grammar here merely demonstrates a familiar point: Traditional instruction in grammar is neither soundly inductive nor expository in a soundly concrete and cumulative way.

Similar problems are predictably caused by matters of usage. For instance, the text may list *shall, will, may, can,* etc. It may then provide a test frame like "Paul _____ study" to make the student decide whether all these auxiliaries could be used with the verb *study*. Again, the thinking response would be, "Surely, 'Paul shall study' would occur only in a theoretical sentence constructed by a textbook author." The student who makes the "wrong" decision at this point is the one who has more of an ear for language than his more docile classmates.

The basic objection to programmed instruction is that like the traditional handbook it favors cut-and-dried answers over balanced discussion. The major task of the English teacher is to develop in his students a feeling for the power, flexibility, and suppleness of the written word. In this task he is not helped by teaching materials that substitute an artificially simplified sequence for the multiple interconnections and the supple rhythms of organized discourse. A true textbook for English is a book like Paul Roberts' *Patterns of English* or Lawrence Perrine's *Sound and Sense*. Quite apart from its command of subject matter, such a book serves as an example of lucid exposition, a model of humane, living prose. It reflects the English teacher's belief that every specific activity in his courses should at the same time serve his larger aim of strengthening the student's familiarity with and respect for living language.

It has become customary for advocates of programmed instruction to state their objective of freeing the teacher from the more mechanical aspects of teaching and allowing him to concentrate on the more human and challenging aspects of his work. How candid such declarations are is hard to judge. Educators are not the only sorcerer's apprentices who find themselves unable to keep the spirits they call forth restricted to their proper place. Just as objective tests have widely replaced genuine examinations, programmed instruction, once introduced, will be difficult to

[25] Blumenthal, *English 3200,* p. 3 ff.

keep from invading those areas of our discipline where it is inappropriate or even harmful. *The English teacher becomes a teacher of non-English to the extent that he relies on workbooks, rulebooks, programmed texts, objective examinations, or any other device that teaches students to substitute fragmented and artificially channeled responses for the full exercise of their linguistic faculties.* Like workbook exercises or objective tests, programmed instruction should be employed in the teaching of English only reluctantly and for clearly limited purposes.

Instructional Television

Whatever the real and alleged educational benefits of programmed instruction, its immediate value to the administrator lies in the solutions it offers to staffing problems that might otherwise become impossible to solve. The same is true for instructional television. Through **closed-circuit television,** a single instructor, with assistants and lay readers, can take the place of ten or twenty fully qualified teachers teaching the same required course. Through the use of videotapes or kinescopes, one master teacher's course can be used to replace countless individual teachers in a district-wide or statewide system—and to replace the master teacher himself through reruns in later semesters.

However, instructional television has advantages other than those of a mere stopgap measure. It can substitute for a course taught live by an instructor with only partial or faulty training a televised course by a teacher whose professional qualifications are beyond doubt. For instance, the Ford Fondation Fund for the Advancement of Education "early became interested in television as a means of extending the reach of the superior teacher to greater numbers of students."[26] Being more public and less improvised than usual classroom teaching, with more time and resources for planning, televised instruction tends to be more carefully thought out and more carefully prepared. It offers graduate assistants or apprentice teachers exceptional opportunities to watch an experienced teacher at work.

More clearly inherent in television as a medium are the exceptional opportunities it offers for graphic demonstration. These possibilities are most impressive in courses in the natural sciences or in the history of art and architecture. The television instructor can show and manipulate objects that students are unable to see in the usual large classroom or lecture hall. He can work pictures and graphs into the natural flow of his presentation without the interruptions and fumblings attending the use of projectors, for instance. He can show legibly and neatly lettered words

[26] John W. Meaney, *Televised College Courses* (The Fund for the Advancement of Education, October, 1962), p. 5.

and phrases without the shortcomings and loss of time of ordinary black-board work.

Since written English is a visual medium, these resources of graphic demonstration can to some extent be exploited in the teaching of punctu-ation, of sentence structure, of rhetorical principles. The difficulties are twofold: The ratio between screen size and size of letters must be such as to assure legibility. As a result, sample sentences and paragraphs must be relatively short; outlines must be relatively uncomplicated. Furthermore, static panels and charts share with filmstrips a soporific effect. The in-structor must be able to build up, mark up, or otherwise manipulate the sample passages he presents. The overhead camera, for instance, makes it possible for the instructor to work with words and phrases lettered on small strips of cardboard and ready to be placed on a frame resting in front of him on his desk. By this method, he can piece together, punctuate, and rearrange sample sentences and short paragraphs. This method fully utilizes screen size. It makes possible a semianimated sequence well suited to demonstrating the workings of sentence structure or to comparing and contrasting related patterns and conventions.

Generally, a course that was previously taught by a teacher lecturing to four hundred students in a cavernous auditorium is likely to gain rather than lose when it is presented to eight hundred students by closed-circuit television. Many college teachers base objections to instructional television on principles that many institutions surrendered much earlier in the conduct of large lecture classes. A survey by a committee of the American Association of University Professors in 1961 indicated that typically when a college puts a large lecture course on closed-circuit television

> the course is precisely like the conventional course which it replaces or parallels except that the lecture sections are larger. Otherwise, the pro-fessor directs the course and delivers the lectures as he would in the conven-tional course; and the regular laboratory and discussion sections are sched-uled and are manned by junior faculty and graduate assistants as they would normally be. The same examinations are used to measure student achievement, and the relative effectiveness of the TV course is judged on the basis of scores made on these tests.

To the more enthusiastic supporter, the televised course is an ex-ploration "compounding the auditory message of the lecture with all the impact of the visual arts and the realia of the ages," conducted by a teacher who "had never, in all his years of teaching, organized a course as well as this one, never made it flow so efficiently from point to point and with such impact of visual illustration." In less lyrical terms, as early as 1958 "there had been reported hundreds of carefully controlled ex-periments testing the effectiveness of television as an instructional de-vice," resulting "almost universally in the finding of 'no statistically significant difference.' " Typically, "no statistically significant difference in achievement is discernible between the performance of groups of television enrollees and matched control groups taught by the same professor in the conventional classrooms."[27]

The basic objection to instructional television is the same as that to the large lecture course: The slow student cannot ask a question of the television set; the bright student cannot talk back to it. No matter what the medium of presentation, in a class of several hundred students, the individual becomes a passive, at times baffled, at times frustrated spectator. The teacher can no longer conduct the kind of dialogue with his class in which he insists on the definition of terms and the substantiation of judgments; brings in examples, precedents, and parallels; and asks, at crucial points, the questions that redirect discussion toward major formal or thematic problems.

Technicians and administrators promoting instructional television realize that the camera lacks **feedback,** that it cuts off interaction between teacher and student. They have explored various possibilities of allowing teaching stimulus to be accompanied by student response. They recommend, for instance, that students work problems and then evaluate their answers with the help of the television teacher. They have developed equipment that allows the instructor to take up student questions, live or delayed, during the program. Though such devices keep up the appearance of exchange between teacher and student, the realistic student knows that in a television class of large size his personal claim on the teacher's time approaches zero. More so than the classroom teacher, the television instructor must be able to anticipate typical student questions and student problems.

One way of overcoming these limitations is to have the work of the television teacher supplemented by assistants who are not mere proctors and paper graders. A basic presentation by the television teacher is followed up by the classroom teacher in discussion and in the supervision of reading and written work. This approach is most likely to be successful with elementary-school teachers, who have long since become used to taking a back seat to teaching experts and to having their own work planned, co-ordinated, integrated, evaluated, and post-mortemized. In the colleges, a variation of this system is likely to reinforce the traditions that allow senior professors to "teach" without doing the actual spadework that makes teaching bear fruit. Having the students meet for discussion and follow-up with a section instructor or assistant suffers from the same drawback as any system whereby large classes are split up into small discussion sections. Ideally,

> the lecturer should himself be available for questioning by his students; he should himself discover their failures and misconceptions; he should run

his whole show as one enterprise and be responsible for conveying his subject to as many men, personally known to him, as possible. . . . teaching by proxy is as impossible as learning by proxy.[28]

Even in classes where superior students are taught by presumably superior lecturers, students tend to identify the section hand as their teacher and to lose interest in the presentation in the large lecture hall. If televised teaching is to be successful, the television teacher must from the beginning address himself to the students as "their teacher," looking at them firmly and directly through the snake eye of the camera, assuming as far as possible all responsibility for explaining the course, making assignments, and commenting on the students' current progress.

Whatever the technician's resources for simulating feedback, and whatever the teacher's ability to establish rapport with the student via the coaxial cable, the average student is likely to feel that "personal contact with the instructor gives you more of an incentive to learn," that "your problems are personal usually and can't be handled by a TV set," and that, in short, "TV is too mechanical." This does not mean that student response is uniformly negative. The more serious and responsible student responds to television teaching, as one might expect, in serious and responsible fashion. The bitter or disappointed student finds in television a ready scapegoat. Here is a sampling of student reactions to a televised college course in remedial English:

> The majority of the students take advantage of the TV class and distract the students' attention who are interested in learning.
>
> Even where the classes are supervised, it is fairly easy to carry on a conversation with a neighbor or write a letter during class.
>
> I like this method of teaching because you can see and hear the instructions.
>
> I think I am learning more this semester not because of the different technique but because I already flunked once.
>
> If one has a question to ask, he has to ask his section instructor. By the time he gets around to seeing the section instructor, he has forgotten the question.
>
> I think I am learning the same amount, because whether it is live teaching or not I don't get anything out of an English course.
>
> The student feels rather cold towards the teacher. The reason for this is that the student and the teacher don't get to know each other. The teacher is to the student just a face and a voice on the TV.
>
> I think I am learning more because it gives me a feeling of being on my own and a great challenge.
>
> If the instructor were in a classroom I would feel that he was talking to me personally, not to a television camera.
>
> Full time live teachers are subject to human distractions thus preventing them from completing their lectures and getting their point across.

28 Jacques Barzun, *Teacher in America* (New York: Doubleday & Company, Inc., 1955), p. 40.

I am learning more (I had a clod last semester).

They cover more material, more thoroughly because they have no interruption.

The amount of learning has no great difference. because it is the same amount of studying.

If this method does fail I think it will be because of the fact that there was no feeling of human relations between the professor and the students, thus giving the student the feeling that it did not matter how he did in the class because the television set could not praise or help him with his problems.

No matter how effective a televised course looks on the monitor screen in the studio, the teacher is unable to meet the kind of requirement described by Gilbert Highet:

> The young are trying desperately hard to become real people, to be individuals. If you wish to influence them in any way, you must convince them that you know them as individuals. The first step towards this is memorizing their faces and their names.[29]

Whatever its effects on students, television instruction in basic ways affects the rewards that attract people to teaching. The instructor inevitably plays the central role in a complex technical collaboration and thus enjoys considerably more attention and recognition than in live teaching. Awed by the technological paraphernalia and the cost of equipment, administrators tend to grant the television teacher released time and privileges he could not hope to obtain for classroom teaching or scholarship. But once preparations have been completed and the teacher takes his place before the glaring lights, television teaching is a lonely task. Robert C. Pooley describes well the role that human contact with the students plays in motivating teachers, "the flash of an eye that reveals a sudden understanding or appreciation," the students

> who have come to my desk at the end of a class hour to argue, to ask questions, or merely to say, "Gee, that was swell." These were my reward; it was for this human response that I went through all the labor of teaching.[30]

For this reward, the hearty if predictable compliments of the television director are a poor substitute. In the words of Jacques Barzun, "it takes two to teach, and from all we know of great teachers the spur from the class to the teacher is as needful an element as the knowledge it elicits."[31]

Among the typical faculty, instructional television creates problems of morale that the administrator listening to the siren song of the television experts ignores at his peril. One of the life-giving illusions and peace-making pretenses in the average English department is that one teacher, once he has passed through his probationary period, is as good as an-

[29] Highet, *The Art of Teaching* p. 36.
[30] "Automatons or English Teachers?" *The English Journal*, L (March, 1961), 173.
[31] Barzun, *Teacher in America*, p. 43.

other. Television teaching creates an elite of teaching experts, selected at least to some extent for qualities of showmanship and organization-mindedness that other teachers are likely to regard with suspicion. Whatever it does for the master teacher thus selected, such a system does not enhance the status of the average teacher as an independent professional. In experimenting with instructional television, administrators must make sure that it does not lead to the development of a large body of second-class faculty. Certainly, *tenured teachers should not be employed as mere proctors or paper readers for their televised colleagues.*

Instructional television is most likely to offer serious competition to conventional classroom teaching when it becomes part of a formidable alliance of televised and programmed instruction:

> The new self-instructional devices such as teaching machines and pro-grammed books offer very important advantages in some of the areas in which television is weakest: drill, follow-up, acceleration, reinforcement, pacing, etc. It would seem natural, therefore, to expect that television and programmed instruction will both be used more effectively when they are used in correlation with one another.[32]

A similar alliance is taking form between advocates of instructional television and those of team teaching:

> At the primary and secondary school level it has been found that by far the most effective system is to include the classroom teachers with the tele-vision instructor in a team teaching arrangement which assures the full participation of classroom teachers in planning, follow-up criticism, and sub-sequent modification of lessons. The classroom teacher who has thus been involved in the planning knows what to expect and how best to use the television presentation in the classroom.[33]

As the result of widespread experimentation with instructional tele-vision over the last few years, the English teacher resisting pressures to participate in such programs can cite more than mere unexamined prejudice in support of his stand. Regardless of the approach employed, the personality of the instructor, or the identity of the institution, certain basic difficulties tend to recur:

1) the difficulty of maintaining student interest, of compelling the students' attention and concentration;

2) the difficulty of co-ordinating materials presented by the lecturer and by the classroom instructor;

3) the difficulty of establishing the necessary organic relationship between lecture, discussion, written work, and criticism of the written work by the instructor;

4) the lack of direct participation by the student and of personal contact with the instructor.

[32] Meaney, *Televised College Courses,* p. 42.
[33] *Ibid.,* p. 28.

In the average general-education class in English, the teacher cannot capitalize on existing interest in his subject; he must create it against odds. This task requires the live teacher, personally acquainted with each student.

Teachers and Teaching Technology

What, to sum up, should the teacher know about the rapidly developing technical resources that are becoming available to educators? As individuals and as a profession, teachers must learn to keep informed on new developments through sources other than the uncritical testimonials of administrators and technicians directly promoting new techniques. Teachers must realize that in recent technological innovations resides "great potential progress as well as considerable possible harm."[34] When the profession clearly understands the challenges presented by these innovations, and is willing to explore and discuss them in an objective spirit, it may be able to maintain control over these developments rather than becoming controlled by them.

In the years ahead, teachers will increasingly have to take a stand on programmed instruction, instructional television, team teaching, and similar devices. Such resources and devices should be judged on how they can help the teacher, adapting them to his own needs and temperament, increase the usefulness and effectiveness of his work. Teachers should neither close their eyes and ears to meaningful experiment nor expect that new methods will produce drastically improved results. As Albert R. Kitzhaber says in his report on the Dartmouth Study of Student Writing:

> With the encouragement of several big foundations, an increasing number of English teachers in schools and colleges are now busily involved with "team teaching," "lay readers," closed-circuit television, overhead projectors, "resource teachers," "teacher aides," etc., in the hope of "scoring a major breakthrough." Most of these devices simply make it possible to teach more students with fewer teachers; or to word it more positively, to make a dwindling supply of qualified teachers go as far as possible. Insofar as they accomplish this end, they offer welcome help to a hard-pressed profession, but none of them show promise of greatly shortening the length of time it takes to teach a student to write well, or to make the task substantially easier for the student.[35]

None of them, one may add, show promise of greatly reducing the time and effort required to make students alert observers of language, mature and responsive readers.

Teachers of English tend to be individualists, wary of groupthink

---

[34] Ralph F. Fuchs, "A Profession in Quest of Itself," *AAUP Bulletin*, XLVIII (June, 1962), 104.

[35] "Cooperative English Program Notes," *PMLA*, LXXVII (December, 1962), ix.

and gadgets. The best of them are most effective when they teach their own classes their own way. No new publishing ventures or technological advances can be a substitute for putting such teachers to work under conditions that enable them to teach with conviction. The most important resource in the teaching of language and literature is the competent and dedicated individual teacher.

A PROGRAM FOR FURTHER STUDY

J. LLOYD TRUMP AND DORSEY BAYNHAM, *Focus on Change: Guide to Better Schools.* Chicago: Rand McNally & Company, 1961.

The result of a study sponsored jointly by a department of the National Education Association and the Ford Foundation. A blueprint for schools in which a scrambled schedule of large lecture classes, small discussion groups, and individual study has replaced the "self-contained classroom." Representative of studies that, though sponsored by influential foundations and professional organizations, give a one-sided, uncritically enthusiastic view of current innovations.

WENDELL I. SMITH AND J. WILLIAM MOORE, *Programmed Learning: Theory and Research.* Princeton, N.J.: D. Van Nostrand Company, Inc., 1962. An Insight Paperback.

A collection of articles on the psychological foundations and educational implications of programmed instruction. Includes important articles by B. F. Skinner, Sidney L. Pressey, and other psychologists.

ARTHUR D. MORSE, *Schools of Tomorrow—Today!* New York: Doubleday & Company, Inc., 1960.

A report describing in some detail experimental uses of team teaching, instructional television, and other instructional innovations. Includes a report on the experiment in the use of closed-circuit television in Hagerstown, Maryland.

LEON C. FLETCHER, *Instructional Television Review.* Menlo Park, Calif.: Pacific Coast Publishers, 1961.

A brochure published by the Educational Television Research Association of Berkeley, California. Part of a "continuing series of up-to-the-minute reports on the increasing use of instructional television in the United States."

MATERIALS FOR ANALYSIS

A. Study a high school textbook that is part of a series making use of new materials in the study of language. For instance, investigate Lou LaBrant, William G. Leary, Donald A. Bird, and Margaret Painter, *Your Language: Book 5* (New York: McGraw-Hill Book Company, Inc., 1960). Report fully on the selection and presentation of the material.

B. Study the changes in successive editions of a well-established traditional handbook of composition, such as the Woolley *College Handbook of Composition* (Boston: D. C. Heath and Company) or the Hodges *Harbrace College Handbook* (New York: Harcourt, Brace and World, Inc.). To what extent do successive revisions of the book reflect modern trends in the study of language?

C. Study an anthology designed to introduce high school students or college freshmen to imaginative literature. Investigate and evaluate in detail the editor's criteria for selecting materials. Comment on the principles of organization followed in the arrangement of selections, and on the nature and adequacy of the apparatus provided.

D. Study recent reviews in *The English Journal* or *College English* of a type of textbook with which you are well acquainted. Investigate the relevance, significance, and consistency of the criteria applied by the reviewers. If you wish, test the fairness and balance of a typical review by comparing it with your own detailed study of the book reviewed.

E. Study a programmed textbook such as Joseph C. Blumenthal's *English 2600* (New York: Harcourt, Brace & World, Inc., 1961) or M. W. Sullivan's *Programmed English* (New York: The Macmillan Company, 1963). Evaluate its effectiveness of presentation, concentrating on information and concepts that, to judge from your experience, are difficult to learn or to teach. Use detailed illustrations.

F. Watch several installments of a televised course in English or the humanities. Discuss in detail the teacher's use of television as a medium. Comment on features of his style and approach that enhance or limit the effectiveness of his presentation.

G. Find a recent article in a professional journal or national magazine that authoritatively takes stock of both the strengths and weaknesses of instructional television, programmed instruction, or other recent innovations in teaching technology. For example, examine relevant articles in the Education Supplement of the *Saturday Review*. Discuss the author's findings, with special attention to their implications for the teaching of English.

A teacher's effectiveness is to some extent affected by the public image of his profession. His success in the classroom depends in part on the role he plays in the eyes of his students and the community. If a parent sends a student to college with stereotyped ideas about college professors as impractical intellectuals and confused do-gooders, he has to that extent inoculated him against much of what college has to offer. If high school students come to see their English teacher as a harmless drudge, they are not likely to develop the respect for his professional competence essential to fruitful classroom work.

nine

Equally important, obviously, is the teacher's image of himself. He has chosen the wrong calling if he cannot develop a feeling of independence, of confidence, of professional pride. There is something pitiful about the English teacher who acts apologetic for devoting his life to education, for believing in the central human importance of language, for insisting on the central human significance of imaginative literature. To gain the respect he deserves, the teacher must first learn to respect himself.

Professional Status

A Definition of Professionalism

In recent years, teachers of English have increasingly begun to think of their calling as a profession, without always being able to change correspondingly their conditions of employment. Of the high school teacher, Robert C. Pooley said some years ago:

the teacher of English is far too often a hired hand, employed to conduct so many classes a day according to a curriculum in the forming of which he has had no hand, and by using books he has had no voice in choosing. His views regarding grammar, composition, speech, and literature are often not consulted.[1]

[1] "The Professional Status of the Teacher of English," *The English Journal,* XLVIII (September, 1959), 309.

College teachers generally enjoy greater freedom from administrative interference; even in large sectioned courses they generally have some voice in the planning of courses and choice of materials. At the same time, their status is adversely affected by the coolie system, which allows many large institutions to employ young teachers during their best and most energetic years, only to pass them over for tenure in favor of candidates with more spectacular publication records.

In the past, concepts of professionalism have often been too one-sided, and at any rate too ineffectual in securing for the teacher of English true professional status. Traditionally, codes of professionalism have stressed the responsibilities of the teacher toward administrator and community, while being largely silent on the responsibilities of the latter toward the teacher. Disproportionate stress has been placed on the teacher's co-operation with the administrator in creating a public image of the school or college as responsive to community standards and expectations. Professional conduct has at times been interpreted to require that the teacher refrain from public criticism of established educational policy and administrative decisions. In effect, such an interpretation deprives the community of the much-needed guidance of people who, by devoting their lives to teaching, have more than anyone else earned the right to advise the community on problems of education. By repeated warnings not to speak as "institutional spokesmen," teachers have been in effect discouraged from speaking as authoritative representatives of their school or college faculty.

A comprehensive definition of professionalism would attempt to do justice both to its intrinsic requirements and the external conditions on which its exercise depends. The first and most essential requirement is competence. One becomes a member of a profession through the kind of specialized, systematic learning and apprenticeship designed to assure broad competence in a professional career. *As a group, a true profession has the means of safeguarding itself against the dilution of standards that results from the employment of unqualified personnel.* In the colleges, retention and promotion as a teacher of English have typically come to depend on the possession of the doctorate, or at least on satisfactory progress toward it. The deficiences of the traditional Ph.D. program are familiar: neglect of the study of modern English, of rhetoric, of the philosophy of education and methods of instruction—areas crucial to the success of the future teacher as an instructor of undergraduates. Few such programs have met the requirement that the future teacher "be invited early in his career to reflect upon some of the problems with which education is confronted, and to ask what solutions he can find."[2] Nevertheless, the granting of advanced degrees is directly under professional

2 Warner G. Rice, "The Preparation of College Teachers of English," *College English*, XXIV (May, 1963), 636–37.

control, and improvements are thus possible through direct professional efforts.

In the schools, minimum standards for admission to the profession are in effect set by **state certification requirements.** In the past, spokesmen for professional organizations have uniformly found these requirements too low. In many states, the minimum training, in semester hours, required of teachers of home economics and physical education is double, or more, that required of teachers of English.[3] Teachers and laymen must exert every possible pressure to discredit the practice of assigning classes in language and literature to "fill out" the schedule of teachers who do not have at least a strong minor in English.

The second major requirement for true professionalism is dedication. The true professional undergoes his training for motives beyond that of the need for making a living. He derives a kind of pride and satisfaction from his work that cannot be measured in financial terms. As Gilbert Highet says in speaking of the rewards of teaching,

> To teach a boy the difference between truth and lies in print, to start him thinking about the meaning of poetry or patriotism, to hear him hammering back at you with the facts and arguments you have helped him to find, sharpened by himself and fitted to his own powers, gives the sort of satisfaction that an artist has when he makes a picture out of blank canvas and chemical colorings, or a doctor when he hears a sick pulse pick up and carry the energies of new life under his hands.[4]

The third requirement for true professionalism is independence. Though the professional hires out his services for a salary or a fee, he performs them subject to professional standards that are not for sale. As H. G. Rickover says about engineering ethics,

> since engineering is a profession that affects the material basis of everyone's life, there is almost always an unconsulted third party involved in any contract between the engineer and those who employ him—and that is the country, the people as a whole. These, too, are the engineer's clients, albeit involuntarily. Engineering ethics ought, therefore, to safeguard their interests most carefully. Knowing more than the public about the effects his work will have, the engineer ought to consider himself an "officer of the court" and keep the general interest always in mind.[5]

As a professional the teacher does not take orders but participates responsibly in the formulation of policy. *If necessary, he asserts professional standards and the public interest against shortsighted or harmful administrative or community decisions.*

The fourth requirement for true professionalism is recognition— that is, the social status that makes it possible for the professional to

---

3 Donald R. Tuttle, "Basic Considerations in Preparing, Certifying, and Assigning Teachers of English," *College English*, XXIV (May, 1963), 619–24.
4 *The Art of Teaching* (New York: Alfred A. Knopf, Inc., 1950), p. 10.
5 *Education and Freedom* (New York: E. P. Dutton & Co., Inc., 1960), pp. 78–79.

perform his function effectively and in accordance with his standards and commitments. The most concrete indication of such status is remuneration that implies a clear acknowledgment of the years and effort invested in achieving professional competence. A less concrete indication is the courtesy of minor privileges and conveniences whose function as a symbolic recognition of service exceeds their monetary value. Proceeding to more intangible factors, the professional is recognized as someone speaking authoritatively on matters within his field, and as someone entitled to a respectful hearing on matters of public concern *outside* his field.

Finally, the professional insists on having his work guided or evaluated only by persons that are his equals in breadth of background, intellectual attainments, and moral stature. The true professional, to use Thoreau's phrase, "has a bone in his back which you cannot pass your hand through." To achieve true professional status, teachers of English must make considerable progress toward academic self-government, professional salaries, and improved self-respect.

The American system of education typically attaches insufficient weight to the element most essential to its success: the teacher's view of what his job is, and of what is needed to get the job done. Administrators tend to pre-empt publicity and prestige; students' rights and interests are jealously protected; the community makes its influence felt in no uncertain terms. In the process, a basic truth is often overlooked: A school not only is no better than its teaching staff; it *is* its teaching staff. As the authors of *Education for College* observe, "a good teacher is the best curriculum." If there are going to be improvements in American education, they are going to be

> carried out by teachers well educated in their subjects, assigned to duties for which they had been prepared, maintaining professional standards and receiving adequate salaries, working in an intellectual atmosphere, and facing a teaching load not completely beyond the bounds of possibility.[6]

Such teachers must, in Jerome Bruner's words, "be free to teach and to learn." They must be reasonably free from the "semiprofessional tasks that keep teachers pinned down."[7] When humdrum chores and petty annoyances kill the teacher's active and excited interest in his subject, the most essential dynamic element in education has been lost. A student imprisoned in the classroom of a bored and harassed teacher would be better off following Robert Louis Stevenson's advice to play truant in the street and the country, there to broaden his "knowledge of life at large, and Art of Living."

[6] Albert R. Kitzhaber *et al., Education for College: Improving the High School Curriculum* (New York: The Ronald Press Company, 1961), p. 39.
[7] *The Process of Education* (Cambridge, Mass.: Harvard University Press, 1962), p. 90.

General Professional Organizations

Physicians and lawyers have strong and unified professional organizations that publicize their aims, help maintain professional standards, and bring their collective influence to bear on public policy. Teachers lack such unified representation.

Of the general professional organizations, one of the most significant from the English teacher's point of view is the **American Association of University Professors,** or AAUP. Though its membership is limited to college faculty, its activities in the past have important implications for the work of all teachers. The Association has set precedents relevant on all levels of instruction by insisting on the "primacy of the faculty in matters the faculty are best qualified to determine." It has vigorously promoted the view that "the direct impact of the knowledge and experience of faculty members should find a larger place than they now have in national educational councils."[8]

Over the years, a central concern of the Association has been the definition and implementation of **academic freedom.** In effective theoretical statements in the Association *Bulletin,* and in carefully considered action in support of individual teachers, the AAUP has kept in focus a crucial point: The first loyalty of scholar, scientist, and teacher is not to a cause, not to his government, not even to mankind, but to truth. To pursue the truth as he sees it, he must be protected from shortsighted public pressure or administrative reprisal. The privilege of academic freedom, safeguarded most concretely by the **right of tenure,** is not an encouragement to irresponsibility. It is based on the belief that in the long run free knowledge will better serve mankind than partial and managed knowledge, however well intentioned.

The right of free inquiry and debate is a precious achievement of the Western tradition. It distinguishes a free society from the gloomy totalitarianisms that have imposed their narrow and twisted patterns upon the minds of twentieth-century men. Such freedom must be protected against many hostile forces: defensive ignorance, short-range self-interest, personal antipathies and frustrations, the sweep of irrational passions. *One primary task of an educational institution is to establish an atmosphere in which intellectual freedom can thrive, in which students can learn to make confident and responsible use of their own minds.*

While the work of the Association has important implications for the future of free research and scholarship, it also has an important bearing on the status of every individual teacher. In order to function as a useful member of society, the businessman needs his reputation for

[8] Ralph F. Fuchs, "A Profession in Quest of Itself," *AAUP Bulletin,* XLVIII (June, 1962), 106–08.

financial integrity; the physician needs the recognition of his professional competence by his peers. The teacher needs his reputation for impartial, dedicated work. Generally, the American teacher has found that in contemporary American society this essential asset is insufficiently protected. Imputations of disloyalty, ranging from crude anonymous slander to subtle innuendo, have been allowed to undermine public confidence in individuals, and to some significant extent in the profession as a whole. In too many cases, unsubstantiated sensational charges, given wide newspaper publicity, have left a permanent feeling of suspicion and doubt. Given these conditions, the AAUP has performed a valuable service in confronting susceptible administrators and trustees with a choice between opportunistic yielding to outside pressures and observing due process, as well as elementary standards of fairness and of truth.

Among general professional organizations open to all teachers, first in numbers and financial strength is the **National Education Association,** or NEA. Open to members from all levels of instruction, and to administrators as well as teachers, it comes close to being *the* professional organization for American educators. Its importance in this role is the greater in view of the limited educational leadership on the national level that can be provided by agencies like the U. S. Office of Education. Through its numerous affiliated organizations, the NEA sponsors innumerable projects, publications, and activities devoted to the improvement of education at all levels. It speaks for a large cross section of American educators on many matters of concern to English teachers, ranging from teaching about communism to the teaching of foreign languages in the public schools.

Associated in the public mind with "progressive education," the NEA has in recent years found it difficult to dam the rising tide of extremist criticism of our schools, and to distinguish it from more thoughtful and responsible criticism of modern educational theory and practice. The spokesmen of the organization have often been educational administrators and professors of education. Key articles in its publications have too often been written in the hazy and grandiloquent jargon that has been the bane of modern educational theorists. ("In a divided world, can we hope to survive as a free people unless our enculturation includes the most significant generalizations, values, and processes drawn from the frontiers of knowledge?") Reports sponsored by the NEA or subsidiary organizations have shown an uncritical acceptance of schemes and slogans, with little regard for the misgivings of classroom teachers. On matters of educational policy, the NEA has not always succeeded in creating an image of itself as encouraging active scholarly debate within its ranks on genuinely controverted questions of great importance. Many teachers have felt that the uncritical enthusiasm and unfailingly "constructive" attitude encouraged by the organization had become a façade for conformity.

For the classroom teacher, it has been difficult to find in the NEA his true professional image. Often, joining the organization has been a thinly veiled condition of employment. Through its affiliated organizations and publications, the NEA has seemed to promote a barren verbal opposition between "subject matter" and "professional" training—as though a balanced concept of professionalism could be possible without a requirement for subject-matter competence. Its spokesmen have customarily thought in terms of "school people" on the one hand and "academic scholars" on the other, thus making more difficult a unified image of the teacher at any level as a teacher-scholar. On the other hand, there has been a blurring of the distinction between teachers and "administrative faculty"—while at the same time the NEA has insisted on administrators being "professionally" trained as administrators.

Whatever the merits of such charges and complaints, they have in practice contributed to the spread, both in the schools and in the colleges, of the **American Federation of Teachers** (AFL–CIO), a teacher's union claiming to offer the teacher more genuine and effective representation than rival groups. Many teachers consider union membership incompatible with their conception of professional status. On the other hand, the AFT has had some success in making administrators and legislators pay respectful attention to teachers' views previously slighted. Union locals have helped teachers obtain remedy for their grievances, but they have also seemed to cultivate grievances as a means of harassing administrations. Union belligerence has often threatened to become merely negative, hindering rather than furthering the development of conditions in which administrators and teachers can work together in mutual respect, toward common goals.

Many teachers are alienated by the extreme outspokenness of union representatives. Union members have at times shown considerable disregard of traditional professional courtesies and timidities. However, whatever their affiliations, teachers must ask themselves whether their traditional reluctance to speak up for themselves has served their cause. Many teachers deplore the emphasis of their schools on the peripheral and nonacademic; they complain of the lack of administrative and public support of what is most important in their work. These complaints, however, are seldom translated into an effective public statement of the teacher's position. Referring to the conditions that make possible a successful and satisfied career for the teacher of English, the executive secretary of the Commission on English of the College Entrance Examination Board said:

Success in alleviating the ills has rarely come from altruistic aim or administrative vision. A certain quarrelsomeness, not the easiest behavior for English teachers, is called for.[9]

Because of widespread indifference on the part of teachers, and because of the widely different interests, assumptions, and affiliations of existing organizations, there is little prospect for rapid progress toward effective professional unity. We are far away from the ideal of "an association of teachers of all ranks and specialties, and serving the interests of teachers before the public—a real and inclusive professional body" that "should endeavor to tell the people what teachers are for, what they do and what they want, and why it seems best to support them more liberally than hitherto."[10] Even so, there is little excuse for the teacher who does not give a share of his time and income to the professional organization of his choice.

Professional Organizations in English

The most prestigious of the professional organizations that concern themselves directly with English is the **Modern Language Association of America,** or MLA. Though it is an organization of college and university teachers in English and foreign languages, it exerts a strong influence on the teaching of English at all levels. Its standards and ideals determine to a large extent the training in English that the future teacher receives in college. Though the most direct purpose of the MLA is to promote scholarship, it has through its committees and special commissions shown an increasing concern with the improvement of teaching at all stages of the student's schooling. Many of its most active and influential members have recognized the futility of the college teacher's declaiming against the public schools and "educationists" without "having any realistic idea of what they were trying to do."[11]

Traditionally, the MLA has discouraged on the one hand a practical, utilitarian, vocational emphasis in the teaching of English and on the other an uncritical preoccupation with the contemporary and up-to-the-minute. It has seen a major aim of the profession in preserving and, where necessary, recovering our humanistic heritage:

This avenue of providing individual enrichment has been the scholar's and the poet's own for centuries. For Matthew Arnold's Empedocles, we are the strangers here, the world is from of old, yet each new man strikes root into

9 Floyd Rinker, "Priorities in the English Curriculum," *The English Journal,* LI (May, 1962), 311.
10 Jacques Barzun, *Teacher in America* (New York: Doubleday & Company, Inc., 1955), p. 256.
11 Brice Harris, "Commentary by the Presidents of Fifteen Sister Organizations on the Occasion of the Seventy-Fifth Anniversary of the Modern Language Association" *PMLA,* LXXIII (December, 1958), Part 2, p. 3.

a far foretime. And humanistic scholarship has been apt to see its best function in enlarging men's view during each generation by the recovery of
vivid interests from that far foretime.

Ideally conceived, **humanistic scholarship** does not mean a passive dwelling on the glories of the past: it "has long distinguished itself from
antiquarianism by insisting upon critical evaluation of things recovered,
and of seeing present relevance in them." Needless to say, the ideal of
humanistic scholarship, broadening, enlightening, and humanizing, has
often been belied by the fragmentation and narrow specialization of
scholarly practice:

> the old graduate school notion that each writing must make some contribu-
> tion to the sum total of knowledge, without care for who should put this
> nebulous sum total together in meaningful fashion, has bred a monstrous
> pile of interesting bit facts, a pile growing so fast, and covering such a wide
> field, that it will soon smother us in a sahara of particles.[12]

To be humanistic in any but a self-congratulatory sense, scholarship must
proceed from the carefully established facts to human significance. When
thus defined, humanism clarifies our purposes and gives balance to our
culture by placing immediate short-range concerns in the context of
man's more permanent intellectual, moral, and aesthetic needs.

PMLA, the quarterly publication of the Association, listed 12,000
individual subscribers in 1961, twice as many as *College English,* and four
times as many as any other journal in the area of English devoted primarily to scholarly investigation. In its statements of editorial policy,
PMLA has explicitly invited work in critical theory and the history
of ideas. In its yearly supplements, it has given space to articles examining recent work in linguistics from the point of view of classroom teachers.
By and large, however, its emphasis, as the chronological arrangement of
its quarterly table of contents suggests, has been on literary history. In addition to critical studies of theme and form in major works, it prints a
substantial amount of traditional scholarship marked by limited objectives, command of a wealth of detail, and extensive documentation:
discussion of limited areas of the vocabulary of *Beowulf* and other early
documents; elucidation of controverted passages from major works;
studies of influences on, and sources of, major and minor works; detailed
exploration of lesser known works in the corpus of major authors.
Paradoxically, much of the material in the scholarly journal for English
teachers that enjoys the largest circulation appeals to highly specialized
interest.

The largest and most representative organization for teachers of
English at all levels is the **National Council of Teachers of English,** or

---

[12] George Winchester Stone, Jr., "The Modern Language Association and the
Shape of Things to Come: 1958–83," *PMLA,* LXXIII (December, 1958), Part 2,
82–83.

NCTE. Through its numerous state organizations and regional affiliates, it sponsors and promotes professional activities of all kinds. In its publications and conventions, it has long provided a forum for teachers concerned with new developments in the teaching of language and literature. Though careful to avoid the appearance of sponsoring a particular school or movement, the NCTE has done much to publicize and gain acceptance for new developments in linguistics. Both in the parent organization and in affiliates like the Conference on College Composition and Communication, attention has focused on English as the keystone of the student's general education.

Among the Council's monthly periodicals, *College English* has long provided college teachers with an opportunity to look at their subject matter from the point of view of the teacher as well as of the scholar. Over the years, it has published numerous articles on the implications of linguistics for the English teacher's work. In its articles on both language and literature, *College English* has effectively avoided becoming identified with a limited manner or point of view. Without cultivating the polemical, it has provided an effective medium for controversy and discussion. Like the other Council periodicals, *College English* through book reviews helps the teacher keep track of the mass of current scholarly studies and new textbooks.

The oldest of the Council's periodicals is *The English Journal,* addressed primarily to high school teachers. Though it prints articles by college-based authorities on secondary-school English, many of its contributions come from practicing high school teachers. Generally, *The English Journal* has been successful in creating an image of the high school teacher as a self-reliant professional. In its department on "The Public Arts," the *Journal* has provided incisive commentary on the popular culture that provides the background and the setting for the English teacher's work. Inevitably, *Journal* reports on high school programs are often idealized; teachers more often write about their successes than their failures. Nevertheless, *The English Journal* furnishes a wealth of suggestions for day-to-day teaching and for the planning of curricula.

The third major journal published by the National Council is *Elementary English,* devoted to the teaching of the language arts in the elementary schools, including the junior high school. This periodical keeps the teacher up-to-date on research in the language arts; it provides accounts of successful classroom practices and bibliographies of books for children. Here the teacher can find authoritative articles on individualized instruction, on the application of linguistics to the teaching of reading, on language activities for the retarded.

The most recent addition to the Council's list of periodicals is *CCC,* the Journal of the Conference on College Composition and Communication. At a time when the freshman course in college was often regarded as purgatory by instructors and as limbo by administrators, the Conference gave to the teaching of composition a much-needed measure of recognition and prestige. It has come to serve as an effective forum for the many college teachers throughout the nation who have always regarded freshman English not as a perfunctory service course but as a crucial part of the student's general education.

An independent professional organization for college English teachers is the **College English Association,** with numerous regional affiliates throughout the country. Its monthly, the *CEA Critic* provides a vehicle for more informal and at times more outspoken comment on professional issues than other professional journals for the college teacher.

In our professional activities—the articles, speeches, discussions, workshops—there is necessarily a certain amount of waste motion. Nevertheless, they provide important opportunities for stock-taking and exploration. Just as the well-taught course broadens the horizon not only of the student but also of the teacher, the presentation prepared for a journal or a conference panel has an enlightening function on the author even when hardly anybody is listening. Many a prospective speaker or journal author has realized with G. C. Lichtenberg that "in writing down things, one notices a great deal which one is not aware of in mere meditation."

Though the number of organizations working to improve instruction in English is large, recent years have seen considerable progress toward co-ordinated effort. The MLA and NCTE have joined with the College English Association (CEA) and American Studies Association (ASA) in setting up the "Cooperative English Program." The aims of the Program are to develop in teachers of English an awareness of their responsibility "in preparing students for participation in a complex democratic society and in transmitting the cultural heritage upon which that society is founded," to formulate "challenging but realistic objectives for each level of schooling," and to demonstrate "the best methods and practices for attaining these objectives." Whatever the long-range results of such programs, they are serving to restore "a sense of unity and common purpose among those who are charged with teaching English on all levels in our schools and colleges."[13]

The Teacher's Role

What, to sum up, is the English teacher's present status as a professional? Within our discipline, some vigorous rethinking and reshaping of the teacher's role is in progress. In the words of a recent past president of the NCTE,

> teachers from one end of the country to the other are beginning to see themselves as members of a group rather than as isolated and individual entities.

[13] Stone, *PMLA,* LXXIII, Part 2, 82–83.

> Teachers in the elementary school are finding a kinship with those at the secondary level; both groups are becoming deeply aware of the college teachers. It is heartening to find that the Milton man and the Chaucer scholar are more and more concerned with the problems of elementary and secondary education.[14]

Our major professional organizations are effectively promoting a concept of the teacher of English as having an informed and balanced grasp of his discipline, and being united with his fellow teachers in other areas of the discipline and at other levels of instruction by a common sense of purpose and of professional pride.

Like teachers in other fields, the teacher of English faces the difficulty of effectively defining his role in society. The teacher's aims are necessarily intangible and uncertain. His basic concern is with the long-range development of the student's mind and personality. This concern must be explained and justified to a public that tends to look for concrete, dramatic, and not too long-delayed results. In the words of Jacques Barzun,

> the teacher and thinker must constantly bear in mind the special conditions that define his craft. He cannot count as aids to his advancement the pain and fear that favor the doctor, nor the apprehensions of loss and disgrace that favor the lawyer. He has on his side only mankind's desire for light— the light that gives all other things their shape; and this, though a strong motive, is easily obscured by more immediate demands. The teacher must consequently sustain it most steadfastly in the very persons who neglect or forget it easily.[15]

Apart from their continued efforts to gain adequate recognition and support, teachers must face the attacks of those who are fundamentally out of sympathy with the goals of a liberal education. To some, the free exercise of intellect is in itself an alien idea; they rightly see in the free play of mind a threat to their own narrow prejudices and antipathies. They would use the schools as a means of inculcating in students their own sense of self-righteousness, their own drastically oversimplified answers to complex problems. Teachers of literature inevitably are a frequent target of attacks from such sources:

> Merely from fear of such attacks, schools have removed enduring books from libraries and classrooms. Many students continue their "education" in a climate hostile to free inquiry, with limited access to important literary documents. Dedicated and able students of English considering public school teaching as a career must find little encouragement in this atmosphere of restriction and fear.

In dealing with such pressures, English teachers as a profession must learn to take the kind of carefully considered and yet effective action

---

[14] G. R. Carlsen, "A Sense of Profession," *College English*, XXIV (November, 1962), 147.
[15] Barzun, *Teacher in America*, pp. 258–59.

outlined by the National Council of Teachers of English in its brochure on "The Student's Right to Read."[16]

Ultimately, what is needed to create an adequate public image of the teacher's role is something that teachers should be well equipped to provide: education. *In large part, the education of the public concerning our professional purposes goes on day by day in our current work.* Today's alumni and legislators are yesterday's students, taking with them, for better or for worse, the picture of schools and teachers that we conveyed to them in the classroom. At the same time, teachers as a profession must learn to explain themselves to their fellow citizens, steering a careful course between timid acquiescence and unproductive polemics. In support of this effort, "it behooves every one of us to make his voice heard."[17]

A PROGRAM FOR FURTHER STUDY

MYRON LIEBERMAN, *Education as a Profession.* Englewood Cliffs, N.J.: Prentice-Hall, Inc., 1956.

> A sober stock-taking of the criteria for professional status and the means of effective professional representation. Notable for its detailed review of the nature and history of the NEA and AFT as major competing organizations and of the arguments concerning their respective merits.

The National Council of Teachers of English, *The National Interest and the Teaching of English: A Report on the Status of the Profession.* Champaign, Ill., 1961.

> A strong plea for national recognition of English as a basic humanistic study for students at all levels. Devoted in large part to the need for assuring adequate professional preparation for teachers of English, and for providing adequate teaching conditions for teachers thus prepared. Designed to help bring about a "national reawakening of interest and activity in English."

KINGSLEY AND ELEANOR WIDMER, *Literary Censorship: Principles, Cases, Problems.* Belmont, Calif.: Wadsworth Publishing Company, Inc., 1961.

> A collection not designed "to persuade anyone to favor or oppose any particular kind of censorship" but reflecting the belief that "the debate should be conducted on an intelligent, informed, and relevant level of discourse." Contains excerpts from a wide range of comment on censorship problems, by authors from Plato and Milton to Justice Douglas and Henry Miller.

The National Council of Teachers of English, *The Students' Right to Read.* Champaign, Ill., 1962.

---

[16] National Council of Teachers of English, "The Student's Right to Read" (Champaign, Illinois: 1962), p. 6.
[17] Henry Nordmeyer, "Faith of an Educator," *PMLA*, LXXVII (May, 1962), Part 2, p. 3.

A small but important brochure designed for the assistance of teachers of English hampered by censorship pressures in their teaching of our literary heritage. Fills an urgent need by outlining concrete steps for teachers and administrators to take when local censorship problems arise.

MATERIALS FOR ANALYSIS

A. Find recent discussions of the nature and limits of academic freedom in the *AAUP Bulletin* and similar sources. Prepare a critical discussion of major problems and principles.

B. Study major articles and editorials in recent issues of the *NEA Journal*. Identify and discuss fully one major current concern of American educators as reflected in the pages of the *Journal*.

C. Report on the current purposes, standards, and activities of major professional organizations in English. Draw on such sources as the annual presidential addresses published in *PMLA*, the presidential addresses and "Counciletters" of the NCTE, and the lead articles of the *CEA Critic*.

D. Study newspaper and magazine accounts of recent censorship cases involving teachers of English. Discuss the assumptions and principles involved. To what extent do accounts in the public press reflect an informed understanding of the teacher's task?

E. Study the image of the American teacher reflected in popular entertainment—motion pictures, television programs, and the like. What stereotypes, if any, are in evidence? How serious are they? How justified?

English is the central discipline in the American system of education. Required courses in high school and college give employment to an army of teachers, teachers of teachers, administrators, testers, textbook authors, and educational pundits. The product of their joint efforts is observed and judged by critics in homes and editorial offices across the nation.

In spite of, or perhaps rather because of the size of this undertaking, its nature remains imperfectly defined. The materials that appear in English textbooks range from retellings of the Greek myths to essays on nuclear fission, from scripts of television dramas to chapters from James Joyce's *Ulysses*. The specialized fields that different English teachers find most relevant to their work range from historical linguistics to psychotherapy, from English Renaissance literature to communication theory. The criteria of success applied to the teaching of English range from the student's ability to spell *believe* to his ability to discuss with some degree of authority the limitations of Herman Wouk as a serious writer.

A Summing Up

Furthermore, within every major area of the discipline of English, vigorous controversies are in progress. They range from debate on the status of a word or the meaning of a passage to fundamental disagreements on theory and method. To be widely accepted, the objectives and limits of instruction in English have to be stated in terms general and edifying enough to allow for diverse individual interpretation.

In recent years, however, teachers of English have come to demand a more clear-cut and unified definition of their discipline. They have attempted to focus on their central responsibilities: to give their students an informed understanding of language and literature, to make them responsible and effective users of the language, to train them as perceptive and discriminating listeners and readers. Increasingly, English teachers have examined their programs to determine what is most essential, most directly relevant to their task as teachers of language, of composition, of imaginative literature. They have shown an increasing willingness to hand back to their colleagues in the social sciences, in a separate speech or journalism department, or in the counseling service those duties that are in varying degrees related to the teaching of English but that, if given space, tend to inflate its content beyond what can be taught competently and in adequate detail. Professional organizations and publications, as well as projects sponsored by a variety of sources, are examining the teaching of English to find its true center of gravity. In the words of George Winchester Stone, Jr.,

> English, the humanistic course required of all students in our schools from the grades to the college, has, as a subject and a discipline, long been drifting toward chaos in our schools. The values of reading the *literature* which forms the magnificent English and American heritage, of achieving precision and effectiveness of style in *writing,* and of knowing the grammatical *structure of English* (the three staples of an English course) would seem to be self-evident. But the subject has tended to become the course in which to teach all things to all students. It has lost focus. To recognize the sequential nature of English studies and to preserve the values of their chief components are important tasks facing today's teachers.[1]

This attempt by the profession to define its premises and goals should not be allowed to give rise to false hopes. Today's English teacher can look forward to a more integrated, more coherent view of his subject—but not a simpler one, nor one making his subject easier to teach. *English is the most challenging and complex of the academic subjects.* Determining its ideal content through analogy with more clearly limited fields is misleading. In trying to develop an adequate rationale for his discipline, the teacher of English must be aware of the fundamental characteristics that set it apart from other subjects with which it might be compared.

Specialist and Generalist

The discipline of English is the teacher's specialty, but it is a specialty only in the broadest, most liberal, and most humane sense of that term. First, the different aspects of the study of language and literature are interrelated in intimate ways. They become meaningful as they converge and bear fruit in the analysis of a passage, the reading of a whole work, the writing of a paragraph or theme. English therefore does not survive rigid compartmentalization.

In discussing a line like "Absent thee from felicity awhile," the teacher is in turn grammarian, historical linguist, literary critic, and cultural historian. He must be aware of how words shift from one part of speech to the other, with the change from the adjective *"absent"* to the verb *"absent"* reflected here in shifting stress. He must know something about the historical development of the second person pronoun

---

[1] *Issues, Problems, and Approaches in the Teaching of English* (New York: Holt, Rinehart & Winston, Inc., 1961), p. v.

and its possible implications regarding the personal or social relationship between speaker and listener. He must be able to explore meter and metaphor, the latter here requesting physical removal from an abstraction ("felicity"). He must recognize the learned quality of that abstract term, partly explainable by its etymology, and also the possible echoes of discussions of felicity as the *summum bonum* in philosophical discourse since Aristotle. The teacher should be able to relate the overstated, hyperbolical quality of the metaphor to prevailing conventions of poetry and drama. He must know something about the author and the literature of his time. To be fruitful in classroom work, this knowledge must have the authenticity that comes only from more than superficial study in the various areas involved.

Obviously, we cannot study and teach everything at once, and from all possible points of view. Though all significant questions about language and literature may in the end be related, we must take them up in some order of priority. Inevitably, a teacher will develop special interests in one or more limited areas. At the least, such specialization should instill in him some of the humility that comes from the rigorous confrontation and uncompromising pursuit of problems that the student interested in "the broad outline" of a subject can evade. When this humility affects the teacher's outlook on teaching and scholarship in general, it becomes a much-needed antidote to glibness, faddishness, and oversimplification.

Though the teacher should thus be a specialist in some area, or areas, of his discipline, he cannot afford to be a specialist only. In English, more so than in other fields, it is not true that a half-trained teacher is better than none. The teacher of composition who marks papers only for mechanical correctness cannot be defended on the grounds that at least he is teaching his student mechanics. By giving his students a distorted view of what is essential to good writing, he may choke off whatever conviction and articulateness they had previously achieved. He may prejudice them against future instruction of a more balanced kind—provided they are fortunate enough to have a second chance. Similarly, the teacher of literature who spends most of his time identifying the historical allusions in the poetry of Dryden is doing a job that in itself needs to be done. But when it is done to the exclusion of what is equally or more important, Dryden is done a perhaps fatal disservice. Too often, the student exposed to such treatment will never again on his own read neoclassical literature, or any earlier literature—or any literature.

Language and literature do not make sense when treated out of context. The specialist is judged in part by his skill in dismantling the whole so that the pieces may be inspected and analyzed. The specialist's superior competence is bought at the price of his looking at one piece of the puzzle at a time. When the specialist enters the classroom as a teacher of English, he must be judged in large part by his skill in putting the pieces back together. He cannot be a party to the erecting of rigid barriers between language and rhetoric, or English literature and American studies. Instead, his teaching will reflect the continuity of his concern with language from details of grammatical structure in everyday speech to questions of theme and over-all significance in works of imaginative literature.

Even so, competence in the major areas of our discipline remains incomplete unless it is motivated by a fundamental concern with the role language plays in our lives, in our culture. Through language, man formulates and structures and integrates his experience. The teacher who is not a perceptive and sensitive observer of human experience cannot hope to deal with language and literature in any but a barren, technical sense.

Obviously, we cannot comment on the use of language in the mass media, in politics, or in public relations without some understanding of people and institutions. We must develop a feeling both for the underlying motives and for the need to create an image of ourselves for ourselves and for others, to choose a role—or a mask. We must become sensitive to how fundamental interests and resentments shape—and are in turn revealed by—language. To develop the student's full imaginative response to a work of literature, we must make him sensitive to the emotions and human perplexities at work in it—the yearning for innocence and simplicity in *The Catcher in the Rye,* the grim pathos of the inexorable passing of time in Arnold Bennett's *The Old Wives' Tale* or in the poems of E. A. Robinson.

Much of what needs to be said about Shakespeare's *Othello* will be said by the historian of language and literature, by the expert on the Elizabethan theater, by the student of literary sources and precedents. However, these experts, as experts, will not answer our most fundamental questions about the play. They will merely enable us to investigate these questions knowledgeably rather than naively. Some of these questions are the role of Othello's dark-skinned alienness; the extent to which his passion cancels out and subverts his reason ("My blood begins my safer guides to rule,/And passion, having my best judgment collied,/ Assays to lead the way . . ."; ". . . thou hadst been better have been born a dog/Than answer my naked wrath!"); the relationship between his passion and his concept of justice ("The justice of it pleases"). We cannot discuss these questions meaningfully unless we have some understanding of the psychological complexities of love and hate, of envy and jealousy, and of our demand for justice.

We often hear it said that literary criticism studies, not the human experience that literature mirrors or reflects, but the "angle of refraction." The critic, as expert, concerns himself not with the experience the writer shapes or transforms but with the conditions and the nature of that transformation. In practice, of course, any account of how a writer shapes, transforms, or evades life operates with assumptions, tacit or acknowledged, about the quality of the life of the author, or of his audience, or of his time. Literature is, in the widest sense of the phrase, a "coming to terms" with life. It is, in Matthew Arnold's words, a "criticism of life," provided we can strip the term *criticism* of its coldly intellectual connotation. Whether he discusses Spenser or Kafka, George Herbert or Sherwood Anderson, the critic cannot afford to be any less passionately concerned with life, any less passionately involved in human experience, than his subject.

The secret of the critic's craft is to preserve this capacity for passionate involvement while at the same time bringing to bear upon his subject a responsible and balanced intelligence. In this respect, the critic must command a balance of commitment and detachment that parallels what John Ciardi has called "a central possession of every good writer—the fact that he can be passionately committed to what he is writing at the same time that one part of his awareness is detached, calculating, and technical."[2] The secret of the successful critic and teacher lies in a balance of sensitivity and imaginative sympathy on the one hand and unsentimental critical judgment and technical competence on the other.

It is not surprising that the teacher of English has numerous points of contact with those sister disciplines that most directly explore the characteristic meanings and patterns of human experience. He shares with the historian of philosophy an interest in those writers whose structuring of experience has a strong intellectual, philosophical dimension. The English teacher interested in the logical structure of discourse travels part of his way with the logician who realizes that logic typically operates through language. The historian of literary style encounters the historian of art and architecture on those frequent occasions when parallels in art and architecture help the student visualize stylistic differences.

Like the teacher of English, the aesthetician seeks to understand that rage for order that is not a rage for order of a purely intellectual kind. The psychologist, unless his interests are confined to a narrow range of controlled experiment, finds in imaginative literature reflections of basic patterns of conscious and subconscious behavior. The anthropologist shares the interest of the linguist in how linguistic structure imposes an order upon experience, and the interest of the critic in the prescientific and preliterary elements in ritual and myth. The historian and social scientist study the patterns of man's living and feuding with his fellows—

2 "On Writing and Bad Writing," *Saturday Review*, December 15, 1962, p. 12.

patterns of concern to the student of the epic, the history play, the novel of manners, the social-problem play, the novel of social protest. The mathematician and the communications engineer share the linguist's interest in the internal structure of signaling systems, of symbolic codes.

The teacher cannot be a qualified observer, let alone an expert, in all these related fields. However, he must at the least maintain an open-minded interest in the more direct contributions they can make to his own work. *Language is an expression of the whole man.* To that extent, every teacher of English is necessarily a generalist. He must come to terms with this basic condition of his craft as best he can.

Subjectivity and Objectivity

The close intertwining of technical questions and general significance in the study of language requires of the teacher the ability to maintain a balanced, comprehensive view. The same is true of other fundamental features of language and literature. According to temperament, English teachers are attracted or frustrated by the recognition that their discipline brings into play a large measure of the personal, the subjective. If they are candid with themselves, they recognize how much their own private history has shaped their attitude toward language, their preferences and commitments in literature. Through the autobiographical and critical writings of major authors, they know the intensely personal involvement of the writer in his work, his struggle to be true to himself rather than to a formula, a theory, a market analysis. They realize that in the authentic use of language something breaks through "the public crust of personality," something that is private, personal, unique.

Nevertheless, to be communicated, the personal must cease to be unique and become shared. The private, to be communicated, must become public. The writer who wants to render the specific, unrepeatable scene, the unique, unprecedented mood, must use words whose meanings can be sensed by the receptive reader. Modern trends in the study of both language and literature have led us to stress their public, objective character. Both linguist and critic prefer to substitute for speculation about what passes in the poet's mind an "objective" analysis of the linguistic utterance, the literary artifact.

In practice, every teacher must to some extent square the circle by recognizing the interaction of the subjective and the objective in language. Typically, *good writing is the expression of forceful, distinctive personality while at the same time it shows a masterful use of language as a common medium.* Style is the man, but it is also the means by which the writer breaks out of the isolation of his personality and establishes a community of meaning with the reader.

Rather than be confused by this paradox, the teacher should strive to make it as fruitful and illuminating as possible in his classroom work. On the one hand, he should develop in his students an interest in the personal world, the distinctive vision, of major authors. The student should consider his reading of a short story by Hawthorne or Joyce, of a poem by Donne or Keats, as a first acquaintance with an author to whom, over the years, he will return, with a pleasure enhanced by growing familiarity with the author's characteristic ways of thinking and feeling. We should take care to give our students access to a range of authors wide enough so that each student can find the one, or the several authors who seem to speak to him directly and powerfully as a person.

On the other hand, the teacher should do justice to the recurrent role in literature of certain constants in human experience. The intense subjectivity of the adolescent, which makes him reject generalizations and advice as presumptuously inappropriate to his unique predicament, becomes part of a recognizable pattern when seen from a distance. Such recurrent themes should not be considered as literary "content" in a narrow sense: The search for pattern and order is as much a recurrent element in human life as the search for love or the need to rationalize and understand experience. Part of the teacher's work is to help the student recognize in strange settings, and shaped by unfamiliar conventions, familiar recurrent patterns of aspiration and disillusionment, yearning and incompatibility, imprisonment in and transcendence of self.

There is always the danger that the search for the human significance of literary works will turn into a facile application of ready-made categories. But the critic who misses that significance will see the study of form become purely technical and the study of literary history purely antiquarian. He will see the interest of contemporary literature come to rest largely on the appeal of novelty or exclusiveness. Ultimately, Chaucer and Shakespeare are classics because in some way they touch on the common essence of our humanity. To develop in our students a lasting concern for language and literature we must emphasize the more permanent sources of significance.

A Balanced View

The teacher of English must typically know how to find the golden mean between opposite extremes. He can take for his model neither the narrow specialist nor the genial amateur. Instead, he must develop his professional competence in a broad general subject. He can neither limit himself rigorously to the objective and concrete nor put his trust in subjective impressions and intuitions. Instead, he must develop his sensitivity to language, combining concrete observation with a grasp of larger relationships.

This ability to take a balanced view is needed not only in the teacher's general approach but also more specifically in his grasp of the major principles that structure his subject. *Study and teaching in our discipline must typically locate a mean between two poles: system and diversity, structure and meaning, function and convention.* The linguist explores the regularities of language; he attempts to formulate the system underlying our linguistic choices. Yet at the same time he makes us more receptive to the diversity of language—the subtlety of grammar and the richness of idiom. At one extreme is the person looking for general rules, impatient with exceptions and complications. At the other extreme is the person exploring the curious detail, the recondite etymology, the unique turn of phrase. The teacher taking a balanced view is open to diversity and detail and yet sees them in a general perspective.

Both linguist and critic can do their most reliable work in the study of structure, staying within the closed circle of language itself. Yet the human significance of language lies in meaning, in its role in human interaction. Basic as is our exploration of the linguistic code itself, our real interest centers in the uses to which it is put. In the study of language, some of the matters most urgently significant are the social dimensions of usage, the dynamics of persuasion. In the study of literature, our knowledge of the technical workings of literary language should help us understand the way it appeals to our attitudes and emotions, the way it offers for our contemplation a view of life.

Like teachers in other fields, the teacher of English makes instruction meaningful by showing the reasons behind his data. He shows the functions served by details and relations. He stresses intention and purpose, showing the why as well as the what and how. Yet both language and literature are to a considerable extent shaped not by logic, or purpose, or function, but convention. Unlike the signals of the Morse code or of mathematics, many features of speech and writing are merely customary, or ceremonial, or vestigial. It is customary to put a comma in "Dayton, Ohio"; it is customary to spell *bellboy* but *bus boy, highway* but *high school*. In a given sonnet by Sidney or Spenser or Milton, the sonnet form may be especially suited to the theme, the prevailing mood, the poet's intention. But at least part of the reason that Sidney and Spenser were writing sonnets is that everybody was writing sonnets. Just as certain conventional features of Bach's music are present both in his *St. Matthew's Passion* and in his *Coffee Cantata,* so certain conventional features of Shakespeare's drama recur in plays quite different in theme and mood. The teacher taking a balanced view of the role of function and convention will not be tempted to make our language practices appear more rational and functional than they are.

Because of its significance and richness, the subject matter of English is not easily subdivided into thirty lessons, to be systematically taught and memorized. There are no short-cuts to the kind of competence in

English that results over the years from challenging and varied work with capable teachers. The teacher who takes his work seriously will have little faith in external expedients and devices. He will have little patience with specialists who magnify their own area of interest at the expense of equally important other areas. He will work best with those of his colleagues who are teachers first and linguists, medievalists, critics, or curriculum specialists second. He will value research and scholarship most when it contributes to a unified and balanced view of the discipline of English.

A PROGRAM FOR ADDITIONAL READING

HAROLD WHITEHALL, *Structural Essentials of English.* New York: Harcourt, Brace & World, Inc., 1956.

> A short and non-doctrinaire modern grammar intended for the student and teacher of "serious written English." Concerned not to erect terminological and methodological barriers in the student's path, the author admirably lives up to his belief that "a bridge of explanation between the old and the new, between the traditional and linguistic approaches to composition teaching, must be erected very cautiously and carefully."

H. A. GLEASON, JR., *An Introduction to Descriptive Linguistics,* rev. ed. New York: Holt, Rinehart & Winston, Inc., 1961.

> Though more rigorously technical than more popular introductions to linguistics, this book is "not directed to prospective linguists alone; rather, widely various academic backgrounds and interests are assumed." Includes an illuminating treatment of recent developments and of different schools of linguistic theory.

ALBERT H. MARCKWARDT, *American English.* New York: Oxford University Press, 1958.

> An account, well suited for the student and general reader, of the growth and development of the English language in America. Emphasis is on "the close interaction of linguistic and cultural factors in the growth of American English." Contains chapters on the American tendency toward euphemistic upgrading of the commonplace and on regional and social variations.

JAMES SLEDD AND WILMA R. EBBITT, eds. *Dictionaries and* That *Dictionary.* Chicago: Scott, Foresman & Company, Inc., 1962.

> Notable for its sobering record of popular preconceptions about language as revealed in editorials and reviews written after the publication of *Webster's Third New International Dictionary.* Introduced by materials on the nature and history of dictionaries, this collection presents the full range of reactions to Webster's Third, from judicious praise to shrill denunciation.

SAMUEL R. LEVIN, *Linguistic Structures in Poetry.* The Hague: Mouton & Co., 1962.

> Highly technical, this brief volume illustrates the extension of structural and transformational analysis to style, that is, relationships felt as distinctive

(compared with the most normal or predictable linguistic patterns) and extending beyond the individual sentence. Employs a formidable theoretical and terminological apparatus to establish the contribution made to the unity and permanence of a poem by parallelism and antithesis; synonyms, antonyms, and semantic clusters; meter, rhyme, alliteration, and assonance.

MALCOLM COWLEY, ed. *Writers at Work: The Paris Review Interviews.* New York: The Viking Press, Inc., 1959.

A famous series of interviews with important contemporary writers. Includes revealing discussions of their craft by James Thurber, Thornton Wilder, William Faulkner, Nelson Algren, and Truman Capote.

DAVID DAICHES, *A Critical History of English Literature,* 2 vols. New York: The Ronald Press Company, 1960.

Unlike more traditional histories of literature, this book "is not meant to be looked up, but to be read" and is unified by one author's personal perspective. A convenient overview of the English literary tradition, with emphasis on major figures. Notable for its balanced restatement, and occasional questioning, of accepted views.

WILLIAM K. WIMSATT, JR. AND CLEANTH BROOKS, *Literary Criticism: A Short History.* New York: Alfred A. Knopf, Inc., 1957.

A history of ideas *about* literature from Plato to modern students of myth and archetype. Devoted to demonstrating the continuity of major themes in the history of literary theory, since "literary problems occur not just because history produces them, but because literature is a thing of such and such a sort, showing such and such a relation to the rest of human experience." Written from the point of view of the modern critic who believes that "'form' . . . embraces and penetrates 'message' in a way that constitutes a deeper and more substantial meaning than either abstract message or separable ornament."

WILLIAM K. WIMSATT, JR., *The Verbal Icon: Studies in the Meaning of Poetry.* New York: The Noonday Press, 1958.

Devoted to a rigorous examination of the problems faced by the critic committed to a view of "literature as a form of knowledge" and to the assumption that "style is a level of meaning." Includes well-known essays on the intentional and affective fallacies written in collaboration with Monroe C. Beardsley.

NORTHROP FRYE, *Anatomy of Criticism: Four Essays.* Princeton, N.J.: Princeton University Press, 1957.

The most prominent among recent attempts at a comprehensive and systematic theory of literature going beyond the "formalistic" categories of the New Criticism. Characteristic of the current trend toward sweepingly synoptic symbolical and thematic analysis of literature in a large anthropological framework, with its dynamic principles identified as ritual, archetype, and myth.

JAMES E. MILLER, JR., ed. *Myth and Method: Modern Theories of Fiction.* Lincoln: University of Nebraska Press, 1960.

Out of the mass of modern critical writing devoted to fiction, this short collection brings together a number of crucial and illuminating theoretical essays. In addition to classic discussions by Henry James, Joseph Conrad, and Percy Lubbock, this volume includes essays on the role of myth and archetype by Richard Chase and Northrop Frye.

WAYNE C. BOOTH, *The Rhetoric of Fiction*. Chicago: The University of Chicago Press, 1961.

A detailed and systematic study of the devices by which the writer of fiction controls the reader's response. Illuminates characteristic problems and effects through carefully developed illustrations. Eminently clear and readable, this book admirably succeeds in avoiding the poses of superficially fashionable critics.

RUSSELL E. LEAVENWORTH, ed. *Interpreting Hamlet: Materials for Analysis*. San Francisco: Howard Chandler, 1960.

A paperback collection illustrating well the range of representative modern approaches to Shakespeare. Includes contributions by Coleridge, A. C. Bradley, T. S. Eliot, G. Wilson Knight, E. E. Stoll, Ernest Jones, and Francis Fergusson.

LEONARD F. DEAN, ed. *Shakespeare: Modern Essays in Criticism*. New York: Oxford University Press, 1957.

A collection of essays on major plays and on important aspects of Shakespeare's work as a whole. Illustrates such contemporary critical concerns as the nature of Shakespeare's audience (Harbage), the dramatic role of his imagery (Spurgeon), the organic relations among different plays (Tillyard).

JOHN DEWEY, *Democracy and Education: An Introduction to the Philosophy of Education*. New York: The Macmillan Company, 1961.

A paperback reprint of a classic on the aims and methods of education. See especially Chapter Twelve, "Thinking in Education," on the relation between subject-matter, thought, and experience.

JEROME S. BRUNER, *The Process of Education*. Cambridge, Mass.: Harvard University Press, 1962.

A brief but influential book growing out of a conference devoted to the exploration of new curricula and methods for the teaching of science. Emphasizes the need for teaching specific topics or skills in "their context in the broader fundamental structure of a field of knowledge."

G. B. HARRISON, *Profession of English*. New York: Harcourt, Brace & World, Inc., 1962.

Reflections on the teaching of English literature by an eminent scholar-teacher, author and editor of many authoritative and successful college texts. Many pertinent warnings against pedantry and self-indulgence; much bracing advice for the prospective teacher.

Index

441

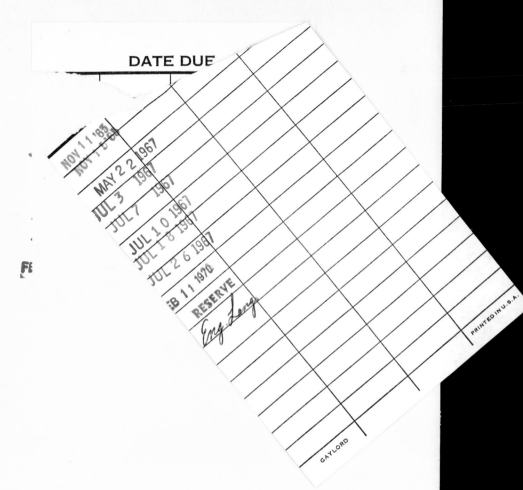

DATE DUE

NOV 11 '65
NOV 1 3 '66
MAY 2 2 1967
JUL 3 1967
JUL 7 1967
JUL 1 0 1967
JUL 1 8 1967
JUL 2 6 1967
FEB 1 1 1970

RESERVE

Eng. Long

PRINTED IN U.S.A.

GAYLORD